WORD
BIBLICAL
COMMENTARY

General Editors
David A. Hubbard
Glenn W. Barker †

Old Testament Editor
John D. W. Watts

New Testament Editor
Ralph P. Martin

WORD
BIBLICAL
COMMENTARY

VOLUME 28

Ezekiel 1–19

LESLIE C. ALLEN

Publishers Since 1798

THOMAS NELSON PUBLISHERS

Nashville

Word Biblical Commentary
Ezekiel 1–19
Copyright © 1994 by Word, Incorporated

Library of Congress Cataloging-in-Publication Data
Main entry under title:

Word biblical commentary.

   Includes bibliographies.
   1. Bible—commentaries—Collected works.
BS491.2.W67   220.7'7   81–71768
ISBN 0-8499-0830-2 (vol. 28) AACR2

Printed in Colombia

The author's own translation of the text appears in italic type under the heading *Translation*, as well as in brief scripture quotations in the body of the commentary, except where otherwise indicated.

The illustrations reproduced on pp. 27, 28, 29, 30, and 37 (Figures 1, 2, 3, 4, and 5) are used by permission of Verlag Katholisches Bibelwerk from *Jahwe-Visionen und Segelkunst* by Othmar Keel. The illustration reproduced on p. 140 (Figure 6) is used by permission of E. J. Brill from *Der Tempel von Jerusalem*, vol. 1 (1970) by Th. A. Busink.

5 6 7 8 9 10 11 12 13 14 15 16 17 18   QWB 09 08 07 06 05 04

To Ken, a brother to look up to

Contents

Editorial Preface

The launching of the *Word Biblical Commentary* brings to fulfillment an enterprise of several years' planning. The publishers and the members of the editorial board met in 1977 to explore the possibility of a new commentary on the books of the Bible that would incorporate several distinctive features. Prospective readers of these volumes are entitled to know what such features were intended to be; whether the aims of the commentary have been fully achieved time alone will tell.

First, we have tried to cast a wide net to include as contributors a number of scholars from around the world who not only share our aims but are in the main engaged in the ministry of teaching in university, college, and seminary. They represent a rich diversity of denominational allegiance. The broad stance of our contributors can rightly be called evangelical, and this term is to be understood in its positive, historic sense of a commitment to Scripture as divine revelation and to the truth and power of the Christian gospel.

Then, the commentaries in our series are all commissioned and written for the purpose of inclusion in the *Word Biblical Commentary*. Unlike several of our distinguished counterparts in the field of commentary writing, there are no translated works, originally written in a non-English language. Also, our commentators were asked to prepare their own rendering of the original biblical text and to use those languages as the basis of their own comments and exegesis. What may be claimed as distinctive with this series is that it is based on the biblical languages, yet it seeks to make the technical and scholarly approach to the theological understanding of Scripture understandable by—and useful to—the fledgling student, the working minister, and colleagues in the guild of professional scholars and teachers as well.

Finally, a word must be said about the format of the series. The layout, in clearly defined sections, has been consciously devised to assist readers at different levels. Those wishing to learn about the textual witnesses on which the translation is offered are invited to consult the section headed *Notes*. If the readers' concern is with the state of modern scholarship on any given portion of Scripture, they should turn to the sections on *Bibliography* and *Form/Structure/Setting*. For a clear exposition of the passage's meaning and its relevance to the ongoing biblical revelation, the *Comment* and concluding *Explanation* are designed expressly to meet that need. There is therefore something for everyone who may pick up and use these volumes.

If these aims come anywhere near realization, the intention of the editors will have been met, and the labor of our team of contributors rewarded.

General Editors: *David A. Hubbard*
Glenn W. Barker†
Old Testament: *John D. W. Watts*
New Testament: *Ralph P. Martin*

Author's Preface

I am grateful to the editors for the opportunity to write this commentary, which stands alongside my earlier *Ezekiel 20–48* and provides a perspective that is consistent with it. The reverse order of writing has given me a strong sense of the wholeness of the book.

I must acknowledge the help of my colleague, James T. Butler, in commenting on a draft of some of my work that impinged on his own, obtaining books from the theological library at Claremont, and being there for me to bounce off my ideas. One of the countless debts I owe my dear wife Elizabeth is her weighing every word I have written and warning of many a trap of careless and infelicitous language. Thanks are due to Fuller Theological Seminary for providing the time and encouragement to study and not least to David Sielaff and his colleagues in the word processing office for their diligent and patient work.

LESLIE C. ALLEN
Fuller Theological Seminary
Pasadena

October 1993

Abbreviations

PERIODICALS, SERIALS, AND REFERENCE WORKS

AB	Anchor Bible
ABD	D. N. Freedman (ed.), *Anchor Bible Dictionary*
AJBA	*Australian Journal of Biblical Archaeology*
AJSL	*American Journal of Semitic Languages and Literature*
ALUOS	Annual of Leeds University Oriental Society
AnBib	Analecta biblica
ANEP	J. B. Pritchard (ed.), *Ancient Near East in Pictures*
ANET	J. B. Pritchard (ed.), *Ancient Near Eastern Texts*
Anton	*Antonianum*
ASTI	*Annual of the Swedish Theological Institute*
ATANT	Abhandlungen zur Theologie des Alten und Neuen Testaments
BA	*Biblical Archaeologist*
BAT	Die Botschaft des Alten Testaments
Bauer-Leander	W. Bauer and P. Leander, *Historische Grammatik der hebräischen Sprache des Alten Testaments* (1922; Hildesheim: Olms, 1962)
BBB	Bonner biblische Beiträge
BBET	Beiträge zur biblischen Exegese und Theologie
BDB	F. Brown, S. R. Driver and C.A. Briggs, *Hebrew and English Lexicon of the Old Testament*
BETL	Bibliotheca ephemeridum theologicarum lovaniensium
BHK	R. Kittel (ed.), *Biblia Hebraica*
BHS	*Biblia Hebraica Stuttgartensia*
BHT	Beiträge zur historischen Theologie
Bib	*Biblica*
BibOr	Biblica et orientalia
BibLeb	*Bibel und Leben*
BibS	Biblische Studien (Neukirchen, 1951–)
BJRL	*Bulletin of the John Rylands University Library of Manchester*
BKAT	Biblische Kommentar: Altes Testament
BMik	*Beth Mikra*
BN	*Biblische Notizen*
BRL	*Biblisches Reallexikon* (Tübingen, 1977)
BSac	*Bibliotheca Sacra*
BTB	*Biblical Theology Bulletin*
BWANT	Beiträge zur Wissenschaft vom Alten und Neuen Testament
BZ	*Biblische Zeitschrift*
BZAW	Beihefte zur ZAW
CAD	*Assyrian Dictionary of the Oriental Institute of the University of Chicago*
CAH	*Cambridge Ancient History*

CahRB	Cahiers de la Revue biblique
CBC	Cambridge Bible Commentary
CBSC	Cambridge Bible for Schools and Colleges
CBQ	*Catholic Biblical Quarterly*
CHB	*Cambridge History of the Bible*
ConB	Coniectanea biblica
ConBOT	Coniectanea biblica, Old Testament
CTA	A. Herdner, *Corpus de tablettes en cunéiformes alphabétiques*
CTJ	*Calvin Theological Journal*
CTM	*Concordia Theological Monthly*
DOTT	D. W. Thomas (ed.), *Documents from Old Testament Times*
EncJud	*Encyclopedia Judaica*
ErFor	Erträge der Forschung
EstBib	*Estudios bíblicos*
ETL	*Ephemerides theologicae lovanienses*
ETR	*Etudes théologiques et religieuses*
ETS	Erfurter theologische Studien
EvQ	*Evangelical Quarterly*
ExpTim	*Expository Times*
FOTL	Forms of the Old Testament Literature
FRLANT	Forschungen zur Religion und Literatur des Alten und Neuen Testaments
FB	Forschung zur Bibel
GB	*Gesenius' hebräisches und aramäisches Handwörterbuch,* ed. F. P. W. Buhl
GKC	*Gesenius' Hebrew Grammar,* ed. E. Kautsch, tr. A. E. Cowley
GTTOT	J. J. Simons, *The Geographical and Topographical Texts of the Old Testament*
HALAT	W. Baumgartner et al., *Hebräisches und aramäisches Lexikon zum Alten Testament*
HAR	*Hebrew Annual Review*
HAT	Handbuch zum Alten Testament
HKAT	Handkommentar zum Alten Testament
HR	*History of Religions*
HSM	Harvard Semitic Monographs
HSS	Harvard Semitic Studies
HTR	*Harvard Theological Review*
HUCA	*Hebrew Union College Annual*
IB	*Interpreter's Bible*
IBS	*Irish Biblical Studies*
IDB	G. A. Buttrick (ed.), *Interpreter's Dictionary of the Bible*
IDBSup	Supplementary volume to *IDB*
IEJ	*Israel Exploration Journal*
Int	*Interpretation*
ISBE	G. W. Bromiley (ed.), *International Standard Bible Encyclopedia,* rev.
JANESCU	*Journal of the Ancient Near Eastern Society of Columbia University*
JAOS	*Journal of the American Oriental Society*

JBL	*Journal of Biblical Literature*
JCS	*Journal of Cuneiform Studies*
JETS	*Journal of the Evangelical Theological Society*
JJS	*Journal of Jewish Studies*
JNES	*Journal of Near Eastern Studies*
JNSL	*Journal of Northwest Semitic Languages*
Joüon	P. Joüon, *A Grammar of Biblical Hebrew*, tr. and ed. T. Muraoka
JPOS	*Journal of the Palestine Oriental Society*
JQR	*Jewish Quarterly Review*
JRAS	*Journal of the Royal Asiatic Society*
JSOT	*Journal for the Study of the Old Testament*
JSOTSup	*JSOT* Supplement Series
JSS	*Journal of Semitic Studies*
JTS	*Journal of Theological Studies*
KAT	Kommentar zum Alten Testament
KB	L. Koehler and W. Baumgartner, *Lexicon in Veteris Testamenti libros*
KEH	Kurzgefasstes exegetisches Handbuch zum Alten Testament
LD	Lectio divina
Leš	*Lešonenu*
NCB	New Century Bible
NICOT	New International Commentary on the Old Testament
NTOA	Novum Testamentum et Orbis Antiquus
NTS	*New Testament Studies*
OBO	Orbis biblicus et orientalis
OBT	Overtures to Biblical Theology
OLZ	*Orientalische Literaturzeitung*
Or	*Orientalia*
OTL	Old Testament Library
OTS	*Oudtestamentische Studiën*
PEFQS	*Palestine Exploration Fund, Quarterly Statement*
PEQ	*Palestinian Exploration Quarterly*
PJ	*Palästina-Jahrbuch*
POS	Pretoria Oriental Studies
RB	*Revue biblique*
REJ	*Revue des études juives*
RevQ	*Revue de Qumran*
RHPR	*Revue d'histoire et de philosophie religieuses*
SBFLA	*Studii biblici franciscani liber annuus*
SBLDS	SBL Dissertation Series
SBLMS	SBL Monograph Series
SBS	Stuttgarter Bibelstudien
SBT	Studies in Biblical Theology
SCS	Septuagint and Cognate Studies
SEÅ	*Svensk exegetisk årsbok*
Sem	*Semitica*
SOTSMS	Society for Old Testament Study Monograph Series
TBT	*The Bible Today*

TBü	Theologische Bücherei
TDNT	G. Kittel and G. Friedrich (eds.), *Theological Dictionary of the New Testament*
TDOT	G. J. Botterweck and H. Ringgren (eds.), *Theological Dictionary of the Old Testament*
THAT	E. Jenni and C. Westermann (eds.), *Theologisches Handwörterbuch zum Alten Testament*
TLZ	*Theologische Literaturzeitung*
TOTC	Tyndale Old Testament Commentaries
TQ	*Theologische Quartalschrift*
TRu	*Theologische Rundschau*
TWAT	G. J. Botterweck and H. Ringgren (eds.), *Theologisches Wörterbuch zum Alten Testament*
TynBul	*Tyndale Bulletin*
TZ	*Theologische Zeitschrift*
UF	*Ugarit-Forschungen*
UUÅ	Uppsala universitetsårsskrift
VT	*Vetus Testamentum*
VTSup	*VT* Supplements
WBC	Word Biblical Commentary
WC	Westminster Commentaries
WMANT	Wissenschaftliche Monographien zum Alten und Neuen Testament
WZ	*Wissenschaftliche Zeitschrift*
ZAW	*Zeitschrift für die alttestamentliche Wissenschaft*
ZDPV	*Zeitschrift des deutschen Palästina-Vereins*

HEBREW GRAMMAR

abs	absolute
acc	accusative
adj	adjective
adv acc	adverbial accusative
c	common
coh	cohortative
consec	consecutive
constr	construct
fem	feminine
fut	future
hiph	hiphil
hithp	hithpael
hoph	hophal
impf	imperfect
impv	imperative
ind	indicative
inf	infinitive

juss	jussive
masc	masculine
niph	niphal
pass	passive
pf	perfect
pilp	pilpel
pl	plural
ptcp	participle
sg	singular
subj	subject

TEXTUAL NOTES

'A	Aquila
Akk.	Akkadian
Arab.	Arabic
Aram.	Aramaic
Arm	Armenian version
B	MT MS, edited by Jacob ben Chayim, Venice (1524/25)
C	MT MS, Cairo Codex of the Prophets
CD	Cairo text of the *Damascus Document*
Egy.	Egyptian
Eth.	Ethiopic language
Eth	Ethiopic version
Gr.	Greek
Heb.	Hebrew
K	Kethib
K^{Occ}	Occidental (western) Kethib
K^{Or}	Oriental (eastern) Kethib
L	MT MS, Leningrad Codex
LXX	Septuagint
LXX*	LXX in its prehexaplaric form
LXX^A	LXX MS, Alexandrian Codex
LXX^B	LXX MS, Vatican Codex
LXX^C	Catena text of the LXX
LXX^L	LXX MSS of the Lucianic recension
LXX^O	Hexaplaric text of the LXX
LXX^Q	LXX MS, Marchalian Codex
MS^G	Heb MS edited by C. D. Ginsburg (1908)
MS^K	Heb MS edited by B. Kennicott (1776–1780)
MS^R	Heb MS edited by J. B. de Rossi (1784–1788)
MT	Masoretic Text
OL	Old Latin
Q	Qere
Q^{Or}	Oriental (eastern) Qere
$4QEz^{a,b}$	MSS of Ezekiel from Qumran Cave 4

11QEz	MS of Ezekiel from Qumran Cave 11
Syh	Syrohexaplaric text
Syr.	Syriac language
Syr	Syriac Peshitta
Tg	Targum
Ug.	Ugaritic
Vg	Vulgate
Θ	Theodotion
Σ	Symmachus

MODERN TRANSLATIONS

KJV	King James Version
NAB	New American Bible
NEB	New English Bible
NIV	New International Version
NJB	New Jerusalem Bible
NJPS	New Jewish Publication Society Version
NRSV	New Revised Standard Version
REB	Revised English Bible
RSV	Revised Standard Version
TEV	Today's English Version

BIBLICAL BOOKS AND APOCRYPHAL BOOKS

Old Testament

Gen	Genesis	Cant	Song of Solomon
Exod	Exodus	Isa	Isaiah
Lev	Leviticus	Jer	Jeremiah
Num	Numbers	Lam	Lamentations
Deut	Deuteronomy	Ezek	Ezekiel
Josh	Joshua	Dan	Daniel
Judg	Judges	Hos	Hosea
Ruth	Ruth	Joel	Joel
1, 2 Sam	1, 2 Samuel	Amos	Amos
1, 2 Kgs	1, 2 Kings	Obad	Obadiah
1, 2 Chr	1, 2 Chronicles	Jonah	Jonah
Ezra	Ezra	Mic	Micah
Neh	Nehemiah	Nah	Nahum
Esth	Esther	Hab	Habakkuk
Job	Job	Zeph	Zephaniah
Ps(s)	Psalm(s)	Hag	Haggai
Prov	Proverbs	Zech	Zechariah
Eccl	Ecclesiastes	Mal	Malachi

New Testament

Matt	Matthew	1, 2 Thess	1, 2 Thessalonians
Mark	Mark	1, 2 Tim	1, 2 Timothy
Luke	Luke	Titus	Titus
John	John	Phlm	Philemon
Acts	Acts	Heb	Hebrews
Rom	Romans	Jas	James
1, 2 Cor	1, 2 Corinthians	1, 2 Pet	1, 2 Peter
Gal	Galatians	1, 2, 3 John	1, 2, 3 John
Eph	Ephesians	Jude	Jude
Phil	Philippians	Rev	Revelation
Col	Colossians		

Apocrypha

1, 2, 3, 4 Kgdms	1, 2, 3, 4 Kingdoms	1, 2, 3, 4 Macc	1, 2, 3, 4 Maccabees
Add Esth	Additions to Esther	Pr Azar	Prayer of Azariah
Bar	Baruch	Pr Man	Prayer of Manasseh
Bel	Bel and the Dragon	Sir	Ecclesiasticus or The Wisdom of Jesus Son of Sirach
1, 2 Esdr	1, 2 Esdras		
4 Ezra	4 Ezra		
Jud	Judith	Sus	Susanna
Ep Jer	Epistle of Jeremy	Tob	Tobit
		Wis	Wisdom

MISCELLANEOUS

chap(s).	chapter(s)
CUP	Cambridge University Press
E	Elohist
ed(s).	editor(s), edited by
H	Holiness Code
id.	*idem*, the same
J	Jahwist
MS(S)	manuscript(s)
P	Priestly Source
tr.	translation, translated by
UP	University Press

In identifying precise portions of material within verses, the standard system of punctuation found in the MT has been used as a basis. The Hebrew text carefully uses accents to divide a verse or sentence into two major divisions and each of the major divisions into smaller subdivisions. In the commentary, English letters refer to the major divisions and Greek letters to the subdivisions. Thus "v 9a" refers to the first half of the Hebrew sentence and "v 9aα" to the first subdivision of the first half. Sometimes phrases or clauses have not been differentiated by accents. In that case, superior numbers are used to demarcate small portions of material, viz. "v 9aα^1."

Main Bibliography

1. Commentaries *(in chronological order; cited by name hereafter)*

Jerome. *S. Hieronymi presbyteri opera I: Opera exegetica 4: Commentariorum in Hezechielem libri xiv.* Corpus Christianorum, Series Latine 75. Turnhout: Brepols, 1974. **Calvin, J.** *Commentaries on the First Twenty Chapters of the Book of the Prophet Ezekiel.* Tr. T. Myers from the French edition of 1565 and the Latin edition of 1617. 1849; repr. Grand Rapids: Eerdmans, 1948. **Ewald, H.** *Die Propheten des Alten Bundes.* Vol. 2. Stuttgart: Krabbe, 1841. **Hitzig, F.** *Der Prophet Ezechiel.* KEH. Leipzig: Weidmann, 1847. **Fairbairn, P.** *Ezekiel and the Book of His Prophecy: An Exposition.* Edinburgh: T. & T. Clark, 1863. **Smend, R.** *Der Prophet Ezechiel.* KEH. 2nd ed. Leipzig: Hirzel, 1880. **Cornill, C. H.** *Das Buch des Propheten Ezechiel.* Leipzig: Hinrichs, 1886. **Davidson, A. B.** *The Book of the Prophet Ezekiel.* CBSC. Cambridge: CUP, 1892. Revised by A. W. Streane, 1916. **Orelli, C. von.** *Das Buch Ezechiel.* 2nd ed. Kurzgefasster Kommentar zu den Schriften des Alten und Neuen Testaments. Munich: Beek, 1896. **Bertholet, A.** *Das Buch Hesekiel.* Kurzer Hand-Commentar zum Alten Testament. Tübingen: Mohr, 1897. **Toy, C. H.** *The Book of the Prophet Ezekiel.* Sacred Books of the Old and New Testaments. New York: Dodd, Mead, 1899. **Kraetzschmar, R.** *Das Buch Ezechiel.* HKAT. Göttingen: Vandenhoeck & Ruprecht, 1900. **Skinner, J.** *The Book of Ezekiel.* Expositor's Bible. New York: Armstrong, 1901. **Jahn, G.** *Das Buch Ezechiel auf Grund der Septuaginta hergestellt.* Leipzig: Pfeiffer, 1905. **Redpath, H. A.** *The Book of the Prophet Ezekiel.* WC. London: Methuen, 1907. **Gaebelein, A. C.** *The Prophet Ezekiel: An Analytical Exposition.* New York: Our Hope, 1918. **Rothstein, J. W.** "Das Buch Ezechiel." In *Die Heilige Schrift des Alten Testaments.* Vol. 1. Tübingen: Mohr, 1922. **Herrmann, J.** *Ezechiel.* KAT. Leipzig: Deichert, 1924. **Cooke, G. A.** *The Book of Ezekiel.* ICC. New York: Scribners, 1936. **Bertholet, A.,** and **Galling, K.** *Hesekiel.* HAT. Tübingen: Mohr (Siebeck), 1936. **Keil, C. F.** *Biblical Commentary on the Prophecies of Ezekiel.* Tr. J. Martin from 1882 German edition. 2 vols. Grand Rapids: Eerdmans, 1950. **Steinmann, J.** *Le Prophète Ezéchiel.* LD 13. Paris: Cerf, 1953. **Fohrer, G.,** and **Galling, K.** *Ezechiel.* HAT. 2nd ed. Tübingen: Mohr (Siebeck), 1955. **Born, A. van den.** *Ezechiël uit de grondtekst vertaald en uitgelegd.* Roermond: Romen & Zonen, 1954. **May, H. G.** "Ezekiel." IB. New York: Abingdon, 1956. 6:39–338. **Ellison, H. L.** *Ezekiel: The Man and His Message.* Grand Rapids: Eerdmans, 1956. **Auvray, P.** *Ezéchiel.* La Sainte Bible. Paris: Cerf, 1957. **Muilenburg, J.** "Ezekiel." In *Peake's Commentary on the Bible.* London: Nelson, 1962. 568–90. **Ziegler, J.** *Ezechiel.* Echter Bibel. Würzburg: Echter Verlag, 1963. **Lamparter, H.** *Zum Wächter Bestellt: Der Prophet Hesekiel.* BAT. Stuttgart: Calwer, 1968. **Stalker, D. M. G.** *Ezekiel: Introduction and Commentary.* Torch Bible Commentaries. London: SCM, 1968. **Zimmerli, W.** *Ezekiel 1: A Commentary on the Book of the Prophet Ezekiel Chapters 1–24.* Hermeneia. Tr. R. E. Clements from 1969 German edition. Philadelphia: Fortress, 1979. ———. *Ezekiel 2: A Commentary on the Book of the Prophet Ezekiel Chapters 25–48.* Hermeneia. Tr. J. D. Martin from 1969 German edition. Philadelphia: Fortress, 1983. **Wevers, J. W.** *Ezekiel.* NCBC. Grand Rapids: Eerdmans, 1969. **Feinberg, C. L.** *The Prophecy of Ezekiel.* Chicago: Moody Press, 1969. **Taylor, J. B.** *Ezekiel: An Introduction and Commentary.* TOTC. Downer's Grove: Inter-Varsity Press, 1969. **Eichrodt, W.** *Ezekiel: A Commentary.* Tr. C. Quin from 1966 German edition. OTL. Philadelphia: Westminster, 1970. **Brownlee, W. H.** "Ezekiel." In *Interpreter's One Volume Commentary on the Bible,* ed. C. M. Laymon. Rev. ed. Nashville: Abingdon, 1973. 411–35. **Carley, K. W.** *The Book of the Prophet Ezekiel.* CBC. Cambridge: CUP, 1974. **Mosis, R.** *Das Buch Ezechiel.* Vol. 1. Chaps. 1,1–10, 44. Geistliche Schriftlesung 18/1. Düsseldorf: Patmos, 1978. **Craigie, P. C.** *Ezekiel.* Daily Study Bible. Philadelphia: Westminster, 1983. **Greenberg,**

M. *Ezekiel 1–20.* AB. Garden City, NY: Doubleday, 1983. **Fuhs, H. F.** *Ezechiel 1–24.* Neu Echter Bibel. Würzburg: Echter Verlag, 1984. **Andrew, M. E.** *Responsibility and Restoration: The Course of the Book of Ezekiel.* Dunedin: University of Otago, 1985. **Gowan, D. E.** *Ezekiel.* Knox Preaching Guides. Atlanta: John Knox, 1985. **Lane, D.** *The Cloud and the Silver Lining.* Welwyn: Evangelical Press, 1985. **Brownlee, W. H.** *Ezekiel 1–19.* WBC. Waco, TX: Word, 1986. **Wilson, R. R.** "Ezekiel." In *Harper's Bible Commentary.* San Francisco: Harper & Row, 1988. 652–94. **Hals, R. M.** *Ezekiel.* FOTL 19. Grand Rapids: Eerdmans, 1989. **Stuart, D.** *Ezekiel.* Communicator's Commentary. Dallas: Word, 1989. **Blenkinsopp, J.** *Ezekiel.* Interpretation. Louisville: Knox, 1990. **Boadt, L.** "Ezekiel." In *New Jerome Biblical Commentary.* Englewood Cliffs, NJ: Prentice Hall, 1990. 315–28. **Vawter, B.,** and **Hoppe, L. J.** *A New Heart: A Commentary on the Book of Ezekiel.* International Theological Commentary. Grand Rapids: Eerdmans, 1991.

2. Texts, Versions, and Textual Studies

Barthélemy, D. *Critique textuelle de l'Ancien Testament.* Vol. 3. *Ézéchiel, Daniel et les 12 Prophètes.* OBO 50.3. Göttingen: Vandenhoeck & Ruprecht, 1992. **Bewer, J. A.** "Textual and Exegetical Notes on the Book of Ezekiel." *JBL* 72 (1954) 158–68. **Boadt, L.** *Ezekiel's Oracles against Egypt: A Literary and Philological Study of Ezekiel 29–32.* BibOr 37. Rome: Biblical Institute, 1980. **Brockington, L. H.** *The Hebrew Text of the Old Testament: The Readings Adopted by the Translators of the New English Bible.* Oxford: Oxford UP, 1973. **Driver, G. R.** "Linguistic and Textual Problems: Ezekiel." *Bib* 19 (1938) 60–69, 175–87. ————. "Hebrew Notes on Prophets and Proverbs." *JTS* 41 (1940) 162–75. ————. "Ezekiel: Linguistic and Textual Problems." *Bib* 35 (1954) 145–59, 299–312. ————. "Glosses in the Hebrew Text of the Old Testament." In *L'Ancien Testament et l'Orient.* Louvain: Publications Universitaires, 1957. 123–61. ————. "Abbreviations in the Massoretic Text." *Textus* 1 (1960) 112–31. **Ehrlich, A. B.** *Randglossen zur Hebräischen Bibel.* Vol. 5. Leipzig: Hinrich, 1912. **Elliger, K.** "Liber Ezechiel." In *Biblia Hebraica Stuttgartensia,* ed. K. Elliger and W. Rudolph. Stuttgart: Würtembergische Bibelstiftung, 1967/77. **Fohrer, G.** "Die Glossen im Buche Ezechiel." *ZAW* 63 (1951) 33–53. **Freedy, K. S.** "The Glosses in Ezekiel 1–24." *VT* 20 (1970) 129–52. **Herrmann, J.** "Stichwortglossen im Buche Ezechiel." *OLZ* 11 (1908) 280–82. **Jahn, L. J. G.** *Der griechische Text des Buches Ezechiel nach dem Kölner Teil des Papyrus 967.* Papyrologische Texte und Abhandlungen 15. Bonn: Habelt, 1972. **Jastrow, M.** *A Dictionary of the Targumim, the Talmud Babli and Yerashalmi and the Midrashic Literature.* London; New York: Trübner, 1903. **Johnson, B.** *Hebräisches Perfekt und Imperfekt mit vorangehenden* wᵉ. ConBOT 13. Lund: Gleerup, 1979. **Joüon, P.** "Notes philologiques sur le texte hébreu d'Ezékiel." *Bib* 10 (1929) 304–12. **Levey, S. H.** "The Targum to Ezekiel." *HUCA* 46 (1975) 139–58. ————. *The Aramaic Bible (The Targums): Ezekiel.* Wilmington, DE: M. Glazier, 1987. **Lust, J.** "Ezekiel 36–40 in the Oldest Greek Manuscript." *CBQ* 43 (1981) 517–33. ————. "Exegesis and Theology in the Septuagint of Ezekiel: The Longer 'Pluses' and Ezek. 43:1–9." In *VIth Congress of the International Organization for Septuagint and Cognate Studies.* SCS 23. Atlanta: Scholars, 1987. 201–32. **McGregor, L. J.** *The Greek Text of Ezekiel: An Examination of Its Homogeneity.* Atlanta: Scholars, 1985. **Reider, J.** "Contributions to the Scriptural Text." *HUCA* 24 (1952/53) 85–106. **Sperber, A.** *The Bible in Aramaic.* Vol. 3. *The Latter Prophets.* Leiden: Brill, 1962. **Tov, E.** "Recensional Differences between the MT and LXX of Ezekiel." *ETL* 62 (1986) 89–101. **Van Dijk, H. J.** *Ezekiel's Prophecy on Tyre: A New Approach.* BibOr 20. Rome: Pontifical Biblical Institute, 1968. **Waltke, B. K.,** and **O'Connor, M.** *An Introduction to Biblical Hebrew Syntax.* Winona Lake, IN: Eisenbrauns, 1990. **Ziegler, J.** *Septuaginta vol. XVI, 1. Ezechiel (2nd ed.) mit einem Nachtrag von D. Fraenkel.* Göttingen: Vandenhoeck & Ruprecht, 1977. **Zorell, F.** *Lexicon Hebraicum et Aramaicum Veteris Testamenti* Rome: Pontifical Biblical Institute, 1954.

3. Major Monographs and Articles

Bettenzoli, G. *Geist der Heiligkeit: Traditionsgeschichtliche Untersuchung des QDŠ-Begriffes im Buch Ezechiel.* Quaderni di Semistica 8. Florence: Istituto di Lingistica e di Lingue Orientali, Universita di Firenze, 1979. **Boadt, L.** "Rhetorical Strategies in Ezekiel's Oracles of Judgment." In *Ezekiel and His Book*, ed. J. Lust. 182–200. **Bodi, D.** *The Book of Ezekiel and the Poem of Erra.* OBO 104. Freiburg: Universitätsverlag, 1991. **Busink, Th. A.** *Der Tempel von Jerusalem von Salomo bis Herodes: 2. Von Ezechiel bis Middot.* Leiden: Brill, 1980. **Carley, K. W.** *Ezekiel among the Prophets: A Study of Ezekiel's Place in Prophetic Tradition.* SBT 2.31. London: SCM, 1975. **Cassuto, U.** "The Arrangement of the Book of Ezekiel." In *Biblical and Oriental Studies.* Tr. I. Abrahams. Jerusalem: Magnes Press, 1973. 1:227–40. **Davis, E. F.** *Swallowing the Scroll: Textuality and the Dynamics of Discourse in Ezekiel's Prophecy.* JSOTSup 78. Sheffield: Almond, 1989. **Fishbane, M. A.** *Biblical Interpretation in Ancient Israel.* Oxford: Clarendon; New York: Oxford UP, 1985. ———. "Sin and Judgment in the Prophecies of Ezekiel." *Int* 38 (1984) 131–50. ——— and **Talmon, S.** "The Structuring of Biblical Books: Studies in the Book of Ezekiel." *ASTI* 10 (1976) 129–57. **Fohrer, G.** *Die Hauptprobleme des Buches Ezechiel.* BZAW 72. Berlin: Töpelmann, 1952. **Fretheim, T. E.** *The Suffering of God: An Old Testament Perspective.* OBT 14. Philadelphia: Fortress, 1984. **Friebel, K. G.** "Jeremiah's and Ezekiel's Sign-Acts: Their Meaning and Function as Non-Verbal Communication and Rhetoric." Diss., University of Wisconsin, Madison, 1989. **Garscha, J.** *Studien zum Ezechielbuch: Eine redaktionkritische Untersuchung von Ez 1–39.* Bern: Lang, 1974. **Gese, H.** *Der Verfassungsentwurf des Ezechiel (Kap. 40–48) traditionsgeschichtlich untersucht.* Tübingen: Mohr, 1957. **Graffy, A.** *A Prophet Confronts His People.* AnBib 104. Rome: Pontifical Biblical Institute, 1984. **Haran, M.** "The Law Code of Ezekiel xl–xlviii and Its Relation to the Priestly School." *HUCA* 50 (1979) 45–71. **Herntrich, V.** *Ezechielprobleme.* BZAW 61. Griessen: Töpelmann, 1932. **Herrmann, S.** *Die prophetischen Heilswartungen im Alten Testament.* BWANT 5. Stuttgart: Kohlhammer, 1965. **Hölscher, G.** *Hesekiel: Der Dichter und das Buch: Eine literarkritische Untersuchung.* BZAW 39. Giessen: Töpelmann, 1924. **Hossfeld, F.-L.** *Untersuchungen zu Komposition und Theologie des Ezechielbuches.* FB 20. Würzburg: Echter Verlag, 1977. **Jeremias, J.** *Theophanie: Die Geschichte einer alttestamentliche Gattung.* WMANT 10. Neukirchen-Vluyn: Neukirchener, 1965. **Joyce, P.** *Divine Initiative and Human Response in Ezekiel.* JSOTSup 51. Sheffield: JSOT Press, 1989. **Klein, R. W.** *Ezekiel: The Prophet and His Message.* Columbia, SC: University of South Carolina, 1988. **Krüger, T.** *Geschichtskonzepte im Ezechielbuch.* BZAW 180. Berlin: de Gruyter, 1989. **Kutsch, E.** *Die chronologischen Daten des Ezechielbuches.* OBO 62. Freiburg: Universitätsverlag, 1985. **Lang, B.** *Kein Aufstand in Jerusalem: Die Politik des Propheten Ezechiel.* 2nd ed. SBS 7. Stuttgart: Katholisches Bibelwerk, 1981. ———. *Ezechiel: Der Prophet und das Buch.* ErFor 153. Darmstadt: Wissenschaftliche Buchgesellschaft, 1981. **Levenson, J. D.** *Theology of the Program of Restoration of Ezekiel 40–48.* HSM 10. Missoula, MT: Scholars, 1976. **Liwak, R.** "Uberlieferungeschichtliche Probleme des Ezechielbuches: Eine Studie zu postezechielischen Interpretationen und Komposition." Diss., Bochum, 1976. **Lust, J.,** ed. *Ezekiel and His Book: Textual and Literary Criticism and Their Interrelation.* BETL 74. Leuven: Leuven UP, 1986. **Messel, N.** *Ezechielfragen.* Oslo: Dybwad, 1945. **Miller, J. W.** *Das Verhältnis Jeremias und Hesekiels sprachlich und theologisch untersucht.* Assen: Van Gorcum, 1955. **Mullo Weir, C. J.** "Aspects of the Book of Ezekiel." *VT* 2 (1952) 97–112. **Parker, R. A.,** and **Dubberstein, W. H.** *Babylonian Chronology 626 B.C.–A.D. 75.* Providence: Brown, 1956. **Parunak, H. V. D.** "Structural Studies in Ezekiel." Diss., Harvard, 1978. **Pohlmann, K.-F.** *Ezechielstudien: Zur Redaktionsgeschichte des Buches und zur Frage nach den älttesten Texten.* BZAW 202. Berlin: de Gruyter, 1992. **Rabenau, K. von.** "Die Entstehung des Buches Ezechiel in formgeschichtlicher Sicht." *WZ* (1955/56) 659–94. **Raitt, T. M.** *A Theology of Exile: Judgment/Deliverance in Jeremiah and Ezekiel.* Philadelphia: Fortress, 1977. **Reventlow, H. G.** *Wächter über Israel: Ezechiel und seine Tradition.* BZAW 82. Berlin: Töpelmann, 1962. **Rooker, M. F.** *Biblical Hebrew in Transition: The Language of the*

Book of Ezekiel. JSOTSup 90. Sheffield: JSOT, 1990. **Rowley, H. H.** *The Book of Ezekiel in Modern Study.* Manchester: John Rylands Library, 1953. **Schmidt, M. A.** "Zu Komposition des Buches Hesekiel." *TZ* 6 (1950) 81–98. **Simian, H.** *Die theologische Nachgeschichte der Prophetie Ezechiels: Form- und traditionskritische Untersuchung zu Ez. 6; 35; 36.* FB 14. Würzburg: Echter Verlag, 1974. **Smith, D. L.** *The Religion of the Landless: The Social Context of the Babylonian Exile.* Bloomington, IN: Meyer-Stone, 1989. **Talmon, S.** "The Textual Study of the Bible— A New Outlook." In *Qumran and the History of the Biblical Text,* ed. F. M. Cross and S. Talmon. Cambridge, MA: Harvard UP, 1975. 321–400. **Vogt, E.** *Untersuchungen zum Buch Ezechiel.* AnBib 95. Rome: Pontifical Biblical Institute Press, 1981. **Westermann, C.** *Basic Forms of Prophetic Speech.* Tr. H. C. White. Philadelphia: Westminster, 1967. ————. *Prophetische Heilsworte im Alten Testament.* FRLANT 145. Göttingen: Vandenhoeck & Ruprecht, 1987. **Willmes, B.** *Die sogenannte Hirtenallegorie Ez 34: Studien zum Bild des Hirten im Alten Testament.* BBET 19. Frankfurt: Lang, 1984. **Wilson, R. R.** "An Interpretation of Ezekiel's Dumbness." *VT* 22 (1972) 91–104. **Woudstra, M. H.** "Edom and Israel in Ezekiel." *CTJ* 3 (1968) 21–35. **Zimmerli, W.** "Das Phänomenon der 'Fortschreibung' im Buche Ezechiel." In *Prophecy.* FS G. Fohrer, ed. J. A. Emerton. BZAW 150. Berlin: de Gruyter, 1980.174–91. ————. *I Am Yahweh.* Tr. D. W. Stott, ed. W. Brueggemann. Atlanta: John Knox, 1982.

Introduction

Bibliography

Boadt, L. "Rhetorical Strategies in Ezekiel's Oracles of Judgment." In *Ezekiel and His Book*, ed. J. Lust. 182–200. ————. "The Function of the Salvation Oracles in Ezekiel 33 to 37." *HAR* 12 (1990) 1–21. **Childs, B. S.** *Introduction to the Old Testament as Scripture*. Philadelphia: Fortress, 1979. **Clements, R. E.** "The Ezekiel Tradition: Prophecy in a Time of Crisis." In *Israel's Prophetic Heritage*. FS P. R. Ackroyd, ed. R. Coggins et al. Cambridge: CUP, 1982. 119–36. ————. "The Chronology of Redaction in Ez 1–24." In *Ezekiel and His Book*, ed. J. Lust. 283–94. **Fechter, F.** *Bewältigung der Katastrophe: Untersuchungen zu ausgewählten Fremdvölkersprüche im Ezechielbuch*. BZAW 208. Berlin: de Gruyter, 1992. **Gosse, B.** "Le recueil d'oracles contre les nations d'Ézéchiel." *RB* 93 (1986) 535–62. ————. "Ézéchiel 35–36, 1–15 et Ézéchiel 6: la desolation de la montagne de Séir et le renouveau des montagnes d'Israël." *RB* 96 (1989) 511–17. **Levenson, J. D.** Review of *Ezekiel 2* by W. Zimmerli and *Ezekiel 1–20* by M. Greenberg. *Int* 38 (1984) 210–17. **Nobile, M.** "Beziehung zwischen Ez 32,17–32 und der Gog-Perikope (Ez 38–39) im Lichte der Endredaktion." In *Ezekiel and His Book*, ed. J. Lust. 255–59. **O'Connor, M.** "The Weight of God's Name: Ezekiel in Context and Canon." *TBT* 18 (1980) 28–34. **Scalise, P. D. J.** "From Prophet's Word to Prophetic Book: A Study of Walther Zimmerli's Theory of 'Nachinterpretation.'" Diss., Yale, 1982. **Tuell, S. S.** *The Law of the Temple in Ezekiel 40–48*. HSM 49. Atlanta: Scholars, 1992.

The Nature of the Commentary

This is the second introduction I have written to a commentary on Ezekiel. The first may be found in the volume *Ezekiel 20–48* (WBC 29, Dallas: Word, 1990), which was written before the present volume. This introduction is a continuation of the former one and so does not repeat some of its basic content.

The editors' preface has briefly indicated the format of the series. I have found that it provides invaluable guidelines for working through the material step by step. The main and sectional bibliographies attest the academic fellowship in which I have been privileged to share. My reading has provided a stimulating circle of commentators and researchers. Each member of this scholarly seminar, so to speak, has made a contribution to the commentary. Those to whom I am especially grateful are Cooke for his careful grammatical observations, Cornill for his pioneering text-critical research, Ehrlich for his knack of looking at the text in a different way, Zimmerli for his labors in form and redaction, and Greenberg for his sense of pervasive literary unity. A host of historical-critical commentaries from Ewald onwards have been used, with earlier scholarship rather meagerly represented by Jerome and Calvin. A number of the judgments in more recent commentaries can be traced back to an earlier time, and some care has been given to crediting authors with their particular innovations. Behind such attributions there sometimes lies the chagrin of finding that a personal insight had been anticipated long ago, only to be forgotten by subsequent scholarship.

Behind the translation lies a number of drafts and changes of mind. It reflects the end product of study, incorporating the conclusions argued for in later sections of the commentary. Two principles underlie the translation. First, I have indulged in an old game I used to play with passages from Demosthenes and Cicero in student days, imagining that they wrote in English and that I had to translate their Greek or Latin back to this original. Second, this quest for naturalness necessarily has often been limited by a demand for closer accord to the Hebrew made by the structural and exegetical comments. The fivefold variety of rendering displayed by the REB in 18:21–28 ("renounces," "mend his ways," "turn," "give up," and "turn his back") captures the stylistic variation of the English language, but at a certain cost. It would not suit a translation for a detailed commentary on the Hebrew text.

As for the grammatical and text-critical observations in the *Notes,* the former speak for themselves. As to the latter, written in response to an editorial mandate to interact with the apparatus of *BHS,* I confess my old-fashioned adherence to the classical tradition. Where the ancient witnesses to the text raise discordant voices, it has been deemed necessary to give priority to the perspective that best accords with the context and with which the origin of secondary readings may be best explained. Qumran has proved unrewarding to the student of the text of Ezekiel, not only because of the paucity of extant fragments but also because they only reflect early forms of the MT. The LXX in its earliest form constitutes the most important witness alongside the MT. In the sophisticated task of assessing differences, the critic must not only explain the contextual superiority of the preferred reading but support it by giving a plausible explanation of the origin of the presumed textual error. One must express personal disappointment at the final report of the Committee of the Hebrew Old Testament Project, sponsored by the United Bible Societies (D. Barthélemy, ed., *Critique textuelle de l'Ancien Testament,* vol. 3). Its conclusions read more like the pleas of a defense attorney for the MT than the verdicts of a judge arbitrating among several textual authorities. Tribute must be paid, however, to its comprehensive reviews of scholarly opinion and presentations of the textual evidence.

These textual annotations represent a second attempt at working on chaps. 1–19. The manuscript of the late W. H. Brownlee's commentary that underlay *Ezekiel 1–19* (WBC 28, Waco, TX: Word, 1986), which this volume replaces, lacked specific sets of textual notes until chap. 16, and it fell to me to produce them. While in this volume I have sometimes been able to quote that work, in general the paucity and predictability of the old notes reveal the inadequacy of attempting textual study without the full support of other perspectives of studying the material. Good textual judgments depend on a broad understanding that only other angles can provide.

These other angles are pursued in the section *Form/Structure/Setting.* Form criticism has proved of inestimable value in clarifying the function and mood of the text. Rhetorical criticism, in the Muilenburgian tradition, has exposed the contours and twists and turns of the material and has also clarified the dimensions of the literary unit. Redaction criticism of a moderate kind has identified the stages of literary development that underlie the present form of the text. This commentary endeavors to stand midway between those of Zimmerli and Greenberg.

To speak in generalizations, the former concentrates on the parts and the latter on the whole. Zimmerli can be accused of creating a canon within a canon, with his concern for a primary text and subsequent commentary (cf. Childs, *Introduction* 369–70; Scalise, "From Prophet's Word" 185–89). Yet, if the proper focus of a commentary is on the final form of a redacted text, it is also legitimate and necessary to inquire how it reached that form. The following essay on the growth and structure of the literary tradition seeks to supply answers, putting together the jigsaw pieces presented in the course of the two commentaries on Ezekiel.

The *Comment* section in the commentary is a step-by-step outworking of conclusions reached in the two previous sections. It shows the correlation between the details of the material and makes smaller exegetical decisions along the way. The *Explanation* section sums up the agenda(s) of the literary unit. Actually it is the best place for the less experienced reader to begin. It often draws concentric circles around the particular unit, the rest of Ezekiel, the OT, and even the biblical revelation as a whole. J. D. Levenson, in the course of a review of Zimmerli's and Greenberg's commentaries, asked whether a commentary should include an element of preaching (*Int* 38 [1984] 212). This commentator would answer that, since these are prophetic texts, his task is to uncover the preaching to their own constituency in which the texts are engaging. To this end the NT references often supplied in the *Explanation* are an attempt partly to take Christian readers back to an understanding of the OT passage and partly to make them realize its spiritual affinity to areas of their own religious world.

Overall, the attitude taken in this commentary is that of a friend to Ezekiel and his book, an honest friend but an understanding one. This empathetic attitude is perhaps an obvious one for a moderately conservative seminary professor to whom the book is part of the canonical scriptures. It is also one that has been learned from several years' experience of attempting to teach Judaism from the inside to Christian classes and to speak up for it in response to suspicion and misunderstanding. If the commentator does not speak up on behalf of Ezekiel and the book that bears his name, no one else will bother to do so.

There is an interim quality about every commentary. After a while one can glance through any example of the genre and determine its date without looking at the front. The bibliography stops at a certain point, and the questions posed to the text reflect a certain period. Nonetheless, this has been a good time to write on Ezekiel. Zimmerli and Greenberg have left readers of their respective commentaries wondering, and the time is ripe for a rapprochement between their approaches, rather than, as some might think, setting up entrenched battle lines between literary and historical-critical claims. Moreover, recent years have been productive ones for research into Ezekiel, as the fruit of the 1985 conference at Louvain, *Ezekiel and His Book* (edited by J. Lust), exemplifies. The time has been opportune to catch up with recent academic contributions and to correlate them with older scholarship.

The Growth and Structure of the Literary Tradition

The dates attached to some of Ezekiel's messages indicate a prophetic ministry that lasted twenty-two years from 593 to 571 B.C. (1:2; 29:17). The visions, signs, and oracles associated with this ministry seem to fall into two groups. The first corresponds to the period from 593 to about 586 and was initially intended for a constituency of upperclass Judeans who had been deported by Nebuchadnezzar in 597 and settled in a labor camp in the Babylonian heartland. To this threatened group Ezekiel had to bring the even more threatening news that Jerusalem was to finally fall and that Judah's political existence was to be terminated. A second group of visions, signs, and oracles was evidently delivered to a wider audience, enlarged by Judeans exiled after the fall of the capital. Now Ezekiel had a happier message. As heir of a prophetic tradition of a stark sequence of judgment and salvation in Yahweh's dealings with the covenant people, he was able to envision return to the land by historicizing the tradition. Darkness was to be followed by the dawn of a new and far better day.

This tradition of judgment and salvation is reflected plainly in the book. Chaps. 1–24 are basically given over to oracles of judgment, while chaps. 33–48 are given over to messages of hope. Ezekiel's public oracles are preserved in a distinctly literary form that stands at a distance from the communal setting in which they were given. His prophetic ministry is subsumed under the reported voice of God. Even the exiles' remarks are refracted through a divine oracle.

> There are only two voices in Ezekiel's book, the prophet's and God's. Those who consult and oppose Yahweh and Ezekiel never speak. The words of the latter are doubly framed; Ezekiel quotes Yahweh quoting them in refutation. (O'Connor, *TBT* 18 [1980] 28)

Two of the people's comments about Ezekiel's public prophesying speak of him as "he" (הוא, 12:26; 21:5[20:49]), but any impression of him as a person in his own right is largely hidden behind his testimony to the God whose word he brings. Apart from his objection to carrying out part of a symbolic act in 4:14 and his anguished cries of intercession in 9:8 and 11:13, little humanity is allowed to obtrude into the message given by the Lord whose dutiful servant he is.

Ezekiel had plenty of time to compile his prophetic reports, which incorporated his oracles of judgment in the seven years until 586 and his oracles of salvation in the period more than twice as long, from 586 to 571. There is no reason to dismiss the plain import of the message-reception formula that characteristically prefaces the oracles that inaugurate literary units, "I received a message from Yahweh." Nevertheless, there are indications that Ezekiel's own work has been amplified by other contributions that are claimed as equally partaking of prophetic authority by continued use of Ezekiel's messenger formula, "This is the Lord Yahweh's message," and divine-saying formula, "so runs the oracle of the Lord Yahweh." For this reader, the book contains persistent evidence of literary units that are made up of three layers: a basic oracle, a continuation or updating that stays relatively close to the basic material, and a closing oracle that stands apart from the earlier two pieces. The conclusion to be drawn is that the first two layers are to be ascribed to Ezekiel and the third to heirs of his work who were concerned to preserve it and adapt it to the needs of a succeeding generation (cf. Clements, "The Chronology of Redaction in Ez 1–24" 290, 292).

No long period of time seems to have elapsed in the composition of the book. While Ezekiel ministered in person to the pre-587 prisoners of war and to the first generation of post-587 exiles, the later adaptations that appear in the book seem to have been made among the second generation of exiles. Nothing in the book reflects return to the land as a historical fact. Nor is there any hint that the Persian empire has succeeded the Babylonian. Whereas Second Isaiah placed the fall of Babylon within the historical setting of the rise of Cyrus in the 540s, the book of Ezekiel is remarkably reticent about any such prospect. Only 21:35–37 (30–32) speaks in guarded tones about its future fall, which was actually to occur in 539 and to lead to Cyrus's edict of 538 permitting Judeans to return to the land. There are two features in the book that may indicate the timing of the later process of redaction. If the dating of the final vision "in the twenty-fifth year of our exile" (40:1), along with the use of the number twenty-five and its multiples in the ensuing measurements of the new temple, implicitly refers to a year of jubilee, the fiftieth year (cf. 46:17), one may imagine a striking implication. Was the end of the exile understood by the second-generation heirs of Ezekiel's message to be due to take place in the early 540s (597–547)? A similar extrapolation may be drawn from some other numerical evidence. The exile is put into a forty-year period in the supplementary 4:6, while the same time frame is applied three times to an exile for the Egyptians in the redactional passage 29:11–13. For the Judeans this would spell out the same endpoint (587–547). It is not difficult to infer that these apparent clues to the time of the return would have stimulated keen interest in the book during the 550s, which resulted in the canonical version of the book of Ezekiel.

It is the book, of course, that has canonical authority, and not the prophet himself, although the oral and literary work of the prophet provides its substance. The book shows evidence of much editorial activity, undertaken by Ezekiel and his successors, in terms of both arranging oracles and supplementing them to speak to later concerns of the exiles. The edited book invites its readers to look back at the prophet's ministry and to apply its challenge and assurance to their own hearts and lives. The intended readers or hearers were living in the closing years of the exile, and by faith we modern heirs of this scripture may stand alongside them and overhear what they heard first. This issue of the setting of the book as a whole is important. Zimmerli, while concerned with the whole book, was inclined to stand beside Ezekiel and then look beyond to the redactional sequel to which the book bears witness. This is a natural procedure, especially since the book urges us to look back at Ezekiel's prophesying. Yet its real invitation is to engage in a re-reading of the record from a later standpoint, and it is only as we endeavor to respond to that invitation that we honor the book.

CHAPTERS 1–24

This first major section is substantially made up of three collections of messages of judgment. There is a pattern of compilation that runs through much of the book: a vision followed by an account of interpreted sign acts (1:1–3:15/3:22–5:17; 8:1–11:25/12:1–20; 37:1–14/15–28). In each of the first two cases there is a continuation with oracles of judgment. The emphasis on divine judgment indicates its continuing value for the exiles. One purpose it must have had was to give meaning to the recent abyss into which the Judeans had been plunged by loss of land and nationhood. This literary purpose in recounting the interpretation of the tragedy in terms of judgment finds indirect confirmation in the oracles of 22:23–31 and 36:16–23, retrospective post-587 oracles in which we overhear Ezekiel explaining in God's name the necessity of such punishment for the Judeans. Such a purpose may also be deduced from the injunction to the exiles never to forget their shameful past that led to their judgment (16:54, reinforced in 36:31; 39:26).

Each of the three judgment collections begins with a report of a momentous event that is precisely dated. The date in 1:1, with its enigmatic reference to "the thirtieth year," has been redactionally brought into line with the chronological system used elsewhere in the book, along with details about Ezekiel necessary for second-generation readers (1:2–3a). The report of Ezekiel's seeing a vision of Yahweh as a God of judgment and hearing his commission as a prophet of judgment in 1:1–3:15 is followed by a divine mandate to engage in ominous sign-acts and an interpretation of the final sign, in 3:16a, 22–5:17, and then by a pair of judgment oracles rhetorically addressed to "the mountains of Israel" in chap. 6 and by a series of content-related oracles that announce disaster for Judah and Jerusalem in chap. 7 (cf. Boadt, "Rhetorical Strategies" 188–90). No mention has yet been made of 3:16b–21, which will be discussed later together with similar material.

The second collection begins with a date that verifies the experience of a second vision and also a consultation by the leaders, which marked the community's recognition of Ezekiel as a prophet. To 8:1–10:22; 11:22–25 has been added a report of a separate temple vision in 11:1–13. It serves to confirm the visionary message of accusation and judgment in a temple setting that appears in chap. 9. The two sign-acts of 12:1–20 duly follow, which forecast the defeat and exile of the people of Jerusalem. At an earlier stage in the history of the book, the sequel was probably a series of judgment oracles against Jerusalem, which pounded nail after nail into its coffin. These are the oracles of 14:12–23 and 15:1–8, which have been combined into a single literary unit, and the single oracle of 16:1–43ba.

The third collection has no initial vision but takes its cue from chap. 8 by prefixing a date to a second visit from the leaders, who are given no comforting word but only a message of judgment (20:1–26, 30–31). Two sign-acts are incorporated into a group of oracles that celebrate a "sword" of judgment (21:1–32 [20:45–21:27]). Further oracles follow, two concerning the coming fall of Jerusalem (22:1–16, 17–22), to which a third was added in confirmation (22:23–31), and then the complex of oracles about Jerusalem's fate in chap. 23, which in its final parts has been augmented from chap. 16. The two oracles of chap. 24 forecast the fall of the now besieged capital. Its initial date is not relevant to the basic structuring of the three collections. Its style does not accord with the dates elsewhere in the book, and it was evidently added at a later stage.

It is obvious from the gaps in the foregoing treatment of chaps. 1–24 that there is other material not yet accounted for. This material breaks the previous pattern and has a pattern of its own, a double agenda of assurance and challenge. It seems to have been editorially inserted, whether by Ezekiel himself or by the redactors of the next generation. The first case is 3:16b–21, which either represents a custom-made digest of 33:1–20 or presses into service an existing variant of it. Post-587 readers are shown that the message of radical judgment sounded in the context still has a certain relevance (cf. Scalise, "From Prophet's Word" 238–39). Two alternatives now faced the exiles, life or death, and from Ezekiel and his book came every incentive to choose the life and salvation Yahweh intended for them. With that opportunity came a spiritual and moral challenge. The God who had judged his people was to be the judge of the willful unbelievers and apostates among his people.

The second instance occurs in 11:14–21, which functions as a literary response to Ezekiel's passionate cry deprecating God's wholesale destruction of his people. One of the prophet's oracles of salvation is placed here to assure exilic readers of Yahweh's positive purposes for them in terms of restoration to the homeland and moral and spiritual renewal. It has a sting in its tail, a warning in v 21 that those whose hearts and habits were opposed to God would encounter due retribution.

A further updating in the second collection of Ezekiel's oracles of judgment occurs in 12:21–14:11. This is a complex of oracles, both pre-587 and post-587, that are concerned with prophecy and the issue of who constituted the people of God. The complex probably arose as backing for Ezekiel's stand against sinister religious features rife in the post-fall community. It boosted his stock by appealing to the historical validation of his old oracles of judgment despite the doubts of those who first heard them. In the setting of the book, this complex reminds exilic readers of the potential of a right relationship with the covenant God and the promise of return to the land; it also warns that certain aberrations could lead to forfeiture and urges repentance. The God who had carried out the radical judgment earlier prophesied by Ezekiel was not to be trifled with. He would carry out any necessary judgment among his people, a relative judgment to be sure, but one to be taken seriously.

The latter part of chap. 16 continues in a similar vein. The oracle in vv 43bβ–58 is Ezekiel's updating of the pre-587 message of judgment. That message had come true, but the post-587 exiles dare not shrug off its recriminations. In a short list of urban centers of vice, Jerusalem trailed miserably behind Sodom and Samaria. The exiles are called to repent of so deplorable a history and, when they returned to the land, to take back with them a spirit of deep regret. The second-generation supplement in vv 59–63 supports Ezekiel's sardonic challenge with an exhortation written from a straightforward and theological perspective. It gives a reminder of the grace of God that was to be manifested in the coming act of salvation and uses it as an extra lever to stimulate repentance over past sins. A strong sense of divine mercy and of human undeservedness must mark future life in the homeland.

The complex of oracles in 17:1–19:14 strikes the same notes of assurance and challenge, while reinforcing the lesson of national judgment. In chaps. 17 and 19, four oracles of judgment have the downfall of the Davidic dynasty as their theme. At their heart is set a second-generation promise of royal restoration that elevates the language of the negative oracles to a glorious reversal and takes its spiritual cue from Ezekiel's oracle concerning the reestablishment of a united kingdom under a restored monarchy (37:15–24a). Such good news had moral implications. Chap. 18, a post-587 call to repentance that Ezekiel had issued to the first generation of exiles, is deliberately inserted into the complex, immediately after the oracle of salvation. It shows that the prospect of salvation must exert a moral magnetic force on its would-be heirs, which they resisted at their peril. Eschatological life and renewal were God's gifts to the repentant.

In the third collection of judgment oracles, one does not have to wait long for the mingled notes of assurance and challenge to be sounded again. The pre-587 oracle of 20:1–26, 30–31 sets before the deportees God's ancient forecast of national exile (v 23). Its terms "nations" and "countries" are echoed in v 32: by now the exile was a reality. Vv 32–44 give the assurance of a second exodus to the promised land and a glorious, God-honoring occupation. Yet there was a somber factor to reckon with. The divine judgment against Dathan and Abiram in the wilderness long ago would find a typological parallel in a partial judgment for the exiles. "Rebels" among them would be barred from entering the land (vv 36–38). Moreover, the exiles who did return must never forget how little they deserved the lavish grace of God, in the light of their own former, now forgiven, sins (vv 43–44).

Later in the collection a simple note of assurance is struck. The oracle against the Ammonites in 21:33–34(28–29) reflects not a pre-587 situation but their taunts against the Judeans when Jerusalem fell (cf. 25:3). It assures of vindication and justice. Moreover, the chronologically later element in vv 35–37(30–32) dares to predict doom, in a loud whisper, for Babylon. At the end of chap. 24, there appears a contextually appropriate hint of better times to come. After the imminent downfall of Jerusalem, Ezekiel would no longer function as a sign of divine judgment (v 24) but as a sign of grace (v 27).

CHAPTERS 25–32

The book of Ezekiel falls into line with the other major prophetic books in devoting a substantial section to a series of oracles against foreign nations. The series falls into two nearly equal halves, chaps. 25–28 and 29–32. The first half pays little attention to dating: only one date occurs, in 26:1. The role of this half is to give assurance to the exiles. The hint at the end of chap. 24 that the tide of suffering would turn with the fall of Jerusalem is developed. Chap. 25 basically consists of two pairs of short post-587 oracles directed against Ammon and Moab, Edom and Philistia. The first is amplified by a further anti-Ammon message in vv 6–7. The emphasis on Ammon recalls the message of assurance in 21:33–34(28–29). In both places Ammon seems to function as a representative symbol of local hostility to Judah. All the oracles in chap. 25 level against their ethnic objects accusations of unjust animosity. The first oracle supplies a sympathetic summary of the tragedy of 587: profanation of the temple, desolation of the land, and exile for the people (25:3). The first consequence functions as an echo of 24:21, where Yahweh declared: "I will profane my sanctuary." In the new context of salvation, the mockery of the nations over Judah's judgment was a reprehensible act.

The same note of sympathetic assurance is struck in the first oracle against Tyre, in 26:2. If the date is correctly transmitted and understood, already during the siege of Jerusalem Tyre was hoping to make political capital out of Jerusalem's downfall (cf. Gosse, *RB* 93 [1986] 554–55). This reason for its judgment is evidently determinative for the collection of oracles against Tyre or its king in

26:1–28:19. In chap. 26 the oracle of vv 4–6 finds an interpretive restatement in vv 7–14. Two later oracles forecasting its eventual fall to Babylon follow in vv 15–18 and 19–21. They must antedate the end of the thirteen-year siege of Tyre in 573. The same can be said of the satirical lament over the ship of Tyre in 27:1–11, 25b–36. It has been skillfully amplified in vv 12–25a with a list of Tyre's trading products and partners, which was adapted into a cargo list for the doomed ship. The oracles in 28:1–10, 11–19 are directed against the king of Tyre. Ezekiel's intent in uttering the anti-Tyre oracles, apart from the first, was probably to quash the last vestiges of optimism among his fellow exiles and to show that resistance to Nebuchadnezzar ran counter to Yahweh's will. Editorially, however, they appear to function as implicit oracles of salvation, taking their cue from 26:2.

The last oracle is addressed to Sidon, in 28:21–23. The supplement in v 24 intends to give the gist of 25:1–28:23 (cf. Fechter, *Bewältigung* 265–69). The description of all Israel's neighbors as showing contempt (שׁאט) deliberately recalls the use of the noun in 25:6, 15, as a frame for these chapters. The exiles are promised that Yahweh would put an end to the harassment of their ethnic neighbors.

What follows in 28:25–26 is the first of three editorial summaries that appear in the book. The context of the punishment of the nations is related to general positive themes to which Ezekiel's teaching pointed: the international vindication of Yahweh in restoring Israel to the land promised to Jacob and the prospect of living secure and productive lives. This was the substance of the God-given hope to which the exiles should cling.

The second half of the collection of foreign oracles in 29:1–32:16 has a different message. Boadt's characterization of chaps. 25–32 as "indirect words of hope" (*HAR* 12 [1990] 5) belongs properly to the first half. The target of all the oracles in this second group is Egypt, to which Judah had appealed for help against the Babylonian attack (cf. 17:15; Jer 37:5, 11). A host of dates are supplied, for each of the basic oracles except 30:1–9. Looking back, one can see the earlier dates in the book marching slowly and inexorably toward the siege of Jerusalem. From this perspective, the redactional date of the beginning of the siege in 24:1 is apposite, and so is the date of 26:1. In the present group of oracles, the dates cluster around the period of the siege, like vultures circling over a dying beast. The last two, in 32:1, 17, fall just beyond the time when news of the fall of the capital reached Ezekiel in exile (cf. 33:21). The date in 29:17 follows the different agenda of its associated oracle.

The basic oracles call into question the hope of the exiles that judgment could be averted by Egyptian help. Thus 29:2–6a, associated with the date 7 January 587, forecasts defeat for the pharaoh Hophra, the chaos monster of the Nile. Vv 6–9a seem to reflect the situation a little later, when he proved unable to sustain his military attack. The redactional supplement in vv 9b–16 continues a message of Egypt's fate of desolation but tones it down somewhat to an exile of forty years (cf. 30:23, 26) and restoration to national mediocrity. This fruit of theological reflection appears to set the fate of Egypt within a wider framework of revelation. In 29:17–21 an oracle dated in 571 and associated with the ending of the prolonged siege of Tyre serves as a confirmation that Egypt would eventually fall. The undated 30:1–9 probably belongs to the same time as 29:1–6a; the oracle speaks of the downfall of Egypt in terms of the day of Yahweh. A later oracle appears in

30:10–12, in which Nebuchadnezzar's conquest of Egypt is promised. Vv 13–19 are about the destruction of Egypt's cities, a literary continuation that echoes the two previous passages.

30:20–26 reflects news of the Babylonian repulse of the Egyptian attack on the besiegers and promises further misfortune for Egypt at Nebuchadnezzar's hands, even exile. The oracle in 31:1–18 about the pharaoh in the role of a cosmic tree that is cut to the ground is dated two months later. It attacks the exiles' continuing obsession that he would resume the attack and drive the Babylonian troops away from the capital. V 18 may function as a literary summary of the chapter. The last two dated oracles are set after the news of the fall of Jerusalem had reached the exiles. They were probably meant to stamp out glowing embers of an optimistic hope that Egypt would not tolerate Babylonian control of Judah. 32:1–16 returns to the motif of the chaos monster, while vv 17–28 compare Egypt with other national has-beens. In a redactional epilogue, vv 29–32, other states are included in Egypt's fate. The reference to "the commanders of the north" in v 30 appears to encompass the Gog war of chaps. 38–39 (Nobile, "Gog-Perikope" 256–57). We seem to be returning to the note of assurance sounded in the first half of the collection of foreign oracles. Predominantly, however, the original tone of accentuating Judah's judgment is maintained. It may be summed up in words from 29:16: "Never again will the community of Israel have [in Egypt] an object of trust to which they turn."

A topic that increasingly confronts the reader of the collection is the grim description of Tyre's and Egypt's dooms in terms of Sheol (26:19–21; 28:8; 31:14, 15–18; 32:18–32). It functions as negative backing to the positive message of life for Israel in the succeeding chapters.

CHAPTERS 33–48

The fall of Jerusalem changed the nature of Ezekiel's prophesying from national judgment to salvation. After the darkness of the old age of radical sin and punishment, a new age was to dawn. The oracles of salvation that celebrate its imminent coming are presented in chaps. 33–48.

First place is given to a combination of assurance and warning, which continues the tone of the series of insertions in chaps. 1–24. In terms of the literary history of the book, these insertions constitute a backward projection that takes its cue from chaps. 33–34. Chap. 33 enshrines at its heart, in vv 21–22, the date when news of Jerusalem's fall reached the prophet. As 24:27 had predicted, it marks the end of the sinister silence of dumbness imposed on the prophet in 3:26–27. It is followed by an oracle of indirect hope for the exiles in vv 23–29, assuring them that they had not forfeited their inheritance of the land. This assurance is qualified by a message of relative judgment for the jubilant exiles in vv 30–33. The continuity and contrast between the two periods of Ezekiel's prophetic ministry are well expressed by the echo of 2:5 in 33:33. At the outset of the book, the fulfillment of radical judgment of God's people was to prove Ezekiel's role as a true prophet to the Judeans deported in 597. By this means they would "know that there has been a prophet among them." Now a new criterion is offered, execution of the relative judgment that would befall irresponsible members of the exiled people. The same qualified assurance occurs in 33:1–20. It is dominated by the motif of life, in vv 10–16. Even as it offers God's gracious gift of life in vv 10–11, it challenges to moral responsibility in vv 12–20. These messages serve as examples of Ezekiel's description as a watchman to warn and preserve the people (vv 1–9).

The same combination of assurance and challenge appears in 34:1–22, in the course of a collection of messages that uses the metaphor of sheep. The oracle in 34:1–16 counterposes the phases of national judgment and salvation. The Judean kings had been bad shepherds who had lost God's sheep. Yahweh was to be the good shepherd who would rescue the exilic strays. Vv 17–22, on the other hand, describe strife among the contemporary flock of exiles and promise divine intervention to effect discriminating judgment on the oppressors and salvation for their victims.

The rest of the chapter consists of successive redactional supplements that develop the sheep imagery. Vv 23–24 theologically round off the earlier messages with a reminiscence of the sign of the scepter in 37:1–24a and its editorial continuation in 37:24b–25. Yahweh would appoint a royal undershepherd for the sheep, who would do good work, unlike the preexilic monarchy. The second supplement in vv 25–30 depicts the land as green pastures, secure and fertile for the returning people. It majors in an eschatological claim of the blessings of Lev 26:1–13. The claim represents a literary reversal. In chaps. 4–6 Ezekiel had appealed to the curses of Lev 26 and claimed that they would be implemented in the coming national judgment. Now there is a corresponding concern to lay claim to the covenant blessings as ingredients of the era of salvation. The final supplement, in v 31, provides a literary conclusion for the unit, rather like 31:18; it defines the covenant relationship in terms of God's flock.

The gift of the land remains the focus of attention in 35:1–36:15. Reversal of past judgment in future salvation marks the complex of two oracles in 35:1–36:8. Underlying both is Ezekiel's oracle against the mountains of Israel in chap. 6. Features from that judgment oracle reappear at the beginning of each of these messages (see Allen, *Ezekiel 20–48* 171–72; Gosse, *RB* 96 [1989] 511–17). Judgment was to veer toward Judah's enemy Edom (35:1–14). This first message is an oracle against a foreign nation that finds a place here as a foil for the restoration of God's people. It is later in origin than the oracle against Edom in 25:12–14: it reflects Edomite incursion into Judean territory. Yahweh reassuringly claims back the land for his people to enjoy (36:1–8). The echo of the blessings of Lev 26:9 in 36:9–11 aligns the passage with the redactional material of 34:25–30. V 12 serves to introduce vv 13–15, in which the curse pronounced on the land in Num 13:36 is lifted.

36:16–23 counterpoints previous judgment of Israel's sins with the prospect of salvation, this time in the direct fashion of 34:1–16. Return from exile is given a theological grounding in the restoration of honor to Yahweh's name, which had been tragically desecrated by his people's exile. Vv 24–31 are a redactional development, a theological meditation on the implications of vv 16–23 that gathers together a number of Ezekiel's themes from elsewhere. It was the necessity of Yahweh's self-vindication that undergirded the promise of restoration—not any merit in Israel. The sins that caused the predicament of exile must arouse a sense of shame and repentance both now and back in the land (cf. 16:52, 58; 20:43–44). Yahweh would give his people a fresh moral start (cf. 37:23). He would create in them a new spirit of obedience (cf. 11:19–20). So the land, earlier defiled by sin according to vv 17–18, would blossom again, and the people, duly cleansed, would be able to live in it again. The land is the renewed focus of the two pieces in vv 33–36 and 37–38, which promise repopulation and fertility for the now ruined land.

The themes of the restored people's sharing in God's spirit and their consequent obedience, promised in v 27, prompted further elaboration. Ezekiel's vision of revived bones and his interpretive oracle of salvation in 37:1–13 are used to elucidate the role of God's spirit, as the repetition of 36:27a in 37:14 shows. Then the obedience of 36:27b, which reappears in 37:24b, has light shed on it by Ezekiel's sign and oracle of 37:15–24a. The passage functions as another literary flashback. It is used to show that a means of establishing authority and order would be provided by the restoration of a united kingdom under its messianic king.

The redactor, after using two of Ezekiel's messages, provides in vv 25–28 a summary of the major themes of the preceding four chapters (cf. Boadt, *HAR* 12 [1990] 15–16). It resumes and advances the positive summary of 28:25–26. It also exhibits a feature we have seen before, echoes of the blessings of Lev 26:4–13. This intertextuality permits a reference to the new temple in vv 26–27, taken from Lev 26:11. The themes of temple, covenant people, king, and land are clearly intended as a heading for chaps. 40–48, which will be used to elaborate them.

Readers have to wait a while, since chaps. 38–39 now intervene. The theme of the account of Gog's invasion and defeat is secure habitation in the promised land. It functions as an extended echo of that motif in 34:25–28, where it is derived from Lev 26:5; it appears in the account at 38:8, 11, 14 and also in 39:26. There would have been good reason to have inserted it at the end of chap. 34. Presumably a sense of the continuity of the established chaps. 34–37 (cf. Boadt, *HAR* 12 [1990] 15–16) prevented such a placement. Instead, it is put after the series of salvation oracles, a second-best position following mention of peaceful habitation in the land at 37:25–26. The promise of secure habitation is put to the test by envisioning a worst-case scenario. If the new Israel was to be safe from its local neighbors (28:26), how about the possibility of another great foreign invasion? Such worries on the exiles' minds are allayed. The Gog account checks the security system and finds it more than adequate.

If the Gog account has been redactionally set in its present position, there is little reason to deny Ezekiel's voice and hand in much of it. It has certainly been reworked. Its three basic parts of 38:1–9; 39:1–5 and 17–20 were first elaborated with a series of parallel treatments at 38:10–16; 39:6–7, 9–10, and 21–22, and further amplified by 38:18–23; 39:11–16. At least the first set of accretions probably goes back to the prophet's own editing. At three points the text stands at a considerable distance from its context: in 38:17, where Gog's invasion is claimed as the fulfillment of older, historically based prophecies; in 39:8, where Gog's defeat is viewed as a similar fulfillment; and in the epilogue of 39:23–29. The redactional epilogue is reminiscent of 28:25–26. Both passages deliberately turn from a subsidiary issue to summarize mainstream concerns. This one rehearses

Yahweh's past judgment of Israel for its sins, which merited exile and must stay fresh in the people's memories. It reaffirms the promise of return to the homeland and recapitulates Israel's prospect of secure habitation. Moreover, it celebrates the coming vindication of Yahweh in the world and his perpetual commitment to his people. If a busy person wanted a reliable digest of the book of Ezekiel, one could not do better than commend the three nutshells of 28:25–26; 37:25–28; and 39:23–29. The only major theme not explicitly mentioned is that of the relative judgment that would discriminate between members of the exilic community. However, the moral responsibility it was meant to instill is included in the conviction that the sins that led to the exile should be taken seriously even after return to the land.

The visions that begin in chap. 40 exhibit a feature that occurred in the salvation oracles, the reversal of a particular judgment in a manifestation of salvation. They function as a reversal of the vision of the old temple and its consequent destruction and Yahweh's abandonment described in chaps. 8–11. As in 8:1, a date is supplied in 40:1, and the fall of Jerusalem is explicitly recalled. Motifs from 8:1–3 are resumed in 40:1–3, and from 8:3–4 in 43:2–5. Chaps. 40–48 fall into three parts. The first, 40:1–42:20, is a visionary tour of the area of the new temple that Yahweh would create for his people ("I will put my sanctuary in their midst," 37:26). Its description has been amplified at an early stage by 40:38–46a, a supplement about rooms adjacent to some of the gatehouses described in vv 6–37, and by 42:1–14, a further supplement about two sets of rooms in the western area described in the course of 41:5–15a. There is another, misplaced, supplement in 41:15b–26 that carefully describes the woodwork of the temple. One expects it to appear after 40:47–41:4, and its misplacement may reflect its comparative lateness.

The account of the visionary tour continues in 43:1–46:24, now associated with extensive divine commands. The divine glory that left the old temple in chaps. 10–11 returns and fills the new temple. Ezekiel is commanded to transmit to the exiles the transcendent holiness of this temple not made with hands, with which the old one is adversely compared, in order to stimulate among them a shaming sense of the distance that lies between Yahweh and their sinful selves. The prophet is ordered to pass on the ensuing regulations for the organization of the temple. The description of the design of the altar in 43:13–17, which paves the way for regulations for its dedication in vv 18–27, may be editorial. Ezekiel is portrayed as cultic founder in 43:18–22 and also later in 45:18–20a; 46:13–14, a not incongruous role for the prophet of priestly lineage. Two short visionary narratives and related commands feature in 44:1–5; v 5 serves as a heading for 44:6–46:18 (or 24).

The regulations that follow fall into three sections, relating to (1) the two-tiered system of priests and Levites in 44:6–16 and the holy lifestyle of the priests in 44:17–31, (2) the economic maintenance of personnel and sacrifices in 45:1–17, and (3) the cultic procedures of rites and offerings in 45:18–46:15. The prime place is given to the issue of temple personnel, to whom degrees of holiness manifest in the description of the temple are applied. The result is the tiers of Zadokite priests and of Levites. This crucial differentiation brings to a climax a literary process of gradual development. 40:45–46a merely mentioned two types of priests, those with altar duties and those with duties in the temple area. Then in 46:19–

20, 24 "priests" are differentiated from "those who serve in the temple area," while in 42:13–14 there is a one-sided mention of "the priests who have access to Yahweh" or "the priests." In 45:4–5 the lower group has assigned to it the title "Levites," in contrast with "the priests who serve in the sanctuary and have access to serve Yahweh." Finally, in the vehement oracle of 44:6–18, the latter are called Zadokite priests, a development that was duly incorporated into 40:46b; 43:19; and 48:11. A key factor behind the assignation of the high priestly family to this role may have been that priests of such exalted rank could best reflect the holiness of God and his temple. This last stage must antedate the restoration of full worship in the rebuilt postexilic temple in 516, where the priests were simply "the sons of Aaron" (Clements, "The Ezekiel Tradition" 130–31). Did Ezekiel advocate only the first stage of 40:45–46a or himself begin to apply gradations in the holiness of the temple to its personnel? The stage of 42:13–14 and 46:19–20, 24 probably reflects Ezekiel's later work, since they are set in contexts that otherwise seem to be so characterized. The redactional full-blown system is evident in 44:6–16 and is made the controlling prescription both here and in other passages that it infiltrated. The outworking of holiness in the lives of the priests described in 44:17–27, 31 may have had a wider application at an earlier stage of the text.

A noticeable feature of the subunit 43:1–46:24 is a particular stratum concerning the נשיא "head of state" that appears in 44:3; 45:21–25; 46:1–12, to which may have been attracted less specific material in 46:10–18 and 45:16–17 and also in 45:8, 9 (see Allen, *Ezekiel 20–48* 253). This type of material is represented among a number of sections that have their own agendas. Ezekiel's use of מלך "king" for Israel's future ruler in 37:24 and the redactional translation to נשיא "head of state" in 37:25b suggests a late origin for it (cf. 34:24). However, it may be significant that the prophet appears to have described preexilic monarchs as both מלכים "kings" (43:7–9) and נשיאים "heads of state" (e.g., 22:6).

The role of 44:28–30 appears to be to anticipate the next section concerning economic maintenance of the cult; it may have been a continuation of 44:6–16, with which it has some similarity. 45:1–8 has been drawn from 48:8–22, which it summarizes. It defines the land holdings of the two grades of temple personnel and of the head of state. The injunction about correct weights and measures in 45:10–12 governs the contributions of vv 13–17, more specifically those of vv 13–14. The last section, 45:18–46:15, contains regulations about the rites and offerings of the temple. Like the previous section, it begins with Ezekiel's role as founder of the new cult in 45:18–20a, which the related 46:13–14(15) may have continued at an earlier stage. In 45:21–25; 46:1–12 the cultic role of the head of state comes to the fore. The material about his use of land in 46:16–18 seems to build a bridge to the issue of apportionment of the land described in chaps. 47–48. The visionary journey that closes the subunit in 46:19–24 has close links with 42:1–14 and so may be assigned to a second stage of Ezekiel's work.

The material devoted to the reoccupation of the land in chaps. 47–48 opens in 47:1–12 with a visionary scene and tour that are more exotic than the previous ones. A careful description of the land's frontiers in 47:13–23 leads into an account of its allocation in 48:1–29 that depends upon the former passage. The issue of temple personnel reemerges within it. A reflection of the third logical stage in the literary development we noticed earlier has been updated to the fourth within v 11. A later supplement that presupposes 48:1–29 appears in the closing vv 30–35. Developing v 16, it honors the new Jerusalem. It provides both a positive reversal of the old city that Yahweh had justly abandoned to its fate and continuity with the restored capital that featured in 16:53, 55, 61.

This attempt to steer a course through the complex material of the book is necessarily tentative. The prophetic book seems to bear witness to a process of literary arrangement and amplification that the prophet himself initiated. Not all the evidence in the text has been set out in this survey. In chap. 10, for instance, Ezekiel's reflections about the cherubim appear to give way to later reflections in vv 9b–12, 16–17, and 22aγb. The intent of the completed book was to prepare the exiles to receive God's gift of new life in the land. The theological summaries of the book in 28:5–6; 37:25–28; and 39:23–29 show an awareness of the complexity of the book and a need to help readers grasp the essential themes. On the verge of the promised land, Ezekiel's messages were re-read as sources of coherence for Israel's bewildering history and as humbling insights into the people's evil potential and into God's sheer grace in taking them back to fellowship with himself. Nor had Yahweh's role as judge ended in 587 B.C. The prospect of a discriminating judgment is repeatedly woven into happier promises and set alongside accomplished threats of past judgment. Beyond such warnings, there is a concern to contrast the national judgment that lay in the past with the prospect of national salvation, as the many cases of deliberate reversal indicate, both within literary units and in the course of the book. The redactors developed the prophet's salvation oracles. They followed his lead in grounding judgment in the covenant curses of Lev 26 by claiming fulfillment of its blessings in the coming age of salvation. They had an eye for theological reflection on themes broached in Ezekiel's oracles of salvation. On a religious plane, they felt impelled to take a definitive stand on the issue of the priesthood of the new temple, in application of the principle of divine holiness. Other priestly interests are manifest in the details of the temple woodwork in 41:15b–26 and of the cleansing of the land in 39:11–16.

Ezekiel's redactors may justly be called disciples. The relatively short time that seems to have elapsed between Ezekiel's own prophetic ministry with tongue and pen and the completed book indicates that they knew him intimately and empathized with his aims. They too probably came from priestly families, and they claimed the same prophetic authority as their master. With literary skill they updated the book for the next generation, keeping alive the prophet's ministry to the people of God.

Ezekiel's Visionary Call   (1:1–3:15)

Bibliography

Adams, R. M. *Heartlands of Cities: Surveys of Ancient Settlement and Land Use on the Central Floodplain of the Euphrates.* Chicago: Chicago UP, 1981. **Albright, W. F.** "The Seal of Eliakim and the Latest Preëxilic History of Judah, with Some Observations on Ezekiel." *JBL* 51 (1932) 77–106. **Allen, L. C.** "The Structure and Intention of Ezekiel 1." *VT* 43 (1993) 145–61. **Auvray, P.** "Ézéchiel i–iii: Essai d'analyse littéraire." *RB* 67 (1960) 481–502. **Barr, J.** "Theophany and Anthropomorphism in the Old Testament." In *Congress Volume, Oxford 1959.* VTSup 7. Leiden: Brill, 1960. 31–38. **Barrick, W. B.** "The Straight-Legged Cherubim of Ezekiel's Inaugural Vision (Ezekiel 1:7a)." *CBQ* 44 (1982) 543–50. **Block, D. I.** "Text and Emotion: A Study in the 'Corruptions' in Ezekiel's Inaugural Vision (Ezekiel 1:4–28)." *CBQ* 50 (1988) 418–42. **Bodi, D.** *The Book of Ezekiel and the Poem of Erra.* OBO 104. Freiburg: Universitätsverlag; Göttingen: Vandenhoeck & Ruprecht, 1991. 82–94. **Budde, K.** "The Opening Verses of the Book of Ezekiel." *ExpTim* 12 (1900) 39–43. ———. "Zum Eingang des Buches Ezechiel." *JBL* 50 (1931) 20–41. **Driver, G. R.** "Ezekiel ii.6: 'Sitting upon Scorpions.'" *JTS* 35 (1934) 54–55. ———. "Ezekiel's Inaugural Vision." *VT* 1 (1951) 60–62. **Ephal, I.** "The Western Minorities in Babylonia in the 6th–5th Centuries B.C.: Maintenance and Cohesion." *Or* 47 (1978) 74–88. **Fretheim, T. E.** *The Suffering of God: An Old Testament Perspective.* OBT 14. Philadelphia: Fortress, 1984. 79–106. **Garfinkel, S.** "Of Thistles and Thorns: A New Approach to Ezekiel ii.6." *VT* 37 (1987) 421–37. **Grave, C.** "The Etymology of Northwest Semitic *sapānu.*" *UF* 12 (1980) 221–29. **Greenberg, M.** "The Use of the Ancient Versions for Understanding the Hebrew Text: A Sampling from Ezek. ii.1–iii.11." In *Congress Volume, Göttingen 1977.* VTSup 29. Leiden: Brill, 1978. 131–48. ———. "Ezekiel's Vision: Literary and Iconographic Aspects." In *History, Historiography and Interpretation: Studies in Biblical and Cuneiform Literatures,* ed. H. Tadmor and M. Weinfeld. Jerusalem: Magnes, 1983. 159–68. **Gruenwald, I.** *Apocalyptic and Merkabah Mysticism.* Leiden: Brill, 1980. **Habel, N.** "The Form and Significance of the Call Narratives." *ZAW* 77 (1965) 297–323. **Halperin, D. J.** "Merkabah Midrash in the Septuagint." *JBL* 101 (1982) 351–63. ———. *The Faces of the Chariot: Early Jewish Responses to Ezekiel's Vision.* Texte und Studien zum Antiken Judentum 16. Tübingen: Mohr (Siebeck), 1988. **Höhne E.** "Die Thronwagenvision Hesekiels: Echtheit und Herkunft der Vision Hes. 1,4–28 und ihrer einzelnen Züge." Diss., Erlangen, 1953. **Houk, C. B.** "A Statistical Linguistic Study of Ezekiel 1, 4–3,11." *ZAW* 93 (1981) 76–85. **Keel, O.** *Jahwe-Visionen und Siegelkunst: Eine neue Deutung der Majestätsschilderungen in Jes 6, Ez 1 und 10 und Sach 4.* SBS 84/85. Stuttgart: Katholisches Bibelwerk, 1977. 125–273. **Kutsch, E.** *Die chronologischen Daten des Ezechielbuches.* OBO 62. Freiburg: Universitätsverlag; Göttingen: Vandenhoeck & Ruprecht, 1985. **Landsberger, B.** "Akkadisch-Hebräische Wortgleichungen." In *Hebräische Wortforschung.* VTSup 16. Leiden: Brill, 1967. 170–204. **Lang, B.** "Die erste und die letzte Vision des Propheten: Eine Überlegung zu Ezechiel 1–3." *Bib* 64 (1983) 225–30. **Lentzen-Deis, F.** "Das Motiv der Himmelsöffnung in verschiedenen Gattungen der Umweltliteratur des Neuen Testaments." *Bib* 50 (1969) 301–27. **Lind, W. A.** "A Text-Critical Note to Ezekiel 1: Are Shorter Readings Really Preferable to Longer?" *JETS* 27 (1984) 135–39. **Long, B. O.** "Prophetic Call Traditions and Reports of Visions." *ZAW* 84 (1972) 494–500. ———. "Reports of Visions among the Prophets." *JBL* 95 (1976) 353–65. ———. "Prophetic Authority as Social Reality." In *Canon and Authority: Essays in Old Testament Religion and Theology,* ed. G. W. Coats and B. O. Long. Philadelphia: Fortress, 1977. 3–20. **Low, A. A. K.** "Interpretive Problems in Ezekiel 1." Diss., Dallas Theological Seminary, 1985. **Marquis, G.** "Word Order as a Criterion for the Evolution of Translation Technique in the LXX and the Evaluation of Word-Order Variants as Exemplified in LXX-Ezekiel." *Textus* 13 (1986) 59–84. **Mettinger, T. N. D.** *The Dethronement of Sabaoth: Studies in the Shem and Kabod Theologies.* ConBOT 18. Lund: Gleerup, 1982. **Newsom, C.** *Songs of the Sabbath Sacrifice: A Critical Edition.* HSS 27. Atlanta: Scholars, 1985. **Nobile, M.** "'Nell' anno trentisimo. . . ' (Ez 1,1)." *Anton* 59 (1984) 393-402. **Ohler, A.** "Die Gegenwart Gottes in der Gottesferne: Die Berufungsvision des Ezechiel." *BibLeb* 11 (1970) 79–89, 159–68. **Olmo Lete, G. del.** *La vocación del líder en el antiguo Israel: Morfología de los relatos bíblicos de vocación.* Bibliotheca Salamanticensis 3:2. Salamanca: Universidad Pontifica, 1973. 289–319, 369–406. **Oppenheim, A. L.** "Assyrian-Babylonian Religion." In *Forgotten Religions,* ed. V. Ferm. New York: Philosophical Library, 1950. 63–79. **Parrot, A.** *Nineveh and Babylon.* London: Thames and Hudson, 1961. **Parunak, H. V.** "The Literary Architecture of Ezekiel's *Marʾot ʾElohim.*" *JBL* 99 (1980) 61–74. **Procksch, O.** "Die Berufungsvision Hesekiels." In *Karl Budde zum siebzigsten Geburtstag.* BZAW 34. Giessen: Töpelmann, 1920. 141–49. **Quiring, H.** "Die Edelsteine im Amtsschild des jüdischen Hohenpriesters und die Herkunft ihrer Namen." *Sudhofs Archiv für Geschichte der Medizin und die Naturwissenschaften* 38 (1954) 193–213. **Roberts, J. J. M.** "The Hand of Yahweh." *VT* 21 (1971) 244–51. ————. "*Ṣāphôn* in Job 26,7." *Bib* 56 (1975) 554–57. **Savignac, J. de** "Note sur le sens du terme SÂPHÔN dans quelques passages de la Bible." *VT* 3 (1953) 95–96. **Scholem, G.** *Major Trends in Jewish Mysticism.* London: Thames and Hudson, 1955. **Sprank, S.,** and **Wiese, K.** *Studien zu Ezechiel und dem Buch der Richter.* BWANT 3:4. Stuttgart: Kohlhammer, 1926. 26–73. **Taylor, S. G.** "A Reconsideration of the 'Thirtieth Year' in Ez. 1.1." *TynBul* 17 (1966) 119–20. **Tucker, G. M.** "Prophetic Superscriptions and the Growth of the Canon." In *Canon and Authority,* ed. G. M. Coats and B. O. Long. Philadelphia: Fortress, 1977. 56–70. **Vogt, E.** "*Sāfôn* = caelum nubibus obductum." *Bib* 34 (1953) 426. ————. "Der Nehar Kebar: Ez 1." *Bib* 39 (1958) 211–16. **Waldman, N. M.** "A Note on Ezekiel 1:18." *JBL* 103 (1984) 614–18. **Weinfeld, M.** "כבוד kabod." *TWAT* 4:23–40. **Westermann. C.** "כבד kbd schwer sein." *THAT* 1:794–812. **Wiseman, D. J.** "Books in the Ancient Near East and in the Old Testament." In *Cambridge Ancient History of the Bible,* ed. P. R. Ackroyd and C. F. Evans. Cambridge: CUP, 1970. 1:30–48. **Wilson, R. R.** "Prophecy and Ecstasy: A Reexamination." *JBL* 98 (1979) 321–37. ————. "Prophecy in Crisis: The Call of Ezekiel." *Int* 38 (1984) 117–30. **York, A. D.** "Ezekiel 1: Inaugural and Restoration Visions?" *VT* 27 (1977) 82–98. **Zadok, R.** "The Nippur Region during the Late Assyrian, Chaldaean and Achaemenian Periods, Chiefly according to Written Sources." *Israel Oriental Studies* 8 (1978) 266–332.

Translation

[1]*In the thirtieth year, in the fourth month, on the fifth of the month, while I was living among the exiles by the Kebar Canal,*[a] *the skies opened,*[b] *and I saw a divine vision.*[c] [2]*"On the fifth of the month" refers to*[a] *the fifth year of King Jehoiachin's period of deportation.* [3]*The priest*[a] *Ezekiel son of Buzi received*[b] *a communication from Yahweh by the Kebar Canal in Chaldea.*

I[c] *felt Yahweh's hand on me there,*[d] [4]*and I saw something to which my attention was drawn. It was a storm wind coming from the north. It consisted of a huge cloud*[a] *and a blazing*[b] *fire; radiance surrounded the cloud.*[c] *Out of it—out of the fire*[d]*—appeared something that gleamed like*[e] *amber.*[f]

[5]*Out of it materialized four figures that looked like living beings. Their appearance was as follows: they had human forms,* [6]*but each one had four faces, and each*[a] *had four wings,* [7]*while their*[a] *legs were straight,*[b] *with feet*[c] *like calves' hooves; they*[d] *gleamed like burnished copper.* [8]*However, human arms and hands*[a] *were beneath their wings on each of their four sides.*[b] [10]*This was what their faces looked like: they each had a human face,*

and the four of them also had a lion's face on the right side, and the four had a bull's face on the left side, and the four had an eagle's face. [11]*Their wings*[a] *were extended upwards; they each had a pair of wings brushing against their neighbor's*[b] *and another pair covering their*[c] *bodies.* [12]*Each moved straight ahead: they could move forward wherever the spirit wanted to go, without changing direction as they moved.*

[13]*Out of*[a] *the living beings appeared what looked like*[b] *burning, fiery coals. The fire*[c] *looked like torches*[d] *moving to and fro between the living beings: the fire had radiance, and from the fire*[e] [14]*what looked like lightning flashes darted hither and thither.*

[15]*As I looked,*[a] *my attention was drawn to a wheel on the ground beside the living beings; there was one for each of the four of them.*[b] [16]*The wheels*[a] *looked like gleaming gold topaz;*[b] *they all four had the same*[c] *shape, and their construction*[d] *seemed to be that each had another wheel inside it.* [17]*When the wheels*[a] *moved forward,*[b] *they could move in the direction of*[c] *any of their four sides, without changing direction as they moved.* [18]*As for their rims, which were awesomely high[?],*[a] *their rims were completely covered with eyes in the case of the four of them.* [19]*When the living beings moved forward, the wheels would move beside them; and when the living beings ascended from the ground, the wheels could ascend too.* [20]*Wherever the spirit wanted to move forward, they would do so,*[a] *and the wheels*[b] [21]*would move forward when they did; and when they stopped, they would stop too. When they ascended from the ground, they*[a] *would ascend alongside them, because the spirit of the living beings*[b] *was in the wheels.*

[22]*Above the heads of the living beings was something shaped like a platform that gleamed like crystal;*[a] *it extended over their heads above them.* [23]*Beneath the platform, their wings kept in formation*[a] *beside their neighbors', while their other pair covered their bodies.*[b] [24]*I could hear the noise made by their wings: it sounded as loud as floodwaters, as loud as the Almighty.*[a] *When they moved,*[b] *there was a tumultuous noise like the sound of an army;*[c] [25]*when they stopped, they would drop their wings.*

[26]*Above the platform over their heads was what looked like lapis lazuli in the shape of a throne, and on the throne-shaped object was what looked like a human form, above it.*[a] [27]*I saw something that gleamed like amber*[a] *from the semblance of his waist upwards, while from the semblance of his waist downwards I saw what looked like fire. There was radiance all around him:* [28]*the surrounding radiance looked like the rainbow that appears in the clouds on a rainy day. That was what the figure who is associated with the glorious presence of Yahweh looked like. At the sight I threw myself down on my face.*

Then I heard a voice: it was somebody speaking. [2:1]*"Human one,"* *he said to me, "stand on your feet so I can speak with*[a] *you."* [2]*The spirit entered me*[a] *and made me stand on my feet. Then I heard somebody speaking*[b] *to me.* [3]*"Human one,"* *he said to me, "I am sending you to the rebellious community of Israel,*[a] *who till this day have rebelled*[b] *against me, both they and their forebears.* [4]*It is to the descendants, whose facial expression is more insensitive and whose wills are more stubborn,*[a] *that I am sending you.*[b] *You are to tell them, 'This is the message of the Lord*[c] *Yahweh,'* [5]*whether*[a] *they listen or fail to do so,*[b] *rebel community as they are, and they will realize that there has been*[c] *a prophet among them.* [6]*You, human one, are not to be afraid of them nor intimidated by their facial expression,*[a] *as well you might when*[b] *nettles and thorns confront you*[c] *and you sit on*[d] *scorpions.*[e] *Do not be afraid of their words nor intimidated by their facial expression, rebel community as they are,* [7]*but speak my words to them, whether they listen or fail to do so, rebels*[a] *as they are.*

[8]*"You, human one, are to listen to what I tell*[a] *you, rather than being a rebel like that rebel community. Open your mouth and eat what I present to*[b] *you."* [9]*I looked, and my*

attention was drawn to a hand stretched out toward me, holding[a] *a book scroll,* [10]*which he unrolled in front of me. It had writing on the front and back, with the heading*[a] *"Laments,*[b] *mourning and woe."*[c] [3:1] *Then he said to me, "Human one,*[a] *eat this scroll and go, speak to the community of Israel."* [2]*I opened my mouth, and he fed me with the*[a] *scroll,* [3]*saying to me, "Human one, give your stomach the opportunity to feed on this scroll I am presenting to you, and let your belly be filled with it." I ate it,*[a] *and it tasted as sweet*[b] *as honey.*

[4]*"Human one," he then said to me, "come, go to the community of Israel, and use my very words in speaking*[a] *to them.* [5]*For if*[a] *you were sent to a people whose speech is incomprehensible,*[b] *whose language is difficult to grasp,*[c] [6]*or*[a] *to a host of peoples*[b] *whose speech is incomprehensible, whose language is difficult to grasp*[c] *and whose words you could not understand—if*[d] *they were the ones I sent you to, they would listen to you.* [7]*But the community of Israel will not be willing to listen to you, because they are unwilling to listen to me, since the whole community of Israel has stern brows and hard hearts.* [8]*I now make*[a] *your face as stern as theirs are and your brow as stern as their brows:* [9]*as hard as diamond,*[a] *which is harder than flint, I am making your brow. You will not be afraid of them nor intimidated by their facial expression, rebel community as they are.* [10]*Human one," he told me further, "take to heart all my words that I speak to you, listening with both ears.*[a] [11]*Then come, go to your fellow nationals in exile and speak to them. Tell them, 'This is the message of Yahweh,' whether they listen or fail to do so."*

[12]*Then the spirit lifted me up, and behind me I heard a noise, a loud, pulsating sound, as the manifestation of Yahweh's glorious presence rose*[a] *from where it was situated.* [13]*The loud, pulsating sound was the noise*[a] *made by the wings of the living beings as they kept in formation*[b] *beside one another, and also the noise made by the wheels alongside them.* [14]*The spirit, then, lifted me up*[a] *and took me off. I was passionately moved*[b] *as I went,*[c] *being under the firm control of Yahweh's hand.* [15]*I came to the exiles in Tel Abib, where they were living.*[a] *I stayed there among them for a week, in a state of disorientation.*[b]

Notes

1.a. Hardly "the grand canal" (e.g., Cooke 4; Fohrer 5). It appears in two Akk. texts as *naru kabāru/i;* the adj is *kabru* "great."

1.b. For the Heb. construction, see Cooke 8.

1.c. The Heb. pl of generalization (Joüon 136j), which recurs in 8:3; 40:2, is to be rendered as sg.

2.a. Lit. "it (was)": for the use of היא "it" in such explanatory notes, see Cooke 8. The reference to the fifth month functions as a cue phrase harking back to the date in v 1 (Herrmann 1; Lang, *Bib* 64 [1983] 225) by means of an abbreviated reference to the last element.

3.a. Or possibly ". . . the priest Buzi." The office may relate to the first or second name in OT usage. The literary convention of referring to a prophet's occupation in a superscription (see *Form/Structure/Setting*) supports the former alternative, which the LXX followed here.

3.b. The inf abs is used idiomatically at the outset of narratives: see Greenberg (41) for examples. V 3 functions along with v 2 as another beginning for the unit (see the *Comment*).

3.c. For MT עליו "upon him," the reading עלי "upon me," implied by LXX Syr and found in thirteen MSS, is generally preferred. The MT suffered assimilation to the third person of v 3a. The first-person echoing of the clause in 3:14bβ supports the emendation; so does the juxtaposition of divine hand and human vision in 8:1b–2, as here in vv 3b–4.

3.d. Since the LXX* regularly lacks שם(ה) "there" in similar contexts, at 3:22; 8:1; 40:1, it has been regarded as an addition (see, e.g., Zimmerli 82). But it is arguable that it is relevant at 3:22; 40:1 (see the *Notes*). Did the LXX* omit here as superfluous (cf. Kraetzschmar 7; Lang, *Ezechiel* 20; Lind, *JETS* 27 [1984] 137)? Or was it added to the text in order to bind together more closely the two separate halves of the verse?

4.a. The second and third nouns are in apposition to the first. The copula inserted before the second in the LXX and also in the Vg and eight MSS is an easier and so inferior reading: Zimmerli (8) draws attention to this tendency in the LXX. The LXX also presupposes the addition of בה "in it," which further clarifies the relation of the cloud to the wind. Ehrlich (*Randglossen* 5:2) interestingly suggested that at an earlier stage it was בא "came" and was a note added to show the parallelism of the wind and cloud.

4.b. The verb מתלקחת, which should basically mean "take hold of itself" and is used of lightning in Exod 9:24, seems to have the idiomatic sense of catching on fire and so burning. G. R. Driver (*VT* 1 [1951] 60 n. 1 and *Bib* 35 [1954] 145) cited Akk. and Syr. parallels for this semantic development in the case of the synonymous stem *ʾḥz*.

4.c. The underlying Heb. text of the LXX evidently had a different order of clauses (see *BHS*), relating the surrounding radiance more clearly to the cloud (לו "to it": ענן "cloud" is masc); at the Gr. level, since νεφέλη "cloud" is fem, κυκλῷ αὐτοῦ "around it" must relate to the neuter πνεῦμα "wind." Ehrlich (*Randglossen* 5:2), related the suffix to אש "fire" by arguing that it is epicene (cf. Greenberg 43). It is more likely that after the specification of the three nouns (ABC) the latter two are defined further in a B'C' order; the *Vorlage* of the LXX had a secondary ABB'CC' order. The difference in order has sometimes been taken as an indication that the clause about the radiance is a gloss that compares its presence in v 27 (Herrmann 1; Hölscher, *Dichter* 46; et al.), but it is structurally fitting in both places (see *Form/Structure/Setting*).

4.d. Ehrlich (*Randglossen* 5:2) suggested that מן "from" has a locative sense, as often in compound prepositions, here and in v 5, and in fact LXX so interpreted. But the thought seems to be that from the perspective of the viewer details gradually materialized from the background as the phenomenon approached and could be seen more clearly. The following מתוך האש "from the midst of the fire" is often taken as an early gloss to make explicit the antecedent of the preceding suffix, but it is universally attested, and a near parallel occurs in v 13, where similar specifying emphasis is laid on the fire, as one reads on.

4.e. For Heb. כעין "like the gleam of," cf. W. McKane, *Proverbs, A New Approach* (London: SCM, 1970) 394.

4.f. For the rendering, see the *Comment*. The LXX adds "and brightness in it," which may have originated in a comparative gloss נגה בית לה "radiance: inside it" which briefly noted the variant בית לה סביב "inside it around" that appears in the MT of v 27a for נגה לה סביב "and radiance to it around" here and in v 27b.

6.a. MT לאחת להם "to each to them" is strangely used in the sense "to each one of them" (cf. Ehrlich, *Randglossen* 5:2; Cooke 12, 24). LXX Vg do not represent להם "to them," and 10:21a, as well as v 6a here, supports the shorter text. The extra word may have originated as a variant of להנה "to them (fem)" in v 5.

7.a. After the fem suffixes relating to the living creatures in vv 5–6 (apart from the intrusive להם "to them" in v 6), there appears in vv 9–12 and 23–25 a series of masc suffixes. They are often taken as evidence of redaction (see *Form/Structure/Setting*). They seem to presuppose a humanoid form for the grammatically fem entities and indicate that חיות "living beings" does not here mean "animals." A parallel phenomenon is the use of fem suffixes for the wheels in parts of vv 16–18, which may indicate their inanimate nature.

7.b. Lit. "(were) a straight leg." In v 23 appears an evidently misplaced gloss on the sg phrase here, a pl adj ישרות "straight," which correctly understands the sg as collective or distributive ("were in each case a straight leg" [Hitzig 6]). The LXX* has a pl adj for the MT's sg phrase, which may imply that the gloss had displaced the text of the MT in its *Vorlage*, unless it is a loose rendering. In MT the marginal gloss was wrongly related to the next column.

7.c. Heb. כף רגליהם here refers to the extremities of the legs, just as in v 7a רגלים, lit. "feet," is used in the extended sense of legs (Vogt, *Untersuchungen* 82 n. 64).

7.d. The subj of the verb is not the legs, in which case a fem verb would be expected, but the living creatures, regarded as male throughout the earlier part of the verse (Hitzig 6). Parunak ("Structural Studies" 125) has observed that whenever כעין "like the gleam" is used in this pericope, it refers to the whole entity under consideration and not just a part of it. Cf. the supernatural figure in 40:3 who looked like copper. Then the application of the phrase to legs in Dan 10:6, in obvious dependence on this passage, does not represent the original intent.

8. a. Q ידי "hands of" is generally followed; K ידו seems to mean "his hands (were [the hands of] a human being)" (Keil 23). The term seems to be used in the wider sense of "arm including hand" (see del Olmo Lete, *Vocación* 24; cf. *HALAT* 370a with reference to Jer 38:12).

8.b. The MT adds vv 8b–9: "and their faces and their wings belonging to the four of them; their wings were brushing against each other. They did not change direction when they moved: each moved straight ahead." Hölscher (*Dichter* 46) and Greenberg (44) have observed that vv 8b–9 and 11–12 are apparently doublets, each supplying some lack in the other.

Lind (*JETS* 27 [1984] 138) argues in favor of a number of longer readings in the MT on the theoretically reasonable grounds that (1) the reading that best explains the origin of the others is to be preferred and that (2) claims of scribal amplification must be explained in terms of objectively demonstrated causes. He is not able to find any such causes here and so retains the present text. In fact, it can be plausibly argued that vv 8b–9 are secondary, as Hölscher went on to claim. It is significant that counterparts in chap. 10 to v 8a (10:21b) and the beginning of v 10 (10:22a*a*) are juxtaposed. The material in vv 8b–9 seems to have originated in a string of marginal comments that have been taken together and incorporated into the text. For this phenomenon in other parts of the MT of Ezekiel, see my article "Annotation Clusters in Ezekiel," *ZAW* 102 (1990) 408–13. The latest elements consist of "and their wings" and "Their wings were brushing against each other," which are absent from the LXX*. Basically חברת אשה אל־אחותה "were brushing against each other" was a correction of the corrupt איש "each [masc!]" in v 11b*a*, with חברת functioning as a cue word (Höhne, "Thronwagenvision" 89; cf. Zimmerli 84). The preceding לארבעתם "to the four of them" in v 8b, already in the LXX, seems to be a variant of the form with a fem suffix, לארבעתן, which occurs twice in v 10 after a form with a masc suffix. These two glosses were taken together and supplied with a subj וכנפיהם "and their wings" in v 8b, but after the division into separate sentences it was repeated at the end of v 9a (Zimmerli 84). The initial ופניהם "and their faces" in v 8b is probably a miswriting of וכנפיהם "and their wings," under the influence of vv 6, 10 (Ehrlich, *Randglossen* 5:4), which in the MT has been left alongside a corrected text but in the LXX stands uncorrected. V 9b consists of two clauses from v 12a, b in reverse order: the order in v 12 is supported by v 17. The reverse order was intended to suggest that the wings were the subj, by highlighting the fem suffix on בלכתן "when they moved": after the fem references to wings in v 11, the clauses were understood in terms of the movement of the wings rather than of the living creatures. All this scribal activity relating to vv 11–12 has been taken together and inserted into the text at a seemingly appropriate point after the mention of faces and wings for each of the four creatures in vv 6 and 8a.

11.a. The MT prefaces with ופניהם "and their faces," which is absent from the LXX*: it is probably to be explained as in v 8 (cf. Lind, *JETS* 27 [1984] 137, who envisages vertical dittography). Greenberg (45) notes that it makes no sense at this point, as the disjunctive accent in the MT virtually admits.

11.b. As we noted above, v 9a has preserved a variant or correction, אשה אל־אחותה "each to its counterpart," in place of the MT "each" (masc!). The LXX and Syr so imply and v 23 supports, while the combination in the MT with איש as subj does not occur elsewhere. Undoubtedly the earlier occurrence of לאיש "to each" influenced the corruption. The first century B.C. Qumran MS 4QEz[b], which usually concurs with the MT, attests a text that lacks איש (Lust, "Ezekiel MSS in Qumran," in *Ezekiel and His Book*, ed. J. Lust, 94–95), presumably after secondary omission of an awkward corrupted element.

11.c. For the rare form of suffix, see GKC 91l; Cooke 25.

13.a. For the MT ודמות "and (as for) the likeness of (the living creatures)," the LXX has καὶ ἐν μέσῳ "and in the midst." 10:2 supports the LXX as to the relative positions of the coals of fire and the living creatures. Both Zimmerli (84) and Greenberg (46) restore ובינות "and between," following Hitzig (9) and others, but the form of the preposition is characteristic of chap. 10 (contrast בין later in this verse). Better is ומתוך "and from the midst of" (Herrmann 3; Fohrer 11; cf. *BHS*), a form that appears in vv 4–5, where the LXX renders as here. It shares four consonants with the term in the MT. The latter may have originated as a comparative gloss that alluded to the combination דמות . . . חיות "the likeness . . . of living creatures" in v 5; it was subsequently regarded as a correction of the graphically look-alike preposition. Driver's attempt to interpret דמות as "midst" (*Bib* 19 [1938] 61) is unconvincing; neither the NEB nor the REB adopted it.

13.b. The MT מראהם "their appearance (was like)" suffers from the fact that the fire, rather than the living creatures, is the evident concern of the context. The LXX implies מראה "something that appeared (like)." Greenberg (46) prefers to read כמראה גחלי "like the appearance of coals" on the evidence of the Syr, noting that this is the standard form in the chapter, as later in this very verse, and that the construction in the LXX is unparalleled. However, as often elsewhere, the Syr's reading looks suspiciously like an easier one that has been assimilated to the context. The MT may have been influenced by v 16b.

13.c. Lit. "it," with reference to אש "fire" (Ehrlich, *Randglossen* 5:5; Zimmerli 84).

13.d. The MT (הלפדים) "the (torches)" has frequently been regarded as a dittograph: the LXX does not represent the article.

13.e. V 13bβ and v 14 seem to be doublets (cf. Kraetzschmar 14–15). Since the LXX* omits v 14, scholarship has judged it to be the intruder (but see Ehrlich, *Randglossen* 5:5, who retained the MT with emendations; Halperin, *JBL* 101 [1982] 355 n. 22, who judges the LXX's shorter text to be due to homoeoteleuton; and Lind, *JETS* 27 [1984] 138). However, the last two words of v 13, יוצא ברק "lightning was coming out," and the first word of v 14, והחיות "and the living creatures," appear to be separate glosses that have been absorbed into the flow of the text, rather like vv 8b–9. It is significant that the LXX omits החיות in v 15. Greenberg (46) observes that in v 14 its position before the inf abs violates Heb. usage. The term may have originated as a rubric gloss, which noted the subject matter of vv 5–14 (Freedy, *VT* 20 [1970] 142). Its presence in both vv 14 and 15 seems to represent double incorporation of the same gloss. In v 14 the context refers to flickering flames rather than to the living creatures, which were immobile supports for the throne. As for יוצא "was coming out," it seems to be an easier variant of רצוא in v 14: the Vg "ibant" presupposes it in v 14, while 4Q405 20 ii 21,22:9 וישבו . . . ויצא presupposes a similar *Vorlage* (cf. Newsom, *Songs* 315). Heb. רצוא appears to be derived from a stem רצא as a byform of רוץ "run" (cf. Ewald 224; Dahood, *Bib* 53 [1972] 395; Θ ἔτρεχον "ran"). Likewise ברק "lightning" looks like an explanation of בזק, a *hapax legomenon* that in the light of later Heb. usage appears to mean "lightning flash" (see A. Cohen, *AJSL* 40 [1924] 163; Jastrow, *Dictionary* 154a). As in v 13, the article may be a dittograph. Behind the omission of v 14 in the LXX* lies a recognition of the interrelatedness of vv 13bβ and 14, and a wrong decision to follow the easy path of the former and to excise the latter. It thus attests a post-MT stage of the text.

15.a. The MT adds החיות "the living creatures," which is not represented in the LXX: see the preceding *Note*. Nor is it present in the parallel 10:9. The omission allows the style to accord with v 4 (cf. 2:9; 8:2, 7, 10; 10:1, 9; 44:4), where what Ezekiel sees is a new entity. Lind (*JETS* 27 [1984] 137) explained in terms of scribal supplying of an object for the verb.

15.b. The MT לארבעת פניו "in respect of his four faces" does not fit the context. The final *waw* is generally attached to the following מראה in v 16, as LXX Syr Vg and the parallel 10:9 suggest: "and the appearance." Then in an original לארבעתם "in respect of the four of them," attested by the LXX, the final *mem* was misread as נ׳, a not uncommon error, and sense was achieved by prefixing *pe* (Zimmerli 85, refining the explanation of Cornill 182).

16.a. See the previous *Note*. The MT adds ומעשיהם "and their construction," unrepresented in the LXX* and in the parallel 10:9. It appears to be an anticipation of the term in v 16b (Lind, *JETS* 27 [1984] 137). As Cornill (182) observed, construction is not comparable with a jewel, but appearance is.

16.b. Heb. תרשיש is a precious stone of uncertain meaning. According to the researches of H. Quiring (*Sudhofs Archiv* 38 [1954] 206–8), it means gold topaz.

16.c. Heb. אחד is masc, while the noun is fem: the same reading appears in the parallel 10:10. Driver (*Bib* 35 [1954] 145–46) assumed the ellipse of אופן: "the likeness of one (wheel)."

16.d. The MT prefixes ומראהם "and their appearance," but the LXX* does not represent it, and it is inappropriate here. It is significant that in the parallel 10:10 the previous clause begins with this very word. Accordingly, it represents a comparative gloss relating to v 16aβ.

17.a. Lit. "they."

17.b. The LXX* does not represent בלכתם "when they moved," but since 10:11 reproduces it (with a different word order), the omission may be stylistic.

17.c. Heb. על, usually "on," is used in the sense of אל "to" (cf. vv 9, 12), as often in Ezekiel, doubtless under the influence of Aram. usage (see Rooker, *Biblical Hebrew in Transition* 128–31).

18.a. The MT וגביהן וגבה להם ויראה להם "and as for their rims, and they had height and they had fear" is problematic. The LXX καὶ εἶδον αὐτά implies for the last clause וארא להם "and I saw them," presumably by assimilation to the verb in vv 4, 15, 27, although the form of the verb corresponds to that found in vv 1, 28. The reading is hardly original: one expects a direct object, as in v 27, or further description with והנה "and behold" (cf. *BHS*), as in v 4; 2:9, for which there is no evidence. The MT should probably be retained in v 18a, if only for lack of a convincing alternative. The initial וגביהן is to be taken as a *casus pendens* (Taylor 57; Waldman, *JBL* 103 [1984] 617–18). Elsewhere יראה means "fear" rather than "fearfulness" (Cornill 183), even in Ps 90:11, to which Smend (13) appealed; but analogy with פחד "fear, object of fear" makes such an extension of meaning feasible. For גבים/גבות in the sense of "rims," cf. גבים in 1 Kgs 7:33.

20.a. The MT adds שמה הרוח ללכת "thither the spirit to go," originally intended as a correction of the earlier שם "there" with cue words הרוח ללכת (Herrmann 3). The correction accords with v 12; the corruption was a simple case of haplography. LXX Syr do not represent the three words.

20.b. The traditional text, supported by all ancient witnesses, adds "would ascend alongside them, because the spirit of the living creatures was in the wheels." The same material reappears in v 21b. What distinguishes it from the repetitive text of the rest of vv 19–21 is its lack of logical continuity with what precedes in v 20a. One expects a reference to the forward movement of the wheels at this point, as occurs in v 21a: mention of the vertical movement of the wheels is premature (cf. Höhne, "Thronwagenvision" 93). Seemingly a copyist's eye jumped to יַנָּשֵׂאוּ "would ascend" in v 21b, and he copied out the rest of v 21b, using a text, which, like that of the LXX, still lacked הָאוֹפַנִּים "the wheels" in v 21b. Subsequently, the missing words were reinserted together with the rest of v 21, but without deletion of the now superfluous six words. The cause of the parablepsis may have been the omission of a 34-letter line, if not of two of 17 letters: for this phenomenon, cf. H. M. Orlinsky (*JBL* 61 [1942] 88–89), who refers to lines in Heb. MSS with about 11–13 or 14, 17, 23, 25, 30, and 35 letters to a line, and to my *Greek Chronicles* (Leiden: Brill, 1974) 2:133–36. For another case of a corrected and undeleted error, see 22:20 and *Note*. Höhne ("Thronwagenvision" 93) took v 20 as a gloss on v 21b that wanted to make clear that the spirit was the same as in v 12, but this seems an unnecessarily drastic explanation of the overlap. He rightly noted that 10:17 reflects not v 20 but v 21.

21.a. The LXX* lacks the MT's הָאוֹפַנִּים "the wheels": see the previous *Note*. It appears to be another rubric gloss, again occurring at the end of a topical section, like הַחַיּוֹת "the living creatures" in vv 14, 15.

21.b. Heb. חַיָּה in vv (20) 21–22 is interpreted as a collective sg "living creatures." Presumably it was used to "emphasize the unity of the ensemble" (Greenberg 48).

22.a. The MT adds הַנּוֹרָא "which is awesome," which is not represented in the LXX*. Probably it was originally intended to relate not to הַקֶּרַח "crystal" (Vogt, *Untersuchungen* 8; Greenberg, 48, who understand—on what basis?—as "dazzling" [= TEV; cf. NAB "glittering"]) but to רָקִיעַ "platform." Kraetzschmar's suggestion (18) to read נִרְאָה "was seen" and to relate it to the platform with reference to 10:1 is worth developing. In the description of the platform at 10:1, נִרְאָה "was seen" occurs in the MT but is not rendered in LXX* Syr. It was probably a gloss referring to the preceding line, where the platform is described as "over the heads of the cherubim": the gloss remarked that it had been seen earlier by Ezekiel, i.e., in 1:22. Here הַנּוֹרָא is its counterpart, corrupted from a comparative gloss הַנִּרְאָה and going with what follows: "which was seen extended over their heads" (cf. Dan 1:15 for the construction). The adaptation to נוֹרָא "awesome" was doubtless influenced by its appearance in theophanic descriptions elsewhere (Gen 28:17; Judg 13:6); its strange use to describe the noun of comparison is a clue to its secondary character.

23.a. The MT יְשָׁרוֹת "straight" is awkward in this context: it is forced to explain in terms of a pregnant construction (Kraetzschmar 18; Cooke 19; Greenberg 48). The LXX has a doublet implying פְּרֻדוֹת מַשִּׁיקוֹת "stretched out, keeping in line": the first term occurs in v 11 and the second in 3:13. The similarity of construction ("each other") and context—the noise made by the wings—in 3:13 suggests that מַשִּׁיקוֹת is the original reading, which 3:13 cites (cf. Ehrlich, *Randglossen* 5:7). As noted above, the MT was intended as a marginal explanatory gloss on v 7a. It was related to the wrong column and taken as a correction of מַשִּׁיקוֹת, with which it shares four consonants. For such intercolumnar confusion, see my *Greek Chronicles* 2:90–104, and *VT* 29 (1989) 68–69, with reference to 21:15, 18. For the meaning of the verb, see *Note* 3:13.a.

23.b. The MT, but not the LXX*, repeats וּלְאִישׁ שְׁתַּיִם מְכַסּוֹת לָהֵנָּה "and each had two covering for them." Greenberg (48) takes the repetition as distributive (cf. GKC 134q), comparing 10:9, and considers that the omission in the LXX represents the translator's simplification. However, one would then have expected the repetition of the object, גְּוִיֹתֵיהֶם "their bodies." So dittography seems to have been responsible. Cornill (185) and others have also judged the LXX correct in not representing the first לָהֵנָּה "for them." If it relates to the living creatures, it clashes with the two masc references within the clause. However, Greenberg (48) has suggested that it is an ethical dative relating to the wings (cf. BDB 115b, 116a). Then it has an intensifying force, and LXX doubtless dropped it as otiose. V 23b has been regarded as a gloss from v 11, since its content seems irrelevant here (e.g., Fohrer 13; Cooke 20). It is possible that it represents a marginal comment on v 11b that supplied a variant reading with an initial לְאִישׁ "to each"—as a correction of the awkward preceding אִישׁ "each"?—and a final masc suffix. Then the common topic of wings encouraged its attachment to and incorporation in v 23a, in the next column.

24.a. The LXX* does not represent כְּקוֹל־שַׁדָּי "like the voice of Shaddai," which is often taken as a gloss from 10:5 (Cornill 185; et al.). However, כְּקוֹל אֵל־שַׁדַּי בְּדַבְּרוֹ "like the voice of El Shaddai when he spoke" looks like an elaboration of the shorter phrase here (Halperin, *JBL* 101 [1982] 355–56 and n. 23). Driver's repointing שַׁדָי as "downpour" (*JTS* 41 [1940] 168) has been criticized by J. Barr (*Comparative Philology and the Text of the OT* [Oxford: Clarendon, 1968] 235).

24.b. The lack of *kaph* before the following קוֹל "sound" indicates that קוֹל does not function in a comparison. The continuation in vv 19 and 21, where בלכם "when they moved" begins one clause and another identically structured verb begins the next, suggests that the same occurs here with asyndeton, contra the Masoretic accent. Tg Vg interpreted thus, and thence Vg-based Catholic versions, such as NAB. The implication of v 25b is that the noise ceased (cf. Tg "their wings became silent"; also 4Q*405* 20 ii 21,22:13 [cf. Newsom, *Songs* 319]).

24.c. The LXX* lacks any representation of קוֹל הֲמֻלָּה כְּקוֹל מַחֲנֶה "a tumultuous noise like the noise of an army," and scholars generally judge the MT secondary. However, the term הֲמֻלָּה is too distinctive to be part of a gloss; it can hardly have been derived from the contextually dissimilar Jer 11:16, the only other place it occurs in the MT. It is cognate with Ug. *hmlt* "people, multitude" and is "noise of some magnitude which can be compared with the hubbub of a military camp or to the thundering feet of an army on the march" (W. McKane, *Jeremiah 1–20* [Edinburgh: Clark, 1986] 250). Dan 10:6 already seems to presuppose the final comparison with its paraphrase כְּקוֹל הָמוֹן "like the noise of a multitude." The omission in the LXX* may be explained in terms of overlooking a 27-letter line or two lines of 13 and 14 letters (cf. *Note* 20.b. above); its representation of בלכתם "when they moved" after כנפיהם "their wings" suggests a partial marginal correction and subsequent insertion into the text at a suitable point. The MT adds vv 24b–25a, "when they stopped they would drop their wings. And there was a noise above the platform that was over their heads"; only C and a few MSS omit. The repetition of v 24b in 25b and the close similarity of v 25a to v 26a raise suspicions. The LXX* at the beginning of v 25 implies והנה קול "and behold a sound" for קול ויהי "and there was a voice/sound" and omits vv 25b–26aα. Halperin (*JBL* 101 [1982] 355 n. 22), like Smend (15) before him, has found in the LXX* merely loss of vv 25b–26aα by homoeoteleuton of על־ראשם "over their heads." But the total evidence suggests a more complex phenomenon, namely that three forms of the text may be disentangled: (1) ויהי קול מעל לרקיע אשר על־ראשם "and there was a voice/sound above the platform that was over their heads," the form of v 25a as it appears in the MT; (2) וממעל לרקיע אשר על־ראשם "and above the platform that was over their heads," the form of v 26a as it appears in the MT; (3) והנה קול ממעל לרקיע אשר על־ראשם "and behold a sound above the platform that was over their heads," the form underlying the LXX*. The MT has a doublet consisting of the first two forms, with v 24b serving as cue words to introduce the variant reading of v 25a. Preference is to be given to the form in v 26aα: the initial *waw* "and" at the beginning of a fresh section accords with vv 5 and 22, while an initial והנה "and behold" (cf. vv 4, 15) or ויהי "and there was" is unparalleled. One may best explain the intrusive קול "sound" as a rubric gloss at the end of a section, such as those that appear earlier in the MT in vv 14, 15, and 21: they served to map out the development of the vision account. It is less likely that it was originally intended to anticipate the "voice" of v 28, although that has evidently become its role in the MT. A minor variant in the two MT readings is מעל ל (v 25a) and ל ממעל (v 26aα), meaning "above." Neither occurs elsewhere in Ezekiel, but the latter is more common and is close to מלמעלה "above" in vv 11, 22, and 26b (cf. למעלה, v 27). The former was probably influenced by מעל "from upon" in vv 19, 21. This piece of evidence supports the priority of v 26aα.

26.a. Lit. "on it above." The LXX* (and Vg) omitted עליו as superfluous; subsequently it was wrongly supplied at the end of v 26a.

27.a. The MT adds כמראה־אש בית־לה סביב "what looked like fire: it had a covering all round," which the LXX* does not represent. It seems to be an intrusion on two counts. (1) It breaks the ABB'A' chiasmus of v 27a–bβ, in which the verbs of seeing and the accompanying similes function as A/A' and the upper and lower parts of the body as B/B'. Greenberg (50) envisages the MT as a more complex chiastic structure that includes v 27bγ, so that the A/A' elements are both longer: each consists of a simile and a circumstantial clause, which in the first instance is "having something with the appearance of fire surrounding it" and in the second case is "and he was surrounded by a radiance." His structural claim is spoiled by his correct judgment that v 27bγ refers not to the immediately preceding context of the lower part of the figure but to the entire figure (cf. v 4). This admission is tantamount to denying that v 27bγ has any role within the smaller A' element. (2) In 8:2, which appears to be a reprise of 1:27, there is general academic support, including Greenberg (166), for the originality of the LXX. As Greenberg himself states, there the LXX "restricts 'fire' to the bottom half of the figure, where alone it should be." Fire is out of place in the description of the upper half. The addition in the MT was probably intended as a comment on v 27bβ, with כמראה־אש "what looked like fire" functioning as introductory cue words (Vogt, *Untersuchungen* 8). The intent of the gloss was to claim that the radiance enveloped the fire (לה "it"). This ancient interpretation accords with Ehrlich's claim (*Randglossen* 5:8) that the masc suffix in v 27bγ relates to the fire, as in v 4, rather than to the figure. Heb. בית, lit. "house," here has the sense of receptacle or covering (cf. BDB

109b); the clipped vocalization is the result of the *maqqeph* (cf. חַמַּת־לְמוֹ in Ps 58:5(4); GKC 9u; but here GKC 130a n. 3 explains as constr and standing for [לְ] מִבֵּית "within").

2:1.a. The preposition אֵת "with" in Ezekiel, as in 1–2 Kings and Jeremiah, is often vocalized with suffixes as if it were the object sign: Cooke (36) judged it a colloquialism.

2.a. The MT adds כַּאֲשֶׁר דִּבֶּר אֵלָי "when/as he spoke to me," which the LXX omits. It adds little to the narrative and indeed cuts across the future aspect of v 1b. Cornill (186) observed that in Ezekiel כַּאֲשֶׁר "as" is used in a temporal sense only in 16:50. The MT seems to represent an explanatory marginal comment on the inexplicit messenger formula in 3:11, which echoes the divine language of 3:10: " Thus the Lord Yahweh has said—as he spoke to me." The comment was related to the wrong column and inserted here, as if it resumed מְדַבֵּר "speaking" in 1:28bβ. In place of this clause, the LXX has two verbs added from 3:14 at the Gr. stage of the textual tradition.

2.b. The hithp form means strictly "speaking to himself." It occurs in contradistinction to the piel ptcp in 1:28; 2:8 and recurs in 43:6 with a divine subj. The vocalization appears to be an artificial device motivated by reverence: cf. Greenberg 62.

3.a. In place of the MT בְּנֵי יִשְׂרָאֵל "sons of Israel," the LXX has בֵּית יִשְׂרָאֵל "house of Israel": the two phrases are often confused (via an abbreviation בְּ according to Cooke 36), and the opposite textual phenomenon occurs in 3:1. Cornill (187) argued in support of the LXX that the following pl qualifiers encouraged the change, but Wevers (51) considers that they may make the MT preferable. Zimmerli (89) has urged that the phrase attested in LXX is the customary one in Ezekiel, occurring 83 times over against 11 according to *Ezekiel 2* 564, and so to be expected in this basic place. He also adduces the impressive argument that the expression "house of rebellion" in vv 5, etc. was based on a primary "house of Israel," and so its presence is expected here—rather than delayed till 3:1. The dominant role of בֵּית יִשְׂרָאֵל "house of Israel" throughout the divine speech (3:1, 4, 7) must also be taken into account. Accordingly, the reading of the LXX is to be judged as preferable. The MT was probably influenced by בָּנִים "sons" in v 4. The variant attested in the LXX was known in the Heb. tradition: it turns up as אֶל־בֵּית יִשְׂרָאֵל "to the house of Israel" in 3:5 (see the *Note* there). The MT adds אֶל־גּוֹיִם "to nations," which LXX lacks. It does not fit the context of Ezekiel's mission to Israel. The Syr attests a sg "nation," which the NRSV has adopted, but it is plainly an attempt to match the MT to the context. The addition surely originated in a marginal reading that supplied a variant for אֶל־עַמִּים "to peoples" in 3:6 and strayed into the wrong column: see *Note* 3:6.b. G. del Olmo Lete's suggestion that the *mem* is enclitic (*Vocación* 296) is unlikely: see *Note* 26:12.b.

3.b. The LXX* lacks the MT's addition פָּשְׁעוּ בִי "revolted against me." In the MT the consequent collocation of clauses is "who have rebelled against me; both they and their forebears have revolted against me to this very day." The combination of the parallel verbs indeed occurs in 20:38, but in the MT אֲשֶׁר מָרְדוּ בִי "who have rebelled against me" is left hanging in the air and otiose after הַמֹּרְדִים "rebelling." The presence of the extra words is less easily explained. The phrase is clearly a doublet; it may have originated as a comparative gloss on מָרְדוּ בִי "they rebelled against me": it occurs frequently in the prophetic literature (Isa 1:2; 43:27; Jer 2:8; 33:8; Hos 7:13; 8:1).

4.a. Ehrlich (*Randglossen* 5:9; cf. Brownlee 26) sensitively noted that the adjectives have a comparative sense in this context.

4.b. The LXX* lacks v 4a, rightly in the judgment of many commentators. Zimmerli (90) stated that in Ezekiel בָּנִים "sons" is not used absolutely for the people in relation to Yahweh, but Greenberg has justly countered that neither is it here, where it refers to the present generation of Israelites, as distinct from their forebears. Vv 3–4a exhibit a chiastic structure. It is not fair to call v 4a a gloss from 3:7 (Fohrer 15): the variation in phrasing is significant, קְשֵׁי פָנִים וְחִזְקֵי־לֵב "hard-faced and strong-hearted" here as opposed to חִזְקֵי־מֵצַח וְקָשֵׁי־לֵב "strong-browed and hard-hearted" in 3:7. The changes in 3:7 seem to exhibit the inversion characteristic of recapitulation (cf. Talmon, *Qumran* 358–61), in which case 3:7 may be understood as presupposing the presence of 2:4a. Its absence from the LXX* may be due to the omission of a line of 36 letters or of lines of multiples thereof (see *Note* 1:20.b.) in the textual history of its *Vorlage.*

4.c. For the authenticity of אֲדֹנָי "Lord" in the messenger formula, see the appendix in Zimmerli, *Ezekiel 2* 556–62, which reverses the policy of deletion he earlier advocated throughout his two volumes. For the LXX evidence, see the discussion of McGregor (*Greek Text of Ezekiel* 75–93).

5.a. The MT inserts וְהֵמָּה "and they," which is lacking in LXX Syr. The function of (וְיָדְעוּ) "and (they will know)" in v 5b in the MT is to introduce the apodosis to the conditional clause (cf. GKC 112ff). However, v 7 (cf. the echo of vv 4b–5aα in 3:11) suggests that the conditional clause be taken with v 4b (Cornill 187; Zimmerli 90; et al.). Probably וְהֵמָּה "and they" arose is a comment on or variant of הֵמָּה "they" in v 3b, clarifying that a fresh clause occurs in the MT.

5.b. Here and in v 7 LXX Syr (also Syr in 3:11) render "be frightened" (see *BHS*), reflecting יֵחְדְּלוּ by metathesis for יַחְדְּלוּ (Cornill 187).

5.c. LXX Syr imply אַתָּה "you" for הָיָה "there has been," which Cornill (187) preferred. However, 33:33, which seems to echo v 5b, supports MT here.

6.a. So the LXX, implying וּמִפְּנֵיהֶם אַל־תֵּחָת for the MT וּמִדִּבְרֵיהֶם אַל־תִּירָא "and of their words do not be afraid" (see *BHS*). The LXX is generally preferred: Zimmerli (90) notes that it avoids the awkward duplicating of אַל־תִּירָא "do not be afraid" and supplies a parallel structure in v 6a and v 6b. For the translator's change in the order of words, see Marquis (*Textus* 13 [1986] 78–80). Did the MT originate in a marginal variant that compared or anticipated the first clause in v 6b, which variant was eventually taken as a correction of וּמִפְּנֵיהֶם אַל־תֵּחָת "and by their faces do not be intimidated" in view of its identical order of object with prepositional prefix and suffix + negative + verb? Then it is a further case of a "cuckoo" invading the textual nest, for which see in principle my articles in *JTS* 22 (1971) 143–50; 24 (1973) 69–78.

6.b. Heb. כִּי, lit. "for," gives the reason that they might be afraid (Ehrlich, *Randglossen* 5:9; cf. BDB 473b–74a). A. Aejmelaeus (*JBL* 105 [1986]]205–7), has argued that here and elsewhere a concessive interpretation is wrong; she suggests that here the clause is either causal or an object clause ("that").

6.c. Heb. אֹתְךָ is lit. "with you, in your presence" (cf. *Note* 2.a.). The double subj is of uncertain meaning. If—and the supposition is reasonable—סַלּוֹן is identified with סִלּוֹן "thorn" in 28:24, then סָרָב must have a similar sense. Hitzig (20) and Greenberg (66) have plausibly interpreted as "nettle," comparing the stem צָרַב "burn"; so does M. Zohary (*Plants of the Bible* [London: CUP, 1982] 162). Traditionally it has been taken as "brier" (KJV). LXX Syr Tg interpreted both nouns in terms of Aram. or late Heb. verbs סָרָב "rebel" and סָלָה "despise." Zimmerli (90) retroverted LXX ἐπισυστήσονται ἐπί σέ κύκλῳ "they will combine to attack you around" to an original סְבָבִים "surround," regarding אֹתְךָ as the object sign. But the order of words hardly suits this reconstruction. It is more likely that the verb סָלָה underlies the LXX and that ἐπί σέ κύκλῳ is a loose rendering of אֹתְךָ (Cooke 36; cf. NRSV). Moreover, it is significant that the first verb in the LXX, παροιστήσουσι "will provoke," is used to render סָרַר "be stubborn" in Hos 4:16: evidently סֹרְבִים was translated in terms of its first two consonants. As Greenberg (66) observes, the following term "scorpions" suggests that metaphorical terms are intended in the first clause.

6.d. Heb. אֶל is used in the sense of עַל, as often in Ezekiel (Driver, *JTS* 35 [1934] 54).

6.e. Hitzig (20) suggested that a type of thorn was intended. Garfinkel (*VT* 37 [1987] 430–37) has argued for a secondary meaning in terms of a plant from the context and from late Heb. metathesized עַרְקְבָן "stinging creeper" and also for the causal clause referring to the prophet's protection, as if by barbed wire.

7.a. In place of בֵּית מְרִי "rebellious house," which appears in vv 5, 6, etc., the MT has simply מְרִי "rebellion." "An abbreviated 'בַ may well have fallen out by pseudohaplography after 'כִ" (Allen in Brownlee [1986] 21). On the other hand, the longer, well attested (see *BHS*) reading may simply be a secondary harmonization; strict uniformity is not obligatory. Greenberg's argument (66) that מְרִי serves to provide a link with v 8, where it is used predicatively of the prophet, deserves consideration.

8.a. In place of אֵת אֲשֶׁר־אֲנִי מְדַבֵּר "what I am speaking," the LXX presupposes אֵת מְדַבֵּר "the one who is speaking," clearly by assimilation to v 2b, where the same verb "hear" precedes. The LXX renders differently there (contra Greenberg, VTSup 29 [1978] 139–40) and so the difference seems to have been in its *Vorlage*.

8.b. Ehrlich (*Randglossen* 5:10) distinguished נָתַן אֶל "give toward, hand over" here and in 3:3 from the standard נָתַן לְ "give to."

9.a. LXX Syr Vg do not represent הִנֵּה "behold" in the MT וְהִנֵּה־בוֹ "and behold in it," and the repetition of הִנֵּה is rare (cf. 37:2; Gen 31:51); moreover, a fem suffix בָהּ is expected after יָד "hand." Was a form בָהּ misunderstood as בֹה (= בוֹ; cf. הַמּוֹנֹה, 31:18) and wrongly modernized as בוֹ? It is possible that וְהִנֵּה originated as a marginal comment relating to the variant in 1:25 attested by LXX and was subsequently taken with the wrong column, displacing וֹ(בֹה); on the other hand, the versions may have dropped the repetitious element.

10.a. As before, אֵלֶיהָ is used in the sense of עָלֶיהָ "upon it" or rather here "over it": the sg כָּתוּב "written" suggests that what follows is a title, which Ezekiel could read at a glance, rather than the contents (Ehrlich, *Randglossen* 5:10–11).

10.b. LXX Tg render קִנִים "laments" as if sg. The unusual pl—generally קִינוֹת—favors the MT.

10.c. The MT הִי is used as an interjection "woe!" in Mishnaic Heb., and LXX Vg so interpret. Here it seems to be used as a noun (Driver, *Bib* 35 [1954] 146, with reference to Σ Tg). An emendation to a noun נְהִי "lament" (Cornill 188, following Olshausen; et al.) is not necessary: cf. Greenberg 67.

3:1.a. The MT adds אכול תמצא אשר את־אשר "what you find, eat," which is not represented in the LXX* and is widely believed to be a gloss. After 2:8b–9, a single command, "eat this scroll," is expected (cf. 3:2). It may be suggested that the words originated as an exegetical and comparative gloss, with a final cue word ("eat: what you find"), on אליך נתן אני אשר את־אשר "what I present to you" in 2:8. The gloss alluded to Jer 15:16, ואכלם דבריך נמצאו "your words were found and I ate them." It eased the transition from "hear what I speak to you" in v 8a to "eat what I present to you" in v 8b by hinting, correctly, that Ezekiel, like Jeremiah, was to find words and eat them. The comment suffered displacement from ואכל "and eat" in v 8 to אכול "eat" in 3:1 and was incorporated into the text here. If so, Greenberg's linking of the omission in the LXX here with its omission of "what I" in 2:8a as redactional parallels (VTSup 29 [1978] 139) is mistaken.

2.a. The MT adds הזאת "this," unrepresented in the LXX*. It is generally regarded as an addition assimilating to vv 1, 3: "this" is correct in the mouth of Yahweh, who holds the scroll, but not on Ezekiel's lips (Ehrlich, *Randglossen* 5:11).

3.a. The MT ואכלה "and I ate" is more naturally pointed ואכלה "and I ate it," as the ancient versions took it.

3.b. Is מתוק "sweet" used as a noun, "(in respect of) sweetness" (*HALAT* 618a), or is the sense "and it turned sweet" (Greenberg 68)? The order of words suggests the former. Ehrlich (*Randglossen* 5:11) suggested pointing as inf constr מתוק (לְמְתוֹק) "(so as to) be sweet."

4a. Heb. בדברי ודברת "and speak with my words" appears to have this sense in the context. Zimmerli (92–93) links with the formula יהוה בדבר "by the word of Yahweh" used in 1 Kgs 13, but the use of the pl here does not favor the connection.

5.a. The MT לא "not" is possible, but it must be considered together with לא in v 6a and אם־לא "if not" in v 6b (see below). The context suggests that it be repointed לֹא (= לוּ) "if" (Ehrlich, *Randglossen* 5:12). For confusion between לא and לו, see *HALAT* 487a.

5.b. Lit. "deep" and so inaccessible to the hearer, incomprehensible (cf. Block, *JBL* 103 [1984] 332 and n. 47): cf. Isa 33:19, which adds משמוע "too (deep) to hear."

5.c. Lit. "heavy." The parallelism suggests that the impact on the hearer is in mind and that it signifies "difficult to grasp." However, in Exod 4:10 it means "clumsy, not fluent." The omission of the phrase in LXX^B (*BHS*) is not relevant: it appears to be an inner-Gr. error (cf. Ziegler, *LXX* 98). The MT reflects the general textual tradition in adding ישראל אל־בית "to the house of Israel," which is hardly in apposition to the "people" of v 5a but evidently intended as a contrast, as if "(not . . .) but to . . . ." The construction is awkward, שלוח אתה "you are sent" doing double duty (Greenberg 68). The phrase surely originated as an old marginal gloss on אל־בני ישראל "to the sons of Israel" in 2:3, recording a seemingly correct variant such as the *Vorlage* of LXX contained. It was wrongly taken with the very similar context of 3:6 in the next column and incorporated into the text.

6.a. See *Note* 5.a. above. Θ ὤφελον "would that" presupposes לָא "if."

6.b. For the variant that strayed into 2:3, see *Note* 2:3.a. Cf. רבים גוים "many nations" in 26:3; 31:6. The two phrases occur as redactional variants in the parallel texts Isa 2:3 and Mic 4:2.

6.c. The omission in the Syr of the two adjectival phrases that occurred in v 5a is typical of the version, and so is probably not relevant for the Heb. text. The repetition is often taken as accidental, but the first phrase and the final clause seem to be an expanded form of Isa 33:19, משמוע שפה עמקי "too deep of lip to hear."

6.d. The MT אם־לא evidently means "surely," with a following conditional clause that lacks a conditional particle: "surely (if) . . ." (Hitzig 23; et al., including Greenberg 69; cf. GKC 149b [but 159b, h render this sense unlikely]). This is a most unnatural and confusing construction. Nor is a sense "but" likely, in accord with Aram. אלא (cf. Syr Tg), although it is theoretically possible (cf. Gen 24:38; Ps 131:2): the antithesis does not come till v 7 (Zimmerli 93). Many read אם "if," but the intrusion of לא is then difficult to explain; moreover, לו rather than אם is typically used in an unreal condition (GKC 159l). It is probable that אם originated as an explanation of לא in the sense לָא "if" (cf. Ehrlich, *Randglossen* 5:12; cf. LXX Vg "and if").

8.a. The pf is performative here and in v 9: see *Note* 22:13.a.; Waltke and O'Connor, *Syntax* 30.5.1d and n. 17; Joüon 112f, g.

9.a. Heb. שמיר means "diamond, adamant" rather than "emery, carborundum," as used to be thought on the basis of a misread Akk. term (see *HALAT* 1445b–46a). The LXX attests ותמיד "and continually" in place of ושמיר. Obviously this is a "cuckoo" type of replacement (cf. *Note* 2:6.a.). Was תמיד originally an exegetical comment on 2:3b (cf. Isa 65:3)?

10.a. The tr. conceals the awkward order of clauses, which Ehrlich (*Randglossen* 5:12) credited to Ezekiel's inelegant diction.

12.a. Most since Cornill (190–91) have adopted a conjectural emendation made by S. D. Luzzato and independently by Hitzig (24), ברום "when . . . arose" for MT ברוך "blessed," as the context seems to demand. The doxology in the MT is "certainly a somewhat peculiar utterance" (Fairbairn 41). Kraetzschmar (32) called the emendation one of the most brilliant conjectures ever made in OT study. As Greenberg (70) observes, the sequel shows that the noise was caused by the movement of components of the mobile throne, rather than being an articulate sound. There is a similar confusion of קול as "noise/voice" in the MT at 1:25. The pervasiveness of the corruption throughout the textual tradition indicates that it took place at an early stage: in fact it was in the old Heb. script that *mem* and *kaph* were easily confused. In chap. 10 רום "arise" is the equivalent of נשא "be lifted up" in chap. 1: this text appears to be the source for the change. Ehrlich (*Randglossen* 5:12) proposed that an accidental dittograph, ברומך, was the midpoint between the MT and the original. However, Kraetzschmar's suggestion (32) that comparison with Isa 6:3 influenced the corruption is more likely. Doubtless the similarity of Ps 72:19 to Isa 6:3 also contributed. One of the Qumran "Songs of the Sabbath Sacrifice," which were heavily influenced by Ezekiel, may preserve an awareness of textual variation in its reading וברכו בהרומם "and (the cherubim) bless as they rise" (4Q405 20 ii 21,22:7; 11QShirSabb 3,4:9). The words are probably to be taken together (with Halperin, *Faces* 52, and against Newsom, *Songs* 306). Halperin (*Faces* 44) has described the error as "truly a Freudian slip of the pen," in view of the deep influence it had on centuries of Jewish mysticism.

13.a. In v 13b וקול "and noise" appears to be a slight error for קול "noise" (*BHK*; cf. Ehrlich, *Randglossen* 5:12), by mechanical assimilation to וקול twice before. The final nominal phrase repeats the one in v 12 and functions as subj. Greenberg (71) takes the *waw* as explicative. To categorize v 13 as a gloss with a final cue phrase (Herrmann 7) ignores the structural significance of the verse (see *Form/Structure/Setting*).

13.b. This verb נשק is distinct from נשק "kiss." It is cognate with Arab. *nasaqa* "string (pearls), join one to another" and Eth. *nesūq* "arranged in order." In the OT it is used synonymously with ערך "order" (L. Kopf, *VT* 9 [1959] 265–67; *HALAT* 690b). Here it has the sense of "keeping in line each in relation to the other" (Driver, *Bib* 35 [1954] 147).

14.a. The change of order and construction in relation to v 12a*a* is occasioned by the factor of repetition: cf. 2 Sam 3:22–23; 1 Kgs 20:17, 19 (Joüon 118g).

14.b. Heb. חמה here means "emotional heat, passion" (*HALAT* 313a).

14.c. The MT מר "bitter," which is not represented in LXX* (cf. Ziegler, *LXX* 100) Syr, does not fit the context. It is clearly related somehow to מתוק "sweet(ness)" in v 3. Was it originally a marginal gloss on 2:8b*β* (cf. 3:3a*γ*) that expounded the metaphor and explained that what was presented to eat was by nature bitter, but surprisingly turned out to be sweet? A clever interplay with מרי "rebellious" in 2:8 may also have been intended. In due course the comment was related to the wrong column by someone who understood חמה ("vehemence" = LXX ὁρμή) as "anger." Within the Gr. textual tradition, μετέωρος "through the air" seems to have nothing to do with מר: it was simply an attempt to make sense of the Gr. term in v 15 (see next *Note*) by applying it first to the spirit's transportation of the prophet.

15.a. The MT שם וישבים המה (K) ואשר־כבר־נהר־אל הישבים "who lived by the Kebar Canal and who lived there" is generally held to be conflated (e.g., Zimmerli 95; Greenberg 71). The rest of the textual tradition supports the MT, except that the Syr, along with two Heb. MSS, omits the second clause. Q ואשב "and I sat," substituted for ואשר "and who," in an attempt to make sense of the conflation, is followed by the Tg; K and Q are both represented by the Vg "and I sat where (they were sitting)," which the KJV followed. The second clause seems to be the earlier one (Cornill 191; et al.), minus the *waw* "and," which was added when the first clause entered the text. Probably אל־נהר־כבר "by the Kebar Canal" was meant as a gloss explaining שם "there" in the light of 1:1, and הישבים originated as a cue phrase ישבי (=המה) ה "they lived" (Lang, *Bib* 64 [1983] 227–28). The LXX has μετέωρος καὶ περιῆλθον "high and I went around" for אביב תל "Tel Abib." The first noun was obviously related to the stem תלל "be high." For the second noun ואסב was apparently read: is this reading linked with Q ואשב, displacing אביב in the *Vorlage* of the LXX?

15.b. Heb. משמים appears to be an elative hiph, "distressed": cf. E. A. Speiser (*JCS* 6 [1952] 81–92), one of whose categories of elative hiph is forms denoting stillness, sometimes resulting from fear. Since the hiph of שמם is transitive apart from Job 21:5 and here, KB 989a took as causative, "causing to be distressed." Ezra 9:3–4 has a polel ptcp, משומם, to which Cornill (192) emended.

Form/Structure/Setting

The literary unit runs from 1:1 to 3:15. The formula of rising up and going to
a different place is one convention for marking the end of a narrative segment,
as in principle R. Alter (*The Art of Biblical Narrative* [New York: Basic Books, 1981]
65) has observed; 3:12, 14–15 clearly reflects this convention. The unit as a whole
consists of a report of a vision, which contains an account of a theophany and
communication of a divine commission of a prophetic vocation. B. O. Long (*JBL*
95 [1976] 359–63) has characterized it as belonging to the type of vision report
that is a dramatic word-vision. In this type the report depicts a heavenly scene or
dramatic action, a supramundane situation that presages a future event in the
mundane realm. The ominous import is conveyed by the divine word. An important use of this kind of vision report is to legitimate prophetic claims, such as
Isaiah's message of judgment in Isa 6 and Zechariah's message of salvation in
Zech 1:8–17. The divine word has the function of commissioning the prophet.
Ezek 1:1–3:15 falls into this category. Long has observed that the dramatic word-
visions in Ezekiel tend to lay heavy stress upon the divine word and treat vision as
mere preparation for word. Moreover, there is often a twofold pattern of the appearance of Yahweh's glory and divine address (40:1–4; 43:1–12; 44:4–31; cf.
8:1–6). He has plausibly suggested that a priestly convention for schematizing
divine vision and instruction underlies this bipartite type of account (cf. Num
20:6–8; cf. M. Weinfeld, *THAT* 4:35–36). It might be added that Yahweh's appearing in glory is often associated with judgment in P (Exod 16:10; Num 14:10;
16:19–21; 17:7–10[16:42–45]). The same pattern of vision and instruction appears
in the visionary call narrative here, the report of a theophany and, in a separate
phase, a commissioning message (cf. Dan 8:15–18).

Prophetic call narratives by Ezekiel's time represented an established tradition, behind which lay older accounts of the call of national leaders such as Moses
in Exod 3–4 and Gideon in Judg 6. Zimmerli (97–100) has distinguished between
two types of prophetic call account, one of which majors in a throne vision, seen
in Isa 6, and the other in the divine word, such as Jer 1:4–10. He has found a
combination of both, in chaps. 1 and 2–3, respectively. However, Long (*ZAW* 84
[1972] 494–500) has disputed Zimmerli's bifurcation. He envisions a single type,
discovering a common source for the features of divine vision and word in older,
ancient Near Eastern and Israelite theophany vision or dream reports, in which
theophany was a legitimating device (e.g., 1 Kgs 3:5–15). He prefers to regard
this tradition as exhibiting not a form but a schema that was used in texts of
various genres. There does appear to be a recurring set of traditional elements
that make up the call reports. These have been variously identified, often with
more difference in nomenclature than in substance (cf. the table in G. del Olmo
Lete, *Vocación* 372–73). For example, N. Habel (*ZAW* 77 [1965] 313) found in
Ezekiel's case six elements: divine confrontation (1:1–28), introductory word
(1:29–2:2), commission (2:3–5), implied objection (2:6, 8), reassurance (2:6–7),
and sign (2:8–3:11). The presence of an objection, however, is doubtful.

Identification of generic elements is not necessarily the same as exposing the
literary structure within which they are used as building blocks. The theophany
account, with its emphasis on seeing, is exceedingly elaborate: it extends from
1:1 to 1:28b*a*. G. del Olmo Lete (*Vocación* 299–300, 307–8) has observed that the

long form וָאֵרֶאה "and I saw" in vv 1 and 28ba—as distinct from the shorter equivalent וָאֵרֶא in vv 4, 15, and 27—provides a frame for the theophany account. V 1 has an introductory role; consideration of vv 2–3a may be deferred to a later point. Thereafter it is possible to divide up the narrative on the basis of subject matter, but commentators have shown no consistency in using this method. Rhetorical criticism is a safer, more objective guide in delineating the limits of the parts that make up this literary whole. H. V. D. Parunak has observed that a chiastic framework is provided in vv 4 and 26–28 ("Structural Studies" 123–24; *JBL* 99 [1980] 63):

A. Storm phenomena
רוח סערה, ענן
"storm wind, cloud"

C′. כעין חשמל
"like gleaming amber," v 27a

B. ונגה לו סביב
"and radiance surrounded it"

B′. ונגה לו סביב
"and radiance surrounded him," v 27b

A′. storm phenomena
ענן, הגשם
"cloud, rain," v 28a

C. כעין החשמל
"like gleaming amber"

Within this outer framework, he suggested that the body of the text consisted of three sections, vv 5–14, 15–21, and 22–25, each of which contains the same key word as occurs in the framework units, כעין "like the gleam of" (vv 7, 16, 22).

It is possible to refine this structural analysis. First, the description of the vision proper begins with v 3b (see the *Comment*) and ends at v 28a, after which v 28ba harks back to v 1 and rounds off the narrative, as noted above. V 28bβ aligns with chap. 2. Second, and more important, Smend (10), followed by Bertholet ([1897] 6) and Kraetzschmar (7), on grounds of subject matter isolated vv 13–14 as a section in its own right. Four stylistic factors support this refinement and even suggest that the section closely aligns with vv 3b–4 and 26–28a. (1) אש "fire" occurs in vv 4, 13 (three times), and 27, independently of the chiastic structure of vv 4 and 26–28a. (2) The weather phenomena of vv 4 and 28a are matched by בזק "lightning flash" in v 14. (3) There is a partial echo of the B/B′ element of vv 4 and 27b in ונגה לאש "and the fire had radiance" in v 13 (cf. the resumptive הנגה סביב "the surrounding radiance" in v 28a). (4) כמראה "like the appearance of" occurs only in vv 13–14 (two times), apart from its fourfold occurrence in vv 26–28a. It is true that Parunak's sectional key word כעין "like the gleam of" does not occur in vv 13–14, but neither does כמראה "like the appearance of" occur in v 4. There seems to be a certain selectivity, rather than uniform repetition of every feature.

When content is aligned with this stylistic evidence, there emerges an impression of an alternating sequence that finally coalesces. A storm theophany in v 4 gives way to a throne theophany in vv 5–12; it reappears in vv 13–14 and then yields to development of the throne theophany in vv 15–21 and 22–24a, 25b before the storm and throne theophanies are finally combined in the climactic vv 26–28a:

storm	3b–4		13–14			
throne		5–12		15–21	22–25	26–28a

With respect to the throne theophany sections of vv 5–12, 15–21, and 22–25, Hals (14) observed a consistent feature, a concluding motif of mobility. This insight enables the reader to see that each of these sections falls into at least two parts, the latter of which is concerned with mobility. In vv 5–12 the description of the living creatures, whose role is later shown to be supporters of the throne, culminates at v 12 in their movement under the control of the רוח "spirit." The preceding vv 5–11 consist of two roughly parallel parts. Vv 5–7 mention their human form (v 5a), their four faces (v 6a) and four wings (v 6b), and also their legs (v 7a), while vv 8–11 (actually vv 8a, 10–11: see the *Notes*) develop these aspects by referring to human arms and hands (v 8a) and by describing the faces (v 10) and wings (v 11). Vv 15–21, which describe the wheels of the throne, fall into two parts, vv 15–18 and 19–21: מעל הארץ "from the ground" in vv 19 and 21 function as an inclusion, echoing the initial בארץ "on the ground" in v 15. Vv 19–21 develop v 12, explaining the movement of the wheels in relation to the creatures, under the joint control of the רוח "spirit." Vv 22–24a, 25b are initially concerned with the רקיע "firmament-platform" above the living creatures in v 22. Thereafter the motif of mobility comes to the fore again. To this end v 23 has a transitional function; vv 24a and 25b describe the noise of the creatures' moving wings.

The second part of the visionary call narrative consists of 1:28bβ–3:11. It majors in Yahweh's verbal revelation to Ezekiel: just as the verb ראה "see" echoes through the first part, so the formula that introduces divine speech, ויאמר אלי "and he said to me," reverberates through this one (2:1, 3; 3:1, 3, 4, 10). It is reinforced by the related verb דבר "speak" in the early stages of the account (1:28bβ; 2:1, 2). There has been a tendency to define the structure of this second part in terms of the occurrence of the vocative בן־אדם "human one," which mostly follows the introductory formula ויאמר אלי "and he said to me" and also stands after ואתה "and you" within divine speech (2:6, 8). Thus Lamparter (38), Zimmerli (106–7), and Greenberg (72–73) envision six sections that also express form-critical features: an introduction in 1:28bβ(or 2:1)–2:2, commission in vv 3–5, reassurance in vv 6–7, ordination in v 8–3:3, recapitulation of the commission in 3:4–9, and a summary in vv 10–11. The cases of ויאמר אלי בן־אדם "and he said to me, 'Human one'" in 3:1, 3 are taken as introducing stages within a larger section. We noted previously Habel's analysis of the passage (*ZAW* 77 [1965] 313) solely in terms of form, concluding with a section 2:8–3:11. The heterogeneity of the material in this section makes it unlikely.

Scholars commonly postulate a section 2:8–3:3, which contains three instances of בן־אדם "human one." The abundance of the address casts doubt on the usefulness of the term as a criterion for structural division. Moreover, the identification of form-critical elements is not necessarily a guide to the literary structuring of a particular unit. Does this long text contain rhetorical clues to its structure? The series of imperatives addressed to Ezekiel, עמד "stand" in 2:1, שמע "hear" in 2:8, and לך־בא "come, go" in 3:4, seems to initiate major stages of development. This criterion by itself suffers from the same defect as the vocative address, since imperatives also occur in 3:1, 3, 10, and 11, and prohibitions feature in 2:6. But an analysis in terms of three sections consisting of 1:28bβ–2:7, 2:8–3:3, and 3:4–11 is supported by evidence of inclusion observed by del Olmo Lete (*Vocación* 316–17). In 2:8 and 3:3, אשר אני נתן אליך "what/which I am presenting to you" forms a framework. Likewise, in 3:4 and 11a the divine assignment to Ezekiel is stated twice, in similar terms.

The stylistic structure of 1:28bβ–2:7 is more difficult to discern. Del Olmo Lete has found an inclusion in the repetition of 2:4b–5a in v 7. Certainly 1:28bβ–2:2a functions as an introduction, whose beginning, מְדַבֵּר קוֹל וָאֶשְׁמַע "and I heard the voice of someone speaking," is repeated at the start of the main part, in 2:2b. The doubled motif of sending in vv 3a and 4a is matched by the twin reassurance not to fear in v 6. The content of vv 4b–5a is repeated in v 7. It seems then that after the introduction there are two coordinated subsections, vv 2b–5 and 6–7, each of which falls into two parts.

In terms of content, the three sections are concerned with the elements of commission, ordination, and confirmation, as del Olmo Lete (*Vocación* 316–17) has observed. The first section includes the element of reassurance in 2:6–7. Del Olmo Lete has noted that the final item in call narratives often consists of resumption of one or more earlier elements, and that confirmation closes the extended call narrative in Jer 1, at vv 17–19.

The unit is concluded by the narrative of 3:12–15, with a change of scene whereby Ezekiel is translated from the site of the vision to the exilic settlement. Parunak has seen a complete chiasm covering 1:1–3:15, in the course of which 3:12 corresponds to 2:1–2, 3:13 to 1:4–28, and 3:14–15 to 1:1–3 ("Structural Studies" 122–37; *JBL* 99 [1980] 62–66; cf. Fuhs 19). His comparison of 3:12 and 2:1–2 includes repetition of divinely related speech, but this parallel precariously depends on the Masoretic doxology in 3:12. Del Olmo Lete (*Vocación* 317) has more reasonably found a further case of inclusion. 3:12–14a aligns with 1:4–28, deliberately echoing the earlier description of theophany, while 3:14b–15 resumes 1:1–3 (more strictly 1:1, 3b) in its references to the exiles (הַגּוֹלָה "the exiles" and בְּתוֹכָם "among them" in v 15) and the pressure of Yahweh's hand (v 14b). One may also partially reinstate Parunak's scheme and see in the spirit's translation of the prophet in vv 12a and 14a a counterpart to the spirit's enabling in 2:2. Then 1:4–2:2 is the initial span of material that is paralleled in 3:12–14a.

While 1:1–3:15 gives the impression of being a literary unit in the light of its form-critical and stylistic coherence, we must ask whether and to what extent redactional activity underlies it. In this regard, one must consider that the account appears to envision only Ezekiel's ministry of judgment and never to transcend it with any hope of a brighter future (cf. Hals 10). However, the intrusive 1:2–3a can hardly be excluded from the category of redaction (see below). As for the vision account, while it is impressionistic, it shows clear evidence of reflection. Accordingly, doubt is cast on Block's explanation of the traditional state of the text as the result of an emotional blurting out of the prophet's immediate observations (*CBQ* 50 [1988] 427–39). As Greenberg (52) has observed,

> the depiction of the various motions and situations of the apparition . . . seems to be based on a combination of observations more complex and varied than the mere approach of the apparition involved in this vision.

Yet this reflective character could well have been inherent in the written account from the beginning. Zimmerli, after reviewing and criticizing earlier redaction-critical efforts (95–97), went on to set out his own presentation (100–106). Most

significantly, he saw an indication of redaction in the variation in gender of suffixes relating to the living creatures and associated grammatical phenomena,
whereby masculine forms appear alongside expected feminine ones. It permitted him to isolate a minimal amount of original material, which uses feminine
suffixes. However, Keel (*Jahwe-Visionen* 215 n. 203) has observed that Zimmerli
retained v 12 (apart from v 12ba) despite its masculine references.

A related issue is the use of feminine suffixes for the (masculine) wheels in vv
16–18. Höhne ("Thronwagenvision" 80–84), following Eichrodt (55–56), attributed both sets of aberrant suffixes to copyists who altered to masculine suffixes
in the case of the creatures under the influence of the (male) cherubim in chap.
10 and erroneously altered to feminine suffixes in the case of the wheels in mechanical assimilation to the feminine suffixes in 1:5–12. The relatively random
inconsistency of these grammatical deviations is probably to be laid at the door
of text criticism, rather than redaction criticism, although they may be retained
as a textual curiosity that has no bearing on exegesis.

Zimmerli (104–5, 127), developing the observations of Sprank (*Studien* 52–
54), also regarded the whole section concerning the wheels, vv 15–21, as
secondary, though already presupposed by chap. 10. His main argument depends
on his redactional view of the material with wrong suffixes in vv 5–12. He also
found marked deviation in content from the rest of the vision: a breaking of the
ascending order of description by reverting to a low element, a switch from an
airborne perspective to the ground, and a concern with technical detail. Keel
(*Jahwe-Visionen* 181 n. 125) prefers to think rather of a concern for minute details, but otherwise he tends to support Zimmerli. He argues that the wheeled
divine chariot in vv 15–21 represents a totally different concept from that of the
throne-bearing creatures that dominates the rest of the vision (*Jahwe-Visionen* 180–
88). If the structural analysis offered above is correct, one could also adduce a
structural argument: that if vv 15–21 were omitted, the resultant pattern would
be simply A/B/A/B/AB. Moreover, Houk (*ZAW* 93 [1981] 76–85) has applied to
the unit two statistical methods of determining authorship and deduced that vv
15–21 are secondary. In fact, he cuts out considerably more than Zimmerli's reconstructed text and envisions a brief primary unit of vv 4–5a, 22, 26–28.

These arguments are much more impressive in terms of their cumulative impact than when considered one by one. In my limited experience, statistical
analysis has sometimes supported and sometimes been at tantalizing variance with
other perspectives. Keel (*Jahwe-Visionen* 143) significantly also regarded the whole
of vv 13–14 as secondary. He worked with a unitary conception of Ezek 1 as closely
linked with ancient Near Eastern iconography. But what if the vision narrative
deliberately employs two basically different cultural conceptions, as the structure
suggests, and vv 15–21 represent the influence of the storm theophany of vv 13–
14? Indeed, Mettinger (*Dethronement* 105) has urged the originality of vv 15–21
because of the link between cloud and chariot in literary descriptions of the storm
theophany in the OT. He cited Pss 104:3; 77:19 (18; גלגל "wheeled vehicle"); Zech
6:1–8; 2 Kgs 2:11. Although vv 15–21 embody reflection, like other parts of the
vision, their redactional nature is not assured.

Zimmerli (126) linked v 7 with the addition of vv 15–21 as implying a single
metal post as part of a metal chariot, instead of a foot or feet. However, Keel

(*Jahwe-Visionen* 178 n. 115, 215) has observed on iconographical grounds that a reference to two literal feet is quite possible and indeed more likely. Overall, while one must leave open the possibility of redaction in this complex vision account, it does possess a degree of coherence that is compatible with a writing down (or dictating) of afterthoughts regarding an overwhelming experience.

As for the rest of the call narrative, 1:28bβ–3:15, it is significant that Zimmerli (106–7) has judged it to be of a primary nature. He has defended the text, repetitious as it often is, against earlier charges of redaction. He has found only 3:13 secondary, largely because of its masculine suffix relating to the living creatures. However, as we saw earlier, the verse has a valuable structural role to play in the overall narrative. To attribute this particular stylistic phenomenon to redactional activity is to create a jigsaw with one missing piece.

The call narrative as a whole clearly functions as a literary introduction to the judgment oracles of Ezekiel. The parallel of Isa 6, which evidently served as a preface to a written collection of Isaiah's oracles delivered during the Syro-Ephraimitic crisis (7:1–8:18 or 9:6[7]; cf. R. E. Clements, *Isaiah 1–39* [Grand Rapids: Eerdmans, 1980] 70–71), suggests that it was combined with a shorter or longer collection of Ezekiel's oracles of judgment, possibly culminating in chap. 7. The call narrative provided supernatural warrant for them (cf. Long, "Prophetic Authority" 12–13, although his attributions of both the Isaiah and the Ezekiel complexes to later tradents is less likely).

The redactional note(s) in 1:2–3a seem(s) to consciously integrate this material into a subsequent larger whole. The style of opening an oracle or collection of oracles with a combination of a message-reception formula and general information about the prophet accords with Hag 1:1; Zech 1:1. However, it would be rash to conclude with Zimmerli (110) that the redactional addition was made in the early postexilic period. It is noteworthy that there is a difference in the style of dating by years in Ezekiel on the one hand and in Haggai and Zechariah on the other. The style of Ezek 1:1, 2 accords with that of the rest of the book in supplying (1) first a cardinal number and then the year in cases of numerals from eleven upwards, and (2) first the year and then an ordinal number in cases of numerals from one to ten, while the examples in Haggai and Zechariah follow an evidently postexilic style of placing the year before a cardinal number (cf. C. Hardmeier, *Prophetie im Streit vor dem Untergang Judas*, BZAW 187 [Berlin: de Gruyter, 1990] 102–4 and n. 36). Moreover, the similarity of Ezek 1:2 to Hag 1:1; Zech 1:1 seems to be fortuitous. In this case, the opening of the unit had evidently been established already and was regarded as sacrosanct. The only way to amplify the text was to clarify the date, by means of an addition that referred to the ground-breaking nature of the eventual oracle with the infinitive absolute (see the *Notes*), and to give some basic personal and topographical details about Ezekiel. The secondary impression of the text upon the reader, including its switch to the third person, suggests that Ezekiel himself was not responsible for vv 2–3a and that the writer belonged to the second generation of exiles for whom such details about the prophet were considered necessary, perhaps under the influence of a literary tradition of superscriptions in which parentage, occupation, and setting were already important (cf. Tucker, "Prophetic Superscriptions" 61, 69).

Here is an outline of the literary unit:

Comment

The prophetic call narrative of 1:1–3:15 is a carefully constructed composition that falls into two parts, an account of Ezekiel's visual encounter with Yahweh (1:1–28b*a*) and a description of his auditory receipt of a prophetic commission (1:28b*β*–3:11).

1   The visual encounter is to be described in vv 3b–28a. Here it is supplied with a brief introduction in which the announcement of the vision in v 4 (וארא "and I saw") is expanded into a longer preliminary statement. It fittingly includes the term וארא "and I saw," which will be resumed in the even briefer closing description of Ezekiel's reaction to the vision in v 28b*a*. There is a reference to the time of the vision and, in general terms, Ezekiel's circumstances when he experienced it.

The reference to "the thirtieth year" is problematic. H. H. Rowley's honest admission "I know of no wholly satisfactory solution" (*BJRL* 36 [1953] 182), which echoes that of Keil (19), originally written in 1868, still holds true. The dating does not conform to the use of Jehoiachin's deportation in 597 B.C. as an initial point, which is found in the rest of the book, including v 2. This fact seems to suggest that it antedates that chronological reference system, which begins in 8:1 and runs at intervals throughout the rest of the book (20:1; 24:1, etc.; cf. the more explicit 33:21; 40:1). Its uniqueness is consistent with the supposition that 1:1–3:15 originally prefaced an independent, short collection of oracles of judgment that appears in chaps. 4–7. York (*VT* 27 [1977] 83–91) has given an overview and critique of the various solutions that have been offered. So has Kutsch, more briefly, in *Daten* 45–46, while Low ("Interpretive Problems" 78–124) has devoted a chapter to it. Only the more significant proposals need be reviewed here. It is possible to relate "the thirtieth year" to Jehoiachin's deportation by text-critical means. Thus W. F. Albright (*JBL* 51 [1932] 96–97) developed a suggestion made earlier by A. Merx, that it refers to the publication of the book in 568 B.C. In order to reach this explanation, he had to make the assumptions that v 3a originally followed v 1a*a* and that in v 2 היא השנה "that is, the year" was a corruption of בשנה "in the year." By these means he was able to reconstruct an initial "In the thirtieth year . . . Ezekiel . . . received a communication from Yahweh . . ." After this editorial introduction, the first-person vision account opens with "In the fifth year . . . , while I was living among the exiles . . ." This reconstruction restores coherence to the text but strangely equates publication of a book with receipt of an oracle (York, *VT* 27 [1977] 89). Moreover, it fails to satisfy the reader with what is a paramount necessity in text-critical work, a convincing explanation as to how so clear a text fell into such disorder. If such a text were extant, it would be branded as a secondary attempt to smooth away difficulties. Kutsch (*Daten* 49–54) also has conjectured that the two dates relate to Jehoiachin's exile: they represent originally independent superscriptions, vv 1, 3b and vv 2–3a. The first introduced the theophany narrative in v 4–28a and belonged to the end of Ezekiel's prophetic ministry, while the second prefaced the call narrative of 1:28b–3:11 that reports the inauguration of his ministry. However, this separation puts asunder what in form-critical terms belongs together.

If one equates the thirtieth year with the royal date in v 2, as the present text obviously intends us to do, it refers to 593 B.C. Working back, one arrives at the year 623. Jewish tradition, represented by the Targum and Jerome, accordingly interpreted in terms of Josiah's reform and the finding of the book of the Torah in the temple in 621 (so Herrmann 10). Nobile (*Anton* 59 [1984] 396–99) has traced links between 2 Kgs 22–23 and the book of Ezekiel. But why this fact should have been so crucial for dating Ezekiel's vision or call remains unexplained. So does the supposition that it could have been regarded as self-evident, with no need of explicit clarification.

Another hypothesis links the thirtieth year with the apparent reference to jubilee year chronology in 40:1. The deportation under Jehoiachin is identified as the halfway point in a fifty-year cycle, five years after which Ezekiel received his call (25 + 5 = 30; Nobile, *Anton* 59 [1984] 399–402).

The most plausible solution, one that requires the fewest assumptions or the least reading into the text, is to relate the tantalizing chronological reference to Ezekiel's age at the time of this experience, an explanation that goes back to Origen. Strictly one requires a fuller text, either the prefixing of בֶּן "son of," the standard idiom for age, which Kraetzschmar (4) proposed to insert, or the addition of לְחַיַּי "of my life," in line with Gen 7:11, as K. Budde (*ExpTim* 12 [1900] 39–40) urged. In *JBL* 50 (1931) 29–30 he tentatively suggested emending שָׁנָה "year" to שָׁנַי "of my years" (cf. *BHK*). However, S. G. Taylor (*TynBul* 17 [1966] 119–20) has drawn attention to the briefer text of Gen 8:13, which in dependence on the more explicit Gen 7:6, 11, merely refers to the year, month, and day, with obvious reference to Noah's age. Here there are no preceding standard references, and it must remain a moot point whether in their absence one may find an unambiguous allusion to the prophet's age. Yet if one works with the assumption that the text has been correctly transmitted and that it is meaningful as it stands, it can least unreasonably be understood as a poor way of expressing age. Our knowledge of the Jerusalem priesthood does not permit us to judge whether the age of thirty was professionally significant (cf. the age of ordination in Num 4; 1 Chr 23:3).

The general location of the vision is indicated by the reference to Ezekiel's belonging to the group of deportees residing near the Kebar Canal. Other texts, 3:23 and 43:3, along with the editorial 1:3a, clarify that the vision occurred at the bank of the canal, which was some distance away from the actual settlement according to 3:15. In the light of Ps 137:1–2; Acts 16:13, it is possible that the place was used for worship, the cleansing presence of water serving to mitigate the uncleanness of a foreign land (cf. Amos 7:17). At any rate the parallel of Daniel's angelophany at the bank of the Tigris (Dan 10:4) suggests that such a location was judged worthy of a visual revelation.

The Kebar Canal is mentioned in two fifth-century B.C. texts relating to the banking firm of Murashu, one of which indicates that it ran in the vicinity of the city of Nippur. Accordingly it can no longer be identified with the major artery *šaṭṭ-en-nil*, which flowed through Nippur (so, e.g., Cooke 4–5; Zimmerli 112). It was part of a complex network of canals that came into being in the Mesopotamian heartland to provide artificial irrigation from the Euphrates and, to a lesser extent, the Tigris for the grain crops and date orchards, and also, in the case of larger watercourses, transportation of these and other goods. In the fifth century the large estate of a royal prince, Prince Manuštanu, was situated in the area between Nippur and the Kebar Canal (cf. Vogt, *Bib* 39 [1958] 211–16 = *Untersuchungen* 26–31; R. Zadok, *Israel Oriental Studies* 8 [1978] 266–332; R. M. Adams, *Heartlands* 176–78, 186–88). Various groups of national exiles were eventually settled in the Nippur area, in a neo-Babylonian program to rehabilitate the region after its depopulation from the wars with Assyria in the seventh century (cf. Zadok, *Israel Oriental Studies* 8 [1978] 326; Ephal, *Or* 47 [1978] 80–82).

The opening of the heavens is an expression that occurs here first and has influenced a number of later visionary and apocalyptic texts, in the sense of glimpsing of a heavenly scene or witnessing the descent of a heavenly being (e.g., 3 Macc 6:18; 2 Bar 22:1; T. Lev. 5:1; Matt 3:16; Acts 7:56; Rev 19:11). It here refers to the preliminaries of a theophany. It is tantamount to the tearing (קרע) of the heavens in Isa 63:19(64:1) and to the spreading open (נטה, הטה) of the heavens like the curtains of a tent in 2 Sam 22:10 = Ps 18:10(9); Ps 144:5 for the same purpose (cf. F. M. Cross, *Canaanite Myth and Hebrew Epic* [Cambridge, MA: Howard University, 1973] 159 n. 59). It thus prepares fittingly for the theophany Ezekiel is about to experience. However, the choice of verb seems to add a particular nuance. In the OT the "windows" or floodgates of heaven were opened to permit the sending down of either blessing (2 Kgs 7:2; Mal 3:10) or judgment (Gen 7:11; Isa 24:18) (see F. Lentzen-Deis, *Bib* 50 [1969] 303). The subsequent content of the vision will make clear that here a revelation of judgment is in view.

The Heb. מראות אלהים might here be interpreted "vision(s) of God," that is, a vision in which God was seen. However, it is a fixed phrase in Ezekiel, occurring also in 8:3; 40:2, in contexts where divinely given visions are in view. This latter meaning is to be adopted here for the sake of consistency. It was a vision "no mortal eye could see without divine help" (Greenberg 41).

2–3a This material has an intrusive ring, as its third-person reference to Ezekiel indicates. One might regard v 2 as a text-critical gloss, as Herrmann (1) and Lang (*Bib* 64 [1983] 225), among others, have done. Its initial cue phrase certainly conforms to a pattern of glosses that appears in the book (cf., e.g., 23:4b). However, the random element that marks such glosses is conspicuously lacking. The content aligns with the system of dating that occurs throughout the book from 8:1 onwards. Thus v 2 is redactional in nature. The use of היא "that is" is the same as in 2 Kgs 25:8: the redactional intent is to provide a consistent synchronism for the dating of v 1, and there is no reason to doubt the chronological equation. According to Parker and Dubberstein's calendrical reconstruction of Nebuchadnezzar's reign (*Babylonian Chronology* 28), it represents 31 July 593. The dating by the deportation of "the king" appears to reflect the political reality that Jehoiachin was still the legitimate monarch and that Zedekiah ruled in Judah only as regent (cf. Zimmerli 114–15). Understandably, it also expresses a conviction among the exiles that the future lay with them rather than with those in the homeland, a conviction that Ezekiel shared and endorsed in his prophetic ministry.

V 3a seems to continue the redactional amplification. It provides a superscription, not for the book, since only one oracle (דבר "word") is in view, but strictly for the unit 1:1–3:15. It reveals an awareness that the ensuing vision is a preparatory part of a larger whole in which the divine word is the significant element. To this end it takes over the message-reception formula that characteristically introduces oracles in the book (see 3:16b and *Comment*). However, it seems also to reflect a placing of this material at the head of a series of oracles (see *Form/Structure/Setting*).

The name *yĕhezqēʾl*, which recurs in 24:24 and is shared by another priest in 1 Chr 24:16, means "May God strengthen." It expresses the prayerful wish of his parents that God would care for the newborn child by endowing him with strength, so that he could face life's vicissitudes with confidence (see J. D. Fowler, *The Theophoric Divine Names in Hebrew*, JSOTSup 49 [Sheffield: JSOT, 1988] 98, 100). A yahwistic form of the name, *yĕhizqiyyāhû* (Hezekiah) "May Yahweh strengthen," was the name of an earlier Judean king, among others (see BDB 306a). In 3:8–9 there is probably a play on Ezekiel's name: he would be given grace to live up to it, as an unpopular prophet.

The location of the prophet when he receives the vision is beside the Kebar Canal, which is further defined as in southern Babylonia ("Chaldea"). The definition of place marks both a narrowing and a widening clarification of the information given in v 1. There the reference to the canal identified it with the settlement to which Ezekiel belonged; here it is the setting of the encounter with Yahweh (see *Comment* on v 1). The designation "Chaldea, land of the Chaldeans" is more specific than "Babylon(ia)," which from the perspective of far-off Judah is generally the location of the deportees (2 Kgs 24:16; Ezra 1:11, etc.; Jer 24:1; 28:4; 29:1, 4), although the present description occurs in Jer 24:5.

3b–4 The experience of Yahweh's "hand" is regularly associated with the personal receipt of a vision in the book of Ezekiel (3:22; 8:1; 37:1; 40:1); in 33:22 it triggers an extraordinary divine action. It has antecedents in earlier descriptions of prophetic experiences. The closest to the examples in Ezekiel is in 2 Kgs 3:15, where Yahweh's hand causes a trance in which an oracle is communicated. The case in 33:22 is comparable with that in 1 Kgs 8:46, where it relates to a physical empowering to run with exceptional speed. In Isa 8:11 it refers to the divine constraint associated with delivery of an oracle (cf. in principle Jer 20:7, 9). In Jer 15:17 it is used more generally in association with the vehement, anti-social consequences of being a prophet; similarly in Ezek 3:14 it is associated with prophetic passion. Roberts (*VT* 21 [1971] 244–51) has related the expression to the usage in ancient Near Eastern and Israelite literature concerning a negative manifestation of supernatural power, especially in sickness or plague (cf., e.g., Exod 9:15). He has traced the prophetic development to a similarity between physical or psychophysical symptoms and the prophetic phenomena. However, Wilson (*JBL* 98 [1979] 325) has observed that the expression belongs to the same set of prophetic terminology as the message-reception formula. So it refers not to external behavior, such as ecstasy or trance, but to divine possession as the means of divine-human communication. Yet it may be noted that divine possession here results in specific manifestation of a vision, which may or may not be regarded as an ecstatic experience, according to one's definition of the word (cf. Wilson, *JBL* 98 [1979] 324 and n. 10). In this case the physical pressure of the divine hand is the harbinger of an experience of a supernatural vision. Chronologically it does not follow the seeing of v 1 but introduces the flashback describing the vision in detail and prepares for the seeing of v 4 (cf. 8:1b–2; cf. Mosis 253 n. 17).

The visionary convention of first announcing the vision with a verb of seeing and then using the transitional והנה "and behold" before presenting the vision segment is followed here (Long, *JBL* 95 [1976] 357). D. J. McCarthy (*Bib* 61 [1980] 332) has described this transitional element in terms of excited perception that conveys a strong emotional tone.

The phenomenon observed by Ezekiel is described in general terms in v 4 as something seen in the distance. Then in the succeeding account, specific details reflect its approach. Storm, cloud, and fire are in the OT regular elements of a storm theophany, a literary tradition that was basically derived from mythological descriptions of the storm or war god in ancient Near Eastern religious contexts and already had a long history of literary usage in Israel. It is from this latter source that Ezekiel evidently took it. The storm god was at home in upper Mesopotamia and east of the Tigris, where rain-based agriculture was practiced, but not on the lower courses of the Tigris and Euphrates, where irrigation agriculture prevailed (Oppenheim, "Assyrian-Babylonian Religion" 67). The storm theophany was employed in Israel to describe the help given by Yahweh to his servant or people against enemies. The full form consists of two elements, a description of Yahweh's coming and then a description of the reaction of the earth to his appearing (cf. Nah 1:3b–6), but often only one element is used, as here. Parallels to the present description are:

> His way is in whirlwind and storm,
> and a cloud is the dust of his feet. (Nah 1:3b)

> Out of the radiance before him
> there passed through his clouds
> hailstones and coals of fire. (Ps 18:13[12]; cf. 2 Sam 22:13)

The storm wind features similarly in 2 Sam 22:11 (= Ps 18:11[10]); Zech 9:14; Job 38:1; 40:6; Ps 77:19(18). So do clouds in Isa 19:1; Pss 77:18(17); 97:2. The radiance of fire or lightning is also an element of the storm theophany in Hab 3:4, 11 (cf. Isa 4:5).

The theological program of the prophets included a strong tendency to engage in ideological reversal, whereby comforting traditions were re-used in a challenging way. One instance of this prophetic reversal was to portray the coming of Yahweh in a storm theophany to Israel as his victim. Thus Micah used the storm-theophany tradition to express divine judgment on the capital of the Northern Kingdom (Mic 1:3–6). Earlier, punishment had been the lot of Israel's enemies, and this old perspective is preserved in Nah 1:3b–8; Hab 3:3–15. It also appears in Ps 97:3–5, where Yahweh's "judgments," to Israel's relief (v 8), are carried out by means of his appearing in the trappings of a thunderstorm:

> Fire goes before him
> and lights up his foes around.
> His lightning flashes light up the world. (vv 3–4a)

One may contrast Ps 50:3–4, which shares the prophetic nuancing:

> Our God comes, unable to keep silent.
> A fire in front of him consumes,
> and around him a storm rages.
> He calls to the heavens above
> and to the earth, in order to try his people.

Ezekiel too, in the light of the context, appears to be drawing on this use of the storm theophany to convey a threat that Yahweh poses to his covenant people.

The "north" is an unexpected item in the description: after the opening of the skies in v 1, one expects the apparition to come straight down. In 2 Sam 22:10 (= Ps 18:10[11]), Yahweh "spread open the skies and came down." However, a meaning "cloudy sky," derived from צפן "hide" (E. Vogt, *Bib* 34 [1953] 426; J. de Savignac, *VT* 3 [1953] 95–96; cf. N. Habel, *Job* [Philadelphia: Westminster, 1985] 371), does not commend itself, if some suitable significance in terms of the standard sense "north" can be perceived. C. Grave (*UF* 12 [1980] 226–27) has argued for an early meaning "clear sky" for Ugar. *spn*, which was then associated with the north wind that clears the sky. If so, such a meaning would be possible here, although again one would prefer a more established meaning. An oft-suggested reference to Mount Casius, earlier Zaphon (= north), as the mountain home of the gods (so, e.g., Jeremias, *Theophanie* 116–17; cf. Ps 48:3[2]) seems hardly to fit the celestial demand of the context. Nor does the proposal that Yahweh is traveling from Jerusalem to Babylonia along the Fertile Crescent (e.g., Bertholet [1936] 5; Fohrer 12), for the same reason. Intriguingly, in Job 26:7 צפון "north" seems to be used where one might expect a reference to the heavens, but in fact it may indicate the sacred mountain, in synonymous parallelism with ארץ "earth," as Roberts (*Bib* 56 [1975] 554–57) has argued. It appears to bear this meaning in Job 37:22 (Habel, *Job* 515).

The celestial source of the theophany in v 1 suggests as a consequence that the northern sector of the sky is in view here, but why should this be specified? Scholars commonly find links between 2:1–3:1 and the call of Jeremiah in Jer 1, and indeed between various passages in the respective books. Thus in a primary part of the Gog-Magog unit, Ezek 38–39, the invader is described as coming from the north (39:2; cf. 38:6, 15), in echo of the "foe from the north" motif that appears in the early oracles of Jeremiah (cf. Keil 20). In the course of the extended call narrative in Jer 1, Yahweh declares that "from the north will be opened up evil" (מצפון תפתח הרעה, v 14). When one recalls that the same passive verb is used of the opening of the heavens in v 1, seemingly in a sinister sense, and that a theophany of judgment is in overall view, the exegetical possibility presents itself that "north" carries overtones of the proclamation of evil that Yahweh brings with him (cf. 2:10; cf. Keil 20–21; Ziegler 12). He comes from a sinister quarter of the sky.

The recurrence of the material of v 4αβb in v 27 has prompted the widespread suggestion that it is a textual gloss or redactional addition from the later description (cf., e.g., Fohrer 7; Zimmerli 82, 101, 125). However, the discipline of rhetorical criticism has encouraged a more positive attitude toward repetition. Here it seems to have important structural significance (see *Form/Structure/Setting*). The radiant aura surrounding the cloud accords with 2 Sam 22:13 (= Ps 18:13[12]), where such an aura precedes Yahweh's appearance in a theophany.

A dominant feature of the vision account is broached in v 4b, an appeal to analogy, whether by means of the preposition "like" or the use of the nouns מראה "appearance" and דמות "likeness." The presupposition of this feature is that the apparition crosses the bounds of the usual and natural. Human experience cannot find plain words to match the phenomena; it can only provide approximations to what is essentially uncanny and mysterious.

The term חשמל, which also occurs in v 27 and 8:2, raises problems for the lexicographer and exegete. There are a number of indications that support the sense "amber," as in the KJV and NRSV. The equivalents ἤλεκτρον in the LXX and *electrum* in the Vulgate point in two separate directions, amber stone and white gold. The latter is an alloy that in Pliny's period was made up of 80 percent gold and 20 percent silver (*Historia Naturalis* 33.23). The search for the right meaning has concentrated on identifying an Akkadian cognate. G. R. Driver (*VT* 1 [1951] 60–62) equated the word with Akkadian *elmešu*, which he understood as "brass" (so the REB), in reliance on R. C. Thompson's *Dictionary of Assyrian Chemistry and Geology* (Oxford: Clarendon, 1936) 76–79. However, serious doubts have been raised as to whether *elmešu* can bear this meaning (see D. Bodi, *Poem of Erra* 90 and n. 41). *CAD* 4.107–8 is inclined to identify חשמל with this Akkadian term, which it leaves untranslated but interprets in the light of its contexts, where it is used as "a quasi-mythical precious stone of great brilliancy and color which one tried to imitate with dyes." *CAD* 4.366–67 does not favor any connection with *ešmaru*, which means silver or a silver alloy. In the neo-Babylonian Poem of Erra, *elmešu* is apparently derived from a tree, in which case its interpretation as amber is assured (Landsberger, VTSup 16 [1967] 196; Bodi, *Poem of Erra* 93; for the linguistic relation between the Akkadian and Hebrew terms see Landsberger, VTSup 16 [1965] 195 and n. 1).

5–12 The blurred mass of wind-driven cloud and differing degrees of brightness gradually resolves itself into a series of distinct elements. The first to materialize and be noticed as the apparition approaches is the group of four living creatures. At this point the storm theophany becomes a throne theophany, as the vision report will eventually clarify (v 26). Separate motifs have here been combined (Jeremias, *Theophanie* 63; Keel, *Jahwe-Visionen* 190). The throne vision had already featured in the account of Isaiah's prophetic call in Isa 6. Isaiah saw Yahweh present in judgment, sitting in council, with the verdict of judgment passed and awaiting execution (R. Knierim, *VT* 18 [1968] 54–57; O. H. Stek, *BZ* 16 [1972] 195–97; Long, *JBL* 95 [1976] 361). At an earlier period Micaiah ben Imlah had seen a vision of the enthroned Yahweh in session with his council of judgment, discussing how the death sentence might be carried out (1 Kgs 22:19–22). In line with this tradition, the throne vision that Ezekiel gradually describes functions as a theophany of judgment. Indeed, this passage became part of a continuing tradition. In second-century B.C. Judah, two more visions were described that spoke in terms of a throne with wheels, in echo of Ezek 1:15–21. In the Book of the Watchers the intent of the vision is to reprove the supernatural Watchers for their sins (1 Enoch 14:3; 15:1–16:3; for the wheels of the throne, see 14:18). Likewise, in Dan 7:9 the wheeled throne has a setting of a divine court of judgment. There seems to be a conscious reminiscence of Ezek 1 in its description of a theophany of judgment upon the kingdoms of the earth.

While it is not a good exegetical procedure to anticipate later material, in this case the reader will be better served by a brief presentation of the general picture that emerges in the description only step by step. Keel (*Jahwe-Visionen* 125–273), building upon earlier work done by L. Dürr and others, has produced a lavishly illustrated study of ancient Near Eastern and Anatolian royal and religious iconography that sheds light on the particular throne imagery reflected here. Four-winged humanoid figures support on their heads a platform that represents the sky, above which sits the enthroned figure of Yahweh. This conception appears to be a fusion of at least two separate, well-attested traditions of religious iconography. In the first tradition two lions, bulls, or cherubs (two-winged animals with human heads) supported a platform above which stood a throne on which the deity sat. The example illustrated here (fig. 1) is an eight-foot-high basalt sculpture from Carchemish in North Syria that dates from the first half of the first millennium B.C. A throne occupied by a bearded god stands on a platform that is supported by two lions held by a bird-headed genius or lesser deity. The second tradition relates to two- or four-winged genii who support with their

Figure 1. An enthroned deity supported by lions

upper pair of wings and/or hands the wings of the sun or sky. Figure 2 shows a seal of the Persian period that reflects this tradition. The upper part of the skybearers' bodies has a human form, while the lower part takes the form of a bull: this feature of bullmen was taken over from the neo-Assyrian and neo-Babylonian depiction of skybearers.

Figure 2. Winged bullmen as skybearers

In Ezekiel's representation, the sky-bearing genii, as if deposed from their divine role (cf. Ps 82), have strikingly taken the place of the thronebearing animal or cherub attendants; they minister to Yahweh as King of kings and Lord of lords. Vv 5–12 focus upon the skybearers and describe their appearance and role.

5–7   As we noted in *Form/Structure/Setting*, vv 5–7 give a basic overall description of the figures. They have a human form (v 5a), four faces (v 6a), four wings (v 6b), and—evidently—two legs (v 7a). They are described as animate beings (חיות "living creatures"). They are "four" in number, a feature that reappears in their faces and wings and later with respect to the wheels. In ancient Near Eastern art thronebearers were only two in number, whereas representations of skybearers, when freed from the constraints of two-dimensional art, could be four (Keel, *Jahwe-Visionen* 248). The four figures, which are usually under the four corners of the platform, reflect the universal power of God. This significance is derived from the four cardinal directions, "the four quarters of the earth" (Isa 11:12). The Assyrian king was grandiloquently entitled *sar kibrāt erbetti* "the king of the four quarters." Ideally, the figures stand on the edge of the whole earth, supporting the sky above; here they have been scaled down in size, but not in value, as bearers of the divine throne. Their predominantly human shape, which distinguishes them from cherubim (cf. chap. 10) that were essentially animal in form, is qualified by the ensuing list of deviations, in respect of their four faces, four wings, and calves' feet. Their four faces find a partial parallel in the four human or animal—representing the same animal—faces of gods and genii in ancient Near Eastern iconography. Figure 3 shows an eighteenth-century B.C. Assyrian representation of a god with four human faces. Moreover, skybearers

Figure 3. A four-faced deity

Figure 4. Two-headed skybearers

could be depicted with two faces, as in figure 4, which shows the top row of
skybearers with two lions' heads on a fourteenth-century B.C. ivory piece found
at Megiddo. The multiplicity of faces seems to signify the omnipresence of the
god and, in the case of skybearers, their vigilance in scanning the earth to protect heaven from violation (Keel, *Jahwe-Visionen* 230, 233).

The four wings, whose function will be described in v 11, can be paralleled in
many ancient representations of skybearers, as in figure 2. The reference to the
legs as straight in v 7a is not clear. It may simply mean that they were stationary
rather than used for locomotion (Barrick, *CBQ* 44 [1982] 549–50). Then the description does not conflict with the skybearers of ancient iconography, who
generally had knee joints, backward pointing in the case of bullmen. In fact,
Ezekiel's creatures seem to be bullmen with respect to their feet. Again, figure 2
is relevant, in which the upper parts of the skybearers' bodies look human, and
the lower parts, culminating in hooves, are bovine. It was a feature of neo-Assyrian
and neo-Babylonian art to represent skybearers as bullmen, with two legs, and

such seems to be the case here (cf. Keel, *Jahwe-Visionen* 215). In that case the older view that the legs were single metal pedestals (so Zimmerli 126) is a misunderstanding.

The comparison of the creatures with "burnished copper" is reminiscent of the appearance of the supernatural guide much later in the book, at 40:3. In both cases it signifies their shining appearance, as befits supernatural beings (cf. כעין "like the gleam"), like the "two men in dazzling clothing" at the tomb of Jesus (Luke 24:4).

8a, 10–11 The next section is roughly parallel with vv 5–7; it covers similar ground in greater detail, with an ABCD/ABC scheme. First, the human appearance of the creatures is illustrated by reference to their arms and hands (v 8a), and then their faces (v 10) and wings (v 11) are described further. Their hands and arms would look as in figure 2, except that there they are raised to support the sky, whereas according to vv 22, 26 the creatures' heads have that function. In this case too we are probably to envision one pair per creature, as the four of them stood in a square (Cooke 13).

Their faces are of four different types. As we noted above, such diversity is unparalleled. Keel (*Jahwe-Visionen* 231, 237) has given examples of humanoid, winged skybearers with two heads, whether of an eagle, lion, bull, or a human being. Here, however, the four types are strikingly combined in each being. As Greenberg (45) has observed, the uneven formulation reflects the order of observation. In each case Ezekiel saw a human face on the front, which reinforced the generally human appearance, then the two animal faces on the left and right sides, and finally, by comparing the other beings, the eagle's face at the back. As the Midrash Rabbah on Exod 15 commented: "The most exalted of all living creatures is the human being; of birds, the eagle; of cattle, the ox; and of wild beasts, the lion. All of these received royalty and had greatness bestowed upon them, and they are set under the chariot of God" (Shemoth 23:13). But more must be said. In their oriental setting these faces are an expression of divine power, reflecting that of the lion and other great earthly beings. Here the creatures are represented as supernatural, in view of v 7b. As supernatural beings, they are mediators of Yahweh's powerful being. Yet, as his supernatural servants, they also represent the concerted best that each of his orders of animate creation can separately contribute to his glory (cf. Pss 103:20–22; 148).

The upward sweep of the upper of the two pairs of wings does not serve to support the sky as in the case of the Near Eastern winged skybearers. The purpose of v 12a appears to be to explain their function in terms of motion, just as the echo of v 12 in vv 19–21 explains the motion of the wheels. The noise of their wings mentioned in v 24a (and 3:13) also suggests that the outspread wings are not static and ornamental, like those of the cherubim above the ark (Exod 25:20; 1 Kgs 6:27), but dynamic and functional. The other pair of wings, as in the case of four-winged skybearers and other divine beings in Eastern art, point downwards and cover the body (see fig. 2), as in the case of the seraphim of Isa 6:2, of which there may well be a complementary echo here.

12 This expression of mobility is the first instance of an increasingly dominant concluding motif in each of the three throne-theophany sections. In the light of v 11a, the movement of the beings seems to have been accompanied by their flapping wings. It has alternatively been explained in terms of the approach of the whole apparition, within which the beings stand completely rigid and immobile (so, e.g., Zimmerli 121). The amount of redactional layering one espies in this vision account determines which explanation should be followed: certainly the presence of vv 15–21 in it dictates at least the propriety of the former for the full form of the text.

The potential direction of movement is governed by the compass points faced by each of the four beings. The actual direction is controlled by the "spirit" that animates them (cf. v 21). The "spirit" of God is sometimes referred to as the manifestation of God in his omnipresence (Ps 139:7), roaming to all points of the compass (Ezek 37:9), and that conception seems to be implied here. The divine spirit is here the organizing force that directs the apparition hither and thither, wherever it wants to go, as the expression of the divine will.

The very notion of movement, whether of the whole apparition or of the beings, strikes a discordant note against their background as either skybearers or bearers of the throne. By their very nature these are essentially static conceptions. In Ezekiel's vision the basic notion has been transformed. The storm theophany of v 4 has been allowed to determine the essential character of the throne vision. In contemporary art the bearers of the sun or sky and the bearers of a god's throne were models of cosmic or supernatural reality, which brought to the believing observer a sense of the sublime. Likewise, the visionary prophet sees a representation of his universal God manifesting himself in cosmic splendor. In Isa 6 a heavenly scene is superimposed upon the earthly temple; here it is superimposed on the theophanic cloud. In apocalyptic vision accounts, the seer is taken to heaven (cf., e.g., 1 Enoch 14:8–25; 2 Cor 12:2–4); here the heavenly comes down to the seer via the literary tradition of the storm theophany. The two traditions, one literary and the other partly visual, have not simply been juxtaposed but combined in such a way that the first has radically influenced the second. The implicit link that encouraged the combination of the traditions may have been the common motif of wings. In the storm theophany Yahweh travels on the "wings of the wind" according to 2 Sam 22:11 (= Ps 18:11[10]); Ps 104:3. If this association of motifs common to both traditions does underlie the combination, then the representation of the throne theophany in this vision account presumably included the motion of the beings' wings as the means of transporting the throne from the beginning and not merely at a later stage. Moreover, the mention of רוח "wind" in v 4 as a constituent element of the storm theophany may have been an influential factor in its reappearance in the sense of "spirit" in the description of the throne theophany at v 12.

13–14 This section reverts to the storm theophany of v 4, although the mention of the living beings or thronebearers echoes the throne theophany of vv 5–12 by way of coordination. The mention of "fiery coals" aligns with the description of the storm theophany of the warrior God in 2 Sam 22:9, 13 (= Ps 18:9[8]; cf. v 13[12]). The "lightning flashes" are reminiscent of the regular element of lightning (ברק), which appears in 2 Sam 22:13 (= Ps 18:13[12]); Pss 77:18–19(17–18); 97:4, as indeed the textual annotation in v 13 may have been observing (see *Note* 13.e.).

Evidently the closer proximity of the apparition enables the fiery mass glimpsed in v 4 to be particularized into a pulsating core, which is compared with moving "torches" (cf. the theophanic description in Gen 15:17); it breaks through the enveloping aura of v 4 with intermittent flashes that resemble lightning. The emphasis on manifestations of fire has a negative connotation. As in Ps 97:3–4 fire serves to burn up Yahweh's adversaries and lightning to inspire dread in the observing earth, so here his coming with such accouterments poses a terrible threat. The nature of that threat will be spelled out when the divine vision is succeeded by the divine word.

15–21 If vv 13–14 majored in storm theophany while relating it to throne theophany by way of the bearers, vv 15–21 primarily continue the throne theophany theme but tie it into storm theophany by describing the throne in terms of a wheeled chariot. Mettinger, as we noted above (see *Form/Structure/Setting;* cf. also Isa 66:15; Hab 3:8), has observed that the divine chariot is an element of the storm theophany. If the throne theophany of Ezek 1, while resting on OT literary foundations, is closely associated with ancient Near Eastern visual art, here it is strongly influenced by the literary presentations of the storm theophany. There is no compelling objection to crediting Ezekiel with this composite picture. From the beginning, the vision account combines the two motifs from different sources, Yahweh's coming in the storm and his enthronement in majesty (Keel, *Jahwe-Visionen* 190, 253). Accordingly, there can be no cavil in principle at the overlap of the two traditions in this section.

The purpose of the wheels emerges from the structural emphasis on "the ground" in vv 15, 19, and 21 (see *Form/Structure/Setting*). The throne on its platform functions as an amphibious vehicle: it not only flies through the sky by means of the wings of its bearers but drives along the ground by means of its wheels. It is a mark of the two distinct sources of the overall imagery that the structural relation between the wheels and the rest of the structure is left unclarified. The apparition lands on the ground, where indeed 3:12 seems to represent it. There is no need for the artificial conception of a supernatural plane on which the apparition rested in the vision (Tg; Kraetzschmar 15; Bertholet [1936] 4; Cooke 16). Indeed, the emphasis on earthly mobility gives to the traveling throne of judgment a sinister potential. We are reminded of the grim message of relentless judgment delivered by Amos, that wherever God's people fled, whether to Sheol or heaven or to the top of Carmel or the bottom of the sea, they would not be able to escape his clutches (Amos 9:1–4; cf. Ezek 5:12).

15–18 This first half of the account of the wheels concentrates on description. The prophet's attention is drawn first to a single wheel of the now close and stationary apparition and then to the three others. Their relation to the thronebearers is loosely described by the preposition "beside." They share in the brightness and magnificence of the whole (vv 4, 27) and of the other parts (vv 22, 26; cf. v 7) by being compared to precious stones.

Their construction in terms of a wheel within a wheel has taxed commentators and indeed has become an idiomatic expression for an involved set of circumstances. It is tempting to explain in terms of an ancient wheel structure, a disc wheel, solid from hub to rim, with a large concentric hub around the axle, so that the wheel seemed to have a smaller one inside it (see figs. 122–26 in Keel, *Jahwe-Visionen* 184–85). However, the intention of v 17, which deliberately anticipates the wheels' four-directional mobility (backwards, forwards, left, and right) in vv 19–21, appears intended to explain v 16b (e.g., O. Procksch, "Die Berufungsvision" 146). Accordingly, it is preferable to revert to the older explanation of a globe-like structure in which two wheels stand at right angles. Keel (*Jahwe-Visionen* 264–65 and fig. 190) has cited an apposite Hellenistic representation of Mithras from eastern Asia Minor or northern Syria, in which the winged god with a lion's face stands on a globe that has two crisscrossing wheels. The supposition of an optical illusion whereby Ezekiel looked through one wheel to another behind it (Smend 12; Procksch, "Die Berufungsvision" 146–47; Cooke 17) has little to commend it. It would be more likely if the prophet were at a distance from the apparition, but his closeness to it seems to be required by v 15.

The first part of v 18 is uncertain. Waldman (*JBL* 103 [1984] 614–18), unwittingly anticipated by Smend (13) and Weinfeld (*TWAT* 4:32), has taken גבה "height" as "majesty," which would provide a good parallel with יראה "awesomeness" and is a possible rendering in the light of Job 40:10. However, the material context and the comparable use of קומה "height" in 1 Kgs 7:32, in the course of a description of wheels, suggest that גבה is used here in this primary sense, with reference to the top edge of the rims. The "eyes" that cover the rims correspond to nail studs fixed all round the rims of wooden wheels, which served as metal tires, like hobnailed boots, so that the wheels did not wear down (see figs. 123, 191, 192 in Keel, *Jahwe-Visionen* 184, 266). Keel has noted that their metamorphosis into eyes has an analogy in Egyptian figurines of the genius Bes, which were studded all over with copper nails in the New Kingdom period but later with eyes (*Jahwe-Visionen* 269 and figs. 193, 194). These eyes reinforce the four faces of the living beings as an expression of divine omnipresence, like "the eyes of Yahweh that range throughout the earth" in Zech 4:10 (cf. Rev 5:6).

19–21 The second half of the section typically concentrates on mobility, in a development of v 12. The description now departs from the order of Ezekiel's perception—we are not to imagine that the apparition, having landed, took off again before the moment of 3:12—and indulges in generalized observation (cf. Greenberg 52). The wheels were somehow linked with the living beings in their movement. The impression is given that there was no direct contact between the wheels and the beings but that the movement of the wheels automatically aligned with the direction taken by the beings. V 17 has already implied that, while the structure was on the ground, whichever being was in the lead, the wheels that were aligned in that orientation moved and then stopped at that being's direction. In vertical, wing-powered movement, the wheels did not fall off but rose with the flying beings. Vv 20–21 amplify v 19 by relating this double movement to the controlling "spirit" of v 12. It controlled the forward movement on the ground (vv 20 [abbreviated]–21a), and also the taking off into the air (v 21b). The change of syntactical construction with reference to the spirit in vv 20–21 serves to highlight its role in an inclusion and climax. The divine spirit that controlled the beings' wings in flight also controlled the wheels on the ground and kept them attached when the apparatus was airborne. The whole was an extension of the omnipresent spirit.

22–25 The renewed emphasis on the living beings in vv 20–21 facilitates a shift to the רקיע that they supported with their heads. The term is a double entendre: it represents both the "platform" or firm surface on which the divine throne rests (v 26) and the firmament of the sky (cf. Gen 1:6–8; Ps 19:2[1]). Here the role of the living beings as skybearers comes to the fore. The gleaming קרח with which it is compared could be either "crystal" (evidently LXX Syr Vg;

cf. Rev 4:6) or "ice" (Tg; Job 6:16; 37:10). Scholars are divided: for example, Zimmerli (122) opts for the former, and Keel (*Jahwe-Visionen* 254–55) for the latter. The use of כעין "like the gleam of" with "amber" in vv 4 and 27, "copper" in v 7, and "gold topaz" in v 16, suggests that a precious stone is to be preferred here.

The overall structure is evidently determined by a compulsion to revert to the motif of mobility that closed the sections vv 5–12 (in v 12) and vv 15–21 (in vv 19–21). Accordingly, the natural continuation with what lay above the firmament-platform has to be deferred, to make room for mention of the flapping wings of the mobile, airborne skybearers beneath it. Again the observation is generalized and reflective: v 25b catches up with the actually stationary position of the apparition. It reverts explicitly to the stage of vv 11–12, adding the factor of the tight formation of the flyers and stressing that only the upper pair of wings was used for flight.

Sight briefly gives way to sound. The new element of hearing in v 24 anticipates the subsequent auditory stage of the encounter that will begin in v 28b and serves to prepare the reader for it. Here, however, what is heard is moving wings. The noise is illustrated by a double set of comparisons. The first, which is echoed in 43:2, here lacks the connotation of the chaotic sea over whose threat God triumphs (Ps 29:3; Isa 17:12–13) and simply represents overwhelming loudness of a threatening nature, like the comparison with an army in the next clause, but here in terms of the roar of rushing water. In the second comparison, "like the voice of the Almighty," the roaring of the God of the storm in claps of thunder seems to have been borrowed from the storm theophany (cf. Ps 29:3–9; Job 37:2–4, although שׁדי "the Almighty" is not used in either case). The archaizing divine term seems to point to the echoing of an old conception. Once again the mingling of storm theophany and throne theophany is exemplified.

26–28a The final, climactic section reverts in its resumption and development of key vocabulary to the theme of the storm theophany, used earlier in vv 4 and 13–14, and combines it with that of the throne theophany. The living beings' joint role as skybearers and thronebearers is now revealed, for not only does the platform supported by their heads represent the sky, but it in turn supports the divine throne. The throne is compared to "lapis lazuli," a brilliant violet blue stone (cf. Keel, *Jahwe-Visionen* 256 and n. 333) that in the vision of Exod 24:10 is used of the platform on which God stood.

When Yahweh appears in a recognizable form in the OT, the human form is regarded as the natural and characteristic one for him to assume (cf. Barr, "Theopany and Anthropomorphism" 32–33). What is elsewhere implicit in references to Yahweh sitting, standing, or the like (Amos 7:7; 9:1; Isa 6:1) is here explicitly stated. In this vision there is hardly any distinction between the way in which the living beings and Yahweh are described as human (דמות אדם "human likeness" in v 5 and דמות מראה אדם "what looked like a human form" here). Both they and he, as supernatural figures, only approximate to a human form; in the latter case the element of approximation is somewhat heightened. Yahweh manifests himself to human beings as a person in the highest form of life generally perceptible to them.

That this revelation is the heart of the theophany vision is shown by the climactic resumption of terms from v 4 and in part from v 13. What had been glimpsed from afar in terms of a homogeneous mass of energy is now seen close up as the nucleus of the power that had permeated the whole. Moreover, what in vv 13–14 had been located inside the group of living beings is now seen on closer examination to be associated with the throne of God. "Fire," "amber," and "radiance" directly reappear, and reference is also made to "cloud."

The phenomena have the effect of veiling God. Ezekiel sees as if in a mirror dimly (Fretheim, *The Suffering of God* 90, 95). The divine figure's lower portion is enveloped in fire, as if by a train, while the upper portion is more clearly delineated and suffused with a rich amber color. The whole figure is enveloped in an aura, so that what is seen is a silhouette surrounded by light (Auvray, *RB* 67 [1960] 484). The (semicircular?) aura, kaleidoscopic in its coloring, is likened to a rainbow amidst dark storm clouds. It is customary to compare a ninth-century colored ceramic depicting the winged god Asshur set in the flaming yellow disc of the sun, drawing his bow and floating among rain clouds (see fig. 5; a colored reproduction appears in Parrot, *Nineveh and Babylon* 227). His head and the upper part of his body are shown in a human shape, while the lower part is clothed with a flared skirt. A remarkably similar conception is described here, although the rainbow is the aura rather than being held in Yahweh's hands. The basic observation made above on v 4 renders it unlikely that Ezekiel would have seen such a representation. There can be no doubt, however, that the intent is the same. The storm theophany and the throne theophany have here been fused, and the rainbow threateningly alludes to the bow of the warrior God (Hab 3:9; cf. Job 20:24), from which the lightning arrows are shot (cf. v 14; 2 Sam 22:15 = Ps 18:15[14]). Can the rainbow be associated with the gracious symbolism of Gen 9:12–17, as a few scholars have claimed? John Calvin's exegetical acumen prevented him from so doing. He peremptorily commented: "What interpreters bring forward about a symbol of reconciliation is altogether out of place" (105; cf. Höhne, "Thronwagenvision" 74, and contrast Eichrodt 58; Vogt, *Untersuchungen* 11; Low, "Problems" 242–43).

In v 28aβ Ezekiel reflectively sums up his description of the divine figure of vv 26b–28aα by associating with it the כבוד ("glory," "glorious presence") of Yahweh. By this specification he consciously relates his theophanic vision to an earlier tradition of Yahwistic revelation. In fact, כבוד יהוה "the glory of Yahweh" is a set phrase in the Priestly source, and it seems to be to this tradition that Ezekiel alludes, where glory is conceived as a blazing fire enveloped in a cloud (e.g., Exod 24:16–17; cf. Weinfeld, *TWAT* 4:28, 32; Westermann, *THAT* 1:808). In particular, some Priestly wilderness narratives mention Yahweh's appearance in glory in order to pronounce judgment (Exod 16:10–12; Num 14:10–12; 16:19–21; 17:7–10). This tradition of a veiled appearance is only one of the traditions on which the vision has drawn, but the priest-prophet Ezekiel cites it as the one most important to him. Here the divine figure seems to be identified with the glory; not unnaturally in other places the term is widened to cover the whole apparition (e.g., 3:12, 23; 43:2).

The vision account closes in v 28bα with a recapitulation of the initial verb "and I saw" (v 1) and with Ezekiel's response. Overwhelmed, he adopts the body language of shocked submission. His reflex is an acknowledgment of Yahweh's revelation of his glorious self. In so reacting to the manifestation of divine glory, the prophet stays within the Priestly tradition (cf. Lev 9:24; Num 16:22; 17:10 [16:45]).

Figure 5. Asshur as a storm god drawing his bow

1:28bβ–3:11   In the second phase of Ezekiel's visionary experience, God reveals himself not so much to his eyes but to his ears. The distinction is not absolute: as the element of hearing was present in 1:24, so the element of seeing resurfaces in 2:9. "There is a kind of sacramentalism evident in the combination of the word and the visible vehicles in and through which the word is . . . 'enfleshed' and conveyed" (Fretheim, *The Suffering of God* 84). The tone of the composition changes from the transcendent to the immanent, from the universal to the particular. The change is necessitated by the increased involvement of Ezekiel, the Judean exile, as he ceases to be an external observer and becomes a participant in the divine purpose. The essential coherence between the vision and the ensuing commission is that the God who has revealed himself in a theophany of judgment turns Ezekiel into a prophet of judgment. Ezekiel's commissioning to the task of prophecy is set out in 1:28bβ–2:7. It is reinforced by the symbolic rite of ordination described in 2:8–3:3 and by the recapitulating confirmation of his task in 3:4–11.

1:28bβ–2:2a   This introductory subsection prepares Ezekiel for the prophetic commission. Now Ezekiel hears not the noise of flapping wings but an unidentified articulate voice that addresses him. The vocative בֶּן־אָדָם "member of humanity," "human one" relates him to the supernatural beings, Master and servants, whose forms were humanlike (1:5, 26) but who by their very likeness were distinct from humanity. A chasm of essence separates Ezekiel from them and especially from the God whom the spoken words eventually reveal the speaker to be (see 2:4). Ezekiel is "a human being and no God" (28:2; cf. Isa 31:3), out of his league in the transcendent scene, as his physical reflex had demonstrated. Even as the voice underlines the difference, it hints that this human being may have a role in the divine plan. The vocative "human one" persistently prefaces the divine messages in this passage of commission and in fact throughout the book of oracles. It serves to characterize Ezekiel as the prophet of divine transcendence, marked by humble awareness of who God is and by a concern that his fellow exiles should share his awareness.

Accordingly, his natural response to the divine vision must not be allowed to prevent his hearing the divine word of commission. The call to stand up (cf. Dan 10:11; Acts 26:16) is an invitation to conscious participation in God's concerns, to be poised for action on his behalf. Ezekiel's weakness is countered by the enabling power of God, "the spirit-power which proceeds from God" (Keil 48). That this term does not refer simply to a subjective vigor or courage that he felt (Greenberg 62; cf. Zimmerli, *Ezekiel 2* 568) is suggested by the next verb, וַתְּעֲמִדֵנִי "and you made me stand," which seems to refer to an objective force that stands on the divine side of reality (cf. 37:10). It is difficult not to relate this force to the empowering of the living beings and wheels in 1:12, 20–21. The lack of an article accords with the stereotyped style of spirit-control in 3:12, 14, 24; 8:3; 11:1, 24a; 43:5, which is presumably the reason for its absence here.

2b–5   Unwittingly Ezekiel is poised and ready to carry out the errand the mysterious voice now assigns to him. The introductory speaking can now give way to the main communication to which v 1bβ referred.

2b–4a   Two topics are in view: the new role Ezekiel is to play and the moral nature of the people of God. First, the verb "send" is emphasized by its double occurrence in vv 2b and 4a. It is a basic and characteristic term in prophetic call narratives (cf. Isa 6:8; Jer 1:7), which identified the human object as the authorized agent of God (cf. Jer 14:14–15). Significantly, Jeremiah's letter to the hostages in Babylon denounced prophets whom Yahweh had not sent (Jer 29:9, 31). Second, there is a concern for the ultimate recipients of the divine message. They are defined not yet as Judean exiles (3:10) but in wider terms as representatives of "the community of Israel" (בית ישראל), which is a standard designation in the book of Ezekiel for the covenant people, used eighty-three times according to Zimmerli (*Ezekiel 2* 564). The scope of the designation extends not only horizontally from the exiles back to the people in the homeland but also vertically in a series of generations (cf. Jer 3:25). Ezekiel's message in 20:1–32 is a virtual commentary on their sinful past and present. Their sin is characterized as rebellion, both as an attitude and as a succession of acts that exemplified it. The Hebrew term for rebelling (מרד) is a theological metaphor derived from a political act, the refusal of subjects to give loyalty to their king (cf. 2 Kgs 18:7; Ezek 17:15). The present generation is defined as worse than their predecessors, both in external behavior and in internal attitude. Externally, they are marked by brazenness. Literally, they are hard-faced (קשי פנים), a variation of the usual "stiff-necked" (קשה ערף, e.g., Exod 32:9), intended to pave the way for the reaction they will present to the prophet according to v 6 (פנים "faces" twice; cf. 3:8a). Internally, they are strong-willed in their opposition to God.

4b–5 Alliteration links prophetic spokesperson, divine speaker, the alternative reactions of the audience, and their basic nature: אמר "say" (twice), אם "if" (twice), and מרי "rebellious." Ezekiel's task is to deliver the prophetic word, which is cited in terms not of its content but of its divine authority, by using the messenger formula that customarily introduces an oracle of judgment. The response of the recipients to the message of their sovereign (אדני "Lord") is strikingly described as immaterial, whether acceptance of the message or—more likely in view of their sinful nature—rejection. The people are described as a "rebel community" (בית מרי), a term that in Ezekiel's oracles is a bitter nickname for the community of Israel. The implicit reason Yahweh sets no store by their response is that the prophetic message would be one of inexorable judgment, in reaction to the people's sin (vv 3–4a). The learning of its truth would require no spiritual intuition. The stark fulfillment of the judgment in their experience would be its endorsement, proving the prophetic authority of Ezekiel (cf. 33:33). A version of the recognition formula is used. The formula is especially characteristic of Ezekiel's oracles, occurring ninety-two times according to Zimmerli (*Ezekiel 2* 564). Apart from 33:33 and here, the reality of Yahweh himself is what is to be taken to heart (see, e.g., 6:7). Here, however, the context warrants a focus on Ezekiel as his genuine spokesperson. One may compare Num 16:28 for this human perspective: "By this means you will know that Yahweh has sent me to do all this and that it was not my own idea" (cf. Zimmerli, *I Am Yahweh* 49–50).

6–7 Ezekiel is fully briefed on the negative reactions of his audience, so that their antagonism would be no shock that reduced him to panic and consequently to abandonment of his prophetic task. He is strongly urged—even ordered—not to succumb to the fear that would be a natural reaction to so daunting an audience as their characterizations in vv 4a and 5aβ had indicated they would be. Unlike Jeremiah at his prophetic call (Jer 1:8, 18), he is not comforted with the promise of Yahweh's presence or enabling: the latter assurance will, however, be given in 3:8–9. At this point, to be forewarned is to be psychologically forearmed. Thorns are a standard metaphor of hostility (cf. 28:24; Mic 7:4), while sitting on scorpions vividly conveys a sense of shock. Their opposition in demeanor and verbal retort was grounded in their basic antagonism to Yahweh, as a "rebel community" (cf. 3:7). It was no reason for Ezekiel to fail to discharge the mandate of vv 4b–5. He must present God's message in a forthright, take-it-or-leave-it fashion.

2:8–3:3 Ezekiel now undergoes a symbolic rite of ordination. Divine word and prophetic narrative of a visionary, symbolic event alternate in a triple sequence of explanation and deed (2:8 + 9–10; 3:1 + 2; 3:3a + 3b; cf. Hos 1:2–3).

8–10 Ezekiel not only had to "stand" (2:1), poised to be sent to speak Yahweh's message of inevitable judgment, he must also "listen" to that message. In this response of compliance, he is categorically singled out from the rest of the people, just as Isaiah in his prophetic call was isolated from his sinful fellow worshipers by a physical sign of cleansing (Isa 6:5–7). Like Isaiah, Ezekiel is set apart by a symbolic act. It is announced by God's strange call to eat what he is about to receive from God. On second thought, the invitation becomes less strange, for it clearly connects with Jeremiah's inaugural experience, whose mouth Yahweh touched with his hand, assuring him that he had just put his words into it (Jer 1:9). Later Jeremiah said:

> "Your words were found
> and I ate them,
> and your words became a joy to me,
> and my heart's delight." (Jer 15:16)

These texts were evidently mulled over by Ezekiel, and they grew into sensory elements of his own call.

Ezekiel does not yet eat, for the ensuing narrative of vv 9–10 concentrates first on what Yahweh offers to him. The narrative reverts to the visionary mode of chap. 1 (cf. 1:4, 15). Under the influence of the sublimity of that vision, as in the case of the voice in 1:28, the mysterious hand he sees is not directly identified as Yahweh's, although it may be inferred from v 10 ("he unrolled") and 3:1 ("he said") that it was. The book scroll, probably made of leather (cf. Wiseman, "Books" 1:32), was unusually inscribed on the back as well as the front and so was totally filled. Ezekiel could observe the sinister title "laments, mourning, and woe" at the top of the scroll as its first length was unrolled. The scroll symbolizes the prophetic oracles Ezekiel was to deliver and presupposes a custom of preserving a prophet's messages in written form (cf. Jer 36:4, 32; 45:1; cf. E. F. Davis, *Swallowing the Scroll* 50–51). The title refers not to the content of the prophetic revelation but obliquely to its effect. Although laments in the literary sense feature in Ezekiel's prophesying (see 19:1, 14; 26:17; 27:2, 32; 28:12; 32:12–16), they are not in view here. Apart from 19:1, 14 they occur in oracles to other nations, whereas his own people are envisioned here. The terms, piled up in an overwhelming manner, feature as a reaction to extreme suffering (cf. 21:11–12, 17[6–7, 12]). They allude to oracles of judgment, such as Ezekiel delivered during the first seven years of his prophetic service, till the fall of Jerusalem in 587 B.C.

3:1–2 Having clarified what Ezekiel was to eat, Yahweh can reissue his initial command and in the same breath interpret the symbolic act as a preparation for a prophetic ministry to God's people. The mention of the target traces an arc back to the initial announcement of 2:3 and serves to establish that the "laments, mourning, and woe," with which the scroll is crammed full, connote the message of intense punishment deserved by his chronically rebellious people (cf. Isa 1:4–6). Ezekiel proceeds to comply with the first order by opening his mouth, and Yahweh feeds him.

3 Here the symbolic drama of word and deed might have ended. But it continues, with a command that the scroll given by God be swallowed down and digested. In the words of the Episcopal Prayer Book collect, he is to "mark, learn and inwardly digest" the divine oracles and make them his own. In the final snatch of narrative, there is nothing left for Yahweh to do. It remains for Ezekiel to comply. He evidently swallows what is still in his mouth and so is able to take another mouthful. In this complying he observes its ironic sweetness. What in terms of content would have been unpalatable as the bread of adversity (cf. *Note* 3:14.c.), in terms of his willingness to receive it as God's word was sweet, like the "heart's delight" of Jeremiah (Jer 15:16; cf. Ps 119:103). He has opened his life to the divine will and undertaken to submit his own will to his Lord's (cf. 24:16–17, 24; cf. John 4:34). He has committed himself to a prophetic ministry that will invoke hostility and rejection, but the privilege far outweighs such hardship (cf. Phil 1:29).

4–11 Yahweh's visionary communication closes on a note of confirmation that echoes much of the foregoing, often in a heightened form (cf. Greenberg 73). Ezekiel's prophetic role to Israel (vv 4b*a*, 11a) and his obligation to Yahweh (vv 4b*β*, 11b) are reaffirmed in a literary framework. The bulk of the confirmation is devoted to preparing him for Israel's negative reception (vv 5–9), while his own obligation to Yahweh is restated (v 10).

4 The basic message "I am sending you to the community of Israel" (2:3) is reaffirmed in terms of its restatement in 3:1, "go and speak to the community of Israel." The restatement shifts the emphasis from Yahweh's appointment to Ezekiel's responsibility, in this new triangular relationship between God, prophet, and people. A key part of this responsibility is to transmit the divine messages accurately: here the injunction of 2:7a recurs.

5–9 The continuation of the basic message in 2:3–4a was concerned with Israel's fundamental rejection of Yahweh, while the context of 2:7a had to do with Ezekiel's hostile reception in the constituency to which he was being sent and with the need for an unflinching commitment to his task (2:6). These two themes are now developed together. The three parties of Yahweh, Ezekiel, and Israel would be split adversarially: Israel vs. Yahweh and Ezekiel.

5–7 Whereas the sinfulness of the community of Israel had been defined vertically in 2:3b–4a, with the effect of intensifying that of the present generation, now in vv 5–7a*a* there is a horizontal contrast, between the community of Israel and other nations. The initial "for" is used subtly, as often in Hebrew (cf. BDB 473b, 474a). Greenberg (68) has seen a simple causal link: the message may be spoken to Israel verbatim because a common language is shared. But if the text of vv 5–6 is understood as in the translation, it introduces an obstacle to the prophet's mission presented in v 7. Then vv 5–7 give an underlying reason why the exhortation that the prophet be faithful to his task is needed. The sense is virtually "despite the fact that."

The nation of v 5 is presumably Babylonia: the first phrase, rendered "whose speech is incomprehensible," occurs in Isa 33:19, where it refers to the dominant nation of Assyria. Correspondingly the "many peoples" of v 6 seem to refer to ethnic groups of exiles who had been concentrated in the Nippur region (cf. Zimmmerli 137). By comparison with God's people, all such would have made the effort to overcome the language barrier and understand what the prophet was saying. Jesus made a similar point concerning the rejection of his miracles in local towns: Tyre and Sidon would have repented, whereas Chorazin and Bethsaida had not. Even Sodom would have survived, had it seen the miracles that Capernaum despised (Matt 11:2, 23)! Within the OT, in the book of Jonah the people of Nineveh are portrayed as responsive to God's word, while the prophet had been recalcitrant.

There is none so deaf as the person who does not want to hear. Israel's unnatural unresponsiveness would not result from a lack of understanding but from a spiritual barrier, a deliberate refusal. Ezekiel's experience would conform to a prophetic tradition represented especially by Isaiah (see Isa 1:19–20; 28: 12; 30:9, 15). It would not be the fault of Ezekiel; it would reflect Israel's attitude toward Yahweh himself. In a recapitulating echo of v 2a, which referred to the present generation of Israel, but now with a comprehensive "whole" that seems to gather Israel past and present into its sweep, their confrontational nature (cf. Jer 3:3; 5:3; Isa 48:4) and stubbornness of will are deplored.

8–9a How then could Ezekiel cope? It was a question that the commissioning of 2:4–7 had not tackled, while the ordination of 2:8–3:3 had dealt only with the equipping of Ezekiel with the divine word. Now the lack is supplied. If Yahweh and Ezekiel are to be united in suffering rejection (v 7a), there would also be a positive side to this solidarity. As Jeremiah in the sequel to the prophetic call was invested with the strength of a fortified city, an iron pillar, and bronze walls (Jer 1:18–19a), so Ezekiel is now steeled to confront his opponents without flinching. By divine enabling he would live up to the prayerful wish embodied in his name (חָזָק[יִם] "stern, hard, strong"; יְחֶזְקֵאל "May God strengthen"). Hardened in sin as the people were, they would meet their match in his resolute hardness in standing firm for God. Like diamond, the hardest substance known, he would resist their browbeating.

9b Thus there would be no room for fear. The first pair of negative commands in 2:6 can now be restated in terms of promises. The closing reference to Israel's nickname, "rebellious community," taken from the end of 2:6, makes a fitting climax to a section that has emphasized their negative response.

10 Ezekiel also had a part to play in this partnership with Yahweh. His prophetic ministry must be in tune with his rite of ordination. Two lessons are drawn. First, the once-for-all command to digest the scroll in 3:3a was to find a constant counterpart in his inner acceptance of God's messages. Second, the command to "hear" in that sacramental rite, which was symbolically interpreted as eating with one's mouth (2:8), must be a watchword for his future ministry.

11 The conclusion functions basically as a parallel to v 4b, in a framework for the divine speech of confirmation. Ezekiel is sent back into the exilic community to which he belonged (cf. 1:1a). The phrase "community of Israel" of v 4b and elsewhere is now grounded in its local Judean representatives among whom he is to exercise his prophetic ministry. (No mention, be it noted, is made of any ministry in Palestine.) The command to echo Yahweh's own words in v 4bβ is varied by use of the synonymous messenger formula, borrowed from 2:4b–5aα. It makes for a more forceful ending, for it brings with it the shoulder-shrugging alternatives that provide a devastating throwaway line. The messages entrusted to the prophet were to be bad news of inexorable judgment. The verdict had already been passed by the divine judge. It was Ezekiel's task to notify those who had been found guilty.

12–15 Ezekiel's visual and auditory encounter with Yahweh is drawn to a close with a final narrative that by its echoes of earlier parts of the story provides a literary winding down (see *Form/Structure/Setting*).

12–13 The translocation of Ezekiel by the spirit is the first of a number of such experiences (see 8:3; 11:1, 24; 43:5; cf. 37:1). V 14 will continue the topic, but first the departure of the apparition is recorded, in terms of sounds heard. It is implied that it had stood stationary on the ground since the point of 1:15. The term יהוה כבוד "the glory of Yahweh," which had been used in 1:28 to describe the enthroned divine figure, is evidently employed here as a literary shorthand to refer to the whole apparition. Its "standing place" (מקום) corresponds to the similar verb עמד "stand" in v 23 and to its use with reference to the stationary apparition in 1:21, 25. The noise is explained in v 13. The noise of the flapping wings corresponds to that heard in 1:24. Only here is there mention of the (squeaking, rumbling) noise of the wheels. Does it refer to a taxiing, as if along a runway, before takeoff? Strictly one expects the wheels to have been heard before the wings. Perhaps the louder noise is explained first, unless the wings flapped even when the apparition was moving on the ground. The stem רעש, here rendered "pulsating sound," is used of the noise of war chariots in Jer 47:3 and of their wheels in Nah 3:2.

14–15 The description of Ezekiel's translation is now resumed. Significantly, the verb נשא "lift up" is used in 1 Kgs 18:12; 2 Kgs 2:16 (cf. Acts 8:39), with reference to a belief that Elijah could be physically removed by the "spirit of Yahweh," while the second verb לקח "take away" occurs in 2 Kgs 2:3 in the same sense, with Yahweh as subject. The language used evokes preclassical prophetic experiences and characterizes Ezekiel with authoritative credentials as an old-world prophet of the stature of Elijah. Since these older passages seem to be in view, the spirit should be understood as Yahweh's, as explicitly in 37:1.

The action of the spirit is associated with a fresh experience of the "hand of Yahweh." In literary terms it echoes the visionary associations of 1:3b, but in meaning the usage recalls supernatural aid involved in the movement of Elijah from Carmel to Jezreel (1 Kgs 18:46). By such language Ezekiel further claims that the dynamic intervention of Yahweh in Elijah's experience had been re-created in his own (cf. Carley, *Ezekiel among the Prophets* 13–16, 28–37). The supernatural phenomenon had an effect on his mind as well as his body, an emotional excitement that gripped him as the subjective effect of Yahweh's strong hand upon him.

The supernatural journey ends at his exilic settlement, which was evidently some distance away from the scene of the vision. It is identified as Tel Abib, which in Akkadian refers to a very ancient mound, a site believed to have been destroyed by the primeval flood (*abūbu*; cf. *CAD* 1:78a). It is psychologically true to life that the excitement of v 14 gives way to the exhaustion of v 15. The overwhelming experience of vision (cf. 1:28b) and call that he had undergone left him "disoriented" for a whole week.

In a rhetorical sense the account has been neatly rounded off. Yet the conclusion also ironically leaves the reader with a sense of incompleteness and suspense. The commissioned prophet is left stunned and withdrawn! He comes to the exiles, the specific targets of Ezekiel's commission in v 11, and yet he is speechless. He has arrived back "among them," where he was to be a prophet (2:5), and he communicates nothing. The time limitation resolves the *non sequitur*. It conveys a sense of an intermission. The narrative halts in its tracks, waiting for a fresh momentum that will surely come.

Explanation

The vision report in chap. 1 has had a profound effect on its readers down the ages. By the time the book of Sirach was written, about 180 B.C., Ezekiel was remembered as the prophet who "saw a vision and described the different parts of the chariot" (Sir 49:8). For centuries the mystical side of Judaism was fired by the vision (cf. Scholem, *Jewish Mysticism* 40–79; Gruenwald, *Merkabah Mysticism* 29–97). The task of exegesis is to put divine revelation in its ancient setting by explaining its cultural context. If modern readers think of a spaceship when they read the vision, and an earlier generation thought of an airship (cf. Gaebelein 22), it is reasonable to ask what Judean exiles in sixth-century Babylonia would have thought of it. Biblical revelation is essentially clothed in cultural dress; its cultural elements, which were intended to convey what is new by what is known, deserve respect. Yet Ezekiel distanced himself from actually identifying what he saw with his own culturally conditioned descriptions, as his constant recourse to analogy indicates (cf. Davis, *Swallowing the Scroll* 84–85).

Modern study has somewhat robbed the vision of its uniqueness and strangeness. For instance, it has focused on the unity between the divine vision of chap. 1 and the divine word of 2:1–3:11, as a double witness to the prophetic role of Ezekiel. By Ezekiel's time the vocation to be a prophet had been graced by a special experience of theophany, a combination of divine vision and audition through which the prophetic commission was issued. The experience to which Ezekiel bears personal testimony in this account was like that of Isaiah in that it was a vision of Yahweh's heavenly throne of judgment (Isa 6:1–5). But whereas in Isaiah's vision the heavenly scene was superimposed upon the temple, here it is projected on a storm theophany. The literary motif of the storm theophany was a separate tradition that connoted the coming of the warrior God to help his people—or, in a prophetic reversal of meaning, to judge them. It is in this latter sense that the storm-theophany motif is used here: the vision combines the two literary motifs of storm theophany and throne theophany, with their common theme of judgment. The throne scene is depicted in a highly developed form strongly influenced by visual art. The nature of Israel's God has been presented via ancient Near Eastern religious iconography. The artistic conceptions of the sky god supported by his divine four-winged, humanoid bearers and of the enthroned god, the platform of whose throne rests upon two animal bearers, are borrowed and blended, in an effort to express the universal dominion and majesty of Yahweh himself. It is this heavenly king who uses the storm theophany to come to earth on a representation of his celestial throne, to appear to the Judean exile Ezekiel.

There is a sustained and increasing emphasis on the mobility of the apparition. The caryatidlike skybearers and thronebearers are no longer static but fly their divine charge from heaven to earth. The wheels, with their orbits of eyes that reflect omnipresence, are the means whereby Yahweh may travel the earth. It is this universal God from whose judgment none can escape that appears to Ezekiel and summons him to deliver his message of judgment.

The vision report adds special weight to the call account (cf. Fretheim, *The Suffering of God* 84–86). It reveals relevant aspects of the God who calls and so of the word that Ezekiel is to deliver. In a metaphorical rite of ordination, he becomes the host of the imbedded word, the inspired bearer of divine revelation. If later in his ministry he functions explicitly as a "sign" of Israel as recipient of judgment (12:6, 11; 24:24), here he is a sign of the judging God, a messenger of inexorable judgment for a sinful people. As such, he is to bear the brunt of their rejection of God. The literary function of this warning is evidently the same as that of Isa 6, before the rejection of Isaiah's ministry is narrated in the ensuing chapters: to affirm that despite his rejection—and even because of it—he is the authentic emissary of God in his role as prophet of judgment. We have little direct evidence of the exiles' rejection of Ezekiel in this role, and this facet of his call is valuable as an indirect witness to it. The exiles' refusal to listen to the prophet also serves to illustrate the sinfulness of the people of God as a "rebel community" and so their ripeness for judgment. In their rejection of Ezekiel we catch an echo of their rejection of Yahweh (3:7; cf. 1 John 3:1).

From the human angle there is a starkness about Ezekiel's call. He is constantly addressed as "human one," but there is something almost inhuman about his response, or lack of it. He is no Isaiah who pleads for a limit to be set on judgment (Isa 6:11). He is no Jeremiah who protests at the prophetic role that is thrust upon him against his will (Jer 1:6). His "not to reason why," his "but to do and die"! He faints in awe of the theophany; he finds sweet satisfaction in pure obedience. This is evidence of a phenomenon that the whole book attests, an affirmation of radical theocentricity. Did priestly rank in ancient Israel tend to inculcate an attitude toward God such as professional military training does toward superior officers (cf. 1 Sam 2:35)? Be that as it may, there is evidence that the absolute "yes" of Ezekiel's response to God took a psychological toll, in the disorientation of 3:15. Theologically, however, Ezekiel's passive subjection conveys an assurance that his oracles are the true, unalloyed word of God.

Prophetic Signs and Their Interpretation (3:16–5:17)

Bibliography

Amsler, S. *Les actes des prophètes.* Essais bibliques 9. Geneva: Labor et fides, 1985. **Brownlee, W. H.** "The Scroll of Ezekiel from the Eleventh Qumran Cave." *RevQ* 4 (1963) 11–28. ————. "Ezekiel's Parable of the Watchman and the Editing of Ezekiel." *VT* 28 (1978) 392–408. **Fishbane, M.** "The Qumran Pesher and Traits of Ancient Hermeneutics." In *Proceedings of the Sixth World Congress of Jewish Studies 1.* Jerusalem: World Union of Jewish Studies, 1977. 97–114. **Fohrer, G.** *Die symbolische Handlungen der Propheten.* ATANT 54. 2nd ed. Zürich: Zwingli, 1968. **Friebel, K. G.** "Jeremiah's and Ezekiel's Sign-Acts: Their Meaning and Function As Non-verbal Communication and Rhetoric." Diss., University of Wisconsin Madison, 1989. **Garfinkel, S.** "Another Model for Ezekiel's Abnormalities." *JANESCU* 19 (1989) 39–50. **Görg, M.** "Ezechiels unreine Speise." *BN* 19 (1982) 22–23. **Illman, K.-J.** *Old Testament Formulas about Death.* Åbo: Åbo Akademi, 1979. **Krüger, T.** *Geschichtskonzepte im Ezechielbuch.* BZAW 180. Berlin: de Gruyter, 1989. 63–138, 341–55. **Lang, B.** "Street Theater, Raising the Dead, and the Zoroastrian Connection in Ezekiel's Prophecy." In *Ezekiel and His Book,* ed. J. Lust. BETL 74. Leuven: University Press, 1986. 297–316. **Layton, S.** "Biblical Hebrew 'To Set the Face' in Light of Akkadian and Ugaritic." *UF* 17 (1986) 169–81. **Lust, J.** "Ezekiel Manuscripts in Qumran: Preliminary Edition of 4Q Ez a and b." In *Ezekiel and His Book,* ed. J. Lust. 90–100. **Malamat, A.** "The Twilight of Judah: In the Egyptian-Babylonian Maelstrom." In *Congress Volume Edinburgh 1974.* VTSup 28. Brill: Leiden, 1975. 123–45. **Reventlow, H. G.** *Wächter über Israel: Ezechiel und seine Tradition.* BZAW 82. Berlin: Töpelmann, 1962. 4–26, 126–30. **Roehrs, W. R.** "The Dumb Prophet." *CTM* 29 (1958) 176–86. **Schmidt, M. A.** "Zur Komposition des Buches Hesekiel." *TZ* 6 (1950) 81–98. **Schult, H.** "Marginalie zum 'Stab des Brotes.'" *ZDPV* 87 (1971) 206–8. **Sherlock, C.** "Ezekiel's Dumbness." *ExpTim* 94 (1982/83) 296–98. **Smit, E. J.** "The Concepts of Obliteration in Ezek 5:1–4." *JNSL* 1 (1971) 46–50. **Talmon, S.** "Pisqah Be'emsa' Pasuq and 11QPsᵃ." *Textus* 5 (1966) 11–21. **Thiering, B. E.** "The Qumran Interpretation of Ezekiel 4,5–6." *AJBA* 1 (1969) 30–34. **Tromp, N.** "The Paradox of Ezekiel's Prophetic Mission: Towards a Semiotic Approach of Ezekiel 3,22–27." In *Ezekiel and His Book,* ed. J. Lust. 201–13. **Uehlinger, C.** "'Zeichne eine Stadt . . . und belagere sie!' Bild und Wort in einer Zeichenhandlung Ezechiels gegen Jerusalem (Ez 4f)." In *Jerusalem: Texte-Bilde-Steine.* FS H. and O. Keel-Leu, ed. M. Kuchler & C. Uehlinger. NTOA 6. Freiburg: Universitätsverlag; Göttingen: Vandenhoeck & Ruprecht, 1987. 111–200. **Wilson, R. R.** "An Interpretation of Ezekiel's Dumbness." *VT* 22 (1972) 91–104. ————. "Prophecy in Crisis: The Call of Ezekiel." *Int* 38 (1984) 117–30. **Wilson, W. G. E.** "Splitting Hairs in Israel and Babylon." *IBS* 4 (1982) 193–97. **Yadin, Y.** *The Art of Warfare in Biblical Lands.* New York: McGraw-Hill, 1963.

Translation

[16]*A week later—I received the following communication:* [17]*"Human one, I appoint you*ᵃ *lookout for the community of Israel. Whenever*ᵇ *you hear a message from my lips, you are to caution them against*ᶜ *me.* [18]*When I tell someone who is wicked,*ᵃ *'You are doomed to die,' and you have not cautioned him, giving the wicked person an explicit caution*ᵇ *against his wicked*ᶜ *behavior in order that he may live,*ᵈ *the wrongdoing of that*

wicked person[c] *will cause his death, but I will hold you responsible for his demise.*[f] [19]*If, on the other hand, you have cautioned the wicked person, but he has failed to give up his wickedness or any of his wicked behavior,*[a] *his wrongdoing will cause his death, but you will have saved your life.* [20]*Moreover, when someone who is virtuous gives up his virtue*[a] *and does wrong, I will put in his path an obstacle that causes his downfall:*[b] *he will die. If you have not cautioned him, his sin will cause his death and no cognizance will be taken of his virtuous deeds*[c] *that he has done,*[d] *but I will hold you responsible for his demise.* [21]*If, on the other hand, you have cautioned the virtuous person*[a] *that as a virtuous person*[b] *he should not sin, and he stops sinning,*[c] *he will certainly live, because he heeded the caution,*[d] *while you will have saved your life." —*[22]*I felt Yahweh's hand on me there.*[a] *"Get up," he told me, "and go out to the plain so I can speak with you there."* [23]*Getting up, I went out to the plain, where I found the glorious manifestation of Yahweh's presence resting, just as*[a] *I had seen it by the Kebar Canal. I threw myself down on my face,* [24]*whereupon the spirit entered me and made me stand on my feet. Yahweh*[a] *spoke with me: "Go home," he told me, "and shut yourself indoors—*[25]*they will actually put*[a] *ropes round you, human one, and tie you up, so that you will not be able to mix with them outdoors—*[26]*and I will make your tongue stick to your palate, and you will be dumb and so unable to relate to them as an agent of punishment, rebel community though*[a] *they are.* [27]*But whenever I speak with you, I will open your mouth and you will tell them 'This is the message of the Lord*[a] *Yahweh.' Anyone ready to listen may listen and anyone who refuses to do so may refuse, rebel community as they are.*

[4:1]*"You, human one, are to take a brick and, setting it in front of you, draw a city*[a] *on it.* [2]*Then set against it siege appliances: erect a siege tower against it, pile up a ramp against it, station against it army encampments, and set*[a] *battering rams all around.* [3]*Also, you are to take an iron baking plate and use it as an iron wall separating you from the city. Stare fixedly at it and regard it as in a state of siege, and besiege it. It is to be a sign for the community of Israel.*

[4]*"You are also to lie down on your left side and let it feel*[a] *the guilt of the community of Israel. You are to bear their guilt for as many days as you lie on it.* [5]*I assign*[a] *you 390*[b] *days corresponding to their years of guilt, during which time you are to bear the guilt of the community of Israel.—*[6]*When you have completed that period, you are to lie down again,*[a] *this time on your right*[b] *side, and bear the punishment*[c] *of the community of Judah; forty days I assign you, a day for each year.—*[7]*Stare fixedly, then, at Jerusalem under siege, with your arm bared, and prophesy against it.* [8]*In fact, I will put ropes round you, to stop you turning from one side to the other until you have completed your period for the siege.*[a]

[9]*"You are also to take some wheat,*[a] *barley, beans, lentils, millet, and emmer,*[b] *and, putting them in a pot, make them into bread for yourself. You are to eat it as many days as you lie on your side, 390 days.* [10]*The food you eat is to be rationed to*[a] *twenty shekels per day: you are to eat it at the same time each day.*[b] [11]*As for water, you are to drink a controlled amount,*[a] *a sixth of a hin, drinking it at the same time each day.* [12]*The form in which you are to eat it is to be that of a barley cake,*[a] *and you are to bake it*[b] *in stools of human excrement,*[c] *in public view."—*[13]*"This," explained Yahweh,*[a] *"represents the unclean way in which members of Israel will eat*[b] *among the nations."*[c]*—*[14]*"No, Lord*[a] *Yahweh," I said. "My throat*[b] *has never been defiled. From my childhood till now I have never eaten a carcass or ravaged animal, nor has expired sacrificial meat entered my mouth."* [15]*"Look," he told me, "I allow*[a] *you cattle dung in place of human stools, and you may prepare your bread on that."* [16]*He also told me, "Human one, I am going to*

break the bread sticks^a in Jerusalem. They will eat rationed amounts of bread^b and also drink controlled amounts of water.^{b 17}My intent is^a that they should be short of bread and water and that they should one and all^b be filled with despair, mortified by their guilt.

^{5:1}"Next, human one, you are to take a sharp sword and use it as a barber's razor,^a applying it all over the hair of your head^b and beard. Then take scales to weigh it, and divide it up. ²A third part^a you are to burn in flames inside the city, when the period of representing the siege is over;^b another third you are to cut up^c with your sword all round the city; and the remaining third you are to disperse to the wind. I will chase after them with drawn sword. ³Then take a small amount of it^a and wrap it in your skirt,^{b 4}but some of this you are to take again and throw into the fire and burn it up. Out of it^a fire will come to the whole community of Israel.^b

⁵"The Lord Yahweh's message is as follows: This^a refers to Jerusalem, which I have put at the center of the other nations, with other countries^b surrounding it. ⁶But it has wickedly^a rebelled against my standards more than the other nations, and against my rulings more than the countries around it, in that they have rejected my standards and failed to follow my rules. ⁷Therefore this is the message of the Lord Yahweh: Inasmuch as you^a have been more insolent^b than the nations around you, failing to follow my rules or put my standards into practice or even^c to meet the standards of the nations around you, ⁸therefore the Lord Yahweh's message is as follows: I for my part^a am your^b adversary; I will carry out acts of judgment^c inside you in full view of the nations. ⁹I will do in you what I have never done before and will not do again, because of all your shocking practices: ¹⁰so parents will eat children^a inside you, and children will eat their^a parents. I will carry out acts of judgment in you and disperse all those of you who are left to every wind. ¹¹Therefore I swear on my life, runs the Lord^a Yahweh's oracle: because you have defiled my sanctuary with all your detestable objects of worship and with all your other shocking practices,^b I for my part will resort to shearing;^c with no pitying^d glance or personal compassion. ¹²A third^a of you will die of plague or perish of famine inside you, another third will fall to the sword around you,^b while the remaining third I will disperse to every wind and chase after them with drawn sword. ¹³My anger will be exhausted; I will sate^a my fury against them,^b and they^c will realize that I, Yahweh, have spoken in my passion, when I exhaust my fury against them. ¹⁴I will make^a you an object of destruction^b for every passerby to see. ¹⁵Then you will become^a an object of scorn and abuse^b to the nations around you, when I carry out in you acts of judgment^c in furious punishment^d—I, Yahweh, have spoken. ¹⁶When I let loose against them^a my baneful arrows,^b which will wreak destruction,^c I will break your bread sticks. ¹⁷I will let loose against you famine and vicious animals, and they will leave you^a childless.^b Moreover, plague and bloodshed will sweep through you, and I will order the sword to invade you.^c I, Yahweh, have spoken."

Notes

17.a. As in v 9, the pf has a performative sense.

17.b. The Heb. juxtaposition of pf consec verbs has a hypothetical sense: cf. GKC 112kk.

17.c. After מפי "from my mouth" in the previous clause, מהמם could mean "(pass on a warning) from me" (BDB 264a; KB 252b). However, the use of מן with the same verb in v 8 with the sense "warn off, against the consequences of" suggests that divine punishment is in view (Ehrlich, *Randglossen* 5:17; *HALAT* 255a). The English translation "before me" in Zimmerli 142 is inadequate for "vor mir" (*Ezechiel 1* 86), which means rather "(caution) against me."

18.a. The noun, serving as a type, is pointed with the article, but hereafter lacks it: see Greenberg 84.

18.b. The MT reflects the general textual tradition in this double mention of warning. Since the second recurs in the parallel 33:8, the first clause is often regarded as secondary. However, Fohrer (23) argued the other way, that the second clause was a comparative gloss from 33:8. If the first clause has been added, the original intention may have been to note the corresponding clause in 3:20. The force of the pf verbs is conditional, with the same function as כִּי "if" in vv 19, 20b, 20a: see Greenberg (84), who gives examples from priestly legal prescriptions. So the focus of the sentence is on the impf verbs of v 18b as main verbs, as in vv 19–21bα.

18.c. The adj does not occur in 33:8 or in LXX Syr here, but the LXX at the comparable point in v 19 reflects a *Vorlage* that is a development of it. Zimmerli (142–43) regards רָשָׁע as always substantival, "wicked one," and only here in the OT used adjectivally, but see *HALAT* 1208b. In general 3:18–21 reflects a fuller, more heavy-handed text than its counterpart in chap. 33, but this style is probably to be understood in recensional rather than text-critical terms, in the light of the LXX's tendency to reflect a text similar to the MT in this section.

18.d. Since Heb לְחַיֹּתוֹ "to keep him alive" does not occur in the parallel version, there has been a scholarly tendency to delete it as secondary here (*BHS*). See the previous note.

18.e. Heb רָשָׁע הוּא may be an Aramaism, "that wicked person": cf. Dan 2:23 and Greenberg 85. But רָשָׁע could be appositional: cf. the apparently appositional usage of צַדִּיק "righteous" in v 21.

18.f. The NRSV achieves inclusive language by treating the Heb. sg forms as collective. In this historically oriented commentary, it seems preferable to retain the references to individual cases, to provide a basis for exegesis.

19.a. Scholars tend to prune the double phrase by excising וּמֵרִשְׁעוֹ "from his wickedness and" in line with 33:9 (*BHS*). Significantly, if somewhat inconsistently, Zimmerli (142) tacitly retained the text. There seems to be a hinging intent in the sequence וְלֹא־שָׁב מֵרִשְׁעוֹ "and he did not turn from his wickedness" and וּבְשׁוּב מִצִּדְקוֹ "and when . . . turns from his righteousness" in v 20. The LXX reflects הָרָשָׁע הַהוּא "that wicked person" (Fohrer 23), with different word division, contra Zimmerli (143) and *BHS*.

20.a. Scholars prefer to read a fem form, as in 18:24; 33:18 (see *BHS*). However, Greenberg (86) has observed a recensional preference for the masc segholate forms, רֶשַׁע "wickedness" and צֶדֶק "righteousness," in contrast to the fem forms used in chaps. 18 and 33, which he notes were dictated by the standard phrase מִשְׁפָּט וּצְדָקָה "justice and righteousness" used in 18:5 (Greenberg 89). His consequent uneasiness about צִדְקָתוֹ "his righteous acts" may be alleviated by the fact that the fem pl relates specifically to concrete acts rather than a state (cf. Ehrlich, *Randglossen* 5:17).

20.b. That is, a fatal "accident" that leads to his premature death. The term מִכְשׁוֹל "stumbling block" was seemingly borrowed from Jer 6:21: cf. the use of the watchman metaphor of Jer 6:17 in v 17. Cf. in principle 1 Kgs 22:20, 34. Calvin (160–61) rightly saw that it refers to the execution of punishment.

20.c. For the defective writing in K, see *Note* 33:13.b.

20.d. The non-representation of אֲשֶׁר עָשָׂה "that he has done" in LXX[B] is judged an inner-Greek aberration by Ziegler, *LXX* 101; cf. 18:24.

21.a. Ehrlich (*Randglossen* 5:17) suggested that in the MT צַדִּיק "righteous one" stands in apposition to the subj: "you as a righteous person (have warned him)" (cf. Brownlee [1986] 47). This eases the construction but is confusing in the context, in which the term, like רָשָׁע "wicked one" elsewhere, refers to the hypothetical character who is the object of warning. More obviously, the noun is in apposition to the acc suffix: see GKC 131m. LXX Syr imply הִזְהַרְתָּ צַדִּיק "you have warned the righteous person." Greenberg (86) suggests that the MT reflects a conflated text: צַדִּיק is a gloss representing the reading underlying LXX Syr as an alternative to הִזְהַרְתּוֹ "you have warned him." However, הִזְהַרְתּוֹ may simply be a case of mechanical assimilation to the verbal form in v 20. The removal of the suffix yields an expected parallelism with v 19. The LXX does betray a belated awareness of the MT: in v 21b it renders נִזְהָר "he was warned" as if it were הֻזְהַרְתּוֹ. Evidently in the history of its *Vorlage* a marginal reading הֻזְהַרְתּוֹ was taken to relate not to the first instance of the verb but to the second, because of the double occurrence of a preceding כִּי "if, because," and took its place.

21.b. The second instance of צַדִּיק "righteous" in the MT seems superfluous. LXX Syr appear to have found it before the main verb ("the righteous person will certainly live"). It can be argued that the diversity of the textual tradition indicates that it is a gloss of some kind (*BHS*). Greenberg (84) adventurously takes צַדִּיק וְהוּא לֹא־חָטָא as an explanatory gloss on לְבִלְתִּי חֲטֹא, which originally meant "so that he does not sin" (cf. 13:22), with צַדִּיק functioning as a cue word: "righteous one: and he did not sin." However, וחוא לֹא־חטא "and he did not sin" seems to function as a structural counterpart to . . . ולֹא־שָׁב "and he did not turn . . ." in v 19. The positioning in LXX Syr is not likely: רשׁע "wicked one" in v 18b hardly suggests it, since it does not reappear in v 19 and is not matched in v 20. Freedy (*VT* 20 [1970] 143) proposed that the superfluous term originated as a rubric gloss to indicate the theme of v 21. This would be more plausible if a parallel example he found in v 18 (*VT* 20 [1970] 147) were more convincing. I cannot delete צדיק with a good conscience because I have no assurance as to how it entered the text.

21.c. The pf is constative, here referring to extended duration (cf. Waltke and O'Connor, *Syntax* 30.ld; Joüon 112e): "did not continue to sin" (cf. Kraetzschmar 33).

21.d. For the extended meaning of נזהר "take warning," see 33:4 and *Note* 33:4.a.

22.a. LXX* Vg omit שׁם "there": see *Note* 1:3.d. It presumably alludes to v 15 and antedates the insertion of vv 16b–21 (Kraetzschmar 39; Hölscher, *Dichter* 54). Probably it was omitted deliberately because it now lacks an adjacent antecedent.

23.a. In front of כבבוד "like the glory," the LXX has "like the appearance and" (see *BHS*), which evidently represents a comparative gloss from 43:3.

24.a. Lit. "he," with implicit reference to Yahweh; רוח "spirit" is fem. Cf. 1:28bβ–2:3. Here the divine speaking of v 22bβ is fulfilled.

25.a. LXX Vg render as passive, presumably taking as niph. But the following active verb and especially בתוכם "among them" suggest an active form, as Hitzig (28) and others have observed; moreover, להם "to them" in v 26 lends further support (Herrmann 26). Comparison with 4:8 is a red herring: the proposal to read נתתי "I have put" and ואסרתי "and I will tie" with Eth (Ehrlich, *Randglossen* 5:14) is to be resisted. Zimmerli (147) has observed that *BHK*'s appeal to the Tg is unwarranted. The pf verb evidently refers to the future: cf. 4:8, 15 and GKC 106n. It seems to be basically performative with a future application: cf. 4:5 and *Note* 4:5.a.

26.a. For the indirectly causal role of כי "for" here and in v 27, see *Note* 2:6.b.

27.a. For the use of אדני "Lord" in the messenger formula here and in 5:5, 7, 8, see *Note* 2:4.c. It should not be deleted with *BHS*.

4:1.a. The general textual tradition adds את־ירושׁלם "Jerusalem," but the specification is unnatural, and it seems to be an early, correct gloss anticipating vv 7, 16 (Hölscher, *Dichter* 61 n. 1; et al.). The particle את can introduce a gloss, as in Isa 7:17, 20 (cf. Driver, "Glosses" 127).

2.a. The MT adds a fifth עליה "against it," unrepresented in LXX* Vg; it may have entered the text by assimilation to the preceding clauses. Zimmerli (148) observes that it breaks the pattern of three-beat clauses. It is possible, however, that a copyist or translator wearied of reproducing yet another עליה. The preceding verbal form ושׂים "and set" deviates from the earlier consec pf forms, but even if LXX Vg attest ושׂמת (*BHS*), the MT may be retained as a harder reading. Friebel ("Sign-Acts" 508 n. 37) correctly observes that Driver (*Bib* 35 [1954] 147–48) misunderstood the various military terms of this verse as parts of a single siege machine.

4.a. Lit. "put on it": cf. the sense of שׂים ב/על "attribute, impute (error, shameful conduct) to" (BDB 963a). Cf. REB "putting the weight of . . . on it." Krüger (*Geschichtskonzepte* 123) interestingly relates the suffix of עליו "on it" to the community of Israel, but the clear sense "on your side" for עלי in v 4b requires the same meaning here. Wellhausen's conjectural emendation ושׂמתי . . . עליך "and I will place . . . on you" (in Smend 29) anticipates the explicit divine action of v 5 (Zimmerli 148). The emendation used to be popular; it was adopted by RSV and NEB, but significantly NRSV and REB have reverted to the MT. The conjecture ונשׂאת "and bear," with deletion of עליו "on it" (Cornill 194; Zimmerli 148; et al.), arbitrarily rewrites the text in line with vv 5b, 6aβ (cf. v 4b).

5.a. For the performative pf here and in v 6b, see *Note* 3:8.a.

5.b. For the number "190" in the LXX, see the *Comment*. The reading is an easier, and so secondary, one.

6.a. Heb. שׁנית "again" is slightly awkward, which may have been why LXX* Syr omit. Greenberg (105) cites Josh 5:2 for its use in non-identical repetition.

6.b. In L (= *BHS*) K, הימונו seems to be an idiosyncratic slip for הימיני "right"; for Q, see *HALAT* 397b.

6.c. Heb. עון seems to mean "guilt" in v 5 but "punishment" here. See the *Comment*.

8.a. For the pointing מצורך, see GKC 85l. Ehrlich (*Randglossen* 16; cf. *BHK*) suggested a vocalization מצרך "your confinement," with reference to the restrictions imposed on the prophet, but cf. 5:2aβ.

9.a. For the Aramaizing ending, see GKC 87e. The pl forms in this list are plurals of result, referring to threshed wheat, podded lentils, etc. (Cooke 64, with reference to GKC 124m).

9.b. This is another, tetraploid species of wheat, regarded as inferior, since the hulled grains could not be freely threshed; the rendering "spelt" (NRSV) is erroneous, since it is a hexaploid variety of wheat that does not grow in Palestine (cf. Isa 28:25; M. Zohary, *Plants of the Bible* [Cambridge: CUP, 1982] 74–75).

10.a. Lit. "by weight." Heb. מִשְׁקוֹל is a variant of the standard מִשְׁקָל, used in v 16; 5:1.

10.b. Strictly, from one hour of the day to the same hour on the next day. In Mishnaic Heb. the phrase מֵעֵת לְעֵת "from time to time" is used in the same sense, as Kraetzschmar (50) observed.

11.a. The meaning "measure" for מְשׂוּרָה is clear from the contexts in which it is used (also v 16; Lev 19:35; 1 Chr 23:29), but its derivation is uncertain.

12.a. The LXX ἐγκρυφίαν "bread baked in ashes" for עֻגַת "round cake" is a contextually sensitive rendering. It is consonant with the use of the preposition בְּ "in." The noun phrase is appositional: Cooke (64) calls it an acc of specification, comparing Lev 6:9(16)b; cf. the construction in 5:1aα. Then the fem suffix on the verb, whose antecedent is the masc מַאֲכָל "food" in v 10, and also the succeeding pronouns agree with the nearer fem noun (Ehrlich, *Randglossen* 16). Greenberg (107), in the interests of claiming a separate oracle consisting of vv 6, 12–15, finds a new topic here, on the analogy of vv 10–11: the barley cake is the logical object, functioning as a *casus pendens* (cf. 32:7b). More probably the verb resumes the instances in v 10, with further clarification, in view of (1) the application in vv 16–17 solely in terms of vv 10–11 and (2) the description of the food of v 12 as לֶחֶם "bread" in v 15, which resumes the very noun used in v 9, to which v 10 refers.

12.b. Heb. הִיא "it" is a *casus pendens:* other examples of a pronoun so construed occur in 9:10a; 30:18b; 33:17b. LXX Syr Vg do not represent: it is an element naturally omitted in translation.

12.c. The omission of צֵאַת "excrement" in the Syr and in v 15 does not warrant its deletion as a gloss, as Fohrer (31) and Freedy (*VT* 20 [1970] 136) have urged. The Syr notoriously abbreviates, and the briefer later reference is quite natural.

13.a. In place of וַיֹּאמֶר יְהוָה "and Yahweh said," the LXX has "and you will say 'Thus says the Lord God of Israel'" (see *BHS*). This reading obviously repeats 3:27aβ, apart from אֲלֵיהֶם "(say) to them"; the divine title, which recurs in the LXX at v 14; 43:18 (and in LXX^A at 20:47[21:3]) is seemingly a misunderstanding of the Heb. via an abbreviation of the tetragrammaton (see Cooke 65). The omission of "to them" suggests that the material was meant to relate to a context where it no longer applied. V 7b is significant, where Ezekiel is told to prophesy against Jerusalem. Was the material in the LXX originally added as an explanatory gloss relating v 7b to 3:27, observing that this was a case where Ezekiel was released from his dumbness? If so, it is not clear why it slipped down to v 13, where it obviously displaced the introductory clause after being understood as a correction of it.

13.b. The MT adds "their bread," which is not represented in the LXX*. It is best understood as a slight amplification influenced by vv 15–16.

13.c. The MT adds "where I will drive them," which again the LXX* does not yet represent. The verb of divinely enforced exile does not recur in the book; it is characteristic of Jeremiah (see Zimmerli 150). Cooke (56) may be correct in regarding Jer 24:9 as the source.

14.a. For the formulaic use of אֲדֹנָי "Lord" in this exclamation of protest, see Zimmerli, *Ezekiel 2* 556, 561–62.

14.b. For this sense of נֶפֶשׁ (NRSV "I . . . myself"), see H. W. Wolff, *Anthropology of the OT* (Philadelphia: Fortress, 1981) 11–14; cf. the parallelism with פֶּה "mouth" in Isa 5:14.

15.a. See *Note* 3:25.a.

16.a. See the *Comment*.

16.b. The MT adds וּבְדָאָגָה . . . וּבְשִׁמָּמוֹן "and with anxiety . . . and with dismay" to the nouns of limitation, although in sense they do not function as coordinated pairs. The omission of the first added term and the transposition of the second in the Syr support their secondary nature. They evidently originated as comparative glosses from the parallel 12:19.

17.a. The Heb. final clause depends on the divine punishment of v 16aα, as a statement of divine purpose (cf. Zimmerli 170). However, Greenberg (108) takes it as a clause of result, claiming this sense in conclusions at 6:6; 12:19; 14:5; 16:63.

17.b. Lit. "each one and his brother."

5:1.a. For the Heb. order of words and construction, see Cooke 65.

1.b. Coordination with "beard" indicates that רֹאשׁ "head" here refers to the hair of the head (Ehrlich, *Randglossen* 5:17, with reference to Num 6:9; 2 Sam 14:26). Thus in v 1b the pl suffix refers to the two clumps of hair.

2.a. The LXX artificially speaks of fourths rather than thirds here and in v 12: in the application of v 12 it counts plague and famine as two separate punishments. This is a harmonizing process that takes its cue from the "four" judgments of 14:21, in which plague and famine are counted separately.

2.b. Fishbane ("Qumran Pesher" 109 and n. 60) understands as "representing the fullness of time of the siege." Then the clause is an interpretation with reference to the whole period of the siege and anticipates the interpretation later in the verse. He rightly observes that a reference to the end of the siege itself does not fit; rather, the phrase appears to develop the temporal references to Ezekiel's enactment of the symbolic acts in 4:3, 8, 9 (cf. 4:6), as Friebel ("Sign-Acts" 495–96 and n. 14) has observed.

2.c. The MT "and you are to take the third—you are to cut." The second verb, marked by asyndeton and lack of an object, functions as a rather awkward circumstantial clause denoting concomitance (Cooke, 65). It is widely held that the text originally read "and the third you are to cut," (וֹ)לקחת "(and) you are to take" being an insertion (Cornill 202 et al.) and also the object sign, which the next clause (and v 12aβ–ba) lacks (Ehrlich, *Randglossen* 5:17; et al.). Greenberg (109) suspects a conflated text. The verb could have entered the text as an erroneous resumption of the form in v 1b or anticipation of that in v 3a.

3.a. For מִשָּׁם "from there," see BDB 1027b.

3.b. A sg form is expected (cf. 16:8); the MT may easily be an aural error, with a false *plene* writing. Greenberg (110) finds a deliberate echo of the wind wrapping in its wings at Hos 4:19; certainly an allusion to it may underlie the MT.

4.a. The antecedent of the masc suffix is not clear. Cooke (58) and Greenberg (110) take it in a neuter sense, referring to the last act of judgment (cf. the LXX, which evidently relates it to the city), but it is more likely that the antecedent is אֵשׁ "fire" (Friebel, "Sign-Acts" 583 n. 207). To regard the clause as a gloss from 19:14 (Cooke 58; et al.) is dubious: the reference and context are completely different. Zimmerli (151), *BHS*, Liwak ("Probleme" 262 n. 7), and Uehlinger (*Jerusalem* 116, 119) are mistaken in stating that the LXX* does not attest the clause. I echoed this mistake in Brownlee (1986) 79–80.

4.b. The LXX represents a secondary tradition of different sentence division, whereby "to the whole community of Israel" has been taken with v 5. It introduces v 5 with καὶ ἐρεῖς "and you will say." Doubtless the reading originated as a misplaced variant of וַתֶּמֶר "and you rebelled," which itself was subsequently interpreted as וְתֹאמַר "and you will say" in the LXX at v 6. This reading has sometimes been preferred (Cornill 202–3; et al., including Zimmerli, 151).

5.a. Although זֶה/זֹאת "this" often points forward, in this context it points back: cf. the cases listed in BDB 261a. For its use in interpretation, cf. Zech 5:3, 6–8.

5.b. The LXX implies (הָ)אֲרָצוֹת "the (countries)," which reads better and could easily have dropped out by haplography (cf. v 6; Zimmerli, 151). For the pl אֲרָצוֹת, characteristic of later Heb., see Rooker, *Biblical Hebrew in Transition* 75–77.

6.a. It is possible to take (לְ)רִשְׁעָה as a fem inf constr, "(so as to) be wicked," and to link it comparatively with what follows: "more wicked than the nations and . . . than the countries" (Hitzig 37; et al., including Zimmerli 151 and Greenberg 111). Significantly, *HALAT* (1207b) is uncertain. More naturally, the two objects indicate that the initial verb is the focus of the comparison (cf. v 7). Then לְרִשְׁעָה means "in respect of wickedness" and so "wickedly" (RSV).

7.a. The suffix is pl.

7.b. The MT הֲמָנְכֶם is already presupposed by the LXX (cf. Cooke 66) and seems to be intended as a denominative verb from הָמוֹן, "be turbulent," perhaps under the influence of הָמוֹן "multitude, tumult" in 7:11–14. Friebel ("Sign-Acts" 504), rendering "your turmoil ([which is] more than the nations')," evidently regards it as a noun, but the syntactical construction is then problematic. Cornill (203), implicitly following Böttcher, and others have conjecturally emended to הַמֶּרְתְּכֶם "(because of) your rebelling," which nicely resumes v 6; but difficulty in explaining how the corruption might have occurred stands in the way of adopting this otherwise attractive emendation. As I suggested in Brownlee ([1986] 88), Driver (*Bib* 19 [1938] 61) was surely correct in comparing מָנוֹן "insolent" in Prov 29:21; Sir 47:23 (cf. *HALAT* 568a) and seeing here an internal hiph form of מֻן that must be pointed הֲמֻנְּכֶן "(because) you are (more) disdainful": cf. the REB "since you have been more insubordinate." Then a stylistic variant of the verb for rebelliousness in v 6 is employed here.

7.c. Some Heb. manuscripts and editions and Syr Arm and two Gr. manuscripts omit the negative; the NRSV has adopted this shorter text, which accords with 11:12: Israel descended to the low level of the nations. The MT, which has the support of the LXX, fits the context (see the *Comment*). The omission was an attempt to avoid apparent contradiction of 11:12 (Keil 89). The double negativity of divine imminent action in vv 8b–9 functions as a stylistic counterpart to the double human failure to act here.

8.a. LXX* Syr do not represent גַם־אָנִי "even I," but it is contextually fitting: cf. v 11b.

8.b. The suffix is fem sg.

8.c. In the context the MT מִשְׁפָּטִים means ethical "standards" (vv 6, 7); it is here used in the sense שְׁפָטִים "acts of judgment" (vv 10, 15; cf. other passages listed in *BHS*). It is not possible to determine which word is represented in the LXX. Kraetzschmar (59) and Greenberg (111) justify the MT in terms of wordplay between crime and punishment, but more probably the latter form is to be read (Cornill 204 et al.): the MT is a case of mechanical assimilation to the term in v 7, induced by the general overlap of vocabulary.

10.a. The ancient versions harmonize the two clauses: Syr Tg have "their children" and the LXX* has simply "parents."

11.a. For the formulaic use of אֲדֹנָי "Lord" in a divine-saying formula, see Zimmerli, *Ezekiel 2* 556, 562.

11.b. The LXX* does not represent the former of the two phrases. Zimmerli (*Ezekiel 2* 556, 562) considers it possibly an addition, comparing 7:20. The pair occurs indubitably at 11:18, 21. Cf. 37:23 and *Note* 37:23.a.

11.c. Heb. אֶגְרַע here seems to be used absolutely with the sense "I will shear, shave" (Herrmann 30; Zimmerli 152; *HALAT* 195b), repeating the imagery but not the vocabulary of v 1. One may compare the rephrasing of v 2 in v 12 and, more appositely, the stylistic variation employed in vv 6–7. The meaning "shave" is common in Aram.: Greenberg (115) notes that it is used for גלח "shave" in the Tg at Judg 16:19; 2 Sam 10:4. This sense does occur in Heb. at Isa 15:2; Jer 48:37, but its primary meaning is "diminish, restrain." The ancient versions found difficulty: ΣVg Tg (cf. Sperber, *Bible in Aramaic* 4B:335) render as if אֶגְדַּע "I will cut down," which occurs as a minority reading in the Masoretic tradition (see *BHK*) and which the NRSV prefers; LXX Syr have "I will reject you" (= NJB), which may represent אֶגְעַל "I will abhor," since the same equivalents occur in both versions at 16:45. The REB "destroy" (cf. NEB "consume") perpetuates Driver's view that the verb in the MT is cognate with Arab. *jara‘a* "swallow down" and used in the sense "utterly destroy" (*Bib* 35 [1954] 148).

11.d. For the meaningless juss of the Heb. verb, if such it is, see GKC 72r; Joüon 80k and n. 2; Waltke and O'Connor *Syntax* 34.2.1c.

12.a. The form שְׁלִשִׁתִיךְ in L and most manuscripts is a slip for שְׁלִישִׁיתֵךְ (*BHK*; cf. *BHS*). For the LXX "fourth," see *Note* 2.a. above.

12.b. The transposition of clauses in the LXX noted by *BHS* is secondary: it artificially separates what was to happen inside and around the city, in order to juxtapose the two actions with the sword (Cornill 205).

13.a. The LXX does not represent this second verb, but Zimmerli (152) has argued well for its authenticity. Probably the translator combined two verbs into one, as in 6:4.

13.b. The MT adds וַהֲנִחֹמְתִּי "and I will get relief," which is not represented by the LXX*. In favor of the piling up of verbs, Greenberg (111) has appealed to the four clauses for spending fury in 16:42. However, the absence from the LXX* suggests that it is not original. Krüger (*Geschichtskonzepte* 70 n. 35), impressed by the Heb. wordplay, has claimed that inability to convey it was the deliberate reason for omission in the LXX*. But more probably it is a variant reading that has entered the text, which originated in a telescoping of וַהֲנִחֹתִי חֲמָתִי by parablepsis from ח to ה (Herrmann 30). Significantly, the Qumran fragment 11QEzek 5:11–17 does not have room for the whole of v 13 as it appears in the MT (Brownlee, *RevQ* 4 [1963] 15; Lust, "Ezekiel Manuscripts" 91).

13.c. For the pl reference, cf. vv 6b, 12. With its second sg verb, the LXX not only reverts to the initial suffix in v 12 but paves the way for the second sg references in vv 14–17.

14.a. The differentiation between pf consec forms in vv 13 and 15 and the simple impf here suggested by Ehrlich (*Randglossen* 5:19) that v 14 should be regarded as a continuation of v 13bβ. However, the resumptive content of v 13bβ is not continued in v 14; moreover, the rather abrupt switch in person suggests that v 14 be taken separately. Krüger (*Geschichtskonzepte* 70) construes it as a final clause, but structurally v 14 seems to belong with what follows (see the *Comment*).

14.b. The MT's similar-looking terms לְחָרְבָּה וּלְחֶרְפָּה "an object of destruction and an object of scorn" appear to reflect a conflated text. The second term, which anticipates v 15, is significantly not rendered in the LXX*, although again Krüger (*Geschichtskonzepte* 74 n. 50) argues that untranslatable wordplay explains the omission. It may be not simply a dittograph (Ehrlich, *Randglossen* 5:19) but originally a variant לְחֶרְפָּה for חֶרְפָּה "object of scorn" after the verb "become" in v 15 (cf. the respective lists with and without *lamed* in BDB 358a), which suffered the fate of incorporation into v 14 with the copula. The next phrase, בַּגּוֹיִם אֲשֶׁר סְבִיבוֹתָיִךְ "among the nations who are around you," is suspiciously similar to v 15a, לַגּוֹיִם אֲשֶׁר סְבִיבוֹתָיִךְ "to the nations who are around you." It is significant that for לְגוֹיִם there is a variant בַּגּוֹיִם "among the nations" represented in many manuscripts and reflected in LXX Vg. Accordingly, the present phrase, which is a firm part of the textual tradition, looks like an early variant anchored with cue words, which has strayed from the margin into a point in v 14 that roughly matches the position of the original in v 15. For בגוים, the LXX strangely has "and your daughters," which reflects בנותיך. As I explained in Brownlee ([1986] 88), this reading appears to be the result of a mechanical telescoping of אשר סביבותיך בגוים into בנותיך (by parablepsis from ו to ו), which was then read as בנותיך. Then the following κύκλῳ σου "around you" in the LXX represents a (pre-hexaplaric?) partial approximation to the MT.

15.a. The MT והיתה "and it (= Jerusalem) will become" is an error for the similar-looking והי(י)ת "and you will become," implied by the ancient versions and demanded by the context of second fem sg references. The discovery of fragments of 11QEzek has brought apparent confirmation by its reading והית (Brownlee, RevQ 4 [1963] 14–15). Ehrlich (Randglossen 5:19) explained the error in terms of pseudodittography (ה/ח).

15.b. For the form גדופה "object of abuse," see Greenberg 116. The MT has another pair of nouns, מוסר ומשמה "a warning and an object of horror." The LXX* represents only one pair of nouns, which, contra Jerome, Zimmerli (153), and BHS, are not the first but the second pair. My explanation in Brownlee ([1986] 88) may stand, with slight amplification. As for στενακτή "giving cause for mourning," Cornill (206) observed that שמם is rendered by στενάζειν "groan" in 26:16, although Ziegler (LXX 212), on apparently good grounds, there prefers a form of στυγνάζειν "be gloomy," read by MS 967. So, whether or not we emend στενακτή to στυγνακτή, it seems to render משמה "an object of horror." Jerome commented that he did not know what the other term, δηλαιστή (LXX^B etc.), meant; nor do we. The variant δειλιαστή "giving cause for fright" in MS 26 undoubtedly preserves or restores the translator's intent: cf. δειλιαίνειν "make afraid" in Deut 20:8 LXX and δειλιᾶν "be afraid" in Isa 13:7 LXX, both for the niph of מסס "melt with fear." Heb. מוסר seems to have been rendered in terms of its presumed first two root letters. Strangely, the Heb. pair of nouns was translated in reverse order. The MT evidently reflects a conflated text, with only the second pair of terms attested by the LXX*. The first pair looks authentic: cf. the pairing in Isa 51:7; Zeph 2:8. How then did the second pair enter the text? It may be suggested that it has something to do with במשורה ובשממון "by measure and with dismay" in 4:16. The first term is rare (see Note 4:11.a.); it was seemingly supplied with an explanatory gloss that understood it as a variant of מוסר "chastisement." The second term, which occurs seldom in Ezekiel, was glossed with the standard משמה. These two glosses once stood in the margin of 4:16, but were at some point inserted as a pair in the wrong side of the column, at 5:15. A shift to the new context was encouraged not only by the pairing of nouns in 5:15 but also by the presence of חרבה "destruction," a synonym of משמה, and of תוכחות "punishment," a synonym of מוסר, in 5:14 and 15b respectively. In the Vorlage of the LXX, the new pair displaced the first pair of nouns, but in the MT, both pairs have survived.

15.c. The MT adds באף ובחמה "with anger and fury and," which is not represented in the LXX* and is probably a later addition in view of the "clumsy repetition" of חמה (Zimmerli 153). The extra material could be a comparative annotation from Jer 21:5, whose context resembles this passage.

15.d. The LXX has "my fury" for חמה "fury," under the influence of v 13.

16.a. The MT בהם "against them," already attested by the LXX, is awkward, as its omission in the Tg shows: v 16 and the early part of v 17 are dominated by second pl references. See Note 16.c. and the Comment.

16.b. The MT הרעב הרעים "of famine, harmful" appears to be a doublet, of which the LXX* represents only הרעב. However, this awkwardly anticipates one of the acts of judgment detailed in v 17 and is probably a scribal error by mechanical assimilation to the verse. Then the LXX is right in presupposing a pointing חצי "my arrows" in place of the MT חצי "arrows of" (Hitzig 39; et al.).

16.c. The MT adds אשר . . . עליכם "which I will send to destroy you, and famine I will increase upon you," which the LXX* leaves unrepresented. The addition is probably made up of two explanatory glosses (Hitzig 39). The first by the use of an impf verb clarifies the pf היה in the previous relative clause, "which are for your destruction," as a fut reference. The second explains "arrows of famine" of the MT as a series of famines and also interprets the awkward בהם "against them" in second person terms. For the form of אסף "I will add," see Joüon 114g.

17.a. The suffixes from here on are second sg. In the LXX all the second person suffixes are sg, in line with v 15.

17.b. The LXX translates "I will take vengeance on you," a rendering also found in 14:15; the change of person may reflect the influence of the verbal form found there.

17.c. LXX Syr add the equivalents of מסביב "around," perhaps in reminiscence of the contextually similar 28:23 (Hitzig 40).

Form/Structure/Setting

This next literary unit consists of 3:16–5:17. The messenger-reception formula in 6:1 will signal the beginning of a further unit. This unit follows the pattern of the previous one in 1:1–3:15: an introductory divine vision (3:22–24a) is followed by a divine speech (3:24b–5:17). In more general terms, the unit exhibits a scheme that is common in the book, in that an initial narrative written in the first person is followed by a divine speech addressed to the prophet (cf. chaps. 14, 20; cf. Zimmerli 154). However, in this case the narrative is prefaced by a divine announcement of Ezekiel's appointment as prophetic watchman and an elaboration of his consequent responsibilities. This structurally unexpected section, 3:16 (or 16b)–21, which is introduced with a message-reception formula in v 16b, warrants separate comment later.

The divine speech of 3:24b–5:17 basically consists of a series of divine commands for Ezekiel to carry out five sign-acts, with interpretation of those acts included or appended in each case (cf. Fohrer, *Symbolischen Handlungen* 47–53). Both the acts and their interpretation are incorporated into the divine command, a late phenomenon characteristic of Ezekiel (see Zimmerli 156). There are a host of what might be understood as structural markers in the text: וְאַתָּה בֶן־אָדָם "and you, human one" at 3:25; 4:1; 5:1, וְאַתָּה "and you" at 4:3, 4, 9, and וַיֹּאמֶר אֵלַי בֶן־אָדָם "and he told me, 'Human one'" at 4:16. We must bear in mind the randomness (in sectional terms) of such features in the divine speech of 2:1–3:11. In this speech those at 3:25; 4:3, 16 do not carry the weight of introducing major sections.

The first section, 3:24b–27, involves a command to undergo a symbolic act of seclusion. That a sign-act is in view here is suggested by (1) the presence of interpretation of the command at v 26aβb and v 27aβb, (2) the reinforcement of the command with divine action in the course of vv 26–27, just as divine constraint reinforces a sign-act at 4:8, and also (3) the specific description of Ezekiel's release from dumbness in 24:27 as a "sign" (מוֹפֵת). The second section, 4:1–3, consists of a double command to depict the siege of Jerusalem in vv 1–3a and an interpretation in v 3b.

The third section, 4:4–8, is primarily a command to depict Israel's guilt, which includes within it interpretation; v 8 features a divine constraint, to ensure the correct fulfillment of the command. In the present form of the text, a second command appears at v 6, whose function must be considered later. The fourth section, 4:9–15, consists of a command to depict the harsh conditions of the coming siege of Jerusalem, which is interpreted in vv 16–17. The command is uniquely modified in vv 14–15, after the prophet's protest. The role of v 13 will be discussed later.

The fifth section, 5:1–17, is the last and longest. A command to depict the fate of the besieged citizens in vv 1–4a has its own interpretation included, in v 2bδ, but most of the section consists of lengthy interpretive comments, in vv 4b–17. The basic interpretation in vv 5–6, which is introduced with a messenger formula, develops, via its accusatory material in v 6, into an oracle of judgment in vv 7–10. There follows in vv 11–13 an elaborated triple proof saying made up of accusation, sentence, and expanded recognition formula, with a closing formula of divine asseveration in v 13b (cf. Zimmerli 38–40). Two supplementary messages of judgment follow in vv 14–5 and 16–17, each of which closes with the asseveration formula. From v 7 onwards, this interpretive material is addressed rhetorically to Jerusalem or to its citizens. In the light of 4:1–3, 7, there can be no question of the prophet's literal presence in Jerusalem.

It is sometimes advocated that the whole unit falls into two parts, the first consisting of the series of commands to carry out sign-acts, which closes at 5:4, and the second made up of oracular material in 5:5–17 (Zimmerli 174; Krüger, *Geschichtskonzepte* 115; earlier Cooke 58 and Eichrodt 80). Zimmerli bases this bipartite division on his adoption of the introductory "and you will say to all the community of Israel," found in the LXX at 5:4b (see *Note* 5:4.b.), and thus differentiates between the earlier personal commands of Yahweh to Ezekiel and the delivery of a public oracle (cf. *BHS*). Greenberg (110, 117–19), however, bases it on the claim that in 5:5–17 all the foregoing acts find a loose interpretation (cf. Smend 33; Kraetzschmar 42, 56; Keil 88; Eichrodt 87–89; Klein 45–46; Friebel, "Sign-Acts" 498–99). Slightly inconsistently, he also considers this section the "script" of the prophesying that Ezekiel was ordered to undertake in 4:7 (120, 123). Earlier, Cooke (58) regarded these verses as a twofold commentary, on the symbolic act described in 4:1–3(5:5–10) and on the act in 5:1–4(5:11–15). In fact, where there is an echo of previous symbolism, it is that of the last command. In particular, vv 10b and 12 show that the main aim of vv 5–15 is to provide an interpretive commentary on the final sign. If v 5 relates to the model of the city, it does so because it has also featured in the last command, at v 2; in vv 8, 10 בתוכך "inside you" clearly alludes to בתוך העיר "inside the city" in v 2. Thus it seems correct to take 5:1–4 closely with vv 5–15 (Fohrer, *Symbolischen Handlungen* 52–53; Reventlow, *Wächter* 24; Hals 28–30).

It is clear to most scholars that the unit is not homogeneous. The question it poses to careful readers is not whether redaction has taken place but how much. Greenberg (86, 93, 119, 125) has a minimal assessment, regarding 3:20bβ as an interpolation from 18:24 or 33:13 and 4:6, 12–15 as an originally separate little unit about the exile that has been worked into siege material secondarily. The first section of the literary unit, 3:16b–21, is commonly taken as a redactional anticipation of chap. 33 (see my review of scholarly opinion in *Ezekiel 20–48* 143–44). It applies to the first period (or both periods) of Ezekiel's prophetic ministry what strictly belonged to the second period. It is sometimes urged that the Masoretic space within v 16 (traditionally called פסקא באמצע פסוק "a space within the verse") shows an awareness that the text was interrupted with an interpolation (Kraetzschmar 36; Cooke 44; Reventlow, *Wächter* 130). However, Greenberg (83) has appealed to Talmon's well-argued proposal in *Textus* 5 (1966) 11–21 that in other texts such spacing indicates that supplementary information was available elsewhere in the Bible or in extrabiblical material. He suggests that in this case it was a reference to 33:1–9.

The difficulty with 3:16b–21 goes beyond structural considerations (see above): its orientation toward repentance and life hardly accords with the message of inescapable judgment that Ezekiel delivered till Jerusalem fell, to which the first unit of 1:1–3:15 unambiguously referred. M. A. Schmidt (*TZ* 6 [1950] 92) claimed that different settings lie behind 33:1–6 and 33:7–9: first the people and then the prophet are addressed. Accordingly, he argued, while the parable of 33:1–6 belongs to the second, post-587, phase of Ezekiel's work, the application in 33:7–9 has been borrowed from the chronologically earlier 3:16–21. Greenberg (91–97) has followed Schmidt: 3:16–21 were only for Ezekiel's ears and conveyed the message that, whether his audience listened or not (3:10–11), his responsibility lay only in proclaiming God's message of judgment, whereas in chap. 33 a positive, public call to repentance comes to the fore. Irrespective of whether positive notes can be removed from or toned down in 3:16–21, the basic premise of a private oracle that originally had a different setting from a public oracle is problematic in this instance. One may compare the continuation of 33:1–9 in vv 10–20, where divine address to the people (vv 10aβ, 11b, 20) is mingled with address to the prophet (vv 10aα, 11aα, 17). Moreover, the "private" 3:20–21 seems to have been inspired by 33:13, 18, part of the continuing public oracle.

The next section, 3:22–27, is also frequently regarded as a secondary insertion because of its affinity with material in 24:25–27 and 33:21–22 concerning a divine promise to remove Ezekiel's dumbness and its fulfillment. It is often taken as belonging chronologically to a time just before Jerusalem fell (e.g., Cooke 44, 46; Eichrodt 348–50; Krüger, *Geschichtskonzepte* 351–52; cf. Zimmerli 159–61, who regards vv 25–27 as secondary and having no historical basis). However, if the section can reasonably be explained in its present context, our duty is to take it as it stands.

For the sections involving symbolic actions in 4:1–5:4, the question of the interpretive setting is crucial. Since Cornill (198), the test to detect secondary material has been to ask whether the siege of Jerusalem or the exile that followed it is in view. Hölscher (*Dichter* 61–62) added the criterion that each of the commands to engage in sign-acts that related to the siege begins with the instruction קַח לְךָ "take for yourself." He thus established a primary group of three poetic sections, 4:1–2 and 9a, 10–11, and 5:1–2. Among others, Zimmerli (155–56) has followed Hölscher's lead, though playing down somewhat his poetic emphasis. Certainly threefold compositions are not unknown in the prophet's ministry: a good case can be made in the Gog-Magog unit of chaps. 38–39 for such a primary series of passages that subsequently received literary amplification (see *Ezekiel 20–48* 204–9). In this case the result is a neat, symmetrical composition, but whether it is necessary is doubtful. However, Cornill's test remains a fair one. Its application sets question marks at least against 4:6 and 13 and suggests that these verses are reinterpretive material that seeks to update primary siege-related messages.

The problem with 5:5–17 is the complexity of its form-critical structure. Two alternative conclusions may be drawn. First, it is possible to explain the complexity in redaction-critical terms and to reduce the primary material to, for example, an interpretive oracle of judgment in vv 5–6a, 8–9, 14–15 (cf. Zimmerli 154; Fuhs 36–38). Or else one may envision development of the form-critical tradition of the judgment oracle to a point of "dissolution" in "this baroque extravagance" marked by "repetition and cumulation" (C. Westermann, *Basic Forms of Prophetic Speech* [Louisville: Westminster/Knox, 1991] 208). Vv 5–17 do give a distinctly literary impression. The more specific interpretive oracle in vv 11–13 may have been interwoven with the more allusive material. But no hiatus in overall setting is discernible, and so no long period of development is required for the present shape of vv 5–17.

The unit may be outlined as follows:

3:16a, 22–24a	Ezekiel's renewed vision
3:16b–21	His later role as prophetic watchman
3:24b–27	God's commands: (1) Seclusion and dumbness alternating with prophesying of judgment
4:1–3	(2) The sign of the siege game
4:4–5, 7–8	(3) The sign of Israel's guilt
4:6	Application to the exile
4:9–12, 14–17	(4) The sign of siege conditions
4:13	Application to the exile
5:1–17	(5) The sign of the fate of the besieged, with extensive commentary

Comment

3:16b–21 On the grounds of the content of this passage, the indication of time in v 16a should be taken with v 22 (Kraetzschmar 37; Bertholet [1936] 13; Hölscher, *Dichter* 54; Zimmerli 142; Lamparter 46). The intent of the deliberate interruption was evidently to bond it closely with vv 22–27 and what follows in the unit, and the reason will need to be carefully sought from the text as it is encountered. We might have expected the passage, as a further divine definition of Ezekiel's prophetic role, to relate to the earlier call narrative, and in general terms it still does. But its particular placing must be taken seriously, as a comment on or qualification of what follows. A unit consisting of 1:1–3:21 is not to be envisioned, with Smend (1) and Davidson (11), nor is it to be isolated as a separate unit, with Greenberg (82).

16b–19 This passage is borrowed substantially from 33:7–9 and prefaced with a message-reception formula, which characteristically opens a new section of prophetic revelation. The reader is directed to *Ezekiel 20–48* 144–48 for basic exegesis: here the focus will be on relating the passage to its new context. It stands in purposeful tension with its present literary environment. At times it initially aligns with what seems alike but provocatively takes a different tangent. The very metaphor of a watchman for Ezekiel's prophetic ministry is a development of Jer 6:17 and echoes its tones of divine concern that his people should not come to harm. The foe who attacks is strangely also the friend who wants those who on moral grounds are necessarily his enemies to escape. The judge who passes the death sentence that Ezekiel has to transmit for flouting the divine will (cf. 2 Kgs 1:4, 6, 16; cf. K. Illman, *OT Formulas* 104–5) is loath to order the execution. Such was the message the prophet was eventually to receive from Yahweh. Yet in v 27 he is told that he would hear a different message. It consisted of the messenger formula "Thus says the Lord Yahweh," which in the light of its earlier usage in 2:4; 3:11 connotes inescapable judgment. Moreover, in v 27 a take-it-or-leave-it attitude, whereby God shrugs his shoulders over Israel's response as immaterial, is conveyed by the mention of their hearing or not hearing (cf. the even more categorical 3:7). Yet in vv 16b–21 the people's response to the prophetic warning, positive or negative, is all important. Here the victims are not abandoned to the same collective doom but segregated into two groups, those who die and those who survive. Indeed, all could escape, for Yahweh's intent, even in the case of the wicked person who pays no heed to the warning, was "to preserve his life." This statement of purpose is of crucial importance, inasmuch as it has been added to the basic text of 33:8, in order to bring to the surface the underlying truth of Yahweh's redemptive will (cf. 33:10–11). Calvin (155) noticed the clash between this life-giving message and the preceding context, observing that "this may seem absurd, because all hope of repentance was taken away beforehand."

At one point the material does not pass through similar terrain to a different goal but indulges in outright contrast. In v 27 the prophet is coerced into delivering his message of doom by Yahweh's opening the sluicegates of communication. Yet here he has the option of warning or not warning the victims of merited doom. He needs the threat of Yahweh's role as *gōʾēl* or avenging next of kin for the unwarned deceased (cf. Num 35:12–21) as incentive to pass on the warning.

Notes of continuity with material elsewhere in this unit are struck. As in v 17, the prophet has a social responsibility to the "community of Israel," which is mentioned in 4:3, 5; 5:4 (cf. 2:3; 3:1, 4), in terms of bearing witness to the doom of Jerusalem. The iniquity (עָוֹן) that causes death echoes the "guilt [עָוֹן] of the community of Israel" in 5:4. Vv 18–19 echo the "guilt" (עָוֹן, here rendered "wrongdoing") experienced by the besieged citizens of Jerusalem in 4:17; but there is a change of perspective, in that collective sinfulness here gives way to the wrongdoing of a sector of the community, just as the communal "wickedness" of 5:6 is here replaced by that in 3:18, 19. Likewise, the punitive death of 3:18, 19 recalls that of the besieged victims of plague in 5:12, who suffer amid the collective punishment of their peers. Here, however, not only is there a way to escape it, but its victim stands for a group whose sufferings are not necessarily shared by the whole community.

These blatant notes of continuity and discontinuity serve to compare and contrast the later, largely positive ministry of Ezekiel among the exiles, after Jerusalem had fallen in 587 B.C., with his pre-fall, negative task. After human hopes had proved false, salvation or life pressed to the fore as God's future intent for the exiles. Yet they had to identify themselves positively with his saving will in order to achieve it. Like Christian in Bunyan's *Pilgrim's Progress,* Ezekiel was made to see that "there was a way to hell even from the gates of heaven, as well as from the City of Destruction"—from the exilic antechamber to the promised land, as well as from Jerusalem.

20–21 These two verses are not present in the prophetic exposition of the parable of the watchman in 33:7–9. Rather, they are inspired by 33:13, 18 (cf. 18:24, 26; in respect of חטאתו "his sin" in v 20b, 18:24 is closer). After the examples of the radically wicked person who either was not warned or, if warned, persisted in his wickedness, now a backsliding believer provides quasi-parallel illustrations either of failure to warn or of repentance after warning. The microstructure of v 18a is not matched in its evident counterpart, v 20a: the reason is simply the different source material that is being drawn upon, in 33:13, which also explains the extra element of unremembered virtues in v 20bβ. The latter is a realistic observation concerning the need to keep virtue current. "Righteousness is not something to be saved up. Righteousness implies a relationship with others, and such a relationship is either present or not" (Andrew 26).

These two verses are more upbeat in tone than the former pair. The initial divine sentence of death (v 18a), which was carried out twice (vv 18bα, 19bα) against the will of the judge, is passed again (v 20a) but executed only once (v 20aβ). In the second scenario it is replaced by a pledge of life (v 21ba). The responsibility of the prophet is still the main concern, but, as before, the responsibility is shared with his audience in a network of possibilities. The gospel-like bad news that had the potential of becoming good news at last joyfully reaches that goal in the climactic mandate of life. The prophet's efforts come to happy fruition, and so does the positive will of God mentioned earlier. In stylistic terms the initial sentence מות תמות "you are doomed to die" in v 18aα is countered by the final affirmation חיו יחיה "he will certainly live" in v 21ba, in an inclusion. God's goodwill and Ezekiel's labors win through in at least one instance in the outworking of the divine-prophetic program, and so the prophet is both encouraged and validated in his difficult task (cf. 33:30–33).

It is significant that 33:13 features not in a context that emphasizes God's offer of life (33:1–11) but in an ardent discussion of the need for Ezekiel's exilic congregation to choose life and pursue a God-honoring ethical path (33:12–20). Its incorporation into the development of the watchman metaphor serves to reinforce the prophet's duty in his post-fall ministry, not simply to broadcast the grace of God for all the people of God but to challenge them to reflect that grace in their lives. Any who failed to do so would "not inherit the kingdom of God" (Gal 5:21), in the form of eschatological return to the land (Ezek 20:33–38). The role of vv 16b–21 in its present context will be considered further in the *Explanation* below.

3:16a, 22–24a   Ezekiel is allowed a week to recover from and think through his overwhelming encounter with the God who revealed himself in majestic theophany. Then he is summoned afresh and undergoes the same awesome experience as before in a further confirmation of his call to be a prophet of judgment to his fellow exiles.

As in 1:3b, the pressure of the divine hand prepares for the double experience of a vision and the message that will accompany it. However, the vision does not immediately follow; somewhat as in 37:1, it awaits a journey to the scene where it will take place. Whereas in 37:1 Ezekiel is transported by the spirit, here he is commanded to make his own way there; a structural counterpart to this command will be provided in v 24b by the command to return home. His destination is the place that will be the venue of a further vision in 37:1–12, where, however, it will be the setting of a message of new life for the spiritually dead rather than of grim judgment. The plain or broad valley refers to part of the wide alluvial plain of Babylonia interspersed with tels and canals. Here it is in the region around Tel Abib, but in a different area from the scene of the initial call. The narrative carefully plots the two visionary occurrences, just as it will draw a line of reference between the next vision and this one in 8:4, between that and the first one in 10:15, 20, 22, and a double line between the vision of 43:3 and those of chaps. 1 and 8. The vision is introduced simply by הנה "behold" (rendered "I found" in the translation). The whole apparition described at length in 1:4–28a is summed up as "the glory of Yahweh," as in v 12. In this case the prophet does not see it coming from afar and then landing but finds it already at rest. The "resting" (עמד, lit. "standing") corresponds to the term "place" (מקום) in v 12b.

Ezekiel's reaction naturally is a repetition of 1:28ba, one of shocked submission to the claims of the one who appeared in majestic theophany. As in 2:2a, he is empowered by the spirit to stand and so assume the prophetic position of a servant standing in the presence of his divine master, like Elijah and other prophets (1 Kgs 17:1; 18:15; 2 Kgs 3:14; 5:16; Jer 15:19).

24b–27 The verbal communication to which the vision has been the solemn prelude begins here. This next phase, like the first at v 22b, is prefaced by a blunt command, now to return home and stay there. Presumably, the delay of the vocative בֶּן־אָדָם "human one" till v 25, with which the immediate usage in 2:3 contrasts, occurs in order to allow the parallelism of the two initial commands to stand out more clearly. The prophet's seclusion, like the symbolic iron plate interposed between the model city and Ezekiel in 4:3, signifies the alienation of Yahweh from his people: fellowship and blessing are no longer dispensed to his covenant partner. Seclusion from the public is in view: Eichrodt (77) has rightly objected to Zimmerli's judgment (159) that, since elsewhere Ezekiel's house is the place of prophesying (8:1; 14:1; 20:1), he is not here prevented from engaging in prophecy.

25 Ezekiel's seclusion is to be sustained from another quarter. He is informed that his fellow exiles will constrain him, giving physical expression to their opposition to the prophet and so to the God he represents. The vocative "human one" seems to interject a note of sympathy, as mention of an addressee's name would in human speech. Ezekiel's house arrest, enforced by tying him with ropes, aligns with the written counsel of an exilic prophet of a different persuasion, that Jeremiah should be put in the stocks for sending the exiles a letter that predicted a long stay (Jer 29:26–28). The note of popular opposition to Ezekiel for his judgment oracles has been sounded in the call narrative, at 2:6; 3:7. Its present significance is to accentuate the estrangement between God and his people, who in rejecting his prophet reject Yahweh, as in 3:7.

26a After the parenthesis of v 25 that describes attendant circumstances, the command of v 24b is reinforced by a divine constraint; similarly, the command of 4:4 will be reinforced by the constraint imposed by God in 4:8. Enforced silence would accompany the enforced seclusion of the prophet. Normal relations between him and his contemporaries were to be broken off. His silence would represent the silence of God in response to their pleas for his intervention on their behalf against the victorious Babylonians. In a psalm of lament, divine silence is associated with distance from the one who prays (Ps 35:22; cf. 22:2–3[1–2]). The prophet is to act out this lack of communication, which is tantamount to a refusal to come to the people's aid: they have forfeited all claim to that. Yahweh has broken off friendly relations with his people.

26b–27 The affliction of the prophet with dumbness would also—unless or until it were suspended—prevent his carrying out his assigned function of prophesying judgment to the "rebellious community." The epithet deliberately recalls the earlier commissioning speech, where it occurred in contexts of Ezekiel's prophetic activity (2:5–8; 3:9). The careful reader is prepared, therefore, for a modifying statement about his prophesying, such as occurs in v 27.

Controversy has been rife over the precise meaning of אִישׁ מוֹכִיחַ in v 26aγ. The presence of אִישׁ "man" points to a role Ezekiel has within the community: one is reminded of אִישׁ נָבִיא "a prophet man" in Judg 6:8. The clue to the meaning of מוֹכִיחַ appears in the immediate context, in the next verse. If v 26 were damaged and illegible, one would have little difficulty in reconstructing its sense with the aid of v 27: the two verses both pose a contrast and indulge in repetition.

To be struck dumb and so unable to function as an אִישׁ מוֹכִיחַ is the opposite of being freed from the affliction and so able to function as a prophet of inexorable judgment. The latter ability is what is signified in v 27aβγ, in the light of the use of the messenger formula and the qualification of the irrelevance of the people's response in 2:4–5a; 3:11. This structural parallelism within vv 26 and 27, in part antithetic and in part synonymous, maneuvers the reader into a narrow and unambiguous meaning for מוֹכִיחַ. It can signify nothing other than (in German) *Strafprediger* (Kraetzschmar 40; Fohrer 25; Vogt, *Untersuchungen* 34; *HALAT* 392a), "proclaimer of punishment." This meaning is congruent with the sense "(divine) punishments" for the cognate noun תֹּ(וֹ)כָחוֹת within the same unit at 5:15 and also in 25:17. The verb הוֹכִיחַ "reprove" is used in a variety of contexts in the OT, but pertinent texts are Hab 1:12, which speaks of Yahweh using the Chaldeans to punish the wicked, and Isa 37:4, in which Yahweh is asked to rebuke the words of Sennacherib. Here the prophet functions as spokesperson for the punishing God.

Hölscher (*Dichter* 57) wanted to understand the prophetic term as "one who warns and admonishes his hearers to repent"; he equated it with the role of watchman in 3:16b–21. He had in mind the use of the verb in wisdom contexts, such as Prov 24:25, and specifically of the participial noun in Prov 25:12. Similarly, Tromp ("Paradox" 210) defined the term as "somebody who reproves and in that way attempts to bring about the conversion of his audience. . . . No prophet any more . . . might talk them out of their disastrous ways." Rather, the people would be "left to their own fate." Greenberg (102) has likewise interpreted the role as "a reprover, one who reproaches wrongdoers with their wickedness and calls on them to mend their ways." Wilson (*VT* 22 [1972] 98–100) has assigned to the term the sense "arbitrator" and understood it of prophetic intervention with God that is here denied. Even if such a meaning is not attested elsewhere (Greenberg 102), it might be regarded as a feasible development from the forensic sense "arbitrating judge" that the participial noun has in Isa 29:21; Amos 5:10. In *VT* 22 (1972) 93–94, 104, Wilson regarded the present passage as an editorial insertion, but in *JBL* 38 (1984) 129 he related it to the beginning of Ezekiel's ministry. Wilson's suggested meaning is attractive, and I expressed a preference for it in *Ezekiel 20–48* 62. It interprets the dumbness as a ban on intercession with God, a ban that is easily understood as operating for seven years, until the dumbness is removed (24:25–27; 33:21–22), and allows it to be concurrent with the prophesying of v 27. However, his suggestion imports an alien notion into the context, which itself sets clear guidelines for the interpretation. Wilson (*VT* 22 [1972] 93) rightly said, though he had his own ax to grind in so saying, that "the author of iii 22–27, xxiv 25–27, and xxxiii 21–22 clearly wants the reader to understand that the dumbness continued from the prophet's call to the fall of the city."

The modification of the silencing of the prophet in v 27 enables him to impart more than what is connoted by the silence. The sign of the withdrawal of divine favor from Israel is punctuated by announcements of Yahweh's active hostility. In a different way this same double message will be communicated in 4:3. There the erection of the iron plate between Ezekiel, as God's representative, and the model of the city connotes God's hiding of his face from Jerusalem; at the same time, however, the prophet is to "set his face" against it, in token of Yahweh's adversarial attitude. Both messages are necessary, and so v 27 adds an essential qualification of the first message. Intermittently the prophet's dumbness would be suspended, to the limited extent that he would be able to deliver oracles of judgment, which would come to pass whatever the hearers' response to them. In fact, the very limiting of Ezekiel's speech to judgment messages underlines the inevitability of judgment (Lamparter 47).

Many commentators have objected to this plain understanding of the text, inasmuch as it involves seven years of relative silence for the prophet. A significant number deny that the present passage belongs to the beginning of Ezekiel's ministry, preferring to telescope the accounts of dumbness in chaps. 3, 24, and 33 and to view them as covering a short period of enforced silence around the time of the fall of Jerusalem. Zimmerli (160) has objected to the present positioning of the passage on the ground that v 27 cannot refer to intermittent speaking because chaps. 24 and 33 imply uninterrupted dumbness up to the point when it was removed. This objection assumes that the two other passages make a comprehensive statement that may be used as evidence to clarify this passage. However, the assumption expects too much from them. It overlooks a basic element of discord between this passage and the other two. If this one is taken at face value, when the prophet speaks, the content of his speaking is to be nothing other than oracles of radical judgment. Yet in chap. 33 the time for such has passed (Greenberg 103). The discrepancy makes room for the present passage to make its own statement with respect to intermittent prophesying. The commentator must tolerate loose ends in comparing the three related passages and not jump to harmonizing conclusions. 3:26–27 as yet knows nothing about a turning point in God's relations with Israel and any possibility of oracles of salvation. It is firmly locked into a perspective of utter judgment.

A "new twist" (Greenberg 102) is given to the divine insistence in 2:3; 3:4, 10–11 that Ezekiel should speak only what he had first heard from Yahweh. "The theme of dumbness is used to underline the point that the word which the prophet speaks is God's, not his own" (Carley 29). "Ezekiel was to be known as nothing but the mouthpiece of Yahweh. When he spoke, it was because God had something to say; when he was silent, it was because God was silent" (Taylor 74).

His speech is to be intermittent and limited to judgment oracles. Greenberg (102–3, 121) has revived this understanding of the text, which was widely held at an earlier period (Smend 27; Keil 66–67; Kraetzschmar 38, 40; Skinner 53); he has won significant support (Lemke, *Int* 38 [1984] 166 n. 2; Tromp, "Paradox" 209–11; Klein, *Ezekiel* 39; Friebel, "Sign-Acts" 454–57; cf. Sherlock, *ExpTim* 94 [1982/83] 296–98). One may note also the view that v 27 relates to intermittent speech but is a redactional addition (Hölscher, *Dichter* 59; Carley 29). The speechlessness Ezekiel is to undergo is to be understood literally rather than in any metaphorical sense (cf. Friebel's discussion in "Sign-Acts" 439–41). The description of its removal as a "sign" (מופת) in 24:27 indicates a verifiable, objective experience. Does it refer to a physiological condition? Friebel ("Sign-Acts" 444–48) has observed that elsewhere the niphal or passive conjugation of אלם "be dumb" that appears in 3:26; 24:27 refers not to physical incapacity but to self-imposed speechlessness due to circumstances (e.g., Isa 53:7; Ps 39:3[2]; cf. Dan 10:15). He interprets the divine imposition of speechlessness in v 26a*a* as possibly "a stylistic way of stating that the divine ability was given to Ezekiel to fulfill this difficult nonverbal behavior over the required extended period of time"

("Sign-Acts" 448). However, this interpretation may place too much weight on what could be an accidental phenomenon, that in other extant cases the niphal of אלם does not refer to physical incapacity. After all, the adjective אִלֵּם refers to a physiological condition. The prior focus on Yahweh's making Ezekiel's tongue stick to his palate deserves to be considered the determinative statement, which prompts an understanding in terms of a physical constraint, rather than merely an enabling of Ezekiel's voluntary abstinence from speech. This judgment is reinforced by the reference in 33:22aγ to Yahweh's opening the prophet's mouth, in the light of which the passive variants of the phrase in 24:27aα; 33:22bα imply divine agency. Tromp ("Paradox" 209) rightly speaks of three agents in the passage who concur in realizing similar programs: (1) the prophet is told to confine himself to his house; (2) he will be bound by others so that he will be unable to go out; and (3) God will bind the prophet's tongue.

A psychological interpretation in terms of the prophet's depression (cf. 3:15b) that is accompanied by God's command to become secluded and silent (Greenberg 121) appears insufficient. There seem to be no compelling objections to construing the passage in terms of the prophet's intermittent delivery of judgment oracles till the city fell seven years later. If the enforced silence appears to be excessively long, it aligns with other phenomena in the book that exhibit lengthy elaboration and inordinate extravagance. The unambiguous references to the call narrative within the passage tie it firmly to its present setting.

4:1–3   Yahweh's address to the prophet continues in 4:1–5:4 with a series of commands to the prophet to carry out symbolic acts. This set of instructions begins with the order to scratch a recognizable representation of Jerusalem. There are a number of Babylonian examples extant of plans engraved on clay tablets, such as of the city of Nippur (ANEP 260) or of a house (Meissner, Babylonien und Assyrien, vol. 2, fig. 154). It is not specified whether such a ground plan or a sketch on a vertical plane with walls and buildings is in view. However, the consequent elaboration of the sign-act with siege representations may indicate a sketch such as often appeared in Mesopotamian victory reliefs (Uehlinger, "'Zeichne eine Stadt'" 141–49; cf. ANEP 366). Next, Ezekiel is somehow to represent a siege being conducted against the city. Did he draw the siege paraphernalia on the brick (Keil 70; Herrmann 32) or depict the objects on other bricks or use primitive models? The first option is unlikely: the flow of the text in vv 1–2 suggests that the pronominal suffixes referring to the brick continue, so that the brick that now, by means of the drawing, represents the city is confronted with other objects tactically placed to represent a siege attack. Moreover, the repetition of the verb "place" (נתן) used of the brick, to refer to some of the siege paraphernalia, points to the same conclusion. Wevers (60) has observed that there would hardly be room on the brick for the total depiction. Ancient Near Eastern bricks varied in size from 10 to 24 inches long and from 6 to 13 1/2 inches wide (K. Galling, BRL 364). The fact that the verb חקק "draw," used in v 1, is not repeated in v 2 suggests that models were used (Uehlinger, "'Zeichne eine Stadt'" 150–52).

The specification of siege equipment that follows reflects the development of siege warfare under the Assyrians, which the neo-Babylonian army took over. A battering ram moved on wheels and was a wooden structure covered with wicker shields. It had a turret with openings, by means of which the operation of the ram could be controlled and also arrows could be fired at the defenders. The destructive feature was its metal ramming rod, the end of which was shaped like a spear head or an ax blade. It was rammed between the stones of the city wall and then would be levered from side to side so that a section of the wall would collapse (see Yadin, *Art of Warfare* 314–17, 391, for description and illustrations). The siege tower was a mobile assault tower from which archers gave covering fire to the troops operating the ram (Yadin, *Art of Warfare* 314, 391). The ramp was built up of earth and covered on its top and sides with stones and bricks or planks, as a surface along which the battering ram was wheeled up to the wall or gates (21:27[22]; Yadin, *Art of Warfare* 315). The identity of the besieging army is not specified, but in the historical context there was only one real possibility, the Babylonians.

3 After this representational assembly of a grim war game, Ezekiel was to use a utensil that was part of home cooking equipment and place it upright between the city and himself. It was a convex iron plate or griddle that was normally placed over the fire, with the edges resting on bricks surrounding the fire; cakes and bread were baked on it (see M. Kellermann, *BRL* 30, for description and illustration). The plate was to act as an iron wall and to be a figurative expression of the severance of normal relations between Jerusalem and the God whom the prophet represented. In the siege that it was to undergo, its fate was sealed: no help would be forthcoming from God. He had withdrawn his favor and hidden his face (cf. 7:22). An iron curtain of alienation divided him from the city. A number of commentators have usefully compared Lam 3:44:

> You have covered yourself with a cloud,
> so that prayer cannot pass through.

Yet if God's answer to pleas for help was an inactive silence (cf. 3:25–26), his attitude was also one of active hostility (cf. 3:27). He had not only withdrawn his help but also would himself prosecute the siege with determination, using the Babylonian army and its expertise as his instruments. Such was the significance of Ezekiel's staring hard at the city and (presumably) moving the models of the besieging forces to represent the siege in action. The fixed staring is similar to Ezekiel's frequent symbolic gesture of turning to look in the direction of the target of an oracle of judgment (cf. 6:2; 21:7[2], where Jerusalem is the target; cf. Jer 21:10).

The scene to be enacted by the prophet is called a "sign to the community of Israel," that is, to those representatives of it who shared Ezekiel's exile, as comparison of 2:3; 3:1, 4, 7 with 3:11 shows. Only here in this series of five sign-acts does the term "sign" appear. The prophets typically engaged in symbolic acts, and they were particularly characteristic of Ezekiel's ministry (cf. Zimmerli 28–29). Their role was to reinforce the prophetic word of interpretation that accompanied them (see *Form/Structure/Setting*). Their precise intention is disputed. Did they actually create the future by prefiguring it (G. von Rad, *OT Theology* [New York: Harper, 1965] 2:96–97)? Or did they function as "street theater," as a teaching aid that dramatically visualized the oral message of the prophet (Lang, "Street Theater" 305)? Krüger (*Geschichtskonzepte* 118–19) has observed that these explanations need not be alternatives but may both be correct: the first relates the sign-act to the spectators before whom it is performed (cf. v 12), while the second relates it to the event symbolized. However, the view that the sign-act is to be distinguished from the oracle, inasmuch as it had special power bestowed upon it to shape the future, is based on its supposed development from acts of magic (cf. Fohrer, *Symbolischen Handlungen* 10, 47–55, 121–24). Such a developmental view is no longer in vogue among anthropologists (cf. Lang, "Street Theater" 302–5; J. W. Rogerson, *Anthropology and the OT* [Atlanta: Knox, 1979] 22–53; Uehlinger, "'Zeichne eine Stadt'" 122–35). Sign and interpretation worked in mutual confirmation. If actions speak louder than words, here they were a megaphone for the prophetic words.

4–5, 7–8 The first two sets of instructions in 4:1–3, 4–8 are interlocked as a pair by their common references to the siege depicted in the first (4:2, 3, 7, 8). This next sign-act is a demonstration of Israel's guilt. Krüger (*Geschichtskonzepte* 129 n. 324) has usefully referred to Isa 59:2 in illustration of the implicit link between this sign and the previous one:

> But your guilty deeds have caused separation
> between you and your God,
> and your sins have hidden his face
> away from you, preventing his hearing.

Again "the community of Israel" is the target of the sign, but now their vertical links of solidarity with past generations come to the fore, as in 2:3. Ezekiel shared the outlook of Jeremiah and the Deuteronomist, that a backlog of sins lay behind the final destruction of the covenant nation. They are indeed a "rebel community" (3:26–27). The outworking of divine judgment was the focus of the first of these twin signs, in vv 1–3; now underlying accusation is made explicit in the second. Together the two signs function like a two-part oracle of judgment that is made up of both accusation and announcement of punishment. Accordingly, this sign relates not to the future but to the meaning of the past.

While in vv 1–3 Ezekiel represented the divine subject of the section that announced punishment in the judgment oracle, here he correspondingly represents the standard subject of the section of accusation. The necessity of Ezekiel's lying on his left side will become clear in v 7, where his right arm is to feature in a further aspect of the complex sign (cf. Friebel, "Sign-Acts" 538 n. 108). Putting his full weight on one side represents the guilt or culpability of the covenant people, which he is to "bear." This bearing is not substitutionary, as if the prophet were atoning for their guilt, but representative. The phrase "bear guilt" has been borrowed from priestly circles, where it has a range of meanings; in this case the sense is closest to the usage in Exod 28:38.

The period of time allotted to this lying is 390 days, with each day encapsulating a year of guilt. A tradition close to that of the Deuteronomistic History is evidently being followed, according to which the period of the monarchy till the end of Zedekiah's regency was just over 433 years, while Solomon's temple stood for some 422 years (cf. J. A. Montgomery and H. S. Gehman, *Kings* [Edinburgh: Clark, 1951] 48–52). In the light of the specific accusation of defiling Yahweh's sanctuary in 5:11 (cf. chap. 8; 43:7–9; 44:6–8), the number is best understood as a general reference to the existence of the first temple. Alternatively, it may relate to the period of disunity of the covenant nation: the Deuteronomist reckoned

393 1/2 years, or 390 in round numbers, for the period from the division of the kingdom till the fall of Jerusalem. Then one may compare the promise of renewed unity in 37:5–24, specifically in 37:22. This alternative provides a better solution for the actual number, but at the cost of losing a reference to a primary concern in the book.

7 The present sign-act is closely associated with the previous one. Evidently Ezekiel was to lie facing the model of the besieged city, which is now interpreted as Jerusalem; his staring, resumed from v 3b, was to occur during the execution of the second stage. Accordingly, vv 1–3a form a preparation for engaging in a coordinated pair of sign-acts. The amplification of the threatening stare with actual interpretive prophesying suggests that it was indeed a variant, expressed in stronger terms, of the gesture Ezekiel commonly adopted in delivering an oracle of judgment (cf. 6:2; Layton, *UF* 17 [1986] 173). In this role Ezekiel performs as a representative of Yahweh, so that in the doubled symbolic activity he represents both the accusing agent of punishment and the accused. The bared arm, with sleeve pulled back, signifies the readiness of Yahweh to act against his people. In Isa 52:10 it relates to Yahweh's fighting for them, but in this negative context it spells danger and threat (cf. Jer 21:5; Ezek 20:33).

8 Just as in 3:26 a divine constraint reinforced Ezekiel's performance of his first sign-act, so another divinely imposed restraint aids the prophet's own activity, or rather lack of it. He would find himself hampered as if by ropes (cf. Pss 2:3; 129:4) and unable to move until he had discharged the dual task of lying opposite the siege model and prophesying. The metaphor echoes 3:25, but here it has a different application. The concurrence of the two sign-acts meant that the prophet's representation of the siege lasted as long as the days of guilt. The immobility reflects the radical and long-term nature of Israel's sin, which will later be portrayed, in different terms, in 20:3–31. The feasibility of so long a performance has been queried. However, it may be that we are to regard the immobility not as totally continuous over a period of 390 days but as a series of continual daily acts of public witness, which were permanent as long as each one lasted, somewhat like the constraint of 3:26 that was punctuated by the prophesying of 3:27.

> Since the actions were intended to communicate a message to the people, all that is required is that they were performed as part of Ezekiel's public ministry, and not necessarily as part of his private, non-prophetic life. (Friebel, "Sign-Acts" 546; cf. Streane in Davidson 33)

The next dating for Ezekiel's prophetic ministry, in 8:1, allows for fourteen months to elapse after that of 1:1–2. Accordingly, there is time for this period of 390 days—and (after the symbolic act of 5:1–4) also a month's vacation before the prophet had to function again! This reckoning assumes that the daily performance of the double symbolic activity did not overlap into chaps. 8–11. The oracles in chaps. 6–7 may reflect a literary placement rather than a chronological one (cf. Friebel, "Sign-Acts" 545 n. 123). Certainly this and the other symbolic actions are most naturally to be understood as actually carried out: "the accomplishment is essential to a true sign-action" (Zimmerli 156). The mention of public spectators in 4:12 so suggests, while Ezekiel's objection in 4:14 presupposes that he was expected to enact Yahweh's instructions (Herrmann 38).

6 The text jumps from guilt to punishment, from accusation that warranted the siege to representation of exile. This phenomenon will be repeated in v 13; it is part of a process of updating Ezekiel's message to fit changing circumstances. It is significant that v 9b has not yet any awareness of v 6. The shift from the context is facilitated by the double meaning of עָוֹן, "guilt" and "punishment," and so the double significance of נשׂא עָוֹן as "bear guilt" and "bear punishment."

The Priestly Num 14:34 has acted as a literary bridge between the day-years of vv 4–5 and those of v 6, inasmuch as there forty years of staying in the wilderness correspond to the forty days of spying out the land and are to be the period in which the people of Israel bear their iniquities (נשׂא עֲוֹנוֹת) in punishment. However, there the forty days related to sin, and the forty years to punishment; a different relationship between the days and years pertains here in v 6. The new development moves from accumulation of longstanding sin in vv 4–5 to actual punishment over a period of time here. The mention of forty years, a round figure for a generation (cf. Num 14:28–31; Amos 2:10; 5:25), accords with the period of exile attributed redactionally to Egypt in 29:11–12. The victims of exile are identified as the "community of Judah," which is evidently a reference to the people of the Southern Kingdom who experienced the exile, who are now singled out from the total covenant community of v 5, somewhat as in 37:16. One may consider the political description "elders of Judah" in 8:1 as applying to the same group elsewhere referred to in more theological terms as "elders of Israel" (14:1; 20:1; Friebel, "Sign-Acts" 530–31). The naturalness of the historical reference to the political community may be illustrated from 25:3, which refers to the exile of the "community of Judah" after referring theologically to the "land of Israel."

The Septuagint, working backwards, made v 8, with its mention of siege, the starting point for a consistent exegesis of vv 4–8, whereby vv 4–5 were understood in terms of bearing punishment. Then the Israelite experience that preceded the Judean exile had to be the exile of the Northern Kingdom, which took place roughly 150 years before that of Judah (LXX, v 4: cf. *BHS*. The actual number is about twenty years less, but a figure that related to 350 [= 390 – 40] years was obviously desired.) In that case the total years of punishment were 190 (LXX in vv 5, 9). This rationalizing reconstruction, whether it derives from the LXX translator or from a preexisting tradition, is akin to the mention of four parts of hair in 5:2 LXX, as opposed to the three in the MT (see *Note* 5:2.a.). As Friebel ("Sign-Acts" 535) has observed,

> Although the meaning of "Israel" as the Northern Kingdom and "Judah" as the Southern Kingdom is semantically possible, the specific usage in the rest of the book opposes such a singular meaning in 4:4–6.

The LXX may have been misled into taking "right" and "left" as references to south and north, instead of simply opposing sides. A number of scholars, mainly of an earlier vintage, for instance Kraetzschmar (42, 47), Fohrer (29–32), and Eichrodt (78, 83–86; cf. *BHK* and *BHS* at v 5; NEB), have followed the LXX down its false trail of harmonization, encouraged by the doctrinaire assumption that symbolic acts must always depict future events (Fohrer, *Symbolischen Handlungen* 110). Interestingly, the Qumran community used the 390 years to describe Israel's extended "exile" from the time of God's giving them into the hand of Nebuchadnezzar until the emergence of the Hasidim (*CD* 1:5–11; cf. Thiering, *AJBA* 1 [1969] 30–34).

It is one thing to define the literary relationship of v 6 to its context and quite another to understand what, if anything, it means in historical terms. Is the command to be put in a post-587 setting, after the siege had culminated in destruction and exile? Or in an earlier period, after the city had fallen and before the exiles had arrived in Babylonia? It may be that we are to think in terms of a further period of forty days during which Ezekiel later lay on his side, in a reinterpreting resumption of his earlier symbolic action (cf. Cooke 53). Certainly the specification of exile as forty years long indicates a setting not beyond the exilic period (Lamparter 52 n. 20).

9–12, 14–17 The next symbolic action in the series of siege-related representations dramatizes the scarcity of food to be experienced by those beleaguered inside Jerusalem. V 9a has a preparatory but obviously public (cf. v 12) function, like vv 1–3a in relation to vv 3b–7. The use of different cereals and legumes implies that only scraps of each would be available to bake into a concoction of bread. There seems to be no thought of uncleanness in mixing different cereals (Hölscher, *Dichter* 61 n. 2; Fohrer 32; Zimmerli 169; contra Smend 31; Bertholet [1897] 21; Eichrodt 86, with reference to Lev 19:19; Deut 22:9–11). As in vv 4–5, Ezekiel is to represent the victims of divine judgment.

9b The interconnectedness of the siege-related signs is further reflected in that the food Ezekiel is to eat during his period of lying down facing the siege model is now described. Presumably the food was to be kept in storage jars and the preparation was to be repeated as necessary in Ezekiel's "off-duty" hours (Friebel, "Sign-Acts" 551 n. 141).

10–11 Ezekiel is to be rationed to one meal a day, consisting of just over eight ounces of bread, hardly sufficient to maintain life. As for water, he is allocated about two-thirds of a quart, to be drunk at one time (cf. *IDB* 4:833–35). The historical actualities of the eventual siege may be illustrated from Jer 37:21, according to which Jeremiah was allowed a loaf of bread per day till the supply ran out, and from Jer 38:6, where one cistern at least had only muddy ooze at the bottom into which Jeremiah sank.

12 The prophet is given instructions as to how the siege food of vv 9–10 is to be baked. He is told that the baking process is to be carried out "in public view." Evidently, it was customary to bake a barley cake, as distinct from one made from more expensive wheat, not in an oven or on a griddle but directly on hot stones (cf. 1 Kgs 19:6) or in the hot embers of a fire (cf. the parallel cited by Greenberg 107). Dried animal dung could provide fuel for the fire, but here, to depict the rigors of the siege, evidently after the animals had been eaten for food, there is to be the revolting substitution of human excrement, which would be in direct contact with the food. Its uncleanness may be illustrated from the instructions for its disposal outside the camp and the divine warrant for them in Deut 23:13–15(12–14). Even worse siege conditions are envisioned in 2 Kgs 18:27 (= Isa 36:12), eating one's own excrement.

14–15 The prophet vehemently protests at the command to bake the food by such a grossly unclean method. It is out of character with the dietary lifestyle to which he has been committed. His natural objection is intensified by his upbringing in a priestly family who scrupulously ate only kosher food. The Christian reader will be reminded of Peter's protest in Acts 10:14 and may use it as a standard against which to judge the even greater degree of a priest's abhorrence.

Animals that had died from natural causes or from attack by wild animals or birds of prey were barred from the diet of priests (Lev 22:8; cf. Ezek 44:31), as well as that of lay Israelites (Exod 22:30[31]; Deut 14:21; cf. Lev 17:15), presumably because the blood could not be drained from the carcass (cf. Lev 17:10–13). Priestly families had access to the meat of certain sacrificial animals, but it had to be eaten within two days; to eat it later was a ritual offense (Lev 7:18; 19:7).

Ezekiel is granted a concession. He is permitted to substitute dried cattle dung as fuel in his public performance of this sign. It thereby loses some of its representational value; presumably the prophet was able to announce the fact of the milder substitution. Evidently the food was thereby prevented from having the effect of making him unclean (Cooke 57; Zimmerli 171).

16–17 This material logically follows on from the instructions for the symbolic action given in vv 9–12, after the interruption of the exchange in vv 14–15. The discontinuity of the exchange is marked by the insertion of an introductory-speech formula. The sign is interpreted in terms of shortage of food and also of water. The interpretation is thus not comprehensive; it focuses on the particular part of the action commanded in vv 10–11 and also by implication on the scanty supply of basic ingredients suggested in v 9. The mention of "guilt" also alludes to the accusation of the community of Israel in the previous symbolic action (vv 4–5). This overlap is consistent with the explicit links forged between the various symbolic actions that have already been observed.

However, a key purpose of the interpretation is evidently to build a literary bridge between the forthcoming siege of Jerusalem and the series of covenant curses in Lev 26 (cf. Reventlow, *Wächter* 25–26; Greenberg 108). The opportunity to do so seems to have dictated which part or parts of the symbolic activity should be singled out for interpretive comment. Yahweh's announcement that he would "break the bread sticks in Jerusalem" appropriately harks back to the phase of the curses that envisioned the Israelites as gathered within their cities, sheltering from the enemy (Lev 26:25). Yahweh was to "break their bread sticks" (Lev 26:26), so that their bread would be issued "in rationed amounts" (בְּמִשְׁקָל "by weight," exactly as here; cf. בְּמִשְׁקוֹל in Ezek 4:10). Moreover, it is possible that the reference to being "mortified by their guilt" has been borrowed from a later phase of the curses, which relates to exile (יִמַּקּוּ בַּעֲוֹנָם in Lev 26:39; cf. וְנָמַקּוּ בַּעֲוֹנָם here), because of the contextual appropriateness of the reference to guilt. At any rate, the echo of Lev 26:26 makes it clear that the siege is to be Yahweh's punishment of Israel for breaking their covenant with him by failing to honor its terms (Lev 26:14–15; cf. Ezek 5:6).

The breaking of bread sticks is a metaphorical reference to the practice of carrying and storing ring-shaped loaves on a long stick or on cords slung over such a stick (cf. Schult, *ZDPV* 87 [1971] 206–8, developing L. Köhler's earlier work; *HALAT* 543a). To break these sticks implies cessation of the bread supply.

13 This divine statement explicitly interprets the sign-act in terms of the conditions of exile. As Krüger (*Geschichtskonzepte* 124 n. 304) has observed, "members [בְּנֵי lit. 'sons'] of Israel" here signifies part of the collective "community [בֵּית 'house'] of Israel." The reinterpretation disturbs the flow from v 12 to v 14 (Herrmann 37; Cooke 55; Zimmerli 149). It is closely related to that which appeared in v 6 earlier. Like v 6, it deliberately and radically reapplies the symbolic action that explicitly relates to siege conditions (Cooke 50; Eichrodt 79) and wants not to contradict the primary application but to suggest that its significance is not thereby exhausted. There is no need to relate vv 12–15 as a whole to the exile, as a separate sign from that of vv 9–11 (Wevers 60; Carley 34; Garscha, *Studien* 90–91; Greenberg 119): the separate introduction that opens v 13 points to the supplementary nature of the verse. The uncleanness of any food eaten in exile is paralleled in Hos 9:3–4, which this verse may echo; it is a consequence of living in an "unclean land" (Amos 7:17).

5:1–4 The last in the series of sign-acts concentrates on the grim fate of the people confined to Jerusalem, which they would undergo during and after the siege. The shift from the city, which featured in 4:1–3, to its inhabitants has been facilitated by the symbolism of siege food in 4:9–12, 14–17 and by the explicit plural references in 4:16–17. The symbolic action of shaving is a development of the metaphor of divine punishment in Isa 7:20, whereby Yahweh was to use Assyria as a razor that would shave off all bodily hair. The metaphor seems to mean that Ahaz would suffer the deep humiliation of being left with nothing (R. E. Clements, *Isaiah 1–39* [Grand Rapids: Eerdmans, 1980] 90; cf. 2 Sam 10:4–5). For a priest to cut his hair was out of character (cf. 44:20), but the text does not take up this perspective.

1–2 As Ezekiel represented the divine punisher in 4:1–3, so he does here, by doing the shaving (cf. 5:11). But by being the one shaved, he assumes the role of the people in the city, as he represented them in 4:9–12, 14–17 (cf. Friebel, "Sign-Acts" 573). The preliminary instructions to the prophet to shave off all the hair on his head and face and to divide it into three parts precede the symbolic action proper. Its description begins in v 2; it has to be done after Ezekiel has completed the earlier siege-related actions. As in the case of each act concerning Jerusalem (cf. 4:7–8, 9), this final one is carefully interlocked with what precedes. The model city under siege of 4:1–2 features again in this symbolic action, as it did in 4:7.

The fate of the citizens was predetermined: there was no future for them in the city. One of the three piles of hair he was to ceremonially set alight on the brick that bears a picture of the city, in a fire of divine judgment. The second pile he was to spread on the ground and the brick and slash with the sword (Friebel, *Sign-Acts* 575). Ominously, it was to occur on the very area where the besieging army took up its position (סביבותיה "around it," v 2; סביב "around," 4:2). Then the God who commands interrupts his instructions with an interpretation couched in terms of his own destructive work, which obviously cites Lev 26:33a*β*. While the citation is not exact, it is semantically equivalent: the Lev 26 text has והריקתי אחריכם חרב "and I will draw after you a sword," while here we read וחרב אריק אחריהם "and a sword I will draw after them." The abrupt change of person results from a contextually unadjusted quotation: older material has been lifted from its source without harmonizing it with its new context (Rooker, *Transition* 62; cf. Greenberg 109). Or, rather, adjustment has been minimally confined to changing a second plural suffix to a third. In the light of this clear parallel, the preceding clause, "you are to scatter to the wind" (תזרה לרוח), is dependent on Yahweh's scattering "among the nations" (אזרה בגוים) in Lev 26:33a . The underlying note of reprisal for covenant breaking, struck just before in 4:16–17, is here repeated and developed. Those who escaped urban destruction in the land could not find respite from Yahweh's destructive power outside it (cf. Lev 26:31–33). The message is corroborated by harnessing it to an evidently recognized tradition.

3–4   A few hairs that belong to the last third are to be retrieved from the ground where they have fallen and carried safely in the loose end of Ezekiel's robe, which could be turned up and used as a bag (cf. Hag 2:12 and in general 1 Sam 25:29). But how safe are these individual hairs? Not very, for some of them are to be taken out and consigned to the fire of judgment that still burned on the brick. There is an ironic toying with the notion of hope of survival for a remnant. "It is . . . aimed at the destruction of all hope of surviving the judgment with a whole skin" (Eichrodt 87; cf. Friebel, "Sign-Acts" 590–91; Krüger, *Geschichtskonzepte* 125). Thus v 3 functions as a background to v 4, which rephrases the pursuing sword of v 2bδ (Greenberg 110). "Although they escape from the fire, the fire will consume them," as Ezekiel said elsewhere (15:7). The last clause of the verse draws a more general conclusion. The fate of Jerusalem and those Judeans who were besieged within its walls had a representative value: it would be decisive for the covenant people as a whole. The initial fire would lead to a conflagration of judgment that was to engulf the whole community of Israel. For the already exiled members of the community to whom Ezekiel ministered, the fate of the citizens of Jerusalem would entail the extinction of hope.

5–17   A long interpretive oracle now follows, formally introduced with the messenger formula, which in 2:4; 3:11 had been the shorthand designation of messages of judgment.

5   The reference to Jerusalem is not merely a specification of the city as a place, which had just featured in the burning episode of v 2. It also connotes the members of the administration and other notable citizens who played a leading, representative role in the ongoing life of Judah, as the mention of "its" rebellion in v 6 shows. Accordingly, there is a focus on those who lived in Jerusalem, which fits well the sign-act of 5:1–4 (cf. Fohrer 35). While the symbolic action of 4:4–5 had accused the covenant community as a whole of a long history of guilt, here there is a concentration on the sinful role of the capital. The accusation is accentuated by setting it against a background of privilege. Jerusalem's wrongdoing is represented as failure to live up to responsibilities that went with such a privileged position. Such accentuation in terms of a quite unexpected negative response to God's earlier gracious treatment is characteristic of earlier prophets: it occurs notably in Hos 11:1–2; Amos 2:6–12; Isa 5:1–4. Here the concentration on Jerusalem is reminiscent of Isaiah's depiction of the capital as having degenerated from its original state as a "faithful city" that was "full of justice" and the home of "righteousness" to a den of corruption and vice (Isa 1:21–23). Yahweh's setting Jerusalem in the middle (בְּתוֹךְ) of the other nations hardly means that it stood on an equal footing with them (Greenberg 110). The qualifying reference to its being surrounded by them gives expression to its centrality (cf. 32:22–26). One may compare the superlative role of בְּתוֹךְ in 29:12; 30:7, with the sense of standing out among others. "Yahweh has chosen Zion" (Ps 132:13). Later in the book, the position of the postexilic community at the "navel" of the earth (38:12; see my *Ezekiel 20–48* 206–7) represents a transference of a Jerusalem motif to the land (cf. Bodi, *Poem of Erra* 219–30). There is an echo of Jerusalem's preeminent role in Zion theology (cf. Krüger, *Geschichtskonzepte* 77). Zion was nothing less than "the joy of all the earth" and "the perfection of beauty" Pss 48:3[2]; 50:2; Lam 2:15; cf. H.-J. Kraus, *Theology of the Psalms* [Minneapolis: Augsburg, 1986] 78–84). The usage of בְּתוֹךְ "in the middle" and סָבִיב "around" is different from that in v 2 (cf. v 12): the terms have been ironically applied to another sphere of thought, enhancing the contrast between God's initial positive purpose and his ultimate negative purpose.

6 The reference to Jerusalem's rebellion (וַתֶּמֶר) recalls the characterization of the covenant people as a rebel community (בֵּית מְרִי), which occurred most recently in 3:27. The capital's privileged role carried with it the priestly duty of custodianship of the Torah (cf. Isa 2:3; Eichrodt 88; Krüger, *Geschichtskonzepte* 78, 80) and also the social duty of administering and living up to its divinely set standards (Isa 1:21). Yet morally Jerusalem had turned into a veritable Sodom of wickedness, as Isaiah provocatively charged (Isa 1:10). The contrast with other nations recalls the disdainful distinction made in 3:5–7, that they would gladly embrace the prophet's message, unlike the community of Israel. Here there is an implication of a kind of natural law possessed by the other nations, such as is implied in the Noachian covenant of Gen 9 and underlies Amos 1:3–2:3 (cf. J. Barton, *Amos's Oracles against the Nations* [London: CUP, 1980] 40–50).

The mention of Yahweh's "standards" (מִשְׁפָּטִים) and "rules" (חֻקּוֹת) corresponds to the regular phraseology in the Priestly source of the Pentateuch, as the list of OT comparative usage in M. Weinfeld's *Deuteronomy and the Deuteronomic School* (Oxford: Clarendon, 1972) 337 shows. More specifically, the clause "they have rejected my standards" seems to be an allusion to Lev 26:3, 15, which speak of the Israelites, in the second plural, as rejecting, rather than walking in, God's rules. The abrupt change to a plural verb reflects lack of adjustment of the literary reference (cf. Reventlow, *Wächter* 7–9; Greenberg 111; Rooker, *Transition* 62; see the *Excursus* following 6:1–14). The implicit understanding of Jerusalem in terms of its citizens underlies the survival of the plural form. Readers who would like to know what specific sins are in view may turn to a virtual commentary on these generalizations that appears in 22:3–12, 25–30.

7–10 The accusatory interpretation develops into a regular judgment oracle that moves from recapitulated accusation (v 7) to announcement of punishment (vv 8–10). Both elements are lavishly introduced by the messenger formula. Strictly, the first is resumed by the second, as, for instance, in Jer 35:18–19 (Liwak, "Probleme" 73). The oracle is rhetorically addressed to Jerusalem and its inhabitants: one is reminded of Yahweh's charge to Ezekiel in 4:7 to stare fixedly at Jerusalem and prophesy against it. The oracle begins with second plural references in v 7, which slightly adapt the third plurals of v 6b; then it continues in vv 8–10 with second feminine singular references to Jerusalem. The stylistic poles of the oracle appear in Jerusalem's failure to "do" (עָשָׂה) Yahweh's "standards" (מִשְׁפָּטִים) in v 7aγ and Yahweh's resolve to "do acts of judgment" (עָשָׂה שְׁפָטִים) in vv 8b, 10bα. The polarization is reinforced in the latter cases by triple use of the verb עָשָׂה "do" with Yahweh as subject in v 9.

The oracle contains three interpretive elements. First, בְּתוֹכֵךְ "inside you" in vv 8b, 10a reflects בְּתוֹךְ הָעִיר "inside the city" in v 2a ; in this case, unlike v 5, there is a direct connection with the enacted symbolism, although סְבִיסוֹתֵיכֶם "around you" (v 7aβ, b) stays within the different orbit of vv 5–6, in keeping with the recapitulative role of v 7. Second, the scattering to every wind of the rest of Jerusalem's inhabitants—the second singular suffix so connotes (Krüger, *Geschichtskonzepte* 79)—in v 10bβ repeats the divine action of v 2bγ with the climactic addition of כֹּל "every." Third, the adversarial intervention of Yahweh (v 8aβ) and his initiation of punishment interpret Ezekiel's representative role in the symbolic action.

7 In the recapitulated accusation, the reference to insolence is a stylistic variation of the rebelliousness mentioned in the basic charge. The earlier contrast with the nations is here expressed in a separate clause concerning the failure of Jerusalem's citizens to comply even with standards divinely assigned to other nations and customarily kept by them (cf. 16:27).

8 A hinge between cause and effect, "therefore," regularly links accusation and announcement of punishment in prophetic oracles of judgment, and the messenger formula also characteristically introduces the announcement of divine reprisal. A formula of encounter, הנני עליך "behold I am against you," occurs here for the first time in the book (cf. Zimmerli 26 and n. 151, which partially updates p. 175). The reactive phrase גם־אני "I for my part," which will recur in v 11, is also characteristic of announcements of punishment (cf. BDB 169b); it traces correspondence between the retributive intervention of Yahweh and the prior activity of the accused. The phrase עשה שפטים "carry out acts of judgment," which is common in the book, was borrowed from Priestly literature (Exod 12:12; Num 33:4; cf. Exod 6:6; 7:4). Ezekiel was able to draw on a rich heritage of prophetic and priestly traditions. Here the phrase, which outside this book is employed with Israel's enemies as victims, strikingly has Jerusalem as its object. Yahweh, Jerusalem, and the nations appeared in different roles in vv 6–7. Mention of the nations as eyewitnesses of the judgment marks a rearrangement of these three entities, in the fateful twist of the kaleidoscope that v 8 represents.

9–10a The grim threat of unique measures may be a reminiscence of the similar Isa 7:17, in the light of the echoing of Isa 7:20 in v 1. Contextually, it reacts to Jerusalem's glaring excess in so failing to live up to its position of privilege above the other nations as to plunge far beneath them (vv 5–7). The retaliatory nature of these measures is reinforced by recalling the accusations leveled against Jerusalem. The failure to meet Yahweh's standards mentioned in vv 6–7 is now summed up as "all your shocking practices." The term תועבה "abomination, shocking practice" employed here is characteristic of Ezekiel. Krüger (*Geschichtskonzepte* 83 n. 97) has observed that 36 percent of all the instances in the OT occur in the book of Ezekiel, which represents only 6 percent of the whole. Here, unlike the usage in v 11, the term functions as an equivalent of general sins or iniquities, as in 18:13, 24; 20:4; 22:2 (cf. Jer 7:10). It expresses that which is emotionally hateful to Yahweh and incompatible with the covenant relationship. The repeated term לכן "therefore, so" permits a gliding from accusation at the end of v 9 to punishment in v 10a. The statement of cannibalism within the family also functions as an experience of the unique punishment of v 9a, which is here presented in terms of human consequences. It appears to be a loose citation of Lev 26:29, which illustrates the rigors of a siege by means of filial cannibalism. Here that threat is stylistically capped with a climactic statement of its paternal counterpart (Liwak, "Probleme" 76).

10b This pair of statements looks back and forward. Its first statement functions in an inclusion, recalling the initial phrase in v 8b. It is also a summary that sweeps together all the actions to be carried out by Yahweh in Jerusalem according to vv 8b–9. However, such actions within the city interpretively cover only the first part of the symbolic action, in v 2aα. Hasty reference is made to the rest by extracting the striking phrase "scatter to the wind" from v 2bγ, with the addition of "every" to the noun by way of climax, and with appropriate change to a first-person verb. The latter adaptation brings the clause closer to the basic statement of divine scattering among the nations in Lev 26:33aα. The reference to the "rest" (שְׁאֵרִית) of Jerusalem's citizens may be an indirect resumption of the ironic actions of vv 3–4, since the term can mean "remnant" (cf. 11:13). This half verse also functions as a heading, giving an overview of the next section, vv 11–13, which will feature the main interpretation of the sign of the hair, detail by detail.

11 Logically, the conjunction "therefore" must refer back to the accusation of "all your shocking practices" at the end of v 9, which the new accusation resumes (and defines). In a similar way the accusation of v 6 was resumed in the charge of v 7aβ–δ, with an intervening "therefore" and a messenger formula. Here the messenger formula is replaced by an oath formula and an accompanying divine-saying formula, which lend certainty to the fulfillment of this new oracle of judgment. The definition of Jerusalem's "shocking practices" or "abominations" (תּוֹעֵבֹת) reflects the term's traditional links with impurity (see, e.g., Lev 18:24–30; Deut 14:3). In priestly thought the sins of the people had the effect of polluting the sanctuary with a miasma of uncleanness, which required removal by sacrifice to save the people from perishing (Lev 15:31; 16:19; Num 19:20). Milgrom (*RB* 33 [1976] 398) has compared this principle to that in Oscar Wilde's novel about the picture of Dorian Gray, which lost its youth as Dorian degenerated and returned to its former beauty at his death. If the Hebrew text is original at this point (see *Note* 11.b.), the presence of pagan objects of worship in the temple (cf. 8:5–6, 9–10) is cited as a blatant example of the defiling abominations committed by the people of Jerusalem.

In reprisal for this attack on his sanctuary and so on himself, Yahweh had to adopt a radical policy of curtailment: the verb now used means both to shave and to curtail. Nor would he have any compunction in so doing. The double clause that qualifies this punishment is a divine formula that will recur five times in chaps. 7–9. It is an adaptation of an expression whose original setting was in the court of law, according to the usage in Deuteronomy (Deut 13:9 [8]), where it refers to the necessity of extreme punishment due to the serious nature of a crime (see, however, Raitt, *Theology of Exile* 50–53). Here Yahweh judges the offenses to be so grave that no lesser plight could befall the citizens of Jerusalem than the inexorable fate depicted in the symbolic action.

12 The burning of one third of the cut hair "inside the city" (v 2) is interpreted as a metaphor for the rigors of a siege, specifically the fatal outbreak of plague and onset of famine (cf. 2 Kgs 25:3). The slashing of the next third of the pile of hair with the sword "around" the model of the city is sufficiently clear as to need little explanation. It found fulfillment in a royal attempt to escape the besieged city (2 Kgs 25:4–7). The fate of the last pile of hair is simply repeated in v 12b from the end of v 2, with the necessary change of the first of the two verbs to the divine first person, to match the second verb. The change of person brings v 12b even closer to its prototype in Lev 26:33a. The divine curse for the people's radical breach of Yahweh's covenant with them was to come tragically true. The triple formula of fatalities caused by plague, famine, and sword in warfare was also used by Jeremiah (e.g., Jer 21:19; 27:13). It recurs in Ezek 6:11, 12; 7:15. The formula, which may have been borrowed from Jeremiah by Ezekiel, is used rather more freely by the latter (see Illman, *OT Formulas* 94–97).

13 The qualification in the treatment of the final portion of hair in vv 3–4 does not find precise interpretation. Instead, there is a more allusive style of interpretation. The multiple references to divine anger surely correspond to the fresh fires of judgment that blazed in v 4. Moreover, the double use of כלה "be exhausted" not only fittingly characterizes the finality of the fate described there but also echoes the sound of כל "all" in v 4b. The fires of judgment would take the form of divine anger, for which fire is a standard metaphor in this book and elsewhere (e.g., 22:20–22, 31; 24:11–13; Jer 7:20; Lam 4:11).

The addition of a recognition formula to the judgment oracle turns it into a proof saying. The purpose of the judgment was to be the recognition and vindication of Yahweh. He is not one to stand idly by while his people engage in gross sin that pollutes his sanctuary. He will deal radically with the moral chaos that has disturbed Jerusalem's special relationship with Yahweh. The recognition formula is expanded with a formula of asseveration, which refers to Yahweh's verdict of judgment, as in 17:21; here the asseveration formula is qualified with the intensive phrase "in my passion." The recognition formula has been further extended with a clause that refers to the execution of judgment as an accomplished fact, as, for instance, in 6:13; 12:15. The fulfillment of Yahweh's word would reveal him as the God who triumphs over wrong and over the perpetrators of wrongdoing.

14–17 There follow two supplementary statements, in vv 14–15 and 16–17, each of which closes with a further formula of divine asseveration. Vv 14–15 resume and develop the announcement of judgment made in vv 8–10, while vv 16–17 resume and develop that of v 12a. Thus vv 14–17 make up a third block of interpretive material, after those of vv 5–10 and 11–13, and seek to coordinate the two earlier ones. Another major function of this block is to amplify the allusions to Lev 26 that have occurred in vv 5–13.

14–15 The reference to the surrounding nations takes the reader back to v 8 and even further back to vv 5 and 7, while לעיני "before the eyes of (every passerby)" is a sinister echo of לעיני הגוים "in the nations' view" in v 8. The recapitulating "when I carry out acts of judgment" harks back to the language of divine intervention in vv 8 and 10. There were to be two more phases of such judgment for Jerusalem to undergo. First, the covenant curse list of Lev 26 envisioned not only siege for Israel's cities but also destruction. The threat that Yahweh would make them objects of destruction (ונתתי . . . חרבה, Lev 26:31) is here echoed in the language of v 14aα, "and I will make you an object of destruction" (ואתנך לחרבה). Like the earlier acts of judgment in v 8, destruction would be subject to the humiliating observation of others. Such humiliation is brought to the surface in v 15. The motif is borrowed from the tradition of the communal lament (Pss 44:14–15[13–14]; 79:4; cf. 89:51–52[50–51]). It does feature in a curse list in Deut 28:37, but only with reference to exiles. In this final reference to the nations, Jerusalem ironically retains its central role of v 5, but all else has changed. It has exchanged the high place of privilege for the low place of contempt. The "furious punishment" is a measure of the intensity of sinfulness that warrants these acts of judgment. Yahweh has given his verdict and pledges that it will be carried out.

16–17 A whole series of afflictions is promised to Jerusalem and its citizens in this vehement recapitulation of v 12a. At first the citizens are mentioned obliquely, as in vv 6b and 13; then they are addressed in vv 16b–17aα¹, as in v 7. There is finally

a renewed turning to Jerusalem, which is addressed in v 17aα²–b, as in the concluding vv 8–10 and also in vv 14–15. A pattern emerges from these twists and turns.

The description of Yahweh's acts of judgment as his arrows may have been
suggested by Deut 32:23, the context of which is not dissimilar. But the main
intent of these closing verses is to capture the bitter flavor of Lev 26. Thus the
breaking of bread sticks, a citation of Lev 26:26, is repeated from the earlier sign
interpretation in 4:16; now it is closer to the original with respect to לכם "you."
The citation is woven into the present context by the mention of famine repeated
from v 12. The letting loose of "vicious animals" that "leave you childless" is obviously borrowed from Lev 26:22, except that for the hiphil form of the initial
verb a piel is used here. The second singular pronoun reaches beyond the city
of Jerusalem to its inhabitants, as it did in v 10 (שאריתך "those of you who are
left"). The mention of plague and sword reaffirms v 12, but they are also meant
to evoke the rigors of Lev 26:25, as the use of the same phrase, "cause to come
upon" (אביא על), in the second case strongly suggests. The reference to bloodshed presumably paraphrases the dying of v 12aα. The alliterative דבר ודם "plague
and bloodshed" seems to be virtually a hendiadys, "a fatal plague." After this vol-
ley of nightmarish woes, which in formal terms mingle divine punishment and its
human consequences, the divine fiat resounds once more, in confirmation: "I,
Yahweh, have spoken."

Explanation

The book continues almost as dramatically as it began, with a renewed vision
and divine commands for Ezekiel to carry out a series of symbolic actions concerning the coming siege of Jerusalem. Interpretive comments are included with
the actions, mostly of a brief nature; the last sign of the frighteningly methodical
disposal of the people in the capital receives an elaborate interpretation that
grounds divine judgment in accusations of dire human sinfulness. "Emphatic expression is . . . given to the unfathomable guilt of the people and the relentless
fury it has evoked in God" (Greenberg 128). The function of this message of
judgment is theodicy. It focuses on coming catastrophe and asks what has been
done to deserve such a fate. Typically an oracle of judgment that serves as an
expression of theodicy "will refer to the catastrophe under some harsh image
and then fill the accusation with the most extreme charges of sin imaginable"
(Raitt, *Theology of Exile* 90–94, esp. 92). The extreme generalizations that mark
most of the accusations, in 5:6–7, 11, as well as 4:4–5, and the radical nature of
the judgment indicate that the purpose of the present message of judgment is to
explain that God's coming action is justified. Thus this second unit of the book
appropriately follows the first, in which Ezekiel's call by the divine judge was narrated and announced.

This purpose serves to shed light on a NT passage. In Romans 1:18–3:26 Paul
explains justification by faith by arguing that "the wrath of God" (Rom 1:18) must
fall upon humanity, both Gentiles and Jews, because "all have sinned" (3:23).
The latter statement is not meant as a truism: human sinning partakes of an outrageous quality, as the apostle's previous impassioned and extreme definitions
make clear. For Paul, as for Ezekiel, there was need for theodicy, as warrant for
the radical work of God.

In the present unit, corroborative weight is lent to the harshness of the divine intervention by appeal to what was evidently an existing tradition, the series of covenant curses in Lev 26. It is difficult to resist Greenberg's conclusion: "All indications are of Ezekiel's dependence upon Lev 26" (127). The relative closeness of the parallels with Lev 26 and the sustained frequency of their presence seem to point to a literary source that was acknowledged as authoritative by the exiles, to which the prophet appealed to support the vehemence of his message (see the *Excursus* that follows chap. 6). The accusation of rejecting God's standards and rules (5:6) leans on the premise of the curses in Lev 26:15. Then the punishments of Lev 26:22, 25, 26, 29, 31, and 33 are echoed in the interpretive material of 4:10, 16, 17; 5:2, 10, 12, 16, 17. This pattern of quotation or allusion that runs through chaps. 4–5 was evidently intended as a powerful argument that God's new and shocking prophetic word was congruent with an older, priestly word concerning the failure of the covenant people and the inevitable reprisals of their Lord. There is a deliberate historicizing of the phases of deterrent curses in terms of an imminent catastrophe.

Another tradition comes to the fore in these chapters, this time as the target of sinister reinterpretation. Zion theology, which finds poetic and cultic expression in the Songs of Zion, Pss 46, 48, 76, 87, was a strong impediment to threats of Jerusalem's downfall. The aura of impregnability afforded by Yahweh's presence in the temple was a sacred canopy under which his people could shelter from all such threats, whether posed by foreign pressure or by prophets of doom. Indeed, as Lam 4:12 later expressed it:

> The kings of the earth did not believe
>   nor any of the inhabitants of the world
> that enemy or foe could enter
>   through the gates of Jerusalem.

Yet Ezekiel affirmed that the battle whose outcome Zion's lore proudly celebrated, for instance in Ps 48:5–7(4–6), would be virtually reenacted, and that this time God's favor would not save Jerusalem (4:1–3; cf. Krüger, *Geschichtskonzepte* 127). The theological basis for the tradition of Jerusalem's security, its unique character, is brought into the open in 5:5—and made the reason for its fall. The central position of divine privilege that Jerusalem held in the world accentuates the egregious nature of the capital's rejection of divine standards. Much is expected of the one to whom much is given (Luke 12:48). The very argument that Amos had used against the Northern Kingdom reappears here, with reference to Jerusalem:

> You only have I known
>   of all the families of the earth;
> therefore I will punish you
>   for all your iniquities. (Amos 3:2)

Ezekiel's engaging in striking symbolic acts continues the strange tradition represented by Isaiah, who walked barefoot and scantily clad for three years as a "sign" against Egypt (Isa 20:3–4), and by Jeremiah, who carried a wooden yoke around Jerusalem, as a token that the residents should surrender to Nebuchadnezzar (Jer 27:2, 12; 28:10). It is not difficult to see the political relevance of Ezekiel's own symbolic actions, concerning the siege and fall of Jerusalem and the fate of those who lived in or had taken refuge in the city. At about the same time that Ezekiel received instructions to perform these signs and give an accompanying commentary, an anti-Babylonian conference of western states was being held in Jerusalem (Jer 27:3), evidently to plot rebellion against an empire that had recently been beset by domestic and provincial difficulties (see Malamat, "Twilight of Judah" 135–37). The conference gave expression to a widespread hope, at home (cf. Jer 28:1–4) and among the exiles (cf. Jer 29:8–9), of a glorious reversal of Judean fortunes, which would include the release of the 597 B.C. prisoners of war. Ezekiel had to spell out to the exiles the emptiness of all such hopes. Rather, Jerusalem's fate under God was to be a military siege that would culminate in destruction and widespread loss of life. Any expectation that was not realistically grounded in moral and religious commitment to Yahweh was doomed to disappointment. The prophet was preparing the exiles for the tragic fall of Jerusalem that occurred a few years later.

There is evidence of redactional amplification of the basic message. The sudden references to exile in 4:6, 13 arouse suspicion in their siege-related contexts. They lack the appropriateness of the references in 5:2bγ, 12bα that follow a natural sequence of siege, destruction, and exile. Surely 4:6, 13 are to be interpreted in terms of an intention to find a new relevance in the adjacent material. Fulfillment in the siege conditions in 587 B.C. did not exhaust its applicability to God's people as victims of his judgment. Those who eventually languished in the ensuing exile were invited to realize that his sentence of punishment was still being served by their generation and that the divinely imposed curse of eating unclean food was as much a mark of exile as it was of the siege. The updating is comparable with the redactional extension of the sin and punishment of the Northern Kingdom to Judah in the book of Hosea (Hos 8:14; 10:11; 12:1[11:12, see REB], 3[2]). Here the hermeneutical widening of the original scope constitutes a warning that divine judgment could not be relegated to the past but that present experience revealed the same somber side of God in his relationship with the Judean exiles. There is no difficulty in seeing Ezekiel's hand at work in these reinterpretations, since his prophetic ministry continued long after 587 and extended into the main period of exile. It is less likely that the hostages of 597 are in view.

A redactional item of a different type is to be found in 3:16b–21. The rest of the material in this literary unit is marked by conformity with the former unit. The message of inescapable judgment to a rebel community, with which Ezekiel was entrusted at his call, is reaffirmed in 3:27. The note of hostile response to Ezekiel's message, which is struck in 2:6; 3:7, is sounded again in 3:25. On a par with such sentiments is the withdrawal of divine favor that Ezekiel represents both in the seclusion and silence of 3:24, 26 and in the iron plate that separates the prophet from the model of the city in 4:3. The sign-acts and their interpretation describe the form that God's judgment is to take and give justifications. The messenger formula that is used as a cipher of judgment in 2:4; 3:11 continues in that function in 3:27; its regular employment in an oracle of judgment at 5:5, 7, 8 serves to echo the earlier usage. The formula of divine asseveration, "I have spoken" (דברתי) in 5:13, 15, 17 reminds the careful reader of the triple mandate to Ezekiel to repeat "my words" (דברי) in 2:7; 3:4 and "my words that I will speak" (דברי אשר אדבר) in 3:10. The commission to prophesy to "the community of

Israel" (2:3; 3:1, 4, 7) is resumed in the sign for such a constituency at 4:3, in the statement of its guilt at 4:4, and in implications for "all the community of Israel" at 5:4 (cf. 3:7).

This flow of continuity is interrupted by 3:16b–21. There is no need, however, to cut the knot of the presence of this section by resorting to "a purely text-critical cause, such as a displaced page" (Reventlow, *Wächter* 130). As was noted in the *Comment*, the section is superficially integrated into its context by the reference to "the community of Israel" in 3:17 and by the mention of "iniquity" (עָוֹן) in 3:18, 19 (cf. 5:4). However, its discontinuity outweighs the continuity, a phenomenon that suggests that redactional splicing has taken place. It is sometimes suggested that the school of Ezekiel wished to emphasize that divine concern for repentance was a feature of Ezekiel's prophetic ministry from the outset. This conclusion has been drawn, for example, by Fohrer (23), Fishbane (*Int* 38 [1984] 134), Hals (24), and Krüger (*Geschichtskonzepte* 353). However, Greenberg's sensitivity to the falsehood of thus imbedding a statement of Ezekiel's later role in a pre-fall context ("falsely," 93) deserves to be taken seriously. Rather, the insertion bears witness to a re-reading of these early chapters from a vantage point of changed conditions. One may compare the way that, in the book of Isaiah, 4:2–6 and chap. 12 reflect a redactional reading of the preceding chapters in a later period, which seeks to apply them to a different setting. In both the ministry and the book of Ezekiel, a turning point comes with the fall of Jerusalem, and a new message of salvation is made possible. However, the old message of judgment continues to have a certain relevance. Ezek 20:33–38; 33:30–33; 34:20–22 are passages that realistically carry a message of partial judgment, in order to affirm the moral challenge that confronts those who are to be saved. The old message of radical judgment had been fulfilled, but its usefulness lived on in the reminder that "God is not mocked" (Gal 6:7). It is in this sense that 3:16b–21 has been abstracted from 33:1–13 and placed at this point. We are meant to notice not how ill-fitting this passage is in a context of absolute judgment but rather how that context needs to be reinterpreted.

We are invited to look back from a later perspective and to re-read the message of inevitable judgment through eyes that have already read the later modifications to the first message. God does not cease to be the judge of the apostate and of the backsliding believer. Ezekiel's later role as watchman certainly involved a call to repentance and so a desire to save the lost among the people of God. But God's will to save in no way cancels out his moral necessity to judge, wherever evil exists among "the community of Israel." "Iniquity" is still abhorrent to him. The vision of the divine judge must still grip those who hear it read, and Ezekiel's call to announce punishment for rebels against the will of God still stands. God's "severity" survives as a real deterrent, even when his "kindness" has come to prevail—"kindness to you, provided that you continue in his kindness; otherwise you too will be cut off" (Rom 11:22).

The categorical imperative that rested on Ezekiel to carry out this task of watchman is reminiscent of that of Paul to "warn everyone and teach everyone" (Col 1:24–29, esp. v 28). This imperative, both prophetic and apostolic, underscores the need for God's people to covet a strong sense of his will in matters of their own hearts and habits.

Yahweh's Campaign against the Mountains of Israel (6:1-14)

Bibliography

Bettenzoli, G. *Geist der Heiligkeit.* Florence: Universita di Firenze, 1979. 184–89. **Beyse, K.-M.** "חמם *hmm.*" *TDOT* 4:473–77. **Boadt, L.** "Rhetorical Strategies in Ezekiel's Oracles of Judgment." In *Ezekiel and His Book,* ed. J. Lust. BETL 74. Leuven: University Press, 1986. 182–200. **Driver, G. R.** "Confused Hebrew Roots." In *Occident and Orient.* FS M. Gaster. London: Taylor's Foreign Press [1936]. 73–82. **Friebel, K.** "Jeremiah's and Ezekiel's Sign-Acts: Their Meaning and Function as Non-Verbal Communication and Rhetoric." Diss., University of Wisconsin Madison, 1989. 607–22. **Haran, M.** "The Uses of Incense in the Ancient Israelite Ritual." *VT* 10 (1960) 113–29. **Holladay, W. L.** "'On Every High Hill and under Every Green Tree.'" *VT* 11 (1961) 170–76. **Krašovec, J.** *Der Merismus im Biblisch-Hebräischen und Nordwestsemitischen.* BibOr 33. Rome: Pontifical Biblical Institute, 1977. **Nielsen, K.** *Incense in Ancient Israel.* VTSup 38. Leiden: Brill, 1986. **Reindl, J.** *Das Ansicht Gottes im Sprachgebrauch des Alten Testaments.* ETS 25. Leipzig: St. Benno, 1970. **Reventlow, H. G.** *Wächter über Israel.* BZAW 82. Berlin: Töpelmann, 1962. 27–34. **Simian, H.** *Die theologische Nachgeschichte der Prophetie Ezekiels: Form- und traditionskritische Untersuchung zu Ez. 6; 35; 36.* FB 14. Würzburg: Echter Verlag, 1974. 117–26, 190–200, 261–72. **Vaughan, P. H.** *The Meaning of "Bāmâ" in the Old Testament: A Study of Etymological, Textual and Archaeological Evidence.* SOTSMS 3. London: CUP, 1974.

Translation

[1]*I received the following communication from Yahweh:* [2]*"Human one, look in the direction of the mountains of Israel and issue a prophecy against*[a] *them.* [3]*Mountains of Israel, you are to say, listen to the declaration of*[a] *Yahweh. Here is a message from the Lord*[b] *Yahweh to the mountains and hills, to the ravines and valleys.*[c] *I am going to order a sword to invade you, and I will destroy*[d] *your local shrines.* [4]*Your altars will be reduced to ruins, and your incense burners*[a] *smashed.*[b] *I will cause your slain to fall in front of your idols*[c] [5]*and scatter your bones round your altars.* [6]*Wherever you live, towns*[a] *will be devastated and local shrines reduced to ruins,*[b] *with the result that your altars will be devastated and ruined*[c] *and your idols smashed and demolished, while your incense burners will be knocked down and your artifacts obliterated;* [7]*and people will lie fallen,*[a] *slain among you. Then you will realize that I am Yahweh,*[8]*when*[a] *your survivors of the sword are present among the nations, when you are dispersed*[b] *among other countries.* [9]*Then your survivors will remember me among the nations where they are held captive, how*[a] *stricken I was by*[b] *their wanton hearts that had lost faith*[c] *in me and by their wanton eyes that had followed their idols. They will regard themselves with disgust*[d] *for*[e] *all their shocking rites.* [10]*Then they will realize that I am Yahweh; I did not threaten without due cause*[a] *to inflict on them such a disaster.*[b]

[11]*"Here is a message from the Lord Yahweh. Clap your hands and stamp your foot, and bemoan*[a] *all the shocking rites*[b] *of the community of Israel,*[c] *who*[d] *are to fall victim to sword, famine, and pestilence.* [12]*Those far away will die of pestilence, those nearby will fall to the sword, while those who escape the one*[a] *or survive the other will die*[b] *of*

famine, and then I will have exhausted my fury against them [13]*and you will realize that I am Yahweh, when their slain lie among their idols round their altars on every high hill, on all the tops of the mountains,*[a] *and under every luxuriant tree and under every leafy terebinth,*[b] *wherever* [c] *they presented fragrant offerings to appease all their idols.* [14]*I will deal them a blow and reduce the country to wrack and ruin*[a] *wherever they live, from the wilderness to Riblah.*[b] *Then they*[c] *will realize that I am Yahweh.*"

Notes

2.a. For the interchange in sense between אל "to" and על "against," cf. *Note* 1:17.c.

3.a The MT adds אדני "Lord," in contravention of the formulaic range of usage in Ezekiel (see Zimmerli, *Ezekiel 2* 556). Mechanical assimilation to the next clause has doubtless occurred.

3.b. For the use of אדני "Lord" in the messenger formula here and in v 11, see *Note* 2:4.c.

3.c. For the K/Q forms, see Zimmerli 179.

3.d. The LXX implies ואבדו "and (they) will be destroyed," probably by assimilation to the pl verbs of v 4a (cf. v 6).

4.a. See *HALAT* 315b–16a.

4.b. The LXX* does not render this verb separately, making both nouns depend on the earlier verb.

4.c. The etymology of Heb. גלול "idol" is uncertain; probably, it literally means a stone block (Cooke 73; Greenberg 132; cf. *HALAT* 185a). It is vocalized by analogy with שקוץ "abhorrent object of worship." MT adds v 5a, "and I will put the corpses of members of Israel in front of their idols," which violates the direct address of the context and is not represented in the LXX*. It appears to be a gloss that cites Lev 26:30 and interprets "your (slain)" in v 4b, which itself echoes Lev 26:30, in human terms instead of relating to the mountains. In Lev 26:30 and context, the suffixes have the former sense. The secondary nature of v 5a is further indicated by closeness of reference to Lev 26:30, over against the loose treatment in v 4b, as in the overall context (Reventlow, *Wächter* 29).

6.a. The rendering "blood-spattered altars" in NEB and REB for ערים "cities" depends on an alternative etymologizing (cf. Driver, *JTS* 41 [1940] 169, following T. H. Gaster) that was criticized by E. W. Nicholson (*VT* 27 [1977] 113–16). Driver judged that the meaning "cities" did not fit a succession of cultic terms, but it echoes the underlying Lev 26:31, 33 and in turn is clearly echoed in 35:4; 36:4, 10.

6.b. For the vocalization, which derives from a rare stem ישם, see Cooke 74. A variant pointing (see *BHS*) associates with the standard stem שמם.

6.c. Heb. ויאשמו employs a byform of שמם "be desolate," as the renderings in Σ Syr Syh Tg appear to confirm (Driver, "Confused Hebrew Roots" 75–77). The LXX attests a shorter text in v 6, omitting the verbs ויאשמו "and be ruined" and ונשבתו "and be demolished," and also the final clause ונמחו מעשיכם "and your artifacts will be obliterated." The first two omissions may reflect simply the translator's unwillingness to render each verb of destruction separately, as evidently in v 4. The last clause could easily have been overlooked by homoeoarcton of ונ and homoeoteleuton of כם. Kraetzschmar (67) and Cooke (74) rightly warned against uncritically following the LXX. In Brownlee (1986) 95, I drew attention to an impressive stylistic pattern that dominates the sentence as it stands in MT: verb + subj/verb + subj/two verbs + subj/two verbs + subj/subj + verb/subj + verb.

7.a. For this sense of the verb, see Ehrlich, *Randglossen* 5:20; Joüon 112a n. 5.

8.a. The MT prefaces with והותרתי "and I will leave," which is generally taken as reflecting a conflated text (e.g., Greenberg 134). The LXX* does not represent it, and it appears to have originated in a comparative gloss derived from the similar 12:16 (Cornill 209; et al.). The deletion is supported by a form-critical factor: see *Form/Setting/Structure*. Simian's failure to recognize the intrusion led him to characterize vv 8–9 falsely as a promise of salvation (*Nachgeschichte* 121; contrast Hölscher, *Dichter* 66). Zimmerli (179) and Liwak ("Probleme" 276 n. 64) have rightly criticized Driver's understanding of בהיות "when . . . are" as "when they fall" (*Bib* 19 [1938] 61; so NEB but not REB).

8.b. The MT בהזרותיכם "when you are dispersed" would normally be בהזרותכם: the suffix has been treated as if ות- were a fem pl ending (cf. 16:31 and GKC 911). It may simply be a case of mechanical assimilation to the ותיכם- endings in vv 3–6.

9.a. Heb. אשר seems to function as a second object after וזכרו "and they will remember," with the sense "the fact that, how": cf. את אשר "how" after זכר in 2 Kgs 20:3 (= Isa 38:3).

9.b. Driver (*JSS* 7 [1962] 96), followed by Greenberg (134; cf. Keil 96), NEB and NRSV, took נשברתי את as "I was brokenhearted, grieved at," comparing Syr. ʾittbr and Akk. itti "with" after verbs expressing anger. The repetition of אֲשֶׁר נַשׁ is suspicious, but the LXX indirectly supports the MT by representing נִשְׁבַּעְתִּי as נִשְׁבַּרְתִּי "I swore." One may not emend to שָׁבַרְתִּי (אֲשֶׁר) "(how) I broke," on the basis of 'Α Σ Θ Tg Vg (*BHK*; Brownlee 98, 100): not only "hearts" but "eyes" must be the awkward object. The conjectural emendation וְשָׁבַרְתִּי "and I will break" (Wellhausen in Smend 39 et al.) has the same defect. Bewer's proposal in *ZAW* 63 (1951) 193, with comparison of 20:43; 36:31, to delete אֹותִי "me" and also אֲשֶׁר נִשְׁבַּרְתִּי as a variant of אֲשֶׁר שְׁבִיתִי "whom I will have taken captive" in a conflated text, with the consequent syntax "I will remember . . . their wanton hearts," is attractive: וְנִשְׁבְּרוּ "and they will be broken" in vv 4, 6 may have influenced the MT.

9.c. The MT אֲשֶׁר סָר "which turned away," unrepresented in the LXX*, is generally taken as a gloss clarifying the pregnant use of זָנָה מֵעַל "fornicate away from": cf. the parallel אַחֲרֵי הַזְּנוּת "that fornicated after" in the next clause. For זָנָה מֵעַל, cf. Hos 9:1.

9.d. For the vocalization, see Jouon 80o. The MT adds אֶל־הָרָעֹות אֲשֶׁר עָשׂוּ "for [= עַל; cf. 36:31] the evils that they did," which the LXX* does not represent. It seems to be a comparative gloss alluding to 20:43 (Cornill 210; et al.).

9.e. The preposition is usually בְּ in this construction; in 36:31 it is עַל. For לְ, cf. its usage with reference to the cause of an emotion (BDB 514b–515a). The attestation of בְּ by LXX Syr Vg appears to reflect an easier reading.

10.a,b. Heb. לֹא אֶל־חִנָּם "not in vain" (a unique phrase; cf. GKC 119ii) and לַעֲשֹׂות לָהֶם הָרָעָה הַזֹּאת "to do this evil to them" are not represented in the LXX*. Zimmerli (180) took them as secondary, deriving from 14:23, but the wording there is by no means close. The MT deserves the benefit of the doubt. Cooke (71) argued that the striking language supports the MT, while Wevers (70) urged that the first phrase is germane to the passage (cf. also Greenberg 135): "the effectiveness of Yahweh's speech is demonstrated by the exiles' confession and self-loathing." Wevers understood the first clause in terms of effective expression, rather than adequate causality.

11.a. Lit. "say 'alas' for." For the form אָח, seemingly "alas," see *HALAT* 28a; cf. *Note* 21:20(15).d. and the discussion in Friebel, "Sign-Acts" 613–15.

11.b. The MT adds רָעֹות "evil(s)," which the LXX* does not represent and is awkward, whether it is an adj or a noun. The reading is best explained by supposing a marginal phrase תֹּועֵבֹות רָעֹות that originally referred to v 9 and sought to compare 20:43. In the gloss, תֹּועֵבֹות functions as a cue word: "For 'abominations' (20:43 has) 'evils.'" The comparative gloss was taken as a correction of תֹּועֵבֹות "abominations" here in v 11 and displaced it. Then the MT bears witness to two separate attempts at similar annotation of v 9, one of which entered v 9 and the other v 11.

11.c. The REB takes בֵּית יִשְׂרָאֵל "community of Israel" as vocative, but (1) it is rather distant from the supposed addressee, and (2) an article is then expected with the preceding phrase or noun.

11.d. The LXX* does not represent אֲשֶׁר "who." With or without it, the continuation is somewhat strange.

12.a. Heb. וְהַנִּשְׁאָר "and the one who is left" is not represented in the LXX*, but the translator may well have regarded it as an otiose synonym of the following term. Hitzig (43) and others have defined it as a gloss that explained the following הַנָּצוּר as "one who survives," in comparison with the interpretation "one who is besieged" (LXX). Freedy (*VT* 20 [1970] 136–37) added that without it the three cola are perfectly matched. However, Driver (*Bib* 19 [1938] 61; cf. Keil 97; von Orelli 29) adequately explained the pair of words in climactic terms as "he who is left over (from the pestilence)" and "he who is preserved (from the sword)."

12.b. The LXX συντελεσθήσεται "will be destroyed" reflects, in place of יָמוּת "will die," not יִתֹּם "will come to an end" (*BHK*; Driver, *Bib* 19 [1938] 61) but יִכְלֶה "will perish" (see Zimmerli 181). The reading is secondary and represents assimilation to 5:12.

13.a,b. The LXX* does not represent the second and fourth of the four phrases, but Cornill (210–11) retained them for their distinctive phraseology, although he jettisoned the first and third phrases. Greenberg (135) has sensitively traced the innovative adaptation of familiar elements throughout the two pairs of phrases (cf. Simian, *Nachgeschichte* 267).

13.c. For the construction, see Jouon 129q.

14.a. The translation endeavors to capture the alliteration of שְׁמָמָה וּמְשַׁמָּה, two nouns meaning "ruin."

14.b. No such place as Diblah or Diblathah is known. Since J. D. Michaelis, the place name is generally taken, via an early ר/ד error that Jerome noted long ago, as originally a reference to Riblah, to which a few late Masoretic manuscripts correct (see *BHK*). Greenberg (137) has aptly compared the error in the LXX of 2 Kgs 25; Jer 52. Then there are two interpretive options: (1) with the MT to take the phrase as comparative, "more (desolate) than the wilderness of Riblah" (Ehrlich, *Randglossen*

5:22; *BHS*; REB), or (2) as is more commonly done, to point the first noun as abs, מִמִּדְבָּר, and to render "from (the) wilderness to Riblah." In the former case the ה ֶ ending is not easily explicable, while in the latter it is a straightforward indication of direction. However, in the second option one would expect מֵהַמִּדְבָּר "from the wilderness" (see *BHS*), although Greenberg (137) has justified the anarthrous noun as a case of poetic style; in prose Smend (40) compared 21:3; 23:42. The contextual emphasis on comprehensiveness (see the *Comment*) favors the second option.

14.c. The second person in the LXX* "assimilates . . . to the formulation of v 13a" (Zimmerli 182).

Form/Structure/Setting

Chap. 6 comprises a separate literary unit, as the message-reception formulas in 6:1 and 7:1 indicate. The unit breaks down into two oracles in vv 2–10 and 11–14, both of which have messenger formulas at their head (vv 3, 11) and begin with commands to engage in expressive gestures (vv 2, 11). The oracles are marked by double recognition formulas, in vv 7 and 10 on the one hand and vv 13 and 14 on the other. Accordingly, these oracles are proof sayings: they are of the bipartite type, with an announcement of judgment and a closing recognition formula that has a temporal clause appended. Both oracles are extended with further statements of judgment, which in turn end with their own recognition formulas. The temporal clauses, consisting of *beth* with infinitive construct, in vv 8 and 13, are instances of a resumptive clause closely linked with its preceding recognition formula ("you/they will know . . . when . . . ."), which may then be capped with a further recognition formula. This construction is not unparalleled in the book of Ezekiel. We have already observed a resumptive temporal clause in 5:13; the fuller style with a further recognition formula occurs in 30:25–26. The MT has understood the nature of the temporal clause in v 13 as an appendage, but the textual intrusion at the beginning of v 8 prevented recognition of the one there.

In the present two oracles, the temporal clauses do not precisely resume material earlier in their respective oracle, but such must be their form-critical role (see the *Comment*). In each case the following new statement or series of statements, which leads on to a further recognition formula, represents an extension of the message, somewhat as in 36:12, but here much more developed, so that one has two pairs of linked proof sayings. Greenberg (137–38) has called the second sections "afterwaves" and aptly compared 12:15–16; 20:42–44.

The two oracles match not only in their overall form but in their initial expressive gestures (vv 2, 11). Parunak ("Structural Studies" 187) has drawn attention to the stylistic patterning that unites the oracles, an ABB′A′ chiastic arrangement in which A/A′ stand for cultic references within vv 1–7 and 13–14, and B/B′ represent references to human suffering in vv 8–10 and 11–12. One may also observe the use of כָּל תּוֹעֲבוֹת "all the abominations" in vv 9 and 11 as a hinge that connects the two oracles.

The announcement of judgment in the first oracle has its own rhetorical artistry in that it begins with חֶרֶב "sword" (v 3) and ends with חָלָל "slain" (v 7), clearly breaking up the common phrase, which appears frequently in chaps. 31–32, חַלְלֵי חֶרֶב "slain by the sword." In v 4b חַלְלֵיכֶם "your slain" also occurs, while תֶּחֱרַבְנָה "will be devastated" in v 6a may be a word play on חֶרֶב in v 3. This pattern indicates two sections, vv 3–5 and 6–7a, which the content supports. This stylistic feature suggests the originality of vv 6–7a, which have been regarded with suspicion simply because in content they elaborate vv 4–5 (Bertholet [1936] 24–25; Zimmerli 183; Bettenzoli, *Geist der Heiligkeit* 185–86). The second oracle echoes the terms "sword" and "slain," in vv 11–13a, and also the falling of vv 4b and 7a in vv 11b–12aβ.

The second oracle is characterized by an intensification indicated by the term כל "all." In the first oracle it occurs only twice, qualifying מושבותיכם "your dwelling places" in v 6 and תועבתיהם "their abominations" in v 9. However, it reverberates through vv 11–14: it qualifies not only the same recurring nouns (in reverse) in vv 11 and 14 but also the series of four nouns relating to pagan cultic places in v 13. Moreover, it seems to be echoed by the exhausting (וכליתי) of Yahweh's anger in v 12. Thus sin and punishment are vehemently highlighted by this device.

The parallels between the two oracles must not cause us to overlook their difference in perspective. The first oracle is rhetorically addressed to the "mountains of Israel," although there is a switch to the people who live in the homeland, which occurs at least by v 5b (for this phenomenon, see the *Comment*). By contrast, the second oracle is evidently addressed to Ezekiel's fellow exiles, as the second plural reference in v 13aα indicates, and the unexiled Judeans are consistently referred to in the third person, initially as בית ישראל "the community of Israel" in v 11. This difference in perspective between the two oracles shows that they originated separately; so does their different representation of Judah's fate, one of which envisions exile and the other not. Reventlow (*Wächter* 33 n. 167) was doubtless correct in considering that the similarity of the material in the former half of the first oracle and the latter half of the second was the prime reason for combining the two in a literary unit. One may add that the similarity indicates that the second oracle may betray awareness and reflection of the first. Vv 13aβ–14 have been regarded as a redactional expansion to tie the chapter together (e.g., Wevers 67; Zimmerli 191), but that conclusion is by no means compelling (see the *Comment*). Bettenzoli (*Geist der Heiligkeit* 186 n. 2) has defended the passage on structural grounds. The use of deuteronomistic language in v 13 is not incompatible with Ezekiel's authorship (see Joyce, *Divine Initiative* 25–26, and in principle Zimmerli, *Ezekiel 2* xv).

The setting for both oracles is Ezekiel's period of Babylonian exile before the fall of Jerusalem. In the first oracle, turning in the direction of the mountains of Israel and direct address by no means require the prophet's presence in Palestine (cf. Brownlee [1986] 96) but are vivid rhetorical features, as in the oracles against foreign nations (25:2–3; 29:2–3). The real addressees of the first oracle, as of the second, are Ezekiel's companions in exile. The ascription of vv 8–10 to a period after the fall of Jerusalem, so that a later oracle of Ezekiel's was subsequently inserted (e.g., Herrmann 43; Eichrodt 96; Zimmerli 190), is not necessary (cf. Greenberg 140–41, and see the *Comment*).

The unit may be outlined as follows:

6:1–10	Oracle against the mountains of Israel
6:2–7	Destruction of the local shrines and their worshipers
6:8–10	Remorse of the deported survivors
6:11–14	Oracle against those in the homeland

6:11–13aα   God's fury spent in fatalities
6:13aβ–14   Death and destruction in reprisal for illicit worship

Comment

1   The narrative message-reception formula strictly introduces the first oracle
in vv 2–10, but it covers also the second in vv 11–14, and so serves as an introduction to a literary unit, as often in the book.

2   The first oracle opens with a divine command to the prophet, typically addressed as "human one" (see 2:1 and the *Comment*), to engage in a symbolic
gesture of staring in the direction of the addressees of the oracle. This pose of
attentiveness is frequently commanded throughout the book (see the *Comment*
on 21:2 in *Ezekiel 20–48* 24–25). It recalls an ancient prophetic practice associated with Balaam (Num 24:1) and Elisha (2 Kgs 8:11), but in such a context as
this one it no longer refers to visual contact but simply to looking in the general
direction of the target of the oracle. The westward look facilitates the eventual
use of second-person references to the far-off recipients in apostrophic fashion:
they are already the focus of the prophet's gaze. It vividly creates a sense of their
role as the object of Yahweh's attention and will, via his prophetic representative.
Indeed, it may well function as an extension of the setting of the divine face
against objects of his judgment (cf. 14:8; 15:7), an idiom that is associated with
both priestly (e.g., Lev 17:10; 20:3) and prophetic (Jer 21:10; 44:11) settings (cf.
Reindl, *Das Angesicht Gottes* 110–19; Layton, *UF* 17 [1986] 177–78). In this connection, it may be significant to observe that the divine phrase occurs in Lev 26:17
(cf. Reventlow, *Wächter* 27–28), since this chapter contains many allusions to Lev
26. It is no obstacle that the verb for "set" is נתן there and שׂים here, since the
verbs are synonymous in this phrase, and chap. 6 characteristically does not echo
Lev 26 in a slavish fashion. There may already be a presentation of the prophet as
herald of judgment on Israel for breaking the covenant, as earlier in chaps. 4–5.

The target of the oracle is "the mountains of Israel," a phrase that appears
frequently in the book of Ezekiel and nowhere else. The term alludes to the land
of Israel, partly as characteristically mountainous terrain and partly in differentiation from the monotonous Babylonian plain in which Ezekiel and his fellow
exiles now lived. It expresses such nostalgia as a native of Switzerland feels who
has to reside in Holland, or a Welshman who must live in East Anglia. It also
expresses the loss of a grandeur that was the gift of God to his people (cf. Vawter
51). Yet the notion of majestic privilege is here blatantly overridden by a message
of judgment. For all its magnificence, the land must suffer as a result of Israel's
sinning.

3   The message proper is impressively delayed by a verbal fanfare of further
introduction. It consists of a call for attention to the divine word, which highlights the confrontation between Yahweh and his audience, and a messenger
formula. The latter element permits further specification of the target in the spec-
tacular variety of its rugged and gentle contours (cf. Deut 8:7), which were soon
to be overtaken by tragedy.

Whether or not there was an allusion to Lev 26 in the symbolic stare of v 2a, it
can hardly be missed in the first words of the actual oracle. The announcement
of Yahweh's imminent intervention by summoning a "sword" of destruction to

Israel's mountains is a deliberate reminiscence of the beginning of Lev 26:25, "and I will bring a sword against you," like that in 5:17. It alludes to the prospect of Israelites' being given over into the hand of an enemy, as that verse concludes. It announces a confrontation ("I . . . you") that will be spelled out in two respects in vv 3bγ, 4–5b, in v 3bγ, which is further broken down in v 4a, and in vv 4b, 5b (cf. Simian, *Nachgeschichte* 191).

In the first clause of Lev 26:30, a further punitive act of God was to be the destruction of "your local shrines"; here that act is claimed as dreadfully relevant (cf. Holscher, *Dichter* 66; Reventlow, *Wächter* 29). The במות, traditionally rendered "high places," were cultic platforms built of stones on which altars were built, and then by extension the sanctuaries within which the platforms stood (see Vaughan, *The Meaning of 'Bāmâ*,' esp. 29–55). They were commonly situated on high ground but could be built in valleys and even inside cities (see 2 Kgs 17:9). Josiah had undertaken the destruction of the local shrines as part of his religious reforms (2 Kgs 23:8, 15, 19), but evidently they were reactivated after his death in 609 B.C. Behind this condemnation of the local shrines may be espied the standpoint of a Zadokite prophet whose family had served for generations in the Jerusalem temple, a standpoint reinforced by the deuteronomic perspective of the temple as the sole legitimate sanctuary (Deut 12). This standpoint wins support from the ensuing references to the pagan nature of the worship carried on at the local shrines all over Israel's territory.

4–5 V 4a spells out the results of Yahweh's intervention in destroying the shrines, by specifying the destruction of their standard contents, altars and incense burners. The second item is significantly specified as the object of destruction in the second clause of Lev 26:30, so that the oracle is still closely following its source, though not slavishly, since the verbs of destruction vary and "altars" are a new, though natural, item. Garscha (*Studien* 94) wrote of the "astonishing closeness of vv 4–7 to Lev 26:23ff." and found (post-Ezekielian) dependence. The term חמן has been clarified by archeological research as an incense burner of some kind. It may have been a small, portable stone stand in which incense was burned or a vessel placed on top of altars (see *IDB* 2:699–700; Nielsen, *Incense* 45). They are consistently regarded as innovative and pagan in the relatively late passages of the OT in which they are mentioned (Isa 17:8; 27:9; 2 Chr 14:4[5]; 34:7), although in certain forms the use of incense was an established part of Israelite ritual from ancient times (see Haran, *VT* 10 [1960] 113–29). They may have been associated with a particular pagan cult (see Beyse, *TDOT* 4:475–77).

Still shadowing the basic text of Lev 26, the oracle of judgment moves from places and paraphernalia of illegitimate worship to include the people who engage in such worship. V 4b, which together with v 5b is expressed in terms of divine intention, clearly alludes to the next clause of Lev 26:30, "I will place your [= the Israelites'] corpses on the corpses of your idols." "Idols" (גלולים), probably basically "stone blocks" (see *Note* 4.c.), are a frequent object of attack in the book of Ezekiel as a deviant focus of worship (cf. Exod 20:4–5). The second plural references that earlier in the oracle referred to the mountains must now have a human sense, as indeed is the case in the rest of the oracle. Zimmerli (183) has argued well for the originality of this shift in address, which for some scholars has been a signal of redaction (see, e.g., Simian, *Nachgeschichte* 118–19). In fact, the shift was caused by the magnetic pull of the basic text of Lev 26, in which the second plural suffixes consistently refer to Israelites (cf. Reventlow, *Wächter* 29 n. 143). The oracle could not resist its attraction for long. Part of the import of v 4b is that the shrines are defiled by the death of the worshipers. This sentiment is continued and stated more blatantly in v 5b (cf. 2 Kgs 23:14, 16, 20).

6–7a There follows an elaboration of the previous message of destruction, which emphatically underlines it. Amplification occurs at the beginning and near the end. First, there is a reference to the devastation of cities, which looks at first sight to be an intruding element: presumably, the cities feature as the centers where local shrines are found. Once more Ezekiel is staying close to the script of Lev 26. Twice it refers to the devastation of "your cities" (vv 31a*a*, 33b*β*; cf. Reventlow, *Wächter* 30; cf. Fohrer 37, who removed vv 5b–7 as a gloss dependent on Lev 26:30–31). In the former instance, "your cities" occurs in parallelism with "your sanctuaries." Cognate terms are used for devastation, a verb תחרבנה here and a noun חרבה in Lev 26:31, 33. The initial phrase בכל מושבותיכם "in all your dwelling places" is a standard expression in priestly legislation (e.g., Num 35:29; see Reventlow, *Wächter* 30 n. 144; Greenberg 132). There is further amplification in the detail of the destruction of religious artifacts at the end of v 6. Here the reference seems to be to images (cf. Isa 41:29).

The elaboration is couched in terms of consequences of Yahweh's intervention. The ruination of the local shrines is again spelled out with reference to altars, idols, and incense burners, in a slightly different order than before. The detailing is made syntactically clearer by being introduced with למען "with the result that." V 7a repeats the human element from v 4b, in terms that are not specifically cultic. The change seems to be deliberate. There appears to be an inclusion at vv 6a*a* and 7a, so that the loss of human life is widened from shrines to cities: in Lev 26:25 בתוככם "among you," which recurs in v 7a here, follows a reference to cities.

Vv 4–7a represent the first part of a bipartite proof saying that moves from announcement of punishment to a recognition formula. More often proof sayings are tripartite, beginning with accusation. In this case the accusation is implicitly included in the statement of judgment: cultic deviation is the offense that causes divine retribution.

7b–8 The recognition formula in v 7b draws to a close the proof saying in its basic form. The object of Yahweh's acts of judgment against the local shrines and those who worship in them is to reestablish a true awareness of the nature of Yahweh, an awareness that had been dimmed by syncretistic rites. Only such drastic treatment would bring about a recovery of the distinctiveness of Israel's traditional God. Israel would find him, but too late (cf. Amos 4:12).

The use of what is customarily a recapitulating element in v 8 at first sight creates a problem. Instead of repeating earlier material, the text proceeds to introduce a new experience (cf. Brownlee [1986] 98). The solution is simply that for prophet and hearers, and indeed for early readers, there is already a knowledge of phases of invasion, destruction, death, and exile, so that the text can flow from phase to phase in the development of a familiar theme of judgment. The motif of exile has already occurred in the sign-act and interpretation of 5:1–17, specifically at 5:3b*β*, 10b*β*, and 12b. The present oracle presupposes a series of acts of selective judgments that for some would culminate in exile. Moreover, the master text of Lev 26 itself makes use of such a series, culminating in the threat "I will scatter you among the nations, and I will chase you with unsheathed sword," a threat that chap. 5 puts to striking use. Both Ezekiel's earlier proclamation and the literary source to which he expressly refers make the reference to exile no surprise. The exile marks no reprieve but is itself "a kind of death" (Calvin 227). Far from presenting a positive hope, vv 8–10 "serve to pile doom upon doom and to emphasize the inevitability of the judgment that God has pronounced upon Israel" (Vawter 54).

9–10 The ensuing punishment not only consists of imprisonment on foreign soil but takes on a specifically mental character, the self-torturing of the Judean prisoners with memories of their irredeemable past. Three verbs give expression to this mental punishment: remembering, regarding with disgust, and realizing. Too late, they would recall with revulsion their cultic deviations and so be brought back to a true sense of Yahweh's being. Such remorse would be their reaction to their former alienation from him. The term "heart" refers to the will; similarly, "eyes" refers to allegiance (cf. Ps 123:2; Ezek 18:6). Yet they had adopted a false allegiance, straying from their original faithfulness to Yahweh (cf. Hos 9:1). They had willingly devoted themselves to that which did not represent the true God and readily responded to the temptation of rival claims. The concept of religious unfaithfulness will be developed in chap. 16. If the text is correct (see *Note* 9.b.), there is an impressive reference to the effect of their unfaithfulness on Yahweh himself. His transcendence did not leave him untouched by grief over his people's defection (cf. Ps 78:40–41; Isa 63:10; Eph 4:30; see further Fretheim, *The Suffering of God* 107–13). They would wake up to this deeply personal aspect of their religious deviations. By all such condemning thoughts they would realize that they deserved the series of punishments outlined by Ezekiel, which by then Israel would have received (cf. 14:23). They would belatedly assent to the will of God and own him just in his catastrophic judgments (cf. Greenberg 134).

11 The messenger formula paves the way for a fresh oracle. Again the message is accentuated by the initial expressive activity in which the prophet is ordered to engage. Comparison with Jer 19:1–3 suggests that a message to the prophet has here been merged with a public message (cf. plural "you" in v 13), so that the former slides into the latter. The phenomenon was encouraged by the characteristic presentation of prophetic oracles in the book as communications to Ezekiel rather than as explicitly relayed through him to an audience.

In this contextual setting, the excited gestures seem to express "indignation tempered by grief and sadness" (Friebel, "Sign-Acts" 610; cf. Eichrodt 96–97; Carley 42). Clapping has a number of associations in the OT. Here, as in 21:22(16); Num 24:10, it seems to signify anger, in reflection of the divine fury of v 12b. The stamping of feet occurs only in 25:6, where it is an expression of malicious joy, but here it must reinforce the emotion displayed in the clapping of hands. The crying of "Ah!" or "Alas!" appears to denote lamentation, in the light of its cause, the accusation and coming punishment of "the community of Israel." The latter term has in view those who were residing in the homeland. Their "abominations" or "shocking rites" will be amplified in v 13aβ–b, although for the reader, via the same term at the end of v 9, they already convey the parallel gamut of illegitimate worship mentioned in vv 4–6. The reader also equates the punishment of falling here with that in vv 4b and 7a. In the present oracle, the means of their falling is defined, by means of the triad "sword," "famine," and "pestilence." While in the first oracle the "sword" is the general term for destructive power that was to overwhelm the inhabitants of the land, in the second message it is but one means at God's disposal. The sinister triad has already occurred at 5:12 in the context of the siege and fall of Jerusalem (see the *Comment* there). Here its range is extended to the land, in the light of the latter half of the oracle. The triad represents methodical disposal, rather like the symbolic act of 5:1–3, although here, unlike there (and 6:2–10), exile is not in view. Echoes of Lev 26 in vv 13–14 suggest that Lev 26:25–26 is in mind, where sword and pestilence are mentioned specifically and famine is described.

12–13aα The series of fatalities is elaborated in v 12a. The terms "far" and "near" idiomatically represent a merism that expresses comprehensiveness; it is one of many ways in which comprehensiveness features in this oracle. The terms are a catch-all pair of categories (cf. 22:5; Jer 25:26; cf. Krašovec, *Merismus* 142). Here the triadic scheme requires an extra category, so that the last vestiges of life may be gleaned after the double grim harvest. All these destructive events in human experience would be Yahweh's way of giving full vent to his anger. As in 5:13a, this statement prefaces the recognition formula. His passionate intervention in comprehensive judgment was the only means by which his people could be taught the demands of his being and so of his covenant requirements. The radical representation of their doom requires that "you," Ezekiel's fellow prisoners of war, should be the recipients of the lesson. The logic nicely coincides with the prophetic actuality: all of Ezekiel's oracles were meant to be heard and appreciated by his immediate audience.

13aβ–14 The statement of recapitulation serves as a joint definition of the "shocking rites" of v 11 and of examples of the destruction that they would engender. The dominant mention of "idols," at beginning and end, and of "fragrant offerings of appeasement," at the conclusion, suggest that Lev 26:30–31 is being echoed. If so, the recapitulation fulfills its function in an oblique sense: it is a reminiscence of the scheme of disobedience and destruction set out in Lev 26. The comprehensive nature of the punishment expressed in vv 11b–12 is echoed in the intermediate material of the recapitulating statement, a series of four expressions of illicit worship that include the qualifier "all" (see also *Form/Structure/Setting*). To achieve this end, the prophet presses into service a pair of phrases current in the late preexilic period, especially in deuteronomistic literature, "under every luxuriant tree" and "on every high hill" (1 Kgs 14:23; 2 Kgs 17:10; Jer 2:20; cf. Holladay, *VT* 11 [1961] 170–76, who, however, suggests dependence on Deut 12:2). The second phrase is varied with a different adjective for "high" (רמה for גדולה, as in 20:28; 34:6). With these phrases are intertwined two others, which seem to be adapted from Hos 4:13.

14 The devastation of the land harks back to Lev 26:32a, 33b (cf. Reventlow, *Wächter* 34). The motif is worked into the oracle by means of three embellishments that indicate comprehensiveness: the rhyming "wrack and ruin," the phrase of geographical totality, and the priestly qualifier "wherever they live." The extent of the land is comparable with its description in the priestly terms of the old political land of Canaan in 47:15–20, in dependence on Num 34:2–12 (see *Ezekiel 20–48* 280–81). Then "the wilderness" is "the wilderness of Zin" (Num 34:3). However, the northern boundary extends further north, to Riblah in the administrative area of Hamath ("Riblah" in Num 34:11 is a different place). The extension is "perhaps for the sake of its painful associations" (Cooke 73), as the site of Jehoahaz's imprisonment in 609 B.C. (2 Kgs 23:33), which marked the end of Judah's earlier bid for independence.

The focus of the comprehensiveness expressed in vv 13aβ–b has been the areas of illicit worship up and down the land, and only secondarily the defiling presence of the "slain" in each area. V 14 appropriately develops this focus. Yahweh's punitive blow against his people results in devastation for the land. Accordingly, representatives of the people may be envisioned in the final recognition formula as still alive to witness this destruction and alert at last to divine reality before the death that has overtaken their fellows reaches them in turn.

Explanation

Cassuto ("Arrangement" 230) rightly observed that the bringing of the sword upon the citizens of Jerusalem in 5:17 serves as a literary hinge for chap. 6, which opens with the same fate for the mountains of Israel (v 3). Greenberg (139) has traced three other links with the preceding unit. The stem שׁמם "be devastated" overflows from 4:17; 5:15 into chap. 6, at vv 4, 6, and 14. After 5:13, the exhausting of Yahweh's anger persists in 6:12. The sinister triad of sword, famine, and pestilence in 6:11–12 echoes 5:12 (cf. 17). The theme of divine retribution is continued in no uncertain terms. It may be added that the exile, which brought further loss of life in 5:3–4, 12, features again in a punitive sense in 6:9–10, now as the scene of bitter remorse for former sins.

Boadt ("Rhetorical Strategies" 188–89) has drawn attention to the thematic development in at least three respects. First, the geographical target widens, and with it the scope of the punishment to include the people at large. Not only Jerusalem is to be the target of God's attack (chaps. 4–5), but the mountains of Israel (6:2–10), in fact the land in all its traditional amplitude (6:14). Second, the accusation receives clearer focus. The "iniquity" of 4:5(–6), 17, which was defined in terms of improper worship at the Jerusalem temple (5:11) is now expanded to cover the pagan rites carried on at the semi-pagan local shrines throughout the land. Third, the recognition formula that appeared in 5:13 now bombards the reader at 6:7, 10, 13, and 14. Yahweh's aim was that his people should rediscover their lost perspective as to the true nature of his being and of his expectations; only such drastic means could achieve this aim. Israel, whether alive or dead, must honor Yahweh's demand that he be acknowledged in all the uniqueness of his being.

At the root of Israel's problems was a breaking of the covenant relationship. In reprisal Yahweh's preordained curses had to come into operation. The growing dependence on Lev 26 as a basic text continues in chap. 6. A cluster of its threats now appear, from Lev 26:25, 30–33. This literary agenda provides an ongoing rationale for Ezekiel's interpretation of the catastrophe that was to sweep over the land in a few years' time. Priestly text and prophetic voice unite in a powerful blend of covenant theology and imminent experience.

The book of Ezekiel testifies that Yahweh's last word had not been spoken. Certainly the exiles' human expectations of a quick return to the land and to the status quo had to be dashed. But the dashing of these hopes and the radical dismantling of a perverse religious institution that pervaded the land eventually provided the opportunity for a new, God-given and God-honoring hope. In due course 35:1–36:15 will expressly give a positive counterpart to chap. 6. Catastrophic judgment had to come, but it would be followed by salvation (see *Ezekiel 20–48* 171–74). If the judgment of 3:22–5:17 subsequently needed to be reaffirmed in partial terms for the heirs of that salvation in 3:16b–21, with equal certainty the glorious reversal which that salvation represented had eventually to be celebrated. The double program is not unknown to readers of the NT. In Rom 11 Paul both celebrated the salvation that had reached the Gentiles and would, he argued, ultimately be embraced by the people of Israel (vv 11–16, 23–32) and sounded a warning of divine rejection against those Christians who did not stay within the scope of God's grace (vv 17–22).

Excursus: The Relation between Leviticus 26 and Ezekiel 4–6

Bibliography

Elliger, K. *Leviticus.* HAT 1:4. Tübingen: Mohr (Siebeck), 1966. **Fohrer, G.** *Die Hauptprobleme des Buches Ezechiel.* BZAW 72. Berlin: Töpelmann, 1952. 144–48. **Kilian, R.** *Literarkritische und formgeschichtliche Untersuchung des Heiligkeitsgesetzes.* BBB 19. Bonn: Hanstein, 1963. **Levine, B. A.** "The Epilogue to the Holiness Code: A Priestly Statement on the Destiny of Israel." In *Judaic Perspectives on Ancient Israel.*, ed. J. Neusner et al. Philadelphia: Fortress, 1987. 9–34. ———. *Leviticus.* Philadelphia: Jewish Publication Society, 1989. **Reventlow, H. G.** *Das Heiligkeitsgesetz formgeschichtlich untersucht.* WMANT 6. Neukirken-Vluyn: Neukirchener Verlag, 1961. ———. *Wächter über Israel.* BZAW 82. Berlin: Töpelmann, 1962. 4–34. **Thiel, W.** "Erwägungen zum Alter des Heiligkeitsgesetzes." *ZAW* 81 (1969) 40–73.

In the course of the second volume of the commentary, *Ezekiel 20–48*, which was written before this one, attention was drawn to passages that bear a close relationship to material in Lev 26, which contains a set of blessings and curses according to Israel's response to the covenant terms. These passages fall into two distinct groups. First, there is 33:27–29, which Ezekiel himself must have delivered after 587 B.C. The other passages appear to be redactional and in fact constitute some of the latest parts of the book: they are 34:25–30; 36:9–11; and 37:26–27, all of which give the impression of together endeavoring to supply comprehensive parallels to the blessings in Lev 26, and also 28:25–26.

Lev 26 concludes the Holiness Code, Lev 17–26. In general terms its core seems to consist of the blessings of vv 3–13 and the curses of vv 14–33; but the homogeneity and age of this material are disputed. Consequently it is difficult to determine its relationship to seeming parallels in the book of Ezekiel. Does one piece of literature depend on the other, and if so, in which direction? Do both depend upon a common source, as Fohrer (*Hauptprobleme* 147–48) considered (cf. Krüger, *Geschichtskonzepte* 100)? Kilian (*Untersuchung* 161–62) judged that the primary layer in Lev 26 was composed by a member of the school of Ezekiel, whose diction was influenced by Ezekielian phraseology (cf. Levine, "Epilogue to the Holiness Code" 19–30; *Leviticus* 275–81). On the other hand, Reventlow (*Heiligkeitsgesetz* 30) took the Holiness Code as a whole, including Lev 26, as preexilic and pertaining to the blessing-curse ritual of covenant renewal at the autumn festival (see R. de Vaux's critique in *RB* 69 [1962] 297–99). Further, he regarded the prophet Ezekiel as an official covenant mediator, who made literary use of the cultic text (*Wächter* 42–44).

Ideally, the Ezekiel commentator needs to expend as much labor on the Holiness Code and its relation to the Priestly literature as on the prophetic text, before venturing to address with confidence the relation between Leviticus and this prophetic book. In the absence of such detailed study, certain assumptions have to be made, and certain convictions that come from immersion in the book of Ezekiel must make a contribution.

As a working hypothesis, one may start with the reasonable proposal of Elliger (*Leviticus* 365–66, 371), that behind Lev 26 stands a preexilic cultic text that was used in the autumn festival, as the mention of "rain" in Lev 26:4 suggests. Elliger endeavored to reconstruct this basic text by taking note of the poetic character of much of the material. He accepted as original as much of the text of vv 3–13 as exhibits parallelism and a 3 + 3 meter, or slight variations thereof, and lack of the prosaic object sign את. In vv 14–39 he added the factor of thematic correspondence with the earlier blessings. He excluded material that seemed to reflect historical reminiscence of the fall of Jerusalem. His primary layer was Lev 26:4, 5b, 6a, 7, 9, 11, 12, 15, 16a*α* (as far as בהלה "terror"), 17, 19, 20, 25a*αβ*, 30b, 31, 32ab*α*, 33a, 37b, 38. He attributed the rest of the material to an exilic (i.e., post-587) redactor.

With such conclusions it is possible to regard all the passages in Ezekiel related to Lev 26, which were mentioned in the first paragraph, as dependent on a redacted text that included at least material from Lev 26:4–38. It is an interesting exercise to apply Elliger's arguments to Ezek 33:27–29, which is set in a post-587 oracle of Ezekiel's and so reflects a fixed historical period. The evidence is set out in Table 1. Ezek 33:27 seems to echo Lev 26:22a (redactional), 25a*α* (primary), and b*α* (redactional), while 33:28(–29) reflects 26:19a (primary) and 26:33b*α* (redactional). A number of these redactional labels are open to question. Kilian, who attributed Lev 26 to a tradent of Ezekiel, also distinguished between primary and secondary layers; in fact he judged all these particular parts primary. He justified Lev 26:22a*α* as expressing the reverse of (an original) v 6b (cf. Reventlow, *Heiligkeitsgesetz* 151). He accepted the whole of v 25, while Reventlow (*Heiligkeitsgesetz* 153) took v 25a*α* (as far as חרב "sword") and b*α* as a 3 + 3 bicolon. In v 33 he excluded only b*β*, while Reventlow (*Heiligkeitsgesetz* 155) regarded v 33b as an original 3 + 3 bicolon. Kilian worked with looser criteria, which did not include poetic factors. V 33b*α* (and *β*) does pass Elliger's poetic tests but failed to gain entry into his basic text because of its repetition of v 32 or v 31a*α*, which he claimed not to be a feature of the original. The rhetorical critic will not share his confidence in this particular criterion; Kilian himself (*Untersuchung* 152) considered repetition at this juncture quite feasible. V 25b*α* (with b*β*) also passes the metrical text, but Elliger (*Leviticus*) judged its language to be prophetic, comparing Amos 4:10; Ezek 28:23. Whether this is sufficient ground for excluding it from a preexilic text, at least in its later preexilic form, is questionable. We are left with v 22a*α*, which is firmly prosaic. If Elliger's basic thesis of a preexilic cultic poem is correct and if Ezekiel did echo v 22a*α*, in line with his other allusions in this passage, it had already become part of an amplified text.

	26:19	26:22	26:25a	26:25b	26:33b
33:27		x	x	x	
33:28	x				x

Table 1. Parallels between Leviticus 26 and Ezekiel 33

The relation of Ezek 4–6 to Lev 26 may now be considered. Chap. 6 is a good place to begin, because of its evident cluster of echoes over a relatively short span. These echoes, which are not of a slavish nature, are five or six in number; a further one appears in the MT at 6:5a, but it is a much later intrusion (see *Note* 6:4.c.). The first, the prophet's setting his face in 6:2aβ, may or may not be an allusion to the divine pose of Lev 26:17aα (primary, according to Elliger): see the *Comment*. In 6:3b אני מביא עליכם חרב "I am about to bring upon you a sword" reflects Lev 26:25aα (primary), והבאתי עליכם חרב "and I will bring upon you a sword," while the "high places" (במות) of 6:3bγ and "incense burners" (חמנים) of 6:4aβ correspond to the references in Lev 26:30aα (secondary). In 6:6aβ הערים תחרבנה "the cities will be devastated" reflects either Lev 26:31aα (primary), ונתתי את־עריכם חרבה "and I will make your cities a devastation," or v 33bβ (secondary), ועריכם יהיו חרבה "and your cities will become a devastation." In 6:8 בגוים בהזרותיכם "among the nations, when you are scattered" recalls Lev 26:33aα (primary), ואתכם אזרה בגוים "and you I will scatter among the nations." These are the references in the first oracle of 6:2–10.

	26:3	26:15	26:22	26:25a	26:26	26:29	26:30a	26:31	26:32a	26:33a	26:33b
4:16					X						
5:2										X	
5:6	X'	X									
5:10						X				X	
5:12										X	
5:14								X			
5:16					X						
5:17			X	X							
6:3				X			X				
6:4							X				
6:6								X			X
6:8										X	
6:13							X	X			
6:14									X		X

Table 2. Parallels between Leviticus 26 and Ezekiel 4–6

In the second oracle, 6:11–14, the "idols" (גלולים) of 6:13aβ link with Lev 26:30aβ (secondary) and the "appealing savor" (ריח ניחוח) of 6:13aβ with Lev 26:31b (primary). In 6:14aβ ונתתי את־הארץ שממה "and I will make the land a desolation" echoes either Lev 26:32a (primary), והשמתי אני את־הארץ "and I myself will desolate the land," or v 33bα (secondary), והיתה ארצכם שממה "and your land will become a desolation."

Two striking phenomena of these links between chap. 6 and Lev 26 are that not only do all of them, apart from the uncertain case in v 2, represent a fairly compact group of material within Lev 26, but also, within the two oracles, they move consecutively through the catalogue of curses. Indeed, Garscha (*Studien* 94–96), because of the "astonishing" closeness to Lev 26, considered 5:16–17 and 6:4–7 a later redactional unit. My own study has not found decisive evidence of subsequent redaction in chap. 6.

As for Elliger's secondary material, Lev 26:33b has been discussed above. V 30a seems to feature no less than three times in Ezek 6. Items from it are interwoven in vv 3–4 into a group of primary references. Elliger (*Leviticus* 368) drew attention to its non-poetic character and attributed it to a "prophetic," accusatory layer that does not fit in a pre-deuteronomistic liturgical piece. Reventlow (*Heiligkeitsgesetz* 154) judged that a poetic original lay behind the present poetic form of v 30a: he suggested two bicola (3 + 3, 3 + 2), with passive verbs in the first bicolon. Kilian (*Untersuchung* 151, 155–56), from his later standpoint, raised no objection to v 30a. He was not impressed with Reventlow's rewriting, perhaps not unnaturally in view of their different approaches to Lev 26. On balance, it does appear that, as in Ezek 33, if the prophet was recalling an existing text, it had already received some amplification, here at the point of v 30a. It is preferable to think in terms of an insertion: it is difficult to see why Reventlow's proposed change should have been made.

The apparent references in chaps. 4–5 fall into at least three groups, 4:16; 5:2; and 5:6–17. In 4:16a הנני שבר מטה־לחם "behold I am about to break the bread stick" and לחם במשקל "rationed bread" are reminiscent of Lev 26:26a (secondary). Elliger, (*Leviticus* 368) was inclined to align vv 25aγ–29 with the "prophetic" layer he also found in v 30a. He considered that its details were borrowed from the experience of the fall of Jerusalem and so postdated it. Kilian (*Untersuchung* 151) drew attention to the contextually unparalleled temporal construction (. . . . בשברי "when I break . . .") in v 26aα as possible evidence of its secondary nature. Reventlow (*Heiligkeitsgesetz* 154) posited a grammatical rewriting and reordering of v 26 and thought that he could find two 3 + 3 bicola. He argued that the curse corresponds to the blessing of v 5b (primary), but Kilian more correctly related it only to v 26b. As to reflection of post-587 B.C. experiences, Reventlow (*Heiligkeitsgesetz* 149) preferred to explain the vivid description in terms of increase in the intensity of curses. It seems that once more an amplification of the basic text is involved. However, it need not be dated after 587: rationing and famine are commonplaces in a siege (cf. 2 Kgs 6:25). The guilt-ridden mortification (ונמקו בעונם) of 4:17bβ may possibly be linked with Lev 26:39, but for present purposes it is better to stay within the confines of Lev 26:4–33 and discount it. The phrase recurs in Ezek 24:23; 33:10 in contexts devoid of allusions to Lev 26.

At 5:2bγ the text jumps from instructions to the prophet for the final sign-act to a first-person interpretation, וחרב אריק אחריהם "and a sword I will draw after them." This will recur in 5:12 and surely harks back to Lev 26:33a, והריקתי אחריכם חרב "and I will draw after you a sword," one of Elliger's primary portions. This parallel in turn suggests that the preceding scattering to the wind (תזרה לרוח) in 5:2bβ echoes the divine scattering among the nations (אזרה בגוים) in Lev 26:33aα (primary): the new feature of the wind was dictated by the symbolism of the context.

There is a literary feel about the interpretive section 5:6–17, but there appears to be no reason either to deny Ezekiel's hand in any part of it or to detach it from his pre-587 ministry of judgment. In 5:6b the sudden switch from second singular mention of Jerusalem to third plural references to its citizens is best explained as due to the constraint of allusion to Lev 26. Indeed, Reventlow (*Wächter* 7) interpreted the preceding כי not as "because" but as introducing a quotation: he referred to GKC 157b and compared the later שנאמר "as it is said." One might relate במשפטי מאסו "my standards they rejected" in v 6bα to that very clause in Lev 26:43bβ, with Reventlow (*Wächter* 8) and Greenberg (111). However, it is set in a passage that may well reflect a later, redactional interest in giving a theological explanation of the exile (cf. Thiel, *ZAW* 81 [1969] 66–67). It is better, then, to refer to another verse that Reventlow went on to cite, Lev 26:3a, אם־בחקתי תלכו "if in my rules you walk," as a basis for 5:6bβ, וחקותי לא הלכו בהם

"and my rules—you have not walked in them," and also to Lev 26:15aα, ואם בחקתי תמאסו
"and if my rules you reject" (מֹשֵׁפֹּטַי "my standards" occurs in v 15aβ), as underlying
5:6bα. We have already seen an example of a change from second person to third in
the echoing of Lev 26:33aβ at Ezek 5:2bγ (= 12bβ). Elliger (*Leviticus* 367), after some
discussion, accepted Lev 26:15 as primary and possessing a 3 + 4, 4 + 3 meter. However,
perhaps surprisingly, he regarded 26:3 as prosaically prolix and so secondary (*Leviticus*
365). This latter conclusion creates a certain difficulty: vv 3 and 15 surely correspond,
and each one needs the other. Moreover, ונתתי "(and) I will give" at the beginning of v 3
requires such an introduction as v 3 provides. Reventlow (*Heiligkeitsgesetz* 146) accepted
v 3, but unfortunately without comment. It may be that we should take a leaf out of
Reventlow's book elsewhere and posit a poetic original. Perhaps the issue is not relevant to the present concern: v 15, at the outset of the curses section, need be the only
source. However, in both verses we must reckon with deuteronomic or deuteronomistic
elements, the phrase שמר ועשה "keep and do" in v 3 and מצות "commands" in vv 3 and
15. We recall that Elliger regarded Lev 26:30 as deuteronomistic in tone. Yet such passages may not on that ground be denied to Ezekiel. An increasing number of scholars
are prepared to find deuteronomistic features in his own oracles (cf., e.g., Zimmerli,
Ezekiel 2 xv; Joyce, *Divine Initiative* 122–24).

The next point of contact occurs at 5:10a, where fathers' eating sons (א בות יאכלו
בנים) thematically aligns with Lev 26:29a, ואכלתם בשר בניכם "and you will eat the flesh
of your sons," a secondary passage that, according to Elliger (*Leviticus* 369), reflects the
587 B.C. experience. However, Reventlow's principle of increasingly dire threats may
be sufficient explanation in this case. Besides, child cannibalism in a siege context appears in 2 Kgs 6:24–30 and so can hardly be restricted to the siege of Jerusalem. Nor
must the 3 + 3 meter be overlooked. The link between 5:10bβ and Lev 33aα concerns
scattering, which has already been discussed in the case of 5:2. So have the two references in 5:12baβ, which repeat elements found in 5:2.

In 5:14aα ואתנך לחרבה "and I will make you [= Jerusalem] a devastation" seems to
be an application of Lev 26:31aα, ונתתי את־עריכם חרבה "and I will make your cities a
devastation," which Elliger (*Leviticus* 368) regarded as primary, presumably before the
object sign was inserted. A cluster of parallels occurs in 5:16–17. The breaking of bread
sticks reappears in 5:16bβ: the reflection of Lev 26:26aα has already been discussed in
connection with 4:16. At 5:17aα ושלחתי עליכם . . . חיה רעה ושכלך "and I will let loose
upon you [pl] . . . vicious beasts and they will leave you [sg] childless" can hardly be
dissociated from Lev 26:22a, והשלחתי בכם את־חית השדה ושכלה אתכם "and I will let
loose on you [pl] wild beasts and they will leave you [pl] childless." Elliger considered
this curse secondary, partly because it corresponds to 26:6bα, which he regarded as
secondary because the 4 + 4 meter of v 6b diverges from the 3 + 3 pattern found in the
context. Reventlow (*Heiligkeitsgesetz* 147, 151), who slightly rewrote v 6b to accommodate it to the regular metrical form, argued that the correspondence between vv 6 and
22 was a factor that favored the primary nature of the latter verse, but he was unable to
restore a feasible original. It seems only fair to align this case with secondary prose
cases already noted. In 5:17bα Yahweh's bringing the sword, which recalls Lev 26:25aα,
repeats an element already found in 6:3bβ.

What may be concluded from this detailed examination of numerous points of contact between Lev 26 and Ezek 4–6? Most of them may be credited to a preexilic cultic
text constituted on Elliger's lines, but slightly longer than he allowed. However, there
are a few cases that bear witness to subsequent literary expansion of the basic text.
These are Lev 26:15aα (Ezek 5:6b), 22aα (Ezek 5:17aα), 26a (Ezek 4:16a; 5:16bα), and
30aaβ (Ezek 6:3bγ, 4aβ, 13aβ). There are no good grounds for denying that by the last
years before 587 B.C. Ezekiel and his fellow prisoners of war were familiar with a text
that had already reached the stage of incorporating these elements, in its development
toward the canonical form.

Judah's Day of the Lord (7:1–27)

Bibliography

Bewer, J. A. "On the Text of Ezekiel 7.5–14." *JBL* 45 (1926) 223–31. **Bogaert, P.-M.** "Les deux rédactions conservées (LXX et TM) d'Ezéchiel 7." In *Ezekiel and His Book*, ed. J. Lust. BETL 74. Leuven: Leuven UP, 1986. 21–47. **Dijkstra, M.** "Legal Irrevocability (*lōʾ yāšûb*) in Ezekiel 7.13." *JSOT* 43 (1989) 109–16. **Driver, G. R.** "Some Hebrew Medical Expressions." *ZAW* 65 (1953) 255–62. **Frymer-Kensky, T.** "Pollution, Purification and Purgation in Biblical Israel." In *The Word of the Lord Shall Go Forth*. FS D. N. Freedman, ed. C. L. Meyers et al. Winona Lake, IN: Eisenbrauns, 1983. 399–414. **Goettsberger, J.** "Ez 7,1–16 textkritisch und exegetisch untersucht." *BZ* 22 (1934) 195–223. **Hillers, D. R.** "A Convention in Hebrew Literature: The Reaction to Bad News." *ZAW* 77 (1965) 86–90. **Lust, J.** "The Use of Textual Witnesses for the Establishment of the Text: The Shorter and Longer Texts of Ezekiel. An Example: Ez 7." In *Ezekiel and His Book*, ed. J. Lust. 7–20. **Masson, M.** "*Sᵉpîrâ* (Ezéchiel vii.10)." *VT* 37 (1987) 301–11. **Seitz, C. R.** *Theology in Conflict: Reactions to the Exile in the Book of Jeremiah*. BZAW 176. Berlin: de Gruyter, 1989. **Tov, E.** "Recensional Differences between the MT and LXX of Ezekiel." *ETL* 62 (1986) 89–101.

Translation

[1] *I received the following communication from Yahweh:* [2] *"Furthermore, you human one*[a]—*here is a message from the Lord*[b] *Yahweh to the country of Israel.*
An end is coming,[c] *the end is coming*
upon the[d] *four corners of the earth.*[e]
[3] *Now the end looms over you*
and I will unleash my anger[a] *upon you,*
passing judgment on you as your ways warrant
and repaying you for all your shocking deeds.
[4] *No pitying glance will I give*[a]
nor any show of compassion,
but I will repay you for your ways,
and your shocking deeds will haunt you,
and then you will all[b] *realize that I am Yahweh.*

[5] *"Here is a message from the Lord Yahweh.*
Calamity after[a] *calamity,*
here it comes.
[6] *An end is coming;*
the end[a] *is coming upon you.*
Here[b] *comes,* [7] *comes*[a] *doom(?)*[b]
upon you, residents of the land.
The time is coming,
the day is near—
tumult, not harvest, shouts[c] *in the mountains.*
[8] *Soon now I will drench you with my wrath*
and exhaust my anger upon you,
passing judgment on you as your ways warrant

and repaying you for all your shocking deeds.
[9] *No pitying glance will I give*
nor any show of compassion,
but [a] *I will repay you for your ways,*
and your shocking deeds will haunt you,
and you will all [b] *realize that I am Yahweh, the one who struck the blow.* [c]

[10] *"Here is the day,*
here it [a] *has come* [b]—
doom(?) has appeared.
Injustice [c] *has burst into blossom,*
insolence into bud . . . [d]
[12] *The time has come,*
the day has arrived. [a]
Let the buyer not be glad
nor the seller be sorry. [b]
[13] *For the buyer will not come back*
to what has been sold, [a]
and both, because of the iniquity each has done,
will fail to hold on [b] *to their lives.*
[14] *They have blown* [a] *on the bugle* [b] *and made everything ready;* [c]
but nobody goes into [d] *battle.* [e]
[15] *Outside lurks the sword;*
inside, plague and famine.
Whoever is in the country
will die by the sword,
and whoever is in the capital
will be devoured [a] *by famine and plague.*
[16] *If any escape* [a]
and stay in the mountains,
they will all be put to death [b]
because of the iniquity each has done.
[17] *Every hand will hang limp,*
and every knee will be wet with urine. [a]
[18] *They will tie sackcloth round their waists*
and will be seized by shuddering,
while every face will be covered with shame
and every head shaved bare.

[19] *"Their silver they will throw out into the streets,*
and their gold will be treated as something unclean. [a]
They will not use it to satisfy their appetites
and to fill their stomachs,
because it has caused them to fall into iniquity. [b]
[20] *They* [a] *turned its* [b] *beautiful ornaments into objects of pride*
and made their shocking images [c] *out of it:*
that is why I will turn it into something unclean for them.
[21] *I will hand it over to foreigners as loot,*
as booty to the wickedest people on earth, [a] *who will desecrate it.*

²²*I will avert my gaze from them,*
while they desecrate my treasury: ᵃ
vandals will enter it ᵇ
and desecrate it, ᵇ ²³ *and cause havoc(?).* ᵃ
For the land is full of bloodshed, ᵇ
and the capital is full of violence.
²⁴*I will send in the worst of the nations,*
who will occupy their houses. ᵃ
I will put an end to their source of pride and power, ᵇ
and their sanctuaries ᶜ *will be desecrated.*
²⁵*Anguish is coming,* ᵃ
and they will try to find safety, to no avail.
²⁶*Disaster will come on the heels of disaster;*
bad news will echo bad news.
They will try to get a revelation from the prophet,
while a ruling will elude the priest,
and counsel the elders.
²⁷*The head of state will wear the garb of consternation,* ᵃ
while the people in the land will be shocked into inactivity.
I will make their way of life the basis ᵇ *of my dealing with them*
and judge them by ᶜ *their own judgment of others.*
Then they will realize that I am Yahweh."

Notes

2.a. LXX* Syr add "say" as a link between the vocative and the messenger formula: אמר "say" could have fallen out after אדם "human." An introduction consisting of the impv "say (to them)" and the messenger formula occurs, for instance, in 12:10, 23, 28, but the messenger formula can stand by itself, as in 26:3. The question is whether the initial vocative demands an impv. In 39:17 the sequence of vocative, messenger formula, and impv appears. Closest to the MT here is 22:18–19, where the vocative and messenger formula occur with an intervening explanatory clause, and 26:2–3, where the vocative is separated from a messenger formula by a causal clause. It is a short step from those instances to this one, and so the MT can be justified as a harder reading.

2.b. For the presence of אדני "Lord" in a messenger formula here and in v 5, see *Note* 2:4.c.

2.c. Comparison with v 6 suggests that בא "is coming" should be inserted. The text is hardly coherent without it: in the MT קץ is seemingly an interjection, "The end!" Its omission in the MT was a simple case of haplography: the ancient versions seem to attest it. The evidence of the LXX is especially significant in view of its tendency to attest a shorter text. For the change of word order in the LXX, see in principle G. Marquis, *Textus* 13 (1986) 59–84.

2.d. Q's masc form of numeral is expected with the fem noun (cf. *HALAT* 463a).

2.e. Or "land," but the use of the phrase in Isa 11:12 (cf. Job 37:3; 38:13) suggests "earth" (Herrmann 49; Hölscher, *Dichter* 67; et al.; REB). In v 21 הארץ means "the earth," but in v 23 "the land." The LXX* puts vv 6aβ–9 before vv 3–6aα; in fact, the prefaced material reflects a different translation than that of chaps. 1–25 (cf. McGregor, *Greek Text of Ezekiel* 95) and was obviously added to fill a perceived gap. It was inserted in the wrong place, presumably because of the recurring τὸ πέρας ἥκει "the end has come" in vv 2 (= v 6aα) and 10. In v 6 (= v 9 in the MT) ἐγώ εἰμί "I am" for אני "I" is characteristic of the translator of chaps. 26–39, as opposed to ἐγώ "I" in v 9 (= v 5), which reflects the usual rendering in chaps. 1–25. Bogaert ("Les deux rédactions" 30) wonders whether the presence of εἰμί was encouraged by the ptcp, but comparison with 20:12 suggests not. Moreover, ושפטתיך "and I will judge you" is rendered with the verb κρινῶ in v 5 (= v 8), but with ἐκδικήσω in v 7 (= v 3); both renderings are used in chaps. 1–25 and 26–39. In addition, Bogaert has observed that the rendering ὁ τύπτων "the striker" for מכה is unparalleled in LXX Ezekiel, although it is common in the LXX elsewhere. Zimmerli (201) correctly notes that the displaced material in the LXX relates to vv 6aβ–9. *BHS* wrongly seems to envision blocks of vv 3–5a and 6–9. See *Form/Structure/Setting*.

3.a. The LXX* reflects אֲנִי "I" for אַפִּי "my anger" (Hitzig 45).

4.a. For the form of the verb, see *Note* 5:11.d. The MT adds עָלֶיךָ "(upon) you," which the LXX* and v 9 lack, as do the instances of the formula elsewhere, e.g., in 5:11; 8:18. It probably entered the text by mechanical assimilation to the clauses in vv 3b and 4b*a*.

4.b. "All" in the translation attempts to represent a change to pl. The sg form in LXX Syr here and in v 9 seems to reflect assimilation to the context (cf. 5:13).

5.a. The MT "evil, one evil" is strange; Rashi's interpretation of אֶחָת "one" as "unique" reads into the text. A minority Masoretic reading (see *BHS*) that is reflected in the Tg is אַחַר "after," with the sense "disaster after disaster" (cf. v 26). The Syr implies תַּחַת "in place of, in exchange for," with the meaning "physical evil for moral evil" (Ehrlich, *Randglossen* 5:22). It is tempting to conjecture with Greenberg (148) that the MT אֶחָת is the result of conflation between two variants, אַחַר and תַחַת. The LXX* does not represent v 5b, or at least represents only הִנֵּה "behold." Consequently, v 5b has been regarded as an explanatory gloss on v 6 (Fohrer 43). But so distinctive a text hardly suggests a gloss, and what its intention might have been is not clear. The fuller text in the MT deserves the benefit of the doubt. For the meaning "disaster" for רָעָה, cf. 6:10; 14:22. Ehrlich's interpretation, cited above, anticipates the moral retribution later in the oracle, but it does not fit the immediate context so well.

6.a. The secondary material in the LXX* offers an abbreviated text that omits six words from הֵקִיץ "it is awakened (?)" in v 6a*β* to הַצְּפִירָה "the doom (?)" in v 7a. The omission may simply represent parablepsis by homoeoteleuton (אֵלֶיךָ . . .) "to you (. . . to you)," if הֵקִיץ was not present in the *Vorlage* (Hitzig 47). The latter term probably originated as an orthographical variant of הַקֵּץ "the end" (Hitzig 47; et al.). It has been variously explained as (1) "it is awakened" (*Θ* Vg), (2) "it has brought the end," a denominative verb from קֵץ "end" (Driver, *Bib* 35 [1954] 148, who did not, however, consider the verb authentic), and (3) "it is ripe," denominative from קַיִץ "ripe summer fruit" (Greenberg 148, implicitly following Bewer).

6.b. The fem verb has as its subj the fem noun in v 7.

7.a. The MT בָּאָה "is coming" may be a dittograph (Wevers 73), but the presence of the two verbs with the same subj in v 10 is an argument in its favor.

7.b. The MT צְפִירָה here and in v 10 is hardly the same term that means "garland, crown" in Isa 28:5, though *Θ* and the Tg identified the nouns. "Doom" ([N]RSV, REB) "is as good a guess as any" (Wevers 73) and at least "an educated guess" (Blenkinsopp 47). See the discussions in Zimmerli (201) and Greenberg (148) and most recently in Masson, *VT* 37 (1987) 301–11, who suggests a meaning "net," as a symbol of exile.

7.c. V 7b*β* appears to bear some relation to v 11b. The secondary text in the LXX* is somewhat closer to v 11b in terms of its repeated οὐδέ "neither . . . nor." Indeed, μετὰ θορύβων seems to reflect מֵהֲמוֹנָם "from tumults" (cf. v 11b; cf. θόρυβος for הָמוֹן in Dan 10:6 LXX). But ὠδίνων "labor cries" may have something to do with הָרָה "pregnant woman" (Cornill 213) or הֵרָיוֹן "pregnancy" (Goettsberger, *BZ* 22 [1934] 206). The MT seems to be intended to mean as the translation renders, הֹד being regarded as a variant form of הֵידָד "shout" at harvest time. To relate הֹד to הוֹד "glory" (*'A Θ* Vg) is no help. In the absence of a better explanation, we can only stay with the MT. It is sometimes suggested that יוֹם "a day of" has dropped out after הַיּוֹם "the day" (Cornill 213; Cooke 78; Driver, *Bib* 19 [1938] 61–62; cf. 30:3; Joel 2:2), which would ease the construction.

9.a. The secondary text in the LXX* as well as the Vg implies כִּי דְרָכַיִךְ "because your ways" in place of the MT כִּדְרָכַיִךְ "according to your ways," in line with v 4. The syntax favors the slight change (cf. Zimmerli 196). The MT seems to have suffered mechanical assimilation to כִּדְרָכַיִךְ in v 8a*γ*.

9.b. See *Note* 4.b. above.

9.c. Heb. מַכֶּה "who struck, striker" is rather abrupt. Greenberg (149) has observed the rare use of a predicative ptcp in a recognition formula besides in 20:12; 37:28, in both cases with an object expressed. However, Zimmerli (196) has noted that the verb occurs without an object in 9:5, 7–8. Cornill (213) and others have emended slightly to הַמַּכֶּה "the striker," assuming haplography of ה and appealing to LXX Syr. A fragment of 11QEz has the same reading as the MT, מכה (see Lust, "Textual Witnesses" 91), but this is hardly surprising, since the Qumran MSS of Ezekiel all reflect a Masoretic type of text.

10.a. The LXX* omits הַצְּפִירָה . . . בָּאָה "comes . . . the doom(?)"; הִנֵּה "behold" is seemingly rendered εἰ καί "even though" (cf. Cornill 214). Perhaps the omission was prompted by inability to render צְפִירָה, on which see *Note* 6.a. above.

10.b. The verb is probably to be accented as pf, בָּאָה: see the *Comment*.

10.c. The MT and LXX take as "rod," but מַטֶּה "perversion, injustice" (9:9) makes a more obvious and widely adopted parallel (Bewer, *JBL* 45 [1926] 227–28; et al.). An interpretation of "rod" in terms of Nebuchadnezzar has little to commend it.

10.d. The MT, in common with the general textual tradition, adds v 11. V 11a, "the violence has grown into a rod of wickedness," appears to be an early series of glosses: הֶחָמָס "the violence" was borrowed from v 23 via 9:9, to explain הַמַּטֶּה in terms of injustice (Bewer, *JBL* 45 [1926] 227–28; cf. the previous *Note*), while on the other hand מַטֶּה־רֶשַׁע "rod of wickedness" (cf. שֵׁבֶט הָרֶשַׁע "the staff of wickedness," Ps 125:3) seeks to justify the interpretation adopted in the pointed text. The intervening קָם לְ "has grown into" (cf. Greenberg 148) may be an attempt to combine the diverse explanations into a clause that seeks the best of both exegetical worlds, paraphrasing v 10bβ, "the rod/injustice has blossomed," though it better reflects פָּרַח "has budded, sprouted" in v 10bγ. The LXX, "and he will break the support of the wicked [= רָשָׁע]" (see *BHS*), obtained what was considered an intelligible meaning by taking לְ as introducing an object. The preceding five letters of its *Vorlage* may have been damaged, and indeed it may have lacked הֶחָמָס "the violence." The translator seems to have associated "rod" with Yahweh's breaking of it, in reminiscence of 4:16; 5:16 (συντρίβειν στήριγμα "break (the) support"; cf. Bogaert, "Les deux rédactions" 30) and so used the verb "break." V 11b, "and not from them and not from their multitude and not from their moaning(?) and (there is) no eminence(?) in them," seems to be a variant of v 7bβ but defies coherent explanation. Greenberg (148) calls it "obscure, with its crazy variations on *h* and *m/n* sounds." The LXX*, "and not with tumult nor with haste" (see *BHS*), is shorter and somewhat closer to v 7. Zimmerli (197) has deduced from the LXX* that the MT consists of two basic expressions and two additions (cf. Cooke 86). Comparison with v 7 suggests that the two basic nouns were הָמוֹן "tumult" and מְהוּמָה "confusion." The last phrase seems to be a variant of the former term via a מ/ב confusion. The series of third pl suffixes lacks an antecedent, while vv 13–27 are full of third pl references. This phenomenon suggests that v 11b somehow originated as a comment on part of that material; certainly the second term may have something to do with הֲמוֹנָהּ "its wealth/army" in vv 12 and 14.

12.a. The LXX ἰδού "behold" seems to reflect a misreading of הִגִּיעַ "has arrived" as הִנֵּה.

12.b. The LXX* does not represent v 12b, "since burning anger rests on all its wealth," and it is often taken as an addition, partly because it interrupts the sequence of v 12a and v 13aα. In content it matches the references to Yahweh's anger in vv 3, 8. The LXX* in fact lacks the three similar refrainlike statements here and in vv 13bα and 14b. The fem sg suffix lacks an obvious antecedent: the land in the heading of v 2a has been addressed directly in vv 2b–9. See the next *Note* for further discussion.

13.a. The MT has "for the seller to what has been sold will not return," while the LXX has "for the buyer to the seller will not return." The MT is credible only if it refers to the institution of jubilee, in which land was restored to its original owners (Lev 25), as Jerome suggested (but see Dijkstra, *JSOT* 43 [1989] 110–11). Unfortunately, this interpretation does not follow on naturally from the basic injunction in v 12aγ: the seller's desisting from mourning can hardly be grounded in his future inability to regain the property. If this is what v 13aα means, its lack of direct connection suggests that it is a gloss (cf. Zimmerli 206, 208). The presence of the clause in the LXX is an encouragement to regard it as a primary part of the text. Yet the form it takes in either tradition yields little sense in the context. Accordingly, one must search for an intermediate reading, which underlies both the MT and the LXX. If the latter's "the buyer" (= הַקּוֹנֶה) is right, then it is plausible to suppose that הַמּוֹכֵר "the seller" originated as a corrupt variant of הַמִּמְכָּר "what is sold," under the influence of הַמּוֹכֵר "the seller" in v 12. Then the variant displaced הַקּוֹנֶה "the buyer" in the MT and הַמִּמְכָּר "what is sold" in the text underlying the LXX. In v 13aβ–bα the MT has three additions, (1) "and still in life," (2) "their life," and (3) "for (the) vision concerning all its army will not be revoked." The first two will be considered in the following *Note*. The third links with v 12b (see *Note* 12.b. above) and also with v 14b, and significantly all of these three similar cases are absent from the LXX*.

Generally חָזוֹן "vision" has been taken as an error for חָרוֹן "burning anger" since Ewald (240), but the opposite may be true. This middle case seems to constitute the original comment, which relates to the "vision" (חָזוֹן) that is sought in v 26. No such optimistic revelatory oracle would be forthcoming, because Yahweh's will had been declared through a pessimistic oracle that would not be revoked. This oracle is identified by its subject matter, "concerning all its army [כָּל־הֲמוֹנָהּ]," with reference to Egypt in 32:12, 16. Alternatively, there may be a reference to כָּל־הֲמוֹנֹה "all his army," referring to Pharaoh in 31:18; 32:31, 32, or indeed to both. The annotator had in mind the Egyptian failure to come successfully to Judah's aid against Nebuchadnezzar (cf. 17:15, 17; 30:21–26). He attributed it to Yahweh's declared and irrevocable will in the matter, which no urgent entreaty could avert. The marginal comment became attached to the previous column because of overlap of vocabulary that caused confusion: יִתְאַבָּל "let/will mourn" occurs in vv 12 and 26, and לֹא יָשׁוּב "will not return, be revoked" occurs in the text at v 13. It may be that the initial placing in the text was in v 12b and that after corruption a correct variant was attached after v 13a. Anyway, the form at present in v 12b is an abbreviated version in which חרון "burning anger" has taken the place of חזון "vision," presumably to give a better contextual link with the anger of vv 3, 8 (cf. Jer 18:20; for the verb שוב with the sense "be averted," see Ps 106:23). There may also have been a reminiscence of Jer 4:8: certainly Jer 4:9 is similar to vv 26–27aαβ. After this corruption, כל־המונה must have been understood as "its wealth" in the context of buying and selling, and the suffix was related to the land of Israel in v 2. A third variant, which came to rest in v 14b, made the anger more explicit as Yahweh's חרוני "my burning anger"), in line with the first person suffixes in vv 3, 8. The term חרון does not occur elsewhere in Ezekiel.

13. b. In place of the MT יתחזקו "will strengthen themselves," the LXX* (supported by the Syr) κρατήσει seems to presuppose a sg hiph form יחזק "will retain (his life)." In the LXX OT, κρατεῖν generally stands for the hiph of חזק, though in 2 Kgdms 3:6 it represents the hithp. For the direct object, cf. Mic 7:18. The two glosses in v 13aβ, which the LXX lacks, ועוד בחיים חיתם "(and) still in life, their life," seem to be attempts to accommodate MT's verbal form. The second, "their life," corrected "his life," while the first dealt with the lack of grammatical connection between verb and noun, by suggesting an adverbial relationship. The reading בעין "in eye" implied by the LXX for the MT בעונו "because of his iniquity" is interesting. Jerome (79) commented on the waw/yod interchange. The reading seems to go back to a form intermediate between the LXX and the MT, בעון "(each) because of the iniquity (of his life)," which may have encouraged the corruption to an intransitive verb in the MT. The MT's present text, איש בעונו "each because of his iniquity," is confirmed by v 16 (cf. 4:17).

14.a. There is impressive ancient support for pointing as an impv (see BHS), but v 14aβ suggests a past tense (Ehrlich, Randglossen 5:23).

14.b. For the uncertain noun, see Zimmerli 198. The LXX renders as above.

14.c. Heb. הכין functions as an inf abs continuing the finite verb (GKC 72z; Joüon 80n). The LXX renders, strangely, κρίνατε "judge." A reading or misreading as ה(ו)כיח (Hitzig 50) is its most plausible basis, though the verb is not so rendered in the LXX OT.

14.d. The lack of representation of הכל ואין הלך ל "(everything) but nobody goes into" in the LXX* is probably to be explained in terms of parablepsis by homoeoteleuton, as I suggested in Brownlee 112.

14.e. For v 14b in the MT, see Notes 12.b. and 13.a. above.

15.a. LXX Tg imply יכלנו "will destroy him" for the MT יאכלנו "will devour him": cf. 5:12; 6:12. In the latter case, the variant is secondary.

16.a. For the construction, cf. GKC 144e.

16.b. The MT כיוני הגאיות כלם המות "like the doves of the valleys, all of them cooing" implies that v 16aβ is the apodosis and that v 16b qualifies v 16a: "they will stay in the mountains . . . , each one for his iniquity." The use of the phrase "each for his iniquity" in v 13 (cf. too 3:18, 19; 18:18; 33:18, 19) and the dire language of v 15 point to a harsher fate, to the punishment of death. In fact, the LXX "I will put to death" appropriately implies הָמֵת, a hiph inf abs, for המות "cooing" (Brockington, Hebrew Text 221). However, in the context it should probably be taken as having an indefinite subj and so being a virtual pass, "will be put to death." The LXX* has no equivalent for כיוני הגאיות "like the doves of the valleys," which looks like an explanatory gloss on the following verbal form, explaining both its meaning and its odd fem gender. Θ (= LXXᴼ) renders a Heb. reading כיונים הגיות "like murmuring doves" (cf. Isa 59:11), which was probably the earlier form of the MT (Cornill 216). MT "valleys" was presumably a miswriting under the influence of "mountains" just before.

17.a. See Ehrlich, Randglossen 5:23–24; Driver, ZAW 65 (1953) 260; and Note 21:12(7).a. in Ezekiel 20–48 19. The LXX interpreted thus, in terms of involuntary micturition. Heb. מים "water" functions as an acc of fullness: cf. GKC 117z. The Tg rendered euphemistically, constrained by a public reading of the text, "will be poured out like water."

19.a. The LXX* leaves unrepresented v 19aγ, "their silver and their gold will not have power to rescue them on the day of Yahweh's anger." In this divine speech the third person reference strikes an alien note, while the closeness to Zeph 1:18a suggests that it is a comparative gloss (Hitzig 52; et al.), with the wording slightly changed to comply with כספם . . . וזהבם "their silver . . . and their gold" in v 18aαβ. The gloss shows a sensitivity to the common context of the "day of Yahweh" motif.

19.b. "It" refers to the silver and gold in vv 19b–21 as a single entity. The suffix relates to the entire phrase: "their stumbling block of [= leading to] iniquity" (Greenberg 153).

20.a,b. For the MT שָׂמָהוּ "one made it" (cf. Σ "each . . ."), LXX Syr Vg imply a pointing שָׂמֻהוּ "they made it," which suits the pl verb in v 20aβ. The suffix is resumptive: "as for its ornamentation, they made it . . . ." The MT is seemingly a consequence of understanding עדיו "its (ornamentation)" as a collective sg suffix relating to the people. In fact, it refers to the silver and gold (cf. Zimmerli 199; in his translation "his" should have been rendered "its" in English).

20.c. The LXX* does not represent the MT's addition of שִׁקּוּצֵיהֶם "their detested things." The asyndeton supports its secondary nature (contrast 11:18 in the MT and the LXX). The gloss may have sought to explain the unusual phrase that precedes (Ehrlich, *Randglossen* 5:24). The inserted copula, for which there is some textual evidence, is not to taken as original (*BHK*) but as a subsequent attempt to integrate the gloss.

21.a. For the superlative force here and in v 24, see Cooke 87, and in v 24, also Joüon 141d.

22.a. Lit. "my hidden, treasured thing, treasure." Comparison with אוֹצָר "store, storehouse" alongside בֵּית אוֹצָר "storehouse" suggests that here it may have the extended sense of "treasury" (see the *Comment*).

22.b. The fem suffixes (cf. K in v 21b) seem to identify God's treasure or treasury as Jerusalem. If expected masc forms are read, בֹּה and וְחִלְּלֻהוּ (cf. Q in v 21b), the way is opened to postulating an original *waw* "and" at the beginning of v 23, which was lost by haplography (see the next *Note*).

23.a. The MT "make [impv] the chain(?)" poses syntactical and semantic difficulties. The LXX took it with v 22, rendering "and they will cause confusion," i.e., . . . וְעָשׂוּ (see the previous *Note*), which completes the poetic line and at least makes sense. The emendation (ה)בַתּוּק "slaughter" (cf. 16:40), proposed by Kraetzschmar (82; cf. Bertholet [1936] 28; *HALAT* 160a), imports a reference to loss of life that does not fit the emphasis on material destruction in the context. See BDB 958b and the discussion in Zimmerli 199–200. Did the clause originate as an early gloss qualifying v 20a and referring to chains being made for the idols with the silver and gold (cf. 1 Kgs 6:21; Isa 40:9)?

23.b. The MT, which prefaces with מִשְׁפָּט "judgment" implies "verdicts of murder" and so judicial murder (Greenberg 154). The LXX* does not represent מִשְׁפָּט; the parallelism and comparison with 9:9 oppose its inclusion. Cornill (220) suggested that it originated as a gloss on the preceding unknown רְתוּק. Was it rather an ironical comparative gloss on v 23bβ, with the city "once full of justice [מִשְׁפָּט]" (Isa 1:21) in mind (cf. Messel, *Ezechielfragen* [Oslo: Dybwad, 1945] 53)?

24.a. The LXX* does not render v 24a, perhaps by oversight, since v 24a and v 24b begin with verbs of similar form (Cooke 83). In favor of the MT, Greenberg (154) has drawn attention to the external parallelism of forms and sounds that marks the two lines.

24.b. For the MT עַזִּים "(the pride of) the strong" the LXX presupposes עֻזָּם "their (proud) might," which accords with usage elsewhere in Ezekiel (24:21; 30:6, 18; 33:28).

24.c. The MT מְקַדְּשֵׁיהֶם is oddly vocalized as piel ptcp, with pejorative intent: "the places that they [rather than God] sanctify" (Greenberg 155). The expected מִקְדְּשֵׁיהֶם "their sanctuaries" is presupposed by LXX Vg Tg (cf. Syr "their sanctuary").

25.a. It is generally urged that a fem form be read, בָּאָה "is coming" or תָבֹא "will come," agreeing with the fem subj (see BDB 891b, with reference to GKC 29e). However, Greenberg (155) has plausibly argued that the *hapax legomenon* is masc with an archaic unstressed –â ending (cf. GKC 90f).

27.a. The LXX* leaves unrepresented the initial וְ הַמֶּלֶךְ יִתְאַבָּל "the king will mourn and." The following נָשִׂיא most naturally means "leader, head of state," with reference to the king, in association with "the people of the land": cf. 45:16, 22; 46:2–3, 8–9. In 12:12; 21:30(25) the term refers to Zedekiah, who is in view here. A reference to government officials (cf. Greenberg 156, appealing to 32:29; cf. too 21:17[12]) is difficult in view of the sg number, which vitiates my view expressed in Brownlee (114) that the MT be retained, following Cooke (84). Probably the noun and verb in the MT function as a gloss explaining the next clause, which was later incorporated into the text with the copula. The poetically anarthrous (so the LXX*) "head of state" was explained as "the king," and the unique metaphorical phrase "wear consternation" was explained in terms of the verb in v 12 (Hitzig 56). Heb. שְׁמָמָה, usually "devastation," is seemingly used in the sense of שִׁמָּמוֹן "horror" (4:16; 12:19). The glossator may also have had in mind 2 Sam 14:2, where "wear [לָבַשׁ] the clothes of mourning" is preceded by the hithp of אָבַל.

27.b. LXX Syr Vg render as if כְּדַרְכָּם "according to their way," to which Cornill (221) and others have emended the MT. Heb. מִדַּרְכָּם (דֶּרֶךְ) seems to mean "on account of" or perhaps (Greenberg 157, with reference to BDB 579a) "out of the repertoire of" and may be kept as the harder reading. In fact, Driver (*Bib* 19 [1938] 27) warned that the versions may have rendered freely.

27.c. The preposition בְּ is attested by the LXX ἐν "in," as opposed to the easier כְּ "according to" found in a score of MSS and implied by the Vg. Cooke (85) fittingly compared 23:24; 44:24(Q). The preposition is used with reference to a standard of measurement or computation (cf. BDB 90b).

Form/Structure/Setting

Chap. 7 is a distinct literary unit, as its initial message-reception formula and the fresh beginning in 8:1 indicate. The unit falls into three two-part proof sayings,

in vv 2–4, 5–9, and 10–27, each of which moves from a forecast of divinely instigated disaster to a closing recognition formula. Moreover, in each case,
announcements of divine "judicial" recompense occur near the end (vv 3aγ, 4bα,
8aγb, 9bα, 27baβ). The first two oracles are introduced by a messenger formula,
in vv 2 and 5. They are also parallel in moving from an impersonal fate to a personal intervention on Yahweh's part. This pattern is repeated to some extent in
the third oracle. There the emphasis on the people's fate eventually gives way to
an expression of divine intervention in vv 20b–24 and 27baβ. Other parallels will
be drawn in the *Comment* section.

The third oracle is lengthy and diverse. Hals (43) has observed that "it seems
to ramble puzzlingly with no detectable continuity." However, Greenberg (158)
has usefully isolated recurring elements in this oracle. He has observed three
cases of parallelism: (1) the futility of commerce in vv 12–13 and the futility of
wealth in v 19; (2) war and death in vv 14–16 and invasion and destruction in vv
21–24; and (3) general demoralization and mourning in vv 17–18 and general
consternation in vv 26b–27. These parallels point to a bipartite structure for the
third oracle, vv 10–18 and 19–27.

This analysis finds support from stylistic factors. In the first half, after v 10
introduces the whole oracle, the two sections of vv 12–13 and 14–16 both end
with the phrase אִישׁ בַּעֲוֺנוֹ "each for his iniquity," while the third section, vv 17–
18, begins and ends with a repeated כֹל "all." In the second half, the first section,
vv 19–20, starts and finishes with נִדָּה "unclean thing," while the second section,
vv 21–24, is shot through with references to desecrating (חלל, four times). The
third section, vv 25–27a, is followed by a conclusion to the oracle in v 27b.

This division of the third oracle agrees somewhat with the proposal of Ewald
(238–41) and Smend (41) that the whole unit be divided into three sections, vv
2–9, 10–18, and 19–27. However, one should rather think in terms of two literary
sections, vv 2–9 and 10–27, each of which falls into two parallel statements, vv 2–4
and 5–9, and vv 10–18 and 19–27.

The structural symmetry that has been uncovered constitutes an objective clue
toward resolving a baffling problem that besets vv 2–9. The earliest extant form
of the LXX lacks vv 6aβ–9 in their proper place. They appear in the wrong place,
before v 3, as a subsequent insertion (see *Note* 2.e.). Moreover, the oracles in vv
2b–4 and 5b–9 are very similar in content. This pair of phenomena could suggest
a conflated text, in which the Greek textual tradition preserved the secondary
material in one place and the Hebrew tradition in another (Tov, *ETL* 62 [1986]
90). However, the LXX evidence is more complex: it does not fall into neat divisions of vv 2b–4 and 5–9; it preserves v 2b separately from vv 3–4, in front of part
of v 6. Zimmerli (193, 201; cf. Cornill 213) has correlated the Greek and Hebrew
evidence by deducing that not only do vv 6aβ–9 constitute a variant of vv
2b[including קֵץ "end"]–4, but vv 5a, 6aα originally functioned as an introduction to the oracle of vv 10–27, which now lacks an introduction because of the
intrusion of the variant to the first oracle.

Not all critical scholars have seen recensional variation or secondary accretion
in vv 2–9. For instance, Fohrer (42) considered rather that the second oracle
represents Ezekiel's expansion and adaptation of the first oracle. Cooke (75) was
inclined to suppose that Ezekiel uttered more than one oracle on the same theme
and that both have been grouped together as a prelude to the longer oracle of vv

14–27, along with vv 10–11 and 12–13, which he regarded as separate oracles. Likewise, Brownlee (105) thought not in terms of "variant recensions of the same material, despite close verbal parallels, but of variations of the original prophecy on different occasions" (cf. too Zimmerli's indecision [206]). In terms of content it is not easy to assign priority: while most scholars have regarded the second oracle as later, Hölscher (*Dichter* 67) viewed vv 2b–4 as a secondary addition rather than as a recensional parallel to vv 5–9 or as the primary oracle that was later supplemented with vv 5–9.

One must take into account not only the closeness of the two oracles but also their differences. V 2b strikes a universal note that is lacking in the second oracle. As for the second oracle, there is extra material in v 7, the first part of which implies that this message is addressed not like the first to אדמת ישראל "the country of Israel" but to the (collective) יושב הארץ "inhabitant(s) of the land." Indeed, the feminine suffixes of the second oracle, from which the masculine form in v 7a stands out, may well represent a mistaken assimilation to the feminine suffixes in vv 3–4 (Davidson 47). Zimmerli (201) has drawn attention to this possibility; in fact, the phenomenon points to the original independence of the second oracle, close as it is to the first.

If one resists the temptation to extrapolate from the Greek evidence conflation of a shorter text that lies behind the MT, the question arises how it came about that vv 6aβ–9 are missing from the earliest extant form of the LXX. Parunak's explanation ("Structural Studies" 197–98) in terms of omission by homoeoteleuton, from הארץ "the earth" in v 2 to הארץ "the land" in v 7, loses too much. Rather, the answer lies in omission of a slightly different amount of material by homoeoarcton. A copyist within the tradition of the Hebrew *Vorlage* used by the Greek translator overlooked vv 6aβ–9 because of the similarity of the initial material in v 6aβb and v 10ab, respectively, which was perhaps set out as separate lines (see *Note* 1:20.b.):

בא הקץ אליך הנה באה באה הצפירה
"Coming is the end to you; behold, coming, coming is the doom(?)."

הנה היום הנה באה יצאה הצפרה
"Behold, the day; behold, coming, coming forth is the doom(?)."

One might lay this oversight at the door of the translator, were it not for the fact that room has to be left for the later omission of the last four words in the latter case (see *Note* 6.a. above). Subsequently, comparison with another Hebrew manuscript led to the loss being made good, perhaps by the translator of chaps. 26–39; however, the extra material was inserted in the wrong place.

Neither here nor in chap. 36, where the LXX papyrus 967 lacks vv 23bβ–38, should one jump to conclusions concerning the original state of the Hebrew text. Both of the first two oracles in chap. 7 seem to go back to the earliest stage of the written text. Their identical core should not blind the reader to their differences, especially the change in address from the land to its inhabitants. Yet their literary combination makes positive use of their similarity, as an opportunity to emphasize their common themes by dint of repetition, a phenomenon that is also evident within the third oracle. The structural parallelism of the chapter appears to be an integral, primary phenomenon, which is sabotaged by the assumption that the second oracle represents an alternative recension or is secondary. The overall structure of the group of oracles may be defined as A/A'/B B'. However, there are also signs of an A/B/B' A' pattern, in which the human dimensions of the second oracle match those in the first half of the third oracle, and the emphasis on place in the first oracle is resumed in the second half of the third.

As in chap. 6, the geographical setting of these oracles is Ezekiel's place of exile: the direct וידעתם "and you will know" in vv 4 and 9 seems to represent the real address of the prophet's fellow exiles, as in 6:13. The oracles clearly belong in the pre-587 period. The oracles of 12:21–25, 26–28 imply that Ezekiel was prophesying on these lines long before 587 B.C. The general nature of their content does not permit further historical precision. They reflect a presentiment of disaster, which is spelled out in the third oracle in terms of the collapse of Judah's social life, which Ezekiel had known so well.

This unit stands out as the first one to consist of a collection of poetic oracles (see the layout in *BHS*). All the previous oracles have been in prose, even if in a heightened, poetrylike style in places. The poetry is sometimes prosaic, but poetry it seems to be. The lines are mainly bicola; tricola appear in vv 4b, 7b, 9b, 10aba, 19aδ–b, 20, 26b, and 27b.

In outline, the unit falls into the following divisions:

7:1	Introductory message-reception formula
7:2–4	The coup de grâce for the country of Israel
7:5–9	The final doom for the inhabitants of the land
7:10–27	The breakdown of Judah's social structures in death (vv 10–18) and in material destruction (vv 19–27).

Comment

2 The oracle of vv 2b–4 is addressed rhetorically to "the country of Israel." The phrase is characteristic of Ezekiel; it occurs only in this book, in nearly a score of instances (see Zimmerli 203). If the term "mountains of Israel" in chap. 6 was emotionally evocative, so too is this phrase. "The term ʾadmat 'soil of' evokes the earth of the alienated homeland lived on by Israel; it is particularly poignant in the mouth of an exile" (Greenberg 145). The land of ancient promise tragically becomes the object of threat and punishment, the victim of crimes committed within its boundaries. Yet this judgment is set in a larger context, "the four corners of the earth." There can be little doubt that the universality of the day of Yahweh is in view. The literary setting of this oracle alongside others that explicitly mention "the day" (vv 7, 10, 12) reveals an awareness that it too contributes to this general theme. Ezekiel is echoing a prophetic convention of judgment that, with Israel as target, went back to Amos (Amos 5:18–20) but that gradually took on overtones of judgment for neighboring nations (see Isa 2:6–21) and for the world at large (see Zeph 1:2–18). Other nations may already have been the sphere of reference for Amos's audience (cf. Amos 1: 3–2:16). The universal nature of the day of Yahweh will again be Ezekiel's concern in one of his oracles against Egypt, in 30:2–9 (see esp. v 3). Yet the chosen corner of Israel would not be exempt from Yahweh's general destruction of a wicked world in the coming cataclysm. As in the remaining oracles of this chapter, the theme of the day of Yahweh is only broached at the beginning of the oracle and not pursued.

In the grim announcement of the coming end, which does not intrinsically belong to the day-of-Yahweh theme, there seems to have been an intention to evoke both the message of Amos to the Northern Kingdom, "The end has come upon my people Israel" (Amos 8:2), and the wording in the priestly tradition of the flood, "The end of all flesh has come before me" (Gen 6:13; cf. Frymer-Kensky, "Pollution, Purification" 409–11). This implicit double basis helps to explain the transition from a universal reference to a narrower scope.

3 "Now" it was to be Israel's turn (cf. Hab 2:16). The "end" was to be no impersonal disaster but the outworking of Yahweh's vehement reaction to an immoral lifestyle. A manifestation of his "anger" would be sent, like his arrows of destruction in 5:16, to ravage the land. It was a just anger, triggered by the behavior of those who lived there, that would thus be exposed for the abhorrent thing it was. The verb rendered "repay for" is literally "lay upon," implying Yahweh's effecting of a natural progression from sin to punishment: "sins boomerang, bringing doom upon the perpetrators" (Brownlee 106). "Chastisement is but sin assuming another form, a form which it inevitably takes" (Davidson 45). As in 5:9, תועבת "abominations, shocking practices" is used as a general term for wrongdoing committed in the homeland and characterizes it as abhorrent to Yahweh and out of keeping with the covenant relationship.

4 The oracle continues along a mental track parallel with chap. 5, forestalling any appeal to the clemency of Yahweh and pronouncing the wrongdoing so heinous as to be beyond its reach (cf. 5:11 and *Comment*). The announcement of v 3b must stand. In v 4bβ, literally, their "abominable deeds will be among you," surviving and, as it were, haunting the land in the form of their disastrous effects. Greenberg (147) has rendered the verb "fester" and compared the way that blood is described in 24:7: "The guilty evidence . . . ever-present, will call down retribution on the culprits." The two clauses of v 4baβ combine these self-generating consequences with Yahweh's own intervention, working alongside the natural process and determining its character and timing.

The oracle of judgment culminates in a recognition formula. After the sustained rhetorical address of the homeland, there is now a turning to speak directly to Ezekiel's fellow exiles. The catastrophe that was to befall their beloved country would be evidence of the reality and nature of Yahweh. When disaster struck, this oracle would enable them to recognize it for what it was, the intervention of the true God and the revelation of his moral authority.

5–7 A renewed messenger formula introduces an oracle similar to the previous one, but the similarities must not be allowed to blind the reader to its distinctive nuances. This version goes its own way in important places, despite its overlap with the first oracle. The announcement of a series of disasters will be repeated in the next oracle, at v 26a. As in v 2, the repeated imminence of "the end" is declared, but now it is reinforced with mention of "doom(?)," and its target is not first the world and then the homeland but, with speech that is more direct and more plain, "the inhabitants of the land." The day-of-Yahweh theme emerges more distinctly. "The day" is shorthand for the day of Yahweh: one may compare the short and long references in 30:3 and also the longer rendering of the LXX below in v 10. The nearness of the day is a traditional element in "day of

Yahweh" passages (cf. 30:3; Joel 1:15; 2:1; Zeph 1:7, 14). Also in 30:3 there is a parallel reference to "the time of the nations." Both there and here the "time" is evidently a fateful time or a set time, the meaning of which is colored by the context as the moment when Yahweh intervenes in climactic judgment. But, unlike the case in v 3, there is not an immediate turning to Yahweh's direct role. Instead, there is a dwelling on the chaos that would be engendered. If the standard interpretation is correct, there is a contrast between shouts of war and happy shouting at harvest celebrations. Then the overthrow of normal social life, upon which the third oracle will focus, finds an anticipation here. The association of "the day" with "tumult" (מהומה) invites comparison with Isa 22:5, where there is mention of Yahweh's "day of tumult," with military overtones.

8 The nearness (קרוב) of the day is now echoed by the imminence (מקרוב "soon") of the outpouring of divine wrath. Unlike v 3, "now" simply reinforces the note of imminence. V 8 consists of two lines in regular poetic parallelism, unlike the more rugged first line in v 3, and is made up of phrases that are common in the book. The effect of the two lines, especially of their counterpointed nouns ("my wrath/anger," "your ways/shocking deeds"), is to draw a logical parallel between gross human wrongdoing and vehement divine reprisal. Stylistically, the parallel is reinforced by wordplay, וכליתי "and I will exhaust" and כל "all (your shocking deeds)," a play that we observed earlier at 6:11–12. With their every move, the people of the land were heading for inevitable checkmate in their challenge of God.

9 The echoing of v 3aγb in v 8aγb begins a three-line duplication of the rest of the first oracle. The denial of clemency and the juxtaposition of divine retribution and natural consequences are repeated, along with the closing recognition formula, which again is seemingly directed to Ezekiel's immediate audience. Now, however, there is a capping with the blow that Yahweh is to inflict, which, in the present literary context, points forward to Yahweh's destructive and remorseless blow against Jerusalem in 9:5. It will find a near parallel in 32:15aβb, "when I strike all who inhabit it [= Egypt], then they will know that I am Yahweh." Only by such a harsh blow (cf. 6:14) could the truth about Yahweh be revealed and lesser claims to know his will be discredited.

10, 12aα The recognition formula in v 9 indicates that a new oracle begins in v 10, as does the parallel between v 10abα and vv 6–7a. However, the oracle is not formally introduced, unlike the first two oracles. The abruptness shows its literary role as a continuation and elaboration of the earlier oracles concerned with the day of Yahweh. This oracle differs from the previous ones in that there is no rhetorical address of the land or its inhabitants. Instead, there is a descriptive account that speaks with less artifice of the disruption and disaster that "they," clearly the Judeans, would undergo. As in the previous messages, the day of Yahweh theme is an initial device that has the function of arresting hearers' attention and is not maintained. The beginning in vv 10 and 12a is similar to the start of the second oracle, while it may be significant that v 11b has elements in common with the end of v 7. A novel feature is that perfect verbs appear in vv 10 and 12aα, as opposed to the imminent future aspect of the participial or adjectival forms that have been associated with the day-of-Yahweh clauses earlier. This phenomenon, with which v 14 (and v 20b) should probably be linked, represents a vivid intensification that coexists with the plainer future references in vv 13 and

15–17 (cf. GKC 106n). The last line of v 10 represents new material that is woven into the introduction. The flowering of injustice and budding of insolence are metaphors for the inevitable maturing of deeds into consequences. The notion corresponds to the haunting presence of shocking deeds in vv 4 and 8. These social vices were ripe for reaping in a harvest of destruction. The accusation of injustice will be repeated in 9:9, with Jerusalem as its target. The charge of "insolence" is not brought elsewhere in the book. It might be linked with גאון "pride" in vv 20, 24 and interpreted as self-assured arrogance that pits itself against God (cf. Deut 1:43; cf. Brownlee 115). However, the poetic parallelism and comparison with 9:9 and also 7:23 leave us in little doubt that it refers to willful infringement of human rights. One may compare the use of the cognate verb in Exod 21:14 for "a premeditated disregard of the law, a presumptuous offense against law and morality" (J. Scharbert, *TDOT* 4:48).

12aβ–13 Normal life would be brought to a halt by the disruptive advent of the day of Yahweh. The example of a commercial transaction is explored (cf. Isa 24:2). Buying and selling, along with the contrary emotions of the excitement of getting something new and of the reluctance to part with familiar property, would prove pointless. The sentiment is a variation of the prophetic futility curse, such as building houses and not living in them (Amos 4:11) or sowing but not reaping (Mic 6:15). Here the initial action is represented obliquely, but dramatically, as an exhortation. The consequent frustration, in terms of an inability to capitalize on the initiated action, is capped with an explanation that death would overwhelm both buyer and seller! This fate is justified with the general charge of "iniquity."

14–16 The topic of coming death, broached in v 13bβ, is expounded in this next section. Again there is vivid use of the past tense initially, to underline the certainty of the event, and the style of the futility curse is ominously continued in a new context of military conflict (cf. Amos 5:3 and S. M. Paul, *Amos* [Minneapolis: Fortress, 1991] 161). The trilogy of doom—sword, plague, and famine—used before in 5:12; 6:11–12, reappears in a format of siege warfare, as in 5:12. Yahweh's military agents who were to wield the sword would be backed by fifth columnists, famine and plague, which would ravage Jerusalem from within. Then, somewhat as in 6:12, the chance of escape is countered by a further onslaught of death. As in Amos 5:18, vain hopes are quashed by the illustration of escaping from a lion or bear only to be bitten by a snake, so here a frying-pan-to-fire experience expresses the theme of wholesale and inescapable death. Once more, as in v 13, its justice is grounded in the general charge of "iniquity," for which it was to be a fair reprisal.

17–18 The closing section of the first half of the oracle reverts to an earlier stage, before death has wiped out the community, but maintains the same emphasis on comprehensiveness. The convention of a reaction to bad news is employed here by means of a series of formulaic terms (cf. 21:12[7]; Isa 13:7–8; Jer 6:24; cf. Hillers, *ZAW* 77 [1965] 86–90). It reflects as in a mirror the severity of the coming disaster. General demoralization and loss of physical control would occur, in reaction to the social breakdown caused by invasion. Moreover, mourning rites of sackcloth and shaved heads would give expression to the people's sense of humiliation and dread (cf. 27:31): v 18 artistically weaves external rites and negative emotions in a chiastic order.

19–20 This initial section of the second half of the oracle matches vv 12–13 in the first. Now, however, the upheaval in Judean society is illustrated in terms of a drastic rejection of silver and gold. The sentiment seems to be an echo of material from two "day of Yahweh" passages, Zeph 1:18, "Neither their silver nor their gold will be able to save them on the day of Yahweh's wrath," and Isa 2:20, "they will throw away their silver idols and their gold idols." Indeed, the reference of an alert glossator to the first reminiscence has been preserved in the MT at v 19aγ. A dire situation from which even money cannot buy escape and the spiritual declension marked by the illegitimate use of divine images are dramatically combined as consequence and cause. The second element corresponds to the phrase איש בעונו "each for his iniquity" in v 13. In fact, the term עון "iniquity" recurs here in v 19, in the phrase "stumbling block of iniquity," which is characteristically employed in the book of Ezekiel to refer to the cultic use of images (see 14:3–4, 7; 44:12; cf. 18:30). Here it is used as an anticipatory summary of the sin of v 20.

The priestly term נדה "menstruation, unclean thing" is a strong expression, such as especially a priest would use, for that which is extremely impure. Menstrual blood was regarded as a major ritual contaminant, though it had no immoral connotations (cf. Frymer-Kensky, "Pollution, Purification" 401–4). Here it functions as a metaphor for that which is abhorrent and so undesired. It expresses a sense of despair and a situation of crisis. There seems to be an underlying thought that food was no longer available, so that money was no longer of use. This scenario is viewed as an indirect result of human wrongdoing in the cultic area. A perversion of that which is precious would eventually make it precious no longer. Yahweh's intervention would radically change the Judeans' view of their misused wealth. The divine ratification of the human assessment is a parallel of sorts to the combination of an automatic process of doom and its expediting at Yahweh's hands, in the first two oracles. God was to be secretly at work in the human situation, using history for his own moral ends.

21–24 A plain statement of this retributive providence in operation is made in this next section, which alternates divine causation and human aggression. As in Hos 2:10–11 (8–9), misuse of Yahweh's gifts would result in forfeiture of them. There is an oscillation of referents for the third plural pronouns and verbs, "they/them/their." Mainly, they relate to the human invaders, clearly the neo-Babylonian army, which had invaded Judah earlier, in 597 B.C., but they also refer to the "they" of the earlier parts of the oracle, the Judeans. Yahweh is revealed as on the side of the new human factor and so as the enemy of his people. The grim threat that he would avert his face from them runs counter to his usual benevolent grace, when he lifted up his face upon them with a smile of blessing (Num 6:26; cf. Ezek 4:3a and the *Comment*). The withdrawal of covenant favor corresponds to the lack of clemency avowed in the two earlier oracles, at vv 4 and 9.

The divine commission to aliens and comparative barbarians who would be no respecters of Judean culture or religion finds mention also in the oracles against Tyre (28:7) and Egypt (30:11; 31:11–12), with reference, explicit or implicit, to the neo-Babylonians. In view of the mention of desecration, it is silver and gold objects of worship that are to be abandoned to the enemy. In line with the accusation in v 23b, but in inverse order, first the invasion of the capital is envisioned, in vv 21–23a, and then that of the land in general, in v 24, as the plural term "sanctuaries" suggests. More precisely, Yahweh's "treasury" appears to be the temple in Jerusalem, in which images were to be found (cf. 8:10), as well as in the

local shrines where Yahweh was worshiped (cf. 6:6, 13). It features as the reposi-
tory of precious objects, here specifically of the silver and gold images of v 20.

The intervening accusation of v 23b, which acts as a pivot in this section, corresponds to the accusation of "iniquity" in v 16, at the end of the parallel section
of the first half of the oracle. The charges of murder and social oppression that
found no resolution in the lawcourts (cf. 9:9) represent the second main sin of
Judah in Ezekiel's eyes (cf. 8:16–17). The final term, חמס "violence," "is cold-
blooded and unscrupulous infringement of the personal rights of others,
motivated by greed and hate and often making use of physical violence and bru-
tality" (H. Haag, *TDOT* 4:482). The sudden shift from one charge to the other
shows how closely connected they were as violations of Israel's joint obligations
to Yahweh, in the realms of cult and society. It is made clear that not only cultic
aberrations defiled the temple: severe threats to human life also had a polluting
effect on the sanctuary at the center of Israel (cf. 5:11 and the *Comment*). The
sacrilege that was to be committed by the invaders at Yahweh's command only
rationalized a state of affairs already present. It would expose the breach that the
Judeans themselves had caused in the sanctity of the temple. The permitted desecration of not only the images but also the temple would ratify its contamination
at Judah's hands.

As we observed above, v 24 seems to refer to the invasion of the land as a whole,
which would include the taking over of homes in Judean towns and villages. In
24:21 גאון עזכם "their source of pride and power" (see *Note* 24.b.; cf. Lev 26:32,
though no intertextuality is evident here) is applied to the temple, as the proud
symbol of Yahweh's positive relation to Judah and an inviolable bastion that gave
protection to Jerusalem (see *Ezekiel 20–48* 61). Here too the parallelism indicates
a cultic application, but now with reference to the many local shrines that came
under attack in chap. 6. The juxtaposition of that which is sacred (מקדש "sanctuary") and divinely caused desecration (חלל), polar opposites, calls into question
the religious faith of Judah as a source of hope.

25–27a This section corresponds to the third section of the first half of the
oracle (vv 17–18). It too features the convention of the community's reaction to
bad news, although in less rigid a format than was used there. Again it seems to
reflect the intensity of the disaster that was to come. Within the literary unit, the
coming of anguish and disaster is an echo of the coming of "the end" in v 2 and
of "the end" and "doom(?)" in v 6. More obviously there is a resumption of the
initial coming of "doom(?)" and "the time" in vv 10–11, at the outset of this oracle.
If שלום "peace, security" is the outcome of Yahweh's smiling face (Num 6:25–26),
the result of the averting of his gaze (v 22) is a lack of such peace. Zimmerli
(209) has observed that the succession of bad news finds graphic illustration in
Job 1–2. Recourse to religious authorities would fail, whether to prophets for an
oracle of salvation or to priests for a ruling as to religious standing or possible
reinstatement (cf. Jer 18:18; Lam 2:9; Amos 8:11–12). Behind their silence lies
the silence of God himself (Lamparter 66 n. 26). Civil authorities, represented
by the elders, would have no policy for success (cf. Lam 2:10). The latter theme is
continued in v 27aβ: the king, here called "head of state" (cf. *Ezekiel 20–48* 194;
Seitz, *Theology in Conflict* 121–31), would have no magic answers (cf. 2 Kgs 19:1).
No wonder then that his subjects, "the people of the land" (cf. *Ezekiel 20–48* 253),
were to be demoralized and irresolute.

No answers would be forthcoming, because sufficient answer could be found in their experience of disaster. It would be their only clue to Yahweh's revelation, a revelation by which he showed himself not their patron but their judge and prosecutor. It was not the answer they wanted, but lack of any other would testify to its truth. In fact, Judah's abhorrent lifestyle, including radical injustice that created its own standards (contrast 44:24), ruled out any other answer. The grim message at the close of the two preceding oracles (vv 3–4, 8–9) is reiterated with unremitting force.

Explanation

This is a frightening chapter. It consists of a group of poetic oracles intended to convince Ezekiel's fellow hostages in the Babylonian heartland that their hopes of returning soon to their homes and families in far-off Judah would not materialize. Their own perception of Yahweh was positive and reassuring. They badly needed to learn that his purposes, grounded in his moral character, were necessarily hostile and ominous (vv 4, 9). The message is driven home in this literary setting by repetition, by using two versions of a basic oracle and capping it with another that reinforced its sentiments at greater length. Each oracle opens with an echo of the tradition of the day of Yahweh. This nightmarish tradition was employed by the prophets to evoke fear in the hearts of heedless or optimistic hearers. It spoke of the sinister intervention of God in disaster. In the first pair of oracles, this tradition is reinforced with forecasts of "the end," with ominous reminiscence of the message of Amos about the fall of the Northern Kingdom and of the primeval flood that blotted out the world. "This is no cautionary warning but a promise of sure extinction. If there is to be a future for Israel, it must come as a new revelation. Here there is none" (Vawter 56). The end of all things was at hand, and it was time for judgment to begin with the people of God (cf. 1 Pet 4:7, 17). Half a century later, Second Isaiah could cancel out the potential threat of the flood (Isa 54:9–10). Not so Ezekiel, in the first half of his ministry. Jerusalem had to fall. The national existence of Judah was to be terminated in a cataclysm of judgment.

The cause of such judgment lay not in the mysterious counsels of God but in the behavior of the people of Judah. It was their chickens that were to come home to roost. It was their covenant-violating "ways" and "shocking deeds" (vv 3–4, 8–9) that would generate an automatic doom. Their "injustice" and "violence" were to ripen into a baneful crop (v 10). From this perspective, Yahweh's role was to oil the machinery of cause and effect and to ensure that it worked efficiently. His judicial punishment was the natural and logical outcome of the covenant people's crimes committed against God and against each other. "Do not be deceived," Ezekiel has to proclaim, like Paul; "God is not mocked, for whatever individuals sow they will also reap" (Gal 6:7). This was not to deny the personal, passionate involvement of God in the retributive process. His "wrath" and "anger" (vv 3, 8) were triggered by abhorrence of their faithlessness, which shut the door on his clemency and favor (vv 4, 9, 22).

The third oracle vividly explores the coming disaster in a double presentation of three scenarios: the breakdown of the norms of Judean society, widespread death that overtook even refugees or material destruction that reached as far as the temple, and the general consternation of the Judeans in the homeland, bereft of help from both religious and secular leaders. A society that did nothing about serious violations of the human rights of its members was doomed. A religious institution in which dishonor was done to the basic revelation of the God whose worship was professed was not worth preserving. As K. Koch (*The Prophets* [Philadelphia: Fortress, 1984] 2:92) has commented,

> Wherever a group of people continually engages in evil behaviour, deadly mechanisms begin to interlock. At the bottom of the pyramid come the spheres of act and corresponding destiny, which are now consummated. Above them are the active powers such as pestilence, famine and sword. Higher up still are the entities of wrath and white heat. And finally comes the burning-glass itself—the personal focus in Yahweh who, in his desire to be known, intervenes in history with ardent zeal and without compassion.

This chapter forms the climax of a series of oracles initiated in chap. 5. It closes the first section of the book, a section that began with the revelation in theophany of the divine judge and the commissioning of his prophet of judgment and then proceeded from sign-acts of the coming fall of Jerusalem to an interpretative oracle of judgment and then to messages of doom for the whole land. Cassuto ("Arrangement" 230–31) has observed that the hinge between chaps. 6 and 7 is the divine anger of 6:12 and 7:3, 8. There are further links with chaps. 5–6, though allusions to Lev 26 are not maintained. As in 6:11–14, there is no reference to exile as a further punishment, unlike chaps. 4 and 5 and 6:1–10. Boadt ("Rhetorical Strategies" 188–89) has traced the links with chaps. 5 and 6: the trilogy of disaster—sword, plague, and famine—that runs through the series of oracles (5:12; 6:11; 7:15), along with the denial of clemency (5:11; 7:4, 9) and the recognition formula (5:13; 6:7, 10, 13, 14; 7:4, 9, 27). The prevalence of the last recurring element reflects the necessity of quashing the hopes of Ezekiel's fellow hostages for a speedy return to their homeland. Behind such hopes lay a conviction that God was on their side and ready to answer their prayers. Ezekiel's message of the coming defeat of capital and country revealed the stark truth regarding God's stance. Judah had put itself outside his mercy and within his punitive reach. "It is a fearful thing to fall into the hands of the living God" (Heb 10:31). Each community of faith in every age must add its sober amen and, forewarned, stay out of the trap into which Judah fell.

The Temple Vision   (8:1–11:25)

Bibliography

Ackerman, S. *Under Every Green Tree: Popular Religion in Sixth-Century Judah.* HSM 46. Atlanta: Scholars Press, 1992. 37–99. **Avishur, Y.** "The 'Duties of the Son' in the 'Story of Aqhat' and Ezekiel's Prophecy on Idolatry (Ch. 8)." *UF* 17 (1986) 49–60. **Balla, E.** "Ezechiel 8,1–9.11; 11,24–25." In *Festschrift R. Bultmann zum 65. Geburtstag überreicht.* Stuttgart: Kohlhammer, 1949. 1–11. **Baltzer, D.** "Literarkritische und literarhistorische Anmerkungen zur Heilsprophetie im Ezechiel-Buch." In *Ezekiel and His Book*, ed. J. Lust. 160–81. **Barthélemy, D.** "'Un seul,' 'un nouveau' ou 'un autre'? À propos de l'intervention du Seigneur sur le coeur de l'homme selon Ez 11,19a et des problèmes de critique textuelle qu'elle soulève." In *Der Weg zum Menschen.* FS A. Deissler, ed. R. Mosis and L. Ruppert. Freiburg: Heider, 1989. 329-38. **Becker, J.** "Ez 8–11 als einheitliche Komposition in einem pseudepigraphischen Ezechielbuch." In *Ezekiel and His Book*, ed. J. Lust. 136–50. **Beentjes, P. C.** "Inverted Quotations in the Bible: A Neglected Stylistic Pattern." *Bib* 63 (1982) 506–23. **Block, D. I.** *The Gods of the Nations.* Jackson: Evangelical Theological Society, 1988. 125–61. ———. "Text and Emotion: A Study in the 'Corruptions' in Ezekiel's Inaugural Vision (Ezekiel 1:4–28)." *CBQ* 50 (1988) 418–42. **Brownlee, W. H.** "The Aftermath of the Fall of Judah according to Ezekiel." *JBL* 89 (1970) 393–404. **Busink, T. A.** *Der Tempel von Jerusalem von Salomo bis Herodes: 1. Der Tempel Salomos.* Leiden: Brill, 1970. **Cogan, M.** *Imperialism and Religion: Assyria, Judah and Israel in the Eighth and Seventh Centuries B.C.E.* SBLMS 19. Missoula: Scholars Press, 1974. **Dijkstra, M.** "The Glosses in Ezekiel Reconsidered: Aspects of Textual Tradition in Ezekiel 10." In *Ezekiel and His Book*, ed. J. Lust. 55–77. **Eissfeldt, O.** "Schwerterschlagene bei Hesekiel." In *Studies in Old Testament Prophecy.* FS T. H. Robinson. Edinburgh: Clark, 1957. 73–81. **Goettsberger, J.** "Zu Ez 9,8 und 11,13." *BZ* 19 (1931) 6–19. **Gordis, R.** "'The Branch to the Nose': A Note on Ezekiel viii 17." *JTS* 37 (1936) 284–88. **Graffy, A.** *A Prophet Confronts His People: The Disputation Speech in the Prophets.* AnBib 104. Rome: Biblical Institute, 1984. 42–56. **Greenberg, M.** "The Vision of Jerusalem in Ezekiel 8–11." In *The Divine Helmsman.* FS. L. H. Silberman, ed. J. L. Crenshaw and S. Sandmel. New York: Ktav, 1960. 143–64. ———. "Prolegomenon." In C. C. Torrey, *Pseudo-Ezekiel and the Original Prophecy.* New York: Ktav, 1970. xi–xxxv. **Gruber, M. I.** "Akkadian *labān appi* in the Light of Art and Literature." *JANESCU* 7 (1975) 73–83. **Gunkel, H.** *Schöpfung und Chaos in Urzeit und Endzeit.* 2nd ed. Göttingen: Vandenhoeck & Ruprecht, 1921. **Gurney, O. R.** "Tammuz Reconsidered: Some Recent Developments." *JSS* 7 (1962) 142–60. **Halperin, D. J.** "The Exegetical Character of Ezek. x. 9–17." *VT* 26 (1976) 129–41. **Haran, M.** "The Ark and the Cherubim: Their Symbolic Significance in Biblical Ritual." *IEJ* 9 (1959) 30–38, 89–94. ———. "The Uses of Incense in the Ancient Israelite Ritual." *VT* 10 (1960) 113–29. **Horst, F.** "Exilsgemeinde und Jerusalem in Ez viii–xi: Eine literarische Untersuchung." *VT* 3 (1953) 337–60. **Hossfeld, F.-L.** "Die Tempelvision Ez 8–11 im Licht unterschiedlichen methodischer Zugänge." In *Ezekiel and His Book.* ed. J. Lust. 151–65. ———. "Probleme einer ganzheitlichen Lektüre der Schrift dargestellt am Beispiel Ez 9–10." *TQ* 167 (1987) 266–77. **Houk, C. B.** "The Final Redaction of Ezekiel 10." *JBL* 90 (1971) 42–54. **Jacobsen, T.** "Toward the Image of Tammuz." *HR* 1 (1962) 189–213. **Jozaki, S.** "A Study on Ezekiel 11:14–21: Some Characteristic Features of Ezekiel's Thoughts." *Kwansei Gakuin University Annual Studies* 6 (1958) 29–41. **Keel, O.** *Jahwe-Visionen und Siegelkunst.* SBS 84/85. Stuttgart: Katholisches Bibelwerk, 1977. **Krüger, T.** *Geschichtskonzepte im Ezechielbuch.* BZAW 180. Berlin: de Gruyter, 1989. 318–24. **Levin, C.** *Der Verheissung des neues Bundes.* FRLANT 137. Göttingen: Vandenhoeck & Ruprecht, 1985. 205–9. **Liwak, R.** "Überlieferungsgeschichtliche Probleme des Ezechielbuches." Diss.,

Bochum, 1976. 110–43, 281–96. **Lohfink, N.** "Beobachtungen zur Geschichte des Ausdrucks יהוה עַם." In *Probleme biblischer Theologie.* FS G. von Rad, ed. H. W. Wolff. Munich: Kaiser, 1971. 275–305. **McCarthy, C.** *The Tiqqune Sopherim and Other Theological Corrections in the Masoretic Text of the Old Testament.* OBO 36. Freiburg: Universitätsverlag; Göttingen: Vandenhoeck & Ruprecht, 1981. 91–97. **McKane, W.** "Observations on the TIḲḲUNÊ SÔPᵉRÎM." In *On Language, Culture and Religion.* FS E. A. Nida, ed. M. Black and W. Smalley. The Hague: Mouton, 1974. 53–77. **McKay, J. W.** *Religion in Judah under the Assyrians 732–609 B.C.* SBT 2:26. Naperville: Allenson, 1973. **Müller, D. H.** *Ezechiel-Studien.* Berlin: Reuther & Reichard, 1895. **Murray, D. F.** "The Rhetoric of Disputation: Re-examination of a Prophetic Genre." *JSOT* 38 (1987) 95–121. **Newsom, C.** *Songs of the Sabbath Sacrifice.* HSS 27. Atlanta: Scholars Press, 1985. **Ohnesorge, S.** *Jahwe gestaltet seine Volk neu.* FB 64. Wurzburg: Echter, 1991. 4–77. **Parunak, H. V. D.** "The Literary Architecture of Ezekiel's *Marᵓôt ᵓĔlōhîm.*" *JBL* 99 (1980) 61–74. **Rose, M.** *Der Ausschliesslichkeitsanspruch Jahwes.* BWANT 106. Stuttgart: Kohlhammer, 1975. 196–213. **Saggs, H. W. F.** "The Branch to the Nose." *JTS* 11 (1960) 318–29. **Schmidt, M. A.** "Zur Komposition des Buches Hesekiel." *TZ* 6 (1950) 81–98. **Sinclair, L. A.** "A Qumran Biblical Fragment 4QEzekᵃ (Ezek. 10,17–11,11)." *RevQ* 14 (1989) 99–105. **Smith, M.** "The Veracity of Ezekiel, the Sins of Manasseh, and Jeremiah 44.18." *ZAW* 87 (1975) 11–16. **Sprank, S.** *Ezechielstudien.* BWANT 3.4. Stuttgart: Kohlhammer, 1926. **Torrey, C. C.** "Notes on Ezekiel." *JBL* 58 (1979) 69–86. **Vincent, L. H.,** and **Stève, A. M.** *Jérusalem de l'Ancien Testament.* Vols. 2–3. Paris: Gabalda, 1956. **Yamauchi, E. M.** "Tammuz and the Bible." *JBL* 84 (1965) 283–90. **Zimmerli, W.** "Jerusalem in der Sicht des Ezechielbuches." In *The Word of the Lord Shall Go Forth.* FS D. N. Freedman. Winona Lake: Eisenbrauns, 1983. 415–26.

Translation

¹*In the sixth year, on the fifth of the sixth*ᵃ *month, I was sitting at home with the Judean elders sitting down in front of me, when Yahweh's*ᵇ *hand descended*ᶜ *on me there.*ᵈ ²*I had a visionary sighting of a figure that looked human.*ᵃ *From his waist down*ᵇ *there was fire, while from the waist up there was a sort of shining glow, like gleaming*ᶜ *amber.*ᵈ ³*He stretched out what looked like*ᵃ *a hand and grasped my hair by the forelock. Then the spirit lifted me up into the air*ᵇ *and brought me in a divine vision*ᶜ *to Jerusalem, to the entrance of the north-facing gateway,*ᵈ *where there was situated*ᵉ *the outrageous image, which invokes divine outrage.*ᶠ ⁴*There too was to be found the manifestation of the presence of the God of Israel, just as it had been revealed to me in the plain.* ⁵*"Human one," he told me, "look north." When I did so, I noticed on the north side of the gate the altar*ᵃ *of that outrageous image, at the point of entry.*ᵇ ⁶*"Human one," he told me, "just look*ᵃ *at what people are doing! They are engaging here in extemely shocking rites,*ᵇ *by functioning as they are*ᶜ *away from my sanctuary. But you will go on to observe rites even more*ᵈ *shocking."*
    ⁷*He brought me to the entrance to the court, where I saw a*ᵃ *hole in the wall.*ᵇ ⁸*"Human one," he told me, "break through the wall."*ᵃ *When I had done so, there was a means of entry.* ⁹*"Go through," he told me, "and observe the shocking rites*ᵃ *in which people are engaging here."* ¹⁰*I went through, and there before my eyes was every*ᵃ *kind of horrible object of worship*ᵇ *and all the idols of the community of Israel, engraved*ᶜ *all over the wall.* ¹¹*Seventy of the elders of the community of Israel were standing in front of the engravings—among them was standing Jaazaniah son of Shaphan*ᵃ*—each holding a censer in his hand, and incense fumes*ᵇ *were wafting up.* ¹²*Then he told me, "Just look, human one, at what the elders of the community of Israel are doing in the dark, each at the recess of his image!*ᵃ *They justify it*ᵇ *with the sentiments that Yahweh cannot*

see,[c] *Yahweh has left the country."* [13]*He also told me, "You have yet to observe rites even more shocking, in which people are engaging."*

[14]*Then he brought me to the entrance of the north gateway leading to Yahweh's temple, where I found women*[a] *sitting, bewailing Tammuz.* [15]*"Just look at that!" he told me. "But you have yet to observe rites even more shocking than seen hitherto."*

[16]*He brought me into the inner court of Yahweh's temple, and by*[a] *the entrance to the nave, between the porch and the altar, I found about twenty-five*[b] *men with their backs to Yahweh's nave and their faces turned to the east, kowtowing in worship*[c] *to the sun.* [17]*"Just look at that, human one!" he told me. "It was evidently not enough for the Judean community, after engaging*[a] *in such shocking rites as they have already engaged in here, to fill the country with violence. Now they have gone further in provoking me to anger:*[b] *here they are putting branches to their noses.*[c] [18]*My reaction will be one of wrath. I will give no look of pity and show no compassion. However loudly they cry out for me to hear, I will not listen to them."*[a]

[9:1]*Then he cried loudly in my hearing, "Come here,*[a] *you who are to be responsible for the city's fate,*[b] *with your weapons of destruction in your*[c] *hands."*[d] [2]*There appeared six men, coming from the direction of the upper, north-facing*[a] *gateway,*[b] *all holding cudgels. With them was another man, clothed*[c] *in linen, who had a writing kit*[d] *at his waist. They came and stood beside the bronze altar.* [3]*Now the manifestation of the presence of the God of Israel had ascended from the cherubim-structure*[a] *it rested on and moved to*[b] *the threshold*[c] *of the temple.*

He cried to the man who was clothed in linen and had the writing kit at his waist; [4]*Yahweh*[a] *told him,*[b] *"Pass through the city of Jerusalem*[c] *and put a cross on the foreheads of the men who have been moaning and groaning*[d] *over the shocking rites perpetrated within it."* [5]*To the others he said, in my hearing, "Pass through the city behind him and start killing, with no*[a] *look*[b] *of pity nor show of compassion.* [6]*You are to assassinate and destroy the old together with*[a] *young people of both sexes, and women together with children. But do not go near anyone marked with a cross. Begin at my sanctuary."
They began with the men*[b] *in front of the temple.* [7]*"Desecrate the temple," he told them, "filling the courts*[a] *with the dead. Go out and start killing*[b] *in the city."*

[8]*During the latter killing, while I was left alone,*[a] *I threw myself down on my face and shouted out, "Oh no, Lord*[b] *Yahweh! Do you mean to destroy all*[c] *Israel who are left, while you drench Jerusalem with your fury?"* [9]*He answered me, "The guilt of the community of Israel*[a] *is quite considerable. The country has been filled with bloodshed, and the city is full of injustice.*[b] *They have excused such behavior with the sentiments that Yahweh has left the country and so cannot see.* [10]*My reaction will be that I shall lack any look of pity and show no compassion. I rule*[a] *them accountable for their conduct."* [11]*Then I noticed the man who was clothed in linen and had the writing kit at his waist, reporting back. "I have acted in accord with*[a] *your command," he said.*

[10:1]*I had a visionary sighting of what looked like lapis lazuli above*[a] *the platform that was over the heads of the cherubim: it was in the form*[b] *of a throne*[c] *above them.* [2]*He told the man clothed in linen the following:*[a] *"Go in between the rotary system,*[b] *under the cherubim,*[c] *and fill your cupped hands with fiery coals from the space between the cherubim and scatter them over the city." As I watched, he went in.* [3]*Now the cherubim were standing on the south side of the temple when the man went in.*[a] *Moreover, a cloud was filling the inner court:* [4] *the manifestation of Yahweh's presence rose from the cherubim-structure and moved to*[a] *the threshold of the temple, and so the temple area was filled with the cloud, and the court was full of the radiance of the manifestation of Yahweh's presence.* ⁵*The sound of the cherubim's wings could be heard as far away as the outer court: it was as loud as the voice of the Almighty God, while he was speaking.* ⁶*When he had commanded the man clothed in linen to take fire from the space between the rotary system, between the cherubim, and he had gone in,*ᵃ *he stood beside a particular wheel,* ⁷*and one of the group of cherubim*ᵃ *extended his hand to the fire that was between*ᵇ *the cherubim and picked up some of the fire. Then he put it in the cupped hands*ᶜ *of the one clothed in linen, who took it and went out.* ⁸*The cherubim were seen*ᵃ *to have what appeared to be human arms and hands*ᵇ *under their wings.* ⁹*I had a visionary sighting of four wheels beside the cherubim, each wheel with a cherub beside it.*ᵃ *In appearance the wheels looked like a gold topaz stone,* ¹⁰*and in appearance*ᵃ *they all four had the same form:*ᵇ *it was as though one wheel was inside another.* ¹¹*When they moved forward, they could move in their four directions without changing direction as they moved, because in whichever direction one of the heads*ᵃ *faced, the other ones followed it without changing direction as they moved,* ¹²*and so did their whole bodies,*ᵃ *their backs, arms, and wings. The wheels were full of eyes all over, in the case of the four of them.*ᵇ ¹³*Now these wheels were what I had heard called a rotary system.*ᵃᵇ ¹⁶*When the cherubim moved forward, the wheels would move beside them; and when the cherubim lifted their wings to rise from the ground, the wheels would not change direction*ᵃ *independently of them.*ᵇ ¹⁷*When the former stopped, the latter stopped too, and when they rose, rose*ᵃ *with them, because they had the spirit of the living beings*ᵇ *in them.*

¹⁸*The manifestation of Yahweh's presence left the temple*ᵃ *and took up a position on the cherubim.* ¹⁹*Then the cherubim lifted their wings and rose from the ground before my eyes, leaving with the wheels alongside them and with the manifestation of the presence of the God of Israel above them.*ᵃ *But it stopped*ᵇ *at the entrance of the east gateway to Yahweh's temple.* ²⁰*They*ᵃ *were the very group of living beings I had seen beneath the God of Israel by the Kebar Canal: now I recognized them to be cherubim.* ²¹*Each had four*ᵃ *faces and four wings, and what seemed to be human arms and hands under their wings.* ²²*The semblance of their four faces was that of the faces which I had seen by the Kebar Canal—both their appearance*ᵃ *and the cherubim themselves,*ᵇ *each moving according to his facial orientation.*

¹¹:¹*The spirit lifted me and brought me to the east gateway leading to Yahweh's temple, the one that faces east.*ᵃ *At the entrance to the gateway I noticed twenty-five*ᵇ *men, among whom I saw Jaazaniah son of Azzur and Pelatiah son of Benaiah, who were public officials.* ²*"Human one," he told me, "these are the men who are making iniquitous plans and hatching evil schemes in this city,* ³*who say, 'No need to build any houses in the near future.*ᵃ *This is the caldron, and we are the meat.'* ⁴*So issue a prophecy against them, issue a prophecy, human one."* ⁵*Then Yahweh's spirit descended upon me, and he told me to say, "The message of Yahweh*ᵃ *is as follows: That is the way you have been talking, community of Israel; I know*ᵇ *the thoughts you are entertaining in your minds.* ⁶*You have caused the death of many people in this city, filling*ᵃ *its streets with the dead.* ⁷*So the message of the Lord Yahweh is as follows: Your dead whom you have put in it are the ones who are the meat, if this is a caldron. But as for you, I will take you out*ᵃ *of it.* ⁸*The sword you fear is the sword I will send in to attack you, runs the oracle of the Lord*ᵃ *Yahweh.* ⁹*I will take you out of it and hand you over to aliens, performing acts of judgment against you:* ¹⁰*you will fall as victims of the sword. On Israelite territory I will execute your judgment, and then you will realize that I am Yahweh.* ¹¹*This city will not*ᵃ *serve as your caldron, nor will you be like meat inside it. On Israelite territory I will execute your judgment,* ¹²*and then you will recognize that I am Yahweh."*ᵃᵇ ¹³*As I prophesied,*

Pelatiah son of Benaiah dropped dead. I threw myself down on my face and called out loudly. "Oh no, Lord[a] *Yahweh," I protested, "you are after all going*[b] *to make a complete end of*[c] *Israel's survivors."*

[14]*I received a communication from Yahweh:* [15] *"Human one, your own brothers,*[a] *the kinsfolk for whom you are responsible,*[b] *and the whole community of Israel in its entirety*[c] *have been described by the residents of Jerusalem as follows: 'They are far away*[d] *from Yahweh; we have been given the right to take over the country.'*[e] [16]*Say then that the message of the Lord Yahweh is as follows: Yes,*[a] *I did send them far away among the nations; yes, I did scatter them in other countries, but I have partially*[b] *taken the place of their sanctuary in the countries they have come to.* [17]*Say then that the message of the Lord Yahweh is as follows: I will go on*[a] *to gather you*[b] *from the peoples, collecting you from the countries you have been scattered in, and I will give you the land of Israel.* [18]*When they come there, they will remove from it all its loathsome religious practices and shocking rites.* [19]*I will give them different*[a] *hearts,*[b] *removing stony hearts from their bodies and giving them hearts soft as flesh,* [20]*so that they can follow my rules and actively meet my standards. So they will become*[a] *my people, while I will become their God.* [21]*But those others whose hearts are devoted*[a] *to loathsome and shocking rites, I pronounce*[b] *accountable for their conduct, runs the oracle of the Lord*[c] *Yahweh."*

[22]*Then the cherubim raised their wings, with the wheels alongside them and the manifestation of the presence of Israel's God above them.* [23]*The manifestation of Yahweh's presence rose from its location inside*[a] *the city and took up a position on the mountain that lies east of the city.* [24]*Thereupon the spirit lifted me and brought me to the exiles in Chaldea,*[a] *in the visionary experience*[b] *given by the spirit of God.*[c] *Then I ceased to experience*[d] *the vision I had seen,* [25]*and I declared to the exiles all the messages Yahweh had revealed to me.*

Notes

1.a. The LXX has "fifth," probably by mechanical assimilation to the fifth day (Cooke 89, following Toy). Smend (49) initiated a preference for the reading of the LXX on the ground that the MT has postponed the date to make room for the periods of 3:16; 4:4–6, but see Zimmerli's discussion (216).

1.b. The MT adds אדני "Lord," in contradiction of the regular formulaic usage: cf., e.g., 1:3. See Zimmerli, *Ezekiel 2* 556, who has found here a possible secondary intrusion.

1.c. There is a variation of the common verb in this formulation, ותהי "and . . . came," as in 1:3, in line with which the LXX and MS[Ken 150] standardized here (Hölscher, *Dichter* 69 n. 1). "Ken[105]" in Zimmerli 216 is an error in the English edition.

1.d. The LXX* regularly omits "there" in this formulation: see *Note* 1:3.d.

2.a. The LXX*'s underlying איש "man" for אש "fire" is generally preferred, as corresponding to אדם "human being" in 1:26: the description in v 2 clearly echoes 1:26–27. The MT probably suffered assimilation to אש later. Greenberg (166) has noted in favor of the change that it provides an antecedent for the following personal suffixes. The LXX also lacks representation of the preceding כמראה "like the appearance of." At first sight the MT might accord with דמות כמראה אדם "a figure like the appearance of a human being" in 1:26 or represent assimilation to the longer phrase (Zimmerli, 216); but it is more likely that the MT attests an addition made after the corruption to אש "fire," relating to the secondary כמראה אש "like the appearance of fire" in 1:27aβ (Herrmann 51), where the whole figure is envisioned as enveloped in fire, rather than only the lower half.

2.b. The MT ממראה מתניו "from the appearance of his loins" here (but significantly not in v 2b) seems to have suffered assimilation to 1:27. Probably the phrase was a comparative comment, meant to indicate that 1:27 so read in both cases. The comment displaced ממתניו "from his loins," attested by the LXX and also found in MS[Ken 96].

2.c. The LXX* exhibits a shorter text, lacking representation of זהר כעין "a shining glow like the gleam of," but it seems to be the result of an arbitrary abbreviation (cf. Zimmerli 217): the distinctive זהר seems inconceivable as a gloss (Cornill 221; cf. M. Görg, *TDOT* 4:46).

2.d. For the rendering, see the *Comment* on 1:4. The longer form החשמלה may be due to its climactic placing in a grandiose description (Joüon 93i).

3.a. Heb. תבנית "structure" is unusual in this context: it appears to have developed the sense of form or shape, akin to its use to refer to images (cf. BDB 125b).

3.b. Lit. "between earth and sky."

3.c. For the pl, which is characteristic of Ezekiel, see *Note* 1:1.c., and for the phrase, see the *Comment* on 1:1.

3.d. The LXX* lacks a counterpart to the fem form הפנימית "inner" in the MT, in which an ellipse of (ה)חצר "the court" is presupposed. The inner court of the temple is mentioned in v 16; 10:3, but the present context suggests that a gate farther from the temple is in view (see the *Comment*). The confusion underlying the LXX between הפנה "facing" and הפנימי "inner" at 40:19, 32 suggests that the MT has a conflated text. The second element is the original one. Did a copyist write הפנא in place of (ה)הפונה and leave the torso uncorrected? Then the MT reflects a later attempt to make sense of the abandoned error by recourse to הפנימית "inner" across the scroll in the next column (v 16) and/ or by equating the position of the "glory" in v 4 with the description in 10:3–4. Cf. the comparable case in 22:20 (Allen, *JSS* 31 [1986] 131–33; id., *Ezekiel 20–48* 32). The Syr represents הַפִּנָּה "the Corner (Gate)," which may be another attempt to interpret the torso, via haplography; it is a topographical improvement on the MT, insofar as it refers to a city gate at the west end of the north wall (cf. *IDB* 2:853a). There is no need to prefix an article to שער "(the) gate" (cf., e.g., *BHS*, but contrast *BHK*): cf. 9:2; 40:28 and GKC 126w; Joüon 138b, c.

3.e. Heb. מושב, which in 2 Kgs 2:19 refers to the "situation" of a city, here reasonably denotes the location of the image (BDB 444a). Ehrlich (*Randglossen* 5:25) envisioned a seated image; also Ackerman (*Under Every Green Tree* 39–40) argues for a rendering "throne." The LXX's nonrepresentation does not appear to be textually significant: cf. Zimmerli 217.

3.f. For the verbal form, see GKC 75qq. The LXX (and Syr) ran together the two final terms with one rendering, in line with its penchant for abbreviation in this context. It is striking, however, that the literalizing 'A Σ Θ and LXX^OL rendered with a single form: one must leave open the possibility that the second term, which is not present in v 5, is a gloss (Cornill 222) on, or a dittograph (Ehrlich *Randglossen* 5:25) of, the first.

5.a. The MT has "on the north side of the gate of the altar that outrageous image," so that Ezekiel's attention is here drawn to the image as if to a novel feature, whereas he had already referred to it in the narrative of v 3b. One way to resolve the problem is to regard the relative clause at the end of v 3 as an anticipatory gloss (Cornill 233; et al.). Another, less drastic, expedient is to dissociate v 5 from v 3 by reading with a slight change: לְשַׁעַר מֶזְבַּח "(north) of the gate, the altar of . . . ." (H. Gunkel, *Schöpfung und Chaos* 141 n. 1; Bertholet [1897] 46; et al.). The same end may be achieved with even less alteration by redividing the consonantal text as לשערה מזבח, with a redundant ה, after ל (Driver, *Bib* 19 [1938] 62; he pointed לשערה "to the gate of," but לשערה "to the gate" is necessary [see my note in Brownlee 126]). Driver compared לשאולה "to Sheol" in Ps 9:18(17); one might also cite as a near parallel אל־צפונה "to the north" in v 14 below. An "altar gate" is not otherwise known, though it might conceivably refer to a gate near the bronze altar that Ahaz moved to the north side of the temple court (2 Kgs 16:14; cf. Ezek 9:2; Hitzig 59). However, this explanation is only viable if a gate to the temple (= "inner" in the MT of v 3) court is in view: see the *Comment*. The LXX has "east gate," misreading המזרח for המזבח, which conflicts with the north-facing gate of v 3. But, indirectly, the LXX supports the MT and shows that the latter's error was perpetrated at an early stage.

5.b. The LXX* does not represent the final location, but it can hardly be dispensed with, as Zimmerli (218) and Wevers (80) have correctly observed. For the *hapax legomenon* ביאה, cf. Akk. *bīʾu* "(drainage) opening (in a wall)" (*CAD* 2:297a).

6.a. Joüon 161b has observed that all the instances of הראית "Have you seen?" in the OT have an exclamatory nuance and that Jerome rendered with emphatic statements. This observation, which relates to vv 12, 15, and 17, surely also applies to this case, where a ptcp is employed.

6.b. The MT adds "(in) which the community of Israel (are engaging here)," unrepresented in the LXX*. Superficially the addition accords with the phrasing in vv 9, 12, 17 (cf. v 13), but one then expects an article with תועבות גדלות "great abominations," such as appears in vv 9 and 17 (Cooke 101). The English versions surreptitiously render as if the article were there. The addition sought to provide a parallel to the other verses and was inspired by references to the community of Israel in vv 10–12.

6.c. Is the implicit subj "they" or "Yahweh"? The latter is preferred by modern versions; and it is found in the Vg and followed by some scholars (Ewald 244; et al.). It looks ahead to Yahweh's subsequent abandonment of the sanctuary. However, Cooke (101), like Kraetzschmar (89) before him, admitted that the lack of an explicit subj to this end is "particularly harsh." It is more natural to continue the human subj with LXX Syr Tg 'A Θ (Bertholet [1897] 46; et al.; see especially Zimmerli 218, 238). Greenberg (169) has observed that elsewhere רחק מעל "be far from" has a human subj in relation to God. See the *Comment.*

6.d. The adj has a comparative force in this context, as the parallel v 15b makes clear (Ehrlich, *Randglossen* 5:26). The LXX stylistically renders עוד תשוב "you will yet again" by ἔτι "further" here and in vv 13 and 15.

7.a. Heb. אחד "one" has virtually the force of an indefinite article.

7.b. The LXX* does not represent v 7b. Greenberg (169) has suggested that it originated as a variant of v 8bβ, with חר "hole" having the meaning "hiding place," and referred to a secret meeting place. The omission has been made part of a larger hypothesis concerning the original text, that the passage about the second sin moved from Ezekiel's being brought to the entrance of the court (v 7a) directly to the divine order to enter (v 9), with which the prophet complied and saw the walls of the open court covered with pictures of idols (Zimmerli 218–19, 240; cf. Cornill 223–24; Fohrer 49; Wevers 81). This simple narrative was complicated into a secret rite by the insertion of v 8, presumably at the pre-LXX stage of the tradition, under the influence of the digging through the wall in 12:5, 7, and by the addition of v 7b at a post-LXX stage. A major plank in this theory is the supposed omission of בחשך "in darkness" from the LXX* in v 12, for which see below. The presumed shorter text has the advantage of conforming more closely to the structure of the other scenarios of sin. The first scenario progresses from specification of the place to which Ezekiel is brought (v 3 // v 7) to a divine order to observe (v 5a // v 9). In the third and fourth scenarios there is a direct movement from a specification of place (vv 14a, 16aα) to a description of the sin (vv 14b, 16aβ–b // vv 5b, 10–11). There is a relative uniformity that offers no counterpart to v 8; but its very relativity should make the reader cautious about regarding this extra element as secondary. Its emphasis on secrecy appears to echo an OT motif associated with venturing outside the norms of Yahwistic worship (see the *Comment*). Driver (*Bib* 35 [1954] 149–50) interpreted vv 7b–8 in a feasible way, which in fact coincides with Jerome's exegesis (95–96): the prophet is told to enlarge the existing hole until it becomes an opening big enough to squeeze through. He explained the omission of v 7b in the LXX* in terms of the translator's missing the distinction between חר "hole" and פתח "opening" and regarding them as synonyms.

8.a. The LXX* does not represent either instance of בקיר "through the wall," but in v 10 renders על־הקיר "on the wall" as ἐπ' αὐτοῦ "on it." Zimmerli (219) supposed that the translator did not understand קיר, but it is certainly translated in 12:5, 7; 13:12, 14, 15. The most natural explanation of the evidence is that the pronoun in v 10 presupposes a rendering in v 8 and that we are to envision in v 8a an inner-Greek omission by homoeoteleuton of εἰς τὸν τοῖχον (after ὄρυξον "dig"), the rendering in 12:5. In v 8ba the phrase was deliberately left untranslated as otiose in Greek. Balla (*Festschrift* 8), followed by Fohrer (*ZAW* 63 [1951] 38) and others, took over Herntrich's notion that בקיר "through the wall" was introduced from 12:5, 7. Since in Ezek 12:5, 7, 12, the LXX renders חתר "dig" by διορύττω, while in the LXX of the Pentateuch ὀρύττω stands for חפר "dig," Balla supposed that here LXX ὄρυξον "dig" and ὤρυξα "I dug" imply an underlying חפר (rather than חתר), which should properly be related to another stem, חפר, meaning "search for, look around for." (*HALAT* 327a considers the meaning "search for" to be a metaphorical extension of "dig" within the semantic range of the one verb חפר.) Balla's linguistic differentiation can hardly bear the weight he attaches to it. One may compare the way in which גבול "border" is rendered by the verb διορίζει "borders" in 47:18, while in 47:20 it is translated ὁρίζει. This variation, which Ziegler (*LXX* 324) unnecessarily obliterates, is especially pertinent in the light of McGregor's contention (*Greek Text* 157–81) that the same translator was responsible for chaps. 1–25 and 40–48.

9.a. The MT adds הרעות "the evil(s)," which is not represented in the LXX*. As in 6:11, it seems to be a comparative gloss, in this case probably harking back to 6:11.

10.a. In place of כל "every," the LXX has μάταια "vain things," which Cornill (224) speculated was an error for πάντα τά "all the." However, it is significant that הבל "vanity," in the sense of idols, is so rendered in Jer 2:5; 8:19. In place of והנה כל "and behold every," the translator may have read or misread והנה הבל "and behold vanity" via dittography and a ב/כ confusion. It is possible that הבל originated as a comparative gloss on סמל "image" in v 5: in Jer 2:5 הבל follows רחקו מעלי "they have departed from me." If so, the note slipped down because of the similarity of vv 6 and 9 and was taken as a correction of the similar-looking (ה)כל.

10.b. The MT has a longer text, "every representation of reptile and animal [תבנית רמש ובהמה], detestable thing." The intervening phrase is not present in the LXX*; its awkward position seems to demonstrate its secondary character. It probably originated in an exegetically correct annotation that cited Deut 4:17–18 in a list of prohibited images. Perhaps the annotator also had in mind Lev 11 and envisioned the artistic representations as consisting of ritually unclean creatures (שֶׁקֶץ). Ackerman (*Under Every Green Tree* 43 n. 224) has proposed that here unclean food is in view, eaten at a *marzēaḥ*, a West Semitic religious feast. The switch from sg שֶׁקֶץ "that which is detestable" to pl גלולי "idols" could support this proposal.

10.c. Heb. מחקה is better taken not as a pual ptcp but as a noun, "engraved work," here used predicatively (Ehrlich, *Randglossen* 5:26; Zimmerli 219, with reference to 23:14; 1 Kgs 6:35).

11.a. The syntactical awkwardness of the Heb. expression, which the LXX* tidied (cf. Zimmerli 220) is doubtless original: "the sentence may just be poorly written" (Allen in Brownlee 127).

11.b. It is possible that ענן "cloud" is a gloss on the *hapax legomenon* עתר "perfumed smoke" (Bertholet [1897] 48; et al.): cf. its use relating to incense in Lev 16:13. The LXX* renders with only one term; however, the pair may deliberately have been translated thus.

12.a. The LXX* (cf. Syr Vg) seems to have rendered איש בחדרי משכיתו בחשך "in the dark, each one in the rooms of his image" as "each one of them in their secret bedroom." "Bedroom" implies חדר משכב, which the Tg also reflects. So the ancient versions attest an exegetical tradition, which may have arisen from relating משכית to מסכה "bed covering" (Isa 28:20). Scholars have endlessly copied each other in stating that the LXX* lacks an equivalent for בחשך "in the dark." However, κρύπτω reflects חשך "darkness": cf. κρύπτειν "hide" for the verb מחשיך "make dark" in Job 38:2 LXX and the sense of secrecy for מחשך "dark place" in Isa 29:15. For the change in word order, see in principle G. Marquis, *Textus* 13 (1986) 59–84. The pl חדרי "rooms," in place of sg, is due to the ambiguity of אִישׁ "each, every": see Greenberg 170. The term seems to have the sense of a small chapel or recess. The notion that the cult "took place also in individual homes" (Zimmerli 242) is not a natural interpretation of the text (cf. Hitzig 61).

12.b. Lit. "because."

12.c. The MT adds אתנו "us," which is lacking in the parallel 9:9, where the present claims are expressly quoted (cf. Ps 94:7), and is not represented in the LXX*.

14.a. For הנשים "the women" it is sometimes urged that נשים be read, but idiomatically the article can be used thus (GKC 126q; Joüon 137n).

16.a. For the acc of place, see Cooke 103; Joüon 126h. Contrast 11:1.

16.b. The LXX* has "twenty," which may better suit כ "about," as a round number. However, Greenberg (172) has observed that twenty-five is a favorite number of Ezekiel's.

16.c. An incomprehensible משתחויתם oddly appears in place of the expected משתחוים "worshiping," which sixteen MSS read (Cornill 226). "A marginal note והשתחויתם 'and you worship' may have been written as a catchword for worship of other gods, alluding to such texts as Deut 11:16; Josh 23:16" (Allen in Brownlee 127). Then it was combined with the standard text. Or was the contaminating factor a comment משחתים "about to be destroyed," inspired by their fate in 9:6 and by the term משחית "destroying" that runs through chap. 9? The MT adds קדמה "to the east," which the LXX* does not reflect. It seems unnecessarily repetitious and may have been a vertical dittograph, assuming a fifteen-letter line.

17.a. Usually the Heb. construction with מן is regarded as logically redundant (see GKC 67t; Cooke 103; Joüon 141i). However, both here and in Isa 49:6 it may be explained in terms of time, with the sense "after." That which is ironically regarded as trifling is not the previous three cultic offenses but the community's separate social ills. These ills are introduced by כי "that," and mention of them reverts to 7:23 (and also anticipates 9:9). The present, fourth cultic sin is regarded as worse than the three earlier ones and the social sin. The deletion of כי . . . חמס "that they have filled the country with violence," proposed by Gunkel (*Schöpfung* 142 n.), has won some scholarly support, but there is no textual support for it.

17.b. The LXX* has no counterpart for this clause, but it fits well in leading up to the sin of sins (Cooke 100). The first verb וישבו "and they have gone further" echoes תשוב "you will go further" in v 15b. The following verb has a structural role in the context (see the *Comment*).

17.c. In the Masoretic tradition, אפם "their nose(s)" (see *Note* 9:1.d.) is regarded as one of the *tiqqune sopherim*, deliberate scribal corrections intended to remove objectionable expressions referring to God, as a replacement for אפי "my nose." McKane ("Observations" 71–75) has accepted this tradition. However, the ancient versions know nothing of this interpretation. The LXX "like those turning up noses, sneering" implies the MT, as does the Tg "bringing shame in front of them." Accordingly, the tradition appears to have originated remarkably late. It seems to have developed from particular interpretations of זמורה "(pruned) branch." See McCarthy's discussion (*Tiqqune Sopherim* 91–97) and the *Comment*.

18.a. The LXX* leaves v 18b unrepresented, and it is often taken as having originated in a repetition of 9:1. On the other hand, it could easily have been lost by homoeoarcton (Greenberg 175). It functions as a literary hinge between sections: cf. Ezra 3:13 (cf. D. J. Clines, *Ezra, Nehemiah, Esther* [Grand Rapids: Eerdmans, 1984] 71).

9:1.a. Heb. קרבו is capable of three interpretations. In the context, it is best taken as qal impv, "come here" (= "come," NAB; "draw near," NRSV), with an unusual vocalization (Ehrlich, *Randglossen* 5:27; et al., with reference to Ps 69:19): cf. GKC 46d; Joüon 44c. It is no objection to this understanding that a third person reference occurs in v 1b: it is idiomatic with אישׁ "each one" in second person contexts, whether future (Amos 4:3) or imperatival (1 Sam 25:13; Zech 7:10; 8:17; cf. Joüon 147d). The form could alternatively be piel impv, "bring here" (NIV), with an indefinite subj referring to unseen attendants, which Greenberg (175), among others, prefers. A third possibility is to take as qal pf, "(they) have come" (= "Here they come," REB), for which Cornill (226) and others have opted: this has in its favor the support of LXX Vg but little else. The ancient versions probably missed the idiomatic nature of v 1b.

1.b. Heb. פקדה in the pl elsewhere has the concrete sense of "overseers, persons in charge." Such a personal sense is presupposed by v 1b (Hitzig 65). The LXX rendered "punishment," and there may indeed be ambiguity in the term: cf. the rendering "executioners" offered by Cooke (103) and Greenberg (174). In the translation above, "fate" is an endeavor to exploit this feature. To take the term as an intensive pl ("punishment," Fohrer *ZAW* 63 [1951] 38) or as hinting at the plurality of the executioners (Zimmerli 223, who renders "the woes of punishment") would each be a less likely option.

1.c. Lit. "his": see *Note* 1.a. above.

1.d. The idiomatic sg is to be rendered pl. "Such words as *hand, head* . . . , where the organ or thing is common to a number of persons, are generally used in the singular" (A. B. Davidson, *Hebrew Syntax* [Edinburgh: Clark, 1896] 17 remark 4). V 1b is often taken as secondary, a variant of the clause at the end of v 2aa (Cornill 226–27; et al.), but it has a firm place both in the textual tradition and in the structure of chap. 9, in which משׁח(י)ת "destruction, destroying" plays a major role.

2.a. Heb. מפנה אשׁר "which is oriented" is a strange construction. Usually in Ezekiel either אשׁר פניו "whose face" or הפנה "which faces" (cf. 8:3) is found.

2.b. For the idiomatic lack of article, cf. 2 Chr 23:20 and see GKC 126w.

2.c. The pass ptcp is here and in v 3 continued with an acc as a retention of a second acc, but in v 11 with a genitive: see GKC 116k, 121d.

2.d. Heb. קסת is a loanword from Egy. *gsty* "scribe's palette": see T. O. Lambdin, *JAOS* 73 (1953) 154. LXX ζώνη "belt" is a rendering that has hitherto baffled scholars: it is evidently the result of confusion with כסת "band" (cf. 13:18, 20).

3.a. The sg כרוב "cherub" here appears to refer to a single, comprehensive entity, like the sg גלגל "wheel structure" in 10:2, etc. The usage seems to reflect differentiation in meaning from the pl forms elsewhere in the account: see the *Comment*.

3.b. The preposition is used in a pregnant sense; see GKC 119ee.

3.c. See *HALAT* 588b. Zimmerli (224, 226, 251) followed KB 553a in rendering "podium" but later abandoned this meaning, in *Ezekiel 2* 490. Keel (*Jahwe-Visionen* 129 n. 4) observed that it would be difficult to jump over a podium (Zeph 1:9; cf. 1 Sam 5:4–5).

4.a. The LXX* omitted the divine name, doubtless regarding it as otiose in the context. Greenberg (176) has found an interesting parallel in Lev 1:1: after a reference to the glory of Yahweh (in Exod 40:35, interrupted by vv 36–38), the divine subj is specified not with the next verb but with the one following. This gradual identification prevented an understanding of these two figures in terms of contrast. R. Rendtorff (*Leviticus* [Neukirchen-Vluyn: Neukirchener Verlag, 1985] 22) has drawn attention to a further example of this phenomenon in Exod 24:16 + 25:1. Ohnesorge (*Jahwe gestaltet* 284 n. 4) has correctly noted the general rule that Yahweh is not specified as subj in the vision narratives, but this instance should be retained as a special case.

4.b. For the defective writing in K, see *Notes* 33:13.b.; 40:6.b.

4.c. Lit. "through the city, through Jerusalem." The LXX* lacks the first phrase, but העיר "the city" is a key term in the account. The phrase may have been lost by parablepsis (Wevers 85). The second phrase is often regarded as an explanatory gloss (Cornill 227; et al.), in which case the gloss displaced the original phrase in the LXX, while the MT exhibits a conflated text.

4.d. The pair of verbs is alliterative, אנה and אנק (cf. 6:14 and *Note* 6:14.a.).

5.a. K על "upon" is a slip for Q אל "not," a mechanical copy of the two cases in v 4b.

5.b. Q "your eye" observes the ruling mentioned in *Note* 1.d. above.

6.a. The MT בחור "young men" requires before it the copula, which may have fallen out by pseudohaplography (cf. Zimmerli 225).

6.b. The MT adds in apposition הזקנים "the elders," wrongly identifying with the group in 8:11–12 instead of that in 8:16. The LXX*, here represented by LXX[106], lacks it; LXX[B] betrays hexaplaric influence (Ziegler, *LXX* 19, 40–41). This explanatory gloss was evidently triggered by זקן "the old" in v 6a. At the end of the verse, the LXX has "inside in the house," in place of "in front of the house." Evidently its *Vorlage* had not לפני חהבית but לביח לפנימה (Hitzig 67). Underlying this strange reading, which corresponds to nothing in chap. 8, was probably something like בפנימת הבית "in the inner (court) of the temple area," which harks back to 8:16. This may well have been a (correct) explanatory gloss that displaced the reading that now appears in the MT.

7.a. The LXX "the streets" (=החוצות) for החצרות "the courts" is an error inspired by 11:6 (Cooke 110). Perhaps what was intended as a comparative gloss displaced the correct text.

7.b. The MT צאו ויצאו והכו "Go out, and they will go out and kill" (or, with weak *waw* ". . . and they went out and killed") cannot be right. The LXX (cf. the Syr) implies צאו והכו "go out and kill," which is required. Since Wellhausen (in Smend 57), ויצאו has been explained as originating in a dittograph of צאו. "MT follows the pattern of v 6b in adding narrative fulfillment to a command, but (a) the normal *waw* consec construction is not employed and (b) והכו has no corresponding element in the command" (Allen in Brownlee 141). Greenberg (178) has observed that the MT violates the unity of place maintained in the vision.

8.a. The MT exhibits a mixed form ונאשאר. Q[Or] and many MSS attest ונשאר "and left," a niph ptcp, which fits the following אני "I" in a circumstantial clause (Hitzig 68). This was combined with another, inferior, reading: ואשאר "and I was left." The main clause begins in v 8b, while v 8a sets the scene for it. The alternative text made the main clause begin with v 8aβ, probably under the influence of the string of first person consec verbs in v 8b. The LXX* omits v 8aβ: perhaps its *Vorlage* or a predecessor of it already had the reading ואשאר and the clause was overlooked by homoeoarcton.

8.b. For the standard presence of אדני "Lord" in this exclamatory protest, see *Note* 4:14.a.

8.c. The LXX* does not represent כל "all." "However, the exaggeration belongs to the fervour of the plea" (Cooke 108; cf. Kraetzschmar 103). It seems to correspond to כלה "complete end" in the parallel 11:13.

9.a. The supplementing of בית ישראל "the community of Israel" with ויהודה "and Judah" makes an ill match. The former is a comprehensive term for God's people, used in 8:6, 10–12, and must have the same significance as "Israel" in 9:8. In 8:17 the political term "community of Judah" has been used. The addition seems to reflect an early desire to draw attention to this reference (Zimmerli, *VT* 8 [1958] 82; cf. Kraetzschmar 103; Herrmann 54), encouraged by the resumption of 8:17bα in 9:9aβ. It is already attested in the LXX.

9.b. The LXX adds "and uncleanness," which represents an incorporated variant טמאה (cf. Cornill 229) for משה "injustice," via a metathesized טמה (Hitzig 68). The variant reflects Jerusalem's "uncleanness" in 22:15; 24:13. Within the Masoretic tradition, there is a variant חמס "violence" (see *BHK*), inspired by 7:23 (cf. 8:17). Cornill insisted that the first term in the LXX, ἀδικίας "injustice," represented חמס, but the latter is rendered ἀνομία in 7:23; 8:17 and ἀδικία only in 45:9, perhaps by the same translator.

10.a. The pf is performative: see *Note* 3:8.a.

11.a. In place of K כאשר "as," which the ancient versions attest, Q ככל אשר "according to all that" intends to make the expression more comprehensive and represents an assimilation to the longer version of this formulation: cf. especially Deut 26:14. "K . . . aligns with 12:7; 24:18; 37:7, 10. Q . . . does not occur in the book" (Allen in Brownlee 141).

10:1.a. For the use of אל in the sense of על, here with the sense "above" (cf. 1:26), see *Note* 2:6.d.

1.b. The MT prefaces with כמראה "like the appearance of," which has no counterpart in the LXX*. It doubtless originated as a comparative gloss on כ(אבן) "like (stone)," noting that the basic 1:26 had כמראה אבן "like the appearance of stone" instead of כאבן. The gloss, after the sense of its purpose was lost, was incorporated into the text at a syntactically feasible point.

1.c. The MT adds נראה "appeared, was seen," which has no counterpart in LXX* Syr. It seems to have been a reader's comment on the platform's being over the heads of the cherubim, to the effect that such had been seen by Ezekiel earlier, viz. in 1:22. The reading turns up in 1:22, in the corrupted form הנורא "terrible" (see *Note* 1:22.a.); its parallel placing gives a clue to its original meaning, or at least perceived meaning. One might more naturally have related the gloss to the throne of 1:26a, as a case of déjà vu. If the MT in 1:22 reflects the original meaning of the gloss, it properly belonged before על־ראש "(which) was seen (over the heads)," but was inserted instead before עליהם "above them." If the evidence of 1:22 reflects a mistaken perception, that perception was the mistaking of נראה עליהם "it was seen above them" as a reference to the platform rather than to the throne, and the mistake was caused by equating על "above (them)" and על־ראש "over the heads." In the MT the accentuation suggests that Yahweh was understood to be the subj (so Keil 133, 135; cf. Becker, "Ez 8–11" 146 n. 42).

2.a. The LXX* does not represent ויאמר "and he said." It is easier to explain this as omission of a redundant item than to account for its insertion. Zimmerli (226) attributes it to the secondary editing of chap. 10, which one would take to mean that the divine command is redactional. However, in both his sections on form and on exegesis (234, 250), he regards the command as substantially original but with reference to the ark in the temple rather than to the celestial conveyance: in v 2 only the phrase מבינות לכרובים "from between the cherubim" is secondary (254). Greenberg (180) plausibly accounts for ויאמר as a means of slowing the narrative and thus lending it solemnity; he gives other examples of this phenomenon.

2.b. The sg גלגל here refers collectively to the wheel structure or set of wheels; one may compare the collective usage in 23:24; 26:10, with reference to war chariots. Cf. כרוב "cherubim-structure" in 9:3; 10:4.

2.c. The MT is at first sight a further instance of the phenomenon just mentioned. However, in chaps. 8–11 the text seems to distinguish quite strictly in semantic terms between the collective sg form and the pl form (see the *Comment*). Accordingly, there is much to be said for reading a pl כרובים, as later in the verse, by assumption of pseudohaplography of יכ before ום, as many scholars since Hitzig (69), including Greenberg (181), have done. The pl forms later in the verse and those in the narrative fulfillment of the command at v 7 provide internal support for this change. An appeal to the LXX *(BHS)* is of little value, since it has harmonistic pl forms in 9:3; 10:4, where the MT has sg forms.

3.a. The MT בבאו האיש is a case of a pronoun with a noun in apposition: "when he—the man—went in." This is a construction not uncommon in later Heb. and in Aram. (Joüon 146e; Rooker, *Biblical Hebrew* 91–92). However, Zimmerli (226) has noted a pattern of metathesis of ו and א with this verb, and this instance is doubtless to be so explained. Alternatively, האיש "the man" was a gloss intended to clarify the suffix (Herrmann 54; Dijkstra, "Glosses" 67–68).

4.a. In the light of 9:3, על is used in the sense of אל "to": see *Note* 1:17.c. As in 9:3, the preposition is used in a pregnant sense, "and (moved) to" (Cooke 119).

6.a. Ehrlich (*Randglossen* 5:31) noted that the inf is continued with finite verbs and the main clause is in v 7. Rather, it begins with the second verb in v 6b.

7.a. Heb. וישלח has an indefinite subj: "and one extended." The following מבינות here seems to include a partitive sense "(one) from among," "(one) of a group": cf. the partitive use of מן "from" (cf. BDB 580b, which with reference to the subj cites Lev 25:33; Dan 11:5) and the sense "among" for בתוך and "from among" for מתוך with reference to a group of persons (BDB 1063b) and likewise for בקרב and מקרב (BDB 899a). It can hardly bear a sense of direction toward the cherubim, for which one would expect אל־בינות, as in v 2. The MT הכרוב "the cherub," idiomatically used for "a cherub" (Becker, "Ez 8–11" 147 n. 44, with reference to GKC 126q–s; Joüon 137m–n), has no counterpart in the LXX*. It appears to be a clarifying, exegetically correct gloss: the rest of the verse shows that the man is not the subj, and the content of v 8 indicates an understanding in terms of a cherub's hand. The LXX* does not represent מבינות לכרובים "from among the cherubim." Zimmerli (226–27) observed that the omission of "the cherub" makes the LXX "unintelligible": it reads first as if the man were the subj and then treats him as object of the activity. While one does not need "the cherub," the accompanying prepositional phrase is required. Did an original ἐκ μέσου τῶν χερουβιν "from the midst of the cherubim" (vv 2, 6) fall out by homoeoarcton before εἰς μέσον (ἐκ/εἰς)? Then the scholarly deduction from the LXX* text concerning the secondary nature of v 7αβγ (Hitzig 70–71; et al.; cf. *BHS*) loses its basis.

7.b. Zimmerli (226), following Herrmann (54), urged that the minority reading לכרובים be read for הכרובים "the cherubim." However, Ehrlich (*Randglossen* 5:31) correctly observed that the *lamed* only appears with compound prepositions such as מבינות "from between" and not with simple ones such as בינות "between" here.

7.c. In differentiation from the cherub's "hand" (יד) in vv 7aα, 8, here כפן "hollow of the hand" is used.

8.a. LXX Syr render "and I saw," reflecting assimilation to the verb at the beginning of v 9.

8.b. Heb. יד "hand" seems to be used collectively. The LXX renders pl, probably reflecting ידי "hands" (= v 21) in its *Vorlage*. In 1:8 a sg appears in the LXX and a pl in the MT. For the rendering "arms and hands," see *Note* 1:8.a.

9.a. The Heb. repetition has a distributive force: see GKC 134l, q. The single rendering in LXX* Syr is the result of haplography (Wevers 89).

10.a. Heb. וּמַרְאֵהֶם is a *casus pendens*, "and as for their appearance" (Cooke 120).

10.b. For the masc אֶחָד "one," as in 1:16, see *Note* 1:6.c.

11.a. In v 11a, although in the LXX the cherubim (αὐτά "they") are twice the subj, the wheels must be in view. Both the preceding context and the evidently parallel 1:17 so indicate. The fact that v 11b does not depend on the wheel description in chap. 1 makes a different subj possible. V 12, especially the differentiating "and the wheels," implies that the cherubim are now in view. Then הָרֹאשׁ must mean not the front wheel (Keil 139; Eichrodt 109; *HALAT* 1088a) but either the head of the (leading) cherub ('A; Jahn 62; Zimmerli 127 [on p. 227 "front wheel" seems to be a mistranslation of *das vordeste*]; Greenberg 181) or actually the leading cherub (Σ; Kraetzschmar 110; Fohrer 57). Of the latter alternatives, which yield a similar overall meaning, the first seems to be the better in the light of the sequel. The directional locking of the wheels (v 11a) is grounded in a parallel locking of the cherubim. The reference in v 12a to the physical parts of the cherubim seems to be connected with the prior mention of רֹאשׁ in the sense of "head." Then the subj of the main verbs in v 11b is the other heads, which as they moved still looked respectively to the right or left or the reverse of the direction of travel. This static posture is then applied to the rest of their bodies. Vogt (*Untersuchungen* 70) has followed GB 645b in taking אַחֲרָיו "after it" with the relative clause, rather than with the following verb: it then supplies a resumptive pronoun for the antecedent הַמָּקוֹם "the place," with reference to the directional aim. Perhaps it should be pointed as an explicit subj אֲחֵרָיו "the others [= heads] in relation to it." The reading הָרֹאשׁ הָאֶחָד "the first head," implied by the LXX (see *BHS*), clearly needs more explanation than a ר/ד error. It surely arose as an explanatory comment on הָאֶחָד (פְּנֵי) "(the face of) the first" in v 14. The comment observed, in line with the corrupted MT, that the faces were not features of an individual cherub's single head but belonged to separate heads. The marginal comment was understandably taken as a correction for the very similar-looking הָרֹאשׁ אַחֲרָיו a little higher up and displaced it. For this type of textual development, see *Note* 2:6.a. This explanation raises a problem: v 14 is not extant in the LXX*, but a comment on it is. This phenomenon is to be explained by the fact that the LXX of Ezekiel at times attests a post-Masoretic texttype: in the history of its *Vorlage*, v 14 once stood but was subsequently deleted, perhaps after comparison with another, more highly regarded examplar, but conceivably simply because in its corrupted form it contradicted 1:10.

12.a. The MT וְכָל בְּשָׂרָם "and all their bodies" is not represented in the LXX*, which may indicate that it originated in a (correct) exegetical gloss. The final four words of v 11 are to be understood in v 12a. In v 12b the switch from suffixes to article is a clue to a syntactical change.

12.b. The MT adds an unconnected אוֹפַנֵּיהֶם "their wheels," which Kraetzschmar (111), followed by Ehrlich (*Randglossen* 5:32) and Greenberg (179), plausibly traced to a variant of הָאוֹפַנִּים "the wheels" at the head of v 12b, which has been incorporated into the text. The LXX* seems to attest the term, so that it must have been an early gloss. The suffixed form was presumably the result of assimilation to the three preceding nouns in v 12a. It may well reflect an understanding of the cherubim's bodies as covered with eyes, as well as the wheels, in line with the verse division in the MT. However, comparison with 1:18 suggests that only the wheels had eyes (Torrey, *JBL* 58 [1939] 71–73).

13.a. The REB has misunderstood v 13. The MT adds v 14, "'Each had four faces': the face of the first was a cherub's face, and the face of the second a human face, and the third a lion's face and the fourth an eagle's face." This material is on the borderline between the concerns of text criticism and of redaction criticism. It seems to make use of cue words, "each had four faces," a sign of a textual gloss, yet a redactional feature in 1:2. The cue words could be a citation of 1:6a and belong with the echoes of chap. 1 already encountered in chap. 10; or they could be a citation of 10:21aα and so a gloss incorporated into the text at a different place, before the interpretive comment of v 15b, rather than after its occurrence in v 20a. The presence of v 14 is to be regarded as a textual issue. There is at this point a break in the parallel treatment of chap. 1: vv 9–12 refer back consecutively to 1:15–18, while vv 16–17 deal equally consecutively with 1:19–21. Yet v 14 harks back to 1:6a and also to 1:10. While this inconsistency could be interpreted in terms of a further redactional layer, its association with the glosses represented in v 15 suggests that it originated in a late gloss. One might also adduce the omission of v 14 in the LXX*, but at an earlier stage in its *Vorlage*, v 14 does seem to have been present, before it was discarded (see *Note* 11.a.). The content of v 14 appears confused: v 14bβγ, like 1:10, envisions four faces for each cherub, in line with the cue words, yet v 14bα strangely speaks in terms of each of the four cherubim having one, unique face. If v 14 is a textual gloss, one expects greater conformity with 1:10 and must conclude that subsequent corruption is to blame (Ehrlich, *Randglossen* 5:32). Harmony with both 1:10 and v 14a dictates for v 14bα an original הָאֶחָד פְּנֵי שׁוֹר וְהַשֵּׁנִי פְּנֵי אָדָם

"the first the face of an ox and the second the face of a man." It is feasible to take the first פְּנֵי "the face of" in the MT as the uncorrected result of a copyist's eye jumping from לְאָחָד "to each" to הָאָחָד "the first." Then וּפְנֵי "and the face of" in the second clause came in as a false harmonization with the corrupted start of the first clause. As for פְּנֵי הַכְּרוּב "the face of the cherub," the unique presence of the article with a genitive noun of an animate type betrays its alien nature. It may well have originated in a subsequent gloss on פְּנֵי הָאָחָד "the face of the first" (Ehrlich, *Randglossen* 5:32), which later still displaced the basic פְּנֵי שׁוֹר "the face of an ox." Whereas 1:10 lists the faces directionally, this annotation takes its cue from the "four" of 10:21 (and 1:6) and lists them numerically. In contrast to the southern orientation of 1:10, the numbering of the faces seems to represent a westerly orientation. The Syr interestingly lacks the first פְּנֵי "the face of" and וּפְנֵי "and the face of," but its clause "one (face) was the face of a cherub" discloses that its text is not pre-Masoretic but post-Masoretic, the result of a later partial attempt to harmonize with 1:10. It is just possible that the MT was intended to signify "the first face . . . the second face," as the Vg interpreted (cf. Becker, "Ez 8–11" 148 and n. 46, with reference to GKC 134o–p; Joüon 138b, 142o).

13.b. The MT also adds v 15 "and the cherubim rose; they were the living creatures I had seen at the Kebar Canal." It is present in the LXX*, but Greenberg (183) speaks for most scholars in describing it as an "awkward anticipation of vss. 19a, 20a below; apparently fragments copied in at the wrong place." Kraetzschmar (112) observed that the past consecutive verb in v 15a does not fit the descriptive nature of the context. This amalgamation of separate glosses into a continuous format within the text is no stranger to the MT of Ezekiel: see my note in *ZAW* 102 (1990) 408–13. Vv 14–15 appear to be a cluster of annotations that relate to vv 19a, 20a, 21a. V 14, an elaboration of v 21a, was wrongly attached to the echoing of v 20a in v 15a, as I suggested above. V 15b had earlier become attached to הַכְּרוּבִים "the cherubim" in v 15a, having floated from its marginal mooring near כְּרוּבִים "cherubim" in v 20. So the gloss of v 15a joined the text first, presumably from the margin, where it functioned as a comment on לְרוּם מֵעַל הָאָרֶץ "to rise from the ground" in v 16; the comment compared v 19a, where their capability was put into practice. As to the origin of the second gloss, it is best understood as a variant reading. It seems to scrupulously delete the bare phrase תַּחַת אֱלֹהֵי־יִשְׂרָאֵל "under the God of Israel." It is significant that in v 22 after רָאִיתִי "I saw" the LXX* adds "under the glory of the God of Israel," which doubtless originated as a more seemly variant of the phrase in v 20: the Tg renders in this very way in v 20. Thus there is evidence of two expedients to render the text in a more seemly way, to expand (LXX*, Tg) or to delete (MT, in v 15b) the divine reference.

16.a. Heb. יָסֹב has been used earlier in the sense of changing direction, in v 11a (= 1:17) with reference to the restricted mobility of the wheels while moving on the ground (cf. 1:15, 19). In 10:11b, however, independently of chap. 1, it seems to refer to the similarly limited directional range of the cherubim in flight. Here it relates differently to the wheels, while the celestial conveyance was in flight. In chap. 1 the two means of mobility, the wheels and the living creatures (via their wings), are not mechanically linked, and theoretically the wheels might have fallen off or pursued an independent course. But no, affirms the present passage, they were locked into the same flight path by the controlling "spirit" of v 17. It seems to be implied here that the wheels rotated even in the air, which may have been deduced from 3:13. One may compare the representation of flying horses, reindeer, bicycles, and vehicles in films: legs and wheels move as if on the ground.

16.b. Lit. "from beside them." The verb יָסֹב "change direction" is used in a different context than that of v 11, as we observed above. The Vg *residebant* "did (not) remain behind" may imply יָשְׁבוּ "did (not) stay (behind)," which was adopted by Cornill (229). However, like Σ, οὐκ ἀπελείποντο "were not left behind," it seems to be a rough paraphrase of the MT. Cf. the NJPS "did not roll away from their side." The LXX* does not represent גַּם־הֵם מֵאֶצְלָם "even they from their side," possibly because the translator could not perceive the novel relationship between the prepositional phrase and the verb. However, in v 16a the LXX* has καὶ αὐτοὶ ἐχόμενοι αὐτῶν "they too beside them," which clearly stands for (or אֶצְלָם) גַּם־הֵם מֵאֶצְלָם and fits well there. Cooke (117) considered the phrase here in v 16bβ an accidental repetition of the one in v 16a, which has been shortened in the MT. Then מֵאֶצְל has a locative sense, as in 40:7. While this proposal fits v 16a, it leaves v 16b too skimpy. If the mention of the wheels' changing direction is correct, it does require its present qualification in this new setting. For the expression in v 16b, cf. וַיִּסֹב מֵאֶצְלוֹ "and he turned away from him" in 1 Sam 17:30. There is a possible clue that the LXX* once contained the material now missing from v 16bβ. For "the wheels" it unnecessarily has "their wheels," which raises the suspicion that αὐτῶν "them" is a relic of a rendering for מֵאֶצְלָם "from beside them," lost within the Gr. tradition. In that case the *Vorlage* read גַּם־הֵם מֵאֶצְלָם twice, in the first case by assimilation to v 16bβ triggered by the double preceding הָאוֹפַנִּים "the wheels."

17.a. While the stem רום "be high" is used for most conjugations, it is replaced by רמם in the niph.

17.b. See 1:21–22 and *Note* 1:21.b.

18.a. The MT has a longer text, מעל מפתן הבית "from upon the threshold of the temple," while the LXX* implies simply מהבית "from the temple," which scholars prefer. Greenberg (183), following Cornill (234), has observed that the verb יצא "go out" leads one to expect מן "from," while מעל "from upon" would be more natural with רום "rise," as in v 4. The MT reflects an exegetical gloss based on v 4 or a comparative note.

19.a. The MT, reflecting the general textual tradition, places this last phrase at the end of the verse. Comparison with 11:22 suggests that it belongs here. In its position in the MT, it reads very strangely: one cannot credit even a redactor with putting it there. Evidently, at an early stage a line of twenty-five letters was accidentally dropped (see *Note* 1:20.b.), and it was replaced in an incorrect position. V 20 harks back to the first sentence of v 19, just as v 8 comments on v 7a: the narrative is allowed to reach a natural resting place before commentary is added. But this delay caused the error to go undetected: v 20 flows naturally from the misplaced v 19bβ.

19.b. LXX Syr have a pl verb, as a logical consequence of the error discussed in the previous *Note*, which removed the antecedent of the sg verb. The parallelism of v 18b and 11:23b supports the MT.

20.a. Here and in v 22 the demonstrative pronoun is attracted into the number of the predicate (Cooke 120–21).

21.a. The MT repeats ארבעה "four," as if distributive, but a longer formulation would then be required (cf. v 9 and Cooke 120–21); besides, one expects then a comparable idiom in the next clause (Zimmerli 228). The proto-Masoretic 4QEzekᵃ seems to have contained the repetition (Lust, "Ezekiel MSS in Qumran" 97; Sinclair, *RevQ* 14 [1989] 104). But the cue phrase in v 14a and the text of LXX* Vg here lack the repetition, which is simply a dittograph. However, the LXX* betrays an awareness of the longer text in the history of its *Vorlage*: in the next clause it has "eight" in place of "four." Evidently, a marginal ארבעה ארבעה "four four," a Masoretic type of variant, was taken as a correction of the wrong numeral (cf. Kraetzschmar 114); the Gr. translator added up the numerical pair.

22.a. The LXX* does not represent מראהם "their semblance," but the text can hardly exist without it (see the next *Note*). The translator may have left it untranslated as a cognate acc. My earlier explanation of it as a gloss from 1:13 (in Brownlee 148) founders on its topical dissimilarity.

22.b. Lit. "and themselves," best regarded as a second object of the previous verb (Cooke 121; Blau, *VT* 4 [1954] 12). This is simply a case of poorly written Hebrew. It is methodologically wrong to reconstruct the LXX καὶ αὐτά "and them" (with reference to the cherubim) as והם(ה) (Cornill 234; et al.). The LXX clearly reflects the same text as the MT, and there is no graphical relationship between it and the presumed original (cf. Bertholet [1987] 60; Barthélemy, *Critique* 3:62). Driver (*Bib* 35 [1954] 150; cf. Rooker, *Biblical Hebrew* 88–90) regarded אותם as the subj of the following verb, appealing to Mishnaic usage, but he seems to have abandoned this notion later: it is not reflected in the NEB. Whether or not את can at times express an emphatic nominative, it does not seem to do so here, contrary to my earlier opinion in Brownlee (148).

11:1.a. The repetition is firmly established in the textual tradition. Ehrlich (*Randglossen* 5:34) and others have deleted as a gloss, and Talmon (*Textus* 1 [1960] 172) found conflation here, but "Hebrew writers do repeat themselves" (Wevers 93).

1.b. The LXX "about twenty-five" may reflect an exegetical identification with the group in 8:16. If so, this equation reflects a different layer of tradition than the LXX* text in 8:16, which has instead "about twenty."

3.a. See the *Comment*.

5.a. Usually the messenger formula includes the title אדני "Lord," as in v 7 (see *Note* 2:4.c.). There is a parallel in 21:8(3).

5.b. The MT ידעתי(ה) "(I know) it" is a sg suffix resuming the pl antecedent, a permissible Heb. construction (see GKC 135p; Joüon 149a). However, dittography of *he* may have occurred (Cornill 236, noting, perhaps unfairly, the non-representation in LXX Vg).

6.a. The pf with weak *waw* is used when "the second verb merely repeats the idea of the first, being synonymous or in some way parallel with it" (Davidson, *Hebrew Syntax* 58[a]).

7.a. The MT הוצאי is generally taken as an error for the widely attested (see *BHS*) אוציא "I will take out." A copyist's eye may have slipped to (ו)הוצא(תי) "(and I will) take out" in v 9, which is set in a similar context, and made an inadvertent error. Keil (147) accepted the MT as a pf with an indefinite subj (cf. Greenberg 185).

8.a. For the formulaic use of אדני "Lord" in a divine-saying formula, see *Note* 5:11.a.

11.a. Heb. לא "not" does double duty: its force extends to v 11aβ. Cf. GKC 152z; Joüon 160q.

12.a. The omission of vv 11–12a in LXX^B seems to be merely due to homoeoteleuton (Ziegler, *LXX* 129; Wevers 95): cf. the comparable loss of 33:25aβ–27a.

12.b. The MT adds "by whose rules you have not walked and whose standards you have not met, but you have acted in accord with the standards of the nations around you," which has no counterpart in the LXX*. It seems to be a later comment borrowed from 5:7, except that there a negative statement appears in the last clause. Greenberg (188) has made the form-critical observation that only here is a recognition formula supplemented with material relating to Israel's sin, rather than to divine activity. The relevance of the comment at this point is not immediately clear. It functions as a general accusation and as justification for the judgment. It must have been triggered by the recurrence of the phrase שפטים עשה שפטים "perform acts of judgment" (v 9b) in 5:8 (see *Note* 5:8.c.: the addition attests a pre-corrupted text there). It also serves as a counterpart to v 20a, which must have encouraged the retention of the comparative note.

13.a. Cf. 9:8 and see the *Note* on 4:14.a.

13.b. The ancient versions understood as a question, by comparison with 9:8. Possibly the MT has suffered loss of an interrogative *he* by haplography (Kraetzschmar 119; et al.). On the other hand, the affirmation may serve as an intensification of 9:8 (cf. Eichrodt 140–41).

13.c. Lit. "(in dealing) with": cf. Jer 5:18 and BDB 478b. Fohrer (59) wrongly construed את as the object sign.

15.a. Lit. "as for . . . , of whom . . ." The extended *casus pendens* is not resolved until the object pronouns of v 16, a phenomenon that bonds the two parts of the oracle with remarkable compactness. Ohnesorge (*Jahwe gestaltet* 59–60) has suggested that אשר "whom" means "because," with reference to Eccl 8:11 (cf. 1 Sam 25:26).

15.b. Heb. אנשי גאלותך "your men of redemption" seemingly has a subjective suffix (Horst, *VT* 3 [1953] 337–38; cf. Brownlee 164). LXX Syr imply אנשי גלותך "your men of exile, fellow exiles (= NRSV)," which has been preferred by some scholars since Ewald (252) and Cornill (237). Ehrlich (*Randglossen* 5:34) observed that for this sense בני "sons" would have been used: cf. בני גולה "exiles" in Ezra 4:1, etc. The ensuing context develops the motif of possession of land, to which the term in the MT alludes: see the *Comment.*

15.c. For this phrase, cf. 20:40 and the redactional 36:10.

15.d. The ancient versions agree with the MT's pointing as an impv, which thus reflects a common exegetical tradition. However, Hitzig (78) revived the proposal of medieval Jewish commentators to repoint as pf, in line with the parallel clause, and most commentators have followed suit. The evidently resumptive causative pf הרחקתים "I sent them far away" on Yahweh's lips in v 16 affords a further internal argument for so doing.

15.e. Heb. היא is used as an anticipatory pronoun: "it, namely the land" (cf. Joüon 146e). Its absence from the similar 33:24b and non-representation in the LXX* have led Bertholet ([1897] 62) and a few others to query its authenticity. On the other hand, Cornill (237) and others have regarded הארץ "the land" as the intruder: it could be a comparative gloss from 33:24. Perhaps the MT has a conflated text, and the LXX* preserves one of the two variants. It is hardly true that היא by itself has no antecedent (Zimmerli 229–30): originally it could have referred to Jerusalem (Herrmann 57; Eichrodt 111; Ohnesorge, *Jahwe gestaltet* 7), as a parallel to the quotation in v 3. However, the phrase more naturally refers to the land (cf. 36:5; Exod. 6:8), and certainly by the textual stage of v 17b, a reference to the land is presupposed. Brownlee (154), disregarding the Masoretic accentuation, made a separate clause: "This is ours."

16.a. Heb. כי is evidently used with an asseverative sense (Hitzig 78; et al., including Zimmerli 230): cf. Joüon 164b. Joüon 172b here takes as concessive, "although," but "כי alone is not capable of introducing concessions of the real [as distinct from hypothetical] type" (A. Aejmelaeus, *JBL* 105 [1986] 199 n. 18). She has found a causal meaning here, presumably by taking v 16b as a further part of the causal clause in a negative sense, as Ewald (251) and Smend (65) did. It is more likely that v 16b has a positive meaning, and so כי cannot be causal.

16.b. Heb. מעט functions as appositional to מקדש, "a little sanctuary": for the combination, cf. עזר מעט "a little help" in Dan 11:34 (Greenberg 190). BDB 590a and *HALAT* 578a take as adverbial, with a similar qualitative sense.

17.a. The initial *waw* "and" after a messenger formula evidently expresses continuity. It is not infrequent in Ezekiel: cf. 17:22; 25:13; 30:10, 13; 32:3.

17.b. The LXX has third pl pronouns throughout v 17, harmonizing with v 16. In the case of נפצותם "you were scattered," this necessitated construing as נפצתם "I scattered them," from נפץ instead of פוץ. That stem does not occur elsewhere in Ezekiel.

19.a. The MT אחד "one, a single" has no clear rapport with the context. The LXX implies אחר "another," which most scholars since Hitzig (79), including Barthélemy (*Critique* 3:67–69), have adopted (cf. 1 Sam 10:9), via a ר/ד error. It aligns with the change of heart in v 19b. The supposition of an original חדש "new" (attested by Syr Tg; cf. v 19a), distorted into אחד via an intermediate חד (Cornill 238; Zimmerli 230), is too speculative, as Liwak ("Probleme" 130) observed. The MT may have been influenced by Jer 32:39. Barthélemy ("'Un seul'" 329–38) supposes that the original reading was deliberately changed because of the perception of a pejorative connotation.

19.b. The MT, in principle reflecting the general textual tradition, adds "and a new spirit I will put within you." The widely attested reading בקרבם "within them" (cf. *BHS*), although adopted by many scholars, smacks of secondary harmonization. If the criterion is to reconstruct the most likely textual development, the MT is to be explained in terms of a comparative gloss from 36:26 (Levin, *Verheissung* 207 and n. 36; Ohnesorge, *Jahwe gestaltet* 11).

20.a. For the ingressive-factitive sense of the verb, see N. Lohfink, "Beobachtungen" 297 n. 79.

21.a. The MT ואל־לב "but to the heart of," though supported by the LXX*, cannot be original: לב "heart" unnecessarily anticipates לבם "their heart," and some indication of a differentiated group of people is required. Hitzig (79) and others have derived from the Tg a reading (ואחרי) "but after" (cf. 20:16; 33:31; cf. the Vg "and after the heart of"). Sperber (*Bible in Aramaic* 4B:336) has cautioned that, although לב is not represented in the Tg, the Tg renders אל "to" as בתר "after" in 16:26, 28, while Cornill (288–89) observed that the textual development from this supposed original is difficult to explain. Cornill himself reconstructed the text as ואלה אחרי "but as for these (who) after," arguing that לב was put into the text too soon and subsequently אחרי fell out. Ehrlich (*Randglossen* 5:38–39) found this reconstruction too radical. He read ואלה אל־לב, with a wordplay on two senses of לב: "but as for those (whose) heart adheres to the 'heart' or essential meaning (i.e. immoral consequences)." More plausibly Greenberg (191) has emended to ואלה ב(שקוציהם) "but as for those (whose) . . . (walk) in (their loathsome rites)," comparing ב הלך "walk in" (vv 12, 20) and לב "heart" (v 19) as the contextual components that have been reused here. He was implicitly following Kraetzschmar (122; cf. *BHK*). Perhaps after ואלה was abbreviated to ואל (cf. BDB 41a), haplography of *lamed* was assumed, in order to avoid the impossible apparent phenomenon of two adjacent prepositions. For the asyndetic relative clause, cf. Joüon 158a–db.

21.b. For the performative pf see, *Note* 3:8.a.

21.c. For the use of אדני "Lord" in the divine-saying formula, see *Note* 5:11.a.

23.a. Hardly "from the middle of" (NRSV). The temple was adjacent to the eastern wall of the city. Cf. the use of בתוך to mean "inside" as an emphatic variant of ב "in," e.g., in Gen 18:24, 26 (cf. Bertholet [1897] 64). One expects מתוך "from inside": the expression מעל תוך is unique. There is a contrast with the mountain outside the city (Toy 117).

24.a. Lit. "to the Chaldeans": see Joüon 93d. Idiomatically, it means "to Chaldea": see BDB 505a and cf. 16:29; 23:16.

24.b. The form מראה "vision" is used here (twice) and in 43:3, instead of the standard fem form.

24.c. Heb. ברוח אלהים "by means of the spirit of God" can hardly qualify the verb of which רוח "spirit" is subj. It seems rather to qualify the "vision," which virtually has a verbal force, "that which was seen (by means of)." In v 5 רוח יהוה "the spirit of Yahweh" occurs; the present phrase may have been influenced by the standard מראות אלהים "divine visions" (1:1; 8:3; 40:2).

24.d. Lit. "(the vision) went up from upon me." See the *Comment*.

Form/Structure/Setting

The next literary unit, an extended vision account, comprises chaps. 8–11. The framework of the vision is firmly set within Ezekiel's prophetic ministry to the Judean prisoners of war in Babylonia, and there is no good reason to doubt this setting. This framework is chiastic, in 8:1–3 and 11:24–25 (Hossfeld, "Die Tempelvision" 156–57). Hossfeld's scheme is preferable to that of Parunak ("Structural Studies" 209) and that of Greenberg (150). Ezekiel's this-worldly context is described in 8:1a and 11:25 (A, A'). The onset of the vision is marked by the descent of Yahweh's hand in 8:1b, while the "lifting" of the vision is stated in 11:24b (B, B'). The prophet is translated by the spirit, away in 8:3b and back in 11:24a (C, C'). The vision proper is contained within 8:4/5–11:23. The initial divine summons to look at a visionary object in 8:5 accords with the opening of vision accounts in Gen 13:14; Zech 5:5. The vision account is made up of three consecutive dramatic word-visions. These depict dramatic actions taken as portents presaging future events in human experience and contain Yahweh's spoken word as an integral element (Long, *JBL* 95 [1976] 359–60, 362). The visions progress verbally and visually from accusation of Jerusalem's cultic sins in chap. 8 to its punishment in chaps. 9–10, so that they are a visionary version of a two-part oracle of judgment (Zimmerli 235). Parunak's structuring in terms of a *rîb* or lawsuit ("Structural Studies" 208–10) is forced. One may compare a similar phenomenon in the sign-acts earlier in the book: of the two sign-acts described in 4:1–8, one reveals divine punishment for the capital and the other grounds the punishment in accusation of the people of God. The vision account, reported eventually to the elders (11:24), is another visual means of communicating the same overall message.

The account in chap. 8 consists of four scenes of aberrant worship observed in the area of the temple (vv 3–6, 7–13, 14–15, 16–18). The scenes vary in length, occupying in *BHS* six, ten, three, and seven lines, respectively. They are structured on similar lines, with four or five stages (cf. Horst, *VT* 3 [1953] 342–44; Rose, *Ausschliesslichkeitsanspruch* 196–97). (1) The spirit or Yahweh brings Ezekiel to a location (vv 3, 7, 14a, 16aα). (2) In the first two vignettes, the prophet is ordered to observe (vv 5a, 9). (3) There is a description of a particular cultic sin, introduced by הנה "behold" (vv 5b, 10–11, 14b, 16aα–b) and, apart from the first scene, specifying the participants (vv 11, 14b, 16aβ). (4) A divine rhetorical question about the observation, addressing the prophet as בן־אדם "human one," follows (vv 6bα, 12, 15a, 17aα): it functions formally as an accusation (Zimmerli 235, with reference to 1 Kgs 20:13, 28). (5) An announcement of worse sights to come is made (vv 6bβ, 13, 15b); in the last scene this is replaced by a declaration of climactic sin (v 17aβ–b). The final stage serves to link the scenes into a consecutive whole.

The accusatory scenes of chap. 8 are linked with the judgment scenes that follow by Yahweh's declaration of punishment in 8:18. This link is reinforced by five others: (1) the rhetorical echo of 8:18b in 9:1aα; (2) the harking back to the "abominations" of chap. 8 in 9:4; (3) the reference to the worshipers of 8:16–17 in 9:6a; (4) the deliberate repetition of the claim of religious independence (8:12) in 9:9; and (5) in 9:10 the repetition of the final note of merciless judgment in 8:18, so that chaps. 8 and 9 have parallel endings.

Chap. 9 is made up of three parts with alternating halves: (1) vv 1–2aα (A) and v 2aβb (B), (2) vv 3b–4 (B) and vv 5–7 (A), and (3) vv 8–10 (A) and v 11 (B). Each of the three parts begins with a cry or a shout, a divine cry (קרא) in vv 1, 3b and a prophetic shout (זעק) in v 8. The A sections of the three parts deal with destruction: משח(י)ת "destruction, destroying" (vv 1, 6, 8) is the key word that stylistically unites them. The B sections deal with the sparing of lives and are significantly briefer (1½, 3, and 1½ lines, as opposed to 2½, 5, and 5½ lines for the A sections). The key word עיר "city," which occurs in all the A sections (vv 1, 5, 7, 9), emphasizes that the destruction of the residents of Jerusalem is in view; it also appears in one of the B sections, at v 4.

The theme of the judgment of Jerusalem is brought to a close in the course of 10:1–7; again the key term עיר "city" occurs, in v 2. Now another, related topic is interwoven in 10:3 (cf. 9:3) and developed in 10:1, 18a, 19ba; 11:23: the gradual departure of Yahweh's presence from the temple and eventually from the city (עיר, twice in 11:23). The momentum of the narrative is remarkably slowed in chap. 10 by increasingly discursive description. This change of pace will require examination under the rubric of redaction.

A further visionary temple scene appears in 11:1–13, with a fresh introductory note of Ezekiel's translation by the spirit (11:1), paralleling that of 8:3b. The passage is framed by an inclusion with reference to Pelatiah (vv 1, 13). Its main part is a personal oracle to Ezekiel (vv 2–12), which in form is both a disputation and a proof saying. A similar combination of forms occurs in the vision of 37:1–14 (see Allen, *Ezekiel 20–48* 184). Graffy (*A Prophet Confronts* 42–46) has defined the disputation in terms of a quotation (v 3aβb), preparatory remarks (vv 4–6), a first refutation (vv 7–10), and another refutation (vv 11–12). It is better to analyze in line with Murray's tripartite structure for a disputation (see *JSOT* 38 [1987] 104–11) and to divide into thesis (v 3aβb), dispute (v 6), and counterthesis (vv 7–11). These three elements are obliquely matched with the three elements of a (tripartite) proof saying. The quotation stands outside the latter scheme; the dispute aligns with its accusatory element, and the counterthesis with its element of passing judgment. The recognition formula of v 10b, which is repeated in v 12aα, falls outside the structure of the disputation.

11:14–21 is clearly intended as a literary response to Ezekiel's prayer in v 13. It opens with its own message-reception formula, which normally begins a new unit, and it is not a vision account. Form-critically the piece is both a disputation and a proclamation of salvation. The analysis of Graffy (*A Prophet Confronts* 47–52) is as follows: a quotation (v 15), the first refutation (v 16), and the second refutation (v 17). Again we should take our bearings from Murray's refinement of the shape of the disputation genre: v 15 constitutes the thesis, v 16 the dispute, and vv 17–20 the counterthesis. Vv 17–20 do double form-critical duty as a proclamation of salvation. V 21 appears to be the final part of an inclusion (Cornill 239), an echoing reference to the people cited in v 15b. The basic vision account of chaps. 8–11 is finally resumed in 11:22.

The foregoing analysis of form and structure of the literary unit has revealed a certain lack of straightforwardness. 11:1–21 represents a notable detour from the basic narrative, while within chap. 10 there is a reflective agenda that contrasts with the brisk pace of chaps. 8 and 9. This evidence raises the issue of redaction in the unit. There are points of tension between 11:1–21 and the main vision account. It is unaware of preceding events, the remarkable death of the sinning population of Jerusalem (9:6–8), the burning of the city (10:2, 7), and the arrival of the glory of Yahweh at the east gateway where 11:1–13 is set (10:18–19). The social sins of 11:2–3, 6 are a different cause for complaint than that in 8:6–17, where the sins were of a cultic nature (but cf. 8:17ba; 9:9). The assumption in 11:15 that Yahweh still dwells in the land stands in tension with earlier claims of the residents of Jerusalem that Yahweh has left the land (8:12; 9:9).

Within 11:1–21, vv 1–13 and vv 14–21 appear to have been mutually independent in origin. The message-reception formula used in 11:14 generally introduces a new literary unit but not always: in 12:8; 21:6(1) it introduces a fresh oracular phase within a unit. Here it is comparable to the formula in 3:16b, introducing a redactional item that deliberately breaks into the context. Moreover, the positive message of vv 17–21 creates tension with the message of judgment of the context, and indeed with the tenor of Ezekiel's pre-587 B.C. prophetic ministry. Greenberg (204) has granted that vv 14–21 "appear . . . to have been an originally independent oracle . . . integrated into the vision." The inner coherence of vv 14–21 has been much doubted: the oracle refers to the exiles first in the third person (vv 15–16), then in the second (v 17), and finally in the third person again (vv 18–20), a phenomenon that is easily explained in terms of redactional amplification. Zimmerli (263) and Wevers (95–97) considered v 17 an addition and vv 18 and 21a subsequent, separate additions. Ohnesorge (*Jahwe gestaltet* 14–59; cf. Hals 69–71) has proposed a more intricate series of developments applied to a basic oracle of Ezekiel's that stopped at the end of v 16, with v 21 functioning as a final redactional link between vv 1–20 and the new context of chaps. 8–11. Similarly, in 1960 Greenberg ("Vision of Jerusalem" 163) opined that "whether all of 11:17–20 originally belonged here . . . may well be doubted"; however, by 1983 he was speaking in terms of a single, probably pre-fall oracle (204).

Attention should be paid to the contribution of form criticism to the question of redaction. The shape of the disputation seems to establish the coherence of the oracle at least as far as v 17. The strange switch to direct address of the exiles in v 17 has been reasonably explained by Liwak ("Probleme" 113 and n. 19), who considered only v 21 an addition. The oracle is addressed to Ezekiel in vv 18–20(21), as in v 15, while in v 16 it is addressed rhetorically to the residents of Jerusalem, and in v 17 it is addressed to the exiles, the real audience of the oracle. The separate introductions in vv 16aα and 17aα keep Ezekiel in view as the addressee of Yahweh, and so bridge the main sections of vv 15 and 18–21. These separate introductions also serve to isolate vv 16aβ–b and 17aβ–b with virtual quotation marks, as directed to different addressees. Graffy (*A Prophet Confronts* 48), who, however, accepted as primary only vv 14–17, has drawn attention to 33:24–29 for the switch in persons. The latter oracle, which focuses on the nonexiled Judeans, mentions them first in the third person (v 24), then in the second (vv 25–26), and finally in the third again (vv 27, 29). Similarly, the present oracle, which focuses on the exiles, speaks of them in the third person (vv 15–16), second person (v 17), and third person (vv 18–20). The references to "nations" in v 16 but to "peoples" in v 17 may simply be due to stylistic variation, while the mention of "the country" (אֶרֶץ) in v 15 but of "the land [אַדְמַת] of Israel" in v 17 is not redactionally significant (cf. 33:24aα over against 33:24aβb–26).

As for the historical and geographical setting, the basic oracle is generally credited to Ezekiel's Babylonian ministry before the fall of Jerusalem, because of the reference to "the residents of Jerusalem" in v 15 (cf. 12:19): the post-fall oracle of 33:24–29 mentions "those who reside in these ruins" (33:24; cf. 36:35). However, Eichrodt (143), following Kraetzschmar (119–20; cf. Bertholet [1936] 41; Brownlee, *JBL* 89 [1970] 395), has argued that

the whole passage in general, and in particular the form in which residents in Jerusalem stake their contested claim, displays such striking resemblances to 33:24ff. that it makes all contrary arguments quite unconvincing. The fact that Jeremiah shows no knowledge of any such hasty repudiations by the Jews remaining in the land of their departed fellow-countrymen must tell against putting it at a date previous to 587. Some still lived on in Jerusalem, even subsequently to the conquest of that city.

The content of other parts of the oracle point to the same conclusion, that it must be assigned to the post-fall period. The formulaic expression used in v 16a, which is universally regarded as part of the basic oracle, is elsewhere in the book used only of the exile that followed the fall of Jerusalem. It occurs in historical retrospect, as here, in 30:19, and in predictions in 12:15 (cf. 6:8); 20:23; 22:15. V 18 implies that the returnees would still find the accouterments of idolatry in the land, and no account need be taken of the disruptive crisis of 587. Moreover, the references to cultic abominations seem to presuppose the oracle in 33:24–29 (especially v 26). The two oracles are complementary in that the one in chap. 33 focuses on those in the homeland, and this one on the exiled Judeans. In here espousing a post-587 date, I must admit my uninformed error in earlier ascribing it to the pre-587 era in *Ezekiel 20–48* 153.

11:1–13 strikes notes of serious discord with the foregoing vision narrative, as we observed earlier. Rothstein (888, 890, 892) supposed that it originally belonged after 8:15, while Bertholet ([1936] 29), implicitly followed by May (118), placed it after 8:18. However, the deliberate grouping of four scenes depicting sins that are cultic in nature does not favor these proposals. Schmidt's suggestion (*TZ* 6 [1950] 88–89) that 11:1–21 originally belonged before 11:24, as a parallel vision to that of 8:1–10:18; 11:22–23, is too speculative. 11:1–13 is best taken as a separate temple vision (Fohrer 58; Eichrodt 119, 134–35; Ohnesorge, *Jahwe gestaltet* 55; cf. Greenberg 199). The notice of translation by the spirit in v 1 accords with 8:3b rather than with any subsequent relocation of the prophet within chaps. 8–10, and this factor supports its independent nature. It is true that Ezekiel is so conveyed in 43:5, within the vision of the new temple, but that is expressly to avoid the prophet's walking over an especially sacred area. There are no good grounds for denying the attribution of the vision account to Ezekiel, as Hölscher (*Dichter* 75) and Hossfeld ("Die Tempelvision" 154) have done. Zimmerli (257) considered that the prophet himself inserted this short narrative. Its redactional relevance lies especially with chap. 9: it echoes its temple-set message of accusation-laden judgment. The mention of "the city" of Jerusalem in 11:2, 6 reinforces a motif of the judgment account in chap. 9, while the accusation of 11:6 echoes that of 9:9. The prophet's outcry against the severity of Yahweh's judgment in 9:8b is repeated in 11:13b.

It is to this cry that vv 14–21 function as a redactionally placed reply, a reply that transcends the fate of Jerusalem to be sealed in 587 B.C. and leaps ahead to reassure the exilic victims of that catastrophe.

> Such an editorial activity reveals a change in setting, from a concern for simply enabling the message to be heard by an unwilling audience to a concern for enabling a willing audience to integrate the apparently disparate aspects of an overall message. (Hals 233)

We must now engage with the rather different issues presented by chap. 10. At this stage of the vision account, the flow of the narrative is increasingly interrupted with commentary of various kinds. Redaction critics have not unnaturally endeavored to penetrate behind such elaborations and find the basic core. Thus Zimmerli (231–34) discovered it in vv 2 (without "between the cherubim"), 4, 7 (without both plural references to the cherubim), 18a, 19aα (and then 11:23).

Other scholars have come to similar conclusions. In establishing criteria for amplification of the presumed earliest form of the text, it is important to distinguish material marked by certain patterns. The most obvious pattern is an introductory וָאֶרְאֶה וְהִנֵּה "and I looked, and behold," to which Horst (*VT* 3 [1953] 352–53) called attention. It is at first glance reminiscent of chap. 1, except that there, in vv 4 and 15, the short form of the verb, וָאֵרֶא, is used. In fact it seems to have been borrowed from the second vision, from 8:7. This introduction occurs in 10:1 with reference to the throne on the platform of 1:26a; it interrupts the flow of the narrative from 9:11 to 10:2. Another example occurs in 10:9a, with reference to the wheels of 1:15. A further case has already occurred in 8:2, at the beginning of the vision account, with reference to the divine figure of 1:27aγb. These three instances are all marked by an insistence, "This is what I actually saw." These self-contained visionary remarks are most naturally understood as subsequent reflective comments made by the prophet himself, which serve as important footnotes to guide the reader to a better understanding of the crucial part of the vision described in 10:2 (see the *Comment*).

A second type of supplementary material occurs in 10:13, 20b: it draws attention to an awareness of the seer. The first identifies גַּלְגַּל "rotary system," so called in the prophetic hearing of 10:2, with the wheels of chap. 1. In the second case the cherubim of 10:19 are recognized as identical with the living creatures of chap. 1. G. R. Driver reasonably commented in connection with v 13 that evident glosses can in fact be the work of the original author; he found one such instance here ("Glosses" 124; cf. Davis, *Swallowing the Scroll* 59, with reference to vv 13 and 20). There seems to be a subtype of this second category in 10:8 and also in 10:5. They are like the case in 10:13, in that a passive verb of observation is used, but now an explicitly personal reference such as "in my hearing" is lacking. The instance in 10:8 begins with וַיֵּרָא "and there was seen" and comments on the cherub's hands in v 7, loosely citing 1:8 by way of comparison. In 10:5 the pertinent verb is נִשְׁמַע "was heard" and there is a harking back to a particular noise heard in 1:24.

The case in 10:20, considered above, leads us to a third and fourth type of material, which must logically precede the second. The third type makes an identification between objects seen in the present vision and those seen in the vision of chap. 1. There are three cases, all involving the phrase אֲשֶׁר רָאִיתִי "which I saw." One occurs in 10:20a, explicitly identifying the cherubim of v 19 with the living creatures seen at the Kebar Canal. Another is found at v 22aαβ; it identifies the faces of the cherubim with those seen in the earlier vision. A similar instance appears in 8:4, where attention is drawn to "the glory of the God of Israel," and it is identified with that seen in the vision of 3:23. Block (*CBQ* 50 [1988] 432) has rightly said of 10:20, 22 that "the text itself seems to identify the recipient of this vision and the author of this text with the author of the first chapter." This third type of material represents further reflective observations made by the prophet. One may compare with it 3:23aγ as an earlier example.

The instances in 8:4 and 10:20a are both distinguished by reference to "the God of Israel," whereas the main narrative refers repeatedly to "the glory of Yahweh." This differentiation is a clue for detecting a fourth type of material, which overlaps with the second and third types in v 20 and with the third type in 8:4. One may fruitfully compare the mixture of types in 43:2–3, where "the glory of the

God of Israel" occurs together with a comparison of 1:24 and also with the third type, and categorize it as reflective comment on the basic statement of 43:4a (cf. also 44:2). There is a further example of the fourth type of material in 9:3, which deliberately anticipates 10:4a, but with a change from "the glory of Yahweh" to "the glory of the God of Israel." The change of verb for rising appears to be purely stylistic (cf. 11:23a). Other cases are in 10:19bβ and 11:22b, which are amplifying references to "the glory of the God of Israel" as positioned above the cherubim.

It will have been noted that the first three types of amplification tend to refer back to aspects of the vision reported in chap. 1. This same feature reappears in a different way in a fifth and final type, which indulges in systematic and detailed citation of chap. 1. It has two concerns, form and function. There are three instances. The first, in 10:9b–12a, has an interest in the form of the wheels (מראה[ם] "[their] appearance") in vv 9b–10 and also in their operation (vv 11–12a) and to this end cites 1:16–18a. A second case may be seen in 10:12b, 16–17, which cites 1:18b–19 in continuation of the earlier case. It too is concerned with form, in v 12b, although the precise term מראה "appearance" does not appear, and with function, in vv 16–17. The last example, in v 22aγb, is much briefer: it refers to the form (מראהם "their appearance," v 22aγ) and function (v 22b) of the cherubim, and in the second part quotes from 1:12a.

These five types of considerable editorial supplementation, which have left telltale signs in the text, are all that may reasonably be claimed. One may not, for instance, include 10:3a, which is an innocent circumstantial clause that has every right to stand in the basic narrative. Nor, above all, may one differentiate the plural כרובים "cherubim" from the singular, collective כרוב "cherub-structure" as a redactional criterion. Rather, the different usage was a feature of the text from the beginning, denial of which causes unnecessary difficulties (see the *Comment*).

How may this manifold activity be explained in terms of the literary history of the text? My work in the latter half of the book disclosed time and time again a threefold pattern running through the material in its present shape of literary units. First, there is a basic text; second, there is an updating or continuation or other literary expansion that stays close to the basic material; and, third, there is a stratum that stands at some distance from the previous stages in its perspective (see, e.g., Allen, *Ezekiel 20–48* 229). The perspective of this third stratum can be of various kinds. The enumeration of cargo in 27:12–25a and the detailing of the interior design and decoration of the new temple in 41:15b–26 seem to come closest to the quotation of consecutive blocks of material from chap. 1 in the fifth type of editorial activity. If one applies this model of a threefold pattern of literary development, the more moderate first four types of reflective reworking may be credited to the prophet himself, along with the basic narrative at an earlier stage. In favor of this proposal is the occasional overlap of types in the same material: the third and fourth in 8:4 and the second, third, and fourth in 10:20–22aαβ (cf. 43:2–3). One may also observe the natural way the fourth type at 9:3 is woven into the text by the presence of the divine name in 9:4 (see *Note* 9:4.a.). That Ezekiel himself was not responsible for 10:12a, and so for the material of the fifth type associated with it, is indicated by its misunderstanding of the difficult 1:18a (see the *Comment*).

The literary revision evident in chap. 10 and also sporadically in chaps. 8, 9, and 11 may be summed up as follows, with indication of the different types found:

8:2 (I), 4 (III, IV); 9:3 (IV); 10:1 (I), 5 (II), 8 (II), 9a (I), 10a, b–12a (V), 12b, 16–17 (V), 13 (II), 19b (IV), 20–22a$\alpha\beta$ (II, III, IV), 22aγb (V); 11:22b (IV). In the earlier discussion there has been no mention of 10:21, which cites 1:6, 8aα. The flow of the material, especially between v 21a and v 22a$\alpha\beta$, seems to indicate that there is a single, continuous section here. However, evidence of the fifth type of revision in 10:22aγb, which cites 1:12a, could suggest that 10:21 is part of a larger block continued in v 22aγb. This view wins favor from the fact that in 10:8, if it has been interpreted aright, the prophet has already explained the hand of the cherub mentioned in v 7. Nevertheless, the reference to the cherubim's faces in v 22aα does seem to require the earlier reference in v 21aα. Certainly citation of chap. 1 has been present in earlier types of reworking of the basic text.

Discussion of stages of redaction centering on chap. 10 raises questions concerning the insertion of 11:1–21. The positive continuation of the negative oracle in 11:1–13 with a positive one in vv 14–21 has a parallel in chap. 20, although in that case there is much closer similarity in the terminology of the two oracles. But the principle is the same, and if 20:32–44 may be credited to Ezekiel's own post-587 updating (see my treatment in *Ezekiel 20–48* 8, 15–16 and also in *CBQ* 54 [1992] 448–62), there is no obstacle to seeing in 11:14–20 or 21 the prophet's relocation of later material, which at an earlier stage may have been positioned in the vicinity of the oracle in 33:23–29. The apparent desire to warn the exiles that is present in 11:21 (see *Comment*) is congruent with Ezekiel's special message of judgment-tinged salvation that is also present in the latter half of chap. 20. Overall, the post-587 impression that 11:14–21 leaves on the reader is reminiscent of 3:16b–21, which was also inserted into a pre-587 context. 11:1–21 still tantalizes the careful reader with unanswered questions, but in its present form this pair of passages shows evidence of careful integration into its context. It is a new patch on old cloth, yet has been purposefully sewn in by an expert literary tailor.

An analysis of the literary unit, which leaves out of account its briefer redactional intricacies, is here presented.

8:1–3bα	Introduction to the temple vision
8:3bβ–18	Four scenarios of cultic sin and Yahweh's vocal reaction
8:3bβ–6	The pagan altar
8:7–13	The idolators in the secret room
8:14–15	The women who worshiped Tammuz
8:16–17	The sun worshipers
8:18	Yahweh's pronouncement of punishment
9:1–11	Judgment and exemption
9:1–2	Summons of the supernatural agents
9:3–7	The two commissions of the agents
9:8–11	Ezekiel's protest and Yahweh's negative reply; the return of the agent of exemption
10:1–22	The burning of Jerusalem commanded; the gradual departure of the glory of Yahweh
10:1–3	The commission of the incendiary
10:4–5	The first stage of the departure of the glory of Yahweh
10:6–7	The equipping of the incendiary
10:8–17	Description of the cherubim and wheels

10:18–19	The second and third stages of the departure of the glory of Yahweh
10:20–22	Further description of the cherubim
11:1–21	Sin and salvation
11:1–13	A further vision of sin and judgment
11:14–21	Positive prospects for the exiles
11:22–23	The final stage of the departure of the glory of Yahweh
11:24–25	Conclusion of the temple vision

Comment

8:1 The purpose of the precise dating, which was a mark of the introduction to the first vision (1:1, 2), seems to have been to provide careful documentation as to the genuineness of the prophetic experience and so to eventually vindicate Ezekiel when his forecast came true. In 24:2 the prophet records a divine instruction to write down the date, for later verification that he was a true prophet (cf. Isa 8:1–4; 30:8). According to the tables in Parker and Dubberstein's *Babylonian Chronology* (28), this date represents 17 September 592 B.C., which was nearly fourteen months after the initial vision. The visit of "elders" to Ezekiel's home will recur in 14:1; 20:1 (cf. 33:31). As explicitly in 20:1 (cf. 14:3), they evidently came with the expectation of receiving a favorable oracle. In each case the prophet could proclaim naught for their comfort. In this instance his response was to be the recounting of the vision as testimony to Yahweh's just judgment (11:25). The recourse of the "Judean elders" (in 14:1; 20:1, 3, "Israel's elders") to Ezekiel reflects his religious authority as a prophet (cf. 2 Kgs 19:2). The office of "elder" refers to the system of self-government established among the exiles, in continuation of the representative institution of leadership traditionally carried on in the homeland. It is also attested in Jer 29:1, with the term "exilic elders." The system continued into the main period of exile and thence into the early postexilic period (cf. Ezra 5:5, 9; 6:7, 8, 14). The Egyptian community in Babylonia in 529 likewise had an assembly of elders recognized by the Persian authorities (I. Ephal, *Or* 47 [1978] 74–80).

The ecstatic experience of the vision is inaugurated by the pressure of Yahweh's hand, as in 1:3. The falling of the hand, as distinct from its coming in 1:3 and in most other cases in the book, gives expression to the suddenness of the event, rather as the verb חזק "be strong" in 3:14 and Isa 8:11 refers to its overwhelming nature. The reference in the narrative epilogue at 11:25 to Ezekiel's reporting the vision to "the exiles," presumably the (still) assembled elders, implies that the ecstatic experience had been trancelike and so an out-of-the-body experience, in terms of 2 Cor 12:2, as Jerome (94, 125–26) perceived. The analogy of dreaming suggests that it may have taken place in a short space of time (Skinner 80). In this respect it seems to correspond with the vision of 37:1–14. In the first vision, on the other hand, the experience of translation (3:14–15), though described as here in v 3, appears to have been a physical one, as in the old texts relating to Elijah (1 Kgs 18:12; 2 Kgs 2:16; cf. Acts 8:39). Here a parapsychological phenomenon is used as a vehicle of divine communication that the prophet may recount in turn to his constituency.

2 The significance of this statement will not be immediately obvious to the reader. It belongs to a network of parenthetical observations scattered through chaps. 8–10. In this particular form it is matched by material in 10:1, 9a (see *Form/Structure/Setting*). There is no reason to deny them to the pen or dictating voice of the prophet, but they stand apart from the basic narrative, at a different literary level. V 2 gives the impression of being an independent little vision report inserted as an important afterthought. A mark of these observations is their reference to elements in the first vision in chap. 1. Inquiry into the reason for the comparison must await comment on chap. 10. Here it may be said that the "glory of Yahweh" at that point becomes a crucial theme of the vision account. In anticipation of that later emphasis, the narrative hastens "to focus attention on its presence" (Greenberg 197) and so to give it pride of place in the overall account. From the very beginning, the divine figure of judgment revealed in chap. 1 brooded over the visionary experience and made his presence felt.

It is sometimes suggested that the supernatural figure in this verse functions as an angelic messenger, like that of 40:3 (Zimmerli 236; Wevers 79). However, the vision in chaps. 8–11 has no room for an angelic interpreter, such as features in chaps. 40–48. It is Yahweh who speaks directly to Ezekiel (see, e.g., 8:6, 18). Moreover, the consistent pattern of references to the first vision in the course of chaps. 8–10 makes it clear that the intent is to represent Yahweh, with radiant contours that evoke 1:27ayb, while דמות "figure" recalls "the figure associated with the glory of Yahweh" at 1:28ay. The resumption of that climactic description at the outset of the narrative, before the vision proper has begun, provides a sublime and disturbing frontispiece.

3abα   The processes of lifting and conveying that in 3:14 were both assigned to the spirit are here allocated separately. The standard expression of forcible possession in terms of Yahweh's hand, which was used in v 1, is here extended into an agency of the initial stage of levitation. Zimmerli (236) interestingly conjectures that the mode of lifting corresponded to the pain and giddiness felt by the prophet. Presumably, Ezekiel's hair had grown sufficiently since 5:1. In an Akkadian text, Nergal, the god of the underworld, similarly seizes an Assyrian prince by his hair before carrying him to his domain (*ANET* 110a). Here, however, the spirit takes over its customary role of transportation.

3bβ**–17**   Four scenarios of cultic sins committed in the area of the temple now follow. These scenarios are composed in a similar pattern, already observed in *Form/Structure/Setting*. A major problem that demands resolution is the course along which the prophet is conducted. The immediate impression given by the consistent verbal statements, first ותבא אתי "and (the spirit) brought me" here and then ויבא אתי "and he brought me" in vv 7, 14, and 16, is that Ezekiel is taken on a direct and inward route into the temple court. This impression is supported by the evidence of the vision of the new temple in chaps. 40–48. There the same verb marks the prophet's arrival at the temple site and his progression from outside the complex of temple buildings to its center (40:1–3, 17, 28, 32, 48; 41:1; 43:5; 44:4). In 46:19 the verb is used of access from the outer court to a path built up to the level of the inner court and regarded as an extension of it. Similarly, this verb characterizes the direction of that path in 42:9. It refers to the access of priests in 42:14 and of worshipers in 44:5; 46:2, 8, 9. On the other hand, the prophet's laterally directed movements are marked by the verbs הוליך "conduct" (40:24; 43:1) and העביר "take over" (46:21; cf. סבב "changed direction," in 42:16, 17, 19). The only exceptions to this careful use of terminology are in 40:35;

42:1, where הֵבִיא "bring" is used of entry into buildings and not of movement toward the middle of the temple complex (cf. בֹא "enter" in 8:9, 10). The bottom line of this comparison with chaps. 40–48 is that one expects the verb to signal a similar inward progression here in a relatively short sequence.

This expectation created by the verb is not immediately matched by the places specified as its directional objects. In particular, there do not seem to be enough gates to fit into the route. The issue is complicated by the references in the MT to "the inner (court?)" in v 3 and to the "altar gateway" in v 5, which must refer to a gateway into the inner court of the temple. There are other grounds for adjusting the Hebrew text so that on the first lap of the journey the prophet has not progressed so far (see *Notes* 3.d. and 5.a.). Greenberg (168–69, 171), who retains the traditional text, relates v 16, of course, to the inner court, vv 3 and 5 to the outer entrance of the gateway in the wall around the inner court, and v 7 perhaps to the south entrance of the same gateway. He finds himself unable to identify the location of v 14, though he mentions a suggestion that it relates to a door to the side structure of the temple.

At this point it will be useful to look at Busink's reconstruction of the palace complex built by Solomon (fig. 6), which at the northern end was occupied by the temple set within its own court. The illustration, reproduced from *Der Tempel von Jerusalem* 1:160, leaves unrepresented gates in the northern wall of the temple and in the corresponding wall of the perimeter of the complex. Sprank, who devoted a long section to the topography of vv 3–17 (*Ezechielstudien* 4–25), conceived of a straight course from the peripheral wall to the center of the temple area. He reckoned that vv 3 and 5 refer to the inner entrance of the north gateway leading into the court of the palace complex, and v 7 to the entrance to the temple court. He dismissed v 14 from consideration, judging vv 14–15 to be secondary, on rather slender grounds.

Sprank was countering earlier proposed routes that involved what he called a zigzag course. Thus Kraetzschmar (87–95) and Rothstein (887–88) judged Ezekiel's location in vv 3 and 5 to be at the inner entrance of the gateway to the temple court, in v 7 at the outer entrance of the same gateway, in v 14 at the inner entrance of the gateway in the perimeter wall of the royal complex, and then in v 16 in the temple court. Sprank's instinct in rejecting this movement out and back in was surely correct. As we have seen, the general usage of the verb referring to Ezekiel's directed movements in chaps. 40–48 speaks in its favor. In fact, when the prophet is made to retrace his steps in the new temple vision, the verb הֵשִׁיב "bring back" is carefully used (44:1; 47:1; cf. 44:5; 46:9), while for outward movement הוֹצִיא "bring out" appears (42:1, 15; 46:21; 47:2; cf. 44:5; 46:12). This principle renders unlikely not only Kraetzschmar's and Rothstein's reconstruction but also Cooke's (91–98). He envisioned in vv 3 and 5 a position in the temple court near the north gateway, in v 7 a movement to the interior of the gateway, in v 14 to the outer entrance of the gateway, where he sees the women in the outer court, then back in v 16 to the temple court. A variation on the same theme was offered by Schmidt (*TZ* 6 [1950] 85–87), who placed the prophet at the outer entrance to the gateway to the temple court in vv 3, 5, and 14 and at the inner entrance to the gateway in the perimeter wall in v 7.

The solution to this topographical puzzle, which Sprank did not quite attain, lies in reconstructing the journey backwards. In v 16 Ezekiel is explicitly located

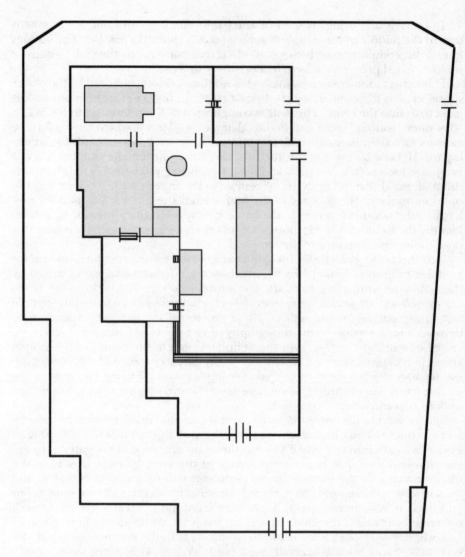

Figure 6. Busink's reconstruction of the palace complex

in the temple court. In v 14 he must be at the outer entrance of the gateway leading directly to the temple, as the text seems to say, and so the gateway set in the wall around the temple court. Then in v 7 "the entrance to the court" must be at the gateway in the perimeter wall of the royal complex. In turn the gateway in vv 3 and 5 must have been a north gateway in the city wall. This is the solution espoused by Zimmerli (236–37, 240), who has been followed by Wevers (79), Vogt (*Untersuchungen* 42–45 and n. 14), and Carley (52–54) and most recently by Ackerman (*Under Every Green Tree* 54–55). Its two advantages are that it posits an ongoing inward movement and it accords with indications in the text itself. Thus v 3 mentions simply Jerusalem as the point of arrival, so that a gateway in the city wall is a natural location for vv 3 and 5. V 7, which refers to "the court" rather than the "inner court" of v 16, then refers to the northern end of the court of the palace complex. V 14 brings Ezekiel and the reader to the gateway in the wall surrounding the temple court, as the text appears to say. This reconstruction supports the adjustments to the MT made in conjunction with other factors in vv 3 and 5: at that stage the prophet must be two gates away from the one giving access to the temple court.

Another issue at stake in 8:3–17 is the nature of the visionary scenes Ezekiel witnessed. Were they meant to constitute a veridical vision, so that a time traveler in the vicinity of the temple on 17 September 592 B.C. could have filmed the events happening as Ezekiel described them by second sight? Probably not: the worship of Tammuz featured in the third scene is a counter indication. Such ritual mourning took place in the fourth month (June–July) rather than the sixth. The god lent his name to the Babylonian term for the fourth month, which the Judeans took over in postexilic times. Although one could explain the discrepancy in terms of a local variation (J. Gray, *IDB* 4:516), there seems to be no need to do so, as Smend (53) observed. As Cassuto ("Arrangement" 231 n. 3) pointed out, the continuation of the vision account in chap. 9 is not meant to refer to the present but is a representation of the destruction that was to occur some five years later. Ezekiel views a series of religious sins that are rhetorically grouped together in the vision but were simply typical of worship carried on at different times in Jerusalem at that period, which he himself may well have seen while he lived there.

Yet can one maintain even this general interpretation? Greenberg, in his "Prolegomenon" to Torrey's *Pseudo-Ezekiel* (xviii–xxvii, xxxiii), has followed Y. Kaufmann and others since Hitzig (65) in arguing that such sins were characteristic of the period of Manasseh in the seventh century but were abolished in the reforms of Josiah toward the end of the century and not revived. Thenceforth, as the evidence of Kings, Jeremiah, and Lamentations shows, unorthodox religious practices were no longer carried on in public, officially sponsored cults, though they did survive in private, clandestine ones. Ezekiel was speaking of Judah's apostasy in terms of Manasseh's; the Chronicler took his cue from Ezek 8 in attributing such apostasy and defilement of the temple to priests and people in Zedekiah's reign (2 Chr 36:14). Only Ezek 8:10–12 may be regarded as a depiction of contemporary paganism. Morton Smith (*ZAW* 87 [1975] 11–16) has challenged Greenberg's thesis on two grounds. First, Kings appears to attribute the final fall of Jerusalem to Zedekiah's wickedness, rather than to Manasseh's sins (2 Kgs 24:19–20). Second, in the account of Jeremiah's clash with the Judean worshipers of the queen of heaven in Jer 44, the suspension of the cult mentioned in v 18 may well refer to the final siege of Jerusalem, rather than to Josiah's reform. If so, in both official and private forms (v 17) the cult persisted down till then, and Ezekiel's reference to cultic sins need not be anachronistic. Smith's case is hardly overwhelming, and anyway the issue is not crucial for our present concern. On balance, however, it seems better to adhere to the commonly held view that Manasseh's cultic aberrations were revived in the reign of Jehoiakim (cf. Zimmerli 245). This view receives support from the religious assessments in 2 Kgs 23:32, 37; 24:9, 19 that Josiah's successors "did evil in the eyes of Yahweh."

3bβ–6   Ezekiel evidently finds himself just inside the city wall of Jerusalem. At least by the seventh century, if not earlier, there was a space between this wall and the north wall of the palace complex (Zimmerli 237; "Jerusalem" 418–20). Perhaps the north gateway is to be identified with the "sheep gate" of Neh 3:1 (Vogt, *Untersuchungen* 42). We are to envision a structure of some size, "like a college lodge," as the Oxford don Cooke (91) commented. At either end of a wide corridor there would have been an "entrance"; in the light of v 5, Ezekiel stood by the south entrance. The "image" (סֶמֶל) he sees at this place is an anthropomorphic idol, to judge by the usage of the term in Phoenician inscriptions. Significantly, the same term occurs in 2 Chr 33:7, 15, seemingly with reference to the Phoenician goddess Asherah, in connection with an image set up in the temple precincts (2 Kgs 21:7). If this cult, abolished by Josiah, was revived after his death, the cult image may have been placed elsewhere (McKay, *Religion* 22–23, 93 n. 27). Here it has pride of place as a guardian figure. The focus of the narrative lies in the religious significance of the image, as an outrage to Yahweh, more literally a provocation to jealousy (קִנְאָ). The sentiment is that which appears in Deut 32:16, 21a (Rose, *Ausschliesslichkeitsanspruch* 210 n. 3):

> They stirred him to jealousy with strange gods; with abominable rites they provoked him to anger. . . . They have stirred me to jealousy with a non-god, provoked me to anger with their nonentities.

Indeed, chap. 8 seems to be citing Deut 32, using these references as a frame at beginning and end: in v 17 the verb הַכְעִיס "provoke to anger" occurs, corresponding to the hiphil form in Deut 32:16 (piel in 32:21). Yahweh's exclusive claims on his people were being fundamentally denied by this evidence of pagan worship in the city of God.

The primary narrative is interrupted by the afterthought of v 4a. It might perhaps better have appeared as a counterpart to the visionary observation of v 5bβ, which is also introduced by הִנֵּה "behold." However, the intent seems to have been deliberate, as Zimmerli (238) suggests, to counterpoint intruder and rightful claimant, the false and the real. Yahweh makes his presence felt by his theophanic presence, as the double "there" indicates. The second "there" is meant in quite general terms. The statement itself is a general one and looks forward, together with 9:3, to the revelation of chap. 10. The opportunity is taken to compare the manifestation with the earlier occurrence in 3:23. Whether כָּבוֹד "glory" refers here simply to the divine figure or, as in 3:23, embraces the throne conveyance is not stated: the comparison with 3:23 and the parallel of 43:2–3 suggest the latter sense.

Throughout the tour described in chap. 8, Yahweh provides a commentary for what Ezekiel sees in his vision. Two of Amos's visions feature a visionary sight, a divine question ("What do you see?"), a pause for an answer, and then a commentary (Amos 7:7–9; 8:1–3). In Jer 1:11–16 there are two similar instances, with the first element lacking. In this vignette and also in the second (v 9), a command to see is followed by a description of the scene and then a shocked question concerning what is seen that leads into commentary. Ezekiel's attention is expressly drawn to what lies on the other side of the gateway and so just outside the wall. He sees an altar associated with the cult of the image erected on the inner side of the gateway. In principle the phenomenon corresponds to Jeremiah's reference to altars "as many as the streets of Jerusalem" (Jer 11:13). The divine reaction refers obliquely to the rites represented by the altar and raises as an objection not simply that they are pagan in nature but that they are being practiced outside the sanctuary. The implication appears to be that, in the eyes of the adherents of this cult, it came under the umbrella of Yahwism and in no way constituted a denial of their basic faith in Yahweh. However, the God of Ezekiel cannot be associated with so liberal a notion. The reference to the temple as the rightful site of worship is an argument against accepting this cultic phenomenon as any true part of Yahwism.

7–10 The reference to "even more shocking rites" in v 6bβ acts as a literary bridge to the next scenario, preparing the reader for an intensification in the scale of religious aberrations. The prophet is brought to a gate in the wall of the palace complex, inside which lay the northern part of the great court of 1 Kgs 7:9, 12. It is probable that this access to the temple was the most frequented: the royal buildings lay to the south and east, while the west was closed by the temple itself (Davidson 55). The regular pattern of the scenarios is interrupted by an incident that draws attention to the secrecy of the particular rite, which will be the concern of the divine commentary in v 12. There seems to be a reference to a large room beside the gateway, evidently built into the wall, but with no obvious door to enter. One may compare the large chamber in Neh 13:5, the hall in 1 Sam 9:22, and the rooms alongside the walls of the outer court in Ezekiel's new temple at 40:17 (see the discussion in Ackerman, *Under Every Green Tree* 67–69). The prophet's attention is drawn to a hole, which he is commanded to enlarge in order to use as a means of entry. By this means he is able to observe the second vignette: evidently the hole would have provided an insufficient view. In this secret room he sees engravings all over the main wall. An annotator has identified the subjects of the engravings with the prohibited images of Deut 4:17–18 and may also have had in mind the ritually unclean creatures of Lev 11. The note is a valuable ancient interpretation, filling out what is left tantalizingly unexplained in the basic text. The figures contrast with the orthodox temple engravings of 1 Kgs 6:29, 32, 35.

11 In the first scenario there was only an indirect reference to worshipers. Now there is a full description. They were none other than the national council of Judah. The number "seventy" is meant to evoke for the reader the traditional institution of Exod 24:1–9; Num 11:16, 24–25. These representatives of the community of faith appear not in a setting of privilege and empowering at Yahweh's hands but in a provocative context of pagan worship. The expression "stand in front of" has the connotation of worship (Herrmann 60). Mention of "Jaazaniah son of Shaphan" may have been intended to indicate a contrast with his father, the devout secretary of state to Josiah (2 Kgs 22:3–14). Three of Shaphan's sons are mentioned in Jer 26:24; 29:3; 36:10–12. He may well have had a fourth, Jaazaniah, "the black sheep of a very worthy family" (Taylor 99). Perhaps too there is an intention to play on the meaning of his name, "Yahweh pays heed" (Ehrlich, *Randglossen* 5:26), and so to suggest how his present behavior belied his name. The group's burning of incense is obviously meant to convey tacit dissonance with the orthodox requirement that only those of priestly rank could offer incense legitimately (Num 16:40; cf. 2 Chr 26:16–19). The burning here comprises a separate offering, independent of other offerings, as an act of worship (cf. Haran, *VT* 10 [1960] 114–24, 129).

12–13 The divine explanation draws attention to the secret nature of the rite. This is a motif of aberrant worship that is especially evident in Deuteronomy as an insidious feature (Deut 13:7; 27:15); it also appears in Job 31:27 as one of Job's denials in his oath of piety. Its combination with defiant justification is reminiscent of Isa 29:15:

> Alas for those who deeply from Yahweh
> hide their plans,
> whose deeds are done in the dark,
> and who say, "Who sees us? Who knows us?"

There it was evidently the foreign policy of Judean statesmen that was under condemnation (cf. Isa 30:1), and there is a hint of shame behind their provocative words. Here a later generation of those statesmen is indulging in pagan rites and making the same brazen claim to self-determination and yet paradoxically expressing their shamefacedness. They ground their convictions in the ancient doctrine that linked Yahweh with the land, a doctrine that now had seemingly lapsed with the defeat of 597 B.C. The sequel to these accusatory scenarios in chaps. 10–11 will ironically show the grain of truth that lay in such a perverted claim: Yahweh was indeed about to leave his temple and land, in an act of judgment upon the lack of faith he found there (Greenberg 200). Their claim that Yahweh had left the country was a boast of impunity, but the coming reality behind the claim would be attended by death and destruction.

14–15 Worse was to come in this tour of impiety. This brief vignette balances the last, long one and paves the way for the climactic one of vv 16–17. It took place on the verge of the temple court, at the entrance to the north gate. Perhaps that was what lent the scenario its heinous quality: approaching holy ground, one found not a return to piety but still more paganism. And in this case the paganism was no longer hidden but overt. A chilling factor from the perspective of Judean exiles in Babylonia was that a Babylonian god was being worshiped on Judean soil. The cult of Tammuz (Dumūzi), which was one of the most popular in Mesopotamia, probably entered Judah under Babylonian influence (McKay, *Religion* 68–69). Scholars used to consider him a dying and rising fertility god, but on inadequate grounds (see Gurney, *JSS* 7 [1962] 153–60; Yamauchi, *JBL* 84 [1965] 283–90). Dumūzi was the husband of the goddess Inanna, who banished him to the underworld. His fate was bewailed in lamentation rites in the month of June–July. Sitting is the posture of mourners (cf. 26:16; Job 2:8; Jonah 3:6). It is likely that the cult appealed especially to women (see Jacobsen, *HR* 1 [1962] 204).

16 Ezekiel is finally brought into the "inner court" of the temple (cf. 1 Kgs 6:36). The place of the last aberration is the open space in the court between the temple porch and the altar of burnt offering, with which Ahaz replaced the old, smaller bronze altar (2 Kgs 16:10–16). It is invested with special sanctity in Jewish tradition (see Greenberg 171). Within the OT it is singled out as the site of the priests' lamentation at a public ceremony of repentance (Joel 2:17). In Matt 23:35 the murder of the priest-prophet Zechariah is regarded as especially abhorrent because it was committed on this spot. Josiah had endeavored to remove the worship of the sun god from the temple court (2 Kgs 23:11–12). The cult was particularly common in Syria and probably spread to Judah from there (see Cogan, *Imperialism* 84–86; McKay, *Religion* 51–53). Turning one's back on Yahweh was a not uncommon metaphor for apostasy (Jer 2:27; 32:33; cf. 2 Chr 29:6). Here it is used literally, yet retains the sense of the metaphor. The worship of the rising sun entailed turning one's back on the temple structure, which itself faced east and which was regarded as Yahweh's home. Thus a situation of intolerable tension between the sun cult and Yahwism is described. The participants may have intended their sun worship as a legitimate extension of their traditional faith (cf. Zimmerli 243–44; McKay, *Religion* 34–35). However, the text engages in deliberate polemic and maintains the incompatibility of the two forms of faith.

17 In a generalizing statement, the divine commentary sums up the earlier religious aberrations and couples them with sin of a social kind. To interpret חמס "violence" as wrong done to God and take it as a definition of the final outrage (Cooke 100) is forcing the text. Appeal to its usage in Job 21:27 and the appearance of the cognate verb with the Torah as object in Zech 3:4; Ezek 22:26 are insufficient arguments. In the book of Ezekiel, both cultic and social sins constitute the basis of divine judgment. In summaries of Judah's wrongdoing, the two types of sin stand side by side (22:4; 33:25–26). Within the short compass of the adjacent chap. 9, both types coexist, the cultic in v 4 and the social, characterized as "very, very great guilt," in v 9. Here the three examples of cultic sin glimpsed earlier in chap. 8 and the implicitly worse social sins of the nation pale beside this last cultic insult to Yahweh. The provoking of Yahweh to anger provides the final scaffolding for a literary framework borrowed from Deut 32:16(21) and first represented in v 3.

The last clause, v 17bβ, has defied extensive exegetical attempts to supply a precise interpretation. Medieval Jewish exposition of זמורה in terms of breaking wind has won some scholarly support (Toy 112; Kraetzschmar 97; van den Born 65; Eichrodt 128; Vawter 69; cf. Zimmerli 244). It has little in its favor beyond providing a suitably insulting meaning. The same may be said of the other rabbinic interpretation, "penis," which McKane ("Observations" 71–75) has accepted, in terms of an idiomatic expression of affront. The former interpretation is closely associated with a reading "my nose," but the very reading seems to have arisen from that homiletical interpretation of זמורה (see *Note* 8:17.c.). Structurally, v 17 corresponds to Yahweh's shocked drawing of Ezekiel's attention to the particular stage of abominations reached and his promise of worse to come, in vv 6, 12–13, 15. The climactic point here reached requires a slightly different order: a brief alerting of Ezekiel is accompanied by a review of previous and other sins and by a statement regarding the present, worst instance. The ABC pattern is varied to ACB. That this is so is shown by the participle שלחים "putting," which matches the participle עשים "doing" in vv 6 and 12; it is missing in the generally brief section of vv 15–16. So the clause is not to be related to the social wrongdoing of v 17ba (contra Gordis, *JTS* 37 [1936] 288; Sarna, *HTR* 57 [1964] 348–49; Greenberg 172–73). Rather, it appears to be a gesture associated with the last pagan rite, a gesture to which all the ire provoked by the rite gets attached. Gestures are symbols of commitment, as the German generals knew well in 1944, when they reluctantly obeyed Hitler's order to adopt the Nazi salute. This particular religious gesture is comparable to the hand-kissing of the mouth in worship of the sun or moon at Job 31:27. The holding of an object to the nose appears in a Syrian representation of a king holding a flower on a stalk in front of his beard, while his right hand is clenched in front of his mouth, as he engages in astral worship (*ANEP* 281; see Saggs, *JTS* 11 [1960] 322, 328). The Akkadian expression *appa labana* denotes a gesture of worship involving both hand and nose. Sometimes the hand holds an object to the nose, as in the Bavian sculpture of Sennacherib worshiping the Assyrian gods, in which the object held by the king is perhaps a branch (see Gruber, *JANESCU* 7 [1975] 78–79).

18 Yahweh's reaction to the blatant behavior of the "Judean community" in v 17 now follows. His coming punishment, which looks forward to chaps. 9–10, is expressed in emotional terms, wrath and mercilessness. The tones of exasperation fittingly follow those expressed earlier, the framing terms "jealousy" or "outrage" and "anger" (vv 3, 5, 17), the piling up of the term "abominations" or "shocking rites" (vv 6, 9, 13, 15, 17), and the associated exclamatory questions (vv 6, 12, 15, 17). The lack of mercy is illustrated in dread terms of Yahweh's refusal to hear entreaties, a not uncommon prophetic motif (cf. Jer 11:11; Mic 3:4; Zech 7:13). There may be a resumptive allusion to the name "Jaazaniah" in v 11: the promise implicit in the name had been forfeited by the conduct of the bearer and his associates.

9:1–11 This next section of the vision account inaugurates the judgment of the "Judean community" (8:17) but focuses its implementation in the "city" of Jerusalem, which is a key word in the section. There is a parallel with Ezekiel's bearing the iniquity of the community of Israel in 4:4–5, in conjunction with his depiction of the coming siege of Jerusalem (4:7–8). The three bipartite subsections noticed in *Form/Setting/Structure*, vv 1–2, 3b–7, 8–11, highlight an unexpected tension in the chapter, between punishment and sparing.

1–2 The loud divine cry ordering punishment drowns out the sinners' potential loud cries for mercy in 8:18b and forms "an ironic contrast" to them (Blenkinsopp 57). The command is issued to a squad of supernatural destroyers. They constitute an example of prophetic reversal of an otherwise positive motif for Israel, the destroying angel of Exod 12:23; 2 Kgs 19:35 (cf. Zech 1:20–21). God's people were no longer on the side of the angels!

The executioners find a cultural parallel in Babylonian literature, the seven gods who feature as agents of the judgment of Erra in the Poem of Erra (Bodi, *Poem* 95–110). The six angels appear from the same direction as the prophet, from the north. Here there seems to be the same echo of Jeremiah's motif of the foe from the north as appeared in 1:4 (cf. Bertholet [1897] 51; et al.). They came through the same gateway as Ezekiel did in 8:16. It is described as "upper": the inner court evidently stood on a higher level than the rest of the precincts, like the new temple court (cf. 40:31). The gateway is commonly identified with the upper Benjamin gate of Jer 20:2, leading to the inner court, though Greenberg (176) considers it a gate in the wall of the outer court. It clearly stood in line with the Benjamin Gate in the city wall (Jer 37:13), which may be the same as the Sheep Gate in Nehemiah. Jotham is said to have built "the upper gate of the house of Yahweh" (2 Kgs 15:35), though whether this one is in view is uncertain, since there was also an upper gate on the south side of the court, to which 2 Chr 23:20 must refer (Zimmerli, "Jerusalem" 420).

Beside the six executioners appears a seventh angel whose only implement is a writing kit. Readers have to wait until v 4 for his role to be disclosed. His linen garment, which serves to distinguish him from his colleagues, can be a mark of priestly rank (cf. Exod 28:42; Lev 6:3[10]; 16:4); accordingly, in 10:6, 7 the Septuagint renders "holy robe," in reminiscence of Lev 16:4. Here, however, as in Dan 10:5; 12:6–7, it seems to demarcate its wearer as an angelic figure (cf. Mark 16:5; Rev 15:6). Linen was generally bleached and so white. The writing kit, which here reflects Egyptian practice, consisted of a wooden palette with hollowed places for cakes of black and red ink and a slot in which pens were kept (*IDB* 4:919; cf. D. J. Wiseman, *CHB* 1:31). It was evidently tucked into the waistline of the linen robe. The angelic group awaits its orders, standing by the "bronze altar," the old Solomonic altar of burnt offering that Ahaz had moved to the north side of the temple court (2 Kgs 16:14).

3a This observation is a deliberate anticipation of 10:4a and wants to insist that the incident of which it speaks had already occurred before that stage in the narrative—and before the present stage. It is not concerned to specify when it occurred but merely links its accomplishment with this context (cf. Becker, "Ez 8–11" 143–44). The God who issues his commands in vv 3b–7 is identified with the glorious figure who was already engaged in the first stage of leaving the temple. The mention of the "shocking rites" of chap. 8 in v 4 and of the arch-sinners of 8:16–17 in v 6 implies that Yahweh's commands are a reaction to the sins revealed in that chapter. Accordingly, the placing of 10:4a at the earlier point of 9:3 makes it clearer that Yahweh's abandonment of his temple is a direct consequence of his people's sins and a parallel punishment to the judgments of chaps. 9–10.

An alternative way of understanding the text involves taking it with what follows, rather than with what precedes (cf. Blenkinsopp 58). Then the verb is not pluperfect but perfect, simply attesting an event prior to the divine cry. In that case, perhaps Yahweh's rising from his throne is the act of the judge in passing sentence (Schmidt, *TZ* 6 [1950] 89 n. 21, with reference to Isa 2:19, 21; Mettinger, *Dethronement* 101). It is more likely, however, that there is here a reminiscence of the Priestly conception of the permanent presence of the glory of Yahweh in the tabernacle, with occasional "emanations" outside it to deliver pronouncements of punishment (Exod. 16:7, 10; Num 14:10; 16:19; 17:7; cf. Mettinger, *Dethronement* 89). Certainly the style of vv 3b–4 (see the *Notes*) evokes a communication of the God who has just revealed himself in glory. Whichever meaning is correct, the relation between 9:3 and 10:4a is left unresolved. Kraetzschmar (100) rightly rejected the harmonistic notion that in between the events of these two verses Yahweh resumed his position on the ark; however, one may not dispose of 10:4a, as he did.

The translation "cherub-structure" renders the singular כרוב "cherub." The singular form appears to be a way of differentiating from the plural כרובים "cherubim," who in the narrative of chaps. 10–11 represent the supernatural "living creatures" of chap. 1 who convey the throne of Yahweh. The use of the singular to differentiate their artistic counterparts from the celestial entities may be because the temple cherubim were a pair, whereas the others were four in number (Greenberg 198–99). It may, however, be because the temple cherubim formed a single structure, with one wing on each side extending horizontally and forming a seat for an invisible throne (cf. Keel, *Jahwe-Visionen* 24–26 and fig. 10, with reference to Haran, *IEJ* 9 [1959] 35–36). The interpretation of this singular form in terms of the cherubim in the holy of holies accords with rabbinic exegesis; it was revived by Müller (*Ezechiel-Studien* 26–29) and followed by Kraetzschmar (100). In 10:2, 4, Zimmerli (250) has interpreted the singular form as a true singular: only one cherub was visible to a person entering the holy of holies. However, Keel (*Jahwe-Visionen* 152) has observed that this representation does not accord with the layout in 1 Kgs 6:23–28, where the two cherubim stand parallel, facing the nave. Further, Zimmerli (232, 254) regards the difference in number as a redactional criterion. The plural redactionally refers to the mobile throne of chap. 1, while the singular in 10:2, 4 relates to a cherub statue in the basic text. In the secondary 9:3a, however, he finds a reference to the mobile throne. Other scholars simply read a plural in 9:3a (see *BHK*; Houk, *JBL* 90 [1971] 51). Greenberg (197) has correctly pointed out that the only meaningful direction of motion to the threshold is from inside outward, and so the singular naturally refers to the wooden figures in the inner sanctuary, and in turn כבוד "glory" relates to his permanent presence within it. The threshold of the temple was located between the porch and the nave of 8:16, at the doors of the nave.

3b–4 The second part of the main narrative begins, like the first, with a divine cry, now addressed to the seventh, linen-clad angel. The initial role of this angel and the function of his writing kit are revealed. He is to use his pen and ink to mark with a cross those who are to be exempted from the general destruction of the population of Jerusalem. The mark, like the sign put on Cain in Gen 4:15, has a protective significance. It is literally the letter *taw* or "t," which in the old Hebrew script was written in the form of a cross or plus sign. The Church Fathers unfairly traded on the reference to a cross, anachronistically understanding it in Christian terms and regarding it as a prooftext for the custom of making the sign of a cross.

The notion of sparing any comes as a surprise after the categorical divine statement of 8:18. The earlier part of the book has already displayed variety in the negative prospects of the Judeans, sometimes implying complete destruction within the land, sometimes permitting for some a short lease on life before death strikes (5:2, 12), and sometimes envisioning exile as a limbo where surviving sinners mourn over their sins (6:9). The sparing of 5:3 has an ironic ring in its context. In the next chapter, 12:16 accords with 6:9, while 14:22 is similar; in 21:8–9(3–4) both innocent and guilty are to be killed. The present passage is striking in that it straightforwardly implies the presence of innocent people in the capital, who were to be spared; perhaps 14:12–20 aligns with it. Different pastoral needs among Ezekiel's fellow prisoners of war presumably shaped these different prophetic responses. The small number of the survivors may be gauged from the proportion of one angel devoted to exemption and six to destruction. His unsummoned appearance in v 2, after the summons to the executioners in v 1, suggests his relatively minor role, at least in his task as a scribe. The survivors serve to enhance the sinful status of their fellow citizens and so the fairness of divine punishment, inasmuch as they voice God's own dismay at the cultic aberrations.

5–7 The narrative now moves into the latter half of the first section. The ruthlessness of 8:18 is to be applied to those who lack the mark of immunity. The executioners are to be unsparing, killing all three categories of the population, the old, the young, and mothers with their children. The sanctuary was no longer to serve as an asylum (cf. 1 Kgs 1:50–53; 2:28–34; 11:15). The slaughter began at God's sanctuary, "for there his holiness had been most profaned and his Torah most defied" (Muilenburg 574). Those who had committed the ultimate sin of 8:16–17 were to be the first to die. V 7 is strictly out of sequence, since the desecrating slaughter had already begun. It functions "as an explicit divine license to commit an unthinkable desecration" (Greenberg 178, following Hölscher, *Dichter* 70 n. 1). The desecration endorses that already committed by the cultic deviants of chap. 8. The killing of the men in front of the temple would formally desecrate the temple itself (cf. 2 Kgs 23:15–16, 20). The command to fill the courts with corpses overlaps with the initial tactical command in v 6aβ to begin at the sanctuary. This second stage covers not only the cultic sinners of 8:16–17 but those of 8:7–14: those in the "inner court" (8:16; cf. 8:14) and at "the entrance to the (outer) court" (8:7) would be included. The final command presumably sweeps within its scope any citizens worshiping illicitly at the city gate (8:3–6). The commands fan out and encompass in reverse the four groups who had engaged in shocking rites in chap. 8.

8 This third verbal communication of the chapter is not a divine command, like the earlier two, but a prophetic plea to God. Ezekiel can remain an onlooker no longer. He passionately projects himself into the visionary situation, as he is left alone (as the only person alive?) in the inner court to imagine the slaughter being perpetrated outside the temple area. This first half of the third part of the narrative picks up the key term מַשְׁחִית(י) "destruction" from vv 1 and 6 and incorporates it into his prayer of intercession. Intercession was a regular part of prophetic ministry: it occurs in a vision account at Amos 7:2, 5. It features in Ezekiel's ministry only here and in 11:13. Its relative absence aligns with the unconditional nature of the doom that is generally reflected in his oracles of judgment (cf. Jer. 7:16; 11:14; 14:7; Greenberg 203). Here Ezekiel protests against the destruction that has been so vividly portrayed as divinely instigated. The pleas of sinners may go unheard (8:18), but there is a chance that a prophet's plea may prevail.

The destruction of the city's population ordered by Yahweh is interpreted in terms of his reaction of anger forecast in 8:18: it is nothing less than the outpouring of his fury (cf. 36:18). Those of Israel who are left are presumably the survivors of the destruction at the hands of the Babylonians in 597 (cf. 2 Kgs 24:14). The population of Jerusalem was a natural concern for the prisoners of war taken to Babylonia, including Ezekiel, since their relatives and even children remained there (cf. 24:21, 25). It is implied that Jerusalem's fate spells the fate of Judeans in the rest of the homeland. The mention of the sinful status of both Judah and Jerusalem in v 9 shows that the capital had a representative role. Whether in his anguish Ezekiel overlooks those to be spared in v 4 (Kraetzschmar 103) or whether he seeks mercy for the sinners is not made clear. The fact that Yahweh's answer in vv 9–10 deals only with sin and sinners suggests the latter explanation.

9 The prophet's protest provides an opportunity for a powerful justification of the destruction at the close of the chapter. "Ezekiel prays, but the answer is in effect: Too late! Sin has reached its full measure" (Blenkinsopp 59). The mercilessness of v 5 is grounded in a fresh statement of the human guilt that must meet with retribution. The guilt is not expressed in terms of the religious sins of chap. 8 that were summarized in 9:4, though they are obviously included in its characterization as "quite considerable." Here the point is being made that the guilt relates not only to Israel's worship but also to their way of life. This other side of their guilt, which was briefly mentioned in 8:17, is now amplified. Jerusalem, as representative of the nation, must suffer for the social sins to be found both in the country at large and in the capital. The charges align with Jeremiah's denunciation of Jehoiakim (Jer 22:13–19; cf. Lam 4:13) and also with Ezekiel's post-587 comprehensive description of the final kings who abused human rights in Jerusalem and of royal officials who did the same both in Jerusalem and in Judah (22:25, 27, 29; see Allen, *Ezekiel 20–48* 31–33, 38–39). The description of objective guilt is reinforced by one of a subjective attitude that repudiated Yahweh's claim on their lives as no longer valid. The double description of the wicked in Ps 94:5–7 is remarkably similar, though it lacks the pointed reference to the defeat of 597:

> Your people, Yahweh, they crush,
> and your inheritance they afflict.
> Widow and resident alien they kill,
> and orphans they murder.
> They say, "Yah does not see,
> the God of Jacob does not realize."

The charges of 8:12 are here quoted. The reversal in order is a feature of literary quotation, while the use of the past tense אמרו "they (have) said" harks back to 8:12 (Beentjes, *Bib* 63 [1982] 508–9). We must take seriously the fact that in 8:12 these sentiments were attributed to the Judean elders. As political leaders they were responsible for the civil wrongs perpetrated in the capital and country, and in their destruction they were to drag down their fellow Judeans.

10   Yahweh continues in the vein of 8:18, גם אני "I for my part," and repeats the note of mercilessness he had sounded there and which in 9:5 he had urged on the executioners who represented him. The divine reaction, it is claimed, was commensurate with the guilt. It was too excessive for a reprieve, such as Amos had obtained in his first two phases of intercession, but significantly not in his third (Amos 7:1–9). In this new context the hard glint in Yahweh's "eye" is an ironic answer to the assertion of v 9 that he cannot see (Greenberg 178). The justice of the punishment is reinforced in the final sentence: the liability they disdained in v 9b Yahweh was simply laying at their door, where it belonged. He was the catalyst whereby deeds matured into their natural consequences.

11   The narrative comes to an interim close and also prepares to advance to its next stage, by the report of the return of the linen-clad angel, who is to feature again in chap. 10. Mention of his writing kit lays emphasis on his earlier role as agent of exemption from destruction. Ezekiel and the reader are implicitly reminded that, if unrepentant sinners could not secure mercy, there were those who stood on the side of God and the prophet whose lives were spared from the solidarity of a comprehensive punishment.

10:1   V 2 will continue the narrative with the new, punitive task of the linen-clad angel to take fire from the divine conveyance borne by the cherubim. This verse, introduced in the style of 8:2; 10:9, pauses to explain that the object mentioned in v 2 is the conveyance of chap. 1; 1:26a is cited, with "cherubim" taking the place of the living beings (חיות). The comment also appears to have a bearing on v 4, where the motif of Yahweh's abandoning the temple is introduced in the primary text (cf. 9:3). Eventually, Yahweh was to move to his conveyance and depart in it (vv 18–19). To this latter end, only 1:26a is cited, and the seated figure of Yahweh in 1:26b is left unmentioned. The mobile throne stands empty, ready for use by the divine king. There seems to be a third intent, perhaps the prime one, in the deliberate reference to chap. 1. There the vision of Yahweh's conveyance signified his character as judge and underscored Ezekiel's call to be a prophet of judgment. Here in v 2 the conveyance provides the fiery coals of judgment that will destroy Jerusalem. So v 1 draws attention to the close connection between the material source of judgment and the vision of chap. 1 and is at pains to observe that the same judgment-laden phenomenon has reappeared in the second vision. The chapter in its final form reflects a dominant need to amplify this observation in a variety of ways.

2 No longer is the angel described as equipped with his writing kit. His role changes from scribe to incendiary. Like Sodom of old, Jerusalem was to be destroyed by fire. The divine command corresponds to the order to kill the population, given to the other six angels in 9:5–7, but now the city itself is to be the object of destruction. Where is the fire to come from? V 1 has already implied that it is to be linked with the divine conveyance of chap. 1. Indeed, "fiery coals" feature there "between [מִתּוֹךְ, emended text] the living creatures" (1:13). It is feasible to suppose that the coals mentioned here, which are to be taken "from between the cherubim" (מִבֵּינוֹת לַכְּרוּבִים), are the very same. However, those scholars who consider that the references to chap. 1 and to cherubim generally in chap. 10 (and also 8:2) emanate from a wrong-headed redactor have been at pains to explain otherwise. The Masoretic reading כְּרוּב "cherub" in the first occurrence in v 2a may be cited in their favor, for the entities who man the conveyance in chaps. 10–11 are elsewhere referred to in the plural, while the singular is reserved for the cherubim-structure associated with the ark in the temple (9:3; 10:4; see *Note* 10:7.a.). However, late in v 2a a plural form appears. Moreover, in the recapitulation of v 2 at v 6 and in the narrative fulfillment at v 7, the plural is found at the corresponding places. Accordingly, the singular form in v 2 is to be emended to a plural (see *Note* 2.b.).

If the fire is given a cultic location in or near the temple, its source is problematic, especially as it is linked with a wheeled object. Zimmerli (250–51), who located the singular cherub in the sanctuary and considered all the plural references secondary, gave vent to his bewilderment in a barrage of questions, among which he speculated that a mobile brazier for the offering of incense was set before the ark in the holy of holies. Eichrodt (134; cf. Vogt, *Untersuchungen* 51), removing reference to the wheels as an accretion, judged the altar of incense in the nave, just outside the holy of holies, to be the source of the fire. Houk (*JBL* 90 [1971] 51), followed by Fuhs (57), harmonized all the singular and plural references to cherubim to plural forms. He thought in terms of wheeled laver stands that had side panels decorated with cherubim (1 Kgs 7:27–37) positioned on the south side of the temple (Ezek 10:4)—and also, he hypothesized, on the north side—and having between them the altar of burnt offering from which the fire came. Keel (*Jahwe-Visionen* 153, 160–61) has rightly rejected these labored explanations. He relates all the references to a single cherub, including the first occurrence in v 2a, not to the ark but to a theophanic phenomenon: Yahweh rides on a cherub (Ps 18:11[10] = 2 Sam 22:11). In this connection he offers a novel meaning for גלגל, which in chap. 10 is usually interpreted "wheelwork" or the like and which in my translation I have rendered "rotary system," to distinguish from (אופן(ים) "wheels." He takes it as a "mass rolled together" or conglomeration, consisting of dark cloud, coals, and lightning accompanying Yahweh's appearing (cf. Ps 18:9–10[8–9], 13–14[12–13]), both in chap. 10 and also in Ps 77:19(18) (NRSV "whirlwind"). Then the redactor(s) adapted or explained these references in terms of the similar vision account in chap. 1. Mettinger (*Dethronement* 100–102) has substantially followed Keel but favors less critical surgery than Keel or Zimmerli: he finds a basic reference to the mobile conveyance of chap. 1 in the singular "cherub" of 9:3; 10:2, 4.

Basic issues in this debate are, first, how far the text can be interpreted in a consistent way and, second, what form that interpretation should take. Where tension occurs, redaction criticism wishes to have its say, but textual criticism may also have a contribution to make. The MT in 10:2 creates havoc by its singular "cherub," and that at least should be adjusted by standard text-critical procedures. Apart from that, the text confronts us with two seemingly separate entities, one associated with a singular "cherub" and the other with the plural "cherubim." Houk would think of an original text with all plural forms, while Zimmerli would conceive of a primary text with a singular and a redacted text with plural forms. So does Keel, but with a radically different interpretation. Of the three interpretations of the source of the fire, Keel's is the most convincing. But it is strange at first sight that he did not find a direct reference to 1:13. After all, 1:13–14, along with 1:4, as I have explained it, uses the motif of theophany, as distinct from the heavenly throne tradition employed in most of the rest of chap. 1. Keel himself (*Jahwe-Visionen* 143) spoke of vv 13–14 as theophanic but considered them an intrusion because they did not align with the dominant motif of the chapter. This view, which ignores the structural dimensions of chap. 1 (cf. my structural analysis in *VT* 43 [1993] 145–51) and confuses redaction criticism with form criticism, predisposed Keel to find no significant reference to 1:13 in 10:2. Moreover, he was doubtless influenced by the fact that elsewhere in chap. 10 "cherubim" appear in undoubtedly redacted contexts.

One may sympathize with the reluctance of Zimmerli, Keel, and other scholars to find references to cherubim a primary feature, for a fundamental objection stands in the way of identifying the mobile cherubim of chap. 10 with the living beings of chap. 1. Both were hybrid beings, but the latter were winged, four-headed humanoids with the feet of calves (and so bullmen). On the other hand, winged cherubim, which represent supernatural protectors, especially of the tree of life, and at times functioned as bearers of a royal or divine throne, had animal bodies and human heads in ancient Near Eastern iconography. Typical examples of cherubim are the Egyptian sphinx, with the body of a lion, and the Mesopotamian entrance guardian, with the body of a bull. Both forms are radically different from the living beings described in chap. 1. It would be extremely difficult to confuse one group with the other. Mettinger (*Dethronement* 99–100) is untroubled by the metamorphosis. He compares August Strindberg's *A Dream Play*, in which a tree in one act appears as a coat hanger in the next. However, Ezekiel's visions do not display such surrealistic confusion elsewhere, and so one does not expect to find it here.

In fact, cherubim have been more broadly defined in the history of scholarship. Vincent (*Jérusalem* 2–3:401) considered that the temple cherubim had human bodies. Unfortunately, his reasoning was based on modern aesthetic standards. He found the notion of human forms in the holy of holies, rather than animal ones, "more worthy and in better harmony with their transcendent role." Busink (*Tempel* 1:269, 285–86) took over Vincent's description but based it on the winged, humanoid genii in ancient Near Eastern iconography. However, Keel (*Jahwe-Visionen* 16–18, 21, 152 n. 46) has observed that such protecting genii flanking a holy object typically faced each other. The ark cherubim had neither this function nor this orientation. They functioned as bearers of the deity, and these always had an animal form and looked forward. In the temple description in 1 Kgs 6:23–28, the gold-covered, olivewood statues of two-winged cherubim stand parallel, looking into the nave. The Chronicles account supports this positioning with an even clearer statement, in 2 Chr 3:13. Therefore, the cherubim in the temple must have had animal forms.

Keel (*Jahwe-Visionen* 16–17) comes to a different conclusion with respect to the cherubim in the wilderness tabernacle. In the Priestly account at Exod 25:20; 37:9, the two-winged cherubim face each other and do not function as bearers of the deity. A different type of cherub is represented there, with a human form. Such cherubim accord with humanoid figures that face an object, such as the tree of life or a divine image, and protect it. Forward-facing figures typically had animal bodies and sideways-facing ones had human bodies. A clear example of a sideways-looking guardian figure with a human body has been found on a bone mirror handle at Hazor. A four-winged cherub, in this eighth-century representation, faces and grasps the tree of life (*ANEP* 854; Y. Yadin, *Hazor* [London: Weidenfeld and Nicolson, 1975] 156–57).

Keel suggested that this Priestly representation may have been dependent on Ezek 10:20, where the cherubim are equated with the living beings of Ezek 1. But what if the Priestly account of the ark in the tabernacle was extant by the period of Ezekiel? The material in P seems to have emanated from different periods: Haran (*Temples* 189–204) has argued that the Priestly account of the tabernacle in the wilderness antedates the reigns of Hezekiah and Manasseh. If the account is earlier than Ezekiel, there is sufficient explanation for the equation of the living beings in chap. 1 with the cherubim in chap. 10, and already in the basic text of v 2 this equation may be seen as implicit. What the various amplifications seek to do is simply to make this presupposition explicit. The divine command of v 2 already envisions such a conveyance as chap. 1 described, with humanoid attendants and wheels of a certain kind.

The naming of the attendants as cherubim occasioned a flurry of explanatory activity; one must ask why the change of term was necessary. The literary means of the change is now apparent: it is plausible to posit dependence on the Priestly account of the tabernacle. It may well be that Ezekiel, versed in this scholastic tradition, considered that the temple cherubim also were of the humanoid type. Anyway, a clear parallel is drawn between the temple cherubim and the "cherubim" of the mobile throne. The intent was seemingly to detract from the significance of the temple cherubim and the associated concept of the protective presence of God grounded among his people. The earthly representation was a temporal shadow of a celestial reality. Two truths had to be proclaimed about this reality. First, it could be manifested differently, in terms of the omnipresent God of judgment, as Ezekiel had earlier experienced in the inaugural vision. Second, this manifestation was not to be tied permanently to time or place. In v 2 the former truth comes to the fore. The theophanic fire of 1:13 is now menacingly present in the inner court of the temple. The mobile cherubim that guard the fire of divine judgment by their presence implicitly overshadow the static models placed inside the temple beside the cultic presence of Yahweh, a notion that v 4 will develop.

Greenberg (180–81) has correctly observed that the wheels extended lower than the attendants, so that there was a space between and under the latter. The angel had to go into the towering structure and fill his "cupped hands" with some of the coals of fire that were to set the city ablaze (cf. Exod 9:8). Houk (*JBL* 90 [1971] 53–54), followed by Fuhs (57), interpreted the fire as purificatory, with reference to Isa 6:6–7, and the means of marking the innocent citizens in chap. 9. He was implicitly developing a suggestion made and rejected by Herrmann (66). His interpretation depends on reordering the present text, so that 10:2–7 (minus vv 4a, 5) originally came between 9:1–2 and 9:3–4. This hypothesis deprives the angel's writing kit of any significance.

3a Ezekiel, who witnessed the angel's entry into the nether parts of the divine conveyance, was presumably standing somewhere in the temple court, to which he had been brought in 8:16. Now the location of the conveyance is established as in the same court, the "inner" court of 8:16, which in v 4b is naturally called simply "the court." More precisely, the cherubim are situated on the south side, which can hardly connote "beneficial" here (Zimmerli 254, in differentiation from the approach of the executioners from the north in 9:2). The cherubim stand well away from the chain of abominations that had occurred at various points to the north of the temple and finally parallel with it (Greenberg 181, who, however, has bunched all the abominations into the temple court, in dependence on the MT).

3b–4 The phenomenon of the cloud filling the court in v 3b is explained and amplified in v 4. The cloud has links both with 1 Kgs 8:10–11 and with Exod 40:34–35. The former passage is often taken as a Priestly accretion from Exodus (see, e.g., Noth, *Könige*, BKAT 9 [Neukirchen-Vluyn: Neukirchener, 1983] 180–81), though Weinfeld (*Deuteronomy and the Deuteronomic School* [Oxford: Clarendon, 1972] 204) and Mettinger (*Dethronement* 88) regard Exod 40:34–35 as a retrojection of the Kings passage. In fact, our passage is slightly closer to Kings, in that the verbs of filling apply both to the cloud and to the glory. There are two important points to be noted. First, there is here a link with a Priestly tradition, which matches the earlier representation of the cherubim. The chapter moves steadily on Priestly lines. Second, there is an echo of Yahweh's taking possession of his completed sanctuary. It is an ironic echo, for here the glory is departing. Yet we cannot miss the significance of juxtaposing v 3a and v 3b. Two traditions are combined here, the Priestly one of the cultic manifestation of Yahweh and the application of the phrase "glory of Yahweh" to the theophanic manifestation of the heavenly throne in Ezek 1:28. The presence of the latter conception is clear from the use of נגה "radiance, bright aura," a key element in chap. 1, at vv 4, 13, 27, and 28, a term that had been borrowed from accounts of storm theophany (e.g., Ps 18:13[12] = 2 Sam 22:13; Hab 3:11). Zimmerli (251), whose concern it was to prune out references to chap. 1 as extraneous, left untouched v 4 with its small but unmistakable testimony to it. There is a sense of transition here, signaled both by the presence of the mobile cherubim in the court and by the movement of the glory of Yahweh from the ark to the threshold of the temple, on its way to joining the cherubim.

Underlying the passage is a complex theological concept of the presence of God, as Greenberg (196) has observed. Hossfeld's criticism of him for so doing ("Die Tempelvision" 160 n. 30) was motivated by his excessive redaction-critical stance. What Fretheim (*Suffering of God* 63) has called the "tabernacling presence" of God could coexist with his self-manifestation in theophany, as 8:4 bears implicit witness. Here the former is strikingly subordinated to, and gives way to, the latter. This may be why גלגל "rotary system" is used in the basic v 2: it has a literary association with the theophanic chariot. In Ps 77:19(18) it means or may be taken to mean "'wheel,' to be understood *pars pro toto* for the chariot" (Mettinger, *Dethronement* 105, following Jeremias, *Theophanie*, 2nd ed., 26 n. 3).

V 4a has already occurred in 9:3a, but this is its primary place. The intensification of divine presence represented by "glory" is here, as in 9:3, a cultic phenomenon. The movement of Yahweh out of and away from the temple is begun. Block (*Gods of the Nations* 129–61) and Bodi (*Poem of Erra* 191–218) have compared the motif of divine abandonment in Ezek 8–11 with the forms it takes in ancient Near Eastern texts. Our text has special links with three roughly contemporary Mesopotamian texts. First, in the story of Esarhaddon's rebuilding of Babylon, the patron deity Marduk's anger at the city for moral and cultic sins is narrated, and then follow his destruction of the city and temples, including his own, and his eventual return to his temple. The departure of other gods from Babylon is mentioned, and his own departure is implied by the subsequent description of his return. Second, the sixth-century Prayer of Adad-guppi briefly relates: "in the sixteenth year of Nabopolassar, king of Babylon, Sin, king of the gods, became angry with his city and with his temple and went up to heaven; the city and the people in it became desolate" (1:6–9). Third, the Cyrus Cylinder, celebrating the Persian conquest of Babylon in 538, mentions Marduk's great anger at the king's cultic aberrations and oppression of his people by forced labor, his departure with the other gods, and the consequent destruction of the temples and city and the annihilation of the population. These cultural examples of the motif provide striking parallels to its use in the context of chap. 8–11. They lend support to Zimmerli's refusal to countenance ("Das Phänomenon" 181–82) or even mention in his commentary the deletion of basic material relating to divine abandonment in 10:4, 18, 19; 11:23, advocated by scholars of the previous generation (Hölscher, *Dichter* 78; Bertholet [1936] 39; Balla, "Ezechiel" 1; cf. Houk, *JBL* 90 [1971] 49, 52).

5 In an afterthought, a comparison is drawn between the cherubim of vv 2–3 and the living beings of the inaugural vision. Like them, they had wings, and their flapping is related to one of the comparisons in 1:24. The simile "as loud as the Almighty" is amplified not only by the addition of "God" but by reference to the divine command of v 2. V 2 is the mainspring of the afterthoughts and redactional comments in chap. 10; it is a revelation on which light was continually sought. In this case v 2 provided an example of the divine voice, which is regarded as loud, as it is explicitly described in 9:1. The flapping of the wings alludes to

their motion, warming the motors up (Mettinger, *Dethronement* 101), as they prepare to leave. The reference to noise heard in the outer court is at first sight
strange, since Ezekiel is standing in the temple court. The outer court is distinguished from the inner court of v 3 and must refer to the court of 8:7, inside the
perimeter wall of the palace complex. Brownlee (150) has plausibly related the
place and the noise to an echo "reverberating from the high walls of the outer
court." Indeed, the palace buildings to the south may have caused the resonance.

6–7 V 2 is now resumed in a brief paraphrase, primarily after the digression
in vv 3–4, in order to prepare for its fulfillment in v 7. The narrative in passing
interprets the "rotary system" in terms of the wheels of chap. 1: a more formal
identification will appear in v 13. The last clause in v 6, "(and) he stood beside a
wheel," begins the next phase of the narrative, which continues in v 7. The execution of the command proves more complex than the command itself: one of
the cherubim hands the fire to the angel. His going out is not merely from the
undercarriage of the celestial conveyance but from the temple court, out into
the city, as in 9:7 (Sprank, *Ezechielstudien* 59 n. 1; Zimmerli, "Das Phänomenon"
181). A veil is drawn over the sequel, as in 9:7, where only the slaughter of the
men in the temple court could be recorded. The reason for this double reticence
is the literary principle of unity of place (Greenberg 193). The narrative takes its
cue from Ezekiel's own location and reports what he was able to observe.

8 Another afterthought is recorded, of the same type as that in v 5 (see *Form/
Structure/Setting*), now concerning the hands of the cherubim. It provides an explanation of the mention of the cherub's hand at the beginning of v 7 and takes
the opportunity to identify the cherubim in yet another aspect with the living
beings in chap. 1, here with reference to 1:8.

9a This is a different type of afterthought, paralleled in v 1 and also in 8:2
and typically consisting of one sentence. As an independent visionary statement,
it seems logically to postdate the kind of comment found in v 8, which is more
smoothly integrated into the flow of the narrative. It is an interruption, however,
that is most naturally to be attributed to Ezekiel himself. It develops the casual
identification of the "rotary system" of v 2 with the wheels of chap. 1. The close
relationship between cherubim and wheels evident from v 2 is explained in a
paraphrase of 1:15.

9b–12a An opportunity is taken to develop the comparison with chap. 1 in a
sustained and more detailed manner. It is difficult to avoid the impression that a
later redactor is at work here. The form of the wheels (vv 9b–10) and how they
function (vv 11–12a) are the objects of intense concern. The purpose of this study
is not only to explain the reference to the wheel at the end of v 6 but evidently to
shed light on a later point in the narrative, v 19a, where the wheels are involved
in the departure of the cherubim. What did these wheels look like? 1:16 supplies
information, both as to their jewel-like gleam and as to their spherical shape; this
information is cited in v 9b–10. How did they work? 1:17–18a is quarried for the
answer. They were constructed to move forward in any of four directions, in dependence on the cherubim. In turn the cherubim were locked into their forward
movement, following the head of the particular cherub that faced in the forward
direction. V 1, where the heads of the cherubim are encountered, with a collective singular, as in the basic 1:26a, provides the cue for mention of the head here.
It had for the redactor the merit of providing clarification of 1:18a and justifica-

tion for the explanation given in 10:12a: reference is found to the physical parts of the cherubim, matching the head. The redactor obviously found difficulty with this half verse. The initial וּגְבֵּיהֶן (with feminine suffix) in 1:18a was construed not as "and their rims," with reference to the wheels, but "and their backs," with reference to the (feminine) living beings, which are now understood as cherubim. The probable reason for this interpretation was a careful differentiation of גביהן from גבתם "their rims" (with a masculine suffix) in 1:18b, which was rightly recognized as the rims of the (masculine) wheels and interpreted as "the wheels" in 10:12b. V 12 provides interesting evidence of the antiquity of the variation in suffixes in chap. 1.

In line with the exegetical decision to relate 1:18a to the cherubim, יראה "fear" was misread or guessed as if it had to do with (arms and) hands. Was it taken as an Aramaic form ידיא "hands"? Then for completeness, there was a rounding out at beginning and end with "bodies" and "wings." Thus all the other parts of the cherubim moved in unison with their individual heads: in particular there is a focus on the three cherubim that were not taking the lead. One fact emerges from this overall interpretation in v 12a, which Herrmann (68) called "fantastic": for all its grammatical care and exegetical ingenuity, it stands at a distance from the basic 1:18a.

13 The text returns to one of Ezekiel's reflective afterthoughts, which at an earlier stage stood next to v 9a. It explains that what the prophet had there been calling "wheels," in line with chap. 1, were properly "a rotary system" in the language of the divine command he had heard and recorded in vv 2 and 6. Kraetzschmar's observation (111) that it should have come after v 6 is hardly fair. V 7 needed logically to come after v 6, but it raised the question of the cherub's hand, which had to be resolved in v 8. Then there could be a return to the issue of the "wheel" mentioned at the end of v 6, first in v 9a and then in the previously adjacent v 13. V 13 sorts out the apparent discrepancy between the reference to both the rotary system and the wheel in v 6.

12b, 16–17 Consecutive use of chap. 1 continues to be made, now from 1:18b–21. Again, the form of the wheels is considered first (v 12b) and then how they functioned (vv 16–17). V 12b is parallel with v 9b and describes their gleaming appearance in terms of the bright eyes that cover the rims, by citing 1:18b. This second block of redactional material has been split into two: v 12b was put with the first block in vv 9b–12a, before v 13, while vv 16–17 were set after it—and eventually at a greater distance by the subsequent intrusion of both v 14 and v 15. Why was the material severed in this way? There was good reason to place v 9b next to v 9a: it follows it in its master text, since v 9a reflects 1:15 and v 9b reflects 1:16a. The redacted text flows on, parallel with that of chap. 1. But the existing v 13 had to be eased into the redactional material at a suitable point. That point was judged to be after the reference in v 12b to "the wheels," which could provide an occasion for mention of their remaining in v 13.

Halperin (*VT* 26 [1976] 131), followed by Keel (*Jahwe-Visionen* 150 n. 40, 269), has suggested that the purpose of 10:9–17 was "to contribute not to the adjacent temple vision, but to the understanding of its own *Vorlage*—the description of the ʾ*ôpannîm* [wheels] in i 15–21" and to interpret the wheels in terms of angels. His premise that vv 9–17 have no contribution to make to the vision is rather hasty. His interpretation has sought to align the material with the understanding of the

ʾôpannîm as a group of angels in late Jewish angelological material. The earliest
evidence of this characterization appears in the Similitudes of Enoch (1 Enoch
61:10), which belongs either to the first century B.C. or to the first century A.D.
Earlier still, in the Songs of the Sabbath Sacrifice found at Qumran, the ʾôpannîm
are animate beings but are not yet regarded as a class of angels (Newsom, *Songs*
309, with reference to 4Q*405* 20 ii 21 22:3 and 4Q*403* lii 15). We have argued
above that exegetically v 12a aligns with v 11 and relates to the cherubim. V 12b
begins a new stage in the redactor's work, and the eyes are a feature of the wheels
alone, as in chap. 1. The present verse division in the MT may well reflect a later
understanding of the wheels in animate terms, encouraged by the corruption in
3:12. Interestingly, in Rev 4:6, 8 the "four living beings" are described as full of
eyes, which at least implies the relating of v 12a to the cherubim, rather than to
animate wheels, as Halperin understands the half verse. In order to maintain his
interpretation, he takes והאופנים "and the wheels" at the beginning of v 12b as a
marginal gloss (*VT* 26 [1976] 137).

The continuation of the redactional material in vv 16–17 uses 1:19–21 to show
the automatic reflex of the wheels to the various movements of the cherubim
and to find it not in any mechanical connection but in the invisible control
wielded by the cherubim by means of their "spirit." This, explains the redactor,
was how the wheels could move alongside the cherubim in v 19. V 16bβ is his own
reaffirmation that the wheels were incapable of independent movement. It corresponds to 1:20aα, which mentions the alignment of wheels and spirit (for the
rest of 1:20, see the pertinent *Notes*). That detail is not directly relevant for the
redactor, whose concern is the subordination of the wheels to the cherubim themselves. His replacement clause is a rough equivalent from his own perspective:
according to 1:21bβ, the spirit was in fact that of the living beings. If proof were
needed, the reference to "living beings" demonstrates that chap. 1 is being used
(Cooke 117).

18–19 The basic narrative is now resumed from v 7. It records a second stage
in the departure of the glory of Yahweh, after the first in v 4a. The empty throne
to which Ezekiel drew attention in v 1 is empty no longer. God's "tabernacling
presence" is over. It is replaced by his presence in a theophany of judgment. The
cherubim function no longer simply as guardians of the fire beneath the throne
but as bearers of the throne of v 1. The "glory of Yahweh" is here a reference to
the resplendent divine figure of 1:28, as it clearly was in v 4 and also in 9:3. However, 8:4 seems to use it more generally of the total revelation of Yahweh on his
mobile throne borne by living beings or cherubim, as in the earlier 3:12, to which
reference is made in 8:4.

The cherubim ascend into the air for the short journey of about fifty yards
across the court to the east gate of the court, going away from the direction of
the temple. The journey could presumably have been accomplished by the wheels
on the ground, but a formal flight served better the motif of divine departure,
which Ezekiel underlines with his subsequent reference to "the glory of the God
of Israel." The division of the departure into separate stages, of which the second
and the third occur in vv 18–19 (cf. v 4), also served to draw attention to the
departure. It is like the slowing down of the normal speed in a movie, so that
each movement in a particular scene can be savored. The use of the verb רום and
its passive surrogate רמם "be (raised) high" in vv 17, 19 is interesting. In the ac-

count of the inaugural vision, הנשא "be lifted up" is used, in a reflective portion, at 1:19, 21. The employment of רום accords with 3:12 (in the original text), where it appears in a narrative of departure, as here. The redactor, unaware of such a stylistic nicety, borrowed רום to use in his reflective material in vv 16–17.

20–22aβ In an afterthought, the prophet makes an explicit identification of the cherubim in vv 18–19 with the living beings of the vision associated with his call. He has come to realize that the living beings were what in the present narrative are called cherubim. Matching features, which corroborate the identification, are supplied in v 21, the four faces and wings and the arms, with allusion to 1:6, 8a. Despite the somewhat confusing reference to cherubim in the divine command of vv 2, 6, they were indeed the living beings described in chap. 1. What clinched the identification was the déjà vu distinctiveness of the faces. It is significant that the cherubim that decorate the temple walls in the eschatological vision at 41:18–19, in a section deriving from later redaction, face one another and so are presumably humanoid. They are described as having two faces, which Wevers (307) and Haran (*Temples and Temple-service in Ancient Israel* [Oxford: Clarendon, 1978] 258 n. 17) have rightly interpreted as a two-dimensional representation of four-faced creatures (cf. Allen, *Ezekiel 20–48* 233, where I followed Galling [in Fohrer 234] and Zimmerli [388] in wrongly speaking of two heads). This description has taken 10:20–21 seriously, with its information about the four faces of the cherubim and their identification with the (humanoid) living beings of chap. 1.

22aγb The redactor responsible for the two conjoined blocks of material concerning the form and operation of the wheels in vv 9b–12a and 12b, 16–17 makes a last, brief reference to form and mode of functioning here. Now not the wheels but the cherubim are in view. Their "appearance" has just been sketched in vv 21–22aβ. How they functioned can be cited from 1:12a. The quotation neatly serves to coordinate appearance and operation, for it traces the importance of the faces in determining direction of movement. The redactor's concern is to investigate why the throne bearers needed to have as many as four faces (v 21). The answer lies in the mobility of the divine conveyance.

11:1–21 The narrative about the departing glory is interrupted by an independent visionary experience in vv 1–13, which in turn is supplemented with a positive message in vv 14–21.

1–13 Mention of the entrance to the east gateway to the temple court in 10:19 prompted a reference to another vision Ezekiel had seen concerning that very place. This vision account is relevant to the basic narrative inasmuch as it overlaps with chap. 9 in its concern for the sin and judgment of Jerusalem (see *Form/Structure/Setting*). The passage is structured in a threefold pattern of narrative and speech. The first two sections contain narrative and divine speech, in vv 1–4 and 5–12, while the third comprises further narrative and the prophet's speech, in v 13. The divine speech consists first of a private communication to Ezekiel (vv 2–4) and then of a public oracle for him to deliver (vv 5aβ²–12).

1 The beginning of the vision account is parallel with 8:3, 5 in referring both to transportation by the spirit to a gateway in Jerusalem and to Yahweh's addressing the prophet. At the entrance to the east gateway to the temple, Ezekiel witnesses a meeting being held that is far from religious in nature. He recognizes from his previous residence in Jerusalem two men, Jaazaniah, who by reason of his patronymic is a different person from that in 8:11, and Pelatiah. He calls them שָׂרֵי הָעָם "officials of the people," a term that otherwise occurs only in postexilic texts, Neh 11:1; 1 Chr 21:2; 2 Chr 24:23. In Jer 29:2; 52:1 "officials of Judah" are differentiated from "officials of Jerusalem," with reference to royal officials who had responsibility for the two administrative areas. Here there is a general appellation, which may reflect the prophet's exilic remoteness (Zimmerli 257).

2–3 It must be Yahweh who speaks, in view of the divine commission to prophesy in v 4. A general characterization of the men is given, citing their involvement in morally evil projects. The first phrase, "making iniquitous plans," and the subsequent mention of "evil" seem to be deliberate echoes of Mic 2:1. Their policy is explained by a resolution in v 3a, which is supported by a metaphorical saying in v 3b. The resolution has been variously interpreted (see Zimmerli 258). The initial echo of the accusation in Mic 2:1–2 provides the clue: there the evil schemes of the powerful were to seize the houses of others, which they coveted (Ohnesorge, *Jahwe gestaltet* 69; cf. Fuhs 60; Fohrer 60; Greenberg 187). These city planners had no scruples in attaining their selfish ends, as the more specific accusation in v 6 will reveal. Their illegal seizure of the property of other citizens made it unnecessary to engage in further building. The epigram in v 3b is harder to interpret. The immediate context and the denial of the validity of the saying in v 11 (cf. v 7) make it clear that a positive, smugly reassuring comment is being made. One can imagine it being said with a knowing grin. The imagery is used differently in 24:3–11, as a metaphor of judgment relating to the siege of Jerusalem: Yahweh would make it hot for the citizens of Jerusalem! Here the thought may be that the caldron protects its contents from the fire (Keil 145; Bertholet [1897] 61). It is more likely, in the light of v 7, that there is an implicit contrast between meat, which corresponds to the best cuts of meat and choicest bones in 24:1 that are put into the caldron, and offal that has no right in the pot (Greenberg 187). The plotters are contrasting themselves with their victims, whose rights to live in the city they have denied.

4 The citation of the proud claims of the powerful elite has launched a disputation to which Yahweh will give a vigorous and reasoned response. The quotation also constitutes an accusation that triggers an oracle of judgment. Ezekiel is commissioned to transmit the oracle. The repetition of the command conveys the deep emotion provoked by the oppression. It is striking that an oracle is issued within a vision: the visionary prophet is characteristically an observer. A parallel occurs in 37:1–14, where Ezekiel becomes a participant in the unfolding of the drama of the dry bones that come to life. Here, however, he remains an observer. His vocal role (v 13) really impinges on the exiles who are listening to the vision account (cf. 11:25). They need to hear reasons why Jerusalem must fall and cannot be spared. The vision is a dramatic means of communicating this unpalatable truth.

5 A fresh segment of narrative appears. Mention of the spirit's falling on the prophet is unique, and it is sometimes suggested that it is a redactional addition (Zimmerli 258; Wevers 93; Ohnesorge, *Jahwe gestaltet* 51). A narrative prelude to the statement that follows is structurally fitting. Elsewhere in the book the spirit relates to the prophet as a means of empowerment (2:2; 3:24) or of the parapsychological feat of translocation (3:12, 14; 8:3; 11:1, 24; 37:1; 43:5). Closely associated with it is the hand of Yahweh as the initiating force in ecstatic experiences (1:3;

3:14, 22; 8:1; 37:1; 40:1). In 33:22 the divine hand is the instrument that releases Ezekiel from dumbness and so enables him to prophesy (cf. Isa 8:11; Jer 15:17). Similarly, the spirit functions here as the stimulus to prophecy, like the "burning fire" that constrained Jeremiah to proclaim the grim word (Jer 20:9). The range of usage of the onrush (צלח) of the spirit in early narratives is worth comparing. The present use corresponds to the onrush of the prophetic spirit (1 Sam 10:6, 10; cf. 1 Kgs 22:24), as opposed to that of the empowering spirit in Judg 14:6, 19; 15:14; 1 Sam 11:6; 16:13. A reason for mentioning the prophetic spirit will emerge later in the verse.

The mention of Yahweh's knowledge of the officials' schemes and feelings of security serves to express their responsibility to a higher, moral power.

> Sheol and Abaddon are visible to Yahweh:
> how much more human minds! (Prov 15:11)

Here the term for "minds" is רוח, the very word used earlier in the verse for the prophetic spirit. There seems to be a conscious polarization between the two mainsprings of speech, the human spirit that expresses itself in self-assured statements of abuse of power and the divine spirit that finds expression in criticizing and countermanding the schemes of its human counterpart. The officials are strikingly addressed as "community of Israel": as officials of the people, they act as representatives. The vocative has an ironic ring. They were certainly not living up to their responsibilities as members of God's covenant people.

6 The role of v 6 is to dispute the thesis propounded by the city leaders. It cannot be valid, because the activity that underlies the thesis is morally wrong. Lives as well as houses were involved in the real estate deals implied in v 3a, just as the disposal of Naboth's vineyard was facilitated by his assassination in the name of legality (1 Kgs 21:1–16). In this case, however, not an individual but large numbers had suffered. Eissfeldt (*Studies* 77–81) showed that חלל "slain" relates not only to the war dead but also to civilians who wrongfully lost their lives by murder or political execution (cf. Deut 21:1–6; Jer 41:9). Accordingly, Zimmerli's strained exegesis, following Horst (*VT* 3 [1953] 341), cannot stand, as Eichrodt (136 and n. 1) observed: he related v 6 to a future divine judgment, caused by the leaders' sin, of filling Jerusalem with corpses slain in war. In terms of an oracle of judgment, v 6 functions as accusation, while in terms of the disputation, it gives reasons for denying the validity of the initial thesis.

7–12a The accusation gives way to a pronouncement of punishment, formally introduced by the linking "therefore" and the messenger formula. Within the disputation it has the role of a counterthesis, as in 33:27–28.

7a The contrary proposition is a restatement of the thesis, which typically inverts the order of clauses (cf. 9:9 and the *Comment*). Those who have a legal and theological right to stay in the city are the people killed for their houses. By a gruesome extension of the metaphor, the meat in the caldron is identified as the corpses of the officials' victims. "The only good Jerusalemite is the dead Jerusalemite" (Taylor 110).

7b–8 But what of the oppressors? They have no right to the city properties they have taken over. So their fate will be to lose their comfortable niche in Jerusalem and to be slain in turn. The rhetorical logic of vv 7–10 depends on a break-up of the stereotyped phrase חֲלָל(י)-חֶרֶב "slain by the sword" (Num 19:16; Isa 22:2; Jer 14:18; Ezek 31:17, etc.). In a sinister word game, one word in the phrase suggests the other. "All who take the sword will perish by the sword" (Matt 26:52). Or in Ezekiel's own striking words in a later oracle, concerning the post-587 occupants of the land, those who "stand by the sword . . . will fall by the sword" (33:26–27). The sword refers to the fall of Jerusalem at the hands of the Babylonians, as v 9 will clarify. The officials were living in a fools' paradise, trying not to think of the fear that had haunted them since the earlier invasion in 597 B.C. That nightmare would come true. The sword would be sent in on Yahweh's orders, commissioned to work out his moral retribution. The divine-saying formula at the end of v 8 serves to mark a minor break in the sequence of thought.

9–10 An amplification of the double punishment of vv 7b–8 now follows. Divine expulsion from the capital would put them in the ruthless power of aliens (cf. 7:21). Thus would the judicial verdict of "guilty" passed against them by the divine judge be carried out (cf. 5:8, 10, 15). This death penalty would be exacted "on Israelite territory." The phrase עַל־גְּבוּל יִשְׂרָאֵל is a shortened variant of the fixed expression בְּכֹל גְּבוּל יִשְׂרָאֵל "in all the territory of Israel." Apart from 2 Kgs 14:25, גְּבוּל יִשְׂרָאֵל does not refer to the border of Israel (M. Ottoson, *TDOT* 2:365). Vv 9–10 have mistakenly been taken as an addition that reads back into the text the execution of leading Judeans at Riblah in Syria in 587 (2 Kgs 25:20–21); then the divine-saying formula in v 8 ended the original oracle, and the repetition of v 7 in v 9 was a mark of redaction (Zimmerli 259; Ohnesorge, *Jahwe gestaltet* 51–52). The oppressors' membership in the community of Israel (v 5) would not save them from a judicial death in Israel. They would suffer the punishment meted out by the God of the land (cf. 6:7, 11–14). The recognition formula in v 10b turns the oracle of judgment into a divine-proof saying. The punishment would be a means to a particular end, the proof of the moral authority of Yahweh, willfully overlooked before his forceful intervention into Judean affairs.

11–12a The oracle is extended in these closing affirmations. This material too has been regarded as secondary, but it should not be impeached on textual grounds (see *Note* 11.a.; v 12b, on the other hand, cannot stay). The form critic does not like continuation after the usually final element of the recognition formula, while the redaction critic is suspicious of repetition (cf. Hitzig 77; et al., including Zimmerli 259; Ohnesorge, *Jahwe gestaltet* 52). For the rhetorical critic, repetition is welcome as an emphatic device characteristic of Hebrew literature. The second role that the oracle has, as a disputation, has determined the presence and content of this further material. In a final twist, the counterthesis of v 7a is rephrased as an outright denial of the thesis in v 3 and related to the future of which vv 7b–10 had spoken. The privilege to reside in Jerusalem was not theirs. Israel's location for the due process of law for deviant members of Israel's community is reaffirmed. There was no lesser means whereby Yahweh could reestablish his authority over them.

13 The segment of narrative introduces the last speech, this time a vocal reaction from Ezekiel. The references to his prophesying and to Pelatiah glance backwards over the unit, citing the verb of v 4 that embraces vv 5–12 and also one of the names of v 1. Evidently Ezekiel carried out the command to prophesy and duly repeated the disputation and proof saying of vv 5–12. The prophet is horri-

fied by the instant demise of Pelatiah (cf. Acts 5:5). It was not a result of his prophesying, which envisions a later fulfillment in terms of invasion and conquest. It
was thus not an event like the death of Jeremiah's rival Hananiah, who died after
a personal oracle to that effect (Jer 28:15–17; cf. Acts 5:9–10). In fact, Pelatiah,
by his quick and premature death, evaded the particular fate decreed by the
oracle. This surprise ending raises questions about the nature of the vision account. Unlike the main temple vision, was it intended as a veridical account? Then
the prophet was exercising the God-given gift of second sight, somewhat like
Elisha in 2 Kgs 5:26; 6:31–33 (Cooke 123; Eichrodt 139–40). However, presumably the veridical nature of the vision did not extend to the prophesying, which
seems to be a voice-over device to express divine judgment, addressed to the exilic
hearers, rather than an integral element of involvement, such as it is in chap. 37.

For Ezekiel the sudden death must have functioned as an omen, as "God's
veto" on the future of Jerusalem and its citizens (Horst, *VT* 3 [1953] 342). It is
probable that the very name "Pelatiah," which means "Yahweh provides escape,"
contributed to the ominous nature of the incident (Goettsberger, *BZ* 19 [1931]
14; cf. Greenberg 189; so earlier Calvin 362). The event tragically belied his name.
But it raised a larger question concerning the Judah-domiciled "Israel" of v 5,
who had escaped the rigors of 597. To this question Ezekiel gives anguished expression in v 13b. It is framed as a statement and so takes a stronger form than
the parallel 9:9, but clearly it has the force of an intercessory prayer or a prophetic lament.

14–21 The anguished prayer of v 13 echoes down the years. This next oracle is
meant to serve as a virtual reply. It has an independent, non-visionary agenda, as
its separate message-reception formula in v 14 attests, but it functions here as a
literary answer that honors the spirit of Ezekiel's petition. The oracle is best interpreted as a post-587 prophecy (see *Form/Structure/Setting*). It is a disputation, like
vv 1–13, but this one blends the counterthesis with a proclamation of salvation. The
thesis, dispute, and counterthesis are distinguished by the separate verbs of saying
(אמר) in vv 15, 16, and 17, as they were in the previous disputation (vv 3, 5, 7).

15 As in 33:24, the non-exiled Judeans console themselves with a theological
claim to the land. In a spirit of one-upmanship, they explicitly contrast themselves with the exiles and raise their own self-esteem at the others' expense.
Yahweh is categorized as God of the land (cf. 1 Sam 26:19; Hos 9:3). A providential conclusion can be drawn, that the exiles have been banished from his
presence, while those left behind still bask in it, enjoying the land as a "sacramental assurance of the favor of Yahweh" (Zimmerli 261). This double assessment in
terms of the possession and denial of territorial rights is made even more of a
put-down for the exiles by the introductory v 15a. It is Ezekiel's own family and
community who are presented as the target of this exclusive way of thinking.
Three concentric circles of kinship are drawn, the first of which is his very own
brothers, members of the nuclear family. The second is a wider circle, the extended family, which significantly relates to the right of a family member to
redeem the land of a relative who had the misfortune to lose it (see Lev 25:25–
26, 29–32; cf. Lev 25:48–49). There was room in the laws of redemption even for
a priestly family like Ezekiel's (Lev 25:32–34). The non-exiled Judeans had failed
to reckon with the right of redemption. This reference casts a beam of hope over
the demeaning thesis and its evaluation. So does the definition of the third and

widest circle, "the whole community of Israel in its entirety." In this context, as in 20:40 (cf. 37:15–23), it seems to refer to the Judean exiles languishing in their Babylonian settlements, characterizing them exclusively as the people of God. The battle lines are drawn up right from the beginning. It is unambiguously affirmed that the Judeans, who have gone through the judgment of exile and stand before God as those who have received the due reward for their deeds, are the ones who have a future with God as his family (cf. Luke 18:14).

16 The initial formal reaction of Yahweh to the land claim of the non-exiles rhetorically addresses them, in the spirit of v 15, which spoke of the exiles as the distant "they." This verbal reaction disputes the thesis. It grants the premise on which the thesis was based, the fact of exile, and even interprets it theologically in terms of an event initiated by Yahweh. For the exiles the old country had been replaced by other countries as their home. However, the dispute adduces a damaging modification of the thesis by claiming that Yahweh is still present with the exiles, though in a reduced form. So they were not "far from Yahweh," as the thesis claimed. This reduced presence is strikingly described in terms of "a partial sanctuary." Reference is often made to Isa 8:14 for elucidation, but the text there seems to require emendation. The formulation may imply that the basis of the exiles' self-confidence was the ability to worship at the ruined temple site in Jerusalem (cf. Jer 41:5). In that case the unexiled Judeans were laying claim to a territorial belief that to worship in the temple carried with it the benefit of continuing as a member of God's people in God's land (see Exod 15:17; Isa 57:13; cf. R. E. Clements, *God and Temple* [Oxford: Blackwell, 1965] 73). The Targum interpreted the present phrase in terms of synagogues, but this is a homiletical rendering: there is no sure knowledge of synagogues until the Hellenistic period in Egypt. We are not told in what ways the limited presence of God among the exiles was apprehended. It may fairly be explained in terms of Jer 29:12–14, in the shorter form of the LXX:

> "You will pray to me and I will hear you,
> and you will seek me and find me,
> when you seek me with all your heart,
> and I will reveal myself to you."

The spiritual presence of God before the exile (and after: cf. chaps. 40–48) required the religious props of temple festivals and sacrifices. But it was available for the exiles apart from the institution of the temple (cf. Dan 6:10).

17 The counterthesis begins in v 17 and continues till v 20. It takes the glorious form of a proclamation of salvation. V 17 has a change of perspective: the exiles, who are the real recipients of the oracle as a whole, are now addressed. Yahweh's personal intention was to return them to their homeland. In so doing, it is implied, he would act as their *gōʾēl* or redeemer, and claim back the land for his people (Liwak, "Probleme" 118–19). What Ezekiel could not do for his family (v 15a), Yahweh himself would undertake for his people. The beginning of the message, v 15a, had raised hopes for the exiles that redemption was part of God's continuing purposes for Israel, which he would accomplish as the spiritual patron of the exiles. There seems at this point to be the beginning of a drawing on the Priestly passage Exod 6:6–8. M. Fishbane (*Text and Texture* [New York:

Schocken, 1979] 132) has observed the sustained usage of this passage in Ezek 20:33–42, with reference to a second exodus. In Exod 6:6 the exodus is represented as Yahweh's redeeming activity, as the exercising of his claim on his people rather than the Egyptians. Here by implication there is to be a new exodus, which would lead to Yahweh's claiming back the land for his exiled people. As in Ezek 20:42, the traditional term ארץ "country" in the basic Exod 6:8 is replaced by אדמת ישראל "the soil/land of Israel," which is characteristic of Ezekiel's oracles and speaks in warm terms of the distant homeland (cf. Zimmerli 203). Usually in Ezekiel there is reference to bringing into the land (20:42; 34:13; 36:24; 37:12, 21; cf. Exod 6:8a). Here it is replaced by the giving of the land, in reflection not only of v 15 above but also of the underlying Exod 6:8b. Ezekiel's hearers would not be unaware that Exod 6:8 promises the land as a מורשה, that which is taken over with full right—the very term that the native Judeans had arrogated for themselves in v 15 with the same verbal construction. The old scripture comes to new life in the setting of exile.

18 The rest of the counterthesis is addressed to Ezekiel, reverting to the perspective of the opening of the oracle, v 15a. V 17 dealt with the second part of the thesis, the issue of the land and its rightful owners. In vv 18–20 the prior part is contested, concerning separation from Yahweh. Fellowship between Yahweh and his repatriated people is promised, under three aspects. The first relates to proper worship. In 20:40–41 there is a reference to the new, acceptable worship to be instituted on God's holy mountain, by contrast with idolatrous worship entertained by some of the exiles (20:32, 39). Here the implicit contrast is with the illicit practices of the Judeans at home, to which the parallel oracle of 33:23–29 plainly refers, in 33:25–26, 29. The noninstitutional spirituality enjoyed by the exiles in v 16b would be translated into a reformation of the religious evidence they would find on their return (cf. 2 Chr 14:2–3[3–4]).

19–20a The second aspect of fellowship that Yahweh and his people would enjoy was to be in terms of general obedience to his will. Both Jeremiah and Ezekiel were aware that the radical deviation of late preexilic Israel from Yahweh's revealed will required an equally radical solution. Ultimately what needed to be removed lay not outside them, as in v 18, but inside, and only God could do that. The heart stands for the will: Israel's hearts had been hard and wanton (2:4; 3:7; 6:9). "Stone hearts" refer to that which is unconscious, immobile, and so unresponsive to God (cf. Exod 15:16; 1 Sam 25:37). By contrast, "hearts of flesh" relate to that which is tender, yielding, and responsive. What was needed was a transformation wrought by God, replacing unresponsiveness with a new compliance to the will of God. This compliance meant obedience to the Torah, the revelation of Yahweh's will for Israel. God had to break in, to do "what the law could not do . . . , in order that the just requirement of the law might be fulfilled" (Rom 8:3–4). The old divine standards were to continue (cf. 20:11, 19), and the human condition was to be eschatologically changed to rise to their sublime level. "The same law *by which* the people were judged becomes the law *to which* they were saved" (Raitt, *Theology of Exile* 182). If v 19 represents a removal of Israel's former unreceptive hearts, v 20a corrects the disobedience deplored in 5:6–7.

20b The third aspect of fellowship with God is the resumption and fulfillment of the former relationship. Whereas Exod 6:6, 8 were echoed earlier, now it is the turn of Exod 6:7. As in that text (cf. Lohfink, "Beobachtungen" 304 n.

100), this covenant between patron God and client people is not logically subsequent to the earlier stages but concurrent with them. The old covenant formulation of Yahweh's commitment to his people in Exod 6:6–8 is here revived and made the object of hope. The motif of God's claim on his people has been incorporated into this re-presentation of his initial pledge of divine patronage. The intrusion does not jar, for the divine claim was to be facilitated by divine enabling.

21 This last verse is difficult to get into precise focus with its context, perhaps because different facets of interpretation are intended, according to the particular context with which one aligns it. Most obviously it forms the latter part of a framework shared by v 15. From this perspective it relates to the impious Judeans left in the land (cf. v 18), whose arrogant claims had sparked the disputation (Cornill 239; et al.). For those who so blatantly rejected God's claims, there could be only judgment, while salvation awaited his true people in exile. The use of the formulaic "put their way upon their heads" in v 21b supports this basic interpretation: it is employed in 9:10 and 22:31 of the pre-587 residents of Jerusalem and in 17:19 of Zedekiah. Yet Hossfeld (*TQ* 167 [1987] 275) has rightly observed that the evidence of pagan worship being entertained by the exiles in 14:1–11 (cf. 20:32) shows that a reference to the exiles is included. Just as in 33:23–29 the denial of the nondeported Judeans' claim on the land because of their immorality posed an implicit challenge for the exiles in 33:30–33, so the present statement functions as a double-entendre that reached beyond sinners in the homeland to embrace sinners in exile.

22–23 The narrative interrupted by 11:1–21 and before that by the afterthoughts and redactional observations in 10:20–22 is now resumed. V 22 functions as more than a recapitulation of 10:19. It has its own role to play in the description of the last stage in the gradual departure of Yahweh's glory. The repetition of v 19 in v 22 serves as a ceremonial backdrop, with the cherubim acting as a guard of honor accompanying the divine king on the fateful journey. It is like a symbolic ceremony marking a colony's independence. It is made plain that a climactic point has been reached in the relationship between Yahweh and his people. The king and his entourage leave the capital. The final stop at the Mount of Olives (cf. Zech 14:4), after flying over the Kidron Valley, accentuates Yahweh's leaving the temple and the holy city. In the ancient Near Eastern motif of a deity's abandoning his temple, the god typically returns to heaven, as indeed Hos 5:15 implies. Here enough has been said in the report of Yahweh's pausing outside Jerusalem: "Behold, your house is forsaken" (Luke 13:35). Anyway, for the watching prophet, the Mount of Olives marked the eastern horizon of the city (von Orelli 44). The literary principle of unity of place, which was observed at work earlier, is evident again. The glory of Yahweh "could be seen by Ezekiel clearly outside the city limits" (Stuart 105).

24–25 As in 3:14–15, the close of the vision is marked by the spirit's transportation of Ezekiel back to the settlement where he lived with his fellow exiles. Here, however, v 24b serves to confirm that his visionary experience had occurred in a trancelike state, unlike the vision of chaps. 1–3. Taylor (113) and Greenberg (191) have compared the "rising" of the vision with the ascent of the divine figure at the close of a theophany (Gen 17:22; 35:13). The elders have been waiting for an oracle (8:1). They now receive it in their capacity as "exiles," as representatives of the exilic community. The prophet returns to consciousness of his natural surroundings and of his mission. The elders heard in the telling of the vision the chilling message of Yahweh's indictment and final judgment of the city to which they had been hoping to return and resume their normal lives.

Explanation

This vivid portrayal of sin and judgment conveys the enormity of both the sins committed in Jerusalem and the divine reprisals that must therefore befall it. "Eye-witnessing . . . here serves theodicy: the prophet sees with his own eyes the depravity of the people and hears judgment pronounced with the culprits in his presence" (Greenberg 200). Or, in Calvin's words (283), "the Almighty must of necessity appear as the avenger of his glory and worship." The portrayal begins and ends with a framework of comings and goings. There are four stages of the prophet's advance into the temple area. As he advances, four separate film clips, as it were, present ever greater sinfulness. Ezekiel "moves from secular space to locations that are progressively more sacred space, . . . from what he considers less reprehensible to more abominable cultic activities" (Ackerman, *Under Every Green Tree* 55). The image and altar at the city gate (8:3b–6), the secret cult at the gate to the palace complex (8:7–13), the open worship of Tammuz at the entrance to the temple court (8:14–15), and the blatant worship of the sun god in front of the temple (8:16–17) are the four scenes to which the prophet is brought in his vision. Some of this religious activity, at least the first act and perhaps the last, would have been justified by its devotees in terms of "poly-Yahwism," to use Rose's striking term (*Ausschliesslichkeitsanspruch* 208), but from the prophet's perspective they were all aberrations and alien to Yahweh's primitive revelation.

Such human comings are matched by divine goings (cf. the slightly different view of Vogt, *Untersuchungen* 53 and n. 26, implicitly followed by Hossfeld, *TQ* 167 [1987] 275; id., "Die Tempelvision" 153). In chaps. 10–11 four stages of Yahweh's departure are depicted, from the holy of holies, where he was enthroned above the ark, to the threshold of the temple (10:4; cf. 9:3), to the mobile conveyance of the cherubim (10:18), then over to the east gateway of the temple court (10:19), and finally beyond the city to the Mount of Olives (11:23). Within this framework it is made clear that Yahweh's departure is accompanied by destruction, presented in two scenes in chaps. 9–10. His celestial agents are ordered to carry out a bloodbath in Jerusalem and to make it a blazing inferno. The description of the sword and fire that the Babylonians would bring to the capital in 587 in terms of the angelic fulfilling of divine commands is reminiscent of the later apocalyptic representation in the book of Daniel of heavenly conflicts that match their earthly counterparts (see Dan 10:13–14, 20–11:1). The prophet's comings in chap. 8 receive a preliminary antithesis in the departure of the angelic execution squad, whose killing begins with the sun-worshipers of 8:16 and continues back through the courts and out into the city, in a reversal of Ezekiel's incoming journey through scenes of cultic sin (9:6–7). There is an echo of this initial angelic departure in that of the celestial incendiary, who receives the fire of judgment from beneath the mobile conveyance that had featured in the theophany of judgment in chap. 1 (see 1:13) and leaves the inner court to do his destructive work in the city (10:2, 7). The exits of 9:7 and 10:7 are matched and transcended by the divine exodus in 10:18–19. Another factor that binds the vision together is the double notation in 8:12; 9:9: "Yahweh cannot see; Yahweh has left the country" (cf. Greenberg 200). God *has* seen, and his showing the prophet in chap. 8 is the proof. Moreover, the excuse that he has left turns into an unconscious prophecy: God does leave, but at his own chosen time.

The conveyance introduced into the vision account in 10:2 provides a coordinating factor: it ties together the destruction of Jerusalem by fire and the eventual departure of Yahweh. Preparation for this double role has been made by the judgment theophany in chap. 1, which is echoed in 10:2. There is a change of terminology from חיות "living beings" to cherubim, which facilitates the theme of the permanent presence of Yahweh above the cherubim in the holy of holies giving way to a merely temporary theophanic presence. This momentous theme was subsequently underscored with a variety of explanatory comments harking back to the vision of chap. 1 and spelling out the identity of the conveyance in this vision with the one that featured there.

The supplementing of the vision with a parallel vision in 11:1–13 provides an opportunity to emphasize the social side of the wrongdoing committed in Jerusalem alongside the cultic sins (cf. 8:17; 9:9) and also to tie the angelic judgment of chaps. 9–10 to earthly actualities. The reiteration of the prophet's reaction of despair (11:12; cf. 9:8) triggers the incorporation of a nonvisionary oracle of hope, a different hope that replaces the lost hope of the sparing of Jerusalem. We are reminded of the deliberate supplementing of oracles of judgment with oracles of salvation later in the book, notably in chap. 20. The intended readers of the book are deported Judeans living in the post-587 period of exile, who looked back to a past judgment. For such, the saga of Yahweh's dealings with his people could be brought up to date. They had a God-given "future and a hope" (Jer 29:11)—and even a present experience of his limited presence. Ahead lay a prospect of much greater fellowship with him and an eschatological enjoyment of the promises of Exod 6:6–8. Lest the recipients of such promises—involving a second exodus, return to the promised land, and inner renewal—act irresponsibly, they are reminded, rather as in 3:16b–21, that if judgment is past, it is not a thing of the past. In a relative sense judgment looms over the heirs of promise, so that hope ever contains a purifying factor (cf. 1 John 3:3). The echoing of 9:6 in 1 Pet 4:17, "For the time has come for judgment to begin with the household of God," widens the issue to the suffering of believers in the eschatological tribulation, but in its own way it wants to affirm their obligation to "do good" (1 Pet 4:19).

The temple vision serves to develop themes broached earlier in the book. The crucial link with the judgment vision of chap. 1 has already been mentioned. Cassuto ("Arrangement" 231) has observed two links with chap. 7: the divine aloofness of 7:22, whereby invaders might raid the temple with impunity, grows into Yahweh's active withdrawal, and the abominations and detestable objects of 7:20 (cf. 5:11) are carefully categorized in chap. 8. Boadt ("Rhetorical Strategies" 188 n. 21) has noticed that the double formula of divine mercilessness in 8:18; 9:5, 10 continues the expressions found in 5:11; 7:4, 9. There are three other links. The outpouring of wrath proposed in 7:8 is portrayed in 9:8 (cf. 8:18), while the social sin of injustice in 7:10 resurfaces in 9:9 and the "aliens" of 7:21 reappear in 11:9. The twin themes of sin and punishment thus receive strong reinforcement in this vision account.

The happy ending to the unit implicitly contrasts the condemned sanctuary of 9:6 with the metaphorical "partial sanctuary" that the exiles found Yahweh to be (11:16). The oracle of salvation does not specifically go on to mention a renewed sanctuary. Apart from 20:40, it is left till 37:26–28 to make that promise. Its own motifs of return to the land and a renewed relationship with Yahweh are deemed worthy of repetition in 36:24–28. The promise at the end of chap. 37 is embodied in a separate vision, the vision of the new temple in chaps. 40–48. In the course of that vision, Yahweh's re-entry through the east gate and the filling of the temple with his glory (43:1–5; cf. v 7) represent a wonderful reversal. Where sin abounded and judgment rightly fell, grace was to superabound in the holy fellowship of God and his people.

Further Signs and Meanings (12:1–20)

Bibliography

Amsler, S. *Les actes des prophètes.* Essais bibliques. Geneva: Labor et Fides, 1985. **Fohrer, G.** *Die symbolische Handlungen der Propheten.* ATANT 54. 2nd ed. Zürich: Zwingli, 1968. **Friebel, K. G.** "Jeremiah's and Ezekiel's Sign-Acts: Their Meaning and Function as Non-verbal Communication and Rhetoric." Diss., University of Wisconsin, Madison, 1989. 623–86. **Giesebrecht, F.** *Die Berufsbegabung der alttestamentlichen Propheten.* Göttingen: Vandenhoeck & Ruprecht, 1897. **Keel-Leu, O.** *The Symbolism of the Biblical World: Ancient Near Eastern Iconography and the Book of Psalms.* Tr. T. J. Hallett. New York: Seabury, 1978. **Krüger, T.** *Geschichtskonzepte im Ezechielbuch.* BZAW 180. Berlin: de Gruyter, 1989. 404–6. **Laato, A.** *Josiah and David Redivivus.* ConBOT 33. Stockholm: Almqvist & Wiksell, 1992. 149–53. **Lang, B.** *Kein Aufstand in Jerusalem.* 2nd ed. Stuttgart: Katholisches Bibelwerk, 1981. 17–27. **Long, B. O.** "Two Question and Answer Schemata in the Prophets." *JBL* 90 (1971) 129–39. **Uehlinger, C.** "'Zeichne eine Stadt . . . belagere sie!' Bild und Wort in einer Zeichenhandlung Ezechiels gegen Jerusalem (Ez 4f)." In *Jerusalem Texte-Bilde-Steine.* Freiburg: Universitätsverlag; Göttingen: Vandenhoeck & Ruprecht, 1987. 136–40. **Uffenheimer, B.** "'And You, Son of Man, Prepare for Yourself an Exile's Baggage' (Ezekiel 12:1–16)." In *Studies in the Bible and in the Ancient Near East.* FS. S. A. Loewenstamm, ed. Y. Avishur et al. Jerusalem: Rubinstein, 1978. 45–54 (Heb.).

Translation

[1] *I received the following communication from Yahweh:* [2] *"Human one, you are living among that rebellious community,[a] who have eyes to see with, but see nothing, who[b] have ears to hear with, but hear nothing, because they are a rebellious community.* [3] *So, human one, you are to make up a pack for exile and then set out for exile[a] in the daytime, with them as spectators. When they watch you going into exile, leaving your present home and going elsewhere, perhaps they will see the truth, though[b] they are a rebellious community.* [4] *While they watch, carry out your pack, made up of such things as you would take into exile. Do it in the daytime. Then in the evening go out yourself, still under their observation,[a] acting as any deportee would.[b]* [5] *While they watch, break through the wall and go out[a] through it.* [6] *Under their continued gaze shoulder your pack,[a] going out[b] at dusk.[c] Keep your face covered so that you cannot see the ground. The reason for doing all this is that I am making you[d] an omen for the community of Israel."* [7] *I did just as I had been instructed. During the day I carried out my pack[a] suitable for exile. In the evening I broke through the wall with my hands.[b] I went out[c] at dusk, shouldering my pack[d] as they watched.*

[8] *Next morning I received a communication from Yahweh:* [9] *"Human one, the community of Israel, that rebellious community, asked you what you were doing, didn't they?* [10] *Say to them,[a]* [11] *I represent an omen for you.[a] They will experience[b] what I have acted out: they will go into exile as prisoners.[c]* [12] *Even[a] the head of state, who is there with them, will shoulder his pack,[b] going out[c] at dusk. He will have had a breach made[d] in the wall through which he may be brought out.[e] He will keep his face covered, because[f] then he will not see anything.[g]* [13] *So I will spread out my net for[a] him; he will be caught in my hunting equipment. I will bring him to Babylon in Chaldea—though he will not*

see it!—and then he will die. [14]*As for all his entourage, who assist him,*[a] *and all his troops,*[b] *I will scatter them to every wind, chasing after them with drawn sword:* [15]*then they will realize that I am Yahweh. When*[a] *I have dispersed them among the nations, scattering them in foreign countries,* [16]*I will leave a few of them unscathed by sword, famine, and pestilence, with the intent that they should declare all their shocking practices among the nations they have reached; so they*[a] *will realize that I am Yahweh.*"

[17]*I received the following communication from Yahweh:* [18]"*Human one, you are to quake*[a] *as you eat your bread, and shudder*[b] *as you drink your water.* [19]*Tell the people of the land this message from the Lord*[a] *Yahweh concerning*[b] *the residents of Jerusalem still on Israelite soil: They will eat their bread anxiously and drink their water with trepidation, anticipating*[c] *its*[d] *territory being desolated and stripped*[e] *of what now fills it, as a result of the violence perpetrated by all who reside there.* [20]*The other cities, now inhabited, will also be laid waste, and the country will become desolate. Then you will realize that I am Yahweh.*"

Notes

2.a. Strangely, the LXX has the equivalent of בתוך תועבותיהם "among their abominations," which is hardly original, not least because the suffix lacks an antecedent. Presumably the suffixed noun once stood in the margin and was foolishly taken as a correction of בית המרי "the rebellious community," with which it has some letters in common. Doubtless the intention of the gloss was exegetical, to supply an object for the seeing and hearing.

2.b. A copula is implied by LXX Syr Tg^MSS Vg and read by some MSS. It could have fallen out by haplography. However, Kraetzschmar (124) observed that Jer 5:21, which probably underlies this clause, lacks it.

3.a. Heb. וגלה "and go into exile" is not represented in the LXX* and since Hitzig (81) has usually been judged a dittograph, on the ground that it anticipates וגלית "and go into exile" in v 3b. However, Driver (*Bib* 35 [1954] 150) defended it by taking the following verb as conditional (cf. REB). Greenberg (209), anticipated by Jahn (73), has also counseled the deletion of יומם "in the daytime" as a mechanical intrusion from v 4a. In Brownlee 170, I commented that "the general nature of גלה ['go into exile'] is significant: it is subdivided into the two stages of bringing out and going out in v 4. The process is initiated during the day: the timing is mentioned because its continuation into the evening (vv 4–6) is in mind."

3.b. Not "see that they are . . ." (cf. NJB, REB). Smend (69) observed that כי, strictly causal "because," does not function here as the object of "will see" but serves as an echo of 2:5–7; 3:27. For the indirect causal sense, see *Note* 2:6.b.; here the clause clarifies the doubt expressed in "perhaps."

4.a. The omission of לעיניהם "before their eyes" in LXX* Syr appears to be stylistic: see Zimmerli 265.

4.b. The construction of כ "like" and abstract noun seems to have been a favorite of Ezekiel's: see the parallel in 26:10 and cf. 33:31. So a repointing to כמוצאי "like those brought out" (Fohrer 63; *BHK*; Brockington, *Hebrew Text* 223; *HALAT* 407b [misprinted in 530a]) is unnecessary.

5.a. The MT והוצאת "and bring out" recurs in principle at vv 6a and 7b, at the same stage of the sign-act and its execution. An ellipse of "your pack" has to be assumed; this is not difficult, since the same occurs with תשא/ישא "place (on your shoulders)" in vv 6a and 12a. The difficulty lies in the fact that there are two stages in the sign-act, the first consisting of the bringing out of the pack, out of the house, in vv 4a and 7a, and the second including going out through the hole, as vv 4b and 12aα explain (cf. Cornill 242). The cases in vv 5b, 6a, 7b must belong to the second stage; להוציא in v 12aβ is in a different category, signifying "to bring (him) out." Accordingly, the qal readings attested by the ancient versions (see *BHS*) are to be adopted in each case, as very many scholars since Hitzig (82) have advised. The latter observed that the misinterpretation depended on a false explanation of להוציא in v 12, as if it meant "to bring it out." Driver (*Bib* 35 [1954] 150) retained the MT in each case, assuming the ellipse of נפשך "yourself," but this makes for a most confusing sequence, especially in v 6a, where two different ellipses have to be assumed. Ehrlich's interpretation of the MT as "defecate" (*Randglossen* 5:40) has no merit. Zimmerli (265) also left the MT unchanged, but at the price of regarding their contexts as redactional. Friebel ("Sign-Acts" 624–25, 628) has not only maintained the MT in these places but emended to a hiph form in v 12a*a*, reading יוֹצִיא "will bring out" for the MT וְיָצָא "and will go out." He has speculated that after making the hole Ezekiel "proceeded back into the house [and] reappeared . . . with the exile bag," which at an earlier point he had taken back into the house ("Sign-Acts" 634 and n. 27). Before him, Smend (70), Ehrlich (*Randglossen* 5:41), and Zimmerli (266) read a hiph in v 12a*a*. It is doubtful whether vv 6 and 12 support Friebel's assumption. V 7, by its narrative order of clauses, implies a hysteron proteron in vv 6 and 12; vv 6 and 7 specify the visibility of the shouldering of the pack, which was evidently lying outside the wall.

6.a. LXX *A* Vg render as a pass verb, "I was carried." So do LXX Vg in vv 7 and 12. This interpretive change may reflect an effort to see wordplay with נָשִׂיא "head of state" in vv 10 and 12, taken as a pass form of noun, "one who is carried." See the *Comment* on v 11.

6.b. See *Note* 5.a.

6.c. Heb. עֲלָטָה, for whose etymology see *HALAT* 787a, occurs only once outside this section (also in vv 7, 12), in Gen 15:17, where it means the period after sunset. "It must here mean dusk, since people could still see what one was doing" (Wevers 100). The LXX in both passages failed to comprehend the term, in Genesis guessing "flame" and here "hidden."

6.d. The pf seems to be performative: see *Note* 3:8.a.

7.a. Cornill (242) and Zimmerli (266) have assumed that the LXX* has no rendering for כְּלִי "my pack." In fact כְּלִי was read as כָּל וְ "all and," with a ו/י confusion and wrong word division (πάντα . . . καί, "everything . . . and").

7.b. Heb. בְיָד "by hand" may be a partial dittograph of בַקִּיר "in the wall": LXX* Syr do not render. Ewald (255) took as "by force," comparing Isa 28:2, but Cooke (131) doubted such a meaning in prose. Ehrlich's emendation to בְיָתֵד "with a tent peg" (*Randglossen* 5:41; cf. *BHK*), comparing Deut 23:14, was linked with his notion of defecation. The MT may be given the benefit of the doubt. The addition of this little detail in reporting Ezekiel's compliance is true to life.

7.c. See *Note* 5.a.

7.d. See *Note* 6.a.

10.a. The MT, followed by the ancient versions, adds incoherently " Thus has the Lord Yahweh said: The head of state, this burden/oracle, in Jerusalem and all the community of Israel who are among them. ¹¹Say." Generally בְתוֹכָם "among them" is conjecturally emended to בְתוֹכָה "inside it," as the context seems to demand. Evidently assimilation to the form in v 12 occurred (see *Note* 11.a. below). According to Smend (69), the emendation was first suggested by J. D. Michaelis. Herrmann (75) bluntly categorized the words rendered "the head of state this burden/oracle" as "incomprehensible." The LXX, which takes מַשָּׂא "burden, oracle" as a synonym of נָשִׂיא "head of state," provides no overall coherence. Σ Vg Tg represent a Jewish exegetical tradition that prefixes עַל: "Concerning the head of state is this oracle (and [concerning] . . .)," and modern versions have adopted this expedient. But nowhere else in Ezekiel does מַשָּׂא "burden" mean "oracle." Herntrich (*Ezechielprobleme* 123) saw a reminiscence of Jer 23:33 אַתֶּם הַמַּשָּׂא (emended, as is customary, with LXX Vg) "you are the burden" and construed "The head of state is this burden," with wordplay between נָשִׂיא and מַשָּׂא. Greenberg (211–12) has adopted this interpretation with reference to the pack carried (נָשָׂא, linked with מַשָּׂא) by Ezekiel. He has seen in it not only a role in a predictive representation of exile but a symbolic sense whereby it stands for the king and people of Jerusalem. His interpretation is closely linked with his view that the pack is "the main prop of the dumb show" (210), which depends on his retention of the hiph forms in vv 5b, 6a, and 7b. Friebel ("Sign-Acts" 625–26 and n. 9) has rendered "This (act of) carrying (refers to) the ruler in Jerusalem and (to) all . . . ," again justifying it by reference to the hiph verbs. The Masoretes obviously intended some such reading, though the word order in v 10b*a* is strange. Freedy (*VT* 20 [1970] 133, 144) has understood v 10b as two separate glosses that have become fused: הַנָשִׂיא "the head of state" originated as a marginal annotation on vv 12–14, while the rest of v 10b*a* was a marginal introduction to vv 3–6, to the effect that the exilic burden carried by Ezekiel referred to an act that would take place in Jerusalem. After the fusion, v 10b*β* was added to make sense, and finally אֱמֹר "say" at the beginning of v 11 resumed the beginning of v 10. Independently, Lang (*Kein Aufstand* 19) has come to a similar but more plausible explanation of v 10b. First, "this burden" was intended as an exegetical elaboration of v 12a*a*, supplying an object for יִשָּׂא "will carry." Second, the rest of v 10b, "the head of state in Jerusalem and all the community of Israel who are among them," was a separate annotation, into which the first one was later interpolated. This latter annotation related to the earlier part of v 12a*a* and made clear that the residents of Jerusalem were also threatened with deportation. A little difficulty surely remains with the presence of הֵמָּה "they" in the relative clause, which can hardly stand alongside בְתוֹכָם "among them," even in a gloss. The latter term should probably be regarded as a later corruption of בְתוֹכָה "within it"; the gloss functions as an explanation of the subj of the verb יֵלְכוּ "they will go (into exile)" in v 11bβ. Lang explains the initial אָמַר "say" in v 11 in the same way as Freedy. Neither has dealt with the messenger formula in v 10aβ. Was its marginal role to explain that, after the prophetic "I" of v 11, a divine "I" is speaking in v 13 or even implicitly from v 12? Garscha (*Studien* 107) and Pohlmann (*Ezechielstudien* 38 n. 136) have objected that v 10 is required to provide an antecedent for the third pl pronouns of v 11 (cf. Zimmerli 268), but in both the historical and literary contexts their identification is obvious.

11.a. The LXX adds "in its midst," which from the flow of the Gr. context evidently goes back to בְּתוֹכָה in its *Vorlage*. It is plausible to regard it as originating in a marginal correction of, or replacement for, בְּתוֹכְכֶם "in their midst" in v 10 (cf. Cornill 243).

11.b. Lit. "it will be done to them." Friebel ("Sign-Acts" 628 and n. 13) renders לָהֶם "by them," an expedient that Hitzig (83) considered and rejected. The role of victims fits שְׁבִי "captivity," which, in line with the underlying verb שָׁבָה "take captive," envisions the people of Jerusalem as objects of aggression.

11.c. Heb. בַּשְּׁבִי "in captivity" has been considered a variant of בַּגּוֹלָה "into exile" (Ehrlich *Randglossen* 5:41; et al.), but it is generally attested, except for the Syr, which characteristically abbreviates and was encouraged to do so here by the fact that it has consistently used *šĕbîtâ* as the rendering for גוֹלָה. The terms do not function as syntactical synonyms.

12.a. The placing of subj before verb implies emphasis.

12.b. See *Notes* 5.a. and 6.a. above.

12.c. The MT (וַיֵּצֵא) "and (he will go out)" can be justified grammatically as a *waw* introducing the apodosis, "in the dusk, then he will go out": see Davidson, *Hebrew Syntax* 56. But it is more likely that the text takes בָּעֲלָטָה "at dusk" with what precedes, whereas v 7, duly emended, suggests otherwise. There is strong textual evidence for reading יֵצֵא "he will go out" (Cornill 243; et al.; see *BHS*). See also *Note* 5.a. above.

12.d. Lit. "they will make a hole." If the reference is to the damage done by the besieging Babylonians (Friebel, "Sign-Acts" 645–46; cf. Garscha, *Studien* 111; cf. the *Comment*), strictly the timing, while future for the prophet, was prior to the earlier actions. The Heb. impf may bear this sense (cf. Joüon 113b). The sg verb in LXX Syr is an easier and so inferior reading; NJPS and NRSV have adopted it, following Ehrlich, *Randglossen* 5:41; et al.

12.e. The implicit object of לְהוֹצִיא "to bring out" is "him," the head of state (Tg; Hitzig 83). The noncausative "to go out" found in LXX Syr has been adopted by many since Cornill (243): it represents a well-meant but unnecessary harmonization with the earlier qal examples of this verb that rightly distinguished between the bringing out of the pack in the first stage of the sign-act and its interpretation and the going out in the second stage. By this criterion, the pack certainly cannot be the object.

12.f. LXX Syr rendered יַעַן אֲשֶׁר "because" as if it were לְמַעַן אֲשֶׁר "in order that": Greenberg (213) has fairly argued, by reference to Abarbanel's exegesis, that paraphrase of the MT is involved. So the widespread emendation advocated since Cornill (244) is unnecessary. The fact that elsewhere the conjunction is construed with a pf or frequentative impf verb is not decisive.

12.g. Heb. לְעַיִן uses the *lamed* of norm, "according to the eye, visibly": cf. 1 Sam 16:7 לְעֵינַיִם "(see) according to the eyes" (Cooke 135, with reference to S. R. Driver, *Notes on the Hebrew Text and the Topography of the Books of Samuel* [Oxford: Clarendon, 1913] 133). The LXX construes the verb as pass, which again since Cornill (243) has encouraged most to repoint as יֵרָאֶה, with reference to the king's disguising himself in his escape from Jerusalem. However, comparison with v 6 suggests that the MT is correct. The MT adds הוּא אֶת־הָאָרֶץ "he (will not see) the ground," a blatant addition, as most since Hitzig (83), including Greenberg (215), have recognized. Now the nonrepresentation in LXX⁹⁶⁷ (= LXX*) supports its secondary nature (Fohrer 65; Zimmerli 267; contra Ziegler, *LXX* 133). The intent of the gloss was evidently to safeguard the active sense of the unpointed verb: it seems to betray an awareness that it might be construed as pass, as indeed LXX did. LXXᴮ reflects this addition, in the form "and he the land will not see," with necessary indication of the verb in translation and after the earlier pass rendering.

13.a. Rather than "over": cf. Prov 29:5 (Ehrlich, *Randglossen* 5:41; Greenberg 214; NIV). See the *Comment*.

14.a. The MT "(source of) his help" may be retained rather than the common emendation since Cornill (244) to עֹזְרָיו "his helpers," with reference to LXX Syr Tg and also to 30:8; 32:21. An etymological link with Ugar *gzr* "warrior" has been postulated (cf. *HALAT* 767a, b; M. Dahood, *Bib* 43 [1962] 226).

14.b. As Smend (71) commented long ago, אֲגַף has been variously aligned with Akk. *agappu* and Aram. אֲגַף "wing," in a military sense, like Latin *ala*, or with Arab. *ǧuff*, *ǧaff* "group," with a prosthetic ʾaleph. *HALAT* 11a opts for the latter derivation.

15.a. For the syntax, see *Form/Structure/Setting*.

16.a. The subj seems to be the new exiles, in line with the previous two verbs (Ehrlich, *Randglossen* 5:42; Cooke 133; Joyce, *Divine Initiative* 153 n. 5), rather than the nations (Bertholet [1897] 67; et al., including Zimmerli 274) or both (J. Hausmann, *Israels Rest* [Stuttgart: Kohlhammer, 1987] 86).

18.a. Elsewhere the noun רעש generally refers to earthquake or to a loud noise, while רגז(ה) can refer more widely to agitation, including that of the emotions. The pair, in the form of noun or verb, often occurs in parallelism; significantly in Job 39:23 both are used of a warhorse quivering with excitement to be off (BDB 1126b).

18.b. The MT, along with the general textual tradition, adds ובדאגה "and with anxiety." As I stated in Brownlee (177), the expression "has been viewed with suspicion [since Herrmann 75] because the parallel clause has only one such qualifying term and this noun recurs with reference to eating, not drinking, in v 19a. Was it a marginal gl[oss] on רעש 'quaking,' generally used of earthquake, in v 18a?" Then the two terms of v 18 refer to physical trembling, while those in v 19a have an emotional force.

19.a. For the use of אדני "Lord" in the messenger formula, see *Note* 2:4.c.

19.b. Not "to," in view of the third person formulation of the oracle: cf. 11:15.

19.c. Heb. למען usually introduces a clause of purpose or even of result. Here, however, its use seems to crystallize the fear of those who eat and drink. Hitzig (84) and Keil (162) (cf. Hölscher, *Dichter* 82) showed a respect for the context in their claim of a causal sense; in fact, the Syr rendered "because." Probably the conjunction is to be aligned with the sense "in view of, on account of" that the preposition has.

19.d. Heb. ארצה "its land" refers to the district or region of Jerusalem: cf. the examples in BDB 76a (2.b, c) and the pl in 1 Chr 13:2; 2 Chr 11:23. The reference to "those who reside in it" appears to hark back to "the residents of Jerusalem" in v 19a. The ancient versions seem to imply ארץ "the land," adopted by Smend (71) and by Cornill (244, with significant reference to 19:7; 30:12; 32:15) and others. Assimilation to those passages may well have occurred. The reading ארצם "their land," found in a few MSS and adopted by Ehrlich (*Randglossen* 5:42) and others, is an easier and so secondary reading.

19.e. The recurrence of the rendering of the LXX at 32:15 supports the MT ממלאה "deprived of its fullness" (Cornill, 244; Zimmerli 276; contra *BHS*). The preposition is used in a privative and pregnant sense: cf. 32:15; Lev 26:43.

Form/Structure/Setting

12:1–20 constitutes a literary unit consisting of two divine commands to engage in sign-acts, together with statements of their interpretation. Each has its own introductory formula of the prophet's reception of a divine message, in vv 1 and 17. Indeed, the two elements of command and interpretation in the first case are demarcated as separate, but consecutive events by a message-reception formula in v 8, rather like that in 24:20, after 24:15. The literary form of prophetic signs and their meaning enveloped within a divine speech was encountered earlier in 3:24b–5:17 (cf. Zimmerli 156–57). Within this unit the second case, in vv 17–20, follows the pattern that appears there. The first case, in vv 1–16, diverges from that pattern in two ways. First, the sequence of divine command and interpretation is interrupted in v 7 by a narrative report of Ezekiel's performance of the command, as in 24:18. Second, use is made in vv 9–11 of a question-and-answer format to link the command and the interpretation. This format occurs elsewhere in the book with this function, in 21:12; 24:19–21; 37:18–19. Long (*JBL* 90 [1971] 129–39) has analyzed this schema both in Ezekiel and elsewhere in the OT and shown that in this book the originally independent schema has been woven into reports of sign-acts. Here, as in chap. 24, it follows a description of the performance of the sign-act. Within vv 1–16, the command to the prophet to engage in the symbolic act in vv 2–6 falls into three parts. Greenberg (217) has observed that the introductory vv 2–3 make up a subunit marked by the device of inclusion, concerning the seeing of the rebellious community. A full statement of the sign follows in vv 4–6a. The two stages of the sign are given in v 4, while in vv 5–6a the three elements of the second stage are supplied. In v 6b the general significance is briefly given. Ezekiel's role as a מוֹפֵת "omen" recalls the need for the community to "see" expressed in vv 2–3, while the fivefold לְעֵינֵיהֶם "before their eyes" throughout vv 3–6a has echoed עֵינַיִם "eyes" in v 2. The report of the performance follows in v 7, echoing the two stages and reiterating two of the three elements in the second stage. The divine interpretation is introduced in vv 9–11bα by a brief recapitulation of the previous key elements: the characterization of "the community of Israel" resident in Babylonia as "a rebellious community" (vv 2, 3), the prophet's role as an "omen" (v 6b), and his performance of the sign-act (v 7aα). A straightforward application of Ezekiel's pantomime of exile, evidently to the people of Jerusalem, is presented in v 11bβ. V 12 applies the details of the second stage of the sign to "the head of state," while vv 13–14 go beyond the sign in describing his subsequent fate and the defeat of his army. V 15a rounds off the purpose of this interpretation that plainly is also an oracle of judgment, with a recognition formula. Thus vv 11–15 function as a two-part proof saying, with the elements of a pronouncement of punishment and a formula of recognition. V 9 might loosely be regarded as contributing the first part of a three-part proof saying, by its accusatory mention of "a rebellious community." Vv 15b–16 are best taken as a supplementary proof saying (Lang, *Kein Aufstand* 18, with special reference to 5:16–17). It supplies the subsequent fate of the exiled people of Jerusalem at Yahweh's hands and the means whereby Yahweh would bring about their recognition of his perspective. This latter proof saying is essentially bipartite, but it contains an accusing reference to the "abominations" of his victims.

The accompanying report, of Yahweh's commission to carry out a sign-act (v 18) and his interpretation, is shorter and much simpler. The symbolism is applied specifically to the residents of Jerusalem (v 19aβ). Again the interpretation also functions as a bipartite proof saying, as the closing recognition formula (v 20b), now addressed to Ezekiel's hearers, discloses. Mention of "violence" in v 19bβ constitutes an accusatory motif. In v 20a the pronouncement of punishment goes beyond the precise dimensions of the sign and its interpretation.

The question of redaction has loomed large in the scholarly study of vv 1–16. The basic issues are whether and to what extent the text steps beyond the expected bounds of the deportation of the people of Jerusalem into the different topic of the flight, capture, and blinding of Zedekiah and applies to the latter topic the elements of the sign-act relating to exile. Thus Herrmann (77) took vv 12–14 as supplementation added by Ezekiel, along with v 6aγ "and you will not see the land" as an anticipatory reference to the blinding of Zedekiah. He noted that vv 12–14 broke the context of vv 11 and 15 that relate to the residents of Jerusalem. Herrmann was developing the view of Giesebrecht (*Berufsbegabung* 167–71; cf. Kraetzschmar 126), who regarded the whole passage as first written down after 587 B.C. by Ezekiel, who incorporated Zedekiah's historical experience into the account. Hölscher (*Dichter* 80–81) found vv 12–14 (and v 10) to be the work of an interpolator, inserted after the fateful royal experience in 587. He included in this redaction the references to evening, darkness (עֲלָטָה), and covering of the face within vv 4–7 as preparatory references to Zedekiah's blindness; in fact, he regarded vv 4–6a, 7aβb as secondary. Fohrer (63–64) reverted to

Herrmann's view, taking vv 12–15 as a second interpretation of the sign-act added
later by Ezekiel and v 10 as a gloss reinterpreting vv 1–11. Zimmerli's treatment
(267–69) is closer to Hölscher's. The references to digging through the wall and
bringing out the pack in darkness (v 5 and within vv 6–7) retrospectively allude
to the breaches made in the wall in 587 and to Zedekiah's escape at night (2 Kgs
25:4; Jer 39:2, 4; 52:7). Vv 10aβ–b, 12–15 are likewise secondary, except the references to shouldering the pack and covering the face within v 12, which were
expressed in the plural at the primary stage. In Zimmerli's wake, Amsler (*Actes*
57) has characterized vv 5, 10, 12–15 as a "re-lecture" or redactional reinterpretation (cf. too Wevers 99). Laato (*Josiah* 152–53) regards vv 12–14 as secondary.

    Lang (*Kein Aufstand* 21–23; *Ezechiel* 25–27) has also found redactional input,
but he has limited it drastically to two short expressions, אֶת־הָאָרֶץ הוּא "he the
land" at the end of v 12b and וְאוֹתָהּ לֹא־יִרְאֶה "but it he will not see" within v
13bβ. I must interject at this point that before reading Lang I came to the same
conclusion concerning the second expression, while regarding the first as a textual addition (see *Note* 12.g.). Lang considers both king and people to lie within
the purview of the sign-act, comparing the associated threat to Jerusalem and
the king in chap. 21 and the double deportation of Jehoiachin and representatives of the people in 597. He takes the two short additions as evidence of a
post-587 reinterpretation of the references to the king, in terms of flight, disguise (covering the head), and blindness. Greenberg (215, 220) has come to
practically the same conclusion as Lang did regarding after-the-event additions
to the text. However, he goes further in that he includes אֶת־הָאָרֶץ "the land" in v
6aα and regards the verb of seeing as originally passive in both vv 6 and 13 (with
LXX, in the second case), in a prediction of Zedekiah's disguising himself in his
attempt to escape. Greenburg allows for the possibility that Ezekiel was responsible for reinterpretive touches alluding to the king's blindness in the light of
events. Similarly Klein (*Ezekiel* 48, 51) finds only the specific references to the
king's blindness, in vv 5, 12, and 13, to be secondary. Uehlinger ("Bild und Wort"
137 n. 125) has characterized only the references to covering the face at night in
vv 6 and 12 to be secondary expansions that refer exclusively to Zedekiah.

    It is clear that the once-dominant view of extensive redaction has been in recent
study not quite demolished but considerably diluted. Since Zedekiah was blinded
not at Jerusalem but at Riblah later (2 Kgs 25:7; Jer 39:7; 52:11), to see references
to his blindness before v 13 is premature and so unlikely. In his attempted escape, the king left Jerusalem through a city gate, not through a breach in the
wall (2 Kgs 25:4; Jer 39:4; 52:7). Surely this was not the "trifling inconsistency"
that Cooke (131) called it, on the assumption of a statement after the event. Certainly the older critical view must be considered correct in the criterion that
originally the sign and its interpretation straightforwardly envisioned deportation and that there seems to be no room for the separate topic of Zedekiah's
series of misdemeanors independent of the people's experience. References to
his escape from the city and disguise, about which the historical sources say nothing, and punishment of blindness have no place here. Not escape but deportation
and becoming prisoners of war are the explicit meaning of the sign (v 11). The
topic of the king's attempted escape is an exegetical red herring that, though as
old as the LXX, has done a disservice to the text. As hinted above, the undoubted
reference to Zedekiah's blindness in v 13 should be credited to the redactor.

Friebel's exegesis in terms of seeing the land of Judah ("Sign-Acts" 643) is forced: Chaldea is more naturally in view. The reference represents a skewing of the basic feature of not seeing the land or ground in vv 6 and 12 (Greenberg 214). The novelty of the interpretation indicates a distance from the basic text so great that it can hardly be credited to Ezekiel's own reworking of it.

But what of the rest of v 13, and v 14, which certainly depart from the sign-act? Here attention should be paid to the setting of the sign and accompanying oracle. V 11 firmly anchors the prophetic revelation among the hostages in Babylonia, in its discrimination between "you," who saw the sign, and "they" in Jerusalem, who were to experience its reality. Moreover, the evident ease in breaking through the wall in vv 6–7 indicates a Babylonian wall of clay brick, rather than a Palestinian house wall that would typically have been built of stone. As to its dating, Lang (*Ezechiel* 56) briefly suggested that chap. 17 is earlier than the sign-acts in chaps. 4–5, 12. In turn Krüger (*Geschichtskonzepte* 404–6) has observed the closeness between 17:16, 20, 21 and 12:13–14 and has argued that the primary interest of the sign-act and its interpretation was not to predict future events but to permit the "seeing" (vv 2–3) of the consequences of the anti-Babylonian policies of Zedekiah, already criticized by the prophet in chaps. 17 and 19. The hostages' failure to take seriously Ezekiel's critique and as yet unfulfilled prophecies of doom prompted a reaffirmation of the fate of the king, within the wider context of the fall of Jerusalem and the deportation of its citizens.

The following sign-act and interpretation in 12:17–20 clearly align with 4:16–17 in content and so presumably with the sign-act of 4:9–12 that depicted for the hostages the rigors of the coming siege. However, Hölscher (*Dichter* 82), implicitly followed by Fohrer (65) and Fuhs (67–68), envisioned a post-587 setting, relating not to the besieged residents of Jerusalem but to those left in the city after the deportation (cf. 33:23–29). This reconstruction depends too heavily on an assumption of historical continuity between the two sign-acts in 12:1–20. As to the geographical setting, the expression "the people of the land," if it is used in v 19 to describe the addressees (rather than those "concerning" whom the oracle is spoken), might be taken as residents of Judah and Jerusalem (cf. 7:27; so Hölscher, *Dichter* 82; Brownlee, 178–79). The issue is clearly germane to the hypothesis of Ezekiel's Judean ministry. Were the evidence stronger elsewhere, the passage could well be used in its support. An exilic provenance is more probable.

The unit may be outlined as follows:

12:1–16	The sign of deportation
12:2–6	Explanation and instructions
12:7	Ezekiel's enactment of the sign
12:8–16	Interpretation
12:17–20	The sign of a meal consumed with anxiety
12:18	Instructions
12:19–20	Interpretation

Comment

1–16 This report of a pair of divine messages received by the prophet covers a period of two days. The former was given on the first day and relates to activities to be carried out both during its daylight hours and in the evening and ensuing dusk. The latter message was given the next morning. A similar time span is specified elsewhere in the book, at 24:18; 33:22. The first message is a command to perform a sign-act relating to the coming exile of the people in Jerusalem. The second is an interpretation of the sign-act. The messages are punctuated by the performance of the sign.

2–3 This introductory part of the first oracle not only gives a brief description of the symbolic act Ezekiel is to carry out but frames it within statements of the lack of understanding of Ezekiel's community of hostages and of the aim to attempt to remove it by means of this enactment. Twice the Judeans already deported are described as "a rebellious house," a designation that recurs in the recapitulation of v 9. The reader of the book is reminded not only of its occurrences in the prophetic commissioning of Ezekiel (2:5–8; 3:9) but also of its dominant role in the first of a block of sign-acts in 3:22–5:4 (3:26–27). The evidence of rebelliousness is a refusal to listen to Ezekiel's presentation of the divine will, just as in the earlier passages doubt had been cast on whether they would be responsive. The implication here is that the prophet had already been endeavoring to communicate his message of judgment, but with scant success. The description of his constituency as blind and deaf seems to be a deliberate reapplication of Jer 5:21. As often, Ezekiel is portrayed as an exilic Jeremiah, just as Jeremiah in turn is portrayed as a southern Hosea by echoes of the earlier prophet. There is probably also a conscious echo of Isa 6:9–10, where Isaiah's prophetic ministry is described in terms of a communication failure that in itself confirms and justifies the message of judgment. As a rejected prophet, Ezekiel was standing in a noble tradition of testimony to God's just punishment of his people. There is an implicit message of assurance for Ezekiel here (cf. 1 Cor 4:2, 4).

The refusal of Ezekiel's neighbors to recognize or listen to God's purposes in contemporary history is challenged with a fresh portrayal (vv 3–7) and proclamation (vv 9–16) of Jerusalem's fate. The hope is expressed in v 3b that the portrayal especially would penetrate the barriers they had created and give them insight. Seeing is used in the cognitive sense of knowing (cf. 21:4, 10[20:48; 21:5]; Zimmerli, *I Am Yahweh* 31; D. Vetter, *THAT* 2:697). In prophetic speech the term אוּלַי "perhaps" is associated with a call to repentance to which the sovereign God might respond favorably and repeal his decree of judgment for the penitent (Jer 26:3; 36:3; Amos 5:15; Zeph 2:3; cf. Joel 2:14; Jonah 3:9; 2 Tim 2:25). Here, however, those addressed are primarily observers, rather than victims, of the coming judgment, although it would dash their hopes of a speedy return. The conditionality is not related to God's sparing them, as a spur to repentance, but to their enlightenment. "Perhaps" is God's sigh, rather than a threat. Whether they chose to see the light or not, the judgment of the covenant nation was inevitable: in the commissioning of Ezekiel the same sentiment was expressed in terms of whether they listened or not (2:7; 3:11; cf. Uffenheimer, "'Son of Man'" 50–51). Greenberg (220) has rightly dissented from Lang's interpretation in terms of political activism (*Kein Austand* 24–25; cf. Uehlinger, "Bild und Wort" 140), whereby Ezekiel was urging the hostages to take last-minute measures to get in touch with the Jerusalem authorities and so avert the city's fate. That fate was beyond hope; its interpretation as divine retribution was still feasible.

An initial description of the sign-act is supplied in v 3a(bα). As in some of the earlier symbolic actions, the first task, here the making up of a pack to take into exile (cf. Jer 46:19), functions as a preparatory feature, rather than being a part of the public demonstration. Ezekiel is to represent the residents of Jerusalem evacuating the capital as deportees. The following verses will break up the process into a series of stages and details, but here two main features are stressed: the beginning of the process is set in the daytime, and Ezekiel is to seize the limelight. He is not told what the pack is to consist of. He knows only too well from personal experience, his own deportation in 597. Deportation of groups and communities was practiced in both the Assyrian and the Babylonian empires. Assyrian victory reliefs depict the process frequently (see *ANEP* 10, 366, 373), and the deportees carry pathetic bundles, survival kits to which their homes had been reduced. In Midrash Rabbah (Lam 1:22) Rabbi Ḥiyya bar Abba, one of the Tannaim, described the bundle of Ezek 12:3 as consisting of three dual-purpose articles, a skin to hold flour (or water, according to another reading) or serve as a pillow, a mat to sit or sleep on, and a bowl to eat or drink from. Ezekiel is to mimic exile by carrying this pack (v 4) on a short journey from his home, "far enough to show what the action meant" (Cooke 130).

4 Further unfolding of the symbolic procedure now appears. It is to fall into two stages, and it is reaffirmed that in both stages Ezekiel is to make himself a public spectacle. As the first stage, he is ostentatiously to carry out his pack during the day. The second stage is the enacting of the start of the actual trek into exile, in the evening, no less conspicuously. Perhaps these two stages evoked the hostages' own last hours in Jerusalem, fearfully responding to unfeeling military orders marked by a "hurry and wait" syndrome. Coolness is the explanation commentators usually give for the timing of the deportation in the evening. Greenberg (210), anticipated by Rothstein (896) and followed by Friebel ("Sign-Acts" 649–50), eschewing historical actuality, has suggested that it evokes calamity and closure, comparing Isa 24:11; Jer 13:16.

5–6a The second stage of the sign-act is elaborated, with three extra details or pairs of details. First, Ezekiel is to break through the wall of his home and step through the hole he has made. Second, he is to go out at dusk and put his pack on his shoulder. Third, he is to keep his face covered and catch no glimpse of the ground. As for the first instruction, in v 5, the damage to the wall is expressed with a plural verb in its interpretive counterpart in v 12. If, as seems reasonable, we are to interpret the sign-act strictly in terms of deportation, the reference must be to the Babylonians breaking through the wall of the besieged Jerusalem, as the prelude to making its residents prisoners (Friebel, "Sign-Acts" 645–46; Uehlinger, "Bilt und Wort" 138; cf. Garscha, *Studien* 111). In terms of history, this climactic event is recounted in 2 Kgs 25:4; Jer 39:2; 52:7. Then, as Friebel has observed, Ezekiel represents at this point not the people of Jerusalem but their enemies. This double role for the prophetic actor has been encountered in the earlier sign-acts in the book, notably in 5:1–2, where he represented both the divine punisher, by shaving, and the people in the city, by being the one shaved. Ezekiel breaks through the wall of his home: קיר customarily has this meaning, and we are to envisage a Babylonian adobe wall made of clay bricks, which could easily be penetrated. Thus is represented the prior capture of the city whose citizens were to be deported, just as in Amos 4:3 the wealthy women of Samaria were to "go out through the breaches" in the walls (Giesebrecht, *Berufsbegabung* 168; Uffenheimer, "'Son of Man'" 48).

In v 6aα leaving the house and shouldering the pack represent the beginning of the trek from the homeland. This second pair of details is expressed less logically: they appear in the opposite order in the account of Ezekiel's performance of the sign in v 7, while v 12 reverts to the order here. Obviously, no difference in meaning is intended. In v 6aβ the third detail is expressed with an added consequence. An interpretation in terms of Zedekiah's dramatic escape from the city with reference to a disguise is to be resisted. It requires a passive verb of seeing in the sense of not being recognized, which is possible only in v 12, where the LXX so rendered, though it virtually imported such a meaning into v 6 by rendering בעלטה "at dusk" as "hidden." To achieve this end by deleting "the land/ground" as a redactional addition (Greenberg 215) is a counsel of despair. Nor is a reference to Zedekiah's blindness relevant: he was only blinded at a later date, after he was captured and taken to Riblah. Uffenheimer ("'Son of Man'" 53) and initially Greenberg (211) interpreted the seeing as a recognition that the land would never be seen again (cf. Jer 22:12). Friebel ("Sign-Acts" 653) has developed this interpretation: the covering of the face figuratively portrays as permanent the exile of the people of Jerusalem. From that point on, the land would no longer be seen. This interpretation has the merit of according with v 12, where, if the MT's conjunction and pointing are maintained, not seeing functions as the explanation of covering the face. Sometimes in the OT covering the face has the connotation of grief (2 Sam 15:30; Esth 6:12) or shame (2 Sam 19:5; Esth 7:8; Jer 14:3–4). A different verb appears here, though that is not an essential factor in the interpretation. Overall, comparison of vv 6 and 12 suggests a symbol of radical loss: the gesture "plaintively hides the lost homeland from the view of the exiles" (Zimmerli 271).

6b Ezekiel's acting out of Jerusalem's downfall and deportation is characterized as a sign to the 597 B.C. exiles, who represented the whole people of God. The term מופת, used here and in v 11, recurs in 24:24, 27, again with reference to the prophet. It is a synonym of the term אות used for the sign-act in 4:3 but brings to the fore the nature of his role as a warning (see S. Wagner, *TWAT* 4:755–56). The word brings to a close the accumulative accent on seeing in vv 2–6: those who have no insight into Yahweh's purposes for his people (v 2) are shown in plain sight (vv 3–5) the separate stages of a warning sign (v 6), to sharpen their perception (v 3). A similar range of vocabulary occurs in Deut 29:1–3(2–4).

7 The prophet narrates that he duly carried out Yahweh's instructions concerning this sign. The two stages of the symbolic action are recorded. Only two phases of the second stage are described, with a telescoping of the literary, overelaborate AB¹CB² structure of vv 5–6aα into a practical AB²C order. The third phase of v 6aβ is not represented, perhaps because of its figurative rather than representative role. One should not reason from the true-to-life incomplete repetition that v 6 has been expanded nor, with Rothstein (896), that a clause has been lost.

8–11 A fresh divine communication is imparted to the prophet early on the morrow. The reader learns that Ezekiel had silently mimed his way through the sign-act and that his intrigued spectators had unavailingly questioned him about its meaning. The prophet is given a basic interpretation in v 11. It passes on to the hostages Ezekiel's dramatic role as an "omen," revealed to him in v 6. If the sign-act was intended to give insight to those with blind eyes, the interpretation was a further attempt to shout its meaning to their deaf ears (v 3). Discrimination is made between "you," the object of the sign, and "they," its subject, clearly the people of Jerusalem who were to share the fate of the already deported hostages, just as Ezekiel had proclaimed earlier in chaps. 5 and 6. They were to lose control of their lives and suffer the fate of exile. In turn the king was to "be brought out" in v 12. The LXX, Aquila, and the Vulgate, by their passive rendering of the verb for "take up, carry" in vv 6, 7, and 12, were sensitively, if wrongly, extending this sentiment of victimization.

12 A detailed interpretation now follows. The careful reader receives two surprises: first, the earlier of the two stages is passed over, presumably as needing no verbal elaboration, and second, not the people but the king features in the application. Zedekiah is referred to as נשׂיא "head of state," as in 7:27. He functions as a representative figure, standing for the people he typifies before God. There is also a sense that not even the king would escape the fate of the community at large. Just as in 21:24–32(19–27) both Jerusalem and the king are threatened in the same oracle, so here their highest ranking citizen takes his place beside the citizens indicated in v 11 (Lang, *Kein Aufstand* 21). Nor must we overlook a further factor. The sign-act and accompanying public oracle were intended as a confirmation of the message in chap. 17 concerning the fate of Zedekiah as a disobedient vassal of Nebuchadnezzar (see *Form/Structure/Setting*). This factor is the main reason for singling him out here.

So there were good reasons for applying the second stage of the sign-act, with its three pairs of details, to Zedekiah. In relation to vv 5–6a, the first two pairs are reversed, but the third is only slightly varied. The reversal was perhaps meant to achieve wordplay between נשׂיא "head of state" and ישׂא "will take up, carry." Who better than he to feature in this action, ominously suited as he was by his description! As we observed in relation to v 5, the switch to a plural in the breaking through the wall now differentiates between Ezekiel's earlier double role, representing both the people of Jerusalem and their enemies. While קיר "wall" usually refers to a house wall, here it is retained with reference to a city wall, usually חומה; indeed, קיר has this meaning in Num 35:4; Josh 2:15.

13–15a The public message that had been put into Ezekiel's mouth about his own role (v 11) has by v 13 shifted into a divine oracle. This phenomenon of alternate voices will recur in the interpretation of another sign-act, at 24:21–24. There is now an echo of Zedekiah's capture and deportation to Babylon, there to die, and of the dispersal and defeat of his army, originally proclaimed in 17:16b, 20–21. Evidently Ezekiel's constituency had been loath to accept his predictions, and the time that had elapsed with no fulfillment of the predictions had confirmed them in their optimistic stand. Now the earlier message is reaffirmed. It is reinforced with a proclamation by sight and sound of the siege of the royal capital and the deportation of its residents, in vv 2–12. There are no references to Zedekiah's attempted escape either here or in chap. 17.

The king would be captured not merely by Nebuchadnezzar's troops but by the divine adversary who masterminded the Babylonian campaign and made it the means of his retribution. Yahweh was the hunter who would trap his prey and give it to his servants to take proudly home. The net is not a sort of giant butterfly net but, as the context of 19:8 makes clear, part of an ambush toward which the frightened victim would be driven to be entangled by netting spread on the ground or to fall into a pit dug under it (cf. Keel-Leu, *Symbolism* 93–94; Greenberg 214). Jerusalem was ironically to be Yahweh's trap. A redactor could not resist inserting a factual reference to Zedekiah's blindness (2 Kgs 25:7; Jer 39:7; 52:11), glimpsing a terrible twist of fate in a different and later "fulfillment" of his unwillingness to see in v 12. Chap. 17 is as silent about his loss of sight as about his attempted escape from Jerusalem. The king's bodyguard and army would be no match for Yahweh's punitive onslaught. A saying that amplifies the echo in 17:21a of 5:2, 12, where the fate of Jerusalem's citizens is in view, here applies narrowly to the soldiery. Dispersed and chased to their deaths, they would be unable to protect their sovereign from divine judgment. By this fate they would recognize at last the work of the divine judge (cf. 17:21b), undoing all their misplaced patriotism and loyalty.

15b–16 The oracle is rounded off by reversion to the theme of general exile announced by the sign-act and by the straight interpretation in v 11. The third-person references naturally relate to the people of Jerusalem, as v 11 used them. Deportation from the capital would result in a fragmentation of their community in exile (cf. 11:16). Nor would that be the sum of their woes. The three furies of sword, famine, and pestilence, with which 5:12; 6:11–12; and 7:15 had threatened Jerusalem, would ravage them further, leaving a mere "remnant" of the community. The motif is not used in any positive or reassuring sense, as if a ship, harried by every wind, at last reaches a safe haven. Rather, with sinister irony, it perpetuates the negativism and suffering, as in 6:9. Their location "among the nations" (v 15b) would be where they come to their spiritual senses and at last feel the burden of "all their abominations" that hitherto had burdened only Yahweh. As Ezekiel in his exile had in God's name accusingly declared the sins or abominations committed in the homeland and the liability to judgment (e.g., 5:9 [see the *Comment* there]; 7:3–4), so they, the accused, in their coming exile would take up his cry in confession. By this grim means Yahweh's way with them would be acknowledged as justified, and he would be vindicated.

17–18 The second of a pair of sign-acts is now commanded, introduced by its own message-reception formula. The symbolic action is related to the one described and interpreted in 4:10–16, forecasting the intense shortage of food and water during the coming siege of Jerusalem. The glosses in the MT at 4:16 (see *Note* 4:16.b.) draw an early and well-motivated parallel between that verse and v 19 here. Here the connection with the siege is indicated by the foreboding threat, as v 19 implies, that was to seize the people of Jerusalem as they ate and drank. Ezekiel is commanded to represent them by acting out that foreboding in an exaggerated physical counterpart, a pitiable trembling that presumably showed itself in spilling his drink and missing his mouth with his food.

Zimmerli (278), followed by Eichrodt (153–54), has diagnosed Ezekiel's condition as a physiological consequence of the strain he felt from his ecstatic prophetic experiences. Greenberg (225) has rightly objected that nothing in the text suggests this origin for the trembling and that comparison with the earlier sign-acts indicates rather that Ezekiel was exercising further dramatic skill. The selection of a meal as the setting for such emotion represents its role as a paradigm of ordinary daily living (cf. Eccl 9:7; Amos 7:12).

19 The interpretation is addressed to "the people of the land." This group, which in the OT usually relates to residents of Judah or Jerusalem, in 7:27; 45:12

is distinguished from the king as the common people (cf. E. Lipiński, *TWAT* 6:190). Here the phrase appears to refer ironically to the prophet's exilic constituency, as former residents of their homeland and now landless (Eichrodt 154–55). It implies that their loss was soon to be shared by the Judean populace at large. The phrase paves the way for subsequent references in the interpretive oracle, first to the "land" (אֶרֶץ) or region of Jerusalem and then to the land (אֶרֶץ again) as a whole. The attempt to understand the land in v 19 as Babylonia (Calvin 407; Vawter 80) is misguided. The physical trembling of v 18 is explained in terms of strong emotion. The foregone conclusion to be drawn from the siege was to dominate the lives of the besieged, casting a terrible shadow of premonition over them. From the vivid perspective of the alleged emotions of the besieged, the fall of Jerusalem is announced afresh. The city and its outlying area (cf. Josh 15:21–61) were to lose their assets in the coming destruction. The interpretation does not miss the opportunity to point a finger at the victims as responsible for their own fate. "Violence," described as an urban sin in 7:23, was to wreak its nemesis.

20 Ezekiel "had threatened destruction to Jerusalem and its citizens: he now adds the other cities which were still inhabited. Lastly, he speaks of the whole land, as if he said that no single corner should suppose itself free from slaughter" (Calvin 408). The devastation of the rest of Judah, especially of its other urban centers, is declared as a future fact. The eventual fulfillment of such catastrophe for Jerusalem and Judah would force upon the attention of the Judean hostages God's role as judge of his people. If the sign and its interpretation failed to do so, the coming of the terrible event to which they pointed would leave no doubt. This future, enforced dawning of truth draws an arc back to the beginning of the unit, vv 2–3. Ezekiel's role as actor and teacher was to attempt to remove present blindness to the purposes of God. To this end the threat that, whether they now wanted to or not, they would soon have no option provides a powerful supporting argument.

Explanation

It is characteristic of the book to follow a vision report, in this case chaps. 8–11, with an account of sign-acts and their interpretation within an oracular setting. Thus the inaugural vision of 1–3:15 was followed by the interpreted signs in 3:22–5:17, and the dry bones of 37:1–14 will be succeeded by the joined sticks of 37:15–28. There are indications that this unit is meant to function as a literary echo and confirmation of 3:22–5:17, just as the preceding vision, by means of its theophany of judgment associated with the cherubim, echoed that of the inaugural vision with its living creatures. Parunak ("Structural Studies" 216) has drawn attention to connecting links. The epithet "rebellious community" in 12:2–3, 9 repeats that of 3:26–27. The motif of dispersion and death in 12:14–16 recalls 5:2, 12. The anxious eating in 12:9 is reminiscent of the shortage of food and the despair in 4:16–17. One might add the use of "abominations" as a general term for sin in 12:16, which evokes 5:9. There are also echoes of elements found in the oracles of chaps. 6 and 7: the lawless violence perpetrated in the capital (7:23) reappears in 12:19, and the destruction of the homeland (6:14) in 12:20. The trilogy "sword, famine, and pestilence" occurs not only in 5:12 but also in 6:11–12 and 7:15. The prophetic wheel of sin and judgment is rotated a second time for readers of the book, to reinforce the message.

Historically the first sign-interpretation had another role, as its closing links with chap. 17 reveal. The message of divine retribution for Zedekiah, involving his capture and permanent deportation, had fallen on deaf ears. The Judean hostages in Babylonia believed fervently in Jerusalem's security. Not to do so would have ruled out their own quick return to their homeland, an intolerable inference. If they had been blind to Ezekiel's earlier oracle, it was because there are none so blind as those who do not want to see. The message is given again, in the wider context of the fall of besieged Jerusalem and the exile of its populace. The vivid portrayal of the sign-act is an endeavor to break through the barriers of self-deception Ezekiel's audience had built to block out the truth (v 3; cf. Mark 8:14–21; Luke 12:54–56). No explicit reference is made to the hostages' own deportation a few years before: in his ominous role Ezekiel may well have mimicked the very procedures they had undergone in their forced evacuation from the capital. If so, a deep sense of déjà vu added emotional weight to the drama. God does not take no for an answer but hammers at the doors of their perception, asking to be let in, so that his will may not only be done but understood and bravely accepted.

The second sign-act intriguingly looks at the home situation through the reactions of those besieged in Jerusalem. The portrayal of strong emotions is meant as a frontal attack on the hostages' attitude. It suggestively countered their willful optimism with grim presentment. It was a further lesson that endeavored to teach the truth about God in this phase of his purposes for his people.

The Validity of Ezekiel's Prophetic Ministry (12:21–14:11)

Bibliography

Brownlee, W. H. "Exorcising the Souls from Ezekiel 13:17–23." *JBL* 69 (1950) 367–73. **Dummermuth, F.** "Zu Ez. xiii. 18–21." *VT* 13 (1963) 228–29. **Filson, F. V.** "The Omission of Ezek. 12:26–28 and 36:23b–38 in Codex 967." *JBL* 62 (1943) 27–32. **Hossfeld, F. L.**, and **Meyer, I.** *Prophet gegen Prophet: Eine Analyse der alttestamentliche Texte zum Thema: Wahre unde falsche Propheten.* BBB 9. Fribourg: Schweizerishes Katholisches Bibelwerk, 1973. 113–43. **Janzen, W.** *Mourning Cry and Woe Oracle.* BZAW 125. Berlin: de Gruyter, 1972. **Liedke, G.** *Gestalt und Bezeichnung alttestamentlicher Rechtssätze.* WMANT 39. Neukirchen: Neukirchener Verlag, 1971. **Lloyd, S.** "Building in Brick and Stone." In *A History of Technology*, ed. C. Singer et al. Vol. 1. Oxford: Clarendon, 1951. 456–94. **Mosis, R.** "Ez 14, 1–11—ein Ruf zur Umkehr." *BZ* 19 (1975) 161–94. ————. "פתה *pth*." *TWAT* 4:820–31. **Polk, T.** "Paradigms, Parables and *Mĕšālîm:* On Reading the *Māšal* in Scripture." *CBQ* 45 (1983) 564–83. **Propp, W. H.** "The Meaning of *Ṭāpēl* in Ezekiel." *ZAW* 102 (1990) 404–8. **Raitt, T. M.** "The Prophetic Summons to Repentance." *ZAW* 83 (1971) 30–49. **Saggs, H. W. F.** "'External Souls' in the Old Testament." *JSS* 19 (1974) 1–12. **Schoneveld, J.** "Ezekiel xiv. 1–8." *OTS* 15 (1969) 193–204. **Schreiner, J.** "Götzendiener wollen Jahwe fragen." In *Segen für die Völker: Gesammelte Schriften zur Entstehung und Theologie des Alten Testaments.* 1970; repr. Würzburg: Echter, 1987. 166–73. **Talmon, S.**, and **Fishbane, M.** "The Structuring of Biblical Books: Studies in the Book of Ezekiel." *ASTI* 10 (1975/76) 129–53. **Tångberg, K. A.** *Die prophetische Mahnrede: Form- und traditionsgeschichtliche Studien zum prophetischen Umkehrruf.* FRLANT 143. Göttingen: Vandenhoeck & Ruprecht, 1987. 103–6. **Vanderkam, J. C.** "The Prophetic-Sapiential Origins of Apocalyptic Thought." In *A Word in Season.* FS W. McKane, ed. J. D. Martin and P. R. Davies. JSOTSup 42 Sheffield: JSOT, 1986. 163–76. **Wold, D. J.** "The *kareth* Penalty in P: Rationale and Cases." In *SBL 1979 Seminar Papers*, ed. P. J. Achtemeier. Missoula: Scholars Press, 1979. 1:1–45. **Zimmerli, W.** "Die Eigenart der prophetischen Rede des Ezechiel: Ein Beitrag zum Problem an Hand von Ez. 14:1–11." *ZAW* 66 (1954) 1–26.

Translation

[21] *I received the following communication from Yahweh:* [22] *"Human one, what do you all[a] mean by this slogan you are using about[b] the land of Israel, 'After a long time elapses, every[c] revelation is a dead letter'?* [23] *Well, tell them this as a message from the Lord[a] Yahweh: I will put a stop[b] to this slogan, and it will be used in Israel[c] no longer. Say to them rather: The time is near, and so is the content[d] of every revelation.* [24] *For no longer will any revelation[a] be spoken in vain[b] nor any divination be devoid of reality[c] in the community[d] of Israel.* [25] *For it is I, Yahweh, who is speaking: whatever word I speak is fulfilled.[a] There will be no further delay.[b] In your lifetime, you rebellious community, I mean to both speak the word and fulfill it. So runs the oracle of the Lord[c] Yahweh."*

[26] *I received a further communication from Yahweh:* [27] *"Human one, I draw your attention to what the community of Israel[a] is saying, 'The revelation he is giving relates to a long time ahead. It is about the distant future he is prophesying.'* [28] *Well, tell them this as a message from the Lord Yahweh: There will be no further delay over any words of mine.[a] Whatever word I speak is fulfilled.[b] So runs the oracle of the Lord Yahweh."[c]*

[13:1]*I received the following communication from Yahweh:* [2]*"Human one, prophesy against Israel's prophets, prophesy*[a] *and tell them:*[b] *Hear Yahweh's pronouncement,* [3]*this message from the Lord Yahweh. Trouble awaits those whose imagination was the inspiration behind their prophesying,*[a] *without receipt of a revelation.*[b] *(*[4]*Your prophets, Israel, have become*[a] *like jackals that haunt ruins.)* [5]*You*[a] *did not climb up to the holes*[b] *in the wall and rebuild it for the community of Israel so they could resist during the fighting on the day of Yahweh.* [6]*You who made worthless revelations and offered false divinations,*[a] *who claimed, 'So runs Yahweh's oracle,' without a commission from Yahweh, and expected the message to be substantiated,* [7]*you did make worthless revelations and speak false divinations, didn't you?*[a] [8]*So the message of the Lord Yahweh is as follows: Because you uttered worthless pronouncements and made false revelations, for that reason I am your opponent, runs the oracle of the Lord Yahweh.* [9]*I will deal a blow*[a] *to the prophets who made worthless revelations and offered false divinations: They will not be included in the assembly of my people nor documented in the register of the community of Israel, nor will they enter the land of Israel. Then you will realize that I am*[b] *Yahweh.*

[10]*"Because*[a] *they have led my people astray*[b] *by promising peace when there has been no peace, and when my people*[c] *built a wall of loose stones,*[d] *they just*[e] *gave it a plaster*[f] *rendering,* [11]*tell those plasterers: 'If drenching rain comes,*[a] *if hailstones*[b] *fall and a storm wind whips up,*[c] [12]*and you are faced with a collapsed wall,*[a] *you will be asked where your rendering is, won't you?'* [13]*So here is the Lord Yahweh's message: In my fury I am going to whip up*[a] *a storm wind, and drenching rain will come because of my anger, and hailstones in destructive fury.*[b] [14]*I will demolish the wall you rendered with plaster and level it to the ground, leaving its foundation exposed.*[a] *Then you will recognize that I am Yahweh.* [15]*I will vent my fury on that wall and on those who gave it a plaster rendering, and then I will say*[a] *concerning you,*[b] *'The wall is gone and its plasterers are gone,'*[c] [16]*that is, Israel's prophets who prophesied about*[a] *Jerusalem and made revelations of peace for it when there was no peace. So runs the Lord Yahweh's oracle.*

[17]*"Now, human one, you are to look in the direction of those women among your people whose imagination is the inspiration behind their prophesying.*[a] *Issue a prophecy against them* [18]*and tell them this as a message from the Lord Yahweh: Trouble awaits those women who get individuals into their power*[a] *by sewing bands*[b] *to put on everybody's wrist*[c] *and by making shawls*[d] *to put on everybody's head, of varying sizes.*[e] *You mean*[f] *to captivate individuals belonging to my people and to sustain your own selves!*[g] [19]*You have desecrated me among my people for*[a] *handfuls of barley and pieces of bread, using your falsehoods uttered to my people, who like to listen to falsehood, to put to death individuals who should*[b] *not die and to restore to life individuals who should not live.* [20]*So the message of the Lord Yahweh is as follows: I intend to counteract your bands, the point at which*[a] *you get individuals into your power.*[b] *I will tear them off your*[c] *arms, and let the individuals you are captivating go free*[d] *and fly away.*[e] [21]*I will also tear off your shawls and rescue my people from your clutches, so that they are no longer within your preying grasp. Then you will realize that I am Yahweh.*

[22]*"Because you have demoralized*[a] *the innocent,*[b] *whom I had no intention of harming, and encouraged*[c] *the guilty rather than getting them to abandon their lifestyle, with their survival in view*[d] *—* [23]*that is the reason you will never again make worthless revelations or practice such divination:*[a] *I will rescue my people from your clutches, and then you will realize that I am Yahweh."*

[14:1]*Some of Israel's elders visited*[a] *me and sat down in front of me.* [2]*I received the following communication from Yahweh:* [3]*"Human one, the minds of these men have turned*[a] *to their idols, and they have focused*[b] *on that which has made them fall into iniquity. Why*[c] *should I let myself be consulted*[d] *by them?* [4]*So speak with them and tell them this as a message from the Lord Yahweh: When any single member of the community of Israel whose mind turns to his idols and who focuses on what makes him fall into iniquity comes to a*[a] *prophet, I, Yahweh, will bring myself to give him an authoritative*[b] *answer,*[c] *in keeping with*[d] *his host of idols.* [5]*My purpose will be to hold the community of Israel responsible*[a] *for their thinking, inasmuch as they have alienated themselves*[b] *from allegiance to me, with all*[c] *their idols.* [6]*Therefore tell this to the community of Israel, as a message from the Lord Yahweh: Turn, turn*[a] *away from allegiance to your idols and turn your attention from all your shocking rites.* [7]*For to every single member of the community of Israel or any*[a] *resident alien within Israel who*[b] *ceases to follow me and adopts another faith,*[c] *mentally turning to his idols and focusing on what makes him fall into iniquity, and then comes to a prophet to consult me through him,*[d] *I, Yahweh, will bring myself to give an authoritative answer.*[e] [8]*I will make that person the focus of my hostility: turning*[a] *him into an omen and a byword,*[b] *I will exclude him from belonging to my people, and then you will realize that I am Yahweh.* [9]*If the prophet is so misled as to deliver an oracle, I, Yahweh, will show him to have been misled:*[a] *I will deal him a blow and fatally remove him from inclusion in my people Israel.* [10]*They will both suffer punishment for their iniquity, inquirer and prophet alike.*[a] [11]*My purpose will be to stop the community of Israel straying from my leadership and sullying themselves with all their rebellious ways, so that they function as my people and I may function as their God. So runs the oracle of the Lord Yahweh."*

Notes

22.a. "All" is added to indicate that the Heb. for "you" is pl.

22.b. Or "in." See *Form/Structure/Setting*.

22.c. The LXX* does not represent כל "every," but its parallel presence in v 23 supports it.

23.a. For the formulaic use of אדני "Lord" in the messenger formula here and in v 28; 13:3, 8, 13, 18, 20; 14:4, 6, see *Note* 2:4.c.

23.b. The pf in the MT is "prophetic": cf. GKC 106n. However, LXX* LXX[OL] and a few MSS imply והשבתי, with a prefixed *waw*, which accords with Ezekiel's style elsewhere (see 11:17 and *Note* 11:17.a.). It could easily have fallen out by partial haplography in a וה וה sequence. The LXX construed the verb as a hiph of שוב, meaning "reverse," a possible but less likely parsing than the pointed MT.

23.c. The LXX implies בית ישראל "house of Israel," which MS[Ken 124] reads, for בישראל "in Israel," an interesting assumption of scribal abbreviation: cf. Cooke 137.

23.d. Heb. דבר "word, declaration, that which is declared" has as its counterpart in the Syr a verb: "(the revelation) will happen." Zimmerli (279) has listed the comparable modern scholarly attempts to supply a match for the verb in v 22bβ, but rightly counseled keeping the MT.

24.a. The MT has constr forms in the case of חזון "revelation" and מקסם "divination," a possible construction that regards the following adj as a noun in each case (see GKC 128w). However, the exegetical intent of this pointing seems to have been to equate these expressions with those relating to false prophets in 13:7. See the *Comment*. Probably the minority pointing as abs (see *BHS*) should be followed, and the qualifying nouns should be taken as predicative (Ehrlich, *Randglossen* 5:42–43).

24.b. Heb. שוא appears to mean here not "false" but "worthless" (Ehrlich *Randglossen* 5:42–43) and so "in vain": see the range of meanings in BDB 996a. 'A rendered εἰκῆ "in vain" and Σ Θ μάταια "vain, empty."

24.c. Heb. חלק, lit. "smooth," seems to have the developed meaning "empty" that it has in Mishnaic Heb. (Ehrlich, *Randglossen* 5:42–43; Greenberg 228; see Jastrow, *Dictionary* 473b–74a). The LXX τὰ πρὸς χάριν "(prophesying) favorably" renders the same stem in Prov 7:5. Cornill's assumption (245) of an underlying חנם "in vain, freely" here is unwarranted.

24.d. The variant "sons," which is widely attested (see *BHS*), is evidence of a common confusion between the two phrases "house of Israel" and "sons of Israel": see *Note* 2:3.a.

25.a. The syntax of v 25a*a* is incertain. The accentuation in the MT implies "For I am Yahweh; I (will) speak what I speak, a word and it will be done." Then the second clause exhibits a deliberately inexplicit *idem per idem* construction (Cooke 136–37; Greenberg 228–29). Cooke, following Hitzig (86) and others, actually regarded דבר "word" as a noun qualifying the preceding relative clause: "what word I will speak." Greenberg invests the final word with the force of a relative clause: "(as) a word that will be done." On the other hand, Zimmerli (279–80; cf. von Orelli 51) construes as "For it is I, Yahweh, who speak. The word that I speak is fulfilled." He makes the good observation that the last five words should be understood in terms of v 28b*a*, which appears to be a parallel statement. With respect to דבר "word," he follows Cooke, but he takes (יעשה)ו not as "and (it is/will be done)" but as introducing an apodosis. Then the initial words are to be regarded as a variation of the concluding statement אני יהוה דברתי "I, Yahweh, have spoken" found in 5:17; 21:22; 30:12; 34:24, which is introduced by כי "for" in 21:37; 26:14. Indeed, the whole sentence is to be regarded as a variation of the larger concluding statement אני יהוה דברתי ועשיתי "I, Yahweh, have spoken and will do (it)" in 17:10; 22:14; 36:36; 37:14 (cf. 24:14) (Zimmerli 281). This variation seems to refer to Yahweh's general, rather than future and specific, activities. The latter are clearly in view in v 25b, which is formulated slightly differently.

25.b. The fem verb has a neuter sense: cf. GKC 122q; Joüon 152c, d. LXX Syr render loosely "I do not delay." The parallelism of v 28 supports the MT, contra Cornill (246), who postulated original divergence between vv 25 and 28 and subsequent assimilation.

25.c. For the formulaic use of אדני "Lord" in the divine-saying formula here and in v 28; 13:6, 8, 16; 14:11, see *Note* 5:11.a.

27.a. The LXX adds the equivalent of המרי "rebellious." Probably this is a case of inner-Greek assimilation to v 25. An addition at the Heb. level would have incorporated בית/οἶκος "house."

28.a. The proposal to move the *'athnach,* so that כל־דברי "all my words" goes with what follows (Ehrlich, *Randglossen* 5:43; *BHS*; Greenberg 229), leaves the preceding neuter verb standing by itself, as in v 25, but at the expense of complicating the following clause in relation to that verse. It is significant that the LXX reflects the MT's punctuation, rendering with a pl verb. The extra material may be explained in terms of the Heb. idiom of construing a pl subj, whether masc or fem, with a fem sg verb (GKC 145k; Cooke 136–37, with reference to 41:25; Zimmerli 283).

28.b. See *Note* 25.a.

28.c. The omission of vv 26–28 in LXX[967] does not appear to be significant for the Heb. text. Most probably it occurred by parablepsis within the Gr. tradition (Filson, *JBL* 62 [1943] 27–32; Lust, "Textual Witnesses" 14–15).

13:2.a. The MT הנביאם "who prophesy" adds nothing to the sense, whereas a repeated הַנָּבֵא "prophesy" accords with Ezekiel's style: cf. 11:4; 34:2; 37:9 (Cornill 246; et al.). The emendation has some support from the LXX, which presupposes והנבא "and prophesy," by assimilation to v 17. Moreover, the combination "prophesy and say" recurs in 21:14, 33(9, 28); 30:2; 36:3. For the origin of the MT, see *Note* 3.a. below.

2.b. The MT לנביאי מלבם "to prophets from their (own) hearts" is an unexpected second definition of the addressees: one expects simply אליהם "to them" (cf. v 17b), which the LXX* represents. For the origin of the MT, see the following *Note.*

3.a. The MT הנביאים . . . רוחם "the foolish prophets who follow their (own) spirits" has a shorter counterpart in the LXX*, "those who prophesy from their hearts." The standard rule of preference for the shorter text seems to apply here. Two alternative, synonymous readings relating to v 3 appear to lie behind the jumble of readings in vv 2–3: (1) הוי על־הַנְּבָאִים מלבם and (2) הוי לְנִבְּאֵי מלבם, both meaning "woe to those who prophesy from their hearts." There are two differences. For the difference of preposition, one may compare ל in v 18 and על in Jer 50:27: the usage in v 18 may point to ל as original, but one must allow for the possibility of stylistic variation and later harmonization. The second difference concerns an abs or constr ptcp: for the latter, see Joüon 129n. In v 2a the MT הַנְּבָאִים "who prophesy" presumably originated as a marginal gloss intended to correct הַנְּבִיאִים "the prophets" in v 3; for the expected ptcp, cf. v 17a. It was wrongly taken as a correction of the original second הנבא "prophesy" in v 2a, doubtless encouraged by the wording in v 17a. In v 2b לנביאי מלבם "to the prophets from their hearts" was earlier לְנִבְּאֵי מלבם "to those who prophesy from their hearts," before the first term was mechanically assimilated to the noun in v 3a. It attests the alternative reading in v 3a and probably aligns with the *Vorlage* of the LXX*; this marginal reading displaced אליהם "to them" in v 2b. In v 3a הנבלים "foolish" may simply represent a misreading of מלבם "from their hearts" in wrong but understandable expectation of an adj after the noun (cf. Cooke 139). Finally, the relative clause is an exegetical gloss, rephrasing the basic text that once stood at the end of v 3a and implicitly contrasting the "spirit" of these prophets with the spirit of true prophecy (cf. Isa 30:1).

3.b. While the context makes the sense clear, the syntax of ולבלתי ראו is difficult. Heb. לבלתי normally makes an inf negative, "so as not to (see)"; here perhaps it means "without (seeing)" (Driver, *Bib* 19 [1938] 63, who compared לבלי "without"). Then one expects an inf rather than the pf in the MT (cf. BDB 116b–117a). KB (132a) advocated repointing as inf abs, רְאֹ. Driver (*Bib* 19 [1938] 63; *Bib* 35 [1954] 150) construed the form in the MT as a verbal noun, "seeing," with the accent on the first syllable: cf. שָׂחוֹ "swimming" in 47:5 (GKC 93x). The initial *waw* is explicative, "and that": cf. BDB 252b. The interpretation of the clause in GKC 152x is unlikely, as GKC 155n acknowledges.

4.a. Heb. היו "have been" has no counterpart in the LXX* (and is absent from MS^Ken 62). For its position and sense, Greenberg (236) has compared 22:18.

5.a. For the switch from third person in v 3 to second, cf. 34:2–3 (Hossfeld and Meyer, *Prophet* 135).

5.b. Since Cornill (247), בפרצות "into the breaches" has often been emended to sg פֶּרֶץ "into the breach," by comparison with the formulation in 22:30; Ps 106:23. Then dittography of ות was to blame (Kraetzschmar 131–32). The ancient versions so attest (cf. *BHS*), but their evidence may reflect a widespread exegetical tradition that assimilated to the common formulation. Elsewhere the pl is פרצים, but in post-bibical Heb. a fem form פרצה is standard (Jastrow, *Dictionary* 1237b–38a). Assimilation is more certainly to blame for the verb "stand" found in LXX Tg, which clashes with עמד "stand, resist" later. Cornill's argument that the text was changed to avoid such a clash is less likely.

6.a. The MT שוא חזו וקסם כזב "they have seen what is worthless and false divination" mixes a verb and a noun. One expects either a pair of verbs or a pair of nouns (cf. vv 7–9). The first expedient was achieved by Driver (*Bib* 35 [1954] 150), who construed חזו as a noun, "vision" (cf. *Note* 3.b. above), in an exclamatory phrase "Oh! Vain vision and false divination!" and the rest of v 6 likewise (cf. the NEB, "Oh, those prophets who say . . ."). Talmon and Fishbane (*ASTI* 10 [1975/76] 150 n. 24) emend to חזון "vision," without intimating how they integrate v 6aα into the rest of the verse. The second expedient, to find two verbs here, is more commonly pursued. Cornill (247) revocalized as two inf abs forms, וְקָסֹם . . . חָזוֹ. The Vg implies וקסמו . . . חזו "they have seen . . . and divined," while the LXX and Tg presuppose ptcp forms, וְקֹסְמֵי . . . חֹזֵי, with a ו/י variant in the first case. Ehrlich (*Randglossen* 5:44) plausibly integrated v 6 with the direct address in vv 5, 7–8 by adopting the latter verbal forms and regarding as vocatives; he noted that the third person references in v 6aγb are idiomatic (cf. GKC 144p and *Note* 22:3.c.).

7.a. The LXX* has no counterpart for v 7b in the MT, "and say 'So runs Yahweh's oracle,' when I have not spoken." Probably the addition represents a comparative gloss on v 6a, for which the first three Heb. words (minus the copula) function as cue words. Comparison was made with Jer 23:21, where in a first person divine context Yahweh's nonsending of false prophets is matched with his nonspeaking. The gloss was subsequently eased into the text at a feasible point, with the addition of *waw*.

9.a. The MT והיתה "and (my hand) will come (upon)" is elsewhere a technical expression relating to an esoteric prophetic experience (e.g., 1:3), which is out of place in this declaration of divine punishment. It is doubtful whether the explanation of the strange usage in terms of sarcasm, given by Kraetzschmar (132) and others is adequate. The LXX implies ונטיתי "and I will stretch out," which is formally expected (cf. 6:14; 14:9, 13) and has generally been adopted since Hitzig (88). Yet how the MT arose is most uncertain. It may have been a comment or correction relating to an adjacent part of the text, which subsequently displaced the right reading here. Was it earlier a masc form והיה belonging to v 11 (see *Note* 11.a.), which was wrongly related to v 9 and adapted in gender?

9.b. The MT adds אדני "Lord," which does not reflect the formulaic practice in Ezekiel: see Zimmerli, *Ezekiel 2* 556–62. It was probably added by assimilation to v 8.

10.a. For the emphatic יען וביען "because and because" in grounds for divine punishment, cf. 36:3; Lev 26:43. Talmon and Fishbane (*ASTI* 10 [1975/76] 133 and n. 21), followed by Greenberg (241), take the causal clause in v 10a as the conclusion of v 9, as in Lev 26:43. But in Ezek 36:3 it is clearly an initial clause.

10.b. Elsewhere the stem is תעה, e.g., in 14:11; here the Aram. form שעה is used.

10.c. Lit. a sg pronoun, with reference to "my people" (Smend 75; et al.).

10.d. See the *Comment*.

10.e. LXX Syr Vg may preserve a variant והמה "and they," in contrast to the earlier pronoun (cf. *BHS*), but the MT והנם "and behold they" fittingly expresses surprise (Ehrlich, *Randglossen* 5:45).

10.f. Heb. תפל is a byform of the stem שפל "coat (with clay)." See the *Comment*.

11.a. For the MT ויפל חיה "and (it) will fall, it was" one expects simply והיה "(it) will come," relating to the rain (cf. v 13b), with *waw* introducing the message, as in v 13aβ. The LXX represents this shorter text. Probably, as I suggested in Brownlee (186), יפל originated as an explanation of the pf נפל in v 12, which refers to the future ("[the wall] will fall"). It was taken as a correction ofוהיה in v 11 and was inserted here, producing a conflated text. In an English translation the juxtaposition of clauses is more naturally replaced by subordination (cf. GKC 159g; Joüon 167b).

11.b. The MT "and you, O hailstones" strangely switches to direct address (cf. v 13b). LXX Vg (cf. Syr) represent a repointing of וְאַתֵּנָה "and you" (cf. v 20a) as וְאֶתְּנָה "and I will give," but a verb is otiose here. D. N. Freedman (in Propp, ZAW 102 [1990] 404 n. 3) has interestingly adopted the interpretation as a verb and coupled it with the next verb: "and I will cause . . . to fall." However, a first person divine reference is out of place here and anticipates v 13. One expects simply a waw before אבני "stones." Did אתנה originate as a correcting or explanatory gloss on the masc form אתם "you" in v 20b? If so, it is difficult to see why the annotation wandered so far. "Hail" is usuallyברד: the term אלגביש, which appears here and in v 13 and also in 38:22, is related to Ugar. ʾlgbt, an unknown commodity, and Akk. algamišu, a type of jewel (HALAT 49b). Driver (Bib 35 [1954] 151) judged the sense to be "(hail)stones hard as rock." The LXX has a second rendering εἰς τοὺς ἐνδέσμους αὐτῶν "to their bundles," which Hitzig (89) rightly explained as a doublet: he compared the rendering of Θ forכפיס in Hab 2:11.

11.c. The MT תבקע, pointed as a piel, is more naturally taken as a niph תִּבָּקַע "break out" (cf. Isa 58:8; 59:5), in line with the pass rendering in the LXX: cf. v 13. Greenberg (238) justifies the MT in terms of the intransitive use of this piel form in midrashic Heb. This is certainly how the present pointing is to be understood, rather than implying the wall as object, as BDB 132a explained, which clashes with the usage in v 13.

12.a. Lit. "and behold the wall will have fallen."

13.a. For the causative piel, cf. Greenberg 238.

13.b. The lack of a verb is supplied by an added ἐπάξω "I will bring" in the LXX. Cornill (249) has been followed by many in emending לכלה "destructively" to תפלנה "will fall," in line with v 11, but the MT can stand.

14.a. The MT and the general textual tradition add ונפלה וכליתם בתוכה "and it [fem] will fall and you will be destroyed in its [fem] midst." Should one change to a masc verb with reference to the wall and understand the suffix in a neuter sense with reference to the fragments of the broken wall (Ehrlich, Randglossen 5:46), in the latter case either repointing as masc (בתוכה, Bertholet [1936] 46) or writing בתוכו (Rothstein 900)? These are methodologically inadequate measures that leave the present text unexplained. It seems to have arisen as a comment on Jerusalem in v 16, interpreting the metaphor of the fallen wall in vv 12, 14a in plain terms. The second word was meant as a comment on לכלה "destructively" in v 13, explaining it as referring to the destruction of the prophets, with help from v 15. The third word either goes with it, meaning "in the midst of the storm wind," or is a corruption ofבתוכחת "in punishments," attested by the LXX (cf. Hitzig 89), a comparative gloss on v 13 that alluded to the parallelism found in 5:15. In BHS the extent of the addition is indicated wrongly.

15.a. The MT ואמר "and I will say" is already attested by the LXX "and I said." Hitzig (89) and others have suggested that it be pointed וְאָמַר, with an indefinite subj, "and one will say," a variation of the pass form in v 12. Syr Tg attest a pass form, clearly by assimilation to v 12.

15.b. Hardly "to you," since the demise of the prophets is envisioned.

15.c. Cornill (249) called the MT ואין . . . אין "there is no . . . and no" a flat expression. He has been followed by many in adopting the reading attested by the Syr,ואיה . . . איה "where . . . and where?" in line with v 12. However, it seems to be a further case of assimilation. Preference for it generally accompanies a redactional view of v 15.

16.a. Not "to" (NIV, REB), since prophets both in exile and in the homeland seem to be in view. Heb. אל is used in the sense of על (here with the sense "concerning"), as in vv 2, 8, 9, 17, 19, 20 (BHS).

17.a. The hithp seems to mean "behave as a prophet" (J. Jeremias, THAT 2:17). Wilson (JBL 98 [1979] 329–36), who also interprets as to act like a prophet, either in word in deed, has observed here and in 37:10 a focus on the prophetic word as the basis of evaluation, so that the hithp form has become synonymous with the niph. Rendtorff (TDNT 6:799) has noted that in 37:10, in differentiation from the niph form in v 7 (and vv 4, 9), it relates to a quasi-magical summons rather than an announcement, which suits the power of life and death exercised by the women prophets in this passage.

18.a. Lit. "hunt down."

18.b. Heb.כסתות, which is found only here and in v 20, is generally related to Akk. kasîtu, kisittu "fetter." In later Heb. the noun means "cushion"; Greenberg (239) so interprets, but it is difficult to fit this meaning into the context. The LXX so renders here, but its translation "belt" forכסת, seemingly taken asכסה, in 9:2 reflects a different interpretation.

18.c. Lit. "joints of hands." For the MT יָדִי "my hands," it is necessary to read יָדִים "hands," implied by Syr Tg and read by a few MSS. The error presumably came about via scribal abbreviation, יְדִי (Cooke 149; Driver, *Textus* 1 [1960] 115). A further shortening to יָד "hand" is attested in LXX Vg.

18.d. Heb. מִסְפָּחוֹת occurs only here and in v 21. The LXX renders in general terms as "coverings." Driver (*Bib* 19 [1938] 63–64) argued by comparative etymologizing that loose flowing or spreading or all-enveloping veils or shawls were in view. In later Heb. the term evidently means "rags" (Greenberg 239).

18.e. Lit. "stature."

18.f. The interrogative *he* is normally pointed without the daghesh, but see GKC 100l; Joüon 102l–m; there is no need to repoint with Cornill (250) and others. The question has the force of a surprised exclamation (Smend 78).

18.g. Heb. לְעַמִּי and לְכֵנָה seem to be used in periphrasis for genitives, "of my people, of yourselves" (Ehrlich, *Randglossen* 5:47). The LXX does not represent לְכֵנָה, probably because it took the adjacent verbs as third pl, rather than second, and so had no room for it.

19.a. Or conceivably "with." Kraetzschmar (136) observed that the *beth* of price is normally seen here but reported that W. Robertson Smith (*Journal of Philology* 13 [1885] 273–87) interpreted of offerings brought to obtain an oracular response.

19.b. For the modal use of the impf, see Joüon 113m.

20.a. Syr Vg Tg render שָׁם . . . אֲשֶׁר, lit. "where," as "by which." Hitzig (91) and others have retroverted as בָּם. Zimmerli (289) has defended the spatial reference of the MT, which is supported by the LXX: the victims are caught as in nets.

20.b. The MT adds לִפְרְחוֹת: see *Note* 20.e.

20.c. The MT along with the general textual tradition attests זְרוֹעֹתֵיכֶם "your arms," but it creates a difficulty inasmuch as v 18 seems to imply that the clients of the women prophets wore the wristbands. Cornill (250) noted that there was no corresponding phrase "off your heads" in v 21aa[1] and conjectured that the phrase "off your arms" was a false addition that took the suffix in v 21 to mean "worn by you," instead of "made by you." Rothstein in *BHK* suggested that זְרֹעֹתֵיהֶם "their arms" be read, and *BHS* has firmly adopted his suggestion. False assimilation to מִסְפְּחוֹתֵיכֶם "your shawls" in v 21 is indeed plausible. There is a bewildering mixture of masc and fem second pl suffixes in vv 19–21. See the *Comment*.

20.d. The MT אֶת־נְפָשִׁים "persons" can hardly be right: such a pl form is not found elsewhere, an article is expected, and the earlier אֶת־תְּנַפֵּשׁוֹת "the persons" needs no repetition. LXX Tg "their souls" implies אֶת־נַפְשָׁם, which deals with the first two difficulties but not with the third. Cornill's brilliant conjectural emendation אֹתָן חָפְשִׁים "them free" (251) has won general acceptance. He cited the well-attested phrase שִׁלַּח חָפְשִׁי "let (slaves) go free" (see BDB 344b, 1019a); the masc is the standard form. The error was due to the two preceding cases of אֶת־הַנְּפָשׁוֹת, which caused wrong word division and the dropping of *heth*.

20.e. Heb. לִפְרְחֹת seems to qualify the setting free of the captivated clients. In v 20a it reappears in the MT in the different context of their being hunted down. It can hardly belong in both places. The lack of a counterpart there in the LXX* and the similarity of the preceding phraseology in vv 20a, b suggest that the term was added there by false assimilation after v 20b was corrupted (cf. Hitzig 92). The stem appears to be Aram., with the sense "fly" ('A Σ Vg), which the LXX "to scattering" and the Tg "to destruction" also reflect. Then it appears to allude to a bird escaping from a snare (Ps 124:7; Hitzig 92). The use of the *lamed* with a ptcp (or a noun "birds") remains difficult (cf. Greenberg 240). Perhaps the composite term means "(let go free) into the state of persons who fly away" (cf. Exod 21:26, 27). Cornill's suggestion that it was a gloss to replace the corrupted חָפְשִׁי "free" (251–52) deserves consideration.

22.a. Since Hitzig (25–52), there has been a tendency to emend to הַכְאִב "harm" in line with v 22aβ, especially because the hiph of כאה does not occur elsewhere. Indeed, *HALAT* (434a) (cf. Ehrlich *Randglossen* 5:46) gets rid of the other (niph) cases of the stem כאה (Ps 109:16; Dan 11:30), regarding them as derived from נכה. However, there appears to be a play on two similar stems (Wevers 110). Greenberg (241) has noted how in Heb. verbs hiph and niph regularly correspond, with act and pass meanings respectively.

22.b. The MT adds שָׁקֶר "falsehood, falsely," for which the LXX* has no counterpart. See *Note* 23.a.

22.c. The *lamed* with inf constr functions as a continuation of the preceding inf in the causal clause: cf. Cooke 150; Joüon 124p. Elsewhere other parts of the verb, rather than an inf, occur in the relevant preceding clause.

22.d. The implicit subj of לְהַחֲיֹתוֹ "to keep him alive" is the female prophets who are addressed: this subj is carried over from the verb in v 22ba, leapfrogging the change of subj in the case of שׁוּב "return."

23.a. Many scholars since Cornill (252) have recommended the conjectural emendation of קסם "divination" to כזב "falsehood," in the light of the parallelism in vv 6, 7, 9, 19. The MT שׁקר, another term for "falsehood," in v 22 is comparable. It doubtless originated as an exegetical gloss on קסם here, as I observed in Brownlee (194); it occurs only here in Ezekiel, and in this chapter is its equivalent, but it is common in Jeremiah (see especially Jer 14:14; Zech 10:2). Here the MT can stand: after the first clause, קסם has a pejorative sense.

14:1.a. The MT ויבא "and one came" is probably a further example of metathesis, to which this verb is particularly prone in Ezekiel (see Zimmerli 300). It was corrupted from the expected ויבאו "and they came," as in 9:2. It is true that the MT is a possible construction (Joüon 150j); that very possibility served to perpetuate the error.

3.a. Lit. "These men have set on their hearts." Schoneveld (*OTS* 15 [1969] 193–98), following M. du Buisson, envisioned an amulet worn over the heart or a tattoo on the breast, but elsewhere the phrase (ה)עלה על־לב relates to thinking (see BDB 749a; cf. 20:32). See Mosis's critique of this thesis in *BZ* 19 (1975) 193 n. 99.

3.b. Lit. "they have set before their faces." The verb נתן "set" is varied with the synonym שׂים in vv 4, 7 (cf. Talmon, *Qumran* 342–43).

3.c. Lit. "Should . . . ?" NAB and NJB idiomatically preface with "Why?" to express the rhetorical nature of the question.

3.d. The niph has a tolerative force (GKC 51c), as with this verb in 20:3, 31; 36:37. The MT "should I be consulted, consulted" is strange. One expects the first verbal form to be that of an inf absol, (ה)הדרשׁ, strengthening an indignant question (GKC 113q). Probably this is a case of mechanical assimilation to the next word (but cf. Greenberg 248).

4.a. Heb. "the prophet": see Cooke (155) for the idiomatic usage.

4.b. בה K "with it" is probably intended to anticipate the following "with the multitude of idols": cf. the Syr "with them." Q בא "when he comes (with),", followed by NJPS and NRSV, makes a minimal improvement by finding a resumption of the previous verb. Since Hitzig (94), בי, which appears in the parallel v 7, has been generally adopted as an emendation, with the presumed support of the Tg, with which Sperber (*Bible in Aramaic* 4B:337) agrees. However, Greenberg's contention that this is not so (247) has merit, especially as the Tg has a rendering for בא, דאתי "for he comes." Nor is it easy to explain a corruption from בי to בה: it could have arisen via an intermediate reading בו, which the LXX may presuppose in v 7, unless it represents בה, by assimilation to the K form here. Yet, in the light of v 7, it is the expected reading, and בה (or בא) can hardly be original. Overall, an emendation to בי is the least objectionable solution. The sense of the preposition is determined by such expressions as speaking in Yahweh's name or swearing by Yahweh (see BDB 90a): "by myself," "on my own authority." It virtually reinforces the reflexive element in the verb (Cooke 155).

4.c. The niph form appears to be of the same type as the verb in v 3, perhaps developed by analogy with it: "allow myself to give an answer." Hossfeld and Meyer (*Prophet* 119) have taken the pf in the sense "I have (already) given an answer," but the clearly parallel expression in v 7, which uses a ptcp, suggests that a fut sense is intended.

4.d. The preposition may connote a standard of measurement (Cooke 155): cf. BDB 90b.

5.a. Ehrlich (*Randglossen* 5:48) has usefully compared the Mishnaic sense of the niph, "be held responsible" (cf. NJPS "hold to account").

5.b. For the niph usage of this verb, cf. Isa 1:4.

5.c. Heb. כלם "all of them" may qualify the subj of the verb, as most modern versions interpret. More probably it reinforces the previous noun, a construction common in Ezekiel (BDB 481b; thus NAB): the phrase appears to be an intensifying counterpart to "with the host of their idols" in v 4 (Smend 81).

6.a. In the light of 18:30, the hiph has an intransitive force, perhaps by way of ellipse of the natural object "yourselves."

7.a. The partitive preposition is here used with a collective sg.

7.b. For the syntactical construction, see Cooke 155.

7.c. Lit. "consecrates himself from after me": cf. the use of the verb to refer to devoting oneself to a pagan god in Hos 9:10. In Lev 22:2 it means "keep oneself religiously separate from [מן]."

7.d. It is more natural to take the client as the subj of the inf: דרשׁ with ב means "inquire of (God)." Then לו means "(coming) to (the prophet)" as agent or medium of the consultation. Greenberg (250) compares דרשׁ אל־המתים "one who consults the dead" in Deut 18:11.

7.e. See *Note* 4.b. above.

8.a. The hiph form is anomalous: the case in 21:21 is a textual error (see *Note* 21:21.b.). A qal form ושׁמתיהו is generally predicated. Did a comparative gloss from v 9, והשׁמדתיהו "and I will destroy him," stand in the margin with reference to its counterpart והכרתיו "and I will cut him off" and encourage a miswriting of the previous verb? The reading with a *šin* found in some MSS, meaning "and I will destroy him," is an attempt to make sense out of the MT.

8.b. Elsewhere a sg משל occurs with the sense "byword." To read a sg form on the alleged evidence of Syr Vg (*BHK, BHS*) is methodologically dubious, especially without an explanation as to how the MT arose. The strange reading "(make you) into a desert and into destruction" in the LXX attests in its *Vorlage* ולמשמה. לשמה. Perhaps this was a copyist's recasting into typical Ezekielian language (cf., e.g., 6:14) of a comparative gloss לשמה ולמשל "as an object of horror and a byword," derived from Deut 28:37. A sg משל is expected here too. In support of the MT, Greenberg (250) has adduced cases of pairs of nouns in which the first is sg and the second pl, at Isa 43:28; 50:6.

9.a. Mosis (*BZ* 19 [1975] 166–69; *TWAT* 4:829–31) has compared the "prophetic" pf forms in vv 4b and 7bβ in statements of future divine reaction that begin with אני יהוה "I, Yahweh." He argued that the same construction is to be found here. Then, as in vv 7bβ–8a, the pf is followed by consecutive pf forms. Following H. E. Smieter, he has attributed to the piel here a factitive force (cf. Joüon 52d; GKC 52g), "show to be misled." Mosis has also plausibly claimed for the piel of פתה in Jer 20:7 the sense "make to be a fool," and for the pual in Jer 20:10 the meaning "let himself be made a fool," by an inadvertent statement or action. Mosis's interpretation has been followed by Fuhs (75) and Klein (*Ezekiel* 111 n. 10).

10.a. Lit. "the like of the inquirer's punishment the like of the prophet's punishment." Cooke (156) observed that in this idiom the present order, whereby the second entity is like the first, is less common.

Form/Structure/Setting

Ewald (254, 257) recognized in 12:21–14:11 a collection of oracular pieces dealing with various aspects of prophecy. He was followed by Smend (67), von Orelli (51), Kraetzschmar (128), Herrmann (76), and Cooke (135), among older scholars, as well as by several more recent commentators, such as Muilenburg (576). Talmon and Fishbane (*ASTI* 10 [1975/76] 131–38) have used structural analysis to establish the validity of this grouping. They compared the collection in Jer 23:9–40, which actually bears the heading "Concerning the prophets." They found the core of the present collection to be a pair of composite oracles, against rival prophets in 13:1–16 and against female prophets in 13:17–23. It is flanked by a pair of oracles in 12:21–25 and 26–28, concerning Ezekiel's prophetic revelation and the people's refusal to accept it, and by a further pair in 14:1–8, 9–11, concerning the seeking and granting of prophetic oracles. One may quibble about the definition of 14:1–11 as a pair of oracles, but vv 1–8 and 9–11 do deal with a pair of topics, respectively, the inquirer and the prophet to whom inquiry is made. In strict terms one could map out the overall symmetry as A + B/A(= a + b)+ B(= a + b)/a + b, but the principle of pairing is beyond dispute. Apart from the prophetic theme that runs through the collection, there are vocabulary links between the double core and the initial pair of oracles. The four expressions that dominate 13:1–16 (or at least vv 1–19, 16), חזה "have a vision" and חזון and מחזה "vision," (ם)קסם "divine, divination," שוא "worthless," and כזב "false," not only recur in vv 19 and 23 but are also anticipated in 12:22–24, 27 in three cases out of the four. A further integrating factor is the common punishment of prophets in 13:9 and 14:9, namely, the blow from the divine hand and exclusion from the people of God.

The first pair of oracles, in 12:21–25, 26–28, are disputations concerning the nonfulfillment of prophecy. Graffy (*A Prophet Confronts* 52–58), in the course of a careful exegetical study, has analyzed their form in terms of quotation (vv 22b, 27aβb) and refutation (vv 23–25, 28). D. F. Murray's threefold structuring of the disputation genre in *JSOT* 38 (1987) 95–121, in terms of thesis, dispute, and counterthesis, suggests a reexamination. In the second and shorter case, the thesis in v 27aβb is followed by a counterthesis in v 28aβ and by a dispute in v 28bα. In the prior and more complex case, the thesis in v 22b gives way first to a parallel counterthesis in v 23bβ and then to a dispute in vv 24–25aα, which in two כִּי ("for") clauses gives the grounds for the counterthesis, and finally to a paraphrase of the counterthesis in v 25aβbα. Beyond the common elements of the genre, the disputations match in several respects: their initial message-reception formulas, the address of Ezekiel as בֶּן־אָדָם "human one," and the use of the messenger formula to introduce the divine responses and of the divine-saying formula to conclude them. Moreover, a shorter version of the restatement of the counterthesis in v 25aβbα reappears in the counterthesis of v 28aβ.

Talmon (*Qumran* 397 n. 204) has found a stylistic phenomenon of inverted recapitulation that binds the two oracles together as a pair in the two matching pairs of statements within vv 25 and 28, namely, אֵת אֲשֶׁר אֲדַבֵּר דָּבָר וְיֵעָשֶׂה לֹא תִמָּשֵׁךְ עוֹד "whatever word I speak is fulfilled. There will be no further delay" and לֹא תִמָּשֵׁךְ עוֹד כָּל־דְּבָרִי אֲשֶׁר אֲדַבֵּר דָּבָר וְיֵעָשֶׂה "There will be no further delay over any words of mine. Whatever word I speak is fufilled." The respective order of the clauses indicates inverted parallelism, so that one mirrors the other.

After the new message-reception formula in 13:1, vv 2–23 divide into two bipartite literary oracles. The first, in vv 2–16, is directed at male prophets and begins and ends with oracular formulas, in vv 2–3aα and 16bβ. The first half is a woe oracle in vv 3aβ–9; it is also a tripartite proof saying. In Ezekiel the woe announcement is used as the first part of a two-part oracle of judgment (cf. *ABD* 6:945–46). The proof saying proceeds from a doom-laden accusation ("Woe . . . ," vv 3aβ–7) to a forecast of punishment that opens with a summary of the accusation (vv 8–9a) and closes with the recognition formula (v 9b). The second half lacks an introduction of its own and functions as a literary continuation of the earlier passage. It is a tripartite proof saying that moves from a reasoning accusation ("Because . . . ," v 10) to a forecast of judgment (vv 13–14a) and the recognition formula (v 14bβ). The judgment is anticipated in vv 11–12 and supplemented with a climactic statement in v 15, while a conclusion to the whole double oracle in v 16 includes elements drawn from both halves. The second literary oracle, in vv 17–23, is directed at female prophets who practice sorcery. The oracular introduction in vv 17–18aα opens with a command of a prophetic gesture. Its first half in vv 18aβ–21 is again a woe oracle that is also a tripartite proof saying, though this time the recapitulating accusation is lacking. It develops from accusation (vv 18aβ–19) to a forecast of punishment (vv 20–21a) and finally to the recognition formula (v 21b). While in the first oracle the two halves were of similar length (9/10 lines in *BHS*), in this case they fall into disproportionate parts (11/3 lines). The second portion, like its counterpart in the first oracle, functions as a literary continuation of the foregoing. Again, like its parallel, it is a tripartite proof saying, whose elements appear respectively in vv 22, 23abα, and 23b.

As for stylistic factors, beyond those represented by form-critical formulas and elements, listed by Hossfeld and Meyer (*Prophet* 129–30), Talmon and Fishbane (*ASTI* 10 [1975/76] 134) have noted how vv 6–9 are dominated by a common vocabulary, variations on חָזָה שָׁוְא "have worthless revelations" and קָסַם כָּזָב "offer false divinations." The four terms operate as an integrating factor for the two composite oracles: they reappear in vv 19 and 23, the final term in v 19 and the other three in v 23. One suspects that only three of the terms are employed in v 23 because the fourth has been used up, as it were, in v 19. V 23, by means of its stylistic echoes, serves as the conclusion for the pair of literary oracles in chap. 13. Parunak ("Structural Studies" 224) has observed the parallelism between the interrogative elements of the accusations in the first halves, at vv 7a and 18b. Another unifying element is the sixfold עמי "my people," distributed at vv 9 and 10, then at vv 18, 19, 21, and 23. Parunak ("Structural Studies" 229–30) has noted that in the second composite oracle, while the sevenfold נפשות "persons" is a key word only for vv 18–21 (cf. too the fourfold צוד, צדד ["hunt"] stems in vv 18, 20, 21), the two halves are united by the repetition of "and I will rescue my people from your clutches" (v 21) in v 23 and by the thematic counterpointing of hunting down or putting to death (vv 18, 19, 20) or demoralizing (v 22) and of keeping alive (vv 19, 22).

14:1–11, after the introductory vv 1–2, consists of a private, explanatory oracle to the prophet in v 3 and commissioning in v 4aα to deliver the public oracle of vv 4aβ–11. There are similar instances of preparatory private oracles followed by public ones in 22:18 + 19–22; 23:2–21 + 22–27, and 36:17–21 + 22–23 (or 32). The public oracle first repeats the private one with an added threat of specific judgment (vv 4aβ–5); then in a development, it envelops that threat in a framework of general appeal and deterrent (vv 6–11) at vv 6 and 11 (cf. Parunak, "Structural Studies" 230–34). Vv 6–11 constitute a call to repentance; they have the formal elements of an admonition (v 6), an accusation (v 7), a threat (vv 8–10), and a promise (v 11) (Raitt, *ZAW* 83 [1971] 35). The overall oracle is also a variant of a judgment oracle. The accusation is sounded three times in similar terms: in the private oracle at v 3, in the threatening first phase of the public oracle at v 4, and in the deterrent, second phase at v 7. For the use of an oracle of judgment to make an eventual appeal, one may compare Isa 28:14–22.

A dominant feature of the whole piece is a host of formulations taken from the realm of cultic law and used to characterize the offender and the fact and form of his punishment (Zimmerli 302–6; earlier in *ZAW* 66 [1954] 8–19). This feature invests the prophetic piece with the solemn air of a priestly ruling uttered with divine authority. The complexity of the piece, as a law-saturated summons to repentance, in which declarations of a positive intent are wrapped round dire announcements of punishment, helps to explain its peculiarities. Thus, its dominant third-person orientation in referring to the human targets of punishment accords with its legal perspective (Zimmerli, *ZAW* 66 [1954] 7). Vv 7–8 constitute a self-contained statement of judgment that is also a two-part proof saying, concluding with the recognition formula. Normally the proof saying is a genre that marks the whole oracle; here it has been subsumed within an individual instance of case law. In fact, here the recognition formula may be regarded as a translation into prophetic terms of the formula of self-designation, "I am Yahweh," that often stands at the end of individual cultic laws in the Priestly legislation and especially in the Holiness Code (see, e.g., Lev 19:11–18, 30, 32, 37). Then in vv 9–10 "in typical case-law style a further subcase appears and requires additional legal elaboration" (Hals 92; cf. Zimmerli 40). Hölscher (*Dichter* 86) and Zimmerli (305) have rightly taken vv 1–11 as an integral piece. There is no need to postulate a redactional addition with Herrmann (87) and Fohrer (76) or a literary supplement made by Ezekiel (Wevers 111).

Stylistically the formulation relating to an inquirer entertaining idolatry and the issuing of a divine response, in vv 3, 4, and 7, bind much of the piece together. So do the solemn ingredients אני יהוה "I am Yahweh" in vv 4 and 7, which are echoed in the recognition formula of v 8. Talmon and Fishbane (*ASTI* 10 [1975/76] 137–38) have drawn attention to the rhetorical relation between offense and penalty in an individual's setting of idols before the face (נתן/שׂים . . . פניו) in vv 3, 4, 7 and Yahweh's setting his face against him and making him an omen (שׂים . . . נתן פני) in v 8. A sustained wordplay runs through the piece and gives added coherence to it: עון "iniquity" (vv 3, 4, 7, 10 [three times]), the verb נענה "allow oneself to answer" (vv 4, 7), and למען "in order that" (vv 5, 11). Human sin leads initially to a dire response of judgment but ultimately encounters positive divine purposes.

As for the settings of the various pieces, 12:21–25 is best understood as relating to Ezekiel's own oracles of Judah's doom and being addressed to his fellow prisoners of war in vv 22 and 25 (Herrmann 78, 83; cf. Fohrer 66; Eichrodt 155; Wevers 103). The evident inclusion of Ezekiel in the collective address in v 22 points to these conclusions. The phrase על־אדמת ישׂראל has often been rendered "on the soil of Israel" or the like, with the implication that the saying was current in Judah concerning such prophets of judgment as Jeremiah and that it had reached the exiles (Zimmerli 281–82; Greenberg 230), or else it surveys a whole history of Israel's response to prophecy (Zimmerli 282, following Janssen). 12:26–28 explicitly relates to Ezekiel's oracles to the exiles but deals with a different type of objection to his prophesying. Again, a pre-587 setting is in order.

The oracles of chap. 13 bear evidence of literary composition and do not necessarily reflect the same setting. The reference to return to the land in v 9 invests the proof saying of 13:2–9 with an exilic provenance, so that Ezekiel's prophetic rivals in exile are in view. The application of the imagery of v 5 to prophets in the homeland at 22:30 (cf. Allen, *Ezekiel 20–48* 33, 39) is no hindrance. It is probable that Ezekiel regarded the exilic prophets as part of a larger group that included counterparts in Judah. But into what period of Ezekiel's ministry does the oracle fit? It is natural to relate the opposing prophetic message to denials that Jerusalem would fall, as in the oracles of Jer 23:16–40. But mention of return to the land aligns with his positive oracles: it is too integrated into its context to take it as introduced by the prophet at a later time or as a redactional insertion, with Eichrodt (167) and Wevers (107). Kraetzschmar (130) helpfully pointed to the preponderance of perfect verbs. Correspondingly, Greenberg (145–46) has contrasted the participles and imperfect forms found in Jer 23 and suggested that the oracle may look back from a post-fall perspective, as in Lam 2:14, which uses verbs in the perfect. There are significant links between vv 3–9 and the oracle in 34:2–16. Both messages are woe oracles containing a rhetorical question, depend on Jer 23, and refer to the day of Yahweh as a past phenomenon, in a backward look at the catastrophe of 587 (Janzen, *Mourning Cry* 76–77). No credence can be given to the older view that differentiated between second and third person references to the prophets, ascribing vv 2, 7, 8 (assumed to be originally second person!) to a pre-587 Babylonian oracle and vv 3, 5, 6, 9 to a post-587 oracle uttered in Jerusalem (Rothstein 898, followed by Cooke 137–38; cf. Fohrer 66).

Zimmerli (*Ezechiel 1* 292 [mistranslated in *Ezekiel 1* 294]), followed by Greenberg (243), has observed that, in the light of Ezekiel's practice elsewhere, the formula of confrontation in v 8 requires continuation with a sentence of punishment such as v 9 provides.

The oracle in vv 10–15 or 16 is a literary continuation of vv 2–9 but does not reflect the same temporal setting. The reference to false optimism points to pre-fall forecasts, while behind the metaphorical language of vv 13–14 there seems to lie an allusion to the fall of Jerusalem as a future event. V 16 is best understood as a post-fall comment that integrates the pre-587 oracle of vv 10–15 into a larger literary whole, consisting of vv 2–16. Its echoes of vv 2 and 10 so suggest: stylistically v 16 provides an inclusion both for vv 10–16 and for vv 2–16.

The oracle against female prophetic sorcerers in vv 17–21 has a focus on their individual clients, which hinders the recovery of a precise setting. The inference of Kraetzschmar (135) and Eichrodt (173–74) that it reflects the complete despair of the post-587 period is not compelling. Zimmerli (298) has more plausibly claimed that the magical practices filled up a vacuum left by loss of the cult in the exilic period. The supplementary passage in vv 22–23 gives the impression of an intention to provide literary symmetry for 13:1–23 (Fuhs 73), not least in the echo of the key vocabulary of vv 2–9 in v 23a. Both that impression and the implicit contrast in v 22 with the post-587 watchman role of Ezekiel according to 3:18; 33:8 point to a post-fall setting, which seems also to be reflected in vv 17–21. Krüger (*Geschichtskonzepte* 459–60) has observed the similarity between the promise to rescue his people from the sorcerers' clutches (vv 21, 23) and 34:10b. Chap. 13 is a literary composition in which earlier oracles have been woven together. It may fairly be attributed to the prophet Ezekiel. An exception should probably be seen in v 4, which with its address to Israel and epigrammatic generalization stands at a distance from its context, and so is to be credited to later redaction.

A clue to the chronological setting of 14:1–11 emerges from the similarity between v 11 and 37:23. On this score Krüger (*Geschichtskonzepte* 460) has plausibly allocated it to the second, positive period of Ezekiel's work; he also compared the use of תעה "go astray" in 44:10, 15; 48:11. The deterrent purpose of v 11 hardly matches the theme of radical and inexorable judgment that runs through his pre-587 oracles (Kraetzschmar 139). Zimmerli (*ZAW* 84 [1972] 512–13) found in the oracle a post-fall situation: he noted the positive ring of the call to repentance in v 6. It is matched in the probably post-587 chap. 18 (vv 30–32). Both v 6 and v 11 have links with the new, saving task of Ezekiel in 33:1–9, 14–15 and their literary anticipation in 3:20–21.

The literary unit may be outlined as follows.

12:21–28	Two disputations about the fulfillment of Ezekiel's oracles
12:21–25	Their certain fulfillment
12:26–28	Their imminent fulfillment
13:1–23	Two two-part oracles attacking false prophecy
13:1–16	Male prophets condemned
13:2–9	Their exclusion from the community
13:10–16	Their exposure as charlatans
13:17–23	Female prophets condemned
13:17–21	The countering of their magic
13:22–23	The termination of their immoral ministry

14:1–11   A two-part oracle condemning lay syncretism and its
                           promotion by prophets

Comment

21–28   Two similar oracles about the fulfillment of Ezekiel's prophesying have
been set together. They are both in the form of disputations and reflect reluctance
among the prophet's fellow exiles to accept his oracles as a valid representation
of the future.

21–22   After the introductory message-reception formula and the address to
the prophet, the community of which Ezekiel forms a part comes under divine
attack for its attitude to prophecy directed against the homeland. The preceding
literary context, though belonging to a separate unit, gives a clear, editorially
intended clue to the type of prophecy meant: in 12:19 אדמת ישראל "the land of
Israel" has been mentioned in connection with the coming siege of Jerusalem
and the devastation of Judah and its other cities, obviously at the hands of
Babylonian invaders. It was such pre-587 oracles that met with resentment from
the targeted constituency. The indignant question that will not tolerate such an-
tipathy has a parallel in opening a dissertation at 18:2. The exiles' frame of mind
is summed up in a משל or popular epigram. Jer 5:12 expresses a similar rejoinder
to prophecies of judgment, uttered by Judeans in the homeland:

> [Yahweh] is insignificant.
> No disaster will come upon us,
> nor will we see sword or famine.

Such an attitude has here been crystallized into a theological slogan. From the
perspective of the people who spoke it, "it sums up the truth about these mania-
cal doom-and-gloom prophets: 'Here is the way it is with you fellows: you talk
tough, but nothing ever happens'" (Polk, *CBQ* 45 [1983] 574). As in 7:26, חזון,
primarily "vision," stands generically for a revealed oracle, with emphasis on the
spoken word. The intent is to dismiss Ezekiel's oracles and to characterize him as
a false prophet who need not be taken seriously. The statement יארכו הימים "the
days grow long" has an imperfect rather than a perfect verb. So it does not claim
that Ezekiel had been prophesying for a long period but, along with the next
clause, represents a generalization that oracles never come true. Nevertheless,
the time lag between Ezekiel's call to be a prophet of judgment in 593 and
Nebuchadnezzar's eventual besieging of Jerusalem in 588 may well underlie the
gibe.

23   In terms of the disputation style, the slogan has represented a preliminary thesis. Yahweh supplies his servant with an authoritative answer. The course
of coming events would be his providential way of silencing these exilic representatives of "Israel." This intervention could be summed up in terms of a
counterthesis. "The days grow long" is adapted into a reversal, "The days have
grown near." In place of the indefinite imperfect verb stands a precise perfect.
The God who prophesied judgment through Ezekiel now stands at the door, judgment in hand. The claim is paralleled in an oracle rhetorically addressed to
Jerusalem, which grounds its coming destruction in its own sin: "You have brought
near your days [of judgment]" (22:4). The second clause of the counterthesis

only partially matches that of the thesis, though the whole corresponds as two cola of two beats. It insists that every judgment oracle will find its target, its wording destined to become fact.

24–25 The dispute that follows the counterthesis underscores it with two good reasons. The first reason picks up the peremptory "no longer" in the introduction to the counterthesis. V 24 has commonly been interpreted in terms of false prophecy and thus often regarded as an irrelevant insertion (see, e.g., Cooke 136; Hossfeld and Meyer, *Prophet* 122). Ehrlich (*Randglossen* 5:42–43; see *Note* 24.a.), implicitly followed by Greenberg (228) and Blenkinsopp (68), suggested that it be understood in relation to the as-yet-unfulfilled oracles of judgment uttered by Ezekiel. Those spoken oracles that still hovered in the air would swoop into human experience and find their promised prey. In terms of Isa 55:11, though oracles of salvation are there in view, God's word would not return to him empty but would accomplish his will. Yahweh would honor his messages of judgment delivered to the exiled representatives of the community of Israel. Here "divination" is used as a neutral term, a synonym of the revealed oracle (cf. 13:6 and the *Comment*). Within the literary unit, this sentiment in v 24 serves as a striking foil to the worthless revelation and false divination of chap. 13. It overlaps in wording but is starkly different in meaning.

A second reason is provided for the counterthesis in v 25a*a*, which is a general theological statement that Yahweh always honors his authentic messages. "God who speaks is not divided against himself. Whenever he opens his mouth, he stretches out his hand to fulfill his words" (Calvin 412). It would not do for the exiles to dismiss the true prophet, for behind him stood one who categorically was both willing and able to make his messages come true. Finally, in the rest of the oracle before the closing divine-saying formula, the counterthesis in v 23 is repeated in a paraphrase that clinches the matter. The reality behind Ezekiel's predictions of judgment would stare the hearers in the face. This generation would be living witnesses to both the spoken word and the grim actuality to which it pointed (cf. Mark 13:30). The "no longer" that featured at the start and midpoint of Yahweh's reply occurs again in this conclusion, as a renewed signal of life-shattering change. The addressing of the exiles as "a rebellious community" accords with usage at 2:5, 7; 3:27 in a description of the prophet's constituency as people who would be unlikely to listen.

26–27 A parallel oracle concerning the nonfulfillment of prophecy is introduced by the message-reception formula and by Yahweh's address. The divine preface to the thesis that this disputation will oppose is less vehement than in the former case, in keeping with the less skeptical tone of the thesis. The more moderate preface includes a differentiation between Ezekiel and his constituency, the exilic representatives of the people of God, who are now referred to in the third person. In contrast to the thesis of v 22, this one represents another group and another time. The thesis pointedly concentrates on the prophet ("he") and so subtly reflects the speakers' shielding themselves somewhat from the divine authority of his oracles. They also distance themselves from his prophecies of judgment by relegating them to a later fulfillment. The chiastic order in the two clauses focuses on this feature. There is not so much complacency here as a sense of relief, such as Hezekiah expressed in Isa 39:8, while voicing his acceptance of Isaiah's oracle, "There will be peace and security in my lifetime." This group did

not share the radical indifference of the elite in Samaria whom Amos characterized as "those who put the evil day far off" (Amos 6:3). The impact of Ezekiel's
oracles is diluted by deferring them to a distant date, though unlike Hezekiah
the recipients have been given no prophetic warrant for so doing. Presumably, a
gap that existed between oracle and fulfillment was construed as ground for a
further respite. The proponents of the thesis reacted like Californians who accept that their region is liable to earthquakes but fail to get their houses bolted
to the foundations or to take other appropriate precautions. Here a belief in a
breathing space constituted a failure to take fully into account the significance of
the predictions of disaster and to make mental and spiritual adjustments.

28 The counterthesis and dispute follow the same lines as those in vv 23–25,
but in a briefer compass. They do give vent, however, to a deliberate emphasis on
the divine origin of Ezekiel's oracles. The doubled human "he" of the thesis is
challenged by mention of "my words (or oracles)," while the reference to
Yahweh's speaking and even the opening messenger formula and the closing divine-saying formula here have a corresponding nuance they lacked in the previous
disputation. The denial of further delay in the counterthesis is now a direct contradiction of the thesis. The fall of Jerusalem was much closer than the exiles
thought: "The time has come, the day is near" (7:7). The argument used to support the counterthesis is again a general appeal to the firm control exercised by
the divine word over human history. The more immediate applicability of this
divine retort to the underlying situation suggests that it was reused and expanded
to fit the different situation of v 22, and this is how the overlap between the two
disputations is to be explained.

13:1–3 The message-reception formula of v 1 introduces a pair of composite
oracles, the former of which extends to v 16, as the divine-saying formula signals.
Within this literary product, one may distinguish vv 2–9 as a woe oracle and a proof
saying. The commissioning of Ezekiel to deliver this message singles out "Israel's
prophets" as its target. The traditional rivalry between establishment prophets and
antiestablishment prophets that is stated in the narrative of 1 Kgs 22 and echoed in
Isa 28:7–10; Hos 4:5; Mic 3:5–8 came to a head in Judah's final period of crisis. Jer
23 and 27–29 bear tragic witness to the equally sincere but radically different voices
that appealed to the people in God's name. Nor was the pre-587 community of
Judean prisoners in Babylonia free of such distressing polarization. Jeremiah's letter to them makes critical mention of deceptive "prophets and diviners," naming
two of them and accusing them of sexual immorality that detracted from the cred-
ibility of their optimistic oracles (Jer 29:8–9, 15, 21–23). In this oracle Ezekiel speaks
from a later, post-587 standpoint (see *Form/Structure/ Setting*). He seems to consciously echo Jer 23 and to apply its accepted prophetic authority to the exilic
context. He addresses a local group of rival prophets who had been active in the
critical pre-fall years, but he regards them as part of a larger group, "Israel's prophets," who included spiritual cousins back in Jerusalem in recent history. The
interjection "woe" in v 3 permits the targets of the oracle to be characterized and
hints at the future disastrous consequences of their activity, which will be spelled
out in vv 8–9a. The characterization draws a lesson from history. Events had shown
that those prophets who delivered messages of hope and reassurance were not inspired by God. Ezekiel echoes Jeremiah's wording, "visions of their own minds,
not from Yahweh's mouth" (Jer 23:16; cf. 14:14; cf. J. W. Miller, *Verhältnis* 93 n. 1).

4 This interruption of the continuation of the accusation in v 5 taxes the exegete. It seems to be a jubilant redactional comment, distanced from the context by its rhetorical address of the community. The same Hebrew term refers to both foxes and jackals (cf. *HALAT* 1341b). Since the former hunt singly and the latter congregate in groups and frequent ruins (cf. Lam 5:18), the choice of rendering is obvious. The ironic point appears to be that the discredited prophets, who envisioned a wonderful future for Israel, have been reduced to mulling over their disappointment, skulking in their ruined hopes. The notion of ruins was derived from the imagery of siege warfare used in v 5.

5 The clear echo of this charge in 22:30, with reference to false prophets in Jerusalem (22:28, which originally stood after v 29), establishes that it is a metaphorical statement referring to the prophetic responsibility of intercession, as the Targum interpreted. Ezekiel had vainly engaged in this task (9:8; 11:13), while Jeremiah had been divinely dissuaded from attempting it (Jer 7:16; 11:14; 14:11–12). In both cases judgment was inexorably fixed. Nonetheless, it was a good instinct for any prophet of judgment to follow and revealed how seriously it weighed on his soul (cf. Amos 7:2, 5, where a synonym of the verb "stand" is used). The optimistic prophets, on the other hand, had no inkling of the coming catastrophe that materialized in 587. So they had lent no such helping hand, in empathy for Israel's distress and in understanding of its cause. Rather, as v 10 will explain, they tried to plaster over the cracks in the wall, blithely unaware that the crisis was of horrendous proportions, a veritable "day of Yahweh," as chap. 7 had interpreted it (cf. 34:12; A. J. Everson, *JBL* 93 [1974] 332–33). The imagery is of siege warfare, specifically of the danger caused by the battering rams that were a feature of Assyrian and Babylonian warfare. They were pushed up ramps constructed against the city wall, to break through the higher, less stoutly built layers of stone (see Yadin, *Art of Warfare* 2:315, 413, 422–25, 434–35; Greenberg 236).

6–7 Yahweh's disowning of the prophets of hope is categorically expressed in Jer 14:14 (cf. 23:21): "I did not send them or command them or speak to them. Lying revelations, vain divinations, and the deceit of their own minds is what they are prophesying to you." Ezekiel adapts such sentiments, with his own negative vocabulary for the nature of their oracles (cf. Miller, *Verhältnis* 105). Divination is strictly the telling of the future by means of devices of various kinds (cf. 21:26 [21]). It is staunchly prohibited in Deut 18:10, 14. However, the addition of the epithet "false" may indicate that Ezekiel judged it by its results rather than by its nature (cf. Vanderkam, "Apocalyptic Thought" 173; cf. the positive usage in Prov 16:10). The same seems to have been true of Micah, who was prepared to credit diviners with divine gifts that they had abused by self-seeking and so were doomed to lose (Mic 3:6–7). In this case the oracles had turned out to be untrue, and so it is reasoned that those who had uttered them were not authentic, commissioned prophets after all. Their sincerity and confidence had been belied by events. The derisive question in v 7 challenges them to admit their error. It rubs their noses in the mess that recent history had left them with. A rhetorical question is a common element in the woe oracle (cf. v 18; 34:2; Janzen, *Mourning Cry* 47 n. 18, 76–77).

8–9 The renewed messenger formula, along with the supporting divine-saying formula, solemnly introduces the divine verdict, while the double "therefore" and the summarizing causal clause attest its reasonableness and justice. Here the divine-saying formula takes on a special quality, in the light of its misuse in v 6:

now a true prophet speaks. The confrontation formula makes a basic declaration of hostility (cf. Jer 23:30–32). It is elaborated in v 9, first in general terms of divine retaliation against these discredited prophets and then in spelling out a triple judgment. The judgment is formally expressed in the third person (cf. Eichrodt 166). It drives a wedge between the words of the phrase used to describe the targets of the oracle in v 2, "Israel's prophets." It would demonstrate that this status was based on spurious claims. Ludwig Köhler (*Hebrew Man* [London: SCM, 1956] 102–3) sought to imaginatively recapture the cultural significance of סוד, here rendered "assembly," by envisioning a campfire circle, where men met together after work to share their news and dreams. Certainly it has a ring of intimacy. Krüger (*Geschichtskonzepte* 459) has plausibly suggested that Ezekiel is transposing Jeremiah's denials that the optimistic prophets ever had a place in Yahweh's סוד or inner council (Jer 23:18, 21). Well then, those who had wrongly claimed this prophetic credential would lose their membership of the סוד at the lower level of the community of faith. The second punishment is exclusion from the roll of Israel's citizens (cf. Ezra 2:2–62; Neh 7:5–64). It was Yahweh's prerogative to maintain this list and to delete the names of those whose lives were diametrically opposed to his covenant (cf. Ps 109:13; "written in the dust," Jer 17:13). Excommunication from the community will be mentioned further in 14:8–9. The third punishment implicitly contrasts the false hopes engendered by the optimistic prophets, for whom Jerusalem could never fall, and the true hope of an eventual return to the land after the full rigors of judgment and exile. True hope as it was, it was conditional, and 20:38 will soberly speak again of its possible forfeiture, in terms of an event of divine demarcation. The eschatological note struck by the third punishment also covers the other two, in the light of the common future verbs. It would be only the true people of God who returned, and God would determine their membership. These three punishments were to vindicate Ezekiel's God as the source of legitimate prophecy and so repudiate any connection with discredited practitioners of the religious art.

10–15 This oracle again deals with the optimistic prophets, but it basically belongs to the pre-587 period. It has been attached to vv 2–9 as a literary continuation, without specification of its targets, in order to explicate the wall metaphor of v 5. Like the previous oracle, it takes over terms used earlier by Jeremiah and so claims continuity with his radical prophetic stand.

10 The rival prophets are accused of leading astray God's people. It is a traditional charge, reflected not only in Jer 23:13, 23 but also earlier in Mic 3:5. As often in the prophetic literature, "my people" has a ring of outrage: as their patron, Yahweh reacts to the victimization of his people. The leading astray is explained in terms of false promises of שלום "peace, security." Again, it was a charge that Jeremiah had made earlier (Jer 6:14 = 8:11; cf. Mic 3:5; cf. Miller, *Verhältnis* 3 and n. 2, 108). For Jeremiah, שלום had a medical metaphorical meaning, "health": he associated it with a superficial cure of the people's wounds at the hands of the optimistic prophets. A reference to superficiality survives in Ezekiel's own recourse to metaphor. He imagines a חיץ, a term that occurs only here in the OT and which in the Mishnah (*m. Šeb.* 3:8) is a rough stone wall, a terrace wall of loose, unmortared stones. What the prophets had done was tantamount to plastering over such a dry wall, giving the impression of a solid, substantial structure. In ancient Mesopotamia, external and internal walls were plastered with a more liquid form of the mixture of clay, water, and chopped straw or dung used for mortar (Lloyd, "Building" 1:461). The people's wall is here envisaged as an external wall in view of its exposure to wind and rain in vv 11 and 13. It represented their own one-sided belief that Yahweh would protect his temple and Jerusalem, out of loyalty to his covenant with them. The optimistic prophets had bolstered such a belief, thereby plastering over the rickety wall. Ezekiel echoed this metaphor in a later oracle, at 22:28. There may be a word-play between תפל (properly טפל) "plaster" and תפל "that which is senseless" (cf. Propp, *ZAW* 102 [1990] 404–8). This possibility is supported by the fact that Jer 23:13, which probably underlies the present passage, refers to תפלה "senseless-ness" manifested by false prophets (cf. W. McKane, *Jeremiah* [Edinburgh: Clark, 1986] 573–74; cf. Lam 2:14).

11–12 One expects an immediate continuation of the formal statement of divine punishment that begins in v 13. Jahn (82) and Zimmerli (290), followed by Wevers (107–8), Carley (83), and Hals (86), have secured form-critical neatness by regarding vv 11–12 as a later addition. Eichrodt (160–61), on the other hand, deleted vv 13–14ba as a subsequent, prosaic addition and kept vv 11–12. The two verses do provide a desired transition from the third-person statements of v 10 to the second-person references of vv (13–)14 via the divine command to the prophet relating to the optimistic prophets in v 11–12. These verses indeed anticipate vv 13–14a, but they leave out from the catastrophe the element of divine causation, so that the ensuing verses are not simply repetitious. As the text stands, there is an impressive movement from the confident speech of the prophets (לאמר "saying," v 10) to the mocking counter-speech of Ezekiel (אמר "tell," v 11), then to the shocked, reactive speech of others (יאמר "it will be said," v 12), and finally to the twofold speech of Yahweh (אמר "says," v 13; ואמר "and I will say," v 15) in the divine sentencing. This pair of verses poses a sardonic question as to the possibility of the wall's collapse. The question closes the accusation, rather like the parallel mocking question in v 7. Here, however, the accusation of shoddy workmanship is viewed from a future perspective. The closest counterparts in the book, in 17:9–10; 26:15, are exclusively oriented toward judgment, rather than accusation.

13–14 The preceding question is capped by a definite forecast of divine punishment along those very lines. There is a new factor of divine agency, which is augmented by references to Yahweh's anger. Popular hope, so assiduously nurtured by the prophets, would be exposed for the sham it was. There seems to be a deliberate echo of Jer 23:19–20: "See, Yahweh's storm, fury, will go forth, and a whirling storm . . . ; Yahweh's anger will not turn back." Only by such drastic means could divine truth be revealed.

15–16 The form-critically supplementary sentence in v 15 returns to the question of vv 11–12 and extends its threat into a forecast of doom for the prophetic plasterers, as well as for their wall. The mocking question posed by other people (v 12) is given an authoritative counterpart, the divine comment on the disappearance of the makeshift structure, prophets and all. The statement strikes a fitting final note, as comparison with Job 8:22; 24:24; Isa 17:14 shows. The literary ending of v 16 returns to the post-fall perspective of vv 2–9. It blends the two separate oracles into a single composition by combining "Israel's prophets" from v 2 with the spurious assurance of peace mentioned in v 10. The piece is given a historical aspect by reference to Jerusalem. It was the capital's survival or fate that was the burning prophetic issue. By the time of v 16, as of vv 2–9, it had been resolved in Ezekiel's favor.

17–19　Among the Judean exiles there were female counterparts to the male prophets of vv 2–16. They had a private rather than a public ministry: their concern was not to interpret political issues but to resolve the personal problems of their clients, like the prophets of Mic 3:5. Moreover, they performed magical spells as a means of prognostication. Ezekiel is directed to engage in a symbolic gesture, as in 6:2 (see the *Comment* there). Here it announces a virtual counterspell that puts the evil eye on these sorcerers. The specification of the object of the gesture permits an initial characterization in terms of a lack of divine inspiration, the same accusation that had been leveled against the male prophets in v 3. The verb for prophesying may allude to the magical activity they indulged in (see *Note* 13:17.a.). The accusation proper after the messenger formula in vv 18–19 begins with the sinister "woe." This inauspicious introduction allows a further characterization of the female prophets, with respect to their magical devices that evidently accompanied the spells. The wristbands and shawls that are mentioned in terms of disparagement here seem to have been worn by the clients, though v 20 suggests otherwise. The prevalence of magical practices in Mesopotamia (see *IDB* 1:283; *ABD* 4:465) doubtless encouraged their use among the exiles, although such a tradition was also known in their homeland (cf. Exod 22:18[17]; Deut 18:10). The female sorcerers' magical powers were evidently widely credited among the exiles. The accusation itself has no doubt about their effectiveness. These women evidently operated under the umbrella of Yahwism and doubtless incorporated his name into their spells, like later Jewish magicians. The nub of the accusation is that they have been driven solely by material considerations (cf. Mic 3:5) and that they have shown no moral discrimination in dispensing their powers of restoration and death. So their operations can be described in negative terms, both as defaming Yahweh's name and as abuse of his people, whom they hunt down or captivate (צוֹדֵד). Yahweh's role of protective patron, which appeared earlier in v 10, resounds through the second half of the chapter, in vv 18, 19, 21, and 23. The references to נְפָשׁוֹת are to living persons, not to "souls" or to the Mesopotamian concept of "external souls," spirit counterparts that personify the inner soul (Saggs, *JSS* 19 [1974] 7–12). It is less speculative to refer v 19 to forms of payment than to offerings that accompanied the spells, as Cooke 147, following W. Robertson Smith, van den Born (87), and Greenberg (244) have interpreted. Contextually, the barley and bread serve to elucidate the reference to sustaining their own lives in v 18b*β*.

20–21　The announcement of divine punishment now follows. Yahweh would neutralize the magical power of the wristbands and shawls, and so set free the victimized members of his people. The reference to "your arms" suggests that the bands were worn by the sorcerers, as opposed to the contrary impression of v 18. Perhaps at some stage in the ritual the objects were transferred from the client to the sorcerer, or vice versa. The metaphor of hunting is imaginatively countered by the notion of the victim's flying away, like a bird freed from a snare (cf. Ps. 124:7). Such liberation would attest the superior power of Yahweh and his concern to vindicate his dishonored name.

22–23　The literary continuation, consciously matching v 10, repeats the earlier accusation of immorality (v 19) in sharper focus. There had been a human willfulness about the sorcerers' diverse treatment of their clients, which ran counter to Yahweh's own moral and redemptive will. Unlike Ezekiel in the second period of his ministry, they had no interest in promoting moral standards in the community, in ensuring that the wicked reform and so inherit the life associated with restoration to the homeland (cf. v 9). There is a clear echo of Jer 23:14, but in this exilic context it stands in contrast to Ezekiel's own perspective (Zimmerli 298). By way of conclusion to the chapter, the divine judgment and recognition formula of v 21 are repeated, along with "never again." The repetition is intertwined with a characterization of the sorcerers in terms of the vocabulary of vv 2–9. Thus public prophets and private practitioners of magic are loosely grouped together under the same fateful condemnation as inadmissible exponents of Yahwism.

14:1–3 The public recognition of Ezekiel as a prophet to the exilic community is indicated by the visit of members of its governing body and their respectful squatting before him (cf. 2 Kgs 4:38; 6:32). Whereas in 8:1; 20:1 they represent the pre-587 group of hostages, here they head up the larger, post-587 Judean community in exile. Ezekiel had by now received accreditation through the fulfillment of his earlier oracles, and it was with not unreasonable expectation of a positive word for the future that the elders came. However, they were to be disappointed. There was no automatic word of salvation for them. The era of promise was not to dawn as an inalienable right of all members of God's people. The private message that Ezekiel receives in v 3 has this implication. It singles out the "men" (אֲנָשִׁים, as in v 1) who had come to Ezekiel as inquirers. These individuals had forfeited any claim they had to a favorable response from Yahweh. They are judged to be halfhearted in their loyalty to him. God could read minds (Ps 7:10[9]; Jer 11:20), and he found inconsistency between their outward recourse to a Yahwistic prophet and their inner disposition. Does the thinking about idolatry that comes into their minds relate to a wistful hankering after preexilic practices in Judah, such as chap. 8 had illustrated (Ehrlich, *Randglossen* 5:47; cf. Eichrodt 179–80)? Similar language is used in 20:32, in another post-587 oracle, and there it refers to an opening of the exiles' minds to the reality and power of the Babylonian gods, now that the catastrophe of Judah's downfall had seemed to expose the weakness of Yahweh. That way madness lay, in the forms of temptation to apostasy and total rejection of Yahweh's claim on their lives. Such doublemindedness lost them their opportunity for a divine oracle in this case, declares Yahweh in an exasperated question. In a comparable vein the psalmist testified after a successful inquiry: "If I had regarded wrong in my heart, the Lord would not have heard me" (Ps 66:18). This private message to Ezekiel, which supplies essential information about his clients, reminds the reader of 1 Sam 16:7, where Yahweh whispers advice to Samuel about Jesse's sons (cf. 1 Sam 9:17).

4–5 Ezekiel is commissioned to explain Yahweh's refusal. The style of the message is heavily influenced by legal terminology. First, the introductory "any single man [אִישׁ אִישׁ] of the community of Israel who . . ." is characteristic of apodictic law (cf. Liedke, *Gestalt* 106–43). It especially occurs five times in the Holiness Code (Lev 17:3, 8, 10; 20:2; 22:18; cf. 17:13); here the shorter formulation of Lev 17:3 is used. In the first four cases, such language introduces a dire offense, and so it does here. In this instance, the offense is to request a prophetic oracle while in the spiritual state of v 3. In the context there is probably also an implicit factor, that the exilic leaders are condemned for the bad example they gave to the people. In v 4b the first phrase אֲנִי יְהוָה "I, Yahweh" is a formula of self-designation that echoes not so much any legal precedent as the usage at the head of an oracular answer (Isa 41:17; 48:17; see Zimmerli, *I Am Yahweh* 15–19). The ensuing promise of an oracle is difficult to square with the outright refusal in v 3, with which v 7 accords. Several expedients have been offered. Ehrlich (*Randglossen* 5:47–48) related the verb נַעֲנֶה not to the stem עָנָה "answer" but to a homonym meaning "humble oneself." He observed that in Mishnaic Hebrew the term can mean "excuse oneself." Here, he suggested, there is a special nuance of this usage, a polite refusal. This explanation would fit, but semantically it is speculative. Bertholet ([1936] 50–51) took v 4b as a question implying denial, assuming loss of the interrogative particle *he* by haplography. This construing would also be grammatically feasible as the text stands. Yet it does not accord with the response given in v 6 or with that in v 8. A common expedient since Hitzig (94) is to take the (emended) בִּי "by myself" as "directly," that is, not through a prophet as an agent. Yahweh would respond not in words but in an act of judgment. It is questionable, however, whether this sense is warranted (see *Note* 14:4.c.). One may profitably compare 20:1–31, where the refusal to give a favorable oracle turns into an oracle of judgment that fundamentally justifies hearers' fate of exile and grounds it in their sin (20:4, 23–24, 30–31). In this case the eventual answer is a double one, first an appeal for repentance (v 6) and then a threat of punishment (v 8). Yahweh ironically promised an oracle: the verbal form underscores his "unilateral control of the revelatory process" (Davis, *Swallowing the Scroll* 151 n. 30). The oracle would be one that was consistent with the propensity of the inquirers to idolatry. The divine aim was to hold the community accountable. The elders came not only as individuals ("these men," v 3) but as representatives of the larger group in which others were infected with the same tendency to take seriously the rival religion around them, hedging their spiritual bets. Yahweh in turn had to take that tendency seriously. The chiastic reversal of idols and thinking (לֵב), which Parunak ("Structural Studies," 231) has noted, neatly concludes vv 4–5.

6 The linking "therefore" and accompanying oracular formulas preface not an announcement of punishment, as so often in the book, but an impassioned call for a change of heart addressed to the community at large. In this case the logical consequence was to begin again the spiritual journey in renewed, wholehearted faith. The call fits well into the second, positive phase of Ezekiel's ministry that prepared the exilic community for return to the land (cf. 18:30; 33:11). The verb דָרַשׁ "seek" in v 3 may have paved the way for this call. There it was used with reference to seeking an oracle ("let myself be consulted"). In prophetic contexts of repentance, it is widely employed in the sense of seeking Yahweh in true faith (Isa 55:6; Hos 10:12; cf. the related בִּקֵּשׁ "seek" in Jer 29:13; Hos 3:5; Zeph 2:3). V 6, then, explains the right way to seek God, as compared to an improper way. As typically in the book of Ezekiel, the call to turn specifies that from which one must turn, here in direct continuity with the negative description of the community in v 5.

7–8 The appeal of v 6 is grounded in the reason of vv 7–8. The specific announcement of punishment elaborated in these verses was meant to serve as a deterrent upon the people at large and to make them think twice about their leaning toward pagan religion. The generic definition of the legal offender in v 7 follows the practice in the Holiness Code exactly, in that resident aliens are included in the community. Of the six references from the Code cited with reference to v 4, all but the first take this longer form. It presumably reflects the stereotyped usage of the preexilic period (Smend 81; et al.; Mosis, *BZ* 19 [1975] 176), unless it refers to resident aliens taken prisoner in 597 (Fohrer, *Hauptprobleme* 245; cf. Kraetzschmar 137). The accusation of an openness to idolatry is also given a wider definition, by spelling out the corresponding loss of spiritual loyalty to Yahweh. The verb נזר is similarly used of devoting oneself to Baal in Hos 9:10. The rest of the accusation and the divine response of a negative oracle largely accord with v 4. V 8 is virtually a statement of that oracle, though the Hebrew presents it as a consequence of its delivery. The announcement of the punishment continues along legal lines. The initial element of divine hostility and the third one of excommunication occur together in texts of the Holiness Code, Lev 17:10; 20:3, 5, 6. What is a legal pronouncement of case law there is in this prophetic context a verdict delivered to specific individuals, the inquiring elders. The hostile stare is an ironic measure-for-measure response to the idolatrous fixation of the accused, mentioned in vv 3, 4, and 7. The sentence of excommunication is expressed in terms of divine activity. In the legal texts it tends to have a passive formulation, with an implication of divine agency, so that the meaning is the same (Mosis, *BZ* 19 [1975] 173). The ultimate curse of excommunication that is invoked is laid down for a variety of offenses in the Priestly literature. It implies a premature death and extinction of the victim's lineage, whether by means of childlessness or by the death of his children, as Wold has argued ("The *kareth* Penalty" 1–25; cf. M. Tsevat, *HUCA* 32 [1961] 192–99). In Lev 20:2–6 this curse is imposed for such types of apostasy as worship of Molech and necromancy, and the present offense of idolatry is clearly related to those two. The resemblance is all the closer in that, apart from Lev 17:10, only the cases in Lev 20:3, 5, 6 share with this case an active verb for the excommunication. Moreover, those three cases also use the singular עם "people," rather than the more common plural form (cf. Zimmerli, *ZAW* 66 [1954] 17). These parallels suggest that in this oracle Ezekiel is not merely clothing a religious offense in legal dress but consciously claiming warrant for it in sacral law, with the forementioned parallels in mind. The turning of the offenders into an omen affords a recognition of the work of God in their fate (see *TDOT* 1:171) and so a means of attaining the intent of the recognition formula. By linking "omen" and "byword" there also emerges a sense of warning (cf. Num 17:25[10]; Jer 29:22), which points forward to Yahweh's deterrent purpose in v 11. For the use of מתוך "from the midst of," Num 19:20 may be compared. It is Ezekiel's "translation" of the synonym מקרב in Lev 20:5–6: the former term is very common in the book, whereas the latter never occurs.

9–10 A related case needed to be included in the ruling. What if a prophet gave a favorable response to such an offender? Human nature being what it is, a prophet might be misled into so doing, as one who "lets himself be induced by the wish to please, or by a calculated compromise . . . treating his client's deadly crime as if it were a venial weakness" (Eichrodt 183). In the protasis, the order כי והנביא "and the prophet if" accords with cultic case law (cf., e.g., Lev 1:2; Liedke, *Gestalt* 24, 142). In the apodosis, a reference to divine deception is traditionally seen. However, Mosis's research has shed new light on the text, especially his comparison of the syntactical construction of vv 4 and 7, with which one expects to find a close parallel here (see *Note* 14:9.a.). Yahweh would bring into the open the mistake made by the prophet by holding him responsible for it and imposing on him, too, the sentence of excommunication. Here the nature of such an act as a divine sentence of death is clearly indicated (cf. Deut 4:3). In summary, the joint liability of both offender and prophetic accomplice is firmly stated: the latter's mistake did not mitigate the former's error. The phrase עָוֹן נָשָׂא in the sense "bear the consequences of iniquity" is yet another element borrowed from cultic law. Significantly, in Lev 20:17 it occurs just after the excommunication formula. Apart from its general usage in terms of liability to divine punishment, it is used specifically of dual responsibility nine times in the cases of adultery and incest in Lev 20:10–20 (contrast Num 5:31). It is probable that these texts have influenced the present passage, so that it constitutes a deliberate reminiscence that borrows from the context of the religious cases in Lev 20:2–6.

11 This selective punishment that exposed blatant compromise and its prophetic fostering was to serve as a deterrent for the rest of the exiles (Hitzig 96; Hölscher, *Dichter* 86). The mingled notes of dire punishment and passionate appeal earlier in the piece here find resolution in the statements of God's ultimate purpose. The worst sinners would be made a public example. Others in the exilic community who harbored a leaning toward paganism but did not draw attention to their inner lie by recourse to a Yahwistic prophet were to be given the opportunity of learning a lesson from the selective punishment and recognizing Yahweh's exclusive claims on their hearts and lives (Kraetzschmar 137). By this means the interim purpose of v 5, to bring home to them the inappropriateness of their divided hearts, would be both accomplished and transcended. A new spiritual decision would halt their proneness to paganism, and they would be spared the fate of excommunication. The closeness of v 11aβba to 37:23 is striking. There the cleansing of the people's defilement with rebellious ways and the realization of the covenant relationship are presented as eschatological ideals that include restoration to the land (cf. 11:20). Here it is implied that the exilic community is called to anticipate that blessed state. They were so to commit themselves to its hope as to purify themselves even now by renewed commitment to Yahweh's leadership (cf. 1 John 3:3). Beside the specter of fatal excommunication from God's people stands a prospect of living up to the covenant relationship.

Explanation

The oracles in this group are interconnected by their common theme of prophecy. Taken as a block, they reflect a post-587 dating. Thereby the popular criticism in 12:22–28 that Ezekiel's prophecies of judgment would not materialize or could safely be relegated to a period beyond the lifetime of the prisoners of war taken in 597 receives a sharp rebuttal. By the same token the counterclaim in this first pair of oracles that the message of doom would come true without delay finds its confirmation in the later standpoint of most of the remaining oracles. The same positive effect is accomplished by weaving the preexilic 13:10–15 into the exilic 13:1–9, 16. By hindsight the simple criterion of the historical fulfillment of prophecy (cf. Deut 18:22; Jer 28:9) could be used as a weapon to prove Ezekiel right. The responses of skepticism (cf. 2 Pet 3:4) and of a more pious but still dangerous deferral (cf. Matt 25:5) were shown to be wrong. So too were the pretensions of prophets of a different ilk, who had opposed oracles of doom that Ezekiel and other prophets in a similar tradition had delivered. The wall of hope built by the people and plastered over by those prophets had by now fallen, and great was the fall of it.

The fall of Jerusalem and the influx of exiles to join the hostages in Babylonia ended neither Ezekiel's prophetic activity nor the need to fight against misrepresentations of Yahweh. Magical practices and fortune telling performed in Yahweh's name, for all their popularity, represented deviation from orthodox Yahwism. Such aberrations could not be countenanced, especially as they were motivated by materialism. Moreover, the temptation, widespread among the exiles, to dilute commitment to Yahweh by taking the claims of Babylonian religion seriously had to be nipped in the bud.

It is clear that the overall concern of this literary unit is not simply prophecy but the relationship between the people and prophecy. It is a feature of the unit to define who belonged to the people of God. Those prophets who had opposed the truth of divine judgment would forfeit the right to communal salvation after the judgment, and indeed to membership of the community of promise (13:9). So too would the exilic leaders who compromised with paganism and yet sought Yahweh's prophetic will, along with any prophet who toadied to them (14:1–11). By contrast Yahweh is presented as the patron of the true people of God, whether misled by false representations or potentially sensitive to overtures to fresh commitment (13:10, 18, 19, 21, 23; 14:11). A further element that binds the different pieces together is the emphatic עוד לֹא "never again" that marks Yahweh's intervention in the Judeans' experience correcting misapprehensions of various kinds. The structural distribution of this phrase, in 12:24, 28; 13:21, 23; 14:11 (two times) is striking. There seems to be an intention to proclaim that, just as surely as Yahweh had intervened by means of the fall of Jerusalem (12:24, 28), so his intent in the exilic situation was both to intervene against the female prophets (13:21, 23) and to restore and purify the community (14:11). Another, minor theme is the drawing of a contrast between Ezekiel's exilic role as preacher of repentance (14:6) and the moral irresponsibility of his religious rivals (13:22).

The intent of the literary unit was to promote Ezekiel's stock, by referring to his successful record in predicting the fall of Jerusalem, in the face of opposition from the people and his prophetic rivals. This legitimation provided support for his crusade against two current and related threats to the faith, sorcery and pagan religion. Such legitimation served to counter the popularity of sorcery and an openness to paganism on the part of exilic leaders, with prophetic backing in the latter case. Against these strong odds Ezekiel was able to make even stronger claims to stand for the truth. The threats of exclusion from the eschatological community align with his stern warnings of selective judgment in the post-fall passage 20:32–38. God could and would cut off sinners from the community of promise—so beware (cf. Rom 11:20–22)! God was cognizant of and sympathetic to the people's secret temptation to pagan religion, and so was providing the way of escape. If, however, they ignored it, the only prospect was to fall (cf. 1 Cor 10:12–13). No one can serve two masters.

The prophet's case was reinforced by reference to two earlier types of religious authority. First, Ezekiel echoed Jeremiah's attacks on false prophets and so claimed to stand in the same, now vindicated, tradition. Jeremiah himself, at an earlier stage of history, had professed to stand in an established tradition of anti-establishment prophets (Jer 28:7–9). Second, Ezekiel found firm warrant for his opposition to religious compromise in the case laws of Lev 20. A similar double recourse to the Torah and to prophetic revelation appears in another unit later in the book, chap. 22 (see Allen, *Ezekiel 20–48* 35–40). In the first oracle, 22:2–16, the future fall of Jerusalem is grounded in the ignoring of Israel's legal traditions, while in the last piece, 22:23–31, its fall, now a fact, is explained as the fulfillment of both Zephaniah's and Ezekiel's prophecies. Here too there is a claim to continuity with the noble traditions of the Torah and the Prophets (cf. Matt 5:17).

As for the relationship of this unit to the prefall visions and messages of judgment in 8:1–12:20, it has a parallel of sorts in the relation of 3:16b–21 to the surrounding 1:1–3:16a, 22–27. Both passages look back from a later vantage point and pertain to the post-fall ministry of Ezekiel. They are a reminder that we, the readers of the book, are looking over the shoulders of the large community of post-587 deportees, rather than the smaller group of post-597 hostages. Heirs of salvation as we also are by grace, like them we must listen afresh to the messages of judgment, lest we fall away from the faith (cf. Heb 3:7–4:13).

Jerusalem's Inevitable Fate   (14:12–15:8)

Bibliography

Baumann, E. "Die Weinranke im Walde." *TLZ* 80 (1955) 119–20. **Day, J.** "The Daniel of Ugarit and Ezekiel and the Hero of the Book of Daniel." *VT* 30 (1980) 174–84. **Dressler, H. H. P.** "The Identification of the Ugaritic Dnil with the Daniel of Ezekiel." *VT* 29 (1979) 152–61. **Margalit, B.** "Interpreting the Story of Aqht: A Reply to H. H. P. Dressler." *VT* 30 (1980) 361–65. **Milgrom, J.** "The Concept of *Maʿal* in the Bible and the Ancient Near East." *JAOS* 96 (1976) 236–47. **Noth, M.** "Noah, Daniel und Hiob in Ezechiel xiv." *VT* 1 (1951) 251–60. **Pohlmann, K.-F.** *Ezechielstudien.* BZAW 202. Berlin: de Gruyter, 1992. 6–11, 159–74. **Ringgren, K. V. H.** "מעל *maʿal.*" *TWAT* 4:1038–42. **Rivlin, A. E.** "The Parable of the Vine and the Fire: Structure, Rhythm and Diction in Ezekiel's Poetry" (Heb.). *BMik* 63 (1975) 562–66. **Schulz, H.** *Das Todesrecht im Alten Testament.* BZAW 114. Berlin: Töpelmann, 1969. 180–81. **Simian-Yofre, H.** "La métaphore d'Ézéchiel 15." In *Ezekiel and His Book,* ed. J. Lust. 234–47. **Spiegel, S.** "Noah, Daniel and Job: Touching on Canaanite Relics in the Legends of the Jews." In *Louis Ginzberg Jubilee Volume.* New York: American Academy for Jewish Research, 1945. 305–55. **Wahl, H.-M.** "Noah, Daniel und Hiob in Ezechiel xiv 12–20(21–3): Anmerkungen zum traditionsgeschlichtlichen Hintergrund." *VT* 42 (1992) 542–53.

Translation

[12] *I received the following communication from Yahweh:* [13] *"Human one, suppose*[a] *a country sins against me by infringing my rights and I deal it a blow, breaking its bread sticks and sending*[b] *famine into it and so depriving it of human and animal life.* [14] *Even if it had living in it these three men, Noah, Daniel,*[a] *and Job, they are the ones who would be saved,*[b] *because of their virtue, runs the oracle of the Lord*[c] *Yahweh.* [15] *Or*[a] *suppose I get wild beasts to prowl the country and they take its children and it becomes desolate and untraveled because of the beasts.* [16] *Even*[a] *if it had those three men in it, then I swear by my life, runs the oracle of the Lord Yahweh, they would not be able to save either sons or daughters. They would be the only ones saved, while the country would become desolate.* [17] *Or suppose I get the sword to invade that country and I command the sword to range the country and I deprive it of human and animal life.* [18] *Even if it had those three men in it, then I swear by my life, runs the oracle of the Lord Yahweh, they would be unable to save either sons or daughters; they are the only ones who would be saved.* [19] *Or suppose I let loose pestilence against*[a] *that country, drenching it with my fury in bloodshed and depriving it of human and animal life.* [20] *Even if it had Noah, Daniel, and Job living in it, then I swear by my life, runs the oracle of the Lord Yahweh, they would not save*[a] *a single son or daughter; they would just save themselves, because of their virtue.*

[21] *"This is the explanatory*[a] *message of the Lord*[b] *Yahweh: All the more so should this be the case now that*[c] *I have let loose against Jerusalem all four of my baneful instruments of judgment, sword, famine, wild beasts, and pestilence, depriving it of human and animal life!* [22] *Surprisingly,*[a] *some survivors will be left in it, sons and daughters who will be brought out alive.*[b] *In fact*[c] *they will come out to you; you will see how they have behaved and conducted themselves, and you will not feel so bad*[d] *about the disaster I have brought on Jerusalem, the totality*[e] *of what I will have brought upon it.* [23] *They*

*will make you feel not quite so bad, when you see how they have behaved and conducted
themselves. You will realize the reasonableness of my doing in it all I did, runs the oracle
of the Lord Yahweh."*

¹⁵:¹*I received the following communication from Yahweh:* ²*"Human one,*ᵃ *out of* ᵇ *all
the various kinds of woody plants,*ᶜ *what becomes of* ᵈ *the wood of the grapevine, the
vine*ᶜ *that is included in the range of woody plants?*ᶠ ³*Is lumber for any constructive use
got*ᵃ *from it? Can one get from it a peg to hang any object on?* ⁴*In fact,*ᵃ *it*ᵇ *is consigned
to the fire as fuel. When its two ends*ᶜ *are consumed by the fire and its middle part is
charred, is it good for any practical purpose?* ⁵*Even when it is whole, it has no constructive use. How much less*ᵃ *does*ᵇ *it have any constructive use when the fire has consumed
it and it is charred!*

⁶*"So this is the message of the Lord Yahweh: As the grapevine functions*ᵃ *among the
range of woody plants,*ᵇ *in that I have designated it to be fuel for the fire, such is the role
I have assigned the residents of Jerusalem.* ⁷*I will set my face against them: they have
escaped one fire only to be consumed by another fire. You*ᵃ *will realize that I am Yahweh
when I set my face against them and* ⁸*make the country desolate because they have in-
fringed my rights, runs the oracle of the Lord Yahweh."*

Notes

13.a. The Heb. syntax is complex. The initial protasis of v 13 is extended in v 14a; the apodosis
occurs in v 14b. Cf. Cooke 156.

13.b. Whereas vv 19 and 21 exhibit a piel of שׁלח "send," here the hiph is used, as often with
reference to the sending of plagues (cf. Zimmerli 310). In Amos 8:11 it is associated with famine, as
here. An emendation to a piel (Herrmann 87; cf. *BHS*) is unnecessary.

14.a. As in 28:3, Q דָּנִיֵּאל seeks to preserve the West Semitic pronunciation of K דָּנִאֵל: cf. Dressler,
VT 29 (1979) 156 and n. 14, with reference to J. C. L. Gibson et al., and Day, *VT* 30 (1980) 181 n. 18,
with reference to E. Lipiński.

14.b. The MT יַנְצִלוּ נַפְשָׁם "would save themselves" is a little strange in its use of the piel, which
elsewhere means to strip off or spoil (cf. BDB 664b): in v 20 a standard hiph occurs. Greenberg's
recourse to the piel-hiph variation of the stem שׁלח "send" in vv 13, 19, 21 (258) assumes that the piel
had a wider use than its remaining attestations in the Heb. Bible (cf. Keil 187; Bertholet [1897] 76).
The LXX implies a shorter text, יִנָּצֵלוּ "would be saved." It is feasible to explain the different readings
by supposing that נַפְשָׁם "themselves" originated in a brief marginal note that served to compare the
different phraseology in v 20 and that its wrongful incorporation into the text necessitated a repointing
as piel (Hitzig 97; et al.). Ehrlich (*Randglossen* 5:49) duly repointed but retained נַפְשָׁם as appositional
to the subj, "they themselves," comparing a not quite parallel case in Isa 46:2. A conjectural emendation to a hiph form in line with v 20 (Bertholet [1936] 50; Cooke 156; Fohrer 77) is not warranted.

14.c. For the standard usage of אֲדֹנָי "Lord" in a divine-saying formula here and in vv 16, 18, 20,
23; 15:8, see *Note* 5:11.a.

15.a. The MT לוּ "if" is generally used of conditions that were unfulfilled or unlikely to be fulfilled
(GKC 159l, x, y; cf. the original לֹא in 3:5, 6). Whether an exception occurs in Gen 50:15 (Greenberg
258) is a moot point. An emendation to אוֹ "or," first proposed by Cornill (254), in line with vv 17 and
19 is attractive. The question must be asked how the reading in the MT arose. Was it a marginal
explanatory note on the unreal condition of v 14a, which was wrongly taken as a correction of the
similar-looking opening of v 15?

16.a. There is ancient support for the prefixing of the copula (see *BHS*), in line with v 18 (cf. vv
14, 20). Perhaps the MT should stand, as the harder reading and in the light of other variations
between the cases (cf. Greenberg 258).

19.a. As often, אֶל is used in the sense of עַל, here with the sense "against."

20.a. The LXX has a pass form "will be left," with "son or daughter" as subj. The translator evidently had his eye on v 22 in using this particular verb. Did he have יִנָּצְלוּ "be saved" in his *Vorlage*?
The reading may have originated as a marginal comment on the verbal phrase in the next clause,
which contrasted the usage in v 14. Then it was taken as a correction of the preceding verb. If so,

both the MT and the LXX exhibit relics of comparative comments, in vv 14 and 20, respectively.

21.a. Heb. כי is lit. "for." The LXX omits it, probably by parablepsis before כה "thus" (Wevers 116). Hitzig (98) and others have taken כי as emphatic, but. cf. its use at the head of the interpretive 32:11–14.

21.b. For the stereotyped אדני "Lord" in the messenger formula, see *Note* 2:4.c.

21.c. Here and in 15:5, as in 2 Sam 4:11, אף and כי retain a separate force, "how much more, when."

22.a. In הנה "behold" "there is a note of surprise" (Zimmerli 310). The Heb. syntax is not clear. Does the main clause begin with v 22a (Smend 85) or with v 22b (Hitzig 98) or at an intermediate point, with הנם "behold they" (Cooke 156; Zimmerli 310)? The structure of the four cases in vv 13–20 suggests the first option: the survival and deportation of some residents of Jerusalem function as an unexpected counterpart to the deliverance and/or nondeliverance in the earlier cases.

22.b. In place of the MT's hoph form, LXX Σ Syr Vg presuppose a hiph ptcp, which has been frequently adopted since Cornill (256). Zimmerli (310), followed by *BHS*, has also dispensed with the article as a dittograph. For the article, see GKC 126w. Greenberg (259) has plausibly defended the pass ptcp in the MT on the ground that the sons and daughters in the illustrative four cases stand for the undeserving. They it is who will now turn out to be the ones who are (not saved but) spared. Then one group is in view in v 22a, the surviving "sons and daughter." See further in the *Comment*, and cf. Jer 38:22.

22.c. Heb. והנם "and behold they" resumes הנה "behold" earlier.

22.d. Lit. "be consoled." LXX^B text 538 106 omit vv 22–23a, seemingly by homoeoteleuton (Ziegler, *LXX* 145). Unfortunately, pap. 967 is not extant at this point. The error appears to have been an inner-Greek one and probably occurred independently in the three MSS. All three belong to different textual families: MS 538 is Lucianic and MS 106 Alexandrian. In Zimmerli (310), as also in his German edition, "108" is an error for "106." Zimmerli, with the redaction critic's suspicion of the repetitious nature of vv 22b–23a, regards the omission as significant for the Heb. text.

22.e. In place of the object sign, על "for" or אל in the sense of על (Rothstein 904; Bertholet [1936] 52) has been proposed. Either would be confusing after הבאתי על־ירושלם "I have brought on Jerusalem." The object sign reflects attraction to the function of הרעה "the disaster" within the relative clause as the object of the verb הבאתי "I have brought" (GKC 117l; Blau, *VT* 4 [1954] 11; T. Muraoka, *Emphasis in Biblical Hebrew* [Jerusalem: University of Jerusalem, 1969] 124). The LXX's longer "all the evil things" for כל "all" is epexegetical, and the shorter MT is to be preferred.

15:2.a. The LXX* (and LXX^L) prefaces with "and you," after the message-reception formula, as in the MT at 7:2; 21:24; 22:2; 27:2; 37:16. Cornill (256) and a few others have adopted this reading. Interestingly, it reflects in its own way continuity with the preceding pericope.

2.b. Heb. מ(כל) expresses separation (Simian-Yofre, "Le métaphore" 237). It has the sense of being singled out from a generic group: see Gen 3:14 (cf. GKC 119w). See further *Note* 2.d. below.

2.c. The sg noun has a collective force here and in v 6; cf. the synonymous pl in v 2b.

2.d. Lit. "the plant of the grapevine becomes what?" The interrogative functions as a predicative noun (cf. BDB 226a): cf. LXX Syr Vg; von Orelli 57; Greenberg 264; Simian-Yofre, "Le métaphore" 237. In the light of the ensuing context, especially v 6, its sole function as firewood is implicitly in view. An interpretation "How is . . . different from" (Tg; Zimmerli 317) does not suit the context. Nor does the similar and widely held interpretation "How is . . . better than," which takes מן as comparative (Ewald 265; et al.).

2.e. The MT, together with Syr Tg, has understood the two halves of the question as synonymously parallel. This seems to be preferable, in that it aligns with the briefer, summarizing v 6aβ. An objection to it is that one expects a fem verb, rather than the masc היה "is (among)" after the antecedent הזמורה "the vine." However, this phenomenon is found elsewhere: cf. Joüon 150b, k. The deletion of הזמורה . . . . בעצי "the vine that is among the woody plants" (Herrmann 90; et al.) takes its cue from the shorter v 6, but it is unnecessary. LXX^B text has no equivalent for הזמורה "the vine," but this is simply due to inner-Greek homoeoteleuton (Ziegler, *LXX* 145): pap. 967 attests it. So there is no warrant to delete it, as Jahn (95) did (cf. *BHS*). LXX Vg took מכל עץ הזמורה together, "out of all the wood of the branches (which . . .)": then "wood" functions as the regular antecedent. Ewald (265–66), Cornill (257), and others have construed thus, finding reference to brushwood, but Hitzig (99) rightly disputed such a meaning for זמורה. On similar lines, Zimmerli has interpreted "than the wood of climbing plants, creepers" (*Ezechiel 1* 325; the English edition [317] mistranslates). Developing such an interpretation, Baumann (*TLZ* 80 [1955] 119–20) explained that Judah, the cultivated vine, had turned into a wild vine in the forest, entering the arena of the nations by its alliance with Egypt. Zimmerli himself (319 n. 6) pronounced Baumann's view an imposition on the text. V 6aβ points to a more general comparison, with all other types of wood. Greenberg (265) takes זמורה as a cut off branch, invoking the verb זמר "prune." This rendering would suit the context, but elsewhere it seems to mean a growing vine branch (Driver, *Bib* 35 [1954] 151); a derivation from זמר "prune" is not certain (cf. Driver; *HALAT* 261b). Driver found reference to two different types of grapevine, the cultivated kind in v 2a and the wild one in v 2b. Hitzig (99) related throughout to the wild vine. See the following *Note*.

2.f. Heb. ב היה has the sense "belong among" (Ehrlich, *Randglossen* 5:50; Greenberg 265). Smend (86), followed by Greenberg (265), rightly understood עצי היער "the trees of the forest" as the class of woody plants.

3.a. LXX Tg presuppose an active verb, by assimilation to v 3b. Greenberg (265) has noted that the MT falls into a pattern of active/pass variation for the verbs עשה "make" in vv 3 and 5 and נתן "give" in vv 4 and 6. There is thus no need to change with Cornill (256) and a few others.

4.a. Heb. הנה "behold" has been understood as introducing a conditional clause (e.g., Fohrer 81; so NAB, NJPS, and REB), but in the light of v 6, v 4a presents a general rule (Hitzig 100; Greenberg 265).

4.b. Simian-Yofre ("Le métaphore" 238–39) has taken as subj יער in the sense of forest and then as subj in v 6aγ both the forest and the grapevine. Irrespective of whether יער bears the sense of forest, neither suggestion appears obvious.

4.c. The LXX by an interesting mistake found a reference to annual pruning, taking קציו "its ends" as cuttings (Cornill 257, following Schleusner) and שני "two" as years (Cooke 158, who noted the converse in 4:5).

5.a. See *Note* 14:21.c.

5.b. For the implicit interrogative sense, see Cooke (158) and GKC 150a.

6.a. There is no need to assume here "strained . . . syntax" (Greenberg 266). In the light of v 2, the verb "to be" should be understood. Then the relative conjunction has a causal sense, as often.

6.b. For the collective sense, cf. v 2a and *Note* 2.c.

7.a. The LXX has a third pl verb, wrongly assimilating to the context.

Form/Structure/Setting

The two oracles of 14:12–23 and 15:1–8, each introduced by its own messenger-reception formula, belong together as a literary unit. Mosis (263 n. 155), Fuhs (79), and Brownlee (214) have drawn attention to their common terminological framework, set in a chiastic order: the infringing of Yahweh's rights (מעל מעל) at 14:13; 15:8b and the desolation of the land at 14:15–16; 15:8a. This deliberate inclusion brackets together two messages that at their conclusions are both concerned with the fate of the residents of Jerusalem (14:21–23; 15:6–8). That the oracles originated separately and were subsequently joined at a literary stage is indicated by the different focus, on survival in the first and on extermination in the second, as in the two oracles of chap. 6.

In genre the paired pieces are proof sayings addressed to Ezekiel's companions in exile. They also have in common a comparative style of arguing that moves from a theoretical situation to a current concern relating to Jerusalem, and from a lesser situation to a more serious one (אף כי "how much more/less when . . . ," 14:21; 15:5). The recognition formula in v 23 shows that 14:12–23 is a proof saying. From v 21 onwards it is a two-part proof saying, with vv 21–23a announcing the coming judgment. More strictly, v 21 announces the divine punishment, and vv 22–23a the human consequences of punishment, which include accusatory references to the behavior of those punished. The messenger formula of v 21 begins the second half of the oracle. The first half is devoted to a hypothetical case of divine judgment, subdivided into alternative scenarios. The language of cultic case law appears in the initial ארץ כי "a country if" (cf. 14:9) and in the repeated או "or" (vv 15 [emended], 17, 19; cf. BDB 15a). Unlike case law, however, different divine punishments, rather than human crimes, are here in view.

The scenarios of judgment pave the way for the specific judgment of the second half of the oracle. The initial premise of sin within v 13a provides the first element of a three-part proof saying in the overall oracle. Fohrer (78) categorized vv 12–23 as a disputation, but Zimmerli (313) has rightly disagreed: the formal structure of a disputation, especially an initial quotation, is lacking. Yet it is clear that contemporary arguments are being challenged in this oracle.

The oracle has a chiastic thematic structure, as Parunak ("Structural Studies" 242) has observed: sin (A, v 13aα), judgment (B, vv 13aβ–20), judgment (B', vv 21–22aα¹), and sin (A', vv 22aα²–23a). The four scenarios in vv 13aβ–20 follow the same pattern of repeated elements, but with variations, which Parunak has set out in a table. Hitzig (97–98), followed by Greenberg (260), noticed that the first and fourth scenarios provide a solid framework for the intervening two: only they name Noah, Daniel, and Job and specify their righteousness. The application of judgment to Jerusalem in section B' echoes the scenarios in combining all the four individual forms of judgment and in repeating the cutting off of life and the mention of sons and daughters. It is closest in its terminology to the initial hypothesis of the last of the four scenarios (v 19), as one might expect from the continuity: the formulation שלחתי אל "I have let loose on" echoes אשלח אל "I let loose on," while להכרית "depriving" matches the term there. Parunak ("Structural Studies" 247–48) has drawn attention to the chiastic ordering of section A': behavior and deeds, the motif of comfort, and Yahweh's bringing retribution on Jerusalem form parallel topics from the edges of the section to the double center.

15:1–8 is another proof saying, unquestionably bipartite, made up of an announcement of judgment (vv 6–7a) and an extended recognition formula (vv 7b–8), which includes a final reason of human sin (v 8bα; see below). It is composed in elevated prose rather than poetry (Zimmerli 318). It resembles the former oracle in devoting its first half to a less threatening generalization, which is then applied concretely in the second half. This parallel must have been a further reason for their being juxtaposed in a literary unit. Again a messenger formula introduces the application. The first half is often described as a parable. However, Hals (99) calls it an analogy, noting that the formulaic characteristics of introducing and concluding a parable are absent. For Simian-Yofre ("Le métaphore" 342–47) it is a metaphor, since it is not a narrative but the description of a situation. The analogy or metaphor is recapitulated as a simile in v 6aβγ. Hals has characterized the function of the oracle as a disputation; however, as before, the precise elements of such a genre are lacking.

As for structure, the skeleton emerges as v 4a, לאש נתן לאכלה "to the fire it is given for consuming," v 6aβ נתתיו לאש לאכלה "I have given it to the fire for consuming," and, in a drawn out application, v 6bα נתתי "I have given" and v 7aγ והאש תאכלם "and the fire will consume them." It is clear then that this negative purpose for the wood of the grapevine is the intended focus of the analogy. These structural bare bones are represented in the analogy at v 4 as a firm fact, which answers the initial question in v 2 as to the purpose of the grapevine wood. This fact is surrounded and reinforced by a barrage of questions that deny a constructive use for the wood: למלאכה "for work" in vv 3 and 4bβ constitutes wordplay with לאכלה "for consuming" (Rivlin, *BMik* 63 [1975] 564). This alliterative term occurs again two times in v 5, once in a negative fact (v 5a) that balances the positive fact of v 4a and again in a supporting exclamatory question (v 5bβ). The key statement of v 4a is supported by partial echoes, אכלה האשׁ "the fire has consumed" within v 4b and אכלתהו אשׁ "fire has consumed it" in v 5ba. The settings of the two oracles are very similar. Chronologically both look forward to the fall of Jerusalem, and so are pre-587. Both are addressed to Ezekiel's companions in exile in their recognition formulas. Zimmerli (318) has gauged from the perfect tense שלחתי "I have sent" in v 21 a precise dating for the first oracle between the capture of Jerusalem and the arrival of the new exiles in Babylonia. Keil's interpretation in terms of divine resolve (188) is not convincing. Possibly the verb has a future perfect sense, "when I will have let loose," as often in temporal clauses, especially of time (cf. Joüon 112i), but the differentiation from the imperfect אׁשלח "I send" in v 19 (cf. vv 15, 17, and also v 13) looks deliberate. A knowledge of the later stages of the siege seems to be presupposed.

Pohlmann (*Ezechielstudien* 6–11, 161; cf. Garscha, *Studien* 270) has suggested for the two parts of chap. 15 a complex history of development. The grapevine illustration arose in the post-587 period as a commentary on the status of the exiled king Jehoiachin (cf. chap. 19), whereas the role of vv 4b–8 and 14:21–23, which also derived from the post-587 period, was to affirm the earlier group of hostages and to disparage the new exiles. Such literary archeologizing differs in its presuppositions from the treatment provided in this commentary.

It has sometimes been doubted whether vv 21–23 are an authentic continuation of vv 13–20, on the grounds of apparent inconsistency between the two parts (cf. S. Herrmann, *Heilserwartungen* 248–52): see the discussion in Zimmerli (313). Likewise, in the second oracle, Hölscher (*Dichter* 92) found a lack of complete correspondence between the analogy and the interpretation. Again, Zimmerli (318) has defended the primary nature of vv 6–7ba. However, it appears to be a different matter with vv 7bβ–8. As noted above, v 8 provides the concluding part of a chiastic framework that secondarily combines the two separate oracles in the literary unit. The intent of vv 7bβ–8 is to provide two stylistic echoes: first, of the second oracle in v 7bβ בשׂומי את־פני בהם "when I set my face against them," varying v 7aα ונתתי את־פני בהם "when I put my face against them," and, second, of the first oracle in v 8 (cf. Hölscher *Dichter* 92; Zimmerli 319–20; Wevers 117). There is no reason, however, to deny Ezekiel's hand in this editorial activity.

Here is an outline of the unit:

14:12–23	The doom of Jerusalem under Yahweh's bombardments
14:13–20	The hypothesis of divine punishment of a sinful country
14:13–14	Fatal punishment by famine
14:15–16	Fatal punishment by wild beasts
14:17–18	Fatal punishment by invasion
14:19–20	Fatal punishment by pestilence
14:21–23	Jerusalem's total bombardment and its justification to the exiles
15:1–8	The doom of Jerusalem in terms of destruction by fire
15:2–5	The analogy of grapevine wood fit only for fuel
15:6–8	Application to the people of Jerusalem

Comment

12–13   The message-reception formula introduces a fresh oracle that in its first half, vv 13–20, presents a theological argument. In the light of the contemporary references in the second half of the oracle, vv 21–23, the intention is to dismiss an expectation that the people of Jerusalem would survive the crisis that threatened them. The argument is presented four times in parallel, slightly different terms, like four heavy hammer blows that crash down on a precious object and smash it to smithereens. This argument is not directed specifically at the historical situation; it stands detached and relates to a hypothetical case that is transparent enough to let the exiles to whom the message is addressed (vv 22–23) realize its import. Each of the four presentations of the case has three sections: a basic hypothesis of (human sin and) divine judgment, development of the hypothesis, and a categorical conclusion that in three out of the four instances is emphasized by a divine oath (Schulz, *Todesrecht* 180). V 13 presents the initial and fullest form of the hypothesis. It postulates a nation that has sinned against Yahweh. Israel is not primarily in view: the case reflects a concept of the universal, providential rule of Yahweh. This concept is part of the prophetic heritage that Ezekiel received from earlier prophets: Amos 1:3–2:3 and Jer 18:6–11 are prime examples.

Yet, like Amos and Jeremiah before him, our prophet was using the concept as a window through which to glimpse obliquely Yahweh's dealings with his own people. There are two indications that the hypothetical nation is really a facade for Israel. First, the term מעל "commit an act of unfaithfulness," which is used as a definition of sinning, elsewhere applies only to Israel, whether only the verb or the noun is used or, as here, the verb with a cognate accusative. The term refers to an infringement of Yahweh's rights, by encroaching on holy ground (2 Chr 26:16–18), meddling with temple customs (2 Chr 29:19; 36:14), taking what belonged to Yahweh (Josh 7:1), or violating an oath taken in Yahweh's name (Ezek 17:18) and especially a promise to uphold the covenant (Lev 26:40, cf. v 15), notably by resorting to idolatry (e.g., Num 31:16) (see Milgrom, *JAOS* 96 [1976] 236–39; cf. Ringgren, *TWAT* 4:1039–41). The second indication that hearers or readers are encouraged to think of Israelites as ultimately in view is the use of terminology expressly associated with covenant curses directed against Israel. As in 4:16; 5:16, the breaking of bread sticks deliberately echoes Lev 26:26. Likewise, in v 15 the prevalence of wild beasts and consequent death of children and the desolation of the land (cf. 6:6, 14) are meant to recall Lev 26:22, 33. In v 17 the introduction of the sword into the land harks back to Lev 26:25, while in v 19 the letting loose of pestilence evokes another part of Lev 26:25. For all these references the *Excursus* on the use of Lev 26 in chaps. 4–6 sought to establish that Ezekiel was appealing to an existing cultic text. Here, then, such Israel-based echoes imply that the apparently hypothetical case contains throughout an exhortation "if the shoe fits—and it does—then wear it." A further indication to the same effect is that Ezekiel's oracles generally apply the triad of sword, famine, and pestilence to Jerusalem's fate (see 5:12 and *Comment*); here the triad is enlarged by a fourth item, the wild beasts, as in 5:17.

14   Though the text shows clear signs of speaking about Israel, the facade of universalism is maintained by mentioning three non-Israelite saints, Noah, Daniel, and Job, in the development of the basic hypothesis. Comparison is often made between vv 13–20 and Jer 15:1–3. There Jeremiah's intercession on the people's behalf is rejected: not even a Moses or a Samuel could avert by his prayers Judah's merited punishment. It is probable that Ezekiel is consciously adapting that oracle, which goes on to specify four different kinds of punishment (pestilence, sword, famine, and captivity) and four types of destruction (sword, dogs, birds, and wild beasts) (Miller, *Verhältnis* 93; Zimmerli 313). However, we should leave open the possibility that the two passages give vent to "parallel insights" (Vawter 88). If there was a link, the switch from Israelite intercessors to non-Israelite saints was necessitated by the universal framework of the case under discussion. Noah is the hero of the flood narrative (Gen 6–9; cf. Isa 54:9), whereas Job is the saint of the ancient story that underlies the book named for him. The foreign and ancient factors of the context indicate that Daniel is not the Judean contemporary with Ezekiel who features in the narratives of Dan 1–6 but the figure in Ugaritic texts, to whom Ezek 28:3 will refer as a model of wisdom in a Phoenician context. Wahl (*VT* 42 [1992] 551–52), following Dressler (*VT* 29 [1979] 157–61), has identified Daniel with the canonical character but at the price of regarding 14:12–20 as a postexilic composition.

Whether the mention of sons and daughters in vv 16, 18, and 20 is a traditional element relating to all three of these characters is a moot point. Since it has been argued that all three both lost their children and saved their children, it is safer to conclude with Greenberg (258) that it does not represent a traditional motif associated with the three figures. Rather, these ancient heroes function as eminently good people, known for their "righteousness" or "virtue," as the text significantly states at the beginning and end of the discussion, here and in v 20. Noah was "a righteous man, blameless in comparison with his contemporaries" (Gen 6:9 [P]; cf. 7:1 [J]). Job was "blameless and upright, fearing God and shunning evil" (Job 1:1; cf. 12:4), and uniquely so (Job 1:8; 2:3). Daniel in the Aqhat epic was a good judge, "judging widows and trying the cases of orphans" (*CTA* 17.5.7–8 and the mutilated 19.1.23–25; *ANET* 151, 153), unlike Jerusalem's judges in Isaiah's time (Isa 1:23). Whether Ezekiel and his fellow exiles had first learned of this figure from Phoenician exiles or Israelite tradition already knew of him we cannot establish. Certainly in later Jewish tradition he features as the uncle and father-in-law of the antediluvian Enoch (*Jub* 4:20).

The insistence that such moral heroes could save no one but themselves seems to be attacking a counterclaim made by the exiles, appealing to a solidarity of virtue that could outweigh the liability of sinners to punishment. Abraham's plea that Sodom be spared if fifty or even ten good persons could be found there (Gen 18:22–33) presupposes such a beneficial solidarity, and the Decalogue (Exod 20:5; cf. 34:7; Deut 5:10) reinforces it. Here the oracle simply rules such a possibility out of court, as inappropriate at this juncture of Israel's history. The ensuing verses repeat the basic "no" again and again. Ezekiel's message is that "there are no party tickets to deliverance" (Taylor 128). In God's name the prophet sized up the situation and categorically denied such a soft option; in the three remaining cases the denial is reinforced by a divine oath. A straight and inevitable line led from sin to punishment, and no reprieve was possible for Jerusalem and Judah. The political inevitability of the fall of Jerusalem was matched by a theological inevitability. Discussion of other possibilities was a monstrous irrelevance, like that of the theological society in hell to which the bishop belonged in C. S. Lewis's *The Great Divorce.*

15–16 The second hypothetical disaster continues in a sinister evocation of Lev 26, now with a double reference. This time a divine oath reinforces the flat denial, as in the two remaining cases. Another regular pattern is established by the citing of sons and daughters as those beyond rescue (cf. vv 18, 20). Spiegel ("Noah, Daniel and Job" 320–21), followed by Greenberg (261), was surely correct in seeing the reflection of a current pressing concern of the exiles here and in vv 18, 20, 22. According to 24:21, the children of the hostages deported in 597 had been left behind, and here Ezekiel prophesies their death rather than the fond reunion of separated family members. Behind the paternal paradigms of "these men" stood real fathers worried about the fate of their dear children. Surely God would hear their prayers and spare these loved ones. No, comes the answer, they themselves were spared by their prior deportation, though they were no Noahs, Daniels, or Jobs, but they could make no claim on God for the sparing of their children.

17–20 The options in God's arsenal continue, first military invasion and then the outbreak of pestilence. Whatever the weapon, its death-dealing force is irresistible. In the latter case, pestilence is linked with bloodshed, as elsewhere in the book (5:17; 28:23; 38:22). No guarantee could be given that a single child would be saved.

21–23a The oracle leaves the sphere of argument and hypothesizing what could or could not happen. It moves over to the real world of Judean cities and countryside laid waste, of Babylonian troops besieging Jerusalem and of the horrors of a sick and starving populace. The change of order whereby the sword is given first place points to military attack as the force that triggered the rest in the historical actuality. Not one of the hypothetical plagues but all four held the capital in their deadly grip, as instruments of divine judgment. How could one entertain theological rationalizations of deliverance in a situation that pointed so clearly to God's punitive hand at work?

The oracle that till now had shouted a vehement "no" at optimistic theologizing now seems to contradict itself. It is prepared to give an assent qualified with reservations to the instinctive question posed by anxious parents in exile. Yet, from another perspective, it brings a logical and necessary conclusion to the earlier discussion. Any debater can see a flaw in vv 14–20. The text argues, evidently seeking to counter religious arguments current among the exiles. Yet it only engages in denial and in reiteration of denial, as to the tenability of the exiles' arguments. Now a proof is provided, a proof that indeed lies in the future and not in the present, but offered for future verification. These very children would arrive in the Babylonian heartland, a living proof of true theology at work. The consequent exposure of Jerusalem's lifestyle over the past few years would show that Yahweh had no option but to destroy that veritable Sodom of a city (cf. 6:9–10; 12:16; 16:48–52). "Ye shall see that it could not be otherwise" (Calvin 82). The exiles would realize that their hopes that the capital's doom would be averted had been misplaced. Such hopes had been fused with family love and buttressed by plausible arguments. Instead, the exiles would be driven to say "yes" to the fall of Jerusalem, at last seeing in it the reasonableness of Yahweh's inevitable reaction. Ironically, the very children who had been the focal point of theological hope for their worried parents would turn out to be agents of a different truth, witnesses to a divine necessity. The home truths of vv 22aa^2–23a, which relate to Jerusalem's fate and the exiles' muted reactions as they witnessed their children's sinfulness, are expressed forcibly by chiastic repetition, which replaces the consecutive repetition of the earlier part of the oracle. Moreover, Greenberg (261) has noted the careful wordplay between חנם (לא) "(not) without due cause" and נחם "be consoled." The survival of beloved children would minimize the sense of shock at the downfall of Jerusalem. However, it would not be a case of human love bringing a measure of consolation. Rather, the factor of consolation is raised to a divine plane, the exiles' coming to understand the will of God and the constraint that triggered his radical action. The children would march as God's subdued prisoners in his victory procession. Their exiled parents would see them as such, not as saved trophies of love and grace given to them in response to their pious prayers. The switch from the positive verb הציל "deliver" that ran through vv 13–20 to יצא "be brought out, come out" in v 22 is highly significant, as Zimmerli (316) has observed, suggesting an echo of Jer 15:1–2.

15:1–2 This next oracle is parallel to the first in a number of respects. Like that one, it begins at a distance from the point it eventually wants to make. After the message-reception formula, there is a musing on a phenomenon of viticulture. Perhaps it was inspired by the exiles' witnessing (or laboring at) the pruning of the grapevines in a nearby vineyard and the collection of the prunings into bundles for firewood. Greenberg (267) aptly refers to the Mishnah (*m. Sanh.* 7:2) and to the Babylonian Talmud, (*t. ʿAbod. Zar.* 18a), which mention bundles of vine stems used for fuel. As for those bundles, Ezekiel queries that there was nothing else one could do with the prunings, was there? The question as to what should be done with them is posed in v 2. There were many trees and shrubs whose wood could be used for constructive ends, but not the grapevine.

3–5 The questions continue, intending to deny any constructive use for grapevine wood. It could not even provide a wall peg. No, the fact was that its only use was one that resulted in its destruction—as firewood. How about, v 4b goes on to posit, when the loose ends of a bundle of grapevine prunings had been burned away and the tighter middle part, to which the air and flames could not get so readily, was left charred by the fire? It was even more obvious then that it had no positive use. It was fit, it is implied, only for burning.

6 The prophetic musing turns out to have been an analogy. It is now telescoped into a simile, to illustrate the fate of the citizens of Jerusalem. The contraction into the confines of a simile helps to show the development of the analogy. There is no mention of the uselessness of the grapevine wood: that topic was only incidental to the analogy. Instead, the focus is on its particular use, as articulated in v 4a. Commentators have tended to see in the wood's uselessness an implicit accusation of the sinfulness of the people of Jerusalem. For example, "What is said about the uselessness of the wood is thereby set before every hearer as the inescapable basis of this judgment" (Zimmerli 318). The real emphasis of the analogy is that it is a fact of life that grapevine wood is useful only as firewood. This is part of the economy of nature in the service of humanity. After pushing uselessness to the fore, commentators have then complained that the application of the analogy makes no mention of the uselessness of the wood. It has no need to do so. As Wevers (117) has stated, though he still wrongly calls the vine's uselessness the point of the analogy and the burning an incidental element (118), "The real comparison is: as the wood of the vine is good for nothing but fuel, so Jerusalem is fit only for the fire." It is debatable what links the prophet's analogy has with the regular covenant metaphor of Israel as the grapevine, which earlier prophets used negatively, in criticism of the nation's purely economic success (Hos 10:1) or of its poor vintage in terms of social ethics (Isa 5:1–7) or of its religious degeneration (Jer 2:21). Here nothing is said about fruit or lack of it. Instead, the focus is on a stage after the grapes have been harvested, when the branches that have fruited are pruned away. The most one can say is that the present analogy is ironic, in its concentration on a negative element of viticulture that did not otherwise feature in theological metaphors. The precise focus is on Yahweh's purpose for the residents of Jerusalem, who stand as representatives of the people of God. A parallel is drawn between the grapevine prunings and the role destined for the capital.

7   God's "giving" (v 6, נתתי; cf. נתן "it is given," v 4) or assigning of such a role shifts into a personal, sinister orientation. It was to mean his "giving" (ונתתי) or setting his face against the citizens in a pose of hostility. The rest of the formulation of vv 4a and 6a inexorably follows, in mention of future consumption by fire. The reference to a previous burning must refer to the captu:e and spoiling of Jerusalem in 597, which left its citizens intact, apart from those deported with Ezekiel. This time their fate was sealed. The backward and forward perspectives in v 7aβ seem to echo the closing part of the analogy, in vv 4–5, on which the text appears to linger intentionally. The half-burnt bundle of prunings, fit only to feed the flames, stands for post-597 Jerusalem waiting for the coup de grâce. The city was by no means "a brand plucked from the burning" (Zech 3:2). No, the fire of 597 was an omen of worse misfortune to come, the beginning of the end. God's task had been done only in part, and he would return to complete his inevitable work of destruction and to consume the city, citizens and all.

The oracle is presented to the 597 deportees as a negative reading of the future of Jerusalem, which would shed light on Yahweh's purpose to judge his people. The literary conclusion in vv 7ba–8 seems to result from Ezekiel's editorial labors. It ties together the two separate oracles of 14:12–23 and 15:1–7ba, inversely echoing Yahweh's hostile orientation in v 7aa and Yahweh's devastation of the land in the earlier case study (14:15, 16) with its basic accusation (14:13). The intent is not only to provide a literary framework for the pair of related oracles but to supply the ingredient of accusation evidently lacking in the presentation of the second oracle. Jerusalem's fate is grounded in its spiritual perfidy. The fall of the capital is carefully explained, not in terms of fatalism but as due to human culpability.

Explanation

Ezekiel waged a constant crusade to convince his fellow exiles of the coming downfall of Jerusalem. Two related attempts are preserved here. The first is evidently a reply to expressions of a contrary hope that were based on a theological argument. It is always tempting to use theology in the service of human desires and emotional attachments. The exiles, with sons and daughters back in the capital, could hardly entertain the thought of the fall of the city and their consequent death. It would mean the rejection of all their prayers, undeserving of rescue though their children might be. The whole issue had to be lifted to a different, unemotional plane, in order that its seriousness might be appreciated. Yahweh's providential working in society, in any society, for moral ends is presented as the crux of the matter. Divine retribution had to be commensurate with widespread evil. This was no time to appeal to a positive solidarity that might conceivably have prevailed against it. All would be swept away by an avalanche of destruction, which for Israel represented the outworking of covenant curses. So any survivors would feature in the realization of Yahweh's moral will as witnesses to his justice. Certainly human righteousness (14:14, 20) could not be used as a shield to protect the ungodly against the establishment of divine righteousness.

The second oracle appeals to metaphor. As Isaiah used agriculture to explain the ways of God (Isa 28:23–29), here Ezekiel applies an aspect of viticulture. The present time allowed no comforting recourse to the covenant picture of the vine lovingly tended and protected by Yahweh (cf. Ps 80:9–20[8–19]). Instead, the divine vinedresser must resort to radical pruning and burning. This message links with Ezekiel's focus on finality in chap. 7: the end was in sight. What our prophet predicated of a doomed Jerusalem, Jesus was to apply threateningly to disaffected followers (John 15:6), while similarly Paul wrote of both Israel and the Gentile-dominated church being broken off from the ideal olive tree of the people of God (Rom 11:17–22; cf. Jer 11:16). Here, Jerusalem had to fall. To the comprehensive instruments of destruction in the first oracle is added a fifth in the second oracle, fire. For the moment, a long and bitter moment for the exiles, the signs of the times could be read in no other way.

Jerusalem, Cinderella and Ugly Sister (16:1–63)

Bibliography

Bloch, R. "Ézéchiel 16: Exemple parfait du procédé midrashique dans le bible." *Cahiers Sioniens* 9 (1955) 193–223. **Bracke, J. M.** "*šûb šᵉbût:* A Reappraisal." *ZAW* 97 (1985) 233–44. **Buis, P.** "Un constat d'adultère pas ordinaire: Ézéchiel 16." *ETR* 53 (1978) 502–7. **Cogan, M.** "A Technical Term for Exposing." *JNES* 27 (1968) 133–35. **Darr, K. D.** "Ezekiel's Justification of God: Teaching Troubling Texts." *JSOT* 55 (1992) 97–117. **Day, J.** *Molech: A God of Human Sacrifice in the Old Testament.* Cambridge: CUP, 1989. **De Vries, S.** "Remembrance in Ezekiel." *Int* 16 (1962) 58–64. **Driver, G. R.** "Difficult Words in the Hebrew Prophets." In *Studies in Old Testament Prophecy.* FS T. H. Robinson, ed. H. H. Rowley. Edinburgh: Clark, 1950. 52–76. _____. "Ancient Lore and Modern Knowledge." In *Hommages à André Dupont-Sommer,* ed. A. Caquot and M. Philonenko. Paris: Adrien Maisonneuve, 1971. 277–86. **Eissfeldt, O.** "Ezechiel als Zeuge für Sanheribs Eingriff in Palästina." *PJ* 27 (1931) 58–66 = *Kleine Schriften.* Tübingen: Mohr (Siebeck), 1962. 1:239–46. _____. "Hesekiel Kap. 16 als Geschichtsquelle." *JPOS* 16 (1936) 286–92 = *Kleine Schriften.* Tübingen: Mohr (Siebeck), 1962. 2:101–6. **Fishbane, M.** "Sin and Judgment in the Prophecies of Ezekiel." *Int* 38 (1984) 131–50. **Fitzgerald, A.** "*Btwlt* and *Bt* as Titles for Capital Cities." *CBQ* 37 (1975) 167–83. **Fitzmyer, J. A.** "A Note on Ez 16, 30." *CBQ* 23 (1961) 460–62. **Galambush, J.** *Jerusalem in the Book of Ezekiel: The City as Yahweh's Wife.* SBLDS 130. Atlanta: Scholars Press, 1992. **Glazier-McDonald, B.** *Malachi: The Divine Messenger.* SBLDS 98. Atlanta: Scholars Press, 1987. **Greenberg, M.** "*Nḥštk* (Ezek. 16:36): Another Hebrew Cognate of Akkadian *naḥāšu.*" In *Essays on the Ancient Near East.* FS J. J. Finkelstein, ed. M. de J. Ellis. Hamden: Archon, 1977. 85–86. **Gunkel, H.** *The Folktale in the Old Testament.* Tr. M. D. Rutter from 1917 German edition. Sheffield: JSOT, 1985. **Halévy, J.** "Recherches bibliques. xxiv." *REJ* 24 (1892) 30–51. **Heider, G. C.** *The Cult of Molek: A Reassessment.* JSOTSup 43. Sheffield: JSOT, 1985. **Kennedy, J. M.** "Hebrew *pithôn peh* in the Book of Ezekiel." *VT* 41 (1991) 233–35. **Krašovec, J.** *Antithetic Structure in Biblical Hebrew Poetry.* VTSup 35. Leiden: Brill, 1984. 96–98. **Kruger, P. A.** "The Hem of the Garment in Marriage: The Meaning of the Symbolic Gesture in Ruth 3:9 and Ezek 16:8." *JNSL* 12 (1984) 79–86. **Krüger, T.** *Geschichtskonzepte in Ezechielbuch.* BZAW 180. Berlin: de Gruyter, 1989. 139–98. **Liedke, G.** *Gestalt und Bezeichnung alttestamentliche Rechtssätze.* WMANT 39. Neukirchen-Vluyn: Neukirchener Verlag, 1971. **Masterman, E. W. G.** "Hygiene and Disease in Palestine in Modern and in Biblical Times: Chapter iv." *PEFQS* 1918. 112–19. **Malul, M.** "Adoption of Foundlings in the Bible and Mesopotamian Documents: A Study of Some Legal Metaphors in Ezekiel 16.1–7." *JSOT* 46 (1990) 97–126. **Miller, P. D., Jr.** *Sin and Judgment in the Prophets: A Stylistic and Theological Analysis.* SBLMS 27. Chico: Scholars Press, 1982. **Nielsen, K.** *Incense in Ancient Israel.* VTSup. 38. Leiden: Brill, 1986. **Polk, T.** "Paradigms, Parables and *Mĕšālîm:* On Reading the *Māšāl* in Scripture." *CBQ* 45 (1983) 564–83. **Renaud, B.** "L'alliance éternelle d'Éz 16, 59–63 et l'alliance nouvelle de Jer 31, 31–34." In *Ezekiel and His Book,* ed. J. Lust. 335–39. **Schottroff, W.** *'Gedenken' im Alten Orient und im Alten Testament.* WMANT 15, 2nd ed. Neukirchen-Vluyn: Neukirchener Verlag, 1967. **Stummer, F.** "אֶמְלָה (Ez xvi 30a)." *VT* 4 (1954) 34–40. **Swanepoel, M. G.** "Ezekiel 16: Abandoned Child, Bride Adorned or Unfaithful Wife?" In *Among the Prophets: Language, Image and Structure in the Prophetic Writings,* ed. P. R. Davies and D. J. A. Clines. JSOTSup 144. Sheffield: JSOT, 1993. 84–104. **Vaughan, P. H.** *The Meaning of 'Bāmâ' in the Old Testament.* Cambridge: CUP, 1974. **Woudstra, M. H.** "The Everlasting Covenant in Ezekiel 16:59–63." *CTJ* 6 (1971) 22–48. **Yaron, R.** "Aramaic Marriage

Contracts from Elephantine." *JSS* 3 (1958) 1–39. **Zipor, M. A.** "Ezechiel 16,7." *ZAW* 103 (1991) 99–100.

Translation

[1] *I received the following communication from Yahweh:* [2] *"Human one, inform Jerusalem of its shocking practices* [3] *and tell Jerusalem this message from the Lord*[a] *Yahweh: Your native country and place of birth was the territory of the Canaanites; your father was an Amorite*[b] *and your mother a Hittite.* [4] *As for the circumstances of your birth, on the day you were born*[a] *your umbilical cord was not cut,*[b] *you were not washed with a view to oiling (?) you,*[c] *you were not rubbed with salt nor were you wrapped*[d] *in swathing cloths.* [5] *No kindly eye ensured any of these things was done out of compassion for you. In fact, you were exposed*[a] *in the countryside, in contempt for your life, on the day you were born.* [6] *I came along, and, noticing you kicking about in your blood,*[a] *I told you in your bloody state*[b] *to live*[7] *and to grow*[a] *as prolifically as a wild plant.*[b] *You did grow: you became tall and started your periods.*[c] *Your breasts*[d] *became firm and your hair became prolific. But you were stark naked.*[e] [8] *I came along again, and, noticing that your time had come, the time for love, I spread over you the edge of my garment and covered your naked body. I pledged myself to you and entered into a marriage covenant with you, runs the oracle of the Lord*[a] *Yahweh, and you became my wife.*

[9] *"I washed you with water, rinsing off your blood, and rubbed oil on you.* [10] *I clothed you in a robe of many colors and put leather*[a] *sandals on you. I wrapped your head*[b] *in fine linen and covered you with rich fabric.*[c] [11] *I gave you jewelry, putting bracelets on your wrists, a necklace at your throat,* [12] *a ring in your nose and earrings on your ears, and a magnificent diadem on your head.* [13] *So you were adorned with gold and silver, while fine linen,*[a] *rich fabric, and multicolored cloth were what you wore. Your food*[b] *was fine flour, honey, and olive oil. You became exquisitely beautiful, fit to be a queen.*[c] [14] *You won international renown for your beauty, because it was perfect as a result of the splendor with which I had endowed you, runs the oracle of the Lord Yahweh.*

[15] *"But you put your faith in your beauty and used your renown to become sexually promiscuous. You lavished your promiscuous favors*[a] *on anybody who came along. To him you came so that they might be his.*[b] [16] *You took some of your clothes, and, making for yourself brightly colored shrines, you were promiscuous as you lay on them.*[a] [17] *You also took your magnificent jewelry, made of my gold and silver I had given you; you used it to make yourself male images, and you were promiscuous with them.* [18] *You took your garments of many colors and used them to cover the images.*[a] *You placed my oil and perfume before them.* [19] *Moreover, my food that I had given you, with which I had fed you in the form of fine flour, oil, and honey,*[a] *you wanted to place before them as fragrant offerings, and this is what happened,*[b] *runs the oracle of the Lord Yahweh.* [20] *You even took your sons and daughters, the ones you had borne me, and sacrificed them to them for food. Were your promiscuous ways not enough,*[a] [21] *that you also slaughtered my sons and gave them up, devoting*[a] *them to the images?*[b] [22] *As well as indulging in*[a] *all your shocking and*[b] *promiscuous ways, you failed to remember your young days—when you were stark naked, you used to kick about in your own blood.*[c]

[23] *"After all such wickedness of yours—woe betide you,*[a] *warns the oracle of the Lord Yahweh—*[24] *you built yourself an enclosure,*[a] *making yourself a stall*[b] *in every square.* [25] *At the corner of every street you built your stall and put your beauty to shocking use, opening your legs for anybody who came along and thus adding to your promiscuous*

ways.^a ²⁶*You made promiscuous overtures to the Egyptians, your neighbors with the big penises,*^a *adding to your promiscuous ways in order to provoke me to anger.* ²⁷*So I reacted by dealing you a blow: I curtailed your quota of land,*^a *letting your enemies have their will*^b *with you, namely the daughters of the Philistines, who were embarrassed*^c *by your lascivious behavior.*^d ²⁸*Then you made promiscuous overtures to the Assyrians, because you were unsatisfied, and you were promiscuous with them,*^a *but still you were not satisfied.* ²⁹*You extended your promiscuous ways to the trading*^a *country of Chaldea,*^b *but even so you were not satisfied.* ³⁰*How angry I became with you,*^a *runs the Lord Yahweh's oracle, when you did all this, just what a headstrong*^b *prostitute does,* ³¹*when you built*^a *your enclosure at the corner of every street and your stall in every square! Yet you have not been like a regular prostitute, in that you have disdained*^b *any payment,*^c ³²*you adulterous wife*^a *who have welcomed strangers*^b *instead of*^c *your husband.* ³³*Every prostitute is given presents,*^a *but you have given your own presents to all your lovers, and you have bribed them with all your promiscuous ways to come to you from everywhere around.* ³⁴*Your promiscuous attitude is contrary to that of those women: you are not solicited, and whereas you give payment, no payment is given to you—you are so contrary.*

³⁵ *"So listen to Yahweh's oracle, you prostitute.* ³⁶*This is the Lord Yahweh's message: Because your sexual profligacy*^a *has been so lavishly demonstrated*^b *and your private parts have been exposed in your promiscuity with*^c *your lovers, and because of*^d *all your shocking idols, and in correlation with*^e *the bloodguilt involved in giving them your sons,* ³⁷*in reprisal I for my part*^a *am going to gather together all your lovers to whom you gave such pleasure.*^b *All those you loved, together with all you came to hate, I will gather from everywhere around to confront you and I will expose your private parts to them, and they will see all your private parts.* ³⁸*I will pass sentences*^a *fit for female adulterers and murderers*^b *and give you over to a death*^c *perpetrated in jealous fury.* ³⁹*I will hand you over to them, and they will overthrow your enclosure, while your stall*^a *will be demolished. They will strip you of your clothes and take away your magnificent jewelry, leaving you stark naked.* ⁴⁰*They will order a crowd to attack you, who will stone you, hack you to pieces*^a *with their swords,* ⁴¹*and burn down your houses, inflicting such punishments on you in the presence of many other women. I will stop you being a prostitute, and you will never again make payments.* ⁴²*Only then will I have sated my fury against you, and my jealous fury will leave you alone; I will then be calm, angry no more.* ⁴³*Because you have not remembered your young days but have upset me*^a *with all this behavior, I for my part now*^b *hold*^c *you responsible for your behavior, runs the Lord Yahweh's oracle.*

"You behaved lasciviously, didn't you,^d *in addition to your other shocking practices?* ⁴⁴*Anyone who likes to quote proverbs would choose for you 'Like mother,*^a *like daughter.'* ⁴⁵*You take after your mother, who rejected her husband and sons. You also take after your sisters,*^a *who rejected their husbands and sons. The mother of you all*^b *was a Hittite, and your father was an Amorite.* ⁴⁶*The bigger of your sisters was Samaria, along with her daughters, who used to live to the north of you. The smaller of your sisters, who lived to the south of you, was Sodom, along with your daughters.* ⁴⁷*You have walked in their tracks and copied their shocking practices, haven't you?*^a *It did not take very long*^b *for your general behavior to become worse than theirs.* ⁴⁸*I swear by my life, runs the Lord Yahweh's oracle, your sister Sodom, along with her daughters, did not behave so badly as you and your daughters.* ⁴⁹*The trouble with your sister Sodom was the pride*^a *she and her daughters took in overeating and in complacent ease, while she gave no support to the poor and needy.* ⁵⁰*They were arrogant*^a *and behaved shockingly toward me. So I*

removed them, when I saw it.[b] [51]*In turn, Samaria did not commit half the sins you have committed. You have engaged in practices more shocking than theirs. In fact, you have made your sisters*[a] *look guiltless by all the shocking things you have done.* [52]*You for your part must bear your humiliation, since you have been an argument in your sisters' defense. They look guiltless in comparison with you, because of the more shocking nature of the sins in which you have indulged. So you are the one who must be ashamed and bear your humiliation,*[a] *because you have made your sisters look guiltless.* [53]*I will rehabilitate them,*[a] *both Sodom and her daughters and Samaria and hers, and I will rehabilitate you*[b] *together with them,* [54]*in order that you may bear your humiliation and feel duly ashamed of all you have done, at the same time bringing consolation*[a] *to them.* [55]*As for your sisters,*[a] *Sodom and her daughters will be restored*[b] *to their original state and so will Samaria and her daughters, while you will similarly be reinstated.* [56]*Your sister Sodom was the topic of your talk,*[a] *wasn't she,*[b] *when you were so proud,*[c] [57]*before your own wickedness was exposed, as it is now*[a]—*the butt of the daughters of Edom*[b] *and all her neighbors, such as the daughters of Philistia,*[c] *who treat you with contempt* [d] *on every side.* [58]*You will bear*[a] *the consequences of your lasciviousness and shocking practices, runs Yahweh's oracle.*

[59] *"Certainly*[a] *the Lord Yahweh's message is as follows: Will I deal*[b] *with you in a way that corresponds with what you have done, you who have despised the oath and so broken the covenant?*[c] [60]*No, I for my part will remember my covenant with you, the one made in your young days, and I will establish*[a] *with you an everlasting covenant.* [61]*You in turn will remember your former behavior and feel humiliated, when you receive*[a] *your big sisters and also*[b] *your little ones and I give them to you as daughters, even though I am not obliged by my covenant with you.*[c] [62]*I for my part will establish my covenant with you and you will realize I am Yahweh,* [63]*in order that you may remember and be ashamed, feeling so humiliated that you will keep your mouth shut in future, when I have absolved you for everything you have done. So runs the oracle of the Lord Yahweh."*

Notes

3.a. For the formulaic use of אדני "Lord" in the messenger formula here and in vv 36 and 39, see *Note* 2:4.c.

3.b. The definite article is not expected with this clearly predicative adj, as the parallel clause and the counterpart of both clauses in v 45 show. It probably came into the text under the influence of the preceding הכנעני "the Canaanite" (Greenberg 274).

4.a. The *casus pendens* is resumed by the verbal continuation (Cooke 166); Bertholet ([1936] 54) took the expression as a variant of the defectively written form in v 3. For the acc retained with a pass verb, cf. Joüon 128b.

4.b. This verb and the next main verb and the last one are probably not pual (*HALAT*, ad loc.) but pass qal (Greenberg 275), since none has a corresponding piel form extant. The LXX "they bound your breasts" reflects not merely a ר/ד error in the case of the noun, but probably also replacement by a slipped marginal note that originally explained שדים "breasts" in v 7 as "your breasts" (cf. *Note* 7.d. below). The verb "they bound" may reflect awareness of a Heb. verb כרר "tie" cognate with Arab. *karra* "wind," here in the form of a pass qal and with an archaic fem sg ending (Driver, "Ancient Lore" 278; cf. *ExpTim* 57 [1945/46] 193). Driver, who considered a reference to the tying of the cord original, suggested as an alternative the reading of MS[K 102], כרך, which he rendered "has been tied," a pass qal כרך. He aligned it with Mishnaic Heb. כרך and Akk. *karāku*, both meaning "wind." His second suggestion had earlier been proposed by Halévy (*REJ* 24 [1892] 30–31). This latter reading was adopted in the NEB (Brockington, *Hebrew Text* 223) and evidently retained in the REB. Barthélemy (*Critique* 3:92) has objected that כרך means to tie with a bandage, not with a knot.

4.c. The Tg rendered this most uncertain term "to be cleansed." Driver ("Difficult Words" 63–64) interpreted as rubbing with oil, taking משעי as an Aram. inf form of a verb שעה cognate with שעע

"smear." V 9 lends support to this interpretation. 'A Θ Vg "for salvation" linked with ישע "save," and Σ "for care" with the postbiblical sense of שעה "look, care." LXX* Syr did not render, presumably out of ignorance.

4.d. The hoph inf abs establishes assonance with the preceding המלח ("salted") (Greenberg 275).

5.a. For this sense of the verb, see Cogan (*JNES* 27 [1968] 133–35), following Ehrlich; Malul (*JSOT* 46 [1990] 100–106).

6.a. The pl accords with the usage in cultic laws with reference to discharge of blood (Lev 12:4–5; 15:19; 20:18; Greenberg 276); a sg occurs in v 22.

6.b. Unlike LXX Syr, the MT repeats the clause, perhaps by repetition of a fourteen-letter line (Allen in Brownlee 218). The Vg rationalized the repetition by taking בדמיך "in your blood" with the verb of saying in the first case and with the impv in the second (cf. Jerome 166; cf. Hitzig 102; Smend 90). The LXX took the phrase with the impv, as its translation in v 22 confirms. Ewald (267, "in spite of your blood") and Cornill (259) followed suit. Of the modern versions, the REB does the same, but the NIV, NJB, and NRSV may be more correct in relating it to the main verb (likewise Zimmerli 323). See the *Comment*.

7.a. The MT רבבה, usually "abundance, myriad," here seems to mean "growth, a grown object" (Greenberg 276). However, the Syr attests ורבו "and grow," and so does the LXX, but without the copula, except for LXXᴬ. The subsequent ותרבי "and you grew" appears to echo such a reading (Cornill 259; et al.). See further in the next *Note*.

7.b. The MT נתתיך "I made you" is represented in the LXX but not in the Syr. Jahn (101), followed by Fohrer (85), Eichrodt (199), and Zimmerli (324), explained it as a consequence of the corruption of the earlier impv to a noun, but its presence in the LXX, which reflects no such corruption, suggests otherwise. Probably a marginal note כצמח השדה נתתיך "I made you like a wild plant" was intended as an exegetical comment. It linked the earlier, negative exposure in the countryside (השדה, v 5b) with positive growth like a plant of the countryside (השדה) and observed that the latter was a divine reversal. This longer comment displaced the comparison; the LXX still attests this stage. Next, the initial impv was adapted to a noun to accommodate the new verb. This stage is reflected in the MT, "I made you a grown object."

7.c. The MT בעדי עדיים "(and you came) into/with adornment of [or: most beautiful] jewels" seems to be meant as an exotic metaphor for the physical development of v 7aα. Ehrlich (*Randglossen* 5:53) and Greenberg (276) have retained MT, but most scholars have followed J. D. Michaelis and found here a reference to the onset of menstruation (עדים, Isa 64:5[6]). Zimmerli (324), with Cooke (166), reconstructed as בעדים "(you reached the stage of [cf. BDB 98a]) menstruation," assuming dittography. This is slightly preferable to Bertholet's suggestion ([1897] 80): בעת עדים "the time of menstruation." The MT was influenced by the clause ואעדך עדי "and I adorned you with jewelry" in v 11. A pl form of the collective עדי "jewelry" does not occur elsewhere. The error is an old one: LXX Syr indirectly reflect it in their rendering "to cities of cities." It represents not merely a ר/ד error but assimilation to ערם ועריה "nakedness and bareness" in v 7bβ (cf. Zipor, *ZAW* 103 [1991] 100).

7.d. Heb. שדים "breasts" need not be corrected to שדיך "your breasts" (Cornill 260; cf. *Note* 4.b. above). It seems to be a high-flown, poetic equivalent of a suffixed noun. Greenberg (277, with a regrettable printing error) has usefully referred to Lam 2:15; 3:41, where a dual suffixless body part occurs alongside a sg suffixed one.

7.e. Predicative nouns are used adjectivally (cf. GKC 141c, d; Joüon 154a).

8.a. For the formulaic use of אדני "Lord" in the divine-saying formula here and in vv 14, 19, 23, 30, 43, 48, and 63, see *Note* 5:1.a. It is omitted in v 58: cf. Zimmerli, *Ezekiel 2* 556.

10.a. Heb. תחש is also used of the cover of the tabernacle in Exod 25:5, etc. It has not been identified with any certainty. It may refer to the hide of the dugong, a herbivorous aquatic mammal, which was used by the Bedouin for sandals (F. S. Bodenheimer, *IDB* 3:252a). Alternatively, it is cognate with Akk. *dušu*, (Sumerian *tu[ḫ]šia*), the leather of goats or sheep dyed and tanned the color of a precious stone *dušu*, which was used for luxury sandals and for decorating harnesses (*CAD* 3:201–2; Greenberg 278, following H. Tadmor).

10.b. Heb. חבש "wrap," when used of clothing, refers to headgear (BDB 289b).

10.c. Heb. משי is some kind of an exotic cloth, for which Egy. and Hittite possible cognates have been found (*HALAT* 609b). Rabbinic tradition identified it anachronistically with silk.

13.a. Q שש "fine linen" repeats the term used in v 10bα. K שש has suffered assimilation to the following משי (Cornill 260; et al.).

13.b. K אכלתי represents the older writing of the second fem pf, while Q gives the later form אכלת. This phenomenon recurs in vv 22a, 31 (2x), 43 (2x), 47, and 51. In vv 22b, 28, and 29, the text exhibits the later form.

13.c. This last clause is not represented in the LXX*. Cornill (261) and others have viewed it as an interpolation. Cornill thought that it destroyed the parallelism of clauses. On the other hand, Cooke (165) regarded it as necessary to bring the story to its climax. Wevers (122) considers its omission in the LXX* an error. Was a twelve-letter line overlooked?

15.a. The MT תזנותיך "your (acts of) harlotry" adds to a sg noun the type of suffix usually attached to a pl noun, here and in vv 22, 33, 34, and 36. However, in vv 20 and 25 this mixed formation occurs only in Q, while K has a sg type of suffix; and in vv 26 and 29 the MT has a sg form of suffix. A similar range of phenomena recurs in chap. 23. See GKC 911; Joüon 94j.

15.b. The MT has here לו־יהי "so that they might be his" and in v 16b לא באות ולא יהיה "not coming things and it/he will not be." These readings appear to be alternatives (cf. Cornill 261–62). The latter was evidently a marginal variant that was subsequently inserted into the text at a point that was judged feasible. The LXX*, which lacks the first case, is a development of this stage. The first and shorter text has been explained by Driver (Bib 35 [1954] 151) as a purpose clause that uses a juss without the copula, as in Job 9:33 (cf. GKC 109i; Joüon 116i): "so that it might become his." Like Keil (204), he took יפיך "your beauty" as the antecedent, which is rather distant (cf. Hitzig 105). Greenberg (280), though he interpreted as an exclamation ("it was his!"), is to be preferred in regarding תזנותיך "your harlotry" as the subj, in line with most medieval Jewish exegetes (cf. Barthélemy, Critique 3:98). Greenberg has noted that the phrase היה ל "become" frequently has a masc verb despite a fem subj (Joüon 150k, l). As for the counterpart in v 16b, which Greenberg (280) has called "hardly coherent," Driver (Bib 35 [1954] 151–52, 312), adapting an earlier proposed emendation made by Cornill, proposed לו באת ולו יהיה "to him you came so that it might become his." The LXX "you will (not) come" lends some support to his interpretation of the first verbal form, in which an expression normally used of a man is strikingly applied to a woman. Again he took "beauty" as the subj of the second verb, an unlikely expedient. If he was right in his slight reconstruction לו באת "to him you came," v 16b does not fit in its present place, but admirably completes v 15. Then the end of v 15 in the MT represents a truncated text that has suffered from parablepsis, whereas the reading found in v 16b constitutes a corrupted form of the longer, original text. In v 15b the Tg represents לא־יהי "so that it will not be," in reversal of the לא/לו error that underlies the MT.

16.a. See Note 15.b. above.

18.a. Lit. "them."

19.a. The Heb. construction is complicated, if not tortuous: a casus pendens that includes an appositional relative clause without אשר "which" (Greenberg 280) and, since לחמי "my food" is still in view in the resumptive ונתתיהו "you gave it," an appositional role for the three specific nouns, "(with which)—namely fine flour, oil, and honey—I fed you." Cornill (262) and others have seen an interpolation here: see Zimmerli 326.

19.b. The Syr does not represent ויהי "and it happened"; one wonders whether it is a fresh variation on the end of v 15. A claim of dittography (Cooke 168; Zimmerli 326; BHS) is not likely. Does the preceding consec pf have the modal sense the impf can bear, "want to" (cf. Joüon 113n)? Then this final statement indicates achievement.

20.a. The question is to be taken with v 21: cf. Josh 22:17–18 (Ehrlich, Randglossen 5:55; Cooke 172; earlier Ewald 268). Cooke was probably right in taking מן as partitive. BDB 590a took it as causal: "because of thy whoredom." The REB construes it as comparative: "Was this slaughtering any less a sin than your fornication?"

21.a. Heb. העביר means to "pass over, offer up," to which 20:31 adds באש "in the fire": see Day, Molech 20, and the Comment.

21.b. Lit. "to them."

22.a. Heb. את here means "besides" (Driver, Bib 19 [1938] 22). The LXX implies זאת "this," which Cornill (263) and others have adopted; for the confusion, cf. 47:17–19.

22.b. The LXX* does not represent תועבותיך "your abominations"; it could easily have fallen out because of its graphical similarity to the next word. Herrmann (93), followed by Zimmerli (326) and BHS, deleted.

22.c. Heb. היית "you were," unrepresented in Syr Vg, is indirectly attested by the LXX in the form חיית "you lived," an echo of v 6b. For the final position of the verb, Greenberg (281) compares 22:18. Syntactically, v 22b can only be taken as in the translation.

23.a. The LXX* does not render this exclamation, lit. "woe, woe to you!" Since Cornill (263), it has often been regarded as a gloss, "a passionate interjection of a reader" (Zimmerli 327). Kraetzschmar (150) urged its retention. It does accord with the passion of v 30aα. In fact, the following divine-saying formula, which the LXX* attests, serves to reinforce the exclamation and so presupposes it.

24.a,b. For the strange pausal form גֵּב in L, cf. עַד in the formula לעולם ועד "for ever and ever." The two terms גב and רמה are significantly differentiated in the text from the במות "shrines" of v 16, though many commentators have identified them, such as Zimmerli (343), in his case as part of his redactional theorizing. The context suggests that secular structures are in view, while the linking of the two terms with prostitution in vv 30–31 must be taken seriously. Heb. גב, as something convex, may here mean a domed tent, like קבה used perhaps for prostitution in Num 25:8. LXX Syr Vg interpreted as "brothel," which Herrmann (93), Hölscher (*Dichter* 95), and Greenberg (281) have accepted. B. Lang (*Frau Weisheit* [Dusseldorf: Patmos, 1975] 137) has taken רמה not as an elevated place or the like but as "house, dwelling place," comparing Akk. *ramû* "put up a dwelling" and Ugar. *rwm* "erect a building." Here he envisions a tent-structure. The Vg again interpreted in terms of a brothel.

25.a. Herrmann (94) and Greenberg (271) have taken v 25b with v 26, in which case v 26b is resumptive.

26.a. As in 23:20, בשׂר "flesh" is a euphemism.

27.a. For this sense of חק "decree, limit," see Liedke, *Gestalt* 164–65.

27.b. For נפשׁ "throat" as the physical seat of desire, see H. W. Wolff, *Anthropology of the OT,* tr. M. Kohl (Philadelphia: Fortress, 1974) 15–17 .

27.c. The LXX τὰς ἐκκλινούσας σε "who were turning you aside (from your way)" (cf. Syr "who were restraining you") may have been motivated by a desire to echo the sound of the Heb. הנכלמות (Cornill 264). It seems rather to represent a *Vorlage* המכלמות, which the translator took as a hiph, "who make (you) ashamed." It was doubtless meant to be a hoph, a less common variant of the niph.

27.d. For the construction, see GKC 131r and cf. 24:13. Greenberg (283) understands זמה as "depravity" here and also in vv 43, 58; 23:27, 29, 35. While it bears that sense in 24:13, its context is sexually oriented in these cases and also in 22:9, 11; 23:44, 48–49.

28.a. The verb זנה "commit fornication" takes a direct object in Jer 3:1 and possibly in Isa 23:17. The construction with "to" in vv 26, 28a and the nonrepresentation of an object in LXX Vg have induced Ehrlich (*Randglossen* 5:56) and others to dispense with the suffix.

29.a. Heb. כנען is here not a proper noun "Canaan" but means "trade," as in 17:4. The LXX*, represented by pap. 967, does render it, contra *BHS*. The omission in LXX^B was caused by homoeoarcton.

29.b. Heb. כשׂדימה is in apposition and idiomatically means "to the land of the Chaldeans, to Chaldea," as in 11:24. See *Note* 24.a.

30.a. The LXX "How can I make a covenant with your daughter?" has in view בת "daughter" and מול "circumcise," interpreted as a sign of the covenant, and reflects the MT; so does Σ, followed by LXX^L and Vg, "With what will I purify your heart?" which understood the verb in terms of purification (Stummer, *VT* 4 [1954] 36). The Tg "How strong was the wickedness of your heart!" took the noun as a feminine variant of לב "heart," like Σ, and derived the verb from מלא "be full," supplying "of wickedness" from vv 23 and 57. The MT אמלה is pointed as a pass ptcp from אמל "be weak" (BDB 51a); accordingly, the NJB translates "How simple-minded you are" and the NIV "How weak-willed you are." Stummer (*VT* 4 [1954] 37–39) rendered "How feverish is your heart," which Zimmerli (328) has tentatively adopted. Stummer took his cue from Σ and the Tg for the noun; following Zorell (*Lexicon* 62), he related the verb to Arab. *malla* "be seized by a feverish excitement" and postulated a byform אמל from a cognate Heb. מלל. He appealed to the interpretation in a Jewish medieval poem on these lines. The NJPS and the NRSV "How sick was/is your heart" have translated in this vein, and so does Greenberg (283), "How hot your ardor is." The interpretation that has the strongest linguistic support is "How I was filled with anger against you," which the alternative renderings in the NJPS and NJB reflect. This interpretation is based on a comparison with Akk. *libbati malu* "be full of anger against," which takes an objective suffix. The same idiom reappears in Aram. מלא לבת "be full of wrath," with an objective genitive (see Driver, *JTS* 32 [1930/31] 366; Cooke 173; Fitzmyer, *CBQ* 23 [1961] 460–62). This option requires a repointing of the verb as אָמְלָה or אֻמְלָה "I was filled": for the final letter, see Joüon 78g. Certainly all the ancient versions except the Tg interpret as a first sg impf. Zimmerli (328) has objected that a note of anger in v 30 occurs too soon. But it accords with the provocation of Yahweh and his partial reaction in vv 26–27 and paves the way for his full reaction initiated in vv 36–37, the performance of which was to sate his anger (v 42).

30.b. Cf. BDB 1020b; Driver, *Bib* 35 (1954) 152. Σ rendered "independent."

31.a. For the vocalization, cf. 6:8 and *Note* 6:8.b. The expected pointing occurs in בעשׂותך "when you did" in v 30. The resumptive nature of the content of v 31a indicates that it is coordinate with v 30b, in fact parallel with v 30a (RSV, NRSV).

31.b. LXX Σ Syr Vg render on the lines of "in gathering (payments)," taking the compared prostitute as subj rather than the "you" of the main verb. Insofar as the LXX recognized the verb קלס in the hithp at 22:5, the rendering may indicate a *Vorlage* ללקט "in gathering" (Cornill 266, who observed that the same Gr. verb is used in Gen 47:14). The MT makes good sense.

31.c. Heb. אתנן is a prostitute's fee (BDB 1072b).

32.a. The syntactical alignment of v 32 with the second-person context is not immediately clear. The LXX took as a separate sentence by adding "is like you" (cf. Σ). It is possible to understand the noun as a vocative. In that case the following clause is to be construed as a relative clause without אשר "who"; for the idiomatic third-person references, see 22:3 and *Note* 22:3.c. A number of scholars since Hitzig (109), including Zimmerli (346), have taken v 32 as a redactional comment. Greenberg (285) regards it as a textual alternative to v 33a in a conflated text.

32.b. For the use of the object sign with an indeterminate noun, cf. Joüon 125h. The LXX seems to imply אתננים "payments" for את־זרים "strangers," doubtless by assimilation to the theme of the context. If v 32 is to be integrated by means of a vocative address, receiving payments does not suit: this is what the addressee does not do (vv 31b; 33b; Wevers 127). Nor is it naturally characteristic of an adulterous relationship. The former objection also applies to the reading מאת־זרים "from strangers" represented in the Syr.

32.c. Or "while under the authority of": cf. 23:5.

33.a. Here and in v 33b נדה and נדן "gift" are used: see Zimmerli (329) and Greenberg (285).

36.a. Heb. נחשתך could conceivably mean "your copper" in the sense of "your money," as the NJB (cf. the LXX) takes it, but the term is not used thus elsewhere and it hardly fits the evidently synonymous parallelism. The Mishnaic use for the bottom of an oven, from which Cornill (266), following A. Geiger and medieval Jewish exegesis, extrapolated a physiological meaning "bottom," is a speculative recourse. Driver (*Bib* 19 [1938] 65) usefully related to Akk. *nuḫšu* "superfluity, luxury," here in the sense of sexual extravagance; he noted that the term often had the connotation of a liquid and so suited the verb. He was anticipated by F. Delitzsch (Cooke 174). Greenberg (285–86; "*Nhštk*" 85–86) interprets more directly in terms of juices that are sexually aroused, comparing Akk. *nuḫsātu*. This would suit the accompanying verb even better. The Akk. term refers to hemorrhage, according to *CAD* 11, 1:141–42; Greenberg claims that it refers more widely to a(n abnormal) genital discharge, usually but not necessarily bloody.

36.b. Lit. "poured out." For השפך the Tg implies חשפך "you uncovered" (Sperber, *Bible in Aramaic* 4B:337). This verb occurs in parallelism with the piel of גלה "expose" at Isa 47:2; cf. the usage in Jer 13:26. Following Geiger, Cornill (266) and others have adopted it, together with a piel form ותגלי "and you exposed," as the Syr rendered. The changes stand or fall according to the understanding of the accompanying noun.

36.c. For this usage, in the sense of אל (*BHS*), cf. vv 26, 28, and 29.

36.d. It is possible to take this preposition as a continuation of the preceding one ("with"; Smend 99; et al., including *BHK* and *BHS*), but the Masoretic accentuation is probably correct in differentiating the phrases, so that three separate accusations are brought.

36.e. Since Ewald (271), the MT וכדמי "and in accordance with the bloodguilt" has generally been rejected in favor of the minority Heb. reading ובדמי "and because of the bloodguilt," with the support of LXX Vg Tg. The latter continues the causality in a straightforward way, but Greenberg (286), implicitly following Smend (99) and Bertholet ([1897] 85), has justly retained the MT as a harder reading, noting Ezekiel's preference for כ "like" in relating offense to punishment.

37.a. The LXX, including the LXX* in the light of the lacuna in pap. 967 and the presence of ἐπί "against" in B, adds "against you," which in view of the following ptcp cannot here represent the confrontation formula (cf. 13:8) but anticipates v 37b, probably by way of exegetical clarification.

37.b. Heb. ערב "be pleasing" is not used elsewhere in a sexual sense. Following H. Graetz, Bertholet ([1897] 85) and others have advocated conjectural emendation to עגבת "you lusted," in line with 23:5, 7, 9. Driver (*Bib* 19 [1938] 65) related ערב to Akk. *erēbu* "enter in," used of a woman who enters the house of a man not her husband. Neither expedient is compelling.

38.a. For משפטי "sentences" the LXX* has a sg form. Kraetzschmar (152) justified the MT in that two sets of criminals are specified. In 23:45 a sg noun appears before each group of criminals. Probably partial assimilation to that passage underlies the LXX*.

38.b. The omission of the second noun in the LXX* was doubtless only an inner-Greek accident, which LXX^c managed to escape.

38.c. Ehrlich (*Randglossen* 5:58), followed by Greenberg (286), justified the MT in the sense "I will make you the object of my bloody anger and jealousy." He compared 35:6, but there the text is probably corrupt (see my note in *ZAW* 102 [1990] 412; *Ezekiel 20–48* 167). LXX Vg imply a *Vorlage* ונתתיך בדם "and I will make you in blood," which seems to have suffered metathesis from ונתתי בך דם "and I will bring upon you blood" (Halévy, *REJ* 24 [1892] 36; et al.; NRSV, REB). The proposal to read on these lines but to delete דם "blood" (Rothstein 908; et al., including *BHK*; cf. *BHS*), by comparison with 23:25, is unnecessary .

39.a. In light of v 25, a sg form, as represented in LXX Vg, is expected in place of the pl of the MT.

40.a. The *hapax legomenon* בתק is well attested in cognate languages: see *HALAT* 160a.

43.a. Greenberg (288) has retained the MT's qal form ותרגזי by continuing the force of the negative and understanding in terms of being agitated by fear: "and were not in dread of me." The ancient versions imply a hiph "and you agitated me," which is generally adopted, ever since Hitzig (111), who compared Jer 50:34. The stem appears in a noun form רגזה "agitation" at 12:18. The previous mention of כל־אלה "all these things" in an evident context of anger at v 30 supports the repointing.

43.b. Heb. הא occurs in Gen 47:23 as an interjection "behold"; it is an evident Aramaism (cf. Dan 2:43). It is supported by LXX Syr, but its position in the sentence is strange (cf. Zimmerli 331). Wevers (129) has observed that, as an equivalent of the normal הנה "behold," it is form-critically fitting.

43.c. The pf seems to be performative: see *Note* 3:8.a. In place of בראש "(I put) on head" one expects בראשך "on your head," as LXX Syr Vg imply: cf. 9:10; 11:21; 22:31. Scribal abbreviation of an obvious element may well have occurred and later been ignored.

43.d. Here and in vv 47 and 56, ולא "and not" introduces a question (Hitzig 111): cf. GKC 150a.

44.a. In כאמה "like her mother" the *mappiq* is not written before *beth*: see Joüon 94h.

45. a. The MT clearly recognizes two pl forms of אחות "sister," אחות in vv 51 (Q), 55 and אחיות in v 52b. Was the former intended as a dual, אחותים? In place of the expected suffixed forms אחותיך or אחיותיך, one finds a defectively written תך ending here and in vv 51 (K) and 52a, b.

45.b. "All" is added in the translation to indicate that the suffix is pl.

47.a. See *Note* 43.d. above.

47.b. Heb. כמעט is used of time, "soon," as in Ps 81:15(14), etc. The intensifying קט is a *hapax legomenon*: *HALAT* 1020a compares Eth. *qʷaṭiṭ* "small." It is not represented in LXX* Syr. For the following *waw*, see Cooke 179. In the text of *BHS*, the annotation "a" should be deleted and "b" changed to "a." Perhaps the editor at some stage intended "a" to accord with note "*a*" in *BHK*. Also in *BHS* ובתועבותיהן is a printing error for וכ'; it is not listed in R. Wonneberger, *Understanding BHS* (Rome: Biblical Institute, 1984) 74.

49.a. Heb. גאון "pride" is explained by the following nouns, whether one repoints it as constr (Ehrlich, *Randglossen* 5:59) or regards them as appositional (Greenberg 289).

50.a. The Masoretic reading וחגבאינה has been assimilated to ותעשׂינה "and they behaved" (Cooke 179).

50.b. Or possibly "as you have seen." Grammatically the verb may be either second person ('Α Σ Θ Vg; see *Note* 13.b. above) or first (LXX Syr Tg). See the *Comment*.

51.a. A pl "your sisters" אחותיך (cf. Q אחותיך) is required. See *Note* 45.a. above.

52.a. Here, in v 54, and also in 39:26, the phrase נשׂא כלמה "bear humiliation" refers to remorse for former sins; elsewhere in the book it relates to punishment (32:24–25, 30; 34:29; 36:6–7; 44:13).

53.a. See Bracke's evaluation of the phrase שׁוב שׁבות in *ZAW* 97 (1985) 233–44. He understands it in terms of Yahweh's reversal of his previous judgment. The noun appears to function as a cognate, internal object of the intransitive verb (cf. Joüon 125q, r), with a genitive noun or suffix relating to the object of the reorientation: "change a changing with regard to." The initial form שׁבית in the MT and the K forms in the rest of the verse evidently derive from שׁבה "take captive," with the sense "captivity," which in this context would not suit the case of Sodom. The forms of שׁבות in Q are the expected ones: cf. לזות "perversity" from לוז. For the K/Q variants, cf. R. Borger, *ZAW* 66 (1954) 315–16.

53.b. In place of K ושׁבית and Q ושׁבות, one expects a verb ושׁבתי "and I will restore," which the ancient versions represent, and this has been generally read since Ewald (273). The error presumably arose by metathesis that occurred within the K form. In place of the anomalously pl noun שׁבו/יתיך one expects שׁבותך. The MT seems to have confused ותך and ותיך endings frequently in this passage.

54.a. The LXX παροργίσαι "to anger" is probably an inner-Gr. error for παρηγορῆσαι "to comfort," a verb that appears as a ptcp in Σ (Cornill 271; P. Katz, *Bib* 35 [1954] 31–32, contra Ziegler, *Bib* 34 [1953] 447).

55.a. In place of the MT אחותיך "and your sisters," a sg ואחותך "and your sister," supported by LXX Syr Vg, would fit "Sodom," but it may stand as a *casus pendens*.

55.b. The form תשׁבן is used two times for the third person to artificially distinguish from the regular form תשׁובינה used for the second person in v 55b (Ehrlich, *Randglossen* 5:60).

56.a. Heb. שְׁמוּעָה, which usually means "report," here presumably means "mention" (BDB 1035a), if not "byword" (Greenberg 290).

56.b. See *Note* 43.d. above.

56.c. A sg גְּאוֹנֵךְ "your pride" is expected, rather than the pl גְּאוֹנַיִךְ in the MT, which never occurs elsewhere in the OT.

57.a. The MT כְּמוֹ עֵת "as at the time of" (= Σ Θ Tg) is strange, but there is no clear alternative. Greenberg (290) assumes that the MT is the equivalent of כְּעַת "now" and takes הֶרְפָּה "reproach" as in apposition to רָעָתֵךְ "your wickedness." Smend (104) observed that one expects Jerusalem rather than her wickedness to be the object of reproach. The translation follows LXX 'A Vg: "as now," i.e., כְּמוֹ עַתָּ, which Hitzig (114) and Cornill (272) adopted. In fact, the LXX interpreted "you are the reproach," which makes good sense, but can hardly be obtained from the MT; as Herrmann (97) commented, the LXX seems to have had the same Heb. consonants in its *Vorlage*. To achieve such a sense, various emendations have been suggested: see the list in Zimmerli (333). If indeed emendation is necessary, the most plausible is כְּמוֹהּ אַתְּ "you like her" (Ehrlich *Randglossen* 5:60).

57.b. The MT אֲרָם "Aram, Syria" does not fit as an enemy in this historical period: "the time of Aram's hostility was much too ancient to be mentioned" (Cooke 178). The Syr implies אֱדֹם "Edom," which also occurs as a minority Masoretic reading, and this has generally been read since Cornill (272). Cf. 25:12; 36:2–15. For the confusion, cf. 27:16.

57.c. Zimmerli (333) regards the reference to the daughters of the Philistines as a gloss inspired by v 27. Its syntactical abruptness, the distance between Edom and Philistia, and the awkwardness of מִסָּבִיב "on every side," seemingly connected with a single nation, certainly raise questions. Edom and Philistia are treated in adjacent oracles in chap. 25.

57.d. For the orthography, see GKC 72p. Joüon 80k derives from a different verb, שׁאט "attack," but see D. Bodi's study of the stem in *Poem of Erra* 69–81, esp. pp. 71–72.

58.a. The pf appears to be prophetic, a "pf of future certainty" (Cooke 178). Σ rendered as fut.

59.a. Heb. כִּי is not rendered in the LXX*: cf. 14:21 and *Note* 14:21.a.

59.b. For the consec pf, see *Note* 11:17.a. A first-person verb is required, as Q and the ancient versions attest, in place of the inappropriate second person form in K, which may simply be a mechanical error, but cf. GKC 44i. Cf. the ambivalent רָאִיתִי "I/you saw" in v 50. In the context וְעָשִׂיתִי is best taken as a question "will I do?" (cf. GKC 150a; Joüon 161a). Calvin (172) was aware of the possibility: "some translate . . . as if it had been said, 'Shall I do with thee as thou hast done?'" It functions as a deliberate counterpart to the negative וְלֹא עָשִׂית "did you not do?" in v 43bβ (see *Form/Structure/Setting*). Taken as a statement, the text refers to Jerusalem's judgment as future, which strains the context. Cf. the flow of Lev 26:44–45.

59.c. C and the LXX (not only "LXX^L 967" [*BHS*]) read "my covenant," but the parallelism supports the MT. Assimilation to v 60 caused the variant.

60.a. Or "maintain." Cf. Elliger, *Leviticus* (Tübingen: Mohr, 1966) 374; Schottroff, *'Gedenken'* 208; *TWAT* 6:1263. Here the evidently new character of the covenant as everlasting suggests the establishing of a new, different covenant: cf. Jer 31:31–34, which may well underlie this passage (Renaud, "L'alliance éternelle" 335–39).

61.a. LXX^967 L Syr represent בְּקַחְתִּי "when I take." Ziegler (*LXX* 157) has equated LXX^B, which follows MT, with the LXX*, but Katz (*Bib* 35 [1954] 34) considered the reading of pap. 967 original. Since Hitzig (115), the variant has been preferred. The MT, which gives a suitable sense (Cooke 181), is to be retained as a slightly harder reading. The use of לקח "take" in the variant accords with the usage in vv 16–18, 20, where it is a preliminary to further action (Greenberg 292). Doubtless that usage encouraged the variant. Here לקח means "receive (as a gift)." Greenberg has compared the sequence in Josh 13:8; 18:7.

61.b. Heb. אֵל, in the sense of עַל, here means "in addition to."

61.c. See the *Comment.*

Form/Structure/Setting

Chap. 16 is a literary unit, as the initial and unrepeated message-reception formula of 16:1 shows. We have to wait until 17:1 for the next. The unit divides into three sections. The basic one runs from v 2 to v 43bα. It continues with—almost drifts into—a second section, vv 43bβ–58. The final section consists of vv 59–63. The basic section is a variation of an oracle of judgment. Thus, a sentence of divine punishment commences in v 35, introduced by a standard link with a preceding accusation, לכן "therefore," and by a summarizing restatement of the accusations and then a resumptive לכן "therefore." Correspondingly, the accusation occurs in vv 15–34. It is announced in v 2, "Inform Jerusalem of its shocking practices." What intervenes is a contrasting motif that is a not infrequent expansion of the accusation in prophetic oracles, a description of the earlier saving acts of God that serves as an incriminating background to the accusation (see Westermann, *Basic Forms of Prophetic Speech,* tr. H. C. White [Philadelphia: Westminster, 1967] 182–83).

The whole oracle of judgment is shaped as a sort of allegory. It is dominated by the metaphor of Jerusalem as a girl who, rescued from death and richly blessed by her benefactor-husband, repays him with infidelity and must lose her life. Allegory is a loose description, for at times the details of the story, parablelike, bear no exact relation to reality, while at other times reality breaks through, leaving the metaphor behind (Zimmerli 335; Hals 109). A better designation would be extended metaphor (Wilson 673; Galambush, *Jerusalem* 11). Gunkel (*Folktale* 128–31) suggested that the allegory goes back to an Israelite folktale. His suggestion needs to be reassessed in the light of Greenberg's criticisms (300–301; cf. Hals 109).

This first oracle fits comfortably into Ezekiel's pre-587 ministry of preparing his fellow exiles for the coming fall of Jerusalem, with its rhetorical address of the personified capital. The same cannot be said of the second oracle, which presupposes the first one and consciously supplements it. Now Jerusalem stands on an equal footing of political desolation with its two sister cities Sodom and Samaria, and only God's future act of restoration can remedy its hapless state (Greenberg 304). This post-587 piece is essentially a call to the exilic community to repent (v 52) in retrospect for preexilic sins worse than the sins of Sodom and Samaria (vv 44–51). It weaves into this theme the coming return from exile (vv 54, 58).

The last section, vv 59–63, is a two-part proof saying announcing God's coming salvation and virtually closing with a recognition formula (v 62b). The actual ending emphasizes a sober concern for Israel's continued repentance (v 63; cf. v 61a*a*). This final piece stands at some distance from the earlier ones. While the earlier two are like chap. 20 in consisting of a pre-fall oracle of judgment and a literary sequel that thematically builds upon it an oracle of salvation with a post-fall background, the last section of chap. 16 is more reminiscent of the generalizing supplements of 34:23–38; 36:24–32; 37:24b–30, which are to be credited to the redactor(s) at work in the second generation of exiles (see Allen, *Ezekiel 20–48* 160, 177–78, 192). Interestingly, in that material the same proof-saying type of oracle of salvation reappears, in 34:25–30; 36:33–36, 37–38; 37:24b–30. Zimmerli, who likewise attributes vv 59–63 to Ezekiel's disciples (353), has commented on the nature of the whole chapter as a kernel element successively supplemented as ideas are developed and expanded (334).

The form-critical structure of each piece has been overlaid with a rhetorical structuring. The form of the basic oracle has already been defined in terms of an expanded accusation (vv 3–34) and an announcement of punishment (vv 35–43b*a*). Each of the two parts has its own introduction, a command from Yahweh to Ezekiel to inform Jerusalem of the accusation in v 2 and then one from Ezekiel to Jerusalem to hear Yahweh's word of judgment in v 35. These two parts are broken into smaller elements by stylistic features. Greenberg (292) has observed the strategic role of the divine-saying formula in demarcating subsections of the first oracle. Thus vv 3–8, 9–14, 15–19, 35–43(bα) close with the formula, and vv 23–29 and 30–34 open with it. By implication vv 20–22, which lack the formula, are isolated as a subsection after the one in v 19 and before that in v 23. Krašovec (*Antithetic Structure* 96–98) has drawn attention to the antitheses that mark the major sections of this first oracle. The foundling's abandonment to death (vv 3–5) is reversed by Yahweh's gift of life (vv 6–14). His love (vv 6–14) is repaid by ungratefulness and unfaithfulness (vv 15–34). She takes off her clothing for her lovers (vv 15–34), while in reprisal they strip it off by force (vv 35–43). Galambush (*Jerusalem* 100–101) has noticed the contrast between Yahweh's doubly passing by (ואעבר) in vv 6 and 8 and the repeated "every passer by" (כל־עובר), first Canaanite gods and then foreign nations, in vv 15 and 25; there is also a parallel between Jerusalem's initial exposure to death in v 4 (cf. דמיך "your blood" in v 6) and her final abandonment to death in v 40 (cf. דם "blood" in v 38).

Parunak ("Structural Studies" 261, 268) and Greenberg (294) have both characterized vv 43bβ and 58 as parallel endings to adjacent pieces, with their double mention of זמה "lasciviousness" and תועבות "shocking practices." They are better taken as an inclusion or framework, so that v 43bβγ has an introductory role (Hitzig 111), as in most modern versions. Its verb עשׂית "you have done" is a keynote of the piece, recurring in vv 47, 48, 51, and 54. One may speak of parallel beginnings in the case of vv 43bβ and 59aβ, where the negative question as to Israel's behavior, ולא עשׂית "and have you not done?" and the positive question as to Yahweh's future behavior, ועשׂיתי "and will I do?" are counterpointed. The resumptive reference to Israel's behavior in v 59aβ, כאשר עשׂית "as you have done," confirms this intention. This counterpointing note runs through the final piece, vv 59–63: Jerusalem broke the covenant, while Yahweh would establish the covenant, and Yahweh would remember his past grace and Jerusalem its past sin. As for the overall structuring of the chapter, Swanepoel ("Ezekiel 16" 93–94) has found a fivefold pattern. God's mercy frames the whole (vv 3–14, 59–63). Jerusalem's sin provides an inner frame (vv 15–34, 44–58). At the center stands the judgment of God (vv 35–43). The double effect is to emphasize the consequences of Jerusalem's sin and the incomparable mercy of God.

The relationship of chap. 16 to chap. 23 deserves some consideration. The latter chapter personifies Judah/Jerusalem as the unfaithful wife of Yahweh. It has a narrower focus in concentrating on Jerusalem's political alliance with Egypt, while secondarily and redactionally it embraces religious sins. The kernel oracle of chap. 16 is concerned solely with Jerusalem, but chap. 23 envisions two sisters, first Judah and Israel (vv 2–27) and then Jerusalem and Samaria (vv 32–34). This broader concern was clearly the inspiration behind the notion of the three sisters, Jerusalem, Samaria, and Sodom, who feature in the supplementary, post-587 messages of chap. 16. The similarities between the two chapters must be correlated with the various literary stages represented in their material (for the development within chap. 23, see Allen, *Ezekiel 20–48* 45–48). At first sight there seems to be a natural overlap between 16:26–29, 37–41 and 23:12, 16, 19, 22–27, verses that belong to the basic oracle of 23:2–27. The prophet was dealing with the same subject matter in both oracles. In fact, it is probable that 23:2–27 is a specific adaptation of 16:2–43bα, prompted by Zedekiah's flirtation with Egypt.

In 16:26 the affair with Egypt is confined to Hezekiah's reign, which suggests that Zedekiah had not yet made overtures to the Egyptians. So there are echoes of the earlier oracle in the later one, though one must leave open the possibility of a little later editing from chap. 23. A fortiori, the links between 16:20–21 and 23:36, 39 are to be understood as the latter's echoes of the former passage: 23:36–49 is comparatively later than 23:2–27. The same applies to the connections between 16:18 and 23:41, 16:38 and 23:45, and 16:40–41 and 23:46–49. The similarity between 16:36–39 and 23:28–30 falls into this category: 23:28–31 and 35 are an editorial framework for the song of the cup in 23:32–34. It is not easy to decide which way the current runs in respect of the closeness of 16:58 and 23:35. Since 23:35 seems to envision the judgment upon Jerusalem as a future event and 16:58 is set in a post-587 literary context, 23:35 probably inspired 16:58.

A related issue is the question of redaction within the kernel oracle. Zimmerli (334–35, 347–48), in the wake of Hölscher (*Dichter* 92–95), has judged that it originally lacked a political orientation and dealt solely with syncretism with the religions of Canaan and the great nations. I was influenced by his viewpoint in *Ezekiel 20–48* 48. However, Krüger (*Geschichtskonzepte* 147–51) has submitted Zimmerli's complex set of redactional supplementation to an intensive critique (cf. Hals 107, 110). In particular he has contended that Zimmerli's interpretation of the "lovers" in vv 37, 39–40 not as foreign nations, as the present context does, but as foreign gods (345, 346) introduces a novel and astounding notion to the book of Ezekiel. Nowhere else is the invasion of Jerusalem credited to the gods of the world powers. If foreign nations are meant, then the announcement of punishment flows on naturally from the political charge of vv 26–29, to which Zimmerli took exception. Ezekiel inherited a developed prophetic tradition in which sexual infidelity was used as a metaphor both for Israel's adoption of Canaanite religion (Hos 1:2; 2:7–15[5–13]; 3:1; Jer 2:20) and for political alliances with foreign powers (Hos 8:9; Jer 2:33, 36). His blending of both themes is an instance of his frequent dependence on earlier prophecy. The very length of the basic oracle may reflect a degree of literary expansion, as Ezekiel transposed the oral message to written form, but its essential shape seems to have been preserved.

The detailed development of chap. 16 may be presented as follows.

16:2–43ba	Jerusalem's resistance to Yahweh's grace and coming retribution
16:2	Ezekiel's accusatory commission
16:3–34	Grace and ingratitude
16:3–5	Jerusalem's pagan and hapless origins
16:6–7	Yahweh's pronouncement of life
16:8–14	Yahweh's commitment to and maintenance of Jerusalem
16:15–22	Jerusalem's turning to Canaanite religion
16:23–34	Jerusalem's turning to foreign powers
16:35	Ezekiel's announcement of Yahweh's punishment
16:36–43ba	Jerusalem's degradation and capital punishment for its sins
16:43bβ–58	Jerusalem's contrition for sins worse than Sodom's and Samaria's
16:43bβ–52	Contrition as a present necessity
16:53–58	Contrition as a future necessity
16:59–63	Yahweh's eschatological renewal of past grace and Jerusalem's contrition for past sins

Comment

2–43bα This initial oracle lays a foundation for the whole chapter. It is rhetorically addressed to Jerusalem and describes it by the metaphor of an unfaithful wife who must receive the legal punishment for her crime. Whereas earlier prophets had used the metaphor for both the religious and political entanglements of Israel in the eighth and seventh centuries B.C., Ezekiel not only combines the two types of aberration but extends the metaphor back in time. So he "provides" Yahweh's covenant partner "with a biography" (Greenberg 299). This biography is presented as an accusation in vv 3–34, and its imminent sequel as a forecast of judgment in vv 36–43bα. Not the covenant nation but its capital is the focus of the oracle. Ezekiel must have been influenced by the description of Jerusalem as a prostitute in Isa 1:21, where, however, infidelity to the moral and social standards of the covenant were in view, rather than religion or international politics.

2–3aα A rhetorical address of Jerusalem in terms of indictment and sentence occurs again in 22:2–16 and begins in a similar formal way in 22:2. There an analysis of contemporary sins is given, whereas here a historical perspective is taken. In this respect the oracle is similar to that of 20:3–31, where a review of Israel's past history is made the basis of a contemporary indictment (20:4, 30). To "inform" or "cause to know" (הודע) is the duty of the priest in communicating Israel's cultic traditions in 22:26; 44:23 (cf. Hos 4:6). When it is used in Ezekiel's oracles of judgment, as here, it takes on a forensic tone (also 22:2; cf. Job 10:2; 13:23), as if in reminiscence of a religious court where priests were the judges (cf. 44:24; Deut 17:9; 19:17). This priest-turned-prophet maintained a priestly role even as he delivered prophetic oracles of judgment in God's name.

3aβ–8 The content of the accusation breaks down into six sections, most of them installments in a continuing story, and this is the first. The first two sections, vv 3aβ–14, major in the preliminary gracious intervention of God, turning an unwanted baby girl into a queen of world renown. To this end a negative word picture of the family background and post-birth experiences of the personified Jerusalem is painted in vv 3aβ–5.

3aβb "Listen, Jerusalem, if you want to know your nature, to see what your behavior is like and to what end you are rushing, inspect your family tree" (Polk, *CBQ* 45 [1983] 575). Jerusalem's background had been completely pagan, a bad omen for its future history. Jerusalem had paganism in its blood. The first part of the eventual accusation, vv 15–22, will implicitly develop the influence of Jerusalem's heredity by describing its adoption of Canaanite religious practices. Ezekiel is exploiting the historical tradition of the Jebusite city-state of Jerusalem, which was not vanquished till the time of David (Josh 15:63; Judg 1:21; 2 Sam 5:6–8). In place of the standard phrase "land of Canaan," mention is made of "the land of the Canaanite" in order to emphasize Jerusalem's pagan origins (Greenberg 274). The Canaanites, Amorites, and Hittites have a firm place in the pentateuchal lists of pre-Israelite ethnic groups, who had to be driven out to avoid Israel's compromising its faith in Yahweh (cf. Gen 15:20–21; Exod 3:8; 23:23–24; Deut 7:1–5). In Num 13:29 (probably J) the Hittites and Amorites are located along with the Jebusites in the hill country. Jerusalem is regarded as Amorite in Josh 10:5, while "Uriah the Hittite" lived in Jerusalem in David's time (2 Sam 11–12; for the extrabiblical background of the two groups, see *ABD* 1:199–202; 3:219–33).

4–5   The oracle moves from place of birth to circumstances of birth, which are equally inauspicious. The passage is framed by an inclusion, "on the day you were born." This is how E. W. G. Masterman (*PEFQS* 1918, 118–19) described the treatment of a newborn baby among the contemporary fellahin:

> As soon as the navel is cut, the midwife rubs the child all over with salt, water and oil, and tightly swathes it in clothes for seven days; at the end of that time she removes the dirty clothes, washes the child and anoints it, and then wraps it up again for seven days—and so on till the fortieth day.

A litany of negative clauses replaces such norms. These omissions are interpreted as a lack of kindly compassion, which by implication had to await Yahweh's intervention to materialize. Exposure of unwanted babies, especially girls, was common in the ancient world (cf. Greenberg 275). This one was abandoned, still attached to the placenta, and left to die. In the ancient Near East, washing, cleaning, and clothing the newborn child had the force of legitimation on the parents' part. By failing to do so they had relinquished all rights to the child (Malul, *JSOT* 40 [1990] 106–10). This part of the story has no historical counterpart, except as a commentary on the Canaanite lifestyle. It serves as a negative foil to Yahweh's positive intervention. To find an allusion to the emigration of Jacob's family from Canaan (Gen 45:6–7; Greenberg 301) is eisegesis.

6–7   Yahweh intervenes for good, rescuing this "little savage" (Eichrodt 205) from certain death and ordaining for her abundant life. God's seeing, here and also in v 8, reverses the lack of a kindly "eye" in v 5. Now at last the baby finds kindness and help. The gory mess in which the newborn was left to wallow has the connotation of ritual uncleanness, like that of menstrual blood (Lev 12:2–8; cf. Luke 2:22–24). The divine decree of empowerment to live and grow, despite such an encumbrance, is reminiscent of the command to be fruitful and multiply in the priestly account of creation (Gen 1:22, 28; ורבו "and multiply" corresponding to ורבי "and grow" here), which in turn is invoked upon Jacob (Gen 28:3; 35:11; cf. 17:2, 6). Malul (*JSOT* 46 [1990] 111–13) has observed that the Akkadian equivalent of the causative form of the verb חיה "live," *bulluṭum* "keep alive," has the connotation of adoption; it is sometimes accompanied by *rubbum* "raise," which accords with the intransitive verb רבה "grow" used two times here. Moreover, to adopt a newborn child while still *ina mêšu* "in its amniotic fluid" or *ina mêšu u dāmêšu* "in its amniotic fluid and birth blood" meant that the baby could not be reclaimed by its natural parents (Malul, *JSOT* 46 [1990] 108–9, 111, 123 n. 86). The comparison with "a plant of the countryside" (שׂדה) ironically echoes the baby's abandonment in the countryside (שׂדה) in v 5: where death lurked for the human outcast, paradoxically an opportunity for life was wrested. Yahweh's passing by hardly alludes to the tradition of God's finding Israel in the wilderness (Hos 9:10; Deut 32:10; cf. Jer 31:2; Krüger, *Geschichtskonzepte* 184). The divine intervention, preparing and preserving it for its destiny, refers to Yahweh's providential watching over the pagan city-state.

The creative command turned into fact, and the baby grew into adolescence and sexual maturity, marked by breasts and pubic hair (cf. Isa 7:20). The onset of menstruation strikes a somewhat negative note that will not be resolved until the washing of v 9, while the nakedness will receive a symbolic resolution in v 8 and an actual one in v 10. What was not done at birth or in the years that followed would eventually be made good when Yahweh had direct dealings with Jerusalem.

8   The woman is the city, preserved and now come of age and reveling in its cityhood. Its privileges are due to Yahweh's prior decree, who had his own plans for its future. The story now joins up with history: in David's reign Jerusalem was incorporated into Israel, becoming its capital city. "You became mine"—the veritable "city of God," as a song of Zion acclaims it (Ps 46:5[4]; cf. Ps 48:2, 9[1, 8]). The union is celebrated as a marriage rite. For a man to spread the hem of his garment over a woman was a symbolic gesture that constituted a proposal of marriage. He thus extended over her both his authority and his willingness to support her (cf. Ruth 3:9; Kruger, *JNSL* 12 [1984] 84–85). Behind the marriage pact lies the divine covenant made with Israel, which received reaffirmation through Jerusalem's becoming Israel's capital (cf. 2 Sam 5:12). Here ברית, the standard word for "covenant," primarily means "marriage pact." Although such a meaning can no longer be found in Mal 2:14, the usage in Prov 2:17 supports such a meaning here (see Weinfeld, *TDOT* 2:255–56; Glazier-McDonald, *Malachi* 100–102). The only parallel for the swearing of an oath in a marriage context occurs in Gen 31:53b, concerning an agreement pertaining to marriage relationships between husband and father-in-law in Gen 31:43–50, 53b–54 (see *ABD* 1:1194–95). The final clause, "and she became mine," evokes the solemn wording of the marriage pact, "She is my wife and I am her husband," which is attested in the Jewish marriage contracts from Elephantine (see Yaron, *JSS* 3 [1958] 2–4; contrast Hos 2:4[2]).

9–14   The second installment largely shows how Yahweh discharged his legal commitment to be responsible for his new wife. This, rather than a wedding ceremony, is now in view. She is cleansed of her ritual and natural impurity with water and oil, to make up for the deprivation that marked her newborn state (v 4). The one who lacked swathing bands and grew up naked (vv 4, 7) is now dressed in the best of clothes, headgear, and footwear. Her royal rank is indicated by the multicolored robe, worn by the royal bride in Ps 45:15(14) (cf. Judg 5:30); to trace parallels with the vocabulary of the tabernacle furnishings is not particularly helpful. A complete set of jewelry is lavished upon her, culminating in a royal diadem. V 13aα pauses to savor these gifts of jewelry and clothing, summarizing them in reverse order. Then the provision of food is mentioned. Fine flour or semolina was included in the food supply of Solomon's household in 1 Kgs 5:2(4:22). Finally, Jerusalem's beauty is celebrated and lingered over in a series of clauses. Under Yahweh's extravagant care, she blossomed into a peerless beauty. Just as handsomeness in Israelite culture was one qualification for kingship (1 Sam 16:12; 2 Sam 14:25), so was beauty for queenly rank. Here Jerusalem's role as a royal capital comes to the fore (Brownlee 228; Krüger, *Geschichtskonzepte* 183). Moreover, the perfect beauty that won international fame evokes the acclaim of Jerusalem in expressions of the theology of Zion, as "the perfection of beauty, the joy of all the earth" (Lam 2:15; Pss 48:3[2]; 50:2). The motif of perfect beauty is reapplied to the great city of Tyre in 27:3, 4, 11. Of course, this affirmation of Zion theology is seriously qualified by the rest of the oracle and by Ezekiel's overall intent to look behind it to a murky past that was more determinative for Jerusalem's grim future. The closing note of this section is the debt that the foundling-wife owed to her patron-husband. All was of grace. As Paul wryly reminded the Corinthian Christians, "What do you have that you did not receive? . . . You are filled, . . . you are rich, . . . you have become kings" (1 Cor 4:7–8; cf. Ezek 31:7–9).

15–19 The narrative takes a scandalous turn in this third installment of the story, as the oracle moves from redemptive grace to accusation and from positive divine acts to Jerusalem's negative reactions. The linchpin of the development is her renown and beauty, which featured in v 14 and now in reverse in v 15. There is a new independence, a wrongful self-confidence that leads to the transfer of her sexual vigor (vv 7–8) to the street. The false trust in her beauty means that the "gift replaces the giver" (Zimmerli 342; cf. 33:13).

This section is dominated by the stem זנה relating to sexual intercourse outside marriage and to prostitution: it occurs four times in vv 15–19 and six times in vv 15–22. In 6:9; 20:30 Ezekiel applies the imagery to the worship of gods other than Yahweh, and it is so used here. The mention of במות "high places" is an early indication (cf. 6:3, 6 and the *Comment*; 20:29). The syncretistic incorporation of Canaanite elements into local worship is in view. The "images" of v 17 (cf. 7:20) and the "fragrant offerings" of v 19 (cf. 6:13) develop the theme. The description of the images as "male" is best understood as a reflex of the sexual metaphor, rather than indicating the exclusion of goddesses. An interpretation as phallic symbols (Ehrlich, *Randglossen* 5:55; et al.) does not suit the reference to clothing them in v 18 (Schottroff, *'Gedenken'* 320). Another dominant motif is the threefold taking of vv 16–18. What Yahweh had given in vv 10–13aα, his consort now grabbed and perverted. The clothes became curtains (cf. Exod 36:8, 35) and also costumes for the images (cf. Jer 10:9). The metal jewelry was melted down into images, whether cast of solid metal or plated. Two other links with earlier endowments are made. First, the rubbing oil of v 9 was diverted to pagan religious use. A new element is added, perfume that involved burning spices as a fumigant (cf. Prov 27:9; Exod 30:37–38; Nielsen, *Incense* 89–94). Doubtless, perfume was added as the second of a standard word pair (cf. 23: 41; Prov 27:9). Since food is specified in the next verse, the reference here to the religious use of incense can hardly refer to meal offerings (cf. Lev 21:1–2). It presumably relates to a concoction used for burning in the incense burners associated with the high places (see 6:4, 6 and the *Comment*). In Isa 57:9 oil and perfumes are associated with the cult of Molech, which is the topic of the next section. Second, the food of v 13aα was turned into meal offerings, properly made of oil, spice, and fine flour and burned on the altar to produce fragrant fumes (cf. Lev 2:1–2). The inclusion of honey, prohibited in the priestly legislation (Lev 2:11), may be a reference to their heterodox nature. The use of meal offerings at Judean high places and in various pagan rites seems to be implied in 2 Kgs 16:4; 18:4; 22:17; 23:5; Jer 1:16, etc. (see M. Haran, *VT* 10 [1960] 117–18).

20–22 The next installment is devoted to a fresh development that is regarded as the ultimate outrage. Reference is made to the cult of Molech that was practiced in the Valley of Hinnom to the immediate south of Jerusalem (cf. 2 Kgs 23:10; Jer 7:31, 32). It involved the sacrifice of children of both sexes. V 21 suggests that this sacrificing occurred in two stages, ritual slaughter and then burning (Cooke 169; Heider, *Cult* 366 n. 722, 374). "Devoting" (העביר; cf. 20:26) is a technical term, short for "devoting in the fire" (20:31 and elsewhere). This new "taking" does not correspond precisely to a gift bestowed by Yahweh, though mention of sons and daughters smoothly follows the marriage of v 8. Ezekiel may have been influenced to set the topic here by the fact that already in Jer 2:23–25; Lev 20:5 (H) the Molech cult is described in sexual imagery. So its mention in this context is natural for himself and his audience.

Emotional outrage is expressed in referring to children whom "you had borne me" and "my sons" and also in the vehement question of vv 20b–21 and in the term "abominations" in v 22. It surfaces too in the closing recapitulation of Jerusalem's "young days" (vv 6–7), before Yahweh's grace had transformed her life. This recapitulation nicely illustrates the purpose of the early stages of the story, to accentuate the accusation as a surprising disappointment (Hals 106). "How could you!" is the implicit message. If Jerusalem had remembered what she was apart from God's grace, she would not have behaved like this. While the accusation of v 22aα sums up vv 15–21, the recapitulation may intend to pinpoint the sins of this particular section, vv 20–21. She who had been at death's door by her parents' whim should have known better than to deliver to death her patron's and her own children.

23–29 An emotional residue lingers in v 23, with its loaded accusing vocabulary and threat of divine reprisal. It seems to echo the divine cry אוֹי לָךְ יְרוּשָׁלַם "Woe to you, Jerusalem," in a context of marital infidelity similar to Jer 13:27. Eventually the account settles to its new topic, to which this fifth installment turns. It explores another aspect of the open marriage, one already described by earlier prophets in sexual terms, alliance with foreign powers (cf. Hos 8:9; Jer 22:20; 30:14; and probably 2:33). Alliance meant dalliance. Jerusalem, as the center of royal administration and so of foreign policy, could reasonably be held responsible. That this dalliance runs parallel to the former one of vv 15–22 is indicated by the repetition of "your beauty" and "any passer by" from v 15. Exactly as in vv 15–22, the stem זנה "be sexually promiscuous" occurs six times. "After" in v 23 has a literary sense rather than a chronological one. It connotes degree: Jerusalem goes from bad to worse. There is an impression of nymphomania, as Jerusalem grows increasingly promiscuous (הרבה "add," vv 25, 26, 29: a parody of the growing of v 7?) but fails to find satisfaction (vv 28, 29). The embarrassment of the Philistine cities at Jerusalem's outrageous behavior in v 27 is a motif that will be exploited later in the chapter. It corresponds to Ezekiel's claim in 5:6–7 that Jerusalem's sin was greater than that of other nations (cf. Amos 3:9–10). The obscenities "open her legs" (v 25) and "big penises" (v 26), the extreme term זמה "lasciviousness" (v 27), and even כל "all" (three times in vv 24–25) contribute to the tone of excess in which Jerusalem's three instances of political affairs are described (vv 26, 28–29). The reference to Chaldea provides an updating of Hosea's and Jeremiah's condemnation of Israel's and Judah's seesawing between Egypt and Assyria (Hos 7:11; Jer 2:18).

After the first of these affairs, Yahweh is driven by exasperation to intervene with an interim punishment, with which Amos 4:6–11 may be compared in principle. That Jerusalem does not learn her lesson but continues in further affairs gives the reader a sense of foreboding as to her fate. There is a historical progression in the political overtures, though links with Assyria predated those with Egypt. Presumably the former's longer control of Judah dictated the order, while Zedekiah's flirtation with Egypt that lies at the base of chap. 23 had not yet occurred. Moreover, in v 28 Judah's subordination to Assyria during Manasseh's long reign is doubtless in view. V 27 shows that Hezekiah's reign is in mind in v 26, specifically his attempt to get Egyptian help for his rebellion against Assyria, which Isaiah condemned in Yahweh's name (Isa 30:1–7; 31:1–3). Sennacherib's annals shed light on v 27:

His [Hezekiah's] towns which I had plundered I took away from his country and gave them (over) to Mitinti, king of Ashdod, Padi, king of Ekron, and Sillibel, king of Gaza. Thus I reduced his country. . . . (*ANET* 288a; Eissfeldt, *PJ* 27 [1931] 58–64)

Here the Assyrian punitive reprisal in 701 B.C. for rebellion and a pro-Egyptian policy is credited to Yahweh's providential control. The "daughters of the Philistines" are the independent cities of Ashdod, Ekron, and Gaza (Fitzgerald, *CBQ* 37 [1975] 171). With v 29 we reach Jehoiakim's three-year submission to Nebuchadnezzar (c. 603–601) and Zedekiah's submission from 597 till the date of this oracle, perhaps with echoes of earlier contacts with Babylon (cf. Greenberg 282). As with earlier prophets, secular options for Judah, a tiny state tossed in the wash of world powers, are left out of consideration. All is subsumed under the prophetic single-minded concept of Yahweh's theological authority, which Judah resists at the cost of its ruin.

30–34 The provocation Yahweh felt at Jerusalem's political affairs was expressed in vv 23–29, not only by the strong language used to describe its policies but also by the reference to angering him in v 26. It is renewed in the emotional outburst of this next section, which corresponds in its tone to the general comment of v 22. Now it is appropriately expanded to a full section, in line with increased provocation. The solid structures of vv 24–25 are recalled and linked with professional prostitution. Hosea had characterized Israel's political switching as the behavior of a "silly and senseless dove" (Hos 7:11) and also their religious promiscuity as "without sense" (Hos 4:11–14), while Jeremiah protested the unnaturalness of Judah's religious deviations (Jer 18:13–15). Here Jerusalem's politics is in view, and scorn is poured on its failure to play out the metaphorical role consistently. The verb שִׁחֵד "bribe" in v 33 links the political reality of the tribute (שֹׁחַד) Judah had to pay as vassal to its imperial overlords (2 Kgs 16:8; cf. מִנְחָה "tribute" in the case of the Northern Kingdom at 2 Kgs 17:3–4; Hos 10:6). Such financial loss hardly fitted the figure of the professional prostitute who trades her favors for fees (אֶתְנַן; cf. Hos 9:1; Mic 1:7). The point being made is not that the illustration breaks down. Rather, Jerusalem, Yahweh's royal consort, gained nothing from her infidelity. She who had been showered with royal wealth squandered it on lovers and had little left. There is an implicit reference to the gold and silver of v 13 (cf. v 17). 2 Kgs 16:8 specifies silver and gold as tribute to Assyria, and 2 Kgs 23:33, 35 as an indemnity (עֹנֶשׁ) to Egypt, while in 597 B.C., according to 2 Kgs 24:13, gold temple vessels were confiscated by the victorious Babylonians. Such impoverishment was proof positive of the folly of playing at international politics. The "adulterous wife" (v 32) who rushed into affairs (v 34, "not solicited") had taken on a role she could not handle properly, to her own advantage. Fierce scorn is expressed finally in the double הֶפֶךְ "contrary" that frames v 34. It is a term that Isaiah had used of Hezekiah's overtures to Egypt (הַפְכְּכֶם "How perverse you are!" [NJB], Isa 29:16), overtures that drained "riches" and "treasures" from Judah but proved a fruitless venture (Isa 30:6–7).

35–43   The judicial sentence that follows falls into an extended passage of cause and effect (vv 36aa^2 + 37–42) and a general summary (v 43a + ba^1). The sentence is formally introduced by a messenger formula (v 36aa^1) and closed by a divine-saying formula (v 43ba^2). By way of transition, v 35 itself, before its summons to hear the sentence, moves from cause to effect by its "therefore" and sums up the overall accusation with the vocative "prostitute."

36   The previous accusations of vv 15–22 + 23–34 are summed up in a triple recapitulation. The second accusation of political affairs comes first, as still fresh in the mind; it picks up the term "lovers" from v 33. Then the first accusation of religious infidelity is mentioned in its two parts, idol worship, which hints at the "images" of v 17 but translates them into Ezekiel's regular term "idols," and then the particularly heinous deviation of v(v 20–)21, child sacrifice. The ensuing portrayal of punishment is mainly angled as reprisal for foreign politics. This perspective serves to counterbalance the representation of the former accusation of indigenous paganism as a development of the introductory vv 3–14, in terms of perversion of Jerusalem's divine rescue and endowment and of reversion to its Canaanite origin.

37–38   The first stage of Jerusalem's punishment fits the crime by involving her international lovers, who are brought from all around, as they had been invited earlier (v 34). The lovers are divided into present lovers, the Chaldeans, and ex-lovers, now rejected (cf. 23:22). The public exposure of the naked body was a symbolic act of legal punishment for adulterers (see Kruger, *JNSL* 12 [1984] 82): it reversed the husband's provision of clothing (v 10) and took away the wife's married identity. In terms of Hos 2:12(10), "I will uncover her immorality in the sight of her lovers" (cf. Jer 13:26; Nah 3:5). Adultery was a capital crime for both men and women (Lev 20:10; Deut 22:22), and so was murder, in this case of Jerusalem's children (v 36). Yahweh, as both cuckolded husband and sovereign judge, would pass the double sentence, with the jealous fury of a husband scorned (cf. Prov 6:34).

39–41a   In the prophetic representation of judgment there is usually "a kind of synergism in which divine and human actions are forged into a single whole or the divine intent of judgment is wrought out through human agency" (Miller, *Sin and Judgment* 138). So here the reprisals of vv 37ba^2–38 were to be carried out by the assembled lovers. The punishment is presented both on the human plane, as a reaping of the baneful crop Jerusalem had sown by playing off one nation against another, and as a providential fate, masterminded by the divine victim of Jerusalem's sins. The final downfall of the city by military means is portrayed as a fitting retribution: the brothels of vv 24–25, 31 are destroyed, and marital assets bestowed in vv 10–13 are lost. The clock was to be put back. Jerusalem would forfeit all the perquisites of royal rank given by the God of Israel. The "crowd" of v 40 is both a legally constituted assembly and an army. In the former role they stone the offender to death, as in Deut 22:21, 24. In the latter role they resort to sword and fire (cf. 2 Kgs 25:9). The hacking of the corpse is unparalleled as a judicial feature. Greenberg (287) compared the quartering of a hanged traitor in old British law. There may simply be a literary mingling of metaphor and reality, a fusion of socio-legal and military roles (cf. 23:47). The witness of other, uninvolved nations ("women") recalls 5:8, 14. In this context it signifies reversal of the international renown of v 14 (cf. v 27; Lam 4:12).

41b–42 Such radical measures as the international humiliation and "killing" of Jerusalem were the only way Yahweh could end the capital's commitment to foreign involvement. V 42 is not an assurance of salvation, as von Orelli (909) and Zimmerli (347) claimed, but "a notice that God will not rest until he has afflicted the extreme penalty" (Greenberg 288). Krüger (*Geschichtskonzepte* 194) has observed in confirmation that the death of Jerusalem has already been announced in vv 40–41. The verse aligns with 5:13 and 24:13 as a grounding of reprisal. There had to be a spending of the jealous fury of v 38, a final resolution of the problem that provoked Yahweh to pain-filled anger in v 26. This glancing back over the earlier material shows that theodicy is the issue at stake in this oracle. Only the final destruction of Jerusalem could wipe clean the slate of accumulated debt owed to its divine patron.

43abα The concluding recapitulation of cause and effect goes back further to v 22. It observes the aggravation of the offense caused by ignoring the benevolence of the divine victim (cf. Judg 8:34). Jerusalem owed everything to God, and to treat him as she had was unconscionable. He could only let justice take its terminal course. As David solemnly stated at the judicial slaying of the Amalekite, "Your blood be on your own head" (2 Sam 1:16).

43bβ–58 This next piece has been composed in conscious dependence on the former oracle. It speaks from a later point in history. There was no longer any need to belabor the punishment of Jerusalem or to project it into the future. The capital's fall from grace was now known to all of Ezekiel's constituency.

43bβ–45 This message starts from the same premise as the first: the pre-Israelite alien family background of the capital. The former oracle had utilized it with a hint of Jerusalem's reversion to type in adopting a Canaanized form of worship, complete with child sacrifice, and in failing to stay within traditional Israelite parameters of loyalty to Yahweh. There was a lot more mileage to be gotten out of the concept, and so the prophet eventually returns to it. In relation to v 3 the reminder "Your mother was a Hittite and your father an Amorite" exhibits the inversion typical of Hebrew recapitulation (cf. Talmon, *Qumran* 358–78, esp. 360). It also serves to put the focus on the mother, emphasizing the female spouse. This permits a pattern to be demonstrated in the way wives treated their husbands and children in this dysfunctional family to which Jerusalem belonged. The personified capital's own behavior is summed up from the first oracle in the strong terms תועבות "abominations, shocking practices" (vv 2, 22, 36) and זמה "lasciviousness" (v 27). This outrageous behavior was no surprise. It was reminiscent of the sexual and religious lifestyle with which Israel tarred the indigenous population of Canaan (Lev 18:25–28; Deut 12:31; 18:9, 12; 20:18).

The proverb defines a person in terms of heredity and upbringing, and so focuses on the next generation (W. McKane, *Proverbs: A New Approach*, OTL [Philadelphia: Westminster, 1970] 29). A fleeting vignette is given of the old mother's lifestyle. In sexual terms she is typified as leaving her husband (not Yahweh, in this case) and in religious terms as sacrificing her sons. This malignant matriarchy continued into the next generation of Jerusalem's "sisters." It is clear that this message, though it starts from the same premise as the first, will develop along a different path. Jerusalem is no longer a foundling abandoned by parents. Nor has it suffered capital punishment. It lives on in the exiles who survived the city's fate. It is a member of a family of three matriarchal women who all bear their mother's ugly likeness. The notion is a development of the two sisters, Judah and Israel or Jerusalem and Samaria, in the preexilic oracles of 23:2–27, 32–34.

46–47 Structurally, this pair of verses expresses in brief what vv 48–51bα will expand into a fuller form (cf. Parunak, "Structural Studies" 262, who excludes v 51bα). Both the abstract and the expansion claim that Jerusalem's sin was worse than that of Samaria or Sodom. These two fallen cities were notorious for their sins that led to their destruction—but fallen Jerusalem was no better! The abstract moves in three stages, first introducing Jerusalem's two ugly sisters and their female brood, next identifying her as a third ugly sister, and finally branding her as the worst of the litter. Samaria, the witch of the north, is called the bigger of the two sisters, not in terms of age but as capital of a nation. Sodom, the witch of the south, historically the older, was a smaller entity, a city-state. Both had satellite cities associated with them, which are called "daughters" (cf. Num 21:25; Ps 48:12[11]; see Fitzgerald, *CBQ* 37 [1975] 172). Both cities were bywords for wickedness. Jerusalem had been compared to them by earlier prophets. In Isa 1:10 Jerusalem is called Sodom, while in Mic 6:16 it is accused of adopting the practices of Omri and Ahab, who both ruled from Samaria (1 Kgs 16:24). Jeremiah had compared the prophets of Samaria and Jerusalem and characterized them as Sodom-like (Jer 3:13–14). In a prose version of the same theme Jerusalem is stigmatized as more guilty than her sister Samaria (Jer 3:11). Ezekiel gathers up such prophetic traditions (cf. too Deut 32:32), especially from Jeremiah, and utilizes them here, in claiming Jerusalem's parity in wickedness and passing to its predominance. The older message needed to be sounded afresh, for a purpose he will disclose later.

48–51bα The theme is forcibly reiterated at greater length and introduced by a divine oath. Jerusalem is furnished with "daughters," or dependent cities, so that the nation of Judah is in view. Now the order "Samaria-Sodom" is stylistically inverted. Yes, Sodom was not so bad as Jerusalem (v 48). Yes, Samaria was not so bad as Jerusalem (v 51a). Yes, Jerusalem was worse than both (v 51b). The inversion that put Sodom first gives an opportunity to expatiate on Sodom's fatal sins, which is done in a relatively minimizing fashion (vv 49–50). The sketch of Sodom's (and Samaria's) sins in v 45bα leads the reader to expect a denunciation on sexual lines, as in Gen 19:1–11. Certainly Yahweh's getting rid of Sodom "when he saw" their behavior (v 50) appears to echo Gen 18:21. Moreover, Sodom's shocking or abominable conduct in v 50 may well be a reflection of homosexuality (cf. Lev 18:22; 20:13; Greenberg 289). But the specification of Sodom's sins highlights the city's arrogance or pride in materialistic comfort and excess, coupled with a lack of concern for the poor. This picture of the urban wealthy who have no concern for the underclass at their door (cf. Luke 16:19–21) may reflect a variant tradition, but it is more likely a projection of the social sins of Jerusalem (cf. Isa 1:17, 23; 3:16; 32:9–14; Jer 22:13–18). "Pride" (גָּאוֹן) significantly recurs in v 56 with reference to Jerusalem. (In dependence on Ezekiel, Sir 16:8 characterizes Sodom's sin as pride.) In Jerusalem's case such sins were compounded by the religious and political sins of vv 15–34.

51bβ–52 The point of this tirade against Jerusalem as the ugliest of three ugly sisters now emerges. This section is a double presentation of a call to repentance framed by accusation. It has an ABA′/ABA structure. The A element reaffirms Jerusalem's peerlessness. It cites the verb used in Jer 3:11 with reference to the

Northern Kingdom's showing itself less guilty (צָדֵק) than Judah. In keeping with a call to Jerusalem and a comparison of cities, now the verb is used with Jerusalem as subject. The A' variation uses a forensic synonym פָלֵל "arbitrate on someone's behalf," here with the sense of providing extenuating circumstances. The B element is a summons to repentance. So the structure runs as follows: (A) Jerusalem made them look guiltless (vv 51bβ, 52aβ); (B) so she must bear her humiliation (vv 52aα¹, 52bα); (A') because she exculpated them (v 52aα²) or (A) because she made them look guiltless (v 52bβ).

The first oracle had mentioned the daughters of the Philistines being ashamed of Jerusalem's lascivious behavior (v 27). This notion of shame is now reused and applied to the Jerusalem that survived in the form of the 587 B.C. exiles. Jerusalem too must come to the point of shamefulness. There appears to be a reminiscence of Jeremiah's complaint that Judah before its downfall had "a harlot's brow, refusing to be ashamed" (Jer 3:3; cf. 6:15; 8:12). In Ezekiel's prophesying, the appeal aligns with his preexilic forecast that Judah's exiled survivors would come to regard their past with revulsion (6:9). The scales would fall from their eyes, and they would at last see themselves as God saw them. This deflated self-awareness for which Ezekiel now pleads was the only spiritually sane course for them to take. It was a call that Ezekiel's editors would reinforce for the exiles in 36:32.

53–54 The final part of the message also consists of twin statements, a brief one in vv 53–54 and an expanded one in vv 55–58. It turns to a positive future, for Sodom, for Samaria (cf. 37:15–22), and, almost as an afterthought, for Jerusalem. There is an ironic handling of the promise of a return from exile. By now Ezekiel's hearers were presumably accustomed to such good news, so that this sardonic variation could have full effect. If Jerusalem was to be restored after plunging to such sinful depths, it was only fair that lesser offenders should participate in restoration and even take precedence. Here Jer 3:11–12 may have been influential, where Israel, less guilty that Judah, is invited to return. The presence of Jerusalem's similarly blessed neighbors would prod her into constant awareness of her sin of deepest dye, as well as gratify them.

Ezekiel affirmed this message in a more straightforward context at 20:43. The restored exiles should never forget their shameful past. In Pauline terms, they should continually thank God that, once slaves to sin, they had been redeemed (Rom 6:17–18). Ezekiel's disciples underlined this truth in 36:31 and 39:26, in the latter case echoing the phraseology of 16:34.

55–58 The elaboration covers similar ground for emphatic reiteration. Vv 56–57 go their own way in glancing at Jerusalem's past and present. Jerusalem, living in her glasshouse, should not have been so ready to throw stones at Sodom. Her complacent gloating was a thing of the past, now that she had suffered Sodom's fate. The verbal ridicule and contempt shown to Jerusalem by her neighbors, the cities of Edom and Philistia, are not the subject of a message of consolation to the Judeans, as in 25:12–17 (cf. 35:1–14; 36:5), but simply just desserts. The exiles dare not complain. Like an ex-boxer whose broken nose and cauliflower ears remain to give away his former profession, they would take back to the land as scars regret and contrition for the radical sinfulness that marked their past. The necessity of repentance in the context of an oracle of salvation, so that salvation is made a presupposition of, or motivation for, repentance—instead

of repentance being a condition for repentance—is striking. It has a later parallel in Isa 44:21–22 and a precedent in Jer 3:12, 14, on which the present passage
may well depend.

59–63 This final, editorial piece stands at some distance from the earlier two,
though in clear continuity with them. It speaks with prophetic authority, as the
initial messenger formula and the final divine-saying formula indicate. It provides a generalizing, theologically reflective conclusion, tying up loose ends of
the former pieces and repeating some of their key lessons.

59–61 First, the ironical tone of vv 53–58 could not be permitted to veil the
real graciousness of God involved in the coming time of salvation, when his people
were brought back to the land. His future deeds would provide a wonderful contrast with what Jerusalem had "done" according to vv 43bβ, 47, 51, and 54. In
between his initial grace and his eschatological grace yawned the chasm of a broken covenant. The pledge and marriage pact of v 8 are here recalled and
interpreted as a figure for the covenant relationship God had made with Israel,
for which Jerusalem is an evident symbol. Jerusalem had been like the last king
Zedekiah, who had despised the divine oath and broken the divine covenant in
his perfidy toward Nebuchadnezzar (17:18–19). In so doing Jerusalem had failed
to remember the desperate situation of her young days (vv 22, 43) and the rescue
to life and love that followed. Not so her faithful consort. He would establish an
"everlasting covenant" with her as the center of a new community, a covenant
that would permanently replace the one that was broken (cf. 37:26). Jerusalem
too would have some remembering to do. God's surprising faithfulness would
provoke her to think back guiltily to her sinful past and so be all the more appreciative of his grace, on the lines of vv 54 and 58. Such grace would include the
gift of the whole land. Sodom and Samaria and their dependencies, restored as
promised in vv 53 and 55, would be subordinated to Jerusalem as capital of a
promised land that included their territory (cf. 47:15–20). The final phrase,
מבריתך, literally "not from your covenant," has a number of possible meanings,
reviewed in Brownlee (251–52). The context suggests that it is another manifestation of divine grace, here transcending the previous relationship. His former
covenant with Jerusalem did not obligate him to give her control of Sodom or
Samaria, but he would magnanimously do so: "this act of grace will not flow automatically, by way of a mechanical deduction, from Jerusalem's covenant"
(Woudstra, *CTJ* 6 [1971] 44; cf. Fishbane, *Int* 38 [1984] 138).

62–63 The piece closes by lingering over the vital truths of vv 60–61 (cf.
Renaud, "L'alliance éternelle" 336). Jerusalem would be reintroduced to Yahweh
and encounter him as the God who graciously renewed the covenant of v 8. His
intent was that her sins should be forgiven but never forgotten. Only a sober
memory of the fate from which she was rescued could keep her from ever brag-
ging again, as in v 56, that she was not like that sinner Sodom (cf. Luke 18:9–14;
Rom 3:19, 27). Instead, it would provide motivation for bearing the fruit of repentance (Matt. 3:8).

Explanation

Ezek 16, or at least vv 1–58, deliberately wears a badge of political incorrect-
ness. It is not surprising that the Targum completely rewrote it, removing any

slur against Jerusalem and turning it into a wholesome presentation of Jewish orthodoxy. Down through the ages its distasteful message has blunted its original intent, though it is pornography only in an etymological sense and has no intent of sexual arousal. In the present climate of thought, its disparaging depiction of the female as victim of social violence is particularly upsetting (cf. Darr, *JSOT* 55 [1992] 114–16). To appreciate the prophetic agenda, we must distinguish between ancient cultural norms of handling marital infidelity and the shocking use to which Ezekiel put them. It was a vehement ploy to communicate the necessity of the fall of Jerusalem, dragging Judah down with it.

The prophet's repeated pre-587 insistence that Jerusalem must be destroyed ran into an immovable object in the form of Zion theology. Doubtless, his fellow hostages insisted more loudly that Jerusalem was sacrosanct, the invincible city of God that "will not be moved" (Ps 46:6[5]). Ezekiel opposed this religious ideology, implicitly in 4:1–3 and explicitly in 5:5–17 (see especially v 5). Now the risqué tour de force in 16:2–43b*a*, which lies at the basis of this composite chapter, represents an irresistible force with which Ezekiel attempted to dislodge the immovable object (cf. Krüger, *Geschichtskonzepte* 174, 197). Isaiah had demanded faith as a necessary catalyst to let Zion theology work (Isa 28:16). Ezekiel too adduces caveats. As in 5:5, he affirms Jerusalem's special status in God's heart (vv 8–14), freely echoing language of the songs of Zion in v 14. However, he sets this truth in the middle of a longer story. It had a sinister beginning and ending, relating to Jerusalem's pagan antecedents and to its failure to measure up to its destiny.

Jerusalem came late into Israel's control. Bad blood lay in its past, the prophet suggests—a hint of the wickedness that led to the pre-Israelite nations being driven out (Deut 9:4–6). Later in the oracle it would be intimated that Jerusalem had reverted to type, by behavior that proved what Christians would call its original sin. The role that was thrust upon Jerusalem, to be the religious and political capital of God's people, is conveyed in the powerful allegory of a foundling, whom Yahweh rescued, married, and marvelously provided for. In the overall message, which is a variation of a standard oracle of judgment consisting of accusation and punishment, the story of divine favor acts as a foil for the following accusation. It was a standard prophetic technique, such as Amos used in Amos 2:9–11, Hosea in Hos 9:10; 11:1; 13:4–5, Isaiah in Isa 5:1–2, and Jeremiah in Jer 2:1–3. The accusation is thereby shown as all the darker, by holding it up to the light of God's grace.

The accusation falls into two parts. Hosea put it more succinctly, in the form of a confession: "Assyria will not save us, and we will no longer call 'our God' what our hands have made" (Hos 14:4[3]). But Ezekiel said it more powerfully, borrowing from Hosea himself and from Jeremiah the metaphor of illicit sex applied both to Canaanized religion and to foreign politics. The language is deliberately repulsive and coarse, to counter mythology with compelling metaphor and to convey the depths of ungrateful infidelity to which Jerusalem had sunk. The metaphor carries the reader on to an inevitable future, the degradation and death that were the legal punishment for adultery. Jerusalem must fall. By such means Ezekiel countered the contemporary value of an ancient theological tradition with the newer, subversive prophetic tradition.

The second piece in vv 43b*β*–58 builds on the first and applies it to a post-587 situation. The exiles who had experienced the downfall of Jerusalem in person or by report must factor it into their spiritual reckoning, urges the prophet. He challenges them, as the living embodiment of Jerusalem, to recognize that its and their sin was "exceeding sinful" (Rom 7:13, KJV), beside which the sins of Sodom and Samaria paled. Whereas the first message defined Jerusalem's sin vertically in relation to God, this one does so horizontally, with respect to two infamous cities. Such a nadir of sinfulness must call forth a response of contrite repentance. Such healthy shame must haunt their coming return to the land, in the form of a deep regret at wounding God so deeply.

The second message dwelt on what had been done by "Jerusalem," now as in Second Isaiah a cipher for the Judean exiles, whereas the first oracle had presented a measure-for-measure punishment for its sins. By contrast, the closing message, which in vv 59–63 editorially develops the first two, celebrates the ending of such correlation in what God was to do in the coming era of salvation. Where sin abounded, grace was to superabound. A God who still loved his people would replace a broken covenant with an unbreakable covenant. Yet, when the dark past was succeeded by so glorious a future, it must ever find a Lenten memorial in the hearts of God's people. There is a glancing forward to 17:19 and the sin of Zedekiah, who despised Yahweh's oath and broke his covenant. The language is reapplied to the exiled "Jerusalem" and used to reinforce a sense of the sinfulness that stained their past. Forgiveness must not mean forgetfulness, which had tragically marked Jerusalem's dark ages (vv 22, 43). The saved know themselves to have been the foremost of sinners (1 Tim 1:15). In that knowledge of unworthiness, they know God's love (vv 2, 62) and are constrained to mirror it in obedience.

The Death and Resurrection of the Judean Monarchy (17:1–24)

Bibliography

Caquot, A. "Le messianisme d'Ézéchiel." *Sem* 14 (1964) 5–23. **Frankena, R.** "The Vassal-treaties of Esarhaddon and the Dating of Deuteronomy." *OTS* 14 (1965) 122–54. **Grayson, A. K.** "Akkadian Treaties of the Seventh Century B.C." *JCS* 39 (1987) 127–60. **Greenberg, M.** "Ezekiel 17 and the Policy of Psammetichus II." *JBL* 76 (1957) 304–9. **Herrmann, S.** *Die prophetischen Heilserwartungen im Alten Testament.* BWANT 85. Stuttgart: Kohlhammer, 1965. 255–59. **Hossfeld, F.** *Untersuchungen zu Komposition und Theologie des Ezechielbuches.* FB 20. Würzburg: Echter Verlag, 1977. 59–98. **Kutsch, E.** "בְּרִית *bᵉrīt* Verpflichtung." *THAT* 1:339–52. **Laato, A.** *Josiah and David Redivivus.* ConBOT 33. Stockholm: Almqvist & Wicksell, 1992. 154–76. **Lang, B.** *Kein Aufstand in Jerusalem.* 2nd ed. Stuttgart: Katholisches Bibelwerk, 1981. 28–88. **Pohlmann, K.-F.** *Ezechielstudien: Zur Redaktionsgeschichte des Buches und zur Frage des ältesten Textes.* BZAW 202. Berlin: de Gruyter, 1992. **Polk, T.** "Paradigms, Parables and *Mᵉšālîm:* On Reading the *Māšāl* in Scripture." *CBQ* 45 (1983) 564–83. **Rabenau, K. von.** "Die Form des Rätsels im Buche Hesekiel." *WZ* 7 (1957/58) 1055–57. **Simian-Yofre, H.** "Ez 17, 1–10 como enigma y parabola." *Bib* 65 (1984) 27–43. **Solomon, A. M. V.** "Fable." In *Saga, Legend, Tale, Novella, Fable,* ed. G. W. Coats. JSOTSup 35. Sheffield: JSOT, 1985. 114–25. **Tsevat, M.** "The Neo-Assyrian and Neo-Babylonian Vassal Oaths and the Prophet Ezekiel." *JBL* 78 (1959) 199–204.

Translation

¹*I received the following communication from Yahweh:* ²*"Human one, tell the community of Israel a cryptic allegory* ³*in a message from the Lord*ᵃ *Yahweh:*
A great eagle
with large wings
and long pinions,
*covered*ᵇ *with plumage,*
with colored feathers,
came to Lebanon.
It took the crown of a cedar,
⁴*plucking off its topmost shoot,*ᵃ
*and carried it away to a trading*ᵇ *country,*
setting it in merchantville.
⁵*Then it took a native seed*ᵃ
and put it in a seed plot.
*Now a shoot,*ᵇ *beside abundant water*
*he set it out, like a willow,*ᶜ
⁶*intending it to grow and become*ᵃ *a grapevine,*
one trailing and low,
with its branches turned toward it
*and its roots staying*ᵇ *beneath it.*ᶜ
It did become a grapevine;

it grew branches and sent out boughs.
⁷But there was another ᵃ *great eagle*
with large wings
and luxuriant plumage.
At once this grapevine
bent ᵇ *its roots in its direction*
and sent out its ᶜ *branches toward it*
to be supplied with water ᵈ—
away from ᵉ *the bed* ᶠ *where it had been planted.*
⁸On a good plot,
beside abundant water,
it had been planted,
but ᵃ*it wanted to grow branches*
and produce fruit
and so become a magnificent ᵇ *grapevine.*
⁹Tell them this message from the Lord Yahweh: Will it flourish? ᵃ
Won't the first eagle ᵇ *tear it out by its roots*
and strip off ᶜ *its fruit* ᵈ *so that it shrivels,*
all the new leaves it has grown shrivel? ᵉ
No need of ᶠ *great force or a large army*
to pull it up, ᵍ *roots and all!* ʰ
¹⁰It is planted now, but will it flourish?
Won't it shrivel away
when it is struck
by the east wind?
On the bed where it is growing it will shrivel."

¹¹I received the following communication from Yahweh: ¹²"Tell that rebellious community, You don't know what all this means, do you? Tell them: Look, the king of Babylon went to Jerusalem and took away its king and officials, bringing them back to Babylon. ¹³Then, taking a member of the royal family,ᵃ he made a treaty with him and required him to enter into an oath; he included in the treatyᵇ the leading people in the country. ¹⁴He wanted the realm to be a lowly one that would not engage in uprising but keep his treaty permanently.ᵃ ¹⁵But the rulerᵃ rebelled against him, sending his envoys to Egypt to obtain horses and a large army. Is he likely to succeed? Willᵇ anyone who is guilty of such conduct get away with it?ᶜ Can he break a treaty and get away with it? ¹⁶I swear by my very life, warns the Lordᵃ Yahweh: The capitalᵇ of the king who gave him royal power, but whose oathᶜ he disregarded and whose treatyᶜ with himᵈ he broke—Babylon is the place where he will die. ¹⁷Not with great military strength and a large army will he deal with himᵃ when war breaks out, when earthworks are piled up and siege structures are built, portending much loss of human life. ¹⁸He has repudiated an oath, thereby breaking a treaty. He actuallyᵃ gave his hand in pledge and yet was guilty of such conduct. So he is not likely to get away with it. ¹⁹This then is the Lord Yahweh's message: I swear by my very life, the repudiated oath to meᵃ and the brokenᵇ treaty made before meᵃ are matters for which I will holdᶜ him responsible. ²⁰I will spread out my net forᵃ him, and he will be captured in my hunting equipment. I will bring him to Babylon, where I will put him on trial forᵇ infringing my rights.ᶜ ²¹All the élite troopsᵃ in his armyᵇ will fall to the sword, while the survivors will be scattered in every direction. Then you will realize that I, Yahweh, gave my word.

²² *"This is the message of the Lord Yahweh: I too will take*ᵃ *from the tall*ᵇ *crown of the cedar a tender shoot,*ᶜ *plucking it from its topmost* ᵈ *shoots. Then I myself will plant it on a high and lofty mountain:* ²³*Israel's high mountain is where I will plant it. It will grow branches and produce fruit and will become a magnificent cedar. Every beast*ᵃ *will live beneath it, while every bird will perch in its shady branches.*ᵇ ²⁴*Then all the trees in the countryside will realize that I, Yahweh, am the one who has reduced the tall tree and raised the low tree, who has shriveled the green tree and given*ᵃ *the shriveled tree new growth. I, Yahweh, have given my word and will act on it."*

Notes

3.a. For the formulaic use of אדני "Lord" in the messenger formula here and in vv 9, 19, and 22, see *Note* 2:4.c.

3.b. Heb. מָלֵא "filled with" functions as a verbal form, with the noun as object. Fohrer (93) proposed a repointing as constr מְלֹא.

4.a. Heb. יְנִיקָה "shoot" occurs only here (cf. Joüon 88Eb for the form); יוֹנֶקֶת in v 22 is the standard form.

4.b. See *Note* 16:29.a.

5.a. Lit. "one of the seeds of the land": זרע is collective.

5.b. Ewald (275) reasonably equated the *hapax legomenon* קָח with Syr. *qûḥâ* "stem, shoot." Akk. *qû*, to which Driver (*Bib* 35 [1954] 312) also appealed, and thence Lang, *Kein Aufstand* 29; Greenberg (310) has no basis: see Barthélemy, *Critique* 3:118. Barthélemy (*Critique* 3:116–17) has rightly queried whether LXX* Syr lack the term, as is generally claimed. The LXX* φυτόν may well mean "plant," rather than "planted," in which case זרע "seed" has been left unrepresented as otiose. This is certainly the case with Syr *nsbt ˀ* "plant."

5.c. Heb. צפצפה is a *hapax legomenon;* it denotes a species of willow in Mishnaic Heb. and Arab. For the syntax, see Greenberg 311. Zimmerli (355), implicitly following Hitzig (117), suggested a more general meaning, "waterside plant," which would ease the construction.

6.a. The MT points as main verbs, "and it grew and became." Ewald (275) proposed repointing with weak *waw* (= NAB), and many scholars have concurred, including Greenberg (311). This expedient avoids repetition in v 6b and accords with the evidently continuing statements of purpose in the second line. It also aligns with the clearly parallel intention of the overlord in the interpretation at v 14.

6.b. For the syntax, see Cooke 186.

6.c. I.e., the eagle, as the contrast in v 7 and the subservience of v 14 suggest (Keil 239).

7.a. Lit. "one," in the sense of "another," if the idiomatic repetition in 19:3, 5; 37:16 may be compared (Keil 237; von Orelli 67–68; Zimmerli 355). Many, including Barthélemy (*Critique* 3:68), emend אֶחָד "one" to אַחֵר "another," claiming LXX Syr Vg in support.

7.b. The context indicates some such meaning, which LXX Syr Tg support. Whether this is the same stem as כפן "be hungry," as Driver (*ETL* 26 [1950] 343–44) argued, is uncertain. BDB 495b compared Arab. *kafana* "spin, wrap (in shrouds)." In later Heb. and Jewish Aram., כפן also means "bend" (Jastrow, *Dictionary* 660b), as evidently here.

7.c. One expects a fem suffix יה. The masc form seems to be a scribal slip after עליו "to him."

7.d. Lit. "so that it (the second eagle) might give water."

7.e. The preposition goes with שלחה "sent out" (Keil 239; Ehrlich, *Randglossen* 5:62). For this suspended order, Greenberg (311) has usefully referred to A. Sperber's list of such cases in *JBL* 64 (1945) 117–18. The attempt to take as comparative, "drink more water than the bed . . ." (Cornill 274; et al.; = NAB, NJPS) is unnecessary and unlikely: see Greenberg 312.

7.f. The pl here and in v 10 is strange and sometimes emended, e.g., by Zimmerli (356), who here blamed metathesis of *waw* and *gimel*. Barthélemy (*Critique* 3:118–20) has explained it in terms of ridges that separate the furrows: cf. the meaning "ascend" for the Arab. and Eth. cognates.

8.a. The relation of v 8a and 8b to each other and to v 7 is not immediately clear. To relate the whole of v 8 to the grapevine's present opportunities can hardly be right, in view of its restriction in v 6. Accordingly, v 8a should point back and v 8b forward. Greenberg (311) has rightly observed that שתל means "plant" rather than "transplant": see *HALAT* 1540a.

8.b. *HALAT* 13b, 17a list as both a noun and an adj. V 23 suggests that it is the latter: for the form, cf. Joüon 89g.

9.a. The verb can have an interrogative force (Keil 240; Ehrlich, *Randglossen* 5:63; Greenberg 313): cf. GKC 150a. But *he* could easily have fallen out by haplography (Hitzig 118), yielding a rhetorical parallel with vv 10 and 15.

9.b. Lit. "he, it."

9.c. The *hapax legomenon* קסס has the sense of (wine) turning sour in Mishnaic Heb.; similarly, the LXX renders "rot," which Greenberg (313) favors. Traditionally the verb has been aligned with קצץ "cut off."

9.d. Bertholet's proposal ([1936] 60) to read פארותיה "its branches" for פריה "its fruit," in line with v 6, is not necessary. "Fruit" echoes the nearer v 8.

9.e. The nonrepresentation of תיבש "it will shrivel" in the LXX* is due to its syntactical reconstruing: see Barthélemy (*Critique* 3:121), who compares the repetition of the verb in v 10. For the syntax of the verb and nouns, see Greenberg (313).

9.f. Lit. "and (that too) without . . ."

9.g. The strange form משאות is evidently an Aramaizing inf of נשא "take away" with an ending borrowed from the *lamed he* type of verb.

9.h. Hardly "from its roots," in view of v 9ba¹; rather, "beginning from its roots."

13.a. Lit. "one of the royal seed," interpreting "seed" in v 5.

13.b. Heb. לקח "took" is usually understood in terms of deportation, but then the order of clauses is strange. Kutsch (*THAT* 1:345), followed by Hossfeld (*Untersuchungen* 78) and Lang (*Kein Aufstand* 55–56), has suggested a sense of taking into a covenant, as in 2 Chr 23:1.

14.a. Lit. "so that it (the treaty) would endure." To take the kingdom as the subj upsets the flow of v 14b. LXX *Σ*, with their transitive verbs, rightly had the treaty in view. Cf. the hiph in Ps 105:10 in the sense of establishing a covenant. C לעבדו "so that it would serve him" (= Tg) is a clarifying replacement.

15.a. Lit. "he."

15.b. For the common interrogative sense of a verb after the conjunction, see GKC 150a and 16:59.

15.c. Lit. "escape."

16.a. For the formulaic use of אדני "Lord" in the divine-saying formula, see *Note* 5:11.a.

16.b. For מקום "place" in the sense of "city," see BDB 880a.

16.c. LXX Syr "my oath . . . my treaty" anticipates v 19.

16.d. The MT takes אתו "with him" with v 16b, but the Vg "which he had with him" rightly takes with "treaty"; cf. Lev 26:44. Cooke's objection (193) that a resumptive pronoun is required has no weight: בתוך־בבל "in Babylon" is the resumptive element.

17.a. Comparison with v 9bβγ, where the army is implicitly Nebuchadnezzar's, has provoked several textual, syntactical, and semantic considerations. Ewald (275–76) treated פרעה "Pharaoh" as appositional to אותו "him" and made Nebuchadnezzar subj, "he will deal with him—Pharaoh—in war." Kraetzschmar (159–60) deleted the name as a false gloss wrongly relating to v 15a; he noted that elsewhere in Ezekiel קהל "army" refers to the Babylonians. Herrmann (104) followed him and claimed that in Ezekiel the verb עשה "deal" with את "with" is always hostile; he actually considered v 17 secondary, interrupting the flow of vv 16 and 18 (106). He interpreted that Nebuchadnezzar would not need a large army to punish Zedekiah. Similarly, Greenberg (*JBL* 76 [1957] 307–9; cf. his *Ezekiel 1–20* 315) has interpreted both vv 9 and 17 as a(n unfulfilled) forecast that Nebuchadnezzar would need only a small army to defeat Zedekiah: (1) פרעה "Pharaoh" is secondary, introduced to overcome the difficulty that a large Babylonian army and a drawn-out siege proved necessary, and referring after the event to Hophra's weak and futile campaign against Nebuchadnezzar; (2) אות־ עשה always means "deal hostilely with" in Ezekiel (7:27; 16:59; 22:14; 39:24; and esp. 23:25, 29), whereas את־ עשה is used for a friendly sense, in 20:44; and (3) as in v 9, ולא "and not" must negate the following adverbial phrases, and not the verb, as it is generally understood. This last point is a good one. The second point has the value of a supporting argument: in Jer 21:2 אות־ עשה has a friendly meaning. Unconvincing attempts have been made to create an unambiguously positive verb. Rothstein (913), following H. Graetz, emended to יושיע "will save," while Driver (*Bib* 35 [1954] 153), followed by the REB, found a supposed Arab. cognate for a stem עשה meaning "protect." As to the source of the evidently intrusive פרעה "Pharaoh," it is perhaps best explained as a comparative gloss supplying a subj for the verb. The annotator confused the רב עם "large army" of v 9 with that desired from Egypt in v 15, misled by the ambiguity of the verbal phrase (cf. Kraetzschmar 160). See the *Comment*.

18.a. McCarthy (*Bib* 61 [1980] 337) observes that הנה "behold" has a concessive sense.

19.a. The suffixes have a loosely objective force, "the oath sworn to me" and "the treaty in which I was invoked as witness" (Ehrlich, *Randglossen* 5:94).

19.b. For the form of the verb, see GKC 67v.

19.c. Heb. ונתתיו "and I will put it (on his head)" loosely employs a masc suffix after two fem antecedents (Smend 112; Greenberg 316). The suffixless emendation ונתתי "and I will put" (Wevers 138) seems to have been anticipated in ancient times: the marginal variant was eased into the text at a suitable point, in v 22, as a quasi-counterpart to the verb in v 5.

20.a. So rightly the NIV here and in 19:8. See *Note* 12:13.a. and *Comment* on 12:13.

20.b. For the acc, see Cooke 193; Greenberg 316. The seeming parallel in 1 Sam 12:7 is textually uncertain. Did על "for" fall out by partial haplography (cf. *BHS*)?

20.c. The LXX* lacks v 20b and also the first phrase of v 21. The error probably occurred within the Gr. tradition, by parablepsis (αὐτοῦ/αὐτοῦ "his"). Removing this material (Cornill 278; et al.) leaves יפלו "(they) will fall" without a pl subj. Fohrer (95), Cooke (190), and Zimmerli (358) accordingly read וכל "and all" in place of בכל "in all," as in the second phrase in 12:14. Cornill observed that this material does not correspond to anything in the allegory, but Bertholet ([1897] 94) retorted that vv 19–21 go beyond the allegory with a further statement, including Yahweh's spreading his net.

21.a. Blau (*VT* 4 [1954] 9) regarded את as an object sign, with the subj perceived as a sort of object, after the niph verb in v 20. It is more likely that it introduces the subj, as in 43:3. Cf. Rooker, *Biblical Hebrew* 88–90. K מברחו (sg) and Q מברחיו (pl) represent a *hapax legomenon* meaning "fugitives," which Σ ΘVg support. 'A and many MSS imply מבחריו "his choice troops," with a pl form as in Dan 11:15; the sg occurs in Ezek 23:7; 24:4–5; 31:16. The Syr "his nobles" and the Tg "his valiant men" also point in the latter direction. Barthélemy (*Critique* 3:122) considers the MT to be the primary reading, before assimilation to a more common term occurred. However, the context requires a word for regular soldiers in v 21aα and then a reference to fugitives in v 21aβ (Zimmerli 358).

21.b. See *Note* 12:14.b.

22.a. For the initial *waw* "and" after the messenger formula, see *Note* 11:17.a.

22.b. The LXX* lacks an equivalent for הרמה "high." The argument that no adj occurs in v 3 (Cornill 278) is not compelling: poetry is typically more succinct than prose. More significantly, LXX* Syr do not represent the MT ונתתי "and I will give," which is "unwanted" (Greenberg 316; cf. 319): see *Note* 19.b. above. It anticipates "and I will plant" in the sequel. It spoils the chiastic order, which seems to deliberately imitate the line in vv 3bβ–4a (cf. Hossfeld, *Untersuchungen* 72).

22.c. LXX* Syr overlook רך "tender," with which יונק "shoot" is to be understood from the preceding noun (Hitzig 120). Cornill (278) conjectured that ἁπαλόν (= 'A Σ Θ) "tender" fell out of the Gr. text after αὐτῶν and before ἀποκνιῶ.

22.d. The LXX* adds καρδίας "heartwood," a misplaced gloss on צמרת "crown". Σ, whose work is not extant here, so rendered in 31:14 and used the synonymous ἐγκάρδιον in v 3 and 31:10. The addition is clearly the product of prehexaplaric revision.

23.a. The MT כל־כנף צפור כל "all birds of every kind [lit. 'wing']" occurs in Gen 7:14 and, without the initial כל "all," in Ezek 39:4, 17. LXX^{AC} implies כל חיה וכל כנף "every beast, and every bird [lit. 'wing']," whereas the LXX*, represented by B 967, and LXX^{OL} reflect the MT, in line with 'A Σ Θ. Again the LXX* has been subject to prehexaplaric revision. Cornill (278) and others, including the RSV, have adopted the variant, observing that birds do not live under trees. Barthélemy (*Critique* 125–26), alert to this objection, has proposed making a break after תחתיו "beneath it" and taking the preceding verb as indefinite, so that the birds are excluded. He regards the early LXX reading as a case of assimilation to the frequent pair "beast-bird." His expedient is artificial and creates an unbalanced pair of clauses, while the variant yields a fine chiastic arrangement (ABC/CBA). Chiasm is a feature of this oracle: two instances have occurred in vv 22aβ–23aα. Probably צפור כל־כנף "bird of every kind" originated as a comparative gloss that was wrongly taken as a correction of חיה וכל כנף "beast and every bird."

23.b. The LXX* has extra material that originated in a Heb. comparative gloss בצלו ישבו "in its shade they will dwell," derived from 31:6. The verb was rendered "be restored," as if from שוב, under the influence of 16:55.

24.a. The final *waw* with weak pf closes a series of parallel, juxtaposed verbs (cf. Joüon 118k).

Form/Structure/Setting

Chap. 17 begins with a message-reception formula that launches a new literary unit. The contents of the chapter are marked by thematic continuity and development, so that the new formula that occurs in 18:1 signals that the former unit consists of chap. 17. In fact, an intervening formula occurs in 17:11, but this has a secondary role of separating interpretation from a previous allegory, as in 21:6(1) after 21:1–5(20:45–49). One may compare its occurrence with interpretation of a sign-act, in 12:8 after 12:1–7 and in 24:20 after 24:15–19. Although there are good reasons for regarding chap. 17 as a literary unit, there are even better ones, which will eventually emerge, for envisioning an overarching unit of chaps. 17–19.

The first of the three pieces in this unit (vv 2–10) is an allegory about two eagles, a cedar, and a grapevine. It is thus a fable, a story in which animals and plants are invested with human characteristics and behavior. The genre was traditionally used as a political cartoon in order to either challenge leadership or affirm it (Judg 9:8–15; 2 Kgs 14:9; Solomon, "Fable" 121). In the overall two-part message of vv 2–10 + 11–21, it is used as an allegory, which is what מָשָׁל in v 2 means in the light of the detailed interpretation that follows. The metaphorical communication is also called a חִידָה or "riddle," not in a technical sense (see Judg 14:10–18) but loosely, as often in the OT, in the sense of a statement that requires elucidation, "whose essence was opaqueness, mystification, enigma" (McKane, *Proverbs* 267). Von Rabenau (*WZ* [1957/58] 1056–57) has found elements of a riddle in the question-and-answer format of vv 9–10 and in the paradox whereby the grapevine abandons its patron.

An initial messenger formula in v 3 has a counterpart in v 9, which also serves to push to the fore the addressees mentioned in v 2. The phenomenon of a doubled messenger formula reminds the reader of a bipartite oracle of judgment, in which accusation and punishment are so demarcated. This impression is supported by a switch from past narrative in vv 3–8 to future consequences, presented largely in the form of questions, in vv 9–10.

The first piece is most probably to be regarded as poetry, as it is laid out in *BHS*. It begins after the messenger formula in v 3; the corresponding introductory material in v 9a, rather strangely including the brief initial question, lies outside the rhythmical scheme. Greenberg's metrical analysis (318) may largely stand, except that the first line in v 6 seems to have a 3 + 3 meter, while the third line in v 7 is 2 + 2 + 2, and v 9b may be defined as 3 + 3, 4 + 4 + 3. Hals (115) prefers to call this material elevated prose, and certainly the difficulty of analyzing vv 9–10 makes one sympathize with this viewpoint. The poem mostly uses 3 + 3 bicola and 2 + 2 + 2 tricola.

The second piece, in vv 11–21, reverts to prose. It has the genre of a tripartite proof saying. The expanded recognition formula in v 21b is preceded by a forecast of divine punishment in vv 19–20, with accompanying human consequences in v 21a. The forecast duly opens with a telltale "therefore," which is followed by a divine oath. One expects to find a corresponding accusation in the initial block of material, vv 12–18. In fact, vv 15b–18 already deal with future human consequences, which are reinforced with an oath and a divine-saying formula in v 16. Past narrative, obviously accusation, occurs in vv 12–15a, after instructions to the prophet to direct a question to the exiles about the meaning of the fable. Is the deviation from a straightforward oracle of judgment due to the other role of the piece as interpretation of the allegory? Yes, there is a close relationship between the two pieces, and the second is tightly controlled by the first. There is consecutive parallelism between the pieces, with correspondence as follows: vv 3aα²–4/

12b, 5/13, 6/14, 7–8/15a, 9/15b–17, and 10/18–21a. The interpretation does not finish at v 15, as many commentators have considered. Details will emerge in the *Comment.* For now it may be observed that, while the form-critical division of vv 12–21 occurs between v 18 and v 19, from a rhetorical perspective the interpretive piece divides after v 17.

The third message, in vv 22–24, is an oracle of salvation that reuses the imagery of the initial poem in a positive sense. Introduced merely by a messenger formula, it is appended to the previous material and presupposes it. It has the form of a positive proof saying, as its extended recognition formula in v 24a indicates. It closes with a formula of affirmation. The echoes of vv 3–10 in this final oracle round off the chapter and provide it with an inclusion (cf. Parunak, "Structural Studies" 270–71; id., *Bib* 62 [1981] 167, who, however, goes further and analyzes the chapter as a chiasm; Parunak also found structural significance in the emphasis on Yahweh in vv 19–21 and 22–24 ["Structural Studies" 274], which Greenberg [320] developed).

The original settings of the three pieces are diverse. The first two oracles are clearly contemporary with each other. If the metaphorical and interpretive oracles of 21:1–10(20:45–21:5) are contemporaneous (Zimmerli 422), surely this pair of oracles is. The "cryptic" allegory could hardly have stood by itself, especially with its false clue of an ostensible reference to Canaan in v 4; Simian-Yofre (*Bib* 65 [1984] 33–40) has detailed the ambiguities of the fable. Evidently Zedekiah was already set on rebelling against Babylon and had appealed to Egypt for military help. Babylonian reprisal, including the siege that began in January 588, lay in a predicted future. Vv 16, 20, and 21 are echoed in the slightly later, but still pre-fall, oracle of 12:2–16; there seems to be no compelling reason to regard these verses as composed after the event. Nor does the proposal to regard vv 16–18 as a "prose" addition (Rothstein 913 and many) commend itself: the context does not appear to be poetry. The material is substantially interlocked into the symmetrical structuring. To delete it would leave a gaping hole (cf. Lang, *Kein Aufstand* 54; Laato, *Josiah* 158). Zimmerli (361) has observed that the description of Babylon in commercial terms reflects the experience of the Judean deportees of 597. The addressees are "the rebellious community" (v 12), the exilic representatives of "the community of Israel" (v 2) among whom Ezekiel exercised his ministry of judgment (cf. 2:5; 12:9).

The third oracle is a literary continuation of the first pair. It reflects a post-587 switch to a positive message for the exiles, now that divine judgment had done its worst. In principle it could be credited either to Ezekiel or to his exilic redactors. The royal eschatological content aligns with 34:23–24; 37:24–25, which (except for 37:24a) are to be assigned to Ezekiel's school (see Allen, *Ezekiel 20–48* 160, 163–64, 191–95). Accordingly, this piece too seems to be a late redaction that crowns the earlier messages of judgment for Judah's last monarch with the good news of God's future grace to the house of David.

The unit falls into the following divisions:

17:1–10	A fable about two eagles, a cedar, and a grapevine
17:3–4	The eagle's removal of a cedar shoot
17:5–8	The grapevine's attraction to a rival eagle
17:9–10	The eagle's likely response

Comment

2–3aα¹/12a Ezekiel is instructed to transmit to the deported representatives of Israel a "riddle" and an "allegory." Riddles excite the curiosity and leave the baffled listeners keen for an answer. What follows is not a true riddle but a fable or theological cartoon that is equally intended to whet the hearers' appetites for the plain oracle that follows. At the head of that oracle the exiles are called, as often, "a rebellious community." The nuance is that spelled out in 12:2, their lack of understanding of Ezekiel's message: "they have ears to hear with but hear nothing." The allegory and the accompanying interpretation are an attempt to penetrate their willful deafness to the prophetic word. The taunting question is like the question-and-answer format that links commands to carry out sign-acts and their interpretations elsewhere in the book (12:9–11; 21:12; 24:19–21; 37:18–19). The repeated instruction to "tell" allows an interval for the audience to reflect on what the fable might mean (Greenberg 314).

3aα²–4/12b The term נשר may refer to either the vulture or the eagle. The abundance of feathers rules out the former, which has a bare neck and head. The coloring points to the golden eagle, which has yellow neck feathers (Greenberg 310). Herrmann (106) suggested that reminiscence of a Mesopotamian colored relief or sculpture underlies the description. The golden eagle, with a wing span up to six or seven feet wide in flight (Brownlee 262), is indeed a "great" bird. This veritable king of birds comes to Lebanon, to engage with a majestic cedar. It seizes a shoot and carries it off to a place known for its commerce. The interpretation of this puzzle, echoing the coming, taking, and bringing of the allegory, calls to mind Nebuchadnezzar's campaign against Jerusalem in 597 and his deportation of the eighteen-year-old king Jehoiachin and also his court to Babylon (see 2 Kgs 24:10–12). Evidently the cedar stands for the Davidic line and Lebanon for its mountain capital.

5/13 The eagle provides a local replacement, which it nurtures from seed to plant (cf. Deut 22:9; Jer 2:21), from seedbed to a well-watered permanent site. The interpretation picks up the detail of taking and, dividing זרע הארץ "the seed of the land" into two clauses, it narrates the appointing of Zedekiah, who was royal "seed," and the making of a treaty with him and "the leaders of the land." The treaty is clearly viewed as beneficial for Judah, a vehicle of stability and opportunity. The mention of an oath alongside the treaty initiates an emphasis that will also appear in vv 16, 18, and 19. It refers to a religious oath of fidelity that a vassal took to his overlord, exposing himself to curses if he reneged. Both terms have Akkadian counterparts. "Treaty" (ברית) corresponds to *adê*, an agreement drawn up in writing by an overlord and imposed on his vassal, who affirmed it with an "oath." This latter term (אלה) is matched by *māmītu* or *tāmītu*, the vassal-oath which, if broken, became an active curse (Frankena, *OTS* 14 [1965] 134–38).

6/14 The eagle's long-term purpose is now presented, in terms of growth, subordination, and loyalty. The plant, a sprawling grapevine, lives up to the eagle's intent with respect to its growth. The interpretation focuses on the purpose and ignores the partial fulfillment. The phrase שְׁפְלַת קוֹמָה "low in stature" is echoed in שְׁפָלָה "lowly" and elaborated in terms of not rising in rebellion. The role of Judah as a vassal kingdom thus comes to the fore; mention of the binding covenant also recalls the assets accruing to Judah as a vassal state of the Babylonian empire. Why is Zedekiah, as representative of the kingdom, described as a grapevine, while his predecessor was a cedar shoot? It possibly reflects Zedekiah's subordinate status, over against Jehoiachin's initial independence. Zedekiah, though son of Josiah, was Nebuchadnezzar's nominee; the natural royal descent flowed through Josiah's firstborn Jehoiakim to his son Jehoiachin.

7–8/15a Hitherto the eagle has been the active agent, and the plant has been the object of its care, only growing as plants do. Now the grapevine develops a mind and activity of its own and gravitates toward a rival eagle, which is somewhat damned by faint praise and by its inactivity, whereby Ezekiel plays down its significance (Brownlee 265). It turns about, in search of more water. V 8 pauses to reflect on the reasoning behind the move. Surely all its needs had been met. Yes, but the grapevine chafed at its enforced lowliness. It wanted to become "magnificent," a high vine on stakes (cf. 1 Kgs 5:5[4:25]) and to grow independently of its master. In the interpretation, the "sending out" (שִׁלְחָה) of branches toward the other eagle is reflected in the "sending" (לִשְׁלֹחַ) of envoys to Egypt. The venture is defined as Zedekiah's act of rebellion, in violation of v 14. The water sought by the grapevine is defined as "horses and a large army," presumably as allied or mercenary forces to aid in resisting Babylonian reprisals for the rebellion of its satellite. Ezekiel is here the heir of Isaiah, who in God's name condemned the anti-Assyrian party at Hezekiah's court who futilely put their faith in Egypt's horses and chariots galore (Isa 31:1–3).

9/15b–17 The fable pauses before continuing in a different vein. The pause, which splits the story into two distinct parts, vv 3–8 and 9–10, is marked by a fresh call to speak God's message, repeated from v 3. The fable turns from past narration and begins to ponder on the poor prospects of the ambitious grapevine. Questions now bombard the hearers (and readers), challenging them to become involved in the issue and to share the prophet's concern, as in chap. 15 (cf. Isa 5:4). The question "Will it flourish?" receives an answer, a long negative counterquestion relating to its fate at the claws of the offended eagle. No more growth for the grapevine: it would lose its roots, fruit, and leaves. Loss of root and fruit is an idiom for total destruction: see Amos 2:9. The allegory, like that in chap. 16 at times, briefly slips from its encoded form into plain reality in contemplating the military ease with which the renegade grapevine would be destroyed.

The interpretation of v 9 in vv 15b–17 begins by repeating the initial question, "Will it/he flourish?" though English idiom now prefers "succeed." It repeats the question in shocked tones, paraphrasing it with two separate questions that raise the prospect of failure for an enterprise that constituted the breaking of a treaty. This expansion of the single question accords with a contrast between the fable and its interpretation, in the proportion of material each uses for the past and for the future. The fable devotes to the grapevine's likely fate only half the space it gives to its history. The interpretation leans heavily toward Zedekiah's doom, expressing it in over twice the amount of material used for past narration. The focus shifts to the punishment it predicts for the royal rebel. The notes of accusation introduced in v 15b correspond to the resumption of the accusation at the outset of the pronouncement of punishment in a judgment oracle, for example in 13:8. The breaking of the covenant mentioned in vv 13–14 initiates a motif to be repeated in vv 16, 18, and 19.

The barrage of ominous questions in v 9bα is introduced by הֲלוֹא "Will not?" a combination of interrogative and negative particles. In 26:15 it introduces the human consequences of divine punishment in a lament type of oracle of judgment. In Hebrew it can idiomatically represent an affirmation (GKC 150e). Not surprisingly, then, it is matched in v 16 by אִם־לֹא "if not, surely," in an oath, after the swearing formula חַי־אָנִי "as I live." Yahweh guarantees Zedekiah's punishment at the hands of Nebuchadnezzar his patron. Roots, fruit, and fresh leaves grown at the eagle's behest are equated with the overlord's gift of kingship and treaty rights, to which Zedekiah had willingly rendered his oath. Now the curses of that oath begin to operate, triggered by his breach of promise. The accusation leveled in the course of v 15b is mentioned once more, with the added factor of the oath of v 13. Both its mention and its position before the treaty fit the new context of Yahweh's curse. The uprooting of the grapevine is equated with deportation to Babylon. The shriveling of its top growth becomes Zedekiah's payment for his perfidy with his life, a punishment that Ezekiel was to repeat in 12:13.

V 17 clearly corresponds to v 9bβγ, as the approximate resumption of its first five words indicates. The problem is that v 9 transparently looks ahead to Nebuchadnezzar's military reaction, while v 17 in the MT refers to Egypt's failure to give Zedekiah the help he had asked for in v 15. This cannot be right, especially in view of the tight correspondence between the fable and its elucidation in other respects. Either in v 9 or in v 17 some adjustment has to be made. Cornill (275) tried to read a reference to Pharaoh into v 9, following the medieval exegetes Kimchi and Rashi, but unconvincingly. A more popular expedient, initiated by Toy (130), has been to delete the military reference of v 9bβ as an intrusion from v 17. However, there is no intrinsic reason for omitting the five words, and one would have expected exact repetition of v 17 in a gloss. The deviation in wording supports its authenticity. The fault must lie in v 17, in the intrusion of פַּרְעֹה "Pharaoh" (see Note 17.a.). Then the reference is, as expected, to Nebuchadnezzar's retaliatory campaign. In the light of the long siege, the anticipated swift capture of Jerusalem turned out to be a rhetorical flourish. Egyptian military aid did cause a temporary Babylonian withdrawal (see Jer 37:5), and doubtless, the glossator had this in mind in adding "Pharaoh." The text itself does envision a siege, describing it as in 4:2 (see the Comment there); 21:27(22). The loss of many (רַבּוֹת) Judean lives ironically counterpoints the not large (רַב) army required and enhances the notion of an overwhelming defeat. The siege and its consequent casualties are a military translation of pulling up the grapevine, roots and all, in v 9.

10/18–21a   The fable warns against drawing a wrong conclusion from the present impunity of the renegade grapevine. The eagle was not its only enemy. Its fate would be sealed by a mysterious new factor, the east wind, which would accelerate the shriveling threatened earlier, in v 9. The interpretation replaces the query as to the grapevine's prospects with a statement of nonimpunity, which had been used in the elucidation at v 15. The accusation leveled there is pushed to the fore: the enormity of Zedekiah's guilt leaves open no other future for him.

His guilt is accentuated by mention of the initial gesture that pledged his allegiance and cooperation (cf. 2 Kgs 10:15; 1 Chr 29:24). The repetition of הנה "behold" (v 10) in v 18 draws a parallel between Nebuchadnezzar's beneficence and Zedekiah's happy acquiescence before he rebelled.

As in v 16, the basic הלוא "will not?" is replaced by אם־לא "if not, surely" in a divine oath. Now, however, the thought implicit in v 16 is expressed. Yahweh's oaths trigger a realization of the self-imposed curses in Zedekiah's oath. The treaty had been made before Yahweh as witness, and so Yahweh would hold him responsible for it. The oath had been sworn to Yahweh, and so he would act as its guarantor. In seeming dependence on this text, 2 Chr 36:13 states that Zedekiah rebelled against Nebuchadnezzar, "who had made him swear by God." Neo-Babylonian vassal treaties have not been preserved. Neo-Assyrian treaties made with subject states in the west did include an oath made by the vassal king, not only to the gods of the overlord but also to his own. Laato (*Josiah* 160–61) has drawn attention to a number of vassal treaties of this kind. Esarhaddon's treaty with Baal, king of Tyre, mentions after the Assyrian gods the gods of Tyre, to whom are assigned deportation of the people and destruction of the country in case of infidelity (see *ANET* 534a). Ashurbanipal's treaty with the Arab tribe of Qedar invokes Asshur and the gods of Qedar (see Grayson, *JCS* 39 [1987] 147–50). The treaty between Ashurnirari V and Mati'ilu of Arpad lists among the invoked gods "Adad of Alep" (see *ANET* 533b). It is reasonable to assume that this custom was maintained in the succeeding empire.

Greenberg's attempt (322) to differentiate between the treaty and oath of v 18 and those of v 19, seeing in the latter a reference to the covenant between Yahweh and Israel, overlooks the close connection between vv 18 and 19 indicated by their common relation to v 10. His appeal to 16:59 confuses two distinct passages and the relation between them. The language of v 19 is comparable to the description of the agreement between Jonathan and David (1 Sam 18:1–4) as "a covenant of Yahweh" (1 Sam 20:8). V 19 only expresses what the growing emphasis on Zedekiah's oath in vv 16 and 18 inferred, that Yahweh was to take seriously his invoked role as divine guarantor of the treaty. The conjunction לכן "therefore" at the head of v 19 draws an immediate conclusion from the accusations made in v 18 (cf. 16:37). The messenger formula is a belated counterpart to the one in v 9, held over because it fits better the present statement of Yahweh's holding Zedekiah responsible. What is said in v 19 could logically also have been said in v 16. The option to put it here is determined by Yahweh's personal involvement avowed in vv 20–21, to which it is an excellent introduction. The east wind of v 10 is an instrument of Yahweh's will. Greenberg (313–14) appeals to Hos 13:15, where the east wind is called "the wind of Yahweh," and to Exod 10:13; 14:21; Ps 78:26, whereas Zimmerli (364) invokes Ps 104:4. V 19 interprets it in precisely this way. Thereby the verdict of some scholars (Rothstein 912; et al., including Zimmerli 363) that v 10 is an alien addition to the poem, perhaps inspired by 19:12, is shown to be misguided (cf. too Lang, *Kein Aufstand* 45–46).

The pronouncement of divine punishment is neatly framed by the same verb, ופרשׂתי "and I will spread out" and יפרשׂ "will be scattered" (Greenberg 316). V 20 restates from a divine perspective v 16 (= 9ba) rather than specifically interpreting v 10ba, but both basic verses have to do with destruction. The capture of Zedekiah by the divine hunter (see 12:13 and the *Comment*) could well link with the touch of the east wind, while the shriveling of the grapevine hints at the fatal outcome of his trial. Zedekiah was actually investigated at Riblah (2 Kgs 25:6), which at least shows that v 10 is not a prophecy after the event (Kraetzschmar 156). Zedekiah's divine capture and death in Babylon are reaffirmed from vv 16 and 20 in 12:13. The description of the royal offense as infringement of Yahweh's rights (מעל) refers to its specific sense as oath violation, if J. Milgrom's thesis is correct (*JAOS* 96 [1976] 237–38). The focus on the fate of Zedekiah's army back in Judah accords with the bed of the grapevine in v 10bβ. The grim prospect of death in combat for the élite troops and rout for the demoralized remainder is repeated loosely in 12:14 to a constituency who had not listened the first time the message was delivered.

21b The intent of this first pair of messages was to lay out a sketch of Zedekiah's just fate before the Judean hostages in Babylon. If this "rebellious community" (v 12) was loath to listen, its realization would finally prove that the fate had emanated from Yahweh, who controlled history by moral principles.

22–24 The text leaps over a chasm of darkness and continues on the far side with hardly a break in its stride. By now Ezekiel's grim word for the future had slipped into a verifying past, and everyone knew too well the truth of God's word of judgment. The last word had not yet been said concerning Israel's monarchy. The fable of vv 1–10 is revisited and extended to a new, positive meaning. The oracle is written in heightened prose that has poetic qualities.

22abα First, vv 3–4 deserved close reexamination: in fact, not only their terminology but their chiastic order is reproduced (cf. Hossfeld, *Untersuchungen* 72). There was a new message from Yahweh for God's people to hear, now an oracle of salvation rather than of judgment. Yahweh, who had stood behind Nebuchadnezzar as the Lord of history and worked out his moral purposes through him (vv 16–21), was to take over that great eagle's earlier role, directly intervening in Israel's affairs. He himself would pluck a tender shoot from the crown of the cedar. The Davidic dynasty that stood permanently under the promise of God (cf. 2 Sam 7; Ps 89) was to produce a scion who would come into his inheritance.

22bβ–23a Now v 8 is recycled. Its two distinct parts are treated together in a new whole. It had spoken about being planted on good, well-watered ground and about the prospect of producing branches, bearing fruit, and generally growing into a magnificent specimen. Yahweh too, in his plans for Israel, had such care and blessing in mind. He was to plant the cedar shoot on the "very high mountain" that Ezekiel had visited in his vision of the new temple (40:2), on "Israel's high mountain" where a returned Israel was to worship him (20:40; cf. too 34:14). Here, on Mount Zion, the cedar would realize the growth that had eluded rebellious Zedekiah. It or he—for none other than a new "David," God's faithful "servant" or vassal (34:24; 37:24–25), is in view—would develop the full potential of the divine promise. Gone would be the period of human vassalage, when the monarchy was reduced to a trailing vine (v 6): a majestic cedar would take its place. In the phrases about the fruit and branches, the verbs of v 8 are inverted, as is common in quotation (cf. Talmon, *Qumran* 361–62). We need not cavil at the idea of a cedar producing fruit. As in Hos 14:9(8), biblical metaphor exercises the privilege of transcending natural realities.

23b Much of the language is derived from 31:6–7. The link with chap. 31 was doubtless made through (the already redactional) 19:11a–b, which depends on

31:3, 5, 9, and 10. Zedekiah's attempts to be independent of Babylon were like the Pharaoh Hophra's aspirations to become a cosmic tree, a Babel-like ambition that was doomed to fail. Here the ancient myth of the cosmic tree is reused in its original positive connotation. The motif "presents the living world as an enormous tree with its roots in the subterranean deep and its top in the clouds, a shelter for every living being" (Allen, *Ezekiel 20–48* 125). The application to royal eschatology, which was facilitated by its attribution to Pharaoh in chap. 31, draws on previous prophetic illustration of the future of the Davidic monarchy in terms of a tree, in Isa 11:1 and Jer 23:5; 33:15 (and later in Zech 3:8; 6:12). The effect is to recall the promises of worldwide rule in the royal psalms (Pss 2:8; 72:8; 89:26[25]; cf. Zech 9:10) and to project them into the eschatological future.

24   The nations have a double role in vv 23–24 (cf. Herrmann 107): here they feature as "all the trees in the countryside." Their description and reaction are an adaptation of 31:15, where they mourn in shock at the cutting down of the Egyptian cosmic tree. The recognition by the other nations that Yahweh has been at work implies not a positive vision of their conversion but an emphatic statement of Yahweh's supremacy, which convinces them against their will (cf. Joyce, *Divine Initiative* 94–97). The expanded recognition formula majors in a claim of the sovereignty of Yahweh. The terminology is taken from the fable. "Low" (שׁפל) comes from v 8, and "shriveled" (יבשׁ) from vv 9–10. Nor should we overlook a contribution from chap. 19: "high" (גבה) seems to echo 19:11, and the verb "shrivel" (הובישׁ) the action of the east wind in 19:12a. Once this perspective is broached, one notices other links with chap. 19: יבשׁ "shriveled" also occurs in 19:12b, while in vv 22–23 שׁתל "plant" occurs in 19:10, 13, and ענף "branches" and פרי "fruit" seem to recall פריה וענפה "fruitful and branched" in 19:10. This is a factor that will repay consideration when we study chap. 19. 21:33 (20:47) has some similarity, but the context is quite different. The interpretation of Hölscher (*Dichter* 102) and Greenberg (317) is surely right, that the reference throughout is to the Davidic line. The perfect tenses of the verbs lend it support, and Greenberg compares the identical objects of contrasted verbs in Deut 32:39. The God who was responsible for destroying the monarchy, on the lines of 17:8–10 and 19:11–12, would restore it. This brief vignette of judgment and salvation fittingly sums up the double message of the literary unit. The oracle is capped with a formula of affirmation (cf. 36:36), one triumphantly longer than the one incorporated in the recognition formula of v 21. What might seem unlikely to happen on the human plane was guaranteed by God's pledge. In fact, the humiliating destruction he had accomplished, in fulfillment of his word, brought its own confirmation of his providential power to restore and glorify.

Explanation

This chapter looks both backward and forward from the standpoint of the exile. Its readers also have the benefit of appreciating Ezekiel's anti-Egyptian oracles in chaps. 29–32, which were probably all uttered later than the first pair of oracles in the present chapter. What the prophet first proclaimed amid the hurly-burly of conflicting politics, concerning the respective rights and prospects of rival kings and strategic possibilities, was now an indisputable fact. The dust had settled, leaving the Judean scene desolate and the royal palace debris. The consequences of Zedekiah's folly in claiming independence with Egypt's help were a matter of historical documentation in the chronicles of Babylon. Ezekiel, however, found a higher agenda. Zedekiah, in breaking his vassal oath to Nebuchadnezzar, had invited retribution from Yahweh, in whose name he had made it. So Yahweh had decreed Zedekiah's downfall and masterminded Babylonian reprisals, working out the very curses Zedekiah earlier recited with invocation of his listening God.

This interpretation of the tragedy of Judah's destruction, monarchy and all, opened the door to a positive future, to which earlier royal and prophetic hopes lent credence. Moreover, appeal could be made to Israel's traditional hymnic declaration of Yahweh's sovereign power of reversal, that he both brings low and sets high (1 Sam 2:7; Pss 75:8[7]; 147:6; cf. Luke 1:52). Those who looked to the past with disappointment are bidden to look upward and onward in expectation of a new "David" whose world rule under God would be "for ever" (37:25). According to Mark 4:30–32, Jesus's call to faith in the greatness of God's coming kingdom, despite its small beginnings, fittingly echoed the cosmic cedar of v 23.

Living the Hope (18:1–32)

Bibliography

Geyer, J. B. "Ezekiel 18 and a Hittite Treaty of Muršiliš II." *JSOT* 12 (1979) 31–46. **Graffy, A.** *A Prophet Confronts His People.* AnBib 104. Rome: Biblical Institute, 1984. 58–64. **Gross, H.** "Umkehr im Alten Testament in der Sicht der Propheten Jeremia und Ezechiel." In *Zeichen des Glaubens.* FS B. Fischer, ed. H. Auf der Maur and B. Kleinheyer. Zürich: Benziger, 1972. 19–28. **Hals, R. M.** "Methods of Interpretation: Old Testament Texts." In *Studies in Lutheran Hermeneutics,* ed. J. Reumann et al. Philadelphia: Fortress, 1979. 271–82. **Hutton, R. R.** "Declaratory Formulae: Forms of Authoritative Pronouncement in Ancient Israel." Diss., Claremont, 1983. **Joyce, P.** *Divine Initiative and Human Response in Ezekiel.* JSOTSup 51. Sheffield: JSOT, 1989. **Junker, H.** "Ein Kernstück der Predigt Ezechiels: Studie über Ez 18." *BZ* 7 (1963) 173–85. **Kilpp, N.** "Eine frühe Interpretation der Katastrophe von 587." *ZAW* 97 (1985) 210–20. **Lescow, T.** "Die dreistufige Tora: Beobachtungen zu einer Form." *ZAW* 82 (1970) 362–79. ———. *Das Stufenschema: Untersuchungen zur Struktur alttestamentlicher Texte.* BZAW 211. Berlin: de Gruyter, 1992. **Lindars, B.** "Ezekiel and Individual Responsibility." *VT* 15 (1965) 452–67. **Matties, G. H.** *Ezekiel 18 and the Rhetoric of Moral Discourse.* SBLDS 126. Atlanta: Scholars Press, 1990. **Milgrom, J.** *The Encroacher and the Levite: The Term ʿAboda.* Studies in Levitical Terminology 1. Berkeley: University of California, 1970. ———. *Cult and Conscience.* Leiden: Brill, 1976. **Nunes Carreira, J.** "Raizes da linguagem profética de Ezequiel: A propósito de Ez 18,5–9" *EstBib* 26 (1967) 275–86. **Rad, G. von.** "Faith Reckoned as Righteousness"; "'Righteousness' and 'Life' in the Cultic Language of the Psalms." In *The Problem of the Hexateuch and Other Essays,* tr. E. W. Trueman Dicken. Edinburgh: Oliver and Boyd, 1966. 125–30, 243–66. **Raitt, T. M.** "The Prophetic Summons to Repentance." *ZAW* 83 (1971) 30–49. **Sakenfeld, K. D.** "Ezekiel 18:25–32." *Int* 32 (1978) 295–300. **Schenker, A.** "Saure Trauben ohne Stumpfe Zaehne: Bedeutung und Tragweite von Ez 18 und 33.10–20 oder ein Kapitel alttestamentliche Moraltheologie." In *Mélanges D. Barthélemy.* OBO 38. Fribourg: Éditions Universitaires; Göttingen: Vandenhoeck & Ruprecht, 1981. 449–70 = *Text und Sinn im Alten Testament.* OBO 103, 1991. 97–118. **Schulz, H.** *Das Todesrecht im Alten Testament.* BZAW 114. Berlin: Töpelmann, 1969. **Tårnberg, K. A.** *Die prophetische Mahnrede.* FRLANT 143. Göttingen: Vandenhoeck & Ruprecht, 1987. 106–10. **Weinfeld, M.** "'Justice and Righteousness'—וצדקה משפט—the Expression and the Meaning." In *Justice and Righteousness: Biblical Themes and Their Influence,* ed. H. G. Reventlow and Y. Hoffman. JSOTSup 137. Sheffield: JSOT, 1992. 228–46. **Westbrook, R.** *Studies in Biblical and Cuneiform Law.* CahRB 26. Paris: Gabalda, 1988. **Wolff, H. W.** "Das Thema 'Umkehr' in der alttestamentliche Prophetie." *ZTK* 48 (1951) 129–48 = *Gesammelte Studien zum Alten Testament.* TBü 22. Munich: Kaiser, 1964. 130–50.

Translation

[1] *I received the following communication from Yahweh:* [2] *"What do you all*[a] *mean by using*[b] *this slogan about*[c] *the country of Israel, 'Parents*[d] *eat sour grapes, but their*[e] *children's teeth feel rough'?*[f] [3] *I swear by my very life, runs the oracle of the Lord*[a] *Yahweh, you will never again use*[b] *this slogan in Israel.* [4] *You see, every person stands in relation to me. The parent as a personal entity and the child as a personal entity relate to me in the same direct way.*[a] *It is the person who sins that will die.* [5] *But the case of a virtuous individual who acts justly and fairly is different.*[a] [6] *I mean one who has never*[a] *feasted on the mountains nor looked up to the idols worshiped by the community of Israel. He does not defile his neighbor's wife, nor does he approach*[b] *a woman during her period.*[c] [7] *He*

wrongs no one: he returns the pledge entrusted to him;[a] *he seizes no property. He gives his own food to the hungry and provides the naked with clothing.* [8] *He does not lend at interest by taking extra for a loan.*[a] *He has no hand in such wrongdoing; he practices honest justice in his dealings with his fellows.* [9] *He meets*[a] *my standards and keeps my rules, putting them*[b] *into practice. This is what it means to be virtuous.*[c] *Such an individual will certainly win life, runs the oracle of the Lord Yahweh.*

[10] *"Suppose he produces a son who is a ruffian*[a] *and a murderer, who commits each one*[b] *of these sins,* [11] *while his father*[a] *refrained from all of them.*[a] *He, however,*[b] *has feasted on the mountains. He defiles his neighbor's wife.* [12] *He wrongs the poor and needy: he seizes properties; he fails to return pledges. He looks up to those idols. He engages in a shocking practice,* [13] *in that he lends at interest by taking extra for a loan. Will such a person win life? He will not:*[a] *after engaging in such shocking practices, he must be put to death,*[b] *with nobody to blame but himself.* [14] *Just suppose he in turn produces a son who, seeing all the sins his father has committed, takes thought*[a] *and does not commit any such sins.* [15] *He has never feasted on the mountains nor looked up to the idols worshiped by the community of Israel. He does not defile his neighbor's wife.* [16] *He wrongs no one: he does not require a pledge, and he acquires nothing illegally. He gives his own food to the hungry and provides the naked with clothing.* [17] *He has no hand in wrongdoing,*[a] *such as requiring interest by taking extra for a loan. He puts my rules into practice and meets my standards. Such a person will not die for his father's iniquity: he will certainly win life.* [18] *In the case of his father, who cheated others of their legal rights and seized the property of fellow Israelites*[a] *and could do no good in his relations with his kinsfolk,*[b] *he had to die for his iniquity.* [19] *'Why,' you ask, 'didn't the son bear any*[a] *of the consequences of the father's iniquity?' His son has acted justly and fairly; he has met my standards and put them into practice, so he will certainly win life.* [20] *It is the person who sins that will die. A son won't bear any of the consequences of his*[a] *father's iniquity, nor will a father bear any of the consequences of his*[a] *son's iniquity. The virtuous will enjoy the consequences of their*[b] *virtue, while the wicked will suffer the consequences of their wickedness.*

[21] *"If, however, the wicked give up all the sins they used to commit and meet my standards and act justly and fairly, they will certainly win life; they will not die.* [22] *None of the rebel ways in which they engaged will be remembered against them.*[a] *Their virtuous behavior will guarantee them life.* [23] *Is the death*[a] *of the wicked what I really want? asks the Lord Yahweh's oracle. Don't I want them to give up their present behavior*[b] *and win life?* [24] *Correspondingly, if the virtuous give up their virtue and do wrong, committing all the same shocking practices as the wicked, will they win life?*[a] *None of the virtuous actions*[b] *they engaged in will be remembered. Their faithlessness and the sin they commit will mean their death.*

[25] *"'The Lord's*[a] *policy is inconsistent,'*[b] *you object. Just listen, community of Israel: Is it my policy that is not consistent? Isn't it rather your behavior that is inconsistent?* [26] *When the virtuous give up their virtue and do wrong, they will die on those grounds.*[a] *They will die for the wrong they have done.* [27] *Again, when the wicked give up the wickedness they used to engage in and act justly and fairly, they will secure their lives.* [28] *Having taken thought and given up all the rebel ways they used to practice, they will certainly gain life; they won't die.* [29] *But the community of Israel objects, 'The Lord's policy is inconsistent.' Is it my policy*[a] *that is not consistent, community of Israel? Isn't it your behavior that is inconsistent?*[b]

[30] *"So*[a] *I will judge you, community of Israel, each on the basis of your behavior, affirms the Lord Yahweh's oracle. Give up your rebel ways, do give them up,*[b] *or else iniquity will*

mean a tragic end for you.^c ³¹*Throw away all your acts of rebellion against me,*^a *and you will get*^b *for yourselves a new heart, a new spirit. Why die, community of Israel?* ³²*I don't want anyone's*^a *death, runs the Lord Yahweh's oracle. So give it all up, and you will gain life."*^b

Notes

2.a. "All" is added to the translation to indicate that the Heb. for "you" is pl.

2.b. The omission in the LXX (see *BHS*) reflects comparative assimilation to 12:22 (Cornill 279). For the Heb. construction with a verbal clause, cf. 1 Sam 11:5, here with ellipse of כי "that," as in Isa 3:15.

2.c. So the NIV renders; cf. NRSV "concerning." Cf. 12:22 and see the *Comment*. The LXX "in the sons of Israel" represents false assimilation to its *Vorlage* in 12:24.

2.d. Lit. "fathers" and later "sons," and similarly in v 4. In vv 5–20, a more literal translation is made, and masc pronouns can hardly be avoided.

2.e. Greenberg (327) has rightly observed that here and in v 20 the article has the force of a possessive pronoun, with reference to Joüon 137f.

2.f. Lit. "be blunt," used of an iron instrument. The verb is here used metaphorically, with reference to the rough acidic coating of the teeth.

3.a. For the formulaic use of אדני "Lord" in the divine-saying formula here and in vv 9, 23, 30, and 31, see *Note* 5:11.a.

3.b. The inf constr is unusually employed as subj of the verb to be: cf. Waltke, *Syntax* 36.2.1b. Cornill (279) and others have suggested repointing as a ptcp, in line with v 2, "anyone who uses," as Syr Tg imply.

4.a. The construction כ(ו) . . . . כ "like . . . (and) like" declares two terms to be identical in the same regard (Joüon 174i). The force of לי seems to be "relate to me": cf. Amos 9:7, "Are you not like the sons of the Ethiopians to me [לי]?" V 4aα must have the same meaning (cf. Davidson 126), rather than referring to Yahweh's lordship over all human life by right of creation. See the *Comment*.

5.a. Lit. "When an individual is righteous . . ." The Heb. construction of vv 5–9 is protasis (v 5a), parenthetical definition (vv 5b–9a), and apodosis (v 9b) (cf. Schulz, *Todesrecht* 168).

6.a. This rendering, borrowed from the REB, usefully encompasses a reference to the preexilic period of the lives of Ezekiel's hearers.

6.b. For the oscillation between pf in v 6abα and impf in vv 6bβ–8, see Joüon 112d n. 2.

6.c. The noun נדה "menstruation" stands in apposition to אשה "woman": see GKC 131c. Mishnaic Heb. has the same construction, doubtless borrowed from here. Ehrlich (*Randglossen* 5:66) suggested that the noun developed a concrete sense.

7.a. The MT חבלתו חוב "his pledge, a debt" exhibits an appositional construction of the type encountered in 16:27 (see GKC 131r), but it is here a more extreme case, in the sense of "his pledge given in conjunction with a debt." The LXX may imply חבלת(ה) חיב "the pledge of a debtor." It is hardly original, as Jahn (123) and Zimmerli (370) have claimed, but a secondary attempt to make sense of an awkward phrase. The Vg conflates the MT and the LXX. Probably חוב "debt" is itself an attempt to wrest sense from a relic חב, which represents a copyist's abandoned mistake whereby he was about to write חבל "he requires (a pledge)," with v 16a in mind. For subsequent elaboration of an abandoned error, see my explanation of והנחתי "and I will deposit" in 22:20, in *JSS* 31 (1986) 131–33; *Ezekiel 20–48* 32. The suffix on חבלתו is objective, "the pledge given to him."

8.a. Whether there is any difference between נשך and תרבית, which both denote interest of some kind, is a moot point. See Greenberg's discussion of possible meanings (330).

9.a. For the piel impf יהלך "he walks," one expects the standard qal pf הלך with the same sense, as we find in v 17 and as the parallel שמר "he keeps" suggests. Most probably after dittography of *yod* the verb had to be construed as a poetic piel.

9.b. In place of the MT אמת "(to do) truth," the LXX implies אתם "them," which fits the context better and is supported by v 19 (Ewald 277; et al.). The sequence משפט אמת יעשה אמת "justice of truth he does" in v 8b encouraged metathesis in the similar לעשות אתם . . . ומשפטי "and judgments . . . to do them." Even Barthélemy (*Critique* 3:127–28) so emends.

9.c. This clause is to be taken as a closing definition parallel to the opening v 5 (Greenberg 346–47) rather than as a declaratory formula (Zimmerli 376, 381). See the *Comment*.

10.a. So the NJPS renders.

10.b. The MT אח is hardly an exclamation, "alas," as it is in 6:11, nor does the sense "brother" fit. It is doubtless an abandoned attempt to write אחד "one," in place of מאחד "only one" (Greenberg 331). For the idiomatic מאחד with a partitive preposition, attested by 'A, see Cooke 203. The parallel כל־אלה "all these things" indicates that it means "each one," rather than "even one (of these things)," as if committing even one of these sins meant losing the status of righteousness, as Greenberg (340) takes it. Some MSS have a fem form, מאחת, in line with Lev 4:2; 5:13, but it is hardly necessary.

11.a. V 11a has been regarded as an inferior variant of v 10b by Bertholet ([1936] 64) and many. The Syr, which does not represent it, is notorious for passing over material it considered otiose. The LXX engages in paraphrase in vv 10b–11a. The pronoun הוא "he" refers to the father, as the subj of v 10a (Keil 252). Clearly in both v 10b and v 11a אלה "these" refers to sins or the like: cf. the similarly resumptive v 14a and also v 13b.

11.b. Heb. כי seems to be asseverative, while גם has an adversative force: "but surely" (cf. Ehrlich, Randglossen 5:67).

13.a. The LXX* "he surely (will not live)" seems to reflect clumsy assimilation to v 9 in its Vorlage, though pap. 967 omits the pronoun. The stylistic variation וחי "and will he live?" reappears in v 24. Cornill (281) rightly preferred the lively MT, comparing 17:15.

13.b. The pass verb, here with a sense of divine agency, is a survival of an old formulation, in the second part of which a human agent of death was exonerated of blame (Hitzig 125; Zimmerli 372, 384, with reference to Lev 20:9, 11, etc.). See the Comment. The variant ימות "he will die" brings into line with the rest of the chapter.

14.a. So von Orelli (71) and others have rendered here and in v 28: cf. BDB 907b. LXX Vg imply וירא "and he feared." Zimmerli (372) has noted that the latter verb occurs seldom in Ezekiel, whereas the former is very common. The nonrepresentation in the Syr seems to presuppose the MT, which it passes over as repetitious (Barthélemy, Critique 3:134).

17.a. Since Ewald (278), the MT מעני "from the poor" has generally been taken as an error for מעול "from wrongdoing," which the LXX implies, as in v 8. The clause in the MT clearly means "from (harming) the poor he turned his hand" (cf. 20:22), but it can hardly be right. The substituted noun may have originated as a comparative gloss relating v 16aa to the longer clause in v 12aa or relating v 17aβ to the interest-free loan to the poor in Exod 22:24(25). In the latter case a marginal מעני "from the poor" displaced מעול "from wrongdoing." In the former case עני "poor" displaced עול "wrongdoing."

18.a. Heb. אח "brother," in the sense of a fellow Israelite, is not attested by the LXX*, but the later עמיו "his kinsfolk" supports it (Barthélemy, Critique 3:128–32).

18.b. The MT עמיו "his kinsfolk" is an ancient term otherwise found in fixed formulas: see Greenberg 332. The LXX "my people" reflects haplography of waw, while Syr Vg Tg "his people" represents a simplification.

19.a. The preposition beth seems to be partitive here and in v 20 (Hitzig 125; et al.).

20.a. See Note 2.e. above.

20.b. It is more natural in English to render the sg references in vv 20–28 as pl. Moreover, it better reflects the fact that alternative types of behavior are in view, rather than the behavior of individuals.

22.a. The lamed expresses a dative of disadvantage. It recurs in the parallel 33:16.

23.a. The verb חפץ "take delight (in)" is construed either with a beth or with a direct object. The construction is mixed in this verse. A minority reading במות "in the death" probably reflects assimilation to v 32 and 33:11.

23.b. A sg noun is widely attested (see BHK, BHS), probably by assimilation to the parallel 33:11. The LXX adds an explanatory adj "wicked."

24.a. The Heb. וחי יעשה "(he) does, will he live?" is not represented in LXX* ("if he does" in pap. 967 [cf. Syh LXX^L] seems to be a prehexaplaric revision, perhaps from Σ) Syr. Since Cornill (282), the words have often been deleted as superfluous. However, Hitzig (126) observed that יעשה "he does" resumes ועשה "and does." It goes closely with . . . ככל "like all . . . ," as the accents indicate (cf. Toy 28). As for the question denying life, which echoes v 13, Eichrodt (234) noted that such an interim pronouncement at this point matches the sequence in vv 21–22, where nonremembrance of previous acts and a final pronouncement follow.

24.b. For the K/Q variation, see Note 33:13.b.

25.a. There is ancient support for the divine name (see BHS) here and in v 29, and also in the parallel 33:17, 20. It may have been replaced to avoid associating it with an offensive charge: cf. Zimmerli, Ezekiel 2 557.

25.b. The Heb. תכן, here in the niph, is commonly taken as "measure" and so here "be correct" (HALAT 1596b). Greenberg (333–34) regards the niph as tolerative, with the sense "(not) determinable" and so "erratic, arbitrary." Fishbane (*Biblical Interpretation* 338 n. 62) finds a similar sense, "acts without principle" (= REB).

26.a. The pl suffix is strange: it appears to refer to giving up virtue and doing wrong as two actions (cf. 33:18). The LXX* (= pap. 967, followed by LXX^L.) ἐν αὐτῷ "by it" simplified by relating to עול "wrong." In LXX^B etc. the phrase is moved to the last clause.

29.a. The noun and accompanying verb are pl, unlike vv 25abβ and 29a. The fault may lie with the verb. Did a variant or corrective pl יתכנו "are consistent," relating to the final verb, displace a sg form and cause a pl pointing of the noun? The sg forms in the LXX may so suggest; there, however, all the cases of דרך "way" in vv 25 and 29 appear in the sg.

29.b. The sg verb in the MT may simply denote lack of congruence due to its distance from its subj (cf. v 13bγ). However, a pl verb may have stood here (cf. *BHS*) and been textually confused with the verb dealt with in the preceding *Note.*

30.a. In the *Vorlage* of the LXX*, לכן "therefore" was overlooked after the similar ending of לתכן (Hitzig 127).

30.b. For the intransitive hiph here and in v 32, cf. 14:6 and *Note* 14:6.a.

30.c. There is more than one way of understanding v 30bβ: (1) "lest they be a stumbling block leading to iniquity" (cf. NJPS, NAB). This accords with the usage in 7:19; 44:12, with which 14:3, 4, 7 may be compared. Then the sg verb can be regarded as attracted to the predicate (Zimmerli 374) or even emended to a pl with the presumed support of the LXX (Cornill 284; et al.; cf. the Tg). Greenberg (334) understands lack of repentance as the implicit subj. This construing regards עון "iniquity" as genitive. However, the context does not favor temptation to sin, as the other contexts imply, but rather calamitous ruin. Accordingly, (2) "lest iniquity be your stumbling block" (Vg; cf. Syr; cf. NRSV, REB, NIV), which is how the Masoretic accentuation construes, is to be preferred, with "iniquity" as subj. It is significant that in the related 3:20; 33:12 the noun מכשול "stumbling block" and the cognate verb respectively are used with reference to a fatal fall.

31.a. The MT "with which [בם . . . אשר] you have rebelled" takes בם as resumptive. Barthélemy (*Critique* 3:137–38) has compared Ezra 10:13 for the style of the MT, but there no cognate noun is involved. One expects "(with) which you have rebelled against me [בי]" with an implicit cognate object, as in 1 Kgs 8:50 (cf. Jer 33:8; Zeph 3:11), as the LXX implies (Hitzig 127; et al.). Cf. the double cognate construction in v 24, where בם "because of them" goes with what follows: did בם arise from a mechanical comparison with v 24?

31.b. For עשה in the sense "acquire (property)," see 22:13; 28:4; 38:12. It is used with a reflexive ל "for (oneself)" in 28:4; Deut 8:17; 2 Sam 15:1; 1 Kgs 1:5. To take it as meaning "make" (BDB 794b) creates unnecessary tension with 11:19; 36:26. Both here and in v 32b the first impv functions as a condition, while the second presents the consequence that fulfillment of the condition will involve (cf. GKC 110f; Joüon 116f). Scholars have missed the construction here, but some have so construed v 32b, at least in their translations (e.g., "that ye may live," Keil 256). Raitt (*ZAW* 83 [1971] 35) has found a promise in the closing "and live." Hals (126) calls it "a motivation, actually a promise." The tension that has been found between the indicatives of the other passages and the impv here in v 31b (e.g., Zimmerli 386) is imaginary. Gaebelein (128–29) went so far as take v 31 as belonging to "the law dispensation" and 36:26 as reflecting "the dispensation of grace."

32.a. For the idiomatic use of the ptcp, see GKC 139d, 144e; Joüon 155h.

32.b. The LXX* shortens v 32, overlooking v 32b in the case of LXX^B and also the divine saying formula in pap. 967. The latter may be an idiosyncrasy: Ziegler (*LXX* 338) has observed that pap. 967 also omits this element in 32:32. Zimmerli (374) unfairly takes the formula as marking a conclusion: in the parallel v 23, it is asseverative (cf. Matties, *Ezekiel 18* 33 n. 35). V 32b is required by the structure of the passage (see the *Comment*). The omission of the imperatives may well be an inner-Greek phenomenon, the result of parablepsis from καί "and" to καί in 19:1.

Form/Structure/Setting

Chap. 18 is set apart as a literary piece by its introductory messenger-reception formula and by its quite different content in relation to chaps. 17 and 19. Consideration will need to be given later to its role in an overarching literary unit consisting of chaps. 17–19. Form-critically it is in general terms a prophetic version of a priestly ruling, as its postulating of cases and its legal terminology indicate. More precisely it is a complex disputation that culminates in an appeal for repentance. The latter feature, in vv 30–32, contains the typical elements of admonition, accusation, and promise (cf. 14:6–14 and see the comparative table in Raitt, *ZAW* 83 [1971] 35). As in chap. 14, it is integrated with a motivating oracle of judgment. Since vv 30–32 represent the intent of the oracle, Tårnberg (*Mahnrede* 110) prefers to call the chapter a complex oracle of admonition and to subordinate the other form-critical elements within that designation.

A disputation is made up of three elements, thesis, counterthesis, and dispute (D. F. Murray, *JSOT* 38 [1987] 95–121). Here the thesis is the slogan reported in v 2. A counterthesis appears in a double formulation at vv 4b–5a, 9ba²: "It is the person who sins that will die, but in the case that an individual is righteous, . . . he will certainly live" (Lescow, *Stufenschema* 18–20; cf. Ewald 277). Lescow noted the correlation of the pronouns הוא "he (will die)" and הוא "he (will live)," which binds together the short and amplified statements. One may draw attention to another factor, the presence of the divine-saying formula at the end of v 9, which demarcates vv 4–9 from what follows. We also have to reckon with a second, related counterthesis, again formulated in two contrasting parts: v 21, "In the case of a wicked individual's turning from all his sin . . . , he will certainly live," and v 24, "But when a righteous individual gives up his righteousness . . . , he will die."

The dispute occurs first in vv 3–4a, a theological denial of the thesis. It continues with vv 10–13 and 14–17, an elaboration framed as a further denial of the thesis, and with vv 18–20, restatements that incorporate an objecting question in v 19a. After the first part of the second counterthesis, v(v) 21(–22), a pair of lively questions appears in v 23. After the second part, an objection is countered with a pair of accusing questions (v 25). In vv 26–29 the second counterthesis is repeated in inverse order and amplified, and the objection of the prophet's constituency is opposed with the same pair of accusing questions as in v 25. The disputation ties well into the general appeal for repentance in vv 30–32. The motif of accusation is developed into a pronouncement of future judgment and then into a series of appeals that includes a further reference to Yahweh's benevolence. Form and content are blended well into a powerfully persuasive combination of argument, challenge, and invitation.

The basic unity of chap. 18 seems assured: the aim of the disputation lies in the closing summons. Fohrer (102), however, deduced from the change of theme at v 21 that two originally separate pieces have been combined. The issue partly depends on whether an underlying setting may be envisioned that necessitated two logically related countertheses. Graffy (*A Prophet Confronts* 58–64) argued on form-critical grounds that the disputation concludes at v 20. It may be asked, however, whether his own definition of a disputation has captured its basic structure or its versatility, especially in the light of Murray's research into the genre cited above. Graffy has also taken into account the overlap of chap. 18 material in chap. 33. He claims that vv 21–32 fit better in 33:10–20 and that the starkness of vv 1–20 invited the addition of a more auspicious message inspired by that passage. In fact, vv 21–32 appear to have been reused in chap. 33 and applied to two separate issues. 33:10–11 reflects material from 18:23, 30–32; it has been supplied with an introduction, the parable of the watchman. Its encouraging message is an opportunity to repent made possible by divine grace for the people who are now all too conscious of their sin. The rest of the material has been used in 33:12–

20 to yield a challenging message of the people's moral responsibility (see Allen, *Ezekiel 20–48* 142–48). This splitting of the content of chap. 18 gives the impression of secondary usage, doubtless at Ezekiel's hands, to fit different settings. In chap. 18 one might loosely say that vv 1–20 teach moral responsibility to the morally unaware, while vv 21–32 preach repentance.

As for the general setting of this oracle, its time and location are clearly exilic. Ezekiel and his constituency are addressed together in v 2. The constituency is defined not only as "Israel" (v 3) but as "the community of Israel" (בֵּית יִשְׂרָאֵל, vv 29–31), which elsewhere refers to the exiled representatives of the covenant nation (cf. 24:21; 36:17–22). The passages just mentioned refer respectively to the pre-fall group of hostages deported in 597 and to the post-fall exilic community. Which is in view here? One's first choice is the former, in view of the tenor of the book to present pre-fall oracles in chaps. 1–24. We have become aware, however, of insertions and updatings that upset this pattern. In fact, study of chap. 19 will show that at an earlier stage chaps. 17–19 were a self-contained unit, into which chap. 18 has been inserted. This does not make it a post-587 oracle, but it does alert us to the possibility of a different temporal setting.

Chap. 18 exhibits a pattern of elements displayed by post-fall messages. The first element is the formulation "no more" (אִם . . . עוֹד) in v 3. It occurs just over forty times in the book, usually in the form לֹא . . . עוֹד. Sixteen cases refer to God's imminent act of radical judgment in fulfilling judgment oracles: eleven refer to the fall of Judah (e.g., 12:23–24) and five to the fall of Egypt and Tyre (e.g., 26:13). Another sixteen cases refer eschatologically to reoccupation of the land, in assurances that the horrors that marked Israel's pre-587 occupation would not recur. Nine instances occur in Ezekiel's own oracles (e.g., 20:39; 36:12–15), and seven are redactional (e.g., 34:28–29; 36:30). Four further cases refer to post-587, exilic conditions: 13:21, 23; 14:11; 34:22. They are all associated with a divine act of relative judgment, which would single out offenders in the exilic community: the fortune-telling women prophets in chap. 13, idolaters and false prophets in chap. 14, and oppressors in chap. 34. Chap. 18 fits well into this setting, especially as it reflects neither postexilic conditions nor the radical judgment of the fall of Judah.

The issue of a relative judgment that would befall Israel has just been broached. The verb שָׁפַט "judge" with divine subject, which occurs in 18:30, is used with the calamity of 587 in view, in 7:3, 8, 27; 11:10–11; 16:38; 36:19. In 34:20, 22 it relates to a judgment to punish Judean oppressors among the exiles and to vindicate the oppressed, whereas in 20:35–36 it pertains to a decisive act of judgment to remove "rebels" from the ranks of the returning exiles and prevent them entering the land. This latter reference aligns with 13:9, where in a post-587 oracle false prophets are doomed to be stripped of their membership of God's people and denied entry into the land. Surely 18:30 and the parallel 33:20 are to be understood in terms of such an act of relative judgment, whose victims were to be egregious sinners among the Judean exiles. The oracles in chap. 33 cluster round the announcement of the fall of Jerusalem in 33:21–22 and mark the formal beginning of Ezekiel's new ministry that superseded his earlier messages of radical judgment.

The polarization of death and life as threat and opportunity for the exiles points in the same direction. On a larger scale it is echoed in the format of the book. Chaps. 33–48 are prefaced with an increasing emphasis on the underworld in the oracles against the nations (26:20–21; 28:8; 31:15–18; 32:18-32). Chaps. 33–37 are framed with references to the life Yahweh wanted Israel to enjoy (33:1–20; 37:1–14) and so are chaps. 33–48 (see 47:9). To live was to be settled in the land of Israel once more, claims 37:12, 14. Zimmerli's reluctance to define life in chap. 18 in terms of an eschatological return to the land as God's saving work for his exiled people (382), even though he assigns the oracle to the post-587 period, is based on the inexplicitness he finds in the oracle. If he had not deleted v 32b, he would have seen that it parallels the future life with the eschatological gift of a new heart and a new spirit in v 31 (cf. 11:19; 36:26).

The oracle contains elements that make it an obvious member of a group of post-587 messages related to the future opportunity to return to the land. What in other texts is presented as an unconditional promise (e.g., 37:1–14) is in a significant number of texts hedged with moral conditions. A coming event of relative but serious judgment was to constitute a divine roadblock that need pose no fear for the persistent righteous but would bar the apostate, including the idolater and the oppressor and those prophets who misused their gifts given for Israel's benefit. It is to this roadblock that the future prospect of death refers. It is an act of excommunication from God's people that meant premature death (cf. 14:8 and the *Comment*). This note of conditionality stands significantly at or near the beginning of the block of salvation oracles (33:1–20 [cf. Kraetzschmar 161], 30–33; 34:17–22). The reason for its presence at this point in the book remains to be seen.

Here is a general outline of the chapter.

18:1–4a	The inadmissibility of the exiles' proverb of transgenerational punishment
18:4b–9	The principle of the present generation's moral responsibility and its eschatological import
18:10–20	Denial of the proverb and affirmation of the principle
18:21–24	The principle of a capacity to change for good or ill and its eschatological import
18:25–29	Defense and affirmation of this principle
18:30–32	An appeal to the community to change for the better and so prepare for eschatological blessing

Comment

2 The exilic community to which Ezekiel belongs receives a strong rebuke from Yahweh through this message. It focuses on a slogan that summed up their attitude. Since they were evidently the ones who gave vent to it, it seems to be a slogan "about" the homeland, as in 12:22, rather than one used "in" it, as one might otherwise render (see the discussion in Joyce, *Divine Initiative* 43, 56). The slogan, a snatch of poetry with a 3 + 3 rhythm, expresses a paradox. Greenberg (328) adduces evidence that eating sour grapes has long been popular in Palestine and Syria; in this context its consequences, at least, are regarded as unpleasant. Perhaps a parallel paradox would be drinking too much alcohol and somebody else waking up with the hangover. The slogan means "The present generation is paying the penalty for the errors or sins of previous generations" (McKane, *Proverbs* 29–30). As he goes on to say, it "serves to express the conviction of every generation that those who preceded them have made a mess of things and that they have to suffer for it." The slogan is expressed in general terms, but the clue that the homeland was its topic helps us to anchor the slogan in the experience of the community who was using it. The fate of the homeland is in view, and so their own fate as displaced persons. In terms of Ezekiel's forecasts and statements elsewhere, the end had come upon it (7:2), it had been destroyed (25:3) and lay desolate (33:24), and they were no longer living there and had to leave it (36:17, 20).

There is a measure of orthodoxy in the slogan. If this disputation had been expressed as a contemporary debate, one might have heard theologians referring to the deferred ("to the third or fourth generation") punishment of Exod 34:7, which was incorporated in the Decalogue at Exod 20:5; Deut 5:9. They could have appealed to Ezekiel's own pre-587 oracles in chaps. 16 and 23, which derived reasons for the inevitable fall of Jerusalem from sins committed in its past. These would make excellent debating points, but there is a sinister edge to the slogan that must make it the target of attack. It implies a denial of responsibility; they had nothing to feel guilty about. Krüger (*Geschichtskonzepte* 392 n. 482) has rightly distinguished the perspective of chaps. 16 and 23 and that of chap. 20. In the pre-fall oracle of 20:3–31, though the coming exile is presented as deferred punishment (20:23), the hostages are represented as walking in their ancestors' footsteps and themselves as reprehensible (20:30–31). Similarly, in Lam 5:7 the lament "Our forebears sinned, and are no more; and we bear their iniquities," though superficially similar to the present slogan, does not shrug off responsibility: in the light of v 16, "we" also sinned. Likewise the Deuteronomistic History, although it grounds the downfall of Judah in a backlog of national sin, especially that of Manasseh (2 Kgs 21:11–15; 23:26; 24:3–4), carefully gives a negative assessment to each king after Josiah (23:32, 37; 24:9, 19). Earlier prophets, such as Hosea and Jeremiah, had spoken in the same double vein (cf. too Matt 23:29–36; Luke 11:45–51). Of course, Ezek 16 and 23, in view of chap. 20 and such condemnations of the present generation as 2:3–4; 3:7, are not to be understood as denials of contemporary responsibility.

The tenor of the chapter suggests that the slogan gave expression to practical nihilism. The exiles saw the present through the prism of the past. The slogan occasioned by Judah's downfall turned into a generalization. Overwhelmed by that recent catastrophe, they saw their whole lives doomed and devoid of purpose. Life was like that, and nothing they did could alter it. Elements in Ezekiel's prophesying might have played a part in encouraging this sentiment. Yahweh's punishment was not only to consist of national defeat but would chase its victims into exile, where he would continue to plague them (5:12). Life would be a misery spent in preoccupation with the past (6:9). That was to view the exile from the pre-587 perspective of judgment. After the watershed of 587, exile looked more rosy. It provided an opportunity to enjoy the limited presence of God (11:16). It was a typological Egypt from which Yahweh would lead his people to the promised land (20:33–42). The different perspectives of judgment and salvation were in line with an already established prophetic tradition and doubtless took their cue from it. In the present oracle the exiles are urged to share such optimism and to view their present and future as time to be lived in relation to God.

3–4a Irresponsibility and nihilism among the exiles, revealed in their slogan, are the targets of the oracle. Behind the vehement, oath-backed "no longer" lies the prospect of a decisive intervention that Yahweh was to make to change things, as in 13:21, 23; 14:11; 34:22, with reference to exilic shortcomings. V 30 discloses that an act of divine judgment was to take place among the community, as in 34:22. In NT parlance, it would separate the sheep from the goats (see *Form/Structure/Setting*; cf. Keil 248–49). Before passing to such eschatological motivation, there is an affirmation of the lines of relationship that radiated out from Yahweh to all the members of the covenant community, "Israel." None of them was exempt from his concern and claim. So each generation in turn came under the divine purview, and no child could hide behind its parent's skirts, whether willfully or as if of no account.

4b–9 The double challenge given to the slogan is a corrective that exposes its sinister connotation. The challenge is an affirmation of moral responsibility before God: sinners and the righteous are polarized, and their respective fates are offered as a deterrent and an incentive. The slogan was wrong in its implications: the morality of the exilic generation of God's people did matter.

4b The first, negative part of this principle is expressed tersely. The use of נפש "person" with a participle is found in priestly deterring statements, such as Lev 7:18, 25; 18:29 (Tårnberg, *Mahnrede* 107 and n. 403), whereas it is combined with the verb חטא "sin" in Lev 4:2, 27; 5:1, 17, 21; Num 15:27 (Graffy, *A Prophet Confronts* 60). The clause as a whole is akin to short pronouncements of capital crimes, such as Exod 21:12, "Whoever fatally strikes a man must be put to death" (see Schulz, *Todesrecht* 70 and n. 300 for further examples). Fishbane (*Biblical Interpretation* 337–41) is surely correct in seeing at this early stage, rather than only in v 20, where the formulation is repeated, Ezekiel's dependence on Deut 24:16. There a criminal ruling is presented that parents should not be put to death for their children nor vice versa, but "every one will be put to death for his own sin" (cf. Deut 7:10). It repudiates the old principle of a vendetta against a murderer's family that survived in the case of regicide (Lindars, *VT* 15 [1965] 455; cf. 2 Kgs 14:1–6). Fishbane has noted the links between the content of Deut 23:20–21; 24:6, 10–15, 17 and that of the moral rulings here in vv 7–8, 13, 16, and 18. He has concluded that these examples are cited because they were already associated with a legal principle that rejected vicarious punishment. In fact, in Deut 24:15 oppression of the poor and needy by withholding their daily wage is discouraged by their complaining to God, with the consequence that the offense would be judged a sin. The parallel Exod 22:23 implies that it would be a fatal sin: God would kill the oppressor after hearing the victim's complaints. Going a little further than Fishbane, one may suggest that for Ezekiel, if not in Deuteronomy itself, that fatal "sin" of oppression was envisioned in the statement of nonvicarious punishment of "sin" in Deut 24:16. Such wrongdoing led to fatal consequences for the perpetrators themselves. In the basic text, death is to be carried out by a human court, as the passive formulation of the verbs indicates. Here Ezekiel has in mind a divine punishment (cf. Exod 22:24). It was to be a premature death that meant exclusion from the promised land, death that would follow the judgment of v 30 (cf. Bertholet [1897] 96–97; Kraetzschmar 162; Herrmann 113; cf. 13:9; 14:8–9; 20:38). Whereas death in 37:1–14 is a metaphor for the unbearably low quality of life experienced by the exiles, here it is a divine ruling that disqualifies those among them whose hearts and habits were alienated from God.

5 The converse of this principle is expressed in vv 5–9 in a strikingly long format that cries out for explanation. The positive form of the principle can be easily detached as "When a man is righteous, he will surely live." It is interrupted halfway through by a definition of the term "righteous": if to be righteous is to do right (1 John 3:7), what sort of deeds does this imply? This accentuation of the positive is of a piece with the call to prepare for life in vv 30–32. A comprehensive picture is painted of the lifestyle of those who await God's gracious restoration to the land. There was much to live for, much to motivate present behavior. Not the numbing past but the prospect of living in the land was to be their focus. Such hope must energize the present generation to respect God and each other, and stop them sinking deeper into the apathy and irresponsibility implied by the slogan of v 2.

The positive principle is expressed in terms of case law (כִּי "when, if"). The overall form of vv 5–9 is a tripartite *tôrâ* or legal ruling. Such a schema characteristically consists of (1) a general introduction that often uses the terms צֶדֶק "righteousness" and מִשְׁפָּט "justice," (2) a central core of cultic and ethical instruction, and (3) a conclusion, most often expressed as a promise. Lescow (*ZAW* 82 [1970] 363–79) has shown that it is found in a variety of contexts, such as in the tithe-related oath of Deut 26:13–14, the confession of piety in Ps 18:21–25 (20–24), the definition of the acceptable pilgrim in the entrance liturgy at Pss 15:2–5; 24:4–5 and the prophetic version in Isa 33:15–16, the related conditional promise of Jer 7:5–7, the conditions for access to the palace in Jer 22:3–4, and the royal profession of loyalty in Ps 101. There is a negative version of this schema in the social analysis of Hos 4:1bβ–3; independently, Westbrook (*Studies* 28–29) has found another in the definition of sins requiring compensation at Lev 5:21–22 (6:2–3). The varied backgrounds of this schema warn against trying to pin down the present instance.

The first, general element of the schema occurs in this verse. To call a person "righteous"

> does not mean that he is sinless, or that he has shown his virtue by conforming perfectly to a comprehensive legal system, but that he is a willing member of the cultic community, who conforms with the ordinances of the community life and thus shows a right attitude towards the covenant relationship. (Eichrodt 239–40)

In sum, it is a term of allegiance and obligation, not of achievement (Hals, "Methods of Interpretation" 272). The term is accompanied by a general statement, acting with justice and righteousness or fairness. This standard is often a royal one in the OT. More relevantly, the phrase "justice and righteousness" is the comprehensive definition of Israel's social ethics given by Amos and Isaiah (Amos 5:7, 24; 6:12; Isa 1:21; 5:7; cf. 9:6[7]). It is echoed in Isa 56:1 in a remarkable later parallel to the spirit of vv 5–9: "Maintain justice and do righteousness, for soon my salvation will come." Righteousness is to treat one's neighbor fairly, while justice is usually understood as reinforcement of that behavior in the lawcourt, though Weinfeld ("'Justice and Righteousness'" 236–46) has reasonably argued that the latter term is wider than the judicial process.

6 The concrete examples given in vv 6–8a fall into five categories, which are mostly negative and in pairs. Israelite law reminds one of parental training of a child. It tended to establish boundaries within which one was free to move but beyond which one must not trespass. Accordingly, vv 10–11b implicitly sum up these examples in terms of sins. This first pair of sins is cultic in nature; it expresses offenses that the priestly side of Ezekiel contemplated with horror. It is a version of the exclusive worship of Yahweh demanded in the first commandment of the Decalogue. Ezekiel had decried worship at local shrines in chap. 6, seeing in it a sinister deviation from orthodox worship at the Jerusalem temple (cf. 8:6). Here communal meals at such mountain shrines are in view (cf. 1 Sam 9:12–13). Clearly, the Babylonian plain where the exiles lived offered no such opportunity, and the prophet has a preexilic sin in mind, as in 22:9. Members of the first generation of exiles are challenged about their behavior back in the homeland. The second of the pair of cultic sins is laid at the door of those who stayed behind in Judah at 33:25, and so it too could have been committed in the homeland. Such exilic accusations as 14:4–7; 20:32, however, show that it might be a feature of the exiles' present lives, as a continuation of an old sin. This sin, too, is particularly abhorrent to Ezekiel, as the use of his characteristic word for "idols" reveals.

The second pair of illustrations impinges on the cultic sphere inasmuch as they deal with sexual acts that caused impurity, which must not invade the sphere of the sacred (cf. 2 Chr 23:19). Two examples are given of what one might call unsafe sex. Adultery is proscribed in the two forms of the Decalogue (Exod 20:14; Deut 5:18), and it is a capital offense in the Holiness Code (Lev 20:10). It is described in terms of defilement here and in 33:26 and also in the legal codes at Num 5:14, 20, 27–29; Lev 18:20. Intercourse during menstruation was an Israelite taboo that transgressed the limits of permissible sexual contact. The sanction against it was the supernatural one of excommunication (Lev 18:19; 20:18; cf. Frymer-Kensky, "Pollution, Purification" 405).

7a Mention of one's neighbor in v 6b has introduced a horizontal solidarity within the covenant community that pervades the rest of the examples and is made explicit at the end of v 8. These next examples form a pair that is introduced by a topical heading. Two illustrations are given of wronging someone (cf. Lev 25:17 [H]); in 34:18–19, 21 it is metaphorically described in terms of strong sheep pushing aside the weaker ones. The first concerns restoration of a collateral pledge after repayment of a debt (Greenberg 329). It is an echo at least of Exod 22:25, which is expanded in Deut 24:10–15. Although no penalty is specified, for Ezekiel, as we have suggested, the death penalty of Deut 24:16 was applicable.

The other sin of גזלה, usually rendered "robbery," is the seizure of property from the helpless poor by the powerful rich (cf. Isa 3:14; 10:2; Mic 2:2; Junker, *BZ* 7 [1963] 175; Westbrook, *Studies* 35–38). It is prohibited in Lev 5:21, 23(6:2, 4; P); 19:13 (H).

7b–8aα The fourth pair of illustrations of good living is positive. They have no specific anchorage in the legal codes but accord with such kindness to the disadvantaged as Deut 24:19–21 and similar texts enjoin. To do good is more than to refrain from wrong. The next pair, though formulated negatively, has the same charitable intent. Interest on a loan to a fellow Israelite is prohibited in Exod 22:24(25); Deut 23:20(19); Lev 25:36–37 (H). The last text is particularly similar. Loaning money was regarded not as a commercial venture but as helping out a brother or sister temporarily in need. The permission to take interest from a non-Israelite in Deut 23:20 and the ban on Jews owning land or belonging to the professions in medieval Europe led to the stereotypes of Shylock the money-lender and of Jewish economic power.

8aβb–9a There is now a return to the generalizing with which the definition of the righteous person opened. Wrongdoing is associated solely with the lawcourt in Lev 19:15 (H), but is defined more widely in Lev 19:35 later. Here it functions as a summary of the inhumanity of vv 6b–8aα. The negative statement is matched by mention of a positive communal spirit at work in human relationships. "Justice" is here used in a wider sense than that of a court of law (Greenberg 330). The final generalization surveys the Torah in a sweeping way characteristic of Ezekiel (5:7; 11:20; 20:13, 19, 21); it seems to depend on Lev 26:3, 15 (H).

9b So the text comes full circle back to v 5. In the context, the short nominal clause "he is righteous" is a logical, resumptive conclusion after the interim definitions (Greenberg 346–47, who compares Num 35:15b–21). Zimmerli's interpretation of it as a declaratory formula (375–76), following von Rad ("Faith Reckoned as Righteousness" 125–29), is closely associated with the erroneous view that the entrance liturgy is the genre underlying these verses. The statement does not occur as a cultic pronouncement; Ps 118:19–20 is hardly sufficient evidence. Nor is it found in sacral law, though a second-person formulation "You are righteous" in Prov 24:24 seems to reflect civil law. Moreover, it has no counterpart in v 13 or v 17, where one might expect it. It has to be extrapolated from such priestly pronouncements as "he is (un)clean" (Lev 13:11, 13), "it is leprosy" (Lev 13:3, 8), or "it is a burnt offering" (Lev 1:17).

The ruling that life will follow in the wake of such virtue is modeled on the death sentence of v 4b; it never serves as a judicial verdict of acquittal. Life was the intended consequence of observing the divine revelation of the Torah according to Lev 18:5, where it means that "Israel will have a secure, healthy life with sufficient goods in the promised land as God's people" (J. E. Hartley, *Leviticus*, WBC 4 [Dallas: Word, 1992] 293). Ezekiel cites Lev 18:5 in 20:13, 21, and he will echo it in 18:19. In chap. 20 the wilderness generation is portrayed as turning their backs on such life and meriting destruction. By implication, the promise of qualified restoration in 20:32–44 represents enjoyment of the promised life. In 33:15, in a context similar to the present one—more exactly, corresponding to 18:21, 27—the prophet speaks of חקות חיים "the rules that make for life" as a precursor of future life. So such a promise aptly follows the formulation of v 9a. The concept of life may also echo the incentive for obedience given in Deut 5:33; 8:1, living and faring well in the promised land. Here in Ezek 18 an eschatological meaning is attached to the term, in the sense that it defines the salvation offered to the exiles, unconditionally in 37:1–13(14); 47:9 but in a qualified form in chaps. 3, 18, and 33 (cf. 13:19, 22). Zimmerli's definition of life as a spiritual promise of God's presence to be enjoyed even in exile (382; cf. von Rad, "Faith Reckoned as Righteousness" 253–66) is inadequate.

In vv 4b–9 the divine antithesis to the exiles' demoralizing slogan has been set out, using a selection of rulings to illustrate what it means to be right with God and with one's neighbors. Echoes of Deut 24 play a key role in justifying and reinforcing the life-or-death alternative. Ezekiel had already used a number of the standards in his pre-587 accusation of contemporary Jerusalem: eating on the mountains, intercourse during menstruation, adultery, and charging interest (22:9–12). The overlap here is natural: the same generation was in view. It serves to reinforce the implied charge that the generation who survived the fall was not so innocent as the slogan claimed. The thrust of the passage, however, is to point forward and to provide a benchmark for the lifestyle of members of a community of hope.

10–17 The slogan of v 2 is now disputed in a precise fashion and given the same eschatological application as in vv 4b–9. The slogan is false, it is claimed, and one may not generalize about bad parents and poor, innocent children. On the contrary, the bad children of good people will die (vv 10–13), while the good children of bad people will live (vv 14–17). The summary in vv 17b–18 shows that the slogan is under attack. It was wrong to extrapolate from the deferred punishment of the recent calamity and a (doubtful) claim of contemporary innocence a nihilistic application to the present and future. Overall, Ezekiel seems to imply that the downfall of Judah, with its strong element of deferment, was a special case in God's purposes. That judgment was now over, and one could look forward to salvation, yet not with presumption. The old divine standards for each generation of Israelites would still apply, not only back in the promised land (11:20; cf. Jer 31:33) but even now as a crucial pledge of good faith.

10–11a A worst-case scenario is presented by way of an appeal to reason. Was it fair that a ruffian or a murderer should have any future in the community (cf. 1 Cor 6:9–10)? The final question "Will such a person win life?" in v 13 reflects the same rhetorical perspective. But these categories also accord with real charges Ezekiel had brought against Jerusalem and Judah in their last days: violence (7:23; 8:17; 45:9) and the shedding of human blood (9:9; 22:3, 4, 6, 9, 12, 27; 36:18).

11b–13 By and large the same standards are applied as in vv 6–8, but now these tests are failed. The first, cultic, set of rulings is split into two, within vv 11 and 12. The second, sexual, pair is reduced to one element. The third, social, pair, with its introductory heading, remains intact, apart from a change in order. Mention of "the poor and needy" reflects the influence of Deut 24:14. The fourth test of charity is omitted as otiose. The fifth pair, relating to interest, is prefaced by an extra, emotional comment, describing the offense as abominable in God's eyes; accordingly, later in v 13 "abominations" is used in a general summary of failure to match up to God's standards (cf. 5:9; 7:3; 22:2). This summary replaces the long positive one in vv 8aβ–9a, though it is set slightly later. The clause "he will not live" is used as an independent promise of death in Gen 31:32; Exod 19:13 (cf. 22:17[18]), but here it points the contrast with v 9 before the eschatological death sentence. Unlike v 4b, a hophal form of the verb is used here, under the influence of Deut 24:16. Both the qal and the hophal appear in old legal texts, generally with reference to divine punishment and human execution respectively (Milgrom, *Encroacher* 5–8; cf. Hutton, "Declaratory Formulae" 121–24). The accompanying clause, literally "his blood will be upon him," regularly accompanies the death sentence of human execution (see Lev 20:16); here it emphasizes the bloodguilt of the accused. Generally, it also serves to exonerate the human executioner. Matties (*Ezekiel 18* 78) has suggested that here it absolves Yahweh from guilt, in contrast to the slogan that blamed God for unjust punishment. This suggestion ties in well with the earlier use of the passive verb: in both cases human factors are transferred to God.

14–17 The second attack on the slogan insists that good children of bad people would enjoy life in the land. A note of brave determination is struck. There is a deliberate breaking free from the bad example of the parent. The insidious cause and effect of which the slogan helplessly complains is broken by a personal decision to march to a different drummer. This note will be struck again later, in speaking of repentance (v 28). The details follow those in vv 6–8 fairly closely, naturally more so than in vv 11–13. The second, sexual pair of standards is only represented by the first item, as in v 11. The third pair, about exploiting others, reproduces v 7a, except that the standard is raised by not taking a pledge at all in security for a debt. Is Deut 24:12 in mind? The fifth pair, concerning interest, is compressed into a single statement and subordinated to the general statement of refraining from wrongdoing in v 8a*β*.

18–19 Vv 10–17 are now summarized. The bad father—more strictly the bad son of a good father—would die, while the good son of a bad father would live. In the former case, a lack of communal spirit is labeled as "not good" and illustrated by an intensification of the third yardstick. Cheating one's fellows of their legal dues (see Westbrook, *Studies* 35–38) is cited. The charge, which Ezekiel leveled against the people of Jerusalem in 22:12, 29, here seems to have in view Deut 24:14–15, where the example of withholding wages is given. The past tense used for the father's death is out of accord with the future references in the rest of the chapter. It has a literary sense, harking back to earlier material. As Ezekiel moves to recapitulate the second lesson, he weaves into it an objection to how the son could escape any vestige of the father's punishment. If the prophet's opponents resented the truth of their slogan, to them it was an acknowledged fact of life (Junker, *BZ* 7 [1973] 177; Greenberg 332, with reference to Calvin 240). His response is simply to reaffirm the claim of vv 14–17, reverting to the general terms of vv 5b and 9a (cf. v 17a*β*). He bends the latter sentiment to the shape of Lev 18:5, "You will keep my rules and my standards by doing which human beings live," reinterpreting life as God's saving gift.

20 The first half of the counterthesis, v 4b, is now emphatically repeated. The implication is drawn in v 20b that moral responsibility does not cross generational lines, in outright denial of the slogan-based protest of v 19a. The contextually novel reference to a father's liability for a son's faults exposes the influence of Deut 24:16 on Ezekiel's thought. It functions as a rhetorical device to drive home the truth of what he is saying (Greenberg 332–33). Finally, the double counterthesis is briefly paraphrased. There is a new pairing of "righteous" and "wicked" that builds a bridge to vv 21–32, which is dominated by this contrast (Greenberg 335). The prophet uses these terms in the sense of a "basic decision for or against Jahweh"; he "values the keeping of the commandments . . . as the sign of a commitment to Jahweh" (von Rad, *Old Testament Theology* [New York: Harper, 1962] 1:393).

21–24 Ezekiel moves to a second counterthesis, which also falls into two halves. The wicked who become righteous will live (v 21), and the righteous who become wicked will forfeit their prospect of life (v 24). These declarations open wider still a door to freedom. If the present generation of exiles is no longer locked into the consequences of bad choices made by its forebears, neither are members of this generation locked into choices they have already made. The accent is still on bad choices: for the prophet, the survivors of the 587 catastrophe were a bad lot (cf. 14:22–23 and the *Comment*), nor were the 597 hostages any better (cf. 20:30–31).

21–22 So an implicit appeal to this largely wicked generation is given the prior place in this new counterthesis, which is elaborated in v 22. Hopefully, the first counterthesis had exposed their moral responsibility, showing that they had let down both God and their neighbors. After such bad news, it was time for good news. There was an opportunity for the wicked to put themselves in the shoes of the righteous who were promised life: vv 5, 9, 19 are echoed here. God would transfer them into that blessed category. Their former disloyalty to the covenant was regrettable, but God would not count it against them (cf. Jer 31:34). Their new right living would be accepted as their passport to the promised land.

23 The implicit reference to God in the passive verb of remembering generates a passionate opening of the divine heart that positively reinforces the first part of the counterthesis. The God whom the exiles' slogan wrongly branded as unjust and uncaring was on their side. They were the ones who were uncaring and unjust, but beyond such inauspicious truth lay a God-given remedy. There was the chance of a new beginning that would let bygones be bygones.

24 The converse must be stated: there was a real possibility that the righteous would lose their inheritance. According to 14:3, 4, 7, there were nominally respectable members of the exilic community who hankered after syncretism. Their "Yahwism plus" amounted to punishable apostasy. The possibility of backsliding is pushed to the fore in 33:12–13 and has sizable space devoted to it in 3:20–21. So it may not be wise to regard this alternative prospect as "supererogatory" (Greenberg 333). It poses a warning—literally in 3:20–21—that had to form part of Ezekiel's post-587 ministry to the exiles. "Let those who think they are standing beware of falling" (1 Cor 10:12). The divine shepherd did not want any of his sheep to be lost.

25–29 The double principle of vv 21 and 24 is now defended and affirmed. The repeated defense in vv 25 and 29 forcefully frames a restatement of the double principle (Zimmerli 385; Parunak, "Structural Studies" 280; Greenberg 336). Its two elements are set in reverse order in vv 26–27, and the second one receives an elaboration parallel to v 22. The elaborations of the principle encouraging the repentance of the wicked show that this is the prime concern. There is no counterpart to the positive reinforcement of v 23: that must await v 32a. Apart from v 23, vv 21–29 fall into a chiastic structure, ABCBA, amplified with emphatic repetition of the C element of v 25 in v 29 (cf. Junker, *BZ* 7 [1963] 178; Joyce, *Divine Initiative* 51).

25, 29 The objection about the first counterthesis in v 19 was slotted smoothly into the argument. These objections, presumably about the second counterthesis as in 33:17, 20, are permitted to protrude, but only to give greater weight to the counterobjections. What is at stake? Jer 18:1–12 provides fruitful parallels and in some form may well have influenced Ezekiel (cf. Miller, *Verhältnis* 95). There the sign of the potter reworking the spoiled clay is interpreted in terms of Yahweh's right to cancel oracles of national judgment and salvation, if the nation in question changes its moral tune. Then Yahweh announces a plan to punish and appeals for repentance, to which the hearers' response is to follow their own plans and do evil. The announcement of divine judgment and the appeal for repentance correspond to vv 30–32 here, while the divine relativity in terms of nations is applied within the community in vv 21–24, 26–28. The divine policy cannot yet refer to judgment, but the contrast between God's "way" and the exiles' "ways" recalls the one between the divine plan and evil human plans in Jer 18:11–12. In both passages the objectors represent a major element of the constituency (here "the community of Israel").

The issue at stake for the objectors is the absolute character of the divine word (cf. A. Rofé, *The Prophetical Stories* [Jerusalem: Magnes, 1988] 169). In a later age the concept of contingency affecting divine sovereignty came to light in the book of Jonah, where Jer 18 is deliberately echoed. It is an untidy and tantalizing notion. In the present context it must have caused mental chaos for those who were asked to unlearn the preexilic prophetic doctrine of an unalterable fate, to which Ezekiel himself had been committed. It made no sense to those who believed its perverted form encapsulated in the slogan of v 2. The divine response to the objection is more than a clever trick of argument. It implicitly points to the intellectual perversion at work in the objectors' theology and traces it to a moral perversion. They had raised a convenient smokescreen to conceal a hidden agenda of willfulness. The charge throws the objectors into the bramble patch of the preceding argument. "Your" inconsistent "behavior" (דרכיכם) echoes "their behavior" (דרכיו) in v 23 and identifies the protesters with the wicked, who, apart from a change of heart and habit, would lose their eschatological place in the sun. The God-given standards that identified the covenant community represented a necessary bridge to a positive future, but tragically the exiles were refusing to cross it.

26–28 The second counterthesis is emphatically repeated: the intent is to preach for repentance rather than to engage in academic debate. The righteous are warned of the truth that, in John Bunyan's parlance, "there was a way to hell even from the gates of heaven." More weight is given to the positive side of the counterthesis, in vv 27–28. A parallel is drawn with v 14, two lives being contracted into one: only a deliberate stopping in one's tracks and reflection can motivate a decision to turn round and go the right way.

30–32 The foregoing statements are implicit appeals to the exilic community to try them on for size and react accordingly. The direct questions of v 25bβγ and 29b have gone further. Developing the bias toward the wicked repenting in vv 21–22 and 27–28, they accuse the community, presumably the majority within it, of failing to be on the side of the angels. Now it is time for a direct appeal.

30 The initial לכן "therefore, so" links the accusation of v 29 with an announcement of punishment (Tårnberg, *Mahnrede* 109). Pre-eschatological judgment is a negative reinforcement of the appeal, corresponding to the positive one of v 23. The criterion of behavior echoes the standard of the radical judgment of 587 (7:3, 8; 24:14; 36:19), but a relative, potentially avoidable judgment is now in view, as in 33:20. In both cases "God is a judge only in the sense that he brings to light whatever already invisibly characterizes a person's nature" (Koch, *The Prophets* [Philadelphia: Fortress, 1983] 2:107). There was to be a rooting out of those who in 20:38 are called "rebels," so that they did "not enter the land of Israel" but lost their lives (cf. Hölscher, *Dichter* 103); the repentant, however, would never forget their former, forgiven "evil ways" (20:43–44; cf. 36:17–19, 22, 25). At this sort of border inspection, there was to be a determination as to where each exile stood in relation to God and to his or her neighbor. Only such

members of the community of faith as Ezekiel had defined earlier would be allowed through. "Behavior" has a negative bias in that it echoes the usage in vv 23,
25, and 29. The appeal for repentance in v 30ba backs up the motif of judgment
by repeating a note of accusation. The term "rebel ways" (פשׁעים) in vv 22 and 28
is applied to the hearers. Those contexts, however, had pointed to a way of escape. If it was not seized, there was a grim alternative, spelled out in v 30bβ as a
fatal stumbling. It is a further negative reinforcement.

31 Yahweh, the object of their rebellion, is the one who, through the prophet,
graciously calls on the exiles to empty their lives of such subversive activity (contrast 20:7–8). God has something better for them. In contrast to the destiny of
death that reinforced the appeal in v 30, an alternative prospect of eschatological
blessing is now presented to support this appeal. It refers to a promise of permanent moral renewal that was to be God's gift along with return to the land (11:17,
19–20; 36:24, 26; cf. Hos 2:15, 19[17, 21] REB; Jer 31:23, 33). Who, faced with
such a choice, would choose the death that had featured in both countertheses?

32 The positive reinforcement of divine goodwill, stated in v 23 and expected
after v 28, is rhetorically delayed till now, since God's kindness is meant to lead
to repentance (Rom 2:4). The carrot follows the stick wielded in v 30a. A NT
parallel with a similar eschatological tone occurs in Heb 6:4–8, 10 amid the ex-
hortations of 6:9, 11–12. In vv 30b–32 the structural relation to the alternatives of
death or life presented in the countertheses has thus far consisted of implicit
references (1) to death in v 30bβ and (2) to life in v 31aβ as prospects for the
hearers (לכם "for you, for yourselves") and then an explicit reference (1) to death
in v 31b, which has been reinforced by v 32a. What the passage requires to round
it off is an explicit reference (2) to life. It is supplied in v 32b, together with the
condition of repentance repeated from v 30ba.

Explanation

Our study of chap. 19 will show that chaps. 17 and 19 are a self-contained unit.
At its center stands the redactional oracle of salvation in 17:22–24, which echoes
but transforms the negative messages that surround it. Into this unit chap. 18 has
been editorially inserted after 17:24, as a supplement to the eschatological oracle
of royal renewal. Such a hope was not merely an intellectual comfort, it is inferred, but a stimulus to an appropriate lifestyle by way of preparation (cf. Hitzig
121, followed by Davidson 132). In NT parlance, "what kind of persons ought
you to be in terms of holy and godly behavior, as you await" such an eschatological
expectation (2 Pet 3:11–12)? And "all who have this hope . . . individually purify themselves" (1 John 3:3).

This editorial intent is in line with the basic purpose of the oracle. Although
Ezekiel cites pertinent theological facets (vv 4, 23, 32), he does not speak as a
systematic theologian but is handling a pastoral crisis. He pursues the watchman
role he was assigned as the basis for his post-587 ministry (33:19; also 3:17–21;
Vogt, *Untersuchungen* 108). It is given the nuance of a reply to the exiles' slogan
about a skewed pattern of cause and effect. The announcement of freedom from
transgenerational retribution and the call to covenantal responsibility enable the
reader to backtrack to the slogan's meaning for its users. It gave expression to a
negative syndrome contaminating the exilic community. A spirit of fatalism was

causing moral and social degeneration. The mushroom cloud of God's retrospective wrath had drifted over their lives. So nothing would change and there was no point in virtue. The vehement claim in v 3 that the slogan would be dropped alludes to a dynamic intervention of judgment (v 30), which, unlike the radical event of 587 B.C., would be relative in its effect but still momentous for the people of God. In the light of 20:35–38, the judgment would be a screening process for eschatological return to the land. Ezekiel evidently regarded it as imminent, rather like the early Church with regard to the Second Coming.

The overall intent was a positive one, as the disproportionately lengthy description of "the righteous" in vv 5–9 indicates. The aim was to provide "social stability in a situation where land, temple and monarchy no longer serve a stabilizing function" and to form a "selective dossier" for the "community under construction" (Matties, *Ezekiel 18* 189, 190; cf. Fishbane, *Biblical Interpretation* 337–38). Various traditions are used to this end. They are passed through the sieve of Deut 24, so as to provide strong teeth for the older rulings, some of which had no serious sanctions. The penalty of death for the disobedient found in Deut 24:16 is given an eschatological dimension, in terms of exclusion from life in the land. To live now in exile is to prepare for this gift from God. Such are the goals and values the prophetic watchman sets before the exilic community, as in God's name he urges them to avoid the danger that would otherwise overwhelm them. In terms of Rom 12:21, the message is: "overcome evil"—the evil of their situation as they perceived it and the evil lifestyle into which their perception had seduced them—"with good." God calls them to a responsible freedom, to be moral masters of their own fate.

The similar denial of the slogan in terms of Deut 24:16, which appears in Jer 31:29–30, has an uncertain literary relationship with our chapter. Its focus on God's new eschatological initiative and its sharp demarcation between (radical) judgment conditions and salvation conditions are close to the present intent. The difference is that here there is a greater, pastorally grounded emphasis on the imminence of that event.

For the Christian reader, besides those texts mentioned at the outset, biblical truths not often heard from the pulpit are pushed to the fore. The Church in every generation must be alerted to a future judgment seat that is to be a sober constraint and incentive in present living (Rom 14:10, 12; 2 Cor 5:10; Gal 6:7–8). The necessity of continuance in the faith and in a lifestyle that commends it is backed by grave provisos from which no believer is exempt (Rom 11:22; 1 Cor 15:2; Col 1:23; Heb 3:14).

Two Elegies for a Doomed Dynasty   (19:1–14)

Bibliography

Begg, C. "The Identity of the Princes in Ezekiel 19: Some Reflections." *ETL* 65 (1989) 358–69. ————. "The Reading in Ezekiel 19, 7a: A Proposal." *ETL* 65 (1989) 370–80. **Brownlee, W. H.** "Two Elegies on the Fall of Judah (Ezekiel 19)." In *Ex Orbe Religionum.* FS G. Widengren. Numen Supplement 21. Leiden: Brill, 1972. 93–102. **Budde, K.** "Das hebräische Klagelied." *ZAW* 2 (1882) 1–52. **Dahood, M.** "Ezekiel 19,10 and Relative *ki.*" *Bib* 56 (1975) 96–99. **Gordon, E. I.** "Of Princes and Foxes: The Neck-Stock in the Newly Discovered Agade Period Stele." *Sumer* 12 (1956) 80–84. **Hammershaimb, E.** "Ezekiel's View of the Monarchy." In *Studia orientalia J. Pedersen dicata.* Copenhagen: Munksgaard, 1953. 130–40. **Held, M.** "Pits and Pitfalls in Akkadian and Biblical Hebrew." *JANESCU* 5 (1973) 173–90. **Jahnow, H.** *Das hebräische Leichenlied im Rahmen der Völkerdichtung.* BZAW 36. Giessen: Töpelmann, 1923. 197–210. **Lang, B.** *Kein Austand in Jerusalem.* 2nd ed. Stuttgart: Katholisches Bibelwerk, 1981. 89–114. **Moran, W. L.** "Gen 49,10 and Its Use in Ez 21,32." *Bib* 39 (1958) 405–25. **Noth, M.** "The Jerusalem Catastrophe of 587 B.C. and Its Significance for Israel." In *The Laws of the Pentateuch and Other Studies,* tr. D. R. Ap-Thomas. Philadelphia: Fortress, 1967. 260–80. Originally published in French in *RHPR* 33 (1953) 82–102. **Oort, H.** "Ezechiel xix; xxi:18, 19v." *Theologisch Tijdschrift* 23 (1889) 504–14. **Pohlmann, K.-F.** *Ezechielstudien.* BZAW 202. Berlin: de Gruyter, 1992. **Seitz, C. R.** *Theology in Conflict: Reactions to the Exile in the Book of Jeremiah.* BZAW 176. Berlin: de Gruyter, 1989. 131–48. **Vogt, E.** "Jojakîn collario ligneo vinctus (Ez 19:9)." *Bib* 37 (1956) 388–89.

Translation

[1] *"You are to utter a lament for Israel's heads* [a] *of state,* [2] *as follows:*
'What was your mother? [a] *She was a lioness* [b]
among the lions! [c]
She crouched [d] *amid the young lions*
and reared her cubs.
[3] *She singled out* [a] *one of her cubs,*
who grew into a young lion.
He learned to hunt his prey,
feeding on human flesh.
[4] *The nations raised a shout* [a] *against him;*
he was captured in their pit, [b]
and they took him with hooks
away to Egypt.
[5] *Seeing she had been frustrated,* [a]
her hopes dashed,
she took another [b] *of her cubs,*
giving him the status [c] *of a young lion.*
[6] *He stalked among the lions,*
having grown into a young lion,
and learned to hunt his prey,
feeding on human flesh.
[7] *He did harm to women by making them widows (?)* [a]

and depopulated his victims'[b] *towns.*
The country and all in it were aghast
at his noisy roaring.
[8]*The nations marched*[a] *against him*
from surrounding districts.[b]
They spread their net for[c] *him;*
he was captured in their pit.
[9]*They put him in a wooden collar,*[a] *in hooks,*[b]
and took him to the king of Babylon,[c]
who put him in prison,[d]
so that his noise would be silenced[e]
on Israel's mountains.

[10]*'Your mother was like a grapevine full of tendrils,*
because[a] *it was planted beside water.*
It was fruitful and full of branches
as a result of the abundant water.
[11]*It grew strong stems*[a]
fit for[b] *rulers' scepters—*
One of them[c] *soared high*
among the clouds.[d]
It was conspicuous for its height,
for its mass of branches—
[12]*But the vine*[a] *was torn up in fury;*
it was thrown to the ground.
Then the east wind
shriveled its tendrils;[b]
they were broken off,
and its strong stem shriveled:[c]
fire consumed it.
[13]*Now it is planted*[a] *in the desert,*
in a dry, parched[b] *region.*
[14]*Fire came out from its own stem,*[a]
consuming its tendrils,[b]
and it did not have a strong stem,
a scepter to rule with.'"
This is a lament, and it has come to function as a lament.

Notes

1.a. The LXX represents a sg via haplography, assimilating to the sg suffix אִמְּךָ on "your mother" in v 2. The pl reflects the content of the lament.

2.a. An exclamatory sense "What a lioness your mother was . . ." (Hitzig 129; and many) is unlikely. Elsewhere מה "what" is used only with adjectives and verbs in this sense. Moreover, the word order opposes it (Brownlee 299). Rather, one must understand it as a question and answer (KJV; Ehrlich, *Randglossen* 5:70). In a lament, an initial exclamation expresses shock at the downfall of the victim, such as "How are the mighty fallen!" (2 Sam 1:19; cf. Ezek 26:17). The question-and-answer format finds a parallel in 31:2–3.

2.b. The MT reflects an artificial pointing to highlight the gender: the standard לָבִיא means "lioness" (Cooke 211; *HALAT* 491b).

2.c. A superlative meaning is conveyed by בין "among," as in Cant 2:2, 3 (cf. the use of בתוך "among" in Ezek 29:12; 30:7).

2.d. The sense opposes the accentuation in the MT, while the *qînâ* meter (3 + 2) is nicely restored (Bertholet [1897] 101; et al.).

3.a. Thus the REB; the context suggests that a cub was taken up from the rest and given a special role (cf. v 5b).

4.a. The MT points as a qal "heard (about him)": Wevers (148) compares 2 Kgs 19:9. Hitzig (129) and most have repointed as a hiph, understanding קול "voice," with the sense "sound an alarm." This yields a more dramatic sense: cf. Isa 31:4. Ehrlich (*Randglossen* 5:70) and others have taken "the nations" as the object of the verb in the sense "summon," with an indefinite subj: see Zimmerli 389.

4.b. Held (*JANESCU* 5 [1873] 173–90) has argued that here and in v 8 שחת means not "pit" but "net," cognate with Akk. *šetu* "net." Lang (*Kein Aufstand* 97–98), however, has contested his claim.

5.a. The MT נוחלה "she (or 'her hope') waited (in vain?)" is uncertain. Wevers' sense "her hope was made to wait, postponed" (148) does not quite fit the context of disappointed hopes. Cornill's emendation נואלה "she acted foolishly" (286–87) has won scholarly support, but Ehrlich (*Randglossen* 5:71) objected that it is unsuitable: the mother subsequently did the same as before! Smend's comparison with Syr. *ʾawhel* "be enfeebled, despair" (123) has received wider backing. Then presumably a second stem יחל must be invoked, with which Driver (*Bib* 19 [1938] 67) claimed Arab. *whl* "be uncertain" to be cognate.

5.b. See *Note* 17:7.a.

5.c. Cf. Driver's rendering "appointed" in *Bib* 35 (1954) 154.

7.a. This colon is a notorious crux. See Begg, *ETL* 65 (1989) 370–77, for a summary of proposed solutions. Isa 13:22, where אלמנות does not mean "widows" but is evidently a dialectal variant of ארמנות "fortresses" (= Θ Tg), has often been judged determinative for this case. However, Greenberg (351) has felicitously revived the suggestion rejected by Hitzig (130), that אלמנותיו means not "his widows" but "the women made widows by him," just as חלליכם "your dead" in 11:6 signifies "those whose death you have caused." LXX Syr "in his boldness" baffled Cornill (288), but Cooke (211) related the rendering to Aram. אלימותא "strength." Greenberg has also suggested that החריב has the connotation "depopulate," as in Zeph 3:6. Then in both cola the consequences of the young lion's eating human flesh (v 6), envisioned as the flesh of males, are in view. The verb וידע "and he knew" does not fit. There is widespread ancient support for a reading וירע, with a common confusion of *resh* and *daleth,* whether from רעה "feed on" (LXX) or רעע (hiph הרע) "do harm to" (*ʾA*) or רצץ = רעע "break" (Tg). The second of these three options is the most fitting.

7.b. Lit. "their" with a reference back to אדם "men" in v 6.

8.a. For the military sense of נתן, basically "give," see Greenberg 352.

8.b. For מדינות "administrative districts," cf. 1 Kgs 20:14–19 and see Zimmerli 389–90.

8.c. Cf. 17:20 and *Note* 17:20.b.

9.a. The Heb. סוגר is cognate with Akk. *šugaru* "wooden collar": cf. the Tg קולרין "collar" and Vogt, *Bib* 37 (1956) 388–89; Held, *JANESCU* 5 (1973) 184–85.

9.b. The MT בחחים may have originated as an explanatory gloss on the previous word (Fohrer 105) or as a comparative gloss from v 4 (Zimmerli 390). The Syr does not represent it.

9.c. Ehrlich's attractive suggestion to repoint as יביאהו (*Randglossen* 5:72) has been adopted.

9.d. The MT has במצדות "in the fortresses." There is a variant with *resh* in place of *daleth:* LXX Syr Vg "prison" implies a Heb. noun *מצר or the like from נצר "guard," while Σ "Egypt," with v 4 in mind, presupposes מצור. Noth ("Jerusalem Catastrophe" 273) compared Akk. *maṣṣartu* "custody."

9.e. The MT עוד "(not heard) any more" is not represented in LXX* Syr (cf. Ziegler, *Bib* 34 [1953] 439). In Ezekiel it is placed right after the verb, except for here, 37:22, where it is secondary, and 39:7. Its deletion would restore a 3 + 2 meter.

10.a. This is another notorious crux. The MT בדמך "in your blood" has a modicum of sense, if דם is credited with the figurative sense of red grape juice (cf. Gen 49:11; Deut 32:14). The LXX "like a flower in a pomegranate" stands for כרמן "like a pomegranate." This is graphically close to the MT and appears to be a degenerate form of it. For a review of suggestions, see Zimmerli 390. His own preference for a niph form of דמה "be like" suffers from a misguided appeal to 27:32 (see Allen, *Ezekiel 20–48* 83). Rashi and Kimchi's hypothesis of a noun *דם "likeness," thus "in your likeness" (cf. the Tg), was revived by Ewald (281) and recently by Barthélemy (*Critique* 3:148–52). The simplest and so most impressive solution is Bewer's proposal in *JBL* 72 (1953) 159: בד(י)ם כ(י) "(like a grapevine [= כגפן] full of) tendrils, because." Wrong word division obscured the fact that the poem's beginning, middle (v 12), and end (v 14) feature the same noun, בדים "tendrils" (cf. too 17:6b). Dahood

(*Bib* 56 [1975] 96–99) gave other examples of defective spelling in Ezekiel and observed that the postulated causal clause provides good external parallelism with the second colon of the next line. He himself claimed a relative sense for כי here.

11.a. The supposition of a pl of majesty (Brownlee, "Two Elegies" 99 n. 3; Lang, *Kein Austand* 91) is unconvincing. The LXX has sg nouns "stem" and "scepter." Hitzig (131) and a number of scholars have so preferred (thus NJPS, NRSV), in line with vv 12, 14. However, secondary assimilation to the latter cases is indicated by the otherwise inexplicable retention of a pl "rulers," which the NJPS and NRSV have unscrupulously rendered as sg. Attention switches to a single (the last) stem in vv 12–13.

11.b. The use of אל "to(ward)" in the sense of ל is strange: Jer 33:4, to which Ehrlich (*Randglossen* 5:72) appealed, is capable of a number of interpretations. One may compare the sense, albeit different, of היה אל "become" (= היה ל) in 40:16; 45:2.

11.c. Lit. "it," with a masc reference to one of the stems (cf. v 12b) that runs throughout v 11aβb. The grapevine, which is fem, reappears in v 12. See *Form/Structure/Setting*.

11.d. For the form, see *Note* 31:3.c.

12.a. Lit. "it," a fem reference to the vine, resumed from v 11aα.

12.b. The LXX indirectly attests בדיה "its tendrils": both here and in v 14 it renders בריה "its chosen ones." A sg noun פריה "its fruit" does not accord with the pl verbs. V 14 shows how easily the two words could be confused (see Cooke 212).

12.c. For the LXX rendering of the first verb, see Cooke (212) rather than Zimmerli (390). An emendation of the second verb from pl to sg (Cooke 210; *BHS*), on the evidence of the LXX and in line with the sg suffix at the end of the line, has the advantage of creating a 3 + 2 line. A pointing וַיֵּבַשׁ is not necessary: a pf with weak *waw* is not unparalleled in the book (Cooke 212; Johnson, *Hebräisches Perfekt* 79).

13.a. The LXX implies שתלוה "they have planted it," by metathesis. The rhetorical echo of the ptcp שתולה "planted" in v 10 justifies the MT.

13.b. The LXX* does not represent the second adj. Cornill (291) counseled its retention in a permissible 3 + 3 line.

14.a. The MT ממטה "from the stem of (its tendrils)" is a consequence of its conflated text. See the next *Note*. One should point מִמַּטֶּהָ "from its stem" (Rothstein 918 [cf. Joüon 96Cf]; cf. מהמטה "from the stem," Cornill 291; מִמַּטֶּה "from its stem," Kraetzschmar 169; מִמַּטֶּיהָ "from its stems," Brockington, *Hebrew Text* 225).

14.b. The pair of terms in the MT בדיה פריה "its tendrils, its fruit" seems to reflect conflation. The LXX lacks the second one. It is probable that the pair represents a cue word and a correction, "for 'its fruit' read 'its tendrils,' " and at an earlier stage was a marginal comment on v 12. Later it was inserted into the text at v 14, displacing בדיה "its tendrils," which functions as the object of the verb.

Form/Structure/Setting

Chap. 19 looks like a literary unit, inasmuch as a new one clearly begins in 20:1–2. However, its opening ואתה "and you" is characteristic of a section within a unit, as in 4:9. It is best understood as originally a continuation of the unit that began with 17:1, into which chap. 18 has been redactionally inserted. This is suggested by the echoes of both 17:1–10 and 19:10–14 in the oracle of salvation in 17:22–24. The genre of the chapter is identified as a (funeral) lament by the inclusion of vv 1 and 14b. It actually falls into two pieces, which share the initial אמך "your mother" as a catchword in vv 2 and 10 but work within the parameters of two separate metaphors, a lioness and a grapevine. The two poems, for such they are, exhibit by and large the standard meter of the funeral lament, 3 + 2. Deviations occur in vv 9ab (3 + 3 + 3 [overloaded?]), 11aβb (2 + 2, 2 + 2 [Zimmerli 391]), 12a (2 + 2). Lang (*Kein Austand* 91) has noted that the 2 + 2 meter is also characteristic of the lament. Ezekiel often used this genre in his oracles against foreign nations, against Tyre in 26:17–18; 27:2–36; 28:12–19 and against Egypt in 31:2–18; 32:2–16.

Whereas in its original setting the lament celebrated the past achievements of a person now dead, the prophets turned it into a forward-looking oracle of judgment.

Its two standard parts of past triumph and present tragedy became a vehicle for expressing the doom of those who seemed to enjoy permanent prosperity. Moreover, at times notes of accusation were worked into the description of initial splendor (28:15–16a; 31:10). The time perspective was characteristically altered: present glory was represented as past, and future doom as already present. The prophet ominously looked back at a past tragedy. This contrast is typically seen in 26:17–18 and 27:32–34, where עתה "now" introduces the second element. In the second lament of chap. 19, it is present in v 13. This specimen actually divides into three parts: past glory in vv 10–11, the onset of disaster in v 12, and present doom in vv 13–14a. The middle section, with its strongly narrative format, is also found in 27:26(–27), where the east wind is again the instrument of destruction, and in 28:17b, where casting to the ground features, as here in v 12. In a looser type of lament in chap. 32, much space is devoted to destruction, 32:3–8, including Yahweh's trapping the Egyptian Leviathan or crocodile with a net, which is similar to vv 4 and 8–9bα in the first lament of chap. 19. This lament falls into two main parts, which subdivide into two smaller sections, the rise and fall of the first young lion (vv 2–3 + 4) and the rise and fall of the second (vv 5–7 + 8–9). The two main parts are marked by consecutive parallelism: vv 3a and 5b–6a correspond, and so do vv 3b and 6b, 4a and 8, and 4b and 9a. The second part expands the features of the first. Its greater size shows its relative importance: by comparison, the first part looks like a rehearsal for it.

As to the setting of these two poems that make up the chapter, one must distinguish between the historical and the literary settings, as often in the oracles of the book. The difference is especially keen here, as the concluding comment in v 14b hints. At an earlier stage in the formation of the book, chaps. 17 and 19 were evidently adjacent. The oracle of salvation of 17:22–24 had a central role, standing head and shoulders above the oracles of judgment that surround it in 17:1–21 and 19:1–14. One may compare the centrality of the fall of Jerusalem in 33:21–22, within a series of oracles that presuppose it in the preceding and following parts of the chapter (see Allen, *Ezekiel 20–48* 151–52). The key role of 17:22–24 is indicated by its echoes of both 17:1–10 and 19:10–14a. The original structure of the two chapters was A/ . . . /A'/ . . . /A. By the time of this literary grouping, the doom predicted in the judgment oracles had already been fulfilled, and they were monuments to God's power and justice. 19:1–14a had become a lament in the literal sense of relating to the past. However, as in 32:16, the editor responsible for 19:14b was aware that a prophetic lament relates to the future. Clearly this was not so in the case of the anticipatory vv 3–4, but it is presumably true of vv 5–9 and of the second lament. So both oracles are pre-587 in origin; they look forward with the characteristic time warp of the lament.

A little more needs to be said about redaction. The reference to a single stem of the grapevine in v 11aβb is most probably to be regarded as a subsequent insertion (Noth, "Jerusalem Catastrophe" 274 n. 22; Zimmerli, 390–91, 398). This material stands out from the rest, with its switch from plural stems to the masculine singular that pervades it before a reversion to feminine forms relating to the grapevine in v 12. Yet it has been made to fit smoothly in some other respects. It anticipates the less vehement references to a single stem in vv 12b and 14. It is metrically acceptable (Zimmerli 391). Structurally it respects the vine/stem alternation that Parunak ("Structural Studies" 289–90) has observed. However, it disturbs the proportion of lines devoted to this alternation (originally 2.1.2.1/ 1.2), by supplementing the single stem-related line with two further ones. These lines were probably added by Ezekiel in a literary adaptation of the oracle: they are already presupposed by the oracle of salvation in 17:22–24.

The chapter falls into the following parts:

19:1	Yahweh's command to lament Israel's rulers
19:2–9	The lament over Jehoahaz and Zedekiah as young lions
19:2–4	Jehoahaz's violent reign and deportation
19:5–9	Zedekiah's violent reign and coming deportation
19:10–14a	The lament over the Davidic grapevine
19:10–11	Its past glory, culminating in Zedekiah's ambitions
19:12	Its coming destruction
19:13–14a	Its exilic fate brought about by Zedekiah
19:14b	The fulfillment of the predictive lament

Comment

The prophetic lament is a variation of the oracle of judgment, a sophisticated way of pronouncing divinely sent destruction upon the addressees. Here Israel's "heads of state" are the subject not only of the first poem but also of the second. The term נשׂיא "head of state" is one that Ezekiel typically uses of Judean royalty, particularly Zedekiah (see the *Comment* on 7:27). In this case the reference to recent and present reigns of such "heads of state" and the attribution to them of lionlike violence and loss of life are paralleled in 22:25 (see Allen, *Ezekiel 20–48* 31–32, 38–39).

2a One of the heads of state is rhetorically addressed. Presumably it is the current king, Zedekiah, as in 21:30–31 (25–26). His "mother," who reappears in v 10, is best taken as the Davidic dynasty. In 17:5–10 the grapevine stands for Zedekiah himself, while the dynasty is signified by the cedar, of which Jehoiachin and the coming king are shoots in 17:3–4, 22–23. The grapevine often stands for the covenant nation in the OT, as it does in chap. 15, but the rest of the oracles in chaps. 17 and 19 point in another direction. Oort (*Theologisch Tijdschrift* 23 [1889] 505) and others have seen here and in v 10 a literal reference to the Judean queen mother Hamutal, the mother of both Jehoahaz and Zedekiah (2 Kgs 23:31; 24:18). This appears to be the "pushing of a metaphor beyond its original intent" (Hals 130). Cooke (206) observed that a personification is most naturally in view in v 10 and so presumably here also. Glory attaches not to a particular woman, however prominent she might have been, but to the Davidic line from which individual kings emerged. This is their "mother" (Zimmerli 394, 397, implicitly following Kimchi and L. Gautier; Pohlmann, *Ezechielstudien* 147, 149, 154). If the kings are like young lions in their violent behavior in 22:25 and later in the oracle, here their lionhood has a glorious aspect, like the title of Christ in Rev 5:5, "the Lion of the tribe of Judah." It is derived from the description of the royal tribe of Judah as a lion in Jacob's blessing (Gen 49:9). There it is said that "he crouches like a lion. Like a lioness, who dare arouse him?" This language and its admiring tone seem to have influenced the beginning of the lament, as a reflection of the traditional grandeur of the Davidic dynasty. The second lament will likewise expand on the grapevine of Gen 49:11 (Bertholet [1936] 70; et al.). As in 31:2–3, an appreciative question elicits the superlative quality of the subject of lamentation.

2b–3   The young males are the individual kings whom the royal house produced, while the cubs are the princes being groomed for royal office or for civil and military leadership. The identification of the first young lion is no mystery: his deportation to Egypt (v 4b) reveals him to be Josiah's son Jehoahaz, who ruled for three short months in 609 B.C. His hunting human prey might be considered an amoral description of royal duties in leonine language but for 22:25, where it is said of Jerusalem's heads of state that they were "like a roaring lion tearing its prey: they devoured lives" (cf. Brownlee, "Two Elegies" 98 n. 1). True, three months were too short to leave an impression of despotism, but the description is essentially a generalization. From Ezekiel's exilic perspective, Judah's kings were all tarred with the same brush (22:6, 25; 45:8, 9). What was true of them as a group might rhetorically be credited to each monarch in turn. The violence that Jeremiah attributed to Jehoahaz's older brother and successor Jehoiakim (Jer 22:13–17; cf. Manasseh in 2 Kgs 21:16) must have deeply impressed Ezekiel in his young years.

4   A stop was put to the young lion's ravages by foreign hunters, Pharaoh Necho II and his army, who captured and deported him (cf. 2 Kgs 23:33–34). Both animals and human captives had hooks or rings put through their noses or lips, through which ropes could be attached (cf. *ANEP* 447, 524; 2 Kgs 19:28; Amos 4:2). This human act is meant to be regarded as a natural process of reaping what one sows in God's world. As an ominous description of a past event within an oracle of judgment, Jehoahaz's fate is comparable with the Northern Kingdom's downfall related in 23:9–10, in an oracle directed to Judah.

5–7   After rehearsing the first king's rise and fall, the lament begins its essential part. There is a glance at the disappointment caused by Egyptian domination, which represented the absolute failure of the policy of independence pursued by Josiah. The identity of the second lion cub has long generated controversy: it is well summarized by Begg (*ETL* 65 [1989] 358–65). The question is resolved at a stroke by considering the genre of the passage. Von Orelli (74–76, implicitly following Oort and implicitly followed by Jahnow, *Leichenlied* 202–4; Fohrer 104, 107; and Lamparter 137–38) rightly observed that the lament is predictive and so must relate to Zedekiah, though he wrongly defined his "mother" as Hamutal. The funeral lament was used by Ezekiel to predict the coming downfall of a living person or extant group. One need not be concerned at the gap in the reigns of the two "young lions" in this schematic presentation of royal history. A prophetic lament requires that the future be described as if it were past. An exception can fairly be made for vv 3–4, but not for this main part of the lament. So the last king of the dynasty is in view, Zedekiah, who reigned from 597 to 587. Jehoahaz's fate functions as an omen of what was in store for him. Theoretically, Zedekiah's immediate predecessor Jehoiachin, now exiled in Babylon, might have been a better choice for this role. Presumably, the high regard of Ezekiel's constituency for him ruled him out. Zedekiah's stalking among lions may be a reference not only to his overtures to Egypt (17:15) but also to the meeting of envoys of western kings he hosted in Jerusalem in 594 to plan a revolt against Babylon (Jer 27:1–11). The man-eating of the first young lion, continued by his successor, is amplified in terms of widow-making, borrowed from 22:25. Literal, culpable wastage of human life is envisioned under the figure of a lion's ravaging communities (cf. Jer 2:15; 2 Kgs 17:25; Greenberg 352). We know hardly anything about Zedekiah's domestic policy. His evident weakness might have condoned all manner of evils (cf. Jer 34:8–22). It is not insignificant that Ezekiel called him "wicked" (21:30[25]).

8–9   Another foreign hunting party soon deals with the problem. See the *Comment* on 12:13 for the net and the pit as means of trapping. Both there and in the underlying 17:20 the net is spread by Yahweh to catch Zedekiah. Editorially, 19:8–9 is to be regarded as a fulfillment of 17:20, which goes on to mention the king being taken by Yahweh to Babylon. V 14b must be taken seriously: the prophetic lament concerning the future eventually came to function as an actual lament relating to the past. These words became historically true. What was indubitably predicted in 17:20 could now be celebrated as fulfilled in the reinterpreted lament. In relating the two passages, the nations are understood as agents of Yahweh, a reasonable notion since in 17:20 God is obviously working through the Babylonians. Such intertextuality indicates that, editorially, Zedekiah is in view both in 17:20 and here. This is early evidence indeed for the identification of the second young lion. A wooden collar, like the hooks, was used both for captured animals and for human prisoners. It was a ladderlike framework that functioned as a restraining device (Gordon, *Sumer* 12 [1956] 82). The tone of finality in the last line of the first lament encourages the impression that this is the last king to reign on Judean soil (Brownlee, "Two Elegies" 97).

10–11   The second lament in vv 10–14a has been used to parallel the first, as the initial catchword indicates. On a larger structural scale, it intends to resume the fable of 17:3–10. Now, however, the grapevine is not a symbol of the individual king Zedekiah but a metaphor for the royal dynasty, like the lioness of v 2. Again Zedekiah appears to be addressed, notwithstanding that later in the lament, within the horizons of the vine metaphor, he is mentioned in the third person. The past glory of the dynasty is described in positive metaphorical terms in vv 10–11aα. They remind the reader of similar language used of Israel's blessings in Ps 80:8–12(7–11), though a territorial element is absent here. The strong stems represent the princes of the royal house: candidates for the throne were ever available. In Ps 110:2 the very phrase, with an initial singular noun, מטה עז, means not "strong stem" but "mighty scepter" of the Davidic king (cf. too Jer 48:17).

The amplification in v 11aβb, already known to the oracle of salvation that closes chap. 17, takes its cue from the single stem relating to Zedekiah later in the poem. It adds an accusatory note of ambition that seems to continue the earlier glorious description of the dynasty, yet has overtones of blame. It echoes chap. 31, a lament for the Pharaoh in terms of an enormous tree that was cut down for its overweening pride, and readers are meant to catch the reference. The details are drawn from 31:3, 5, 9, 10. There is an irony about the allusion. Zedekiah's craving for independence—historically that of his ministers, but as king he had to bear the blame—was a wagon hitched to Egypt's falling star (17:15).

12   The lament moves prophetically to the demise of the dynasty, stating it as a firm fact. The two initial verbs are divine passives, and חמה "anger" reinforces the reference to God, who responds vehemently to the vine he had earlier favored. We cannot avoid associating the term on Ezekiel's lips with Yahweh's passionate moral retribution (cf. 13:13). The stark shift of the original lament has been helpfully explained by the insertion in v 11. Greenberg's appeal to 28:17 (353) shows how good a redactional fit the insertion is, rather than its originality. The whole grapevine, now including its single soaring stem, is torn off its supports and dashed to the ground. The element of divine causality is reinforced by the reference to the east wind, which is Yahweh's instrument of destruction, as in 17:10. Here we must note the recurrence of a phenomenon observed in v 8. In the basic lament, the blasting by the east wind refers to the future. When it was incorporated in its written form, the predictive lament had shifted to an actual lament because its content was now history (v 14b). The reader is meant to trace a sequence between the plainly future reference of 17:10 and this now backward-looking reference. The future shriveling of 17:9b and its past counterpart in 19:12a,b have the same editorial connotation. God's threat had come true, and so vv 10–14a, like vv 2–9, are a testimony to fulfilled prophecy. In deuteronomistic terms Yahweh's hand matched his mouth (1 Kgs 8:24).

The grapevine's strong stem, the present occupant of the Israelite throne as Ezekiel spoke, was to be, and in fact was, shriveled with the rest of the vine. The mention of fire harks back to the divine fury by way of inclusion (cf. 22:21, 31; 38:18–19). In a remarkable parallel, a royal psalm that saw the end of the dynasty looming lamented the burning of Yahweh's fury like fire (Ps 89:47[46]).

13–14 The lament moves characteristically to the ignominious "now," which reverses the glorious "then" of vv 10–11. Parunak ("Structural Studies" 288) has usefully cited D. H. Müller's observation that vv 13–14a are meant to resume vv 10–11a in a tragic inclusion. The echoing of earlier vocabulary in a different con-text accentuates the reversal. The royal family is now (to be) "planted" (שְׁתוּלָה) in exile (cf. Jer 38:22–23). The "tendrils" (בַּדִּים, בַּדֶּיהָ) that signified a healthy vine are described as scorched and lifeless. The supply of royal "scepters" or indi-vidual kings had come to an end. Where there had been water aplenty, desert and drought and even fire dominated. We need not be concerned by the illogi-cality of a grapevine being consumed and then transplanted: a metaphor has to stretch to cover human realities. The negativity of the closing line mournfully matches that of the previous lament, and both express negation of normality that fits well the close of a lament (Jahnow, *Leichenlied* 131, 206).

The blame for the end of the royal house is laid firmly on Zedekiah. Like the fire coming out of the royal bramble in Jotham's fable (Judg 9:15; Hammershaimb, "Ezekiel's View" 136), fire issued from the last "stem" and destroyed the tendrils of the vine. The judgment that Zedekiah brought on himself by rebelling against Babylon was to engulf the dynasty. There is more in the last line than meets the eye. While the first lament evoked the lioness of Gen 49:9, the second echoes not only the vine of Gen 49:11 but also the scepter of Gen 49:10. In 21:30–32(25–27) Ezekiel rhetorically addressed a personal oracle of judgment to Zedekiah, order-ing him in God's name to give up his crown. That oracle closes with a taunting echo of Gen 49:10, reinterpreting its coming ruler as Nebuchadnezzar bringing divine judgment (see Allen, *Ezekiel 20–48* 28). The same message seems to underlie v 14a (cf. Moran, *Bib* 39 [1958] 423–24). No, the "scepter" would "not depart from" the royal house of Judah—"until" God's final judgment came. V 14a and 21:32(27) reinforce each other in a startling prophetic reversal of earlier promise.

Explanation

This shocking chapter gives a particular analysis of the general announcement of the "end" that, according to chap. 7, loomed for Judah in the tragic events of

587. There the head of state was merely mentioned as unable to cope with the crisis (7:27). Here the focus is on the crumbling of the Davidic throne. For all its positive traditions, its destiny was to be inglorious. The prophetic lament is here an ideal vehicle for first expressing and then denying one particular popular hope. If Zion theology was attacked in chap. 16, here it is the turn of Davidic theology (cf. Lam 4:12, 20). Ezekiel tolls the bell for Zedekiah and for the Davidic dynasty. The last king would be captured and deported, while by implication the dynasty would perish. Jehoahaz's deportation at the hands of a world power must be seen as an omen of a similar fate for Zedekiah, the cub from the same litter of the dynastic lioness. The shameless oppression that marked the royal house was to lead to the withdrawal of divine promise, not least that of Gen 49:9. The second lament reverses Gen 49:10–11 and stresses destructive wrath. The two laments with their different emphases are to be read together for the total message. An accusatory note of soaring pride has been skillfully woven into the latter lament, to reinforce the necessity of the divine verdict.

V 14b is a hermeneutical key to the editorial significance of the chapter. History had overtaken prophecy. What has been predicated of the future in a prophetic lament was now verified as valid. Hindsight could now interpret its past tenses literally. From this perspective, chap. 19 serves to confirm what had been unambiguously future threats in chap. 17. Yahweh's word had come true. By the eclipse of royal sovereignty, God's moral sovereignty could be celebrated. Nor was that all. In the complex of chaps. 17 and 19, the central place is given to the salvation oracle of 17:22–24. Where there was a real and undeniable end, there was to be a new beginning. Where judgment had to do its deadly work, salvation was eventually to revive the ancient promises. Room is made for a new, positive version of the vine fable and the vine lament, promising new glory that would transcend the old. Readers who look back and around with despair are bidden to look forward with messianic hope. They—and we—are given "a lamp shining in a dark place, until the day dawns" (2 Pet 1:19).

Index of Authors Cited

Index of Principal Subjects

Index of Biblical Texts

A. Old Testament

B. New Testament

C. Apocrypha

D. Pseudepigrapha and Early Patristic Work

E. Dead Sea Scrolls and Related Texts

F. Rabbinic and Mishnaic Materials